HISTORY

OF

TIFT COUNTY

By Ida Belle Williams

Southern Historical Press, Inc.
Greenville, South Carolina

This volume was reproduced
from a personal copy located in
the Publishers private library

All rights reserved. No part of this publication may be reproduced,
stored in a retrieval system, transmitted in any form, posted
on the web in any form or by any means without the
prior written permission of the publisher.

Please direct all correspondence and book orders to:
SOUTHERN HISTORICAL PRESS, Inc.
1071 Park West Blvd.
Greenville, SC 29611

Copyright 1948 by:
    Tift County Historical Society
New material Copyright 2025:
    Southern Historical Press, Inc.
ISBN #978-1-63914-672-7
Printed in the United States of America

HENRY HARDING TIFT
Founder of Tifton

DEDICATION

With admiration we dedicate this volume of the Tift Coun story to the memory of the founder of Tifton, an unselfi lder, a generous contributor to all good causes, a great bei tor, a great man—HENRY HARDING TIFT.

Editorial Staff of The History of Tift County

Top row—Ida Belle Williams, Editor-in-Chief, author of History of Tift County; Elizabeth Pickard Karsten, assistant editor and author of chapter, "Pioneers."

Bottom row—J. L. Williams, assistant editor, author of True Tales of the Wire Grass. Bob Herring, assistant editor.

APPRECIATION

I wish to emphasize my appreciation of everyone who helped me in the compiling of the *"History of Tift County."* It is impossible to name everyone, but among the number are the following: Mr. J. L. Williams, Mrs. Elizabeth Pickard Karsten, and Mr. Bob Herring, all of the editorial staff of Tift County History; Mrs. N. Peterson, Mrs. Dan Sutton, Mr. C. C. Guest, Miss Laura Guest, Mr. H. Carmichael, Mrs. Bob Herring, Mrs. Briggs Carson, Sr., Mrs. Peggy Herring Coleman, Mr. A. B. Phillips, Mrs. Weetie Tift Rankin, Mrs. Robert Heinsohn, Mr. H. D. Webb, Mrs. D. M. Braswell, Miss Corrinne Tucker and her students, the Tifton High School commercial department; Miss Elmina McKneely, Mrs. Frank Corry, Sr., Mrs. D. B. Harrell, Mr. L. E. Bowen, Sr., Dr. L. A. Baker, Mrs. Paul Fulwood, Sr., Mr. Paul Fulwood, Sr., Miss Billy Jean Pearman, Mrs. R. E. Jones, Miss Eulala Tyson, Mrs. Elizabeth Turlington White, Miss Jean Colley, Mr. Phillip Kelley, the Chamber of Commerce, Mrs. W. L. Harman, Mrs. J. G. Fulwood, Mr. Y. Sutton, Mr. Elias Branch, Mr. John Henry Hutchinson, Mr. Earle Smith, Mr. Fred Shaw, Mrs. Louise Griner, Dr. Sanders, Dr. S. W. Martin, Mr. George King, Mrs. Ralph Johnson, Miss Leola Greene, Mr. Ben McLeod, Mrs. Hazel Whittington Fowler, Miss Mary Lillian Willis, Mrs. Maude Thompson, Mr. George Branch, Mrs. Susie T. Moore, Mrs. R. Eve, Judge Eve, Major Steve Mitchell, Miss Cassie Goff, Mrs. Katherine Tift Jones, Mr. Frank Smith, and all other members of the Tift County Historical Society. I found the task of writing the "History of Tift County" very interesting.

We extend sincere appreciation to the following for donations received by Judge R. Eve, for and in behalf of Tift County Historical Society: E. P. and L. E. Bowen, T. W. Tift (Egan, Ga.), City of Tifton, County of Tift, Mrs. Pearl Myers, Mrs. Robt. A. Balfour (nee Debbie McCrea, Thomasville), Harry Hornbuckle, Mrs. Susie T. Moore, Mrs. Lillian Britt Heinsohn (nee Lillian Britt, Thomasville), A. B. Phillips, Joe Kent, Sr.

IDA BELLE WILLIAMS.

For permission to use copyrighted material, I am grateful to the following:

McCall Corporation, for "Adopting a Rural School," by Myra G. Reed.

Mrs. Lillie Clements, for Judge J. B. Clements's "History of Irwin County." Published by Foote and Davies.

Oklahoma Press, for Debo's "Road to Disappearance" and Caughey's "McGillivray of the Creeks;"

Mrs. Lillie Martin Grubbs, for her book, "History of Worth County," published by the J. W. Burke Co.

Columbia University Press, for Phillips' "History of Transportation in the Eastern Cotton Belt to 1860;"

E. Coulter, for his book, "A Short History of Georgia," published by University of North Carolina Press;

American Historical Society, for Cooper's "History of Georgia;"

R. P. Brooks, for his "History of Georgia," published by Atkinson, Mentger and Company;

Mrs. Lucian Lamar Knight, for Lucian Lamar Knight's "Georgia Landmarks, Memorials, and Legends," published by Byrd Printing Company;

I am also indebted to the Smithsonian Institute for Swanton's "Early History of the Creek Indians and their Neighbors;"

Oklahoma Historical Society, for "Chronicles of Oklahoma," June 1932;

White's "Statistics of Georgia," published by T. Williams, copyrighted;

Jones's "History of Georgia," published by Houghton, Mifflin and Company, copyrighted;

to the entire staff and files of the Tifton Gazette, to Miss Leatrice Foreman, librarian of Tifton High School, to the Herrings for J. L. Herring's "Saturday Night Sketches," and to Carnegie Library, Atlanta, for Watkin's Digest.

IDA BELLE WILLIAMS

Appreciation

of

The Tift County Historical Society

is expressed

to

Ida Belle Williams, M.A.,

Editor-in-Chief

of

The History of Tift County

Miss Williams has for fifteen years taught English in the Tifton High School, of which, for the last five years, she has been the capable and beloved principal. Her feature articles on many subjects have long appeared in the press. Her present work adds another blossom to her bouquet of achievements.

By Elizabeth Pickard Karsten for the Tift County Historical Society.

TABLE OF CONTENTS

	Page
Chapter I Footsteps of the Creek Indians	1
Chapter II Footsteps of "Pale Faces"	13
Chapter III Footsteps of Early Settlers	18
Chapter IV The Founding of Tifton	23
Chapter V Wire Grass in the Eighties	30
Chapter VI "The Gay Nineties"	34
Chapter VII The Early Nineteen Hundreds	53
Chapter VIII Tift County	61
Chapter IX Agricultural School	66
Chapter X Progress from 1910-1917	78
Chapter XI "World Earthquake"—World War I	86

	Page

Chapter XII
The Turbulent Twenties -- 90

Chapter XIII
The Depression -- 96

Chapter XIV
World War II—Second "World Earthquake" ------------------ 111

Chapter XV
Post-War Events—Atomic Era ---------------------- ------------ 126

Chapter XVI
Small Towns -- 132
    Brighton—Brighton Community—Mr. and Mrs. Elbert Fletcher—Mr. and Mrs. Henry Sutton—Mr. and Mrs. Jonathan Walker—Brookfield—Bishop Arthur Moore—Chula—"A Lone Soldier in Gray"—Eldorado—Excelsior District—Harding—Mr. and Mrs. Dan Fletcher—Mr. and Mrs. John Goff—Mr. and Mrs. Jacob Hall—Mr. and Mrs. Azor Paulk—Omega—Ty Ty.

Chapter XVII
Tifton and Tift County Education ------------------------------ 162
    Introduction—Annie Bell Clark School—G. O. Bailey, Jr.—W. L. Bryan—Mrs. J. E. Cochran—A. H. Moon—R. E. Moseley—Jason Scarboro—John C. Sirmons—Ida Belle Williams—Mrs. Dan Sutton—Miss Follis—Miss Shaw—Abraham Baldwin Agricultural College and Preceding Institution—Abraham Baldwin—Tift County Industrial School—W. R. Smith—R. F. Kersey—W. L. Harman—Charles Harman—Faculty of Tift County Schools 1946-47—Superintendents of Education (Tift County)—Present County Board of Education—M. H. Mitcham—Charles Luther Carter—Charles F. Hudgins—W. T. Bodenhamer—Alton Ellis—Mrs. Nicholas Peterson—Conclusion.

Chapter XVIII
Churches -- 204
    Brookfield Baptist Church—First Baptist Church of Tifton—Chula Baptist Church—Ty Ty Baptist Church—Zion Hope—Bessie Tift Chapel—The Tifton Primitive Church—St. Anne's Episcopal Church—Hickory Springs Church—Brookfield Methodist Church—Chula Methodist—Harding Methodist Church—Mt. Calvary Methodist Church—Oak Ridge Methodist Church—Tifton Methodist Church—Church of Nazarene—New River Church—Presbyterian Church—Salem Church—Turner Church.

Chapter XIX

Page

Clubs ---226
  Boy Scouts—Gun Lake Country Club—Tifton Lions Club—Primrose Garden Club—Tifton's First and Second Kiwanis Club—Chamber of Commerce—Tifton Garden Club—The Country Club—Garden Center—Parent-Teacher's Association—United Daughters of the Confederacy—Tifton County Welfare—Tifton Masonic Lodge No. 47—Tifton Shrine Club—Veterans of Foreign Wars—Woodmen of the World—Tifton Junior Woman's Club—Tifton Music Club—Twentieth Century Library Club—Rotary Club—Tift County Post 21 The American Legion.

Chapter XX

Who's Who in Tift County ---258
  S. J. Akers—L. S. Alfriend—G. O. Bailey, Jr.—L. E. Bowen, Sr.—Elias Branch—W. P. Bryan—Annie Bell Clark—Ethel Clements,—Josie Clyatt (Mrs. Jim Clyatt)—Nathan Coarsey—Peggy Herring Coleman—George P. Donaldson—Judge R. Eve—Paul Dearing Fulwood, Sr.—Ruth Vickers Fulwood (Mrs. P. D. Fulwood, Sr.)—Mrs. J. J. Golden—Leola Judson Greene—Mrs. W. S. Harman—Dr. W. H. Kendricks—Joseph Kent—George Harris King—Harry Kulbresh—Bishop Arthur Moore—Susie T. Moore—R. C. Patrick—Mrs. J. A. Peterson, Sr.—Mrs. Nicholas Peterson T. E. Phillips, Sr.—Dr. Franklin Pickett—Mrs. J. W. Poole—D. C. Rainey—Mrs. W. T. Smith—Mrs. Dan Sutton—John Y. Sutton—Amos Tift—E. L. Webb—Ida Belle Williams—J. L. Williams.

Chapter XXI

Some of the Tift County Boys Who Made the Supreme
  Sacrifice in World War II ----------------------------------270
  Garland Anderson—Tilton Edward Belflower—Winford Elijah Evans—Reuben G. Funderburk—Russell Leonard Garner—Ollie E. Gibbs—Ralph Gibbs—Curtis Mathews—Charles William Mathews—Alvin McKinney—Sidney Neighbors—Charles Edwin Patton—Robert B. Powledge—Frederick E. Sears—George Sutton—Pfc. Durward Lee Willis.

Chapter XXII

Wire Grass Journalism ---279
  J. T. Maund—Ty Ty Echo—B. T. Allen—Tifton Gazette—Quaint Writing in Gazette of 1892—John L. Herring—John Greene Herring—Bob Herring—Leola Judson Greene—Gus Pat Adams—Omega News—Lucy Maude Thompson—"A Wire-Grass Easter" (from Saturday Night Sketches")—The Tifton Free Press—J. L. Williams—Elizabeth Pickard Karsten.

Chapter XXIII

Tift County Agriculture ---292
  Agriculture—Tobacco in Tift County—Mrs. Paul Fulwood, Sr.—Paul Dearing Fulwood, Sr.

Chapter XXIV

Page

Industries --306
    The Southern Cotton Oil Company—Armour Enters Tifton Territory—Tifton Cotton Mills—Tifton Coca-Cola Bottling Company.

Chapter XXV

Miscellaneous—Part I ---309
    Facts compiled by the Chamber of Commerce—The Bench and the Bar—Tifton County Representatives and Senators—Mayors and City Managers of Tifton—Airport—Stephen A. Youmans—Frank Henry Smith—George Washington Coleman—Tifton Post Office—Union Road—Chase Salmon Osborn—Christie Bell Kennedy—Florence Karsten Carson—An Appreciation of Tifton—Tift County Officers—Coastal Plain Experiment Station—Silas Starr.

Chapter XXVI

Miscellaneous—Part II --341
    Negro Pioneers—Negro Citizens—Negro Churches—Joe Reeves.

Chapter XXVII

True Tales of Wire Grass Georgia ---------------------------------348
    Tifton's First Tornado—Tribute to J. L. Herring—Tifton's First Radio Station—Tifton's First Automobile—Tifton's First Filling Station—When Tifton Was Dry—The Key Man of Tifton in 1899—The Progressive Minister—The Horned Negro of Tifton—Candidates Running for Office—How the First Session of Tift County Court Was Paid For—City Election for Mayor—When Tifton Had Seventeen Lawyers and One Preacher—Big Hog Dan Walker—Grammar School Block When the Circus Came to Tifton—John H. Sparks—The Vamberg Shows—When Life Began for Me.

Chapter XXVIII

Tift County Pioneers—Appreciation --------------------------------363
    B. T. Allen—Joseph J. Baker—William W. Banks—Mary Evelyn Town Banks—Annie Fogler Bennett—Frederick G. Boatright—George Washington Bowen—Enoch Piercel Bowen—Irwin W. Bowen—Isaac Stephen Bowen—Branch Family—Elias Branch—Britt Family—Edward Buck—Thomas Carmichael—Briggs Carson, Sr.—Charlotte Carson—Captain Lemuel Chesnutt and Family—Samuel Clyatt—Churchwells—James E. Cochran—Abraham Conger—Abraham Benjamin Conger—Virgil Francis Dinsmore—John Duff—Raleigh Eve—Fletchers—Daniel Fulwood—C. W. Fulwood—James S. Gaulding—Jack Gaulding—Greene Family (James, John, Leola)—Gibbs Family—J. J. Golden—Dr. John Goodman—Katherine Tift Jones—C. C. Guest—R. E. Hall—W. T. Hargrett—W. L. Harman—W. H. Hendricks—J. L. Herring—C. B. Holmes—B. C. Hutchinson—J. H. Hutchinson—J. L. Gay, Jr.—George W. Julian—Kent Family—Belle Willingham Lawrence—W. H. Love—J. T. Mathis—Dr. John

Arch McRae—Perryman Moore—Susie T. Moore—Sylvester Murray—Tillou Bacon Murrow—Irvine Myers—Henry Myers—B. H. McLeod—McMillan Family—Silas and Duncan O'Quinn—Overstreets—Padrick Brothers—Thomas J. Parker—Jacob Marion Paulk—Anne Catherine Register Paulk—Dr. John A. Peterson—Dr. Nichols Peterson—J. J. L. Phillips—John A. Phillips—T. E. Phillips—Florence Willingham Pickard—William L. Y. Pickard—J. L. Pickard—John Milton Price—S. G. Slack—Jason Scarboro—Matthew Sylvester Shaw—Edna Cox Shaw—Fred Shaw—Luther Smith Shepherd and Larkin G. Maynard—George Alfred Brannon Smith—Robley D. Smith—W. T. Smith—Walter Crawford Spurlin—Nelson Tift—Henry Harding Tift—E. H. Tift—Bessie Willingham Tift—Henry Harding Tift, Jr.—Amos Tift—Thomas Willingham Tift—W. O. Tift—W. H. Timmons—E. L. Vickers—Jonathan Walker—The Warrens—William Wiley Webb—Whiddon Family—C. A. Williams—Cecelia Matilda Baynard Willingham—Margaret Willingham Wood—E. E. Youmans.

TIFT COUNTY HISTORY

Illustrations

	Page
Henry Harding Tift	v
Judge Raleigh Eve	xix
Editorial Staff	xxi
Commissary Established in 1872	24
Camp Fire Girls of the "Gay Nineties"	35
Abraham Baldwin Agricultural School	69
Tift Theater	97
Mrs. Susie T. Moore, Mrs. Nichols Peterson, Mrs. Paul Fulwood, Sr.	100
Tifton Street Scenes; Entrance to Fulwood Park and Home of Mr. and Mrs. Paul D. Fulwood, Sr.; Woman's Club and Public Library; Street Scene Shriners' Parade	108
Tifton Frozen Foods, Tifton Cotton Oil Company	112
Air View of Omega	153
Tifton Grammar, Junior High, and Senior High Schools	163
Tifton High Band and Glee Club	167
One-Room School attended by Bishop Arthur Moore, Omega School, Brookfield School	181
E. L. Patrick, R. G. Harrell, W. D. Doss, M. H. Evans, J. C. Branch	185
First Corps of Tift County Teachers	187
Mercer Mitcham, C. B. Culpepper, Edna Bishop	191
Tifton Presbyterian Church, Bessie Tift Chapel, Brookfield Methodist Church, First Baptist Church of Tifton, First Methodist Church of Tifton, St. Anne's Episcopal Church of Tifton	206
Baptism Scenes	208
Altar at St. Anne's Episcopal Church	213
Tift County's Diversified Agriculture	294
Scenes in Tift County	298
Scenes on Farms in Tift County	304
Scene in Mrs. Pauline Kent's Yard, Home of Mrs. Elizabeth Pickard Karsten, Sawmill of 1872, Amos Tift, Mary Carmichael	318
J. M. Walker, Leon Clements, Earl D. Gibbs, W. Jelks Warren	330
W. C. McCormick, A. B. Phillips, Chester A. Baker	334
U. S. Post Office, Courthouse, Bank of Tifton, Confederate Monument in Fulwood Park, Tift County Hospital	336
C. A. Sears, Frank Smith, P. D. Fulwood, Sr., R. M. Kennon, J. F. Newton, A. C. Tift	338
With Tift Colored Folk	342
Captain Owen Lemuel Chesnutt, G. W. Crum, P. D. Phillips, Patrick Thomas Carmichael, Henry Hardy Britt	375
C. W. Fulwood, Briggs Carson, Sr., Dr. Jasper Brooks, J. L. Herring, Dr. N. Peterson, John Henry Hutchinson	382
William Lowndes Yancey Pickard	449
Mrs. H. H. Tift and Sons, Mrs. H. H. Tift, Mrs. Florence Willingham Pickard	473
Thomas Willingham Tift	485

THE HISTORY OF TIFT COUNTY

CHAPTER I.

Footsteps of the Creek Indians

Let us stroll in beautiful Fulwood Park, Tifton, Georgia. It is the spring of 1947. The colorful azaleas, native and exotic, bordering the walks, and fragrant roses are blooming. The majestic long-leaf pines—a remnant of an ancient forest that probably whispered messages to Lower Creek Indian maidens and lovers on this spot—are still whispering and sighing. The magnolias, rare camellia plants, weeping willows, hollies, leafy branches of various oaks, dogwood blossoms, and sweet tunes of our Southern birds are announcing spring in Tift County.

Boy Scout log cabins and rustic bridges over natural streams, trickling through the woodland, give their human-interest touch and picturesqueness. April breezes are spreading rustic odors of pine straw and perfume from rose vines and native yellow jasmines garlanded over trellises.

Now as we stroll, let us listen to the tramp, tramp of feet of the past in Wire Grass Georgia! First came the footsteps of the animals and the aborigines. Wolves, bears, tigers, catamounts, deer, and wild turkeys tramped through this spot, the present Fulwood Park, during the forest days before and after the sound of the axe and while the nimble-footed "red men" with their bows and arrows hunted game.

The Lower Creek Indians stepped in this section of Georgia. There is proof that Indians lived in what is now Tift County. Indian pottery was found eight miles from Tifton on Dan King's farm. A number of Indian relics have been found on W. L. Lawson's place, near Tifton. A very rare arrowhead was dug up in the old Pickard yard, where Mrs. Elizabeth Karsten now lives.

Let us discuss some of the facts about the makers of the footsteps. According to Swanton, the Creek Confederacy had forty-seven tribes, composed of families and clans with a population estimated at 20,000. The Handbook of American Indians in Bulletin 30, Bureau of Ethnology, referred to in Cooper's "Story of Georgia," Vol. I, page 46, holds that in ancient days the Creeks occupied the greater portion of Alabama and Georgia, residing chiefly on the Coosa and Tallapoosa Rivers, and on the Flint River.

"They claimed," says the bulletin, "the territory on the east from the Savannah to St. Johns Rivers and all the islands thence to Appalachee Bay and from this line nowthward to the mountains.

"They sold to Great Britain at an early date this territory between the

Savannah and Ogeechee Rivers, and all the islands up to the tidewater, reserving for themselves St. Catherine, Sapelo, and Ossabaw Islands and from Pipemakers Bluff to Savannah.

"The towns were classified as Upper Creeks, on Coosa and Tallapoosa Rivers, Alabama, and Lower Creeks, on middle or lower Chattahoochee River, on the Alabama-Georgia border."

Muskogee was the Indian name for these people, and Creek, the English. There are two theories for the cause of the latter name: many people believe that the Indians' fondness for rivers and streams is responsible; Swanton agrees with Prof. V. W. Crane's idea that Creek is a condensation of Ocheese Creek Indians, Ocheese being an old name for the Ocmulgee, upon which many of these Indians were living when the English first contacted them.

According to Swanton in "Creek Indians and Their Neighbors," the upper Creeks lived on Coosa, Tallapoosa, and Alabama Rivers and in the neighboring country, and the lower Creeks, on the Chattahoochee and Flint. Tradition gives the origin of these Indians in the west, but Swanton asserts that Muskogee tribes had completed their migration before De Soto's arrival.

Colonel Benjamin Hawkins, former Indian agent for United States Government, said, "They have a tradition among them that there is in the fork of the Red River, West of Mississippi, two mounds of earth; that at this place, the Cussetuhs, Conetuhs, and Chickasaws found themselves; that being distressed by wars and red people, they crossed the Mississippi; and directing their course eastwardly they crossed the falls of Tallapoosa above Tookaubatch, settled below the falls of Chattahoochee, and spread out from thence to Ocmulgee, Oconee, Savannah, and down on the seacoast towards Charleston. Here they first saw white people, and from hence they have been compelled to retire back again to their present settlement."[1]

Their towns were divided into white and red; the former for peace; the latter for war, which the Great Warrior determined.[2] When the micco and counsellors believed the town had received an injury, the Great Warrior lifted the hatchet against the offending nation. The micco and counsellors, however, could avoid war by negotiation. If the Great Warrior, still persisting, left for war, his followers joined him in battle, after he fired his gun and set up the war whoop. Not more than one-half the nation ever went to war at the same time or took "the war talk."

Their superstitions were numerous.[3] These Indians believed that a rattlesnake would give good luck if he crawled into a camp during a ball game and that a wolf would punish the irreverent. The musical title, "night wanderers," for the wolf, reminds one of the kennings in "Beowulf." The

---
1. White's "Statistics of Georgia," p. 28.
2. Loc. Cit.
3. Debo's "Road to Disappearance"—page 238.

Creeks respected plants as well as animals. Children were not allowed to play with corn cobs because the corn represented an old lady, who was sensitive.

In the fall to prevent colds, they used leaf-colored water.[4] "For four mornings in succession they drank the leaf-flavored medicine in four sips, facing east and then dipped in it four times." Since mist to them was pure water, the women used it for hair tonic. Their beauty parlors were vine-clad nooks in the woods, where Indian maids spread their hair under the dripping sap of grapevines to give luxuriance. These maids called leaves "tree hair."[5]

Angie Debo in "Road to Disappearance," refers to superstitions given by an aged Creek woman, Monie Coker, p. 299. Pointing a finger at the rainbowbow will make the finger crooked. Blindness and falling teeth are the penalty for not spitting four times after one sees a falling star. If a hunter will bury some of the hair from the right foot of a squirrel he had killed, he will kill more squirrels. Pups if given wasps four mornings will develop into ferocious watch dogs.

Superstitions concerning infants are: if an infant eats the tongue of a mocking bird, he will grow into a mimic; if someone scratches the baby with a quail's toes, the latter will become fast and nimble; if the child drinks liquid from an old well, he will be a good singer.

Their religion was closely related to their superstitions. The Creeks attached much significance to superior beings' directing human affairs.[6] Each tribe had its conjurors and magicians, which the Indians consulted about health, hunting, and war. They called on all spirits, good and bad to help them in difficult undertakings. They regarded signs and dreams as important. Creeks looked upon fire as sacred and paid the author of it a kind of worship. At the time of full moon they observed several feasts and ceremonies, which it would seem were derived from some religious origin.[7]

According to James Adair the Indians worshipped "the Great, Beneficent, Supreme, Holy Spirit of Fire, who resides, as they think, above the clouds and on earth among unpolluted people." With the "red men" this Great Spirit was the sole author of light, heat, and all animal and vegetable life. The Creeks considered the sun as a visible representative of the Great Spirit, ruler of heaven and earth, whom they called[8] "The Great Fire above, and fire, to them an emanation from the sun, was sacred." The fire was rekindled but once a year with a solemn ceremony; it was wicked act to put out the flames in the meantime.

Connected with the Creek's religion was an annual festival, Booksketau,

---
4. Ibid., lines 1 and 2, p. 299.
5. Debo's "Road to Disappearance," p. 200.
6. Hewat, page 78, Swanton's "Early History of the Creek Indians and Their Neighbrs."
7. Loc. Cit.
8. **Walter G. Cooper's "Story of Georgia"** Vol. 1, p. 46.

which the Indians celebrated in the month of July or August. In some towns the festival lasted eight days: in other towns, four days. Colonel Benjamin Hawkins said,[9] "This happy institution of the Booksketau, restores a man to himself, to his family, and to his nation. It is a general amnesty, which not only absolves the Indians from all crimes, murder only excepted, but seems to bury guilt itself in oblivion."

Colonel Hawkins also gave an account of the marriage customs. A man who wanted a wife did not propose in person, but, like Miles Standish, courted by proxy. The lover sent his sister, mother, or some other female relative to the female relatives of the chosen red maid. The representatives consulted the girl's brothers and maternal uncle, and sometimes the father. The last consultation was a mere courtesy, as his approval or disapproval was not important. If the suitor received a favorable answer, carried by his representatives, he would send a blanket and clothing to the women in the girl's family.

After these formalities, the lover could go to his fiancee's home at any time he chose. When he had built a house, made and gathered a crop, hunted and brought home the meat, and presented all these things to the maid, the ceremony ended. The two were then considered married—in other words, the woman was bound.

Now as we feel the vibrations of the "red men's" footsteps, let us sit in the park on a bench under the vigorous green needles of the ancient pines, some of which are two-hundred-forty years old, and watch on the screen of time flashes from the Creek nation.

First, Creek characters flash in the preview. Indian men, with long, coarse, black hair and regular features, enter, wearing animal skins. Some of the leaders are wearing bands of feathers or metal on their heads and ornaments in their noses. The countenance of these men is "open, dignified, and placid, yet the forehead and brow so formed as to strike you instantly with heroism and bravery; the eye, though small, is active and full of fire. Their countenance and actions exhibit an air of magnanimity, superiority, and independence."[10]

Now we have a snow scene.[11] Indian women low, but well proportioned, wearing heavy skin blankets, are hurrying toward their wigwams. Like the men, these squaws have long, black, coarse hair. Following this group are young Indian maidens in short skirts, made of deer skins, and shawls of animal skins.

Spring is here. Indian girls wearing aprons of strings, with pieces of metals dangling from the ends dance across the stage. Now follows another group of dancing maids, carrying turkey feather fans and wearing in their hair ornaments of beads, feathers, copper, and colored stones.

---

9. White's "Statistics of Georgia," p. 33.
10. William Bartram, Cooper's "History of Georgia" Vol. I, p. 49.
11. John R. Swanton's "Early History of the Creek Indians and Their Neighbors."

Now the first main scene flashes. Lower Creek Indians are darting here and there in the dense woods, looking for game. A close-up view shows "men of dark, reddish color, strong, well-proportioned, active and capable of enduring great physical suffering."[12] They hunt game on the low coastal plains and fish in small streams. In the early fall they gather their scanty crops of grain; it does not take much food to satisfy them.

* * * * * *

An Indian lover happily stoops, planting beans and setting poles for the vines to climb on. The happy expression is due to the fact that he killed a bear and sent a pan of bear oil to the beautiful Indian maid whom he wished to marry. Her acceptance of the oil, an equivalent of the English "yes," was the first step in the betrothal; he then was at liberty to hoe her cornfield. Days pass. He now eagerly watches the growth of the beans, for their entwining around the pole will symbolize the union.

Now here comes the bride! Nature is the priest that performs the ceremony. The groom breaks an ear of corn and gives half to the maiden. Instead of a ring ceremony, the groom presents a piece of venison to the bride, and she gives him an ear of corn.[13]

The guests have danced and feasted, and the girl's uncle is leading the couple to their bed. He exclaims,[14] "This is your bed, lie in it."

This marrige is binding until the Green Corn Dance.[15] If the husband or wife is dissatisfied, the marriage can be annulled.

The setting now is for the Green Corn Festival. This woodland scene is far from habitation. It consists of a large square, with four large log houses, each house forming a side of the square.[16] "The houses are of logs and clay and a sort of wicker-work, with sharp topped sloping roofs." Attached to every house is a thick, notched mast, resembling the old-style war club; on each mast is a pile of tall canes, from which black and white feathers droop.

In the center of an outer square is a very high circular mound, which the Indians formed from the earth accumulated yearly by removing the surface of the sacred square.[17] "At every Green Corn Festival the sacred square is strewn with soil yet untrodden; the soil of the year preceding being taken away, but preserved as above explained. No stranger is allowed to press the new earth of the sacred square until its consecration is complete."

Now the head chief in every town is given the signal to extinguish all fires. The first ceremonial is beginning—lighting the new fire of the year.

---

12. Brook's "History of Georgia." p. 17.
13. Scene based on points from "McGillivray of the Creeks" by Caughey, p. 12.
14. Ibid., p. 12, line 40.
15. Ibid., p. 13.
16. Description of Green Corn Dance taken from John Howard Payne's letter in Continental Monthly reproduced by John R. Swanton in "Chronicles of Oklahoma," June 1932. p. 176.
17. Ibid., p. 177.

An Indian is bringing a square board with a hollow in the center; now he is pouring on it dust from dry leaves or trees. Five Indian chiefs are whirling the stick until friction produces a flame. Now they are carrying the fire to the center of the sacred square; over this fire the "red men" set the holy vessels of pottery, and on a bench, the drinking gourds with a handle. Now the Indians are brewing the black drink.

Indian chiefs, motionless as statues are standing around the sides and corners. Every building is full of silent Indians. Those on the back rows are seated in the Turkish fashion, but those in front have their feet on the ground.[18] "All are turbaned, all fantastically painted, all in dresses varying in ornament, but alike in wildness." An Indian chief, wearing a tall black hat with a large silver band and peacock feather is imposing looking. Many of the Indians are wearing eagle plumes, which indicate that they have slain a foe.

Listen to the strange, low, deep wail! Voices in unison are holding notes a long time. Ah, there is a second wail, "shrill like the sound of musical glasses." Now a third wail in another key! The statue-like figures form two diagonal lines opposite each other. One, by one each figure approaches the huge bowls where the black drink is brewing.

Men with whitened long-handled gourds filled with pebbles are seated on mats; whereas those who have been sitting are forming in circles around the fire. Led by a chief, they begin movements from the left. As the procession moves, the solemn "red men" chant to the rhythm of rattling gourds —a surprisingly harmonious sound until some of the dancers interrupt at regular intervals with a chorus like the shrill yelp of a dog.[19] "The dance seems to bear reference to the fires in the center;" the head chief as he approaches the flame, lifts his hand over the flame as if invoking a benediction and every dancer follows his example. Each stately dancer carrying a feather fan gives two taps each with the heel and toe of one foot, then of the other, making a step forward and fanning himself as each foot taps on the earth. The dance increases to a rhythmical run and the dancers vary their cries to suit the motion. Suddenly the Indians give a shrill whoop and stop abruptly. Most of them, however, are rushing down a steep, narrow ravine, canopied with foliage, to the river, into which they plunge.

Now they are returning to the sacred square. An aged chief uttering a low, broken sound, alleluliah, to which the others respond, leads a procession of Indians. In a few minutes they will close with a war whoop.

A fire blazes in the darkness of the wild woods. Eerie forms around the cauldron suggest witches' scenes in "Macbeth." Four weird figures are stirring the cauldron and humming the incantation while the others are dancing. Now they[20] are using "a small kettle-drum with a guitar-like handle."

---
18. Ibid., p. 180.
19. Ibid., p. 181.
20. Ibid., p. 195.

Screen flashes a group of squaws, dressed in long, gaily-colored gowns and bright shawls, draped like mantles. They are wearing innumerable beads on their necks, tortoise-shell combs in their hair, and massive, long silver earrings in their ears. Some of the dancers are wearing under their robes and on their calves large squares of thick leather[21] "covered all over with terrapin-shells close together and perforated and filled with pebbles, which rattle like so many sleigh bells. These they keep silent until their accompaniment is required for the music of their dances." Broad vari-colored ribbon bands streaming from the back of each head to the ground and brilliant glass, coral, and gold beads dangling give the dancers[22] "an air of graceful and gorgeous, and at the same time, unique wildness."

The procession winds around a central fire and stretches out until it extends in three circles and a half. The shortest line halts and faces the men sitting chanting. The last group includes the dancers who wear terrapin leg bands, which rattle to the rhythm of the chants. At the end of each line are two women—one elderly, the other, not young—carrying a little notched stick, floating two feathers and circling around the rest. These two squaws break away from the line and make a circuit outside, while the three circles march slowly round and round, and turn at a given signal to face the men, who face the emblem of the deity, the central fire.

* * * * * * *

Aunt Nancy Luke, an Irwin County woman, whose husband is off fighting Indians, sees five red skins coming toward her in single file. For a moment her eyes reflect horror, as the brave woman pictures torture and death for herself and children. Suddenly regaining self possession as the Indians approach, she invites them to dinner. They follow to the dining room where the sight of food whets their appetite. The "red men" flop on the benches around the table and eat every particle of clabber, corn bread, and potatoes.

As the Indians rise from the table, Aunt Nancy again expects death, but they march into the yard and begin the war dance. As they point to the house, she shudders, for to her they seem to be planning her death. After observing carefully, however, the expression in their eyes and the gesticulations, she decides that the Indians are thanking her for the dinner. Now they form a line and march toward the gate.

* * * * * * *

Cows are stampeding.[23] Pioneer settlers are following the cows, which seem to know when the Indians are approaching and stampede in the opposite direction. Taking what they can in their arms, men, women, and children are following the cattle . . It is night, weary from tramping in the swamp the people lie down . . . Morning dawns and the families again follow the Indian forecasters, the lowly cows, which are valuable protec-

---

21. Ibid., p. 192.
22. Loc. Cit.
23. "History of Worth County" by Lillie Grubbs.

tors. Upon reaching home these people find that the "red men" have ransacked the places.

* * * * *

Aunt Betsy Story, with a bundle in her hand, is walking toward the cow pen to spend the night.[24] The cow pen is the safest spot, for "Old Susie" has scented Indians many times a quarter of a mile away and broken the gate down in her haste to go in the opposite direction.

* * * * *

After several guards among the "pale faces" have mysteriously disappeared, a daring young man has agreed to stand on guard in a spot in the wire grass. Alone in the forest, he hears the grunt of a hog, and looking down in the bushes sees an animal creeping along. Suddenly the man aims and fires. Out of a hog's hide rolls a dead Indian.

* * * * *

Screen flashes a scene in 1814. Quills are moving at Fort Jackson. A treaty with the Lower Creeks is being signed by Indians as representatives of various towns. It has been duly signed by Major-General Jackson, who was responsible for the defeat of the Indians on August 9, 1814. In the War of 1812 between Britain and the United States many Indians sided with Britain. The signing of the treaty is being witnessed by two Indian agents, an officer in the United States Army, three interpreters, and others.

In this treaty Creek Indians have ceded to the United States for Georgia, by virtue of the agreement of 1802, the lands between the western line of Wayne County, bounded on the south by the Florida line, and on the north by lines starting from the Chattahoochee River near Fort Gaines and running due east to a point northeast of Isabella, and thence forty-five degrees northeast to the Ocmulgee River, and thence, following the Ocmulgee to the Altamaha River near Jesup, where it intersects the western boundary line of Wayne County.[25] (The present site of Tift County was in the northern part of the section acquired.)

* * * * *

It is February 12, 1825. General William McIntosh, chief of the Lower Creek Indians, for his people is signing at Indian Springs the treaty which gives the United States Government all lands lying west of the Flint River. The initial ceding of the land was effected by the treaty at Washington, on November 14, 1805.

* * * * *

Flashes are now coming from the late spring of 1836. Creeks from the section around the Chattahoochee River are passing through the Wiregrass Country. Original Irwin County is being devastated by the savages. Gruesome shadows are cast on the background of a dense forest of pines. Men and boys are rushing back and forth, fighting the flames. Pale and trem-

---

24. Irwin County woman referred to in The Tifton Gazette.
25. Dr. Walter Martin's "History of Tift County" published by the Tifton Gazette.

bling, the women and children cringe within the circle of light. Savage yells are renting the air.

* * * * * *

Scene shifts to August 1836. A company of "pale faces" are fighting Indians in the Bushy Creek Swamps. "Pale faces" retreat. Two other companies are following the Indians to a spot five miles below the first battlefield. White men are surrounding the swamp; now they are opening fire. One by one the Indians slink out of the swamp defeated.

A squad of Indians is raiding the house of William Parker (located not far from what is now Lakeland). They are taking more than $300, clothing and food. Captain Knight, commander of a large brave company, is pursuing the red men and overtaking them near Alapaha River, not far from Gaskin Mill Pond. Indians are completely routed. During this skirmish a white man, Mr. Peters, is wounded severely.

Indians throw their guns and plunder into the river and jump into the water. One red man throws his shot gun into the river and tries to throw a shot bag after it. The bag is caught by a limb and hangs over the water.

Having driven the Indians beyond the river, Captain Knight marches his men toward Brushy Creek. As the soldiers arrive they hear a volley of arms. Hastening toward the swamp from which the sound came, the company sees that the battle is over. They learn that the volley was a tribute to Pennywell Folsom, who had fallen during the Brushy Creek engagement. They learn, too, that the Indians have killed Edward Shanks and Ferrell, and wounded Edwin Henderson. Robert Parrish's arm has been broken by a bullet. Twenty-two of the Indians have been killed and numbers wounded.

Leaving the Companies who have fought in the Battle of Brushy Creek, Captain Knight leads his men away to another battlefield (to what is now Clinch County) and overtakes the Indians at Cow Creek. Three Indians are killed and four taken prisoners. Brazelius is dangerously wounded.

A "pale face" rescues the shot bag which lodged on the limb of a tree when thrown toward the river. Upon opening the bag, the white man discovers the money which a "red man" stole from William Parker. The shot gun which is fished from the river is sold for the price—then fabulous—of forty dollars.

(According to Fred Shaw's manuscript about Tift County, the Brushy Creek Battle ended the fighting with "red men" in this section. Supposition is that these defeated Indians joined forces with the Florida Seminoles.)

The following is an excerpt from Shaw's manuscript, which gives facts from old copies of the Ocilla Dispatch and the Valdosta Times:

Of the three companies that took part in the Battle of Brushy Creek there is a record of only the killed or wounded. Of Captain Knight's company, which numbered one hundred and twenty men coming from all parts of Southwest Georgia, the following were among the members:

Bryan J. Roberts, Moses Giddens, John Studstill, Aaron Knight, Guilford Register, David Clements, William Giddens, John Roberts, Zeke Parrish, Nathan Roberts, John McMillan, Robert Parrish, John McDermid, George Henedge, Jeremiah Shaw, Daniel Sloan, John Lee, Moses Lee, James Patten, W. J. Roberts, Isben Giddens, Jacob Giddens, Elbert Peterson, John Knight, Thomas Giddens, Harmon Gaskins, John Gaskins, William Gaskins, Sim Lee, Frederick Giddens, James Parrish, Martin Shaw, Archie McCranie, Alexander Patterson, James Edmondson, David Mathis, Thomas Mathis, Levi Shaw, William Peters, Jonathan Knight, and Brazelius Staten.

Although this immediate section was left in peace after the Indians were driven into Florida, the red skins immediately began making trouble for the people of North Florida and extreme South Georgia. Feeling against the Indians was at a high pitch and military companies from both states joined in an effort to break the power of the savages.

The following pay roll of one of the companies contains the names of many men whose descendants now live in Tift and adjoining counties:

Of Captain H. W. Sharp's Company of Florida Volunteers in the Indian War of 1836. The following is the amount due each officer and soldier:

1. Archibald McCranie, Capt., $124.93; 2. John Lindsey, 1st Lieut., $45.79; 3. John McCranie, 2nd Lieut., $42.27; 4. J. D. Hancock, Ensign and 4th Lieut., $26.43; 5. Martin Shaw, $19.75; 6. Daniel McCranie, Jr., $35.50; 7. Joseph Anderson, $5.75; 8. James J. Burman, $5.05; 9. Thomas Belote, $2.38; 10. William Coane, $3.75; 11. Samuel Connell, $8.75; 12. Peter Connell, $12.00; 13. Ebin Deloach, $26.75; 14. General Deloach, $23.25. 15. William Durrance, $12.00; 16. D. J. Durrance $3.75; 17. Martin Folsom, $7.25; 18. Elijah Folsom, $12.25; 19. Wm. H. Fountain, $6.50; 20. Randall Fulford, $11.50; 21, J. B. Goulding, $23.25; 22. Daniel Griner, $14.50; 23. William Griner, $6.00; 24. Samuel Griner, $2.66; 25. Richard Golding, $13.00; 26. Anderson Golding, $1.98; 27. William Gaskins, $5.25; 28. Jeremiah Hancock, $15.00; 29. Henry Hancock, $8.75.

30. Durham Hancock, $8.75; 31. Jordan Hancock, $5.75; 32. James T. Hancock, $2.38; 33. Lewis Harrell, $2.38; 34. William Kirby, $9.75; 35. Daniel Kinard, $12.00; 36. Arthur Lindsey, $8.75; 37. Joshua Lovett, $15.75; 38. McKeeny McLeod, $5.75; 39. Malcom McCranie, $21.50; 40. William McCranie $21.75; 41. Niel E. McCranie, $16.75; 42. John D. McCranie, $5.75; 43. Daniel McCranie, Sr., $15.00; 44. John McDermit, $27.75; 45. Norman McDonald, $26.00; 46. Malakiah Monk, $11.75; 47. William Monk, $9.00; 48. Rice Mathis, $7.25; 49. C. J. O'Neal, $2.00; 50. R. N. Parrish, $9.50; 51. A. A. Parrish, $10.50; 52. James Parrish, $16.50; 53. E. W. Parrish, $11.50; 54. Joseph Parrish,

$5.50; 55. Alexander Patterson, $15.55; 56. West Rountree, $17.20; 57. Thomas Rooks, $14.00; 58. D. C. Smith, $5.25; 59. Jona R. Varner, $5.25; 60. S. G. Williams, $13.50; 61. E. J. Williams, $7.50.

When a transcript of the pay roll was printed in *The Tifton Gazette*, J. L. Herring commented in part as follows (Sept. 23, 1898): "The following transcript of an old and interesting document was found by Mr. O. F. Sheppard's 12-year-old daughter, May, on the street near his residence one day last week . . .

"Besides being interesting as a relic of the Creek war of 1836, it contains the names of many of the fathers and grandfathers of the men who are now among the most honored citizens of Berrien . . .

"It should be a matter of no small pride to their descendants that so many volunteers of this Florida company were from what is now Berrien, attesting, in no small degree, to their bravery and daring."

* * * * * * *

Creeks are departing for their new home west of the Mississippi, where the United States Government is sending them. An old squaw on a ship disconsolately fumbles with her last reminder of her home in the east, a little bundle of her possessions. She opens and closes—opens and closes—the bundle. Tears roll down her cheeks, as she sings the pathetic notes,[26] "I have no more land; I am driven away from home, driven up the red waters; let us all go, let us all die together, and somewhere upon the banks we will be there."

Officials of a tribe of Creeks are walking in single file, carrying the sacred plates.[27] Another tribe is carrying the large conch shells which the Indians had used in the black drink during the Green Corn Festivals. A group is guarding some of the "town fire" from this beloved home in the East, so that they can keep the old home-fires burning in the West.

Oweeta, a beautiful Creek maiden, is roaming for the last time in her beloved woodland.[28] Sad things have happened since she has roamed in this spot. The "pale faces" have seized the Indian lands, and the poor Creeks can do nothing. William McIntosh, the chief of her tribe, has been murdered for signing a treaty.

She wanders down by the waters of Labothacossa at Indian Springs, Georgia, until she reaches a weather-beaten rock, where there is an outline of an arrow-pierced heart. Here she has spent many hours with her lover, Kotoomi, on this trysting rock; but now her people must leave—must leave their homes and journey to the West. How her heart aches to leave these beautiful hills and valleys, the whispering leaves, and the murmuring waters of the old stream as it ripples over rocks.

---

26. Debo's "Road to Disappearance" page 105 lines 35-36, page 106 line 1.
27. Ibid.
28. Scene based on "The Legend of the Bleeding Heart," by Josephine Jones, Atlanta Journal.

12   HISTORY OF TIFT COUNTY

Kotoomi had whispered, "The wild forest lands will continue on the other side of the big river—we'll have freedom in the West."

"Alas, the forest of the West will never be the forest of the East!" Oweeta exclaims sobbing, recalling his words, as she kisses the old rock, dear to her heart, and sadly turns to join the crowds of departing Indians.

* * * * * *

As the Creeks reach their new land, some of them prophesy with tears;[29] "We . . . are facing the evening of our existence and are nearly at the end of the trail that we trod when we were forced to leave our homes in Alabama and Georgia."

* * * * * *

Screen flashes Pleasant Porter, chief of Creeks at the end of the nineteenth century. He is the son of a white man and a squaw of the Perryman family. Standing before a Senate committee in 1906, Porter eloquently gives a farewell message:[30]

"The vitality of our race still persists. We have not lived for naught. We are the original discoverers of this continent, and the conquerors of it from the animal kingdom, and on it first taught the arts of peace and war, and first planted the institutions of virtue, truth, and liberty. The European nations found us here and were made aware that it was possible for men to exist and subsist here. We have given to the European people on this continent our thought forces—the best blood of our ancestors having intermingled with (that of) their best statesman and leading citizens we have made ourselves an indestructible element in their natural history. We have shown that what they believed were arid and desert places were habitable and capable of sustaining millions of people. We have led the vanguard of civilization in our conflict with them for tribal existence from ocean to ocean. The race that has rendered this service to the other nations of mankind can not utterly perish."

---

29. Debo's "Road to Disappearance" p. 106, lines 12-13-14-15.
30. Reproduced in "Road to Disappearance" by Debo, lines 16-30, page 377, from Creek Tribal Records, 35664; 59 Cong., Sen. Rep. No. 5013. I 627f.

CHAPTER II.

FOOTSTEPS OF "PALEFACES"

As the footsteps of "red men" fade, let us listen to near and distant tramps of early "palefaces" in our section of the new world. The first Europeans to leave tracks in the wire grass region were Hernando De Soto and his men. With soldiers, horses, hogs, weapons, handcuffs, chains, neck collars, and implements for digging gold, these Spaniards landed at Tampa Bay, Florida in 1539.

According to Lucian Lamar Knight in "Georgia Landmarks, Memorials and Legends," Vol. I, Sec. II, p. 1, these cavaliers, wearing handsome armor and bringing horses caparisoned, resembled more a cavalcade of knights than an adventurous band seeking treasures in the wilderness. "This little army," Jones, the historian said, (Vol. I, p. 38) "was composed of men accustomed to wars, skilled in the use of weapons and inured to hardships. Scarcely a gray head appeared among them." Twelve priests, eight clergymen, four monks, to convert the Indians, and men of letters to describe the events of the march were in the group.

The purpose of the expedition was to discover the wealth of the new world. After planting the flag of Spain in what is now Tampa, and claiming the country in the name of Charles V, De Soto marched northward.

In 1540 he and his men marched from Tallahassee, Florida, to Decatur, Georgia, on through original Irwin County to Laurens; he probably did not touch what is now Tift County.

Historians do not agree as to De Soto's route, but they generally concede that he came through Wire Grass Georgia.

The following is the itinerary according to Jones's "History of Georgia," Vol. I, p. 66.

March 3, 1540—Left Anhayea (Tallahassee).
March 7, 1540—Crossed a deep river (Ocklockony).
March 9, 1540—Arrived at Capachiqui.
March 21, 1540—Came to Toalli in Irwin County near the Ocmulgee.
March 24, 1540—Left Toalli.
March 25, 1540—Arrived at Achese, located in Wilcox County, near what is now Abbeville, on the Ocmulgee River.
April 1, 1540—Departed from Achese.
April 4, 1540—Passed through the town of Altamaca.
April 10, 1540—Arrived at Ocute in Laurens County.
April 12, 1540—Left Ocute. Passed through a town, whose lord was called Cofaqui, and came to the province of another land, named Patofa.
April 14, 1540—Departed from Patofa.
April 20, 1540—Lost in a pine barren. Six days consumed in fording two rivers (source of the Great Ogeechee).

April 26, 1540—Set out for Aymay, a village reached at nightfall.

April 28, 1540—Departed for Cutifachiqui (Silver Bluff on the Savannah River, 25 miles below Augusta).

May 3, 1540—Left Cutifachiqui (Cherokee, Georgia, probably in Franklin County).

May 15, 1540—Arrived at Xualla (Nacoochee Valley, near Mount Yonah).

May 20, 1540—Arrived at Gauxule (Coosawattee, Old Town in Murray County).

May 22, 1540—Arrived at Conasauga (New Echota in Gordon County).

June 5, 1540—Arrived at Chiaha, Rome, Georgia.

July 1, 1540—Departed from Chiaha.

The opinion of several historians is that De Soto devastating homes and crops, as he passed through settlements, was intensely cruel to the Indians. "Red men" at a village near the spot where Abbeville is now, entertained him despite his rude manner.

According to Dr. Walter Martin,[1] historian, the Spanish were sole claimers of this Southeastern section of the United States throughout the sixteenth century, during which time the Catholic friars converted many Indians to the Catholic faith. Spanish missions grew up in certain sections of South Georgia, and the priests at that time went into the forest trying to save the "red men's" souls.

After the Spanish and later the French, who sailed along[2] "the island-fringed edge of Georgia," came the footsteps of the English. Let us flash back to 1629 when[3] "Charles I gave to Robert Heath a grant of land, beginning south of Virginia at 36° and extending to 31° at the north tip of Cumberland Island." This region, which included all the territory from the mouth of the Chowan River in North Carolina almost to the present Georgia-Florida boundary line was named Carolina.[4] Our section of South Georgia was then a part of English Carolina rather than Spanish Florida.

The English and Spanish were then about to cross swords for territory. While these countries were disputing in 1733, came the footsteps of the great founder of Georgia, Oglethorpe. The Spanish at this time reclaimed all territory south of the Georgia Colony, the boundaries of which were the Savannah and Altamaha Rivers. The present South Georgia territory had reverted to the Spanish. Our section[5] "remained Spanish until 1763 when, at the close of the French and Indian Wars, England was given all territory east of the Mississippi River. Even Florida became English and for

---
1. "History of Tift County," published in The Tifton Gazette.
2. Coulter's "A Short History of Georgia," p. 4.
3. Ibid., p. 8.
4. Martin's "History of Tift County," published in Tifton Gazette.
5. Ibid 4.

the first time our section of South Georgia actually became a part of Georgia." St. Mary's River was the southern boundary line of Georgia.

Although at different times South Georgia was like a seesaw with Spain on one end, and England on the other, the rightful owners were the Indians until the United States Government effected treaties with the "red men."

To return to the footsteps of Oglethorpe, in 1729 he was chairman of a committee to investigate the debtor prisons. One reason for his keen interest was the fact that one of his friends was in one of the prisons. The investigation was the cause of the release of 10,000 prisoners, many of whom had little hope for the future after their release. Oglethorpe, therefore, suggested sending some of these debtors to America. After the charter was drawn and twenty-one persons, constituting a Board of Trustees, were appointed, the selection of people from reputable families was effected. These[6] "sober, industrious, and moral persons appeared before the trustees, signified their final desire to go and signed articles of agreements." Between one hundred fourteen and one hundred twenty-five men, women, and children stepped on the gangplank of the ship Anne, and later, on January 13, 1733, landed at Charleston, South Carolina.

On February 12, 1733, later designated as the birthday of Georgia, Oglethorpe and his people made footprints eighteen miles from the mouth of the Savannah River on a bluff, then occupied by Yamacraw Indians, a banished tribe of the Creeks, some of whom lived in what is now Tift County, and their chief was Tomochichi. Oglethorpe also found there the wife of John Musgrove, Mary, who being able to speak English, served as an interpreter. Here four tents in a picturesque grove of pines, and moss-draped magnolias and live oaks sheltered these colonists, who made the first settlement in the mainland of Georgia.

Thus[7] "Georgia had been set up not for debtors alone. The Trustees had a much broader vision; there was a place for fortunate Englishmen as well as unfortunate Englishmen; and there was even room for foreigners, with the state of their fortune no barrier to their entry."

* * * * * *

Now as we watch flashes of the "red men" on the screen of time, let us observe scenes presenting "pale faces" who have left tracks on our historical soil.

The screen flashes an event of 1735, when Oglethorpe returns from England, where he carried Tomochichi, his wife, Senauki, his nephew, and five Creek Chiefs with their attendants. On May 18, at ten o'clock in the morning, Oglethorpe finds that Mr. Wiggan, the interpreter, with the chief men of all the Lower Creek Nation has come for an alliance with the new colony.

---
6. Coulter's op. cit. p. 21.
7. Ibid., p. 23

Oglethorpe receives them in one of the new houses in Savannah. Several Indian chiefs speak and present gifts. Tomochichi, mico, now comes in with the Indians of Yamacraw, all of whom bow low to Oglethorpe, who with ingenious tact has won the friendship of the red people.

Tomochichi speaks: "I was a banished man; I came here poor and helpless to look for good land near the tombs of my ancestors, and the trustees sent people here; I feared you would drive us away, for we were weak and wanted corn; but you confirmed our land to us, gave us food and instructed our children. We have already thanked you in the strongest words we could find, but words are no return for such favors; for good words may be spoken by the deceitful and by the upright.

"The chief men of all our nation are here to thank you for us; and before them I declare your goodness, and that here I design to die; for we all love your people so well that with them we will live and die. We do not know good from evil, but desire to be instructed and guided by you, that we may do well with and be numbered amongst the children of the trustees."[8]

* * * * *

It is 1742. Oglethorpe's troops composed of regulars, Indians, and provincial troops are marching up and down the road which the colonist regiment cut through the center of St. Simons Island from Fort St. Simons to Frederica.

(Oglethorpe suffered defeat at St. Augustine with the Spaniards, and then marched his despondent men back northward. He lay ill of fever for two months at Frederica. Aware that the Spaniards were preparing to descend on Georgia, Oglethorpe strengthened his forts on the coast, maintained good relations with Indians, and called for assistance from the South Carolina troops, who refused. On July 4, 1742, Spaniards stood off St. Simons Sound, preparing to land on the island. They ran by Fort St. Simons with no difficulty and landed near Frederica.)

Screen flashes events of July 7.[9] Oglethorpe and his men are attacking the Spaniards as they march in a mile of Frederica. He captures the Spanish commander and kills or captures the most of the troop. The remnant retreat while Oglethorpe's Highlanders and others follow. Georgians reach an open glade and conceal themselves, while Oglethorpe returns to Frederica for reenforcements.

Another Spanish troop, arriving, attacks the ambushed Georgians, who flee. Oglethorpe meets these men on his return.[10] "A group of Highlanders under Lieutenants Southerland and Mackay suddenly execute a flank movement, get in the rear of the Spaniards and ambush another glade about

---

8. Tomochichi's speech from Political State of Great Britain Vol. 47 is reproduced in Cooper's History of Georgia, Vol I, page 157.
9. Scene based on facts from Coulter's op. cit., p. 46.
10. Ibid., p. 46.

two miles from Fort St. Simons." Spaniards march out into this glade, stack their guns, and prepare to rest on their laurels of victory. The Highlanders open fire, rush in to the open, and before the attack is over kill or capture two hundred Spaniards.

(This fight was later called the Battle of Bloody Marsh. According to Coulter in "A Short History of Georgia," page 46, this battle, though a minor engagement, helped to unnerve the main Spanish force and led to its ultimate return to Florida.)

CHAPTER III

FOOTSTEPS OF EARLY SETTLERS

The screen flashes events of 1800 through the "sixties." The time now is 1800. Listen to the reverberations of the axe, while "pale faces" in jeans and brogans are cutting down trees and clearing the land for shanties and farms. The scene shifts. Now several families, forced on account of dangerous Indians to work together in the Tallassee Country, are building their houses in a stockade. ("Tallassee is the name applied to this country by our Legislature in the Act of December 28, 1794. In various other places in the state papers where mention is made of this country it is called Tallassee, but Mr. Jefferson in his message to Congress 1802 calls it the Tallahassee Country. It embraces all of Southeastern Georgia except the counties of Glynn and Camden; the larger part, if not the whole of Southern and Southwestern Georgia was comprehended in it; much likewise of Middle Florida"—("Digest of the Laws of Georgia"—Watkins).

These men are representatives of the immigrants from Virginia, South Carolina, Maryland, and North Carolina.

Now men with their guns are hunting wild deer, birds, and turkeys. These men are not pleasure seekers; the forest is the main source of food except for the little farms, mere gardens, which these farmers till in groups on account of lurking bears, catamounts, and wolves.

It is midnight in Wire Grass Georgia. Vibrations of an unearthly howl startle a woman in a log cabin. A close-up shows terror in her eyes, as she awakens, dazed, and shakes her husband who is sleeping by her. She, in a sweeping yellow homespun gown, and he, in his long night shirt, jump out of bed and seize their guns. These immigrants are not yet accustomed to the howls of wolves in the forest.

Screen flashes events of 1803. There is a buzz in the Georgia Legislature. The Land Lottery Act, which provides for surveying of new lands at public expense, has just passed. The land is to be divided into lots of equal size, each of which is to be given a number. The numbers after being recorded will be written on individual slips, which are placed in a box.

It is 1818. The Act of the Georgia Legislature creating three new counties, Early on the west, Irwin in the center, and Appling on the east, are approved. The counties include the land obtained from Creeks in 1818 and Cherokees by the United States in the treaties of August 1814, at Fort Jackson, at the Cherokee Agency July 8, 1817, and at the Creek Agency on the Flint River, January 22, 1818.

(Irwin at this time embraced what is now Worth, Wilcox, Turner, Ben Hill, Tift, Colquitt, Thomas, Cook, Brooks, Berrien, Lowndes, Echols, Clinch, Lanier, Atkinson, Coffee, Ware, Charlton, Jeff Davis, Bacon, Pierce, and Brantley.)

Scene shifts, but the time is still 1818. According to the provision of the Act of 1818, based on the Land Lottery Act of an early date, Irwin has been surveyed into sixteen land districts and 6,500 lots. The drawing is being held, and a small grant fee, required from each grantee. Each man over eighteen years of age and a resident of the United States for at least three years can draw once. Extra provisions have been made for orphans, widows, and veterans.

Flashes come from Irwin County 1840-1850.

A farmer is loading his wagon with a bale of cotton, chickens, eggs, beeswax, tallow, and hides. While the wagon creaks along a sandy road, he slaps the lines on the old ox's back and hollers, "Git up, Sambo!" This farmer is taking his produce to the nearest town.

His return home after the long journey is a rare event to his family. His wife and children run to meet him and help bring in the packages. Gleefully the little boys and girls tear holes in the packages and peek at sugar, coffee, tobacco, and salt. Finally there are screams of delight; the wife has found a few yards of lace, ribbon, and calico, and the children, a few sticks of peppermint candy.

Mrs. Farmer is weaving on the loom the customary pattern of cloth, checks, for tablecovers, bedspreads, and children's dresses. Cotton has been carded and wound into thread, which came in large hanks from the reel. The thread after being dyed with home-grown indigo, pomegranate, walnut, or logwood and copperas is ready for the loom.

This scene is a log-rolling. The whole community has come to help Mr. Farmer get his land ready for plowing. Trees have been cut into convenient lengths of fifteen feet. Men have been divided into groups of nine, and the prize poles, carried by leaders, have been driven under the ends of the logs, which have been raised. Log-sticks of hickory or blackgum have been thrust under logs, which are being carried by four sturdy partners to a heap, where armfuls of limbs, bark, and lightwood are being thrown between spaces by the lads. Now the boys are lighting the pile; a fire is roaring in the forest.

Lads are carrying to the thirsty men drinking gourds in wooden buckets of water. The large brown jug is there, too, for the older men.

With ropes women are pulling down a quilting frame from the joists, where it hangs when not in active service. Now they are quilting and gossiping around the frame.

The dinner horn sounds a welcome message to the hungry men, who rush to the water shelf on the front porch. Admiring glances from the ladies do not hinder the hand scrubbing. Now the men are ushered into the sand-covered kitchen, where dinner is spread. The odor of collards and ham whets the appetites. After the blessing, the first shift enjoys eating collards, cornbred, chicken and rice, ham, pork, potato custard, pies, and cakes. Now the remainder of guests and the homefolk have their chance at the log-rolling dinner.

Boys and girls are singing on the way to a dance:
"Old Dan Tucker he got drunk
Fell in a fire and kicked up a chunk;
Red hot coals got in his shoe
Oh, good granny how the ashes flew.

"Cotton-eyed Joe with a tune from the South
Everywhere I go I hear his big mouth
I'd been rich a long time ago
If it hadn't been for knock-kneed Cotton-eyed Joe

"Irwin County gals, won't you come out tonight,
Come out tonight, come out tonight?
Irwin County gals, won't you come out tonight
And dance by the light of the moon?"

Garlands of wild flowers and branches of pines enliven this drab room in a loghouse, for it is a festive occasion, a dance. Men are smoking, or chewing and spitting tobacco juice, and the ladies are dipping snuff while watching the young folk play twistification to the accompaniment of

"Oh, come along, my pretty little miss
Come along my honey!
Oh, come along my pretty little miss
And don't go home till Monday.
You are my sugar and tea;

You are my darling;
And now I'll turn my sugar and tea
And now I'll turn my darling."

Fiddlers are tuning up. Now they are playing this song while the leader calls the couples to the floor:

"I wouldn't marry a pore gal
And I'll tell you the reason why;
Her neck is long and skinny,
And I'm afraid she'll never die.
Get along home, Cindy, Cindy;
Get along home, Cindy, Cindy;
Get along home, Cindy, Cindy;
There'll be room for a million more."

"Partners on the floor!" Four couples are arising. "First couple to the right; balance!" Lads and lassies are dancing before their opposites. "Swing." They are joining hands and swinging around. "Swing your corners!" Partners are swinging the nearest, right and left. "All promenade!" Partners are joining hands and promenading to their places. The four couples have made the circuit. "Gents to the right; ladies stand!" "Swing or cheat." Girls are turning their backs to partners. "All promenade!" Ladies to the center; right hands cross. Partners are circling. "Left hand back! Reverse." "Right hand to your partners; balance opposite!" "Swing!" "Balance your partner!" "Swing!" "Promenade All!" "Honor your cotillion; seat your partners."[1]

February 25, 1856. The Georgia Legislature has just passed the act to make a new county, Berrien, from Lowndes, Coffee, and Irwin.

The Sixties. A disconsolate woman in homespun stands on the steps of a log house. Her husband, one of the Irwin County Cowboys, in jeans and brogans has shouldered his gun and is ready to join the Grays. The woman's face is tear-stained, and her hands show marks of toil. The man has deep worry-lines on his brow and his lips are tight. A little boy in a homespun apron runs down the steps, grabs his father's leg, and squeezes it. Henry puts his arms around Nancy, kisses her goodbye, then picks up his little son, who is crying. Quickly the man puts the child down and says, "Be a man and take care of your mamma," then turns away.

[2]A band is playing "Dixie," as Company A, the first company of soldiers from Irwin, the Irwin County Cowboys, with J. Y. McDuffie, captain; George Willcox, first lieutenant; J. J. Henderson, second lieutenant; Wil-

---

1. "Saturday Night Sketches"—Herring.
2. History of Irwin County—J. B. Clements, p. 117.

liam Mathis, orderly sergeant, and Jacob Clemens, corporal, are marching off to battle. Women are waving their handkerchiefs with one hand and drying their tears with the other. Looking into the group of seventy soldiers, Nancy spots her husband, who bravely marches with the colors, and waves as long as she can see him.

1865. Weeds have grown high in the field, near the log cabin while Nancy has struggled with a garden to keep her children from starving. A little spot of butterbeans, potatoes, and cabbage is almost parched. Green corn stalks have lost their vigor and turned a dead brown. A weary Confederate soldier limps slowly up a winding path, almost closed by weeds. Dog fennels and wiregrass have grown in the yard, where flowers used to bloom. Nancy peeks through the shutters and glimpses her husband. She leaps to the front door and rushes to meet him. He grabs Nancy and takes her in his arms.

CHAPTER IV

FOUNDING OF TIFTON

A two-story building, formidable for its time, a commissary, where the clerk sold everything from fertilizer to earbobs, or "yearbobs," as the natives called them, stood at a little piney-woods flag station in the northwestern corner of Berrien County. It was the day of all days—Saturday. In oxcarts men and women with their children had ridden miles to sell produce, trade at the commissary, which was as important to them as Atlanta stores are to us now, and listen to the buzz of the sawmill, a curiosity in this community. Another attraction for the traders was the thrilling sight of an engine, puffing down the Brunswick and Albany Railroad nearby.

The two siren voices of the mill village were the train and mill whistles, which proclaimed the achievement of Tifton in the seventies. The latter whistle was the community clock, which regulated the habits of the population: folk awoke, ate, and slept by its sound.

The train whistle was an oddity, announcing an important arrival, so alluring that the entire community followed the signal and met the train. The crew, under no modern strain, leisurely stepped from the cars, enjoyed greeting the spectators, delivered or received packages, discussed crops or the weather, and exchanged "yarns." During the summer the train crew frequently stopped long enough for a watermelon cutting. Disregarding time tables, these men were in no hurry to leave Tifton.

The Brunswick and Albany was the first train many people in the wiregrass ever saw. It was Mr. Elias Branch's introduction to passenger and freight cars. When a little boy he came to Tifton from Chula and climbed a post to view the train. The engine puffing near his retreat frightened him so that he fell off the post.

To return to the pioneer traders, women dipping snuff and men chewing tobacco, sat on the front porch of the commissary, their rendezvous, between spells of trading, and gossiped. These families were identified by their patterns of calico, which previously had been bought in bolts for raiment. Babies in swaddling clothes, old women, and girls of the courting age were alike true to the calico scheme.

Between tobacco and snuff expectoration, the old folks from different families exchanged tales about "the good old days" and later ate their lunches of cheese, crackers, and sardines. Suddenly during their gossiping the buzz of voices ceased. The captain, owner of commissary and sawmill, was approaching. All classes, no matter how rough, held in high esteem this quiet, dignified man, who courteously recognized them, but who, like the Spectator, had little to say to anyone. Everybody stretched his neck to glimpse Captain Tift; this title was not only an expression of respect, but was an echo of the days when he piloted a Flint-River boat.

Commissary which Henry Harding Tift built in 1872

The captain had appeared and disappeared; the rural folk had exchanged their produce, traded, seen the train, listened to the sawmill and eaten their lunches. It was time to leave. Men untied oxen, which had waited under trees, and filled the carts with packages and families. Then the long journeys through the piney woods! These people would reach home before dark to escape the turpentine negroes, who were under the influence of "moonshine."

Tifton with its sawmill, commissary, and railroad was to the Wire Grass "Georgia Crackers" a cynosure. For days before and after the trip, they would discuss the mill village. "A happy woman, like a happy nation, has no history." Even in the seventies Tifton had made history. According to tradition, this tract of land had been traded for a shotgun; at another time, for a saddle, then for an ox. There is no tradition, however, about the fact that Tifton is located in the Sixth District of what was originally Irwin County and on parts of land numbers 290-291-308-309. The original Irwin County, from which Berrien was made, was surveyed into districts approximately twenty-three square miles, and the districts then were subdivided into lots seven eighths of one mile square, or 529 of such lots to the district. The lots were disposed of by the state by means of drawing, and a small grant fee exacted from the drawer.

It is certain that a man with some capital and a dream of a vast fortune, Abbott H. Brisbane, of Irwin County, after the original drawers had failed to pay the grant fees, paid them and took title to lots covering a vast territory, including the land where Tifton now stands. In 1840 Jones Lee, a resident of the Flint-River section, organized a company with the intention of attempting to build a railroad from Mobley's Bluff, then head of navigation on the Ocmulgee, to Albany, on the Flint.

"This company," according to U. B. Phillips in History of Transportation in the Eastern Cotton Belt pp. 273-274, "is notable chiefly for its irresponsible character and its experience with a gang of Irish laborers. A. H. Brisbane, its engineer agent, and later its president and general factotum, was a personage worthy of a place in literature. In some way, whether by service, courtesy, or presumption he had acquired the title of general. He had a peculiar gift of plausibility, a talent for oratory, and a passion for eulogizing all men and affairs with which he was associated. The climate of Irwin County, then in portions oppressively hot and malarious in actuality, was bracing and healthful in his description and sure to attract people over his railroad to summer resorts on the route. The gangs of Irish immigrants, which by some hook or crook he had enticed into the piney woods wilderness to grade his moneyless railroad were in his words 'several parties of the choicest white laborers'."

Late in 1841 when the grading of the road was two-thirds complete, the directors of the Ocmulgee and Flint River Railroad managed to save themselves from complete bankruptcy by borrowing five thousand dollars from the city of Savannah. "Brisbane now hit upon a new idea. He appealed to the Catholic prelates for charity on behalf of the starving Irish laborers, whom the company was unable to pay or feed. Aid came in response from Bishop England at Charleston and Bishop Hughes, of New York. This, however, was hardly a sound basis for railroad progress." (Loc. Cit.)

By 1843 the company was hopelessly in debt, but "Brisbane, with his talent, was still able to describe the situation as hopeful. But a short while afterwards the starving Irish mutinied and beat Brisbane with stones and cudgels. Brisbane fled for his life, and that is the end of the Ocmulgee and Flint River Railroad story. Not a rail was ever laid upon it." (Ibid., pages 274-275.)

Many of the Irish laborers settled in the wire grass country, and from this source many of our best citizens have come. Take for example J. M. Duff, Tifton's postmaster for several years; Brisbane brought Duff's father to South Georgia. Other descendants of these laborers have proved too that Brisbane was partly right when he called his railroad gangs "several parties of the choicest white laborers."

Discouraged probably for the first time in his life, the "general" attempted to get rid of his worthless land holdings. On February 28, 1844, he sold to Abbott B. White for $200—less than five cents an acre—ten lots in the Sixth District of Irwin County. Nelson and A. F. Tift bought the same land, then in Berrien county, on May 5, 1860. H. H. Tift later bought this tract of 4,900 acres for $10,000 from his uncles, Nelson and A. F. Tift.

Henry Harding Tift worked for five years as a marine engineer on lines operating between New York and Southern coast ports. In 1869 Nelson Tift, needing an expert machinist in the N. and A. F. Tift Manufacturing Company of Albany, Georgia, wrote his nephew, Henry Harding Tift and persuaded him to come South. From the beginning the young man was an asset to his uncle's business. Tift's alertness and efficiency were rewarded when the young man was made general manager of the manufacturing company. Soon, however, envisioning possibilities in another direction, Henry left his uncle to come to the piney woods of Berrien County. Crossing the Flint River was for him and this wire grass section of Georgia another crossing of the Rubicon.

In 1872 when he came to Berrien County to build his sawmill, Tift "picked up" his shanty and rode. The shanty was conveyed on a flat car, and his machinery, bought from Thomas Henry Willingham, was drawn by eight oxen from the village, Willingham, near Macon. (An interesting romantic touch is associated with the machinery because the former owner of it was the father of Bessie Willingham, who later became Mrs. H. H. Tift.) For several months Henry had to live a "rough and tumble" life, but the power to endure was a marked trait of his character.

In the beginning Tift named his village Lena for his sweetheart far away in Connecticut. George Badger, who worked at the sawmill, resolving to be the first to honor the founder of the village, climbed a pine tree and nailed a placard with bold letters TIFTON, a condensation of Tift's Town.

The news of the sawmill was received with great interest at Riverside, a little station a few miles away. The merchants of Riverside, tired of waiting for the trade that never came, decided to move east. Soon after the completion of the mill, John Higdon and William S. Walker moved their store to the mill village, which the railroad recognized as a loading station. A little later a Jew store at Riverside was also moved to Tifton.

A steady growth at the mill continued for the next few years. Each year, in fact, showed such a marked improvement that in 1879, Captain Tift bought an engine and built his first tram road. In the meantime there had been business changes in Tifton. The Jew had gone. In 1876 Jack Turner, who came to Tifton from Brookfield and went into partnership with James Fletcher, succeeded Higdon and Walker, who had moved their store to Alapaha.

One of the distinctive marks of the seventies was the continued growth of the Brunswick and Albany Railroad. Upon the success of the railroad depended the success of the mill. The lumber and naval stores business had increased so much that in 1879 the number of trains had doubled. A train was operated every day except Sunday. Before 1879 the train went to Albany on Mondays, Wednesdays, and Fridays; to Brunswick, on Tueslays, Thursdays, and Saturdays. The name of the railroad had been changed from the Brunswick and Albany to the Brunswick and Western.

The transportation of passengers and freight was a small part of the railroad business at that time. The growing lumber and naval stores business vitally affected the Brunswick and Western Railway. A time book kept by W. F. Barkuloo, of Brunswick, now in the hands of his nephew, O. V. Barkuloo, of Tifton, gives the following records for February 24, 1879:
Brunswick and Western Passengers

Brunswick to Hazlehurst	1—	$1.50
Brunswick to Waynesville	1—	1.25
Brunswick to Albany	1—	5.00
Waynesville to Waycross	1—	1.75
Waynesville to Satilla	1—	.50
Randolph to Waycross	2—	1.00
Waycross to Alapaha	1—	2.50
Waycross to Riverside	1—	3.50
Waycross to Waresboro	2—	1.00
Willacoochee to Brookfield	1—	1.00
Brookfield to Riverside	1—	.50
Riverside to Ty Ty	1—	.50
Ty Ty to Albany	2—	3.00
		$22.00

On the same day the train carried the following freight at the rate stated:

Waynesville	$ 3.68
Prentice	3.02
Pearson	2.33
Alapaha	9.00
Hoboken	1.20
Tifton	8.74
Sumner	10.62
	$38.59

On February 27, 1879 the report of the Western trip of a lumber train is:

Left Brunswick _____ 2:00 a.m.
Arrived Riverside _____ 10:20 a.m.
Left Riverside _____ 11:00 a.m.

Cars number 6, 44, 29, 8, 17, 45, 23, 5, 46, 16, 4, 47, 18, 12, 3, from Brunswick to Riverside.

Loaded at Tifton 9 for (i.e. consigned to) D. C. Bacon. 6 for Cook Brothers.

Time loading 2¼ hours.

The loading time of two hours seems unusually long until one realizes that Tifton had no sidetrack then. When Mr. Tift was ready to ship lumber, he blew a whistle that called to the mill all hands, who with the train crew loaded the cars.

In 1879 Tifton was still merely a spot in the road. Ty Ty, although smaller than it is now, was the metropolis of this part of the wiregrass.

The salient topic for conversation during part of this period was the famous Little River wreck. The passenger train west-bound on the Brunswick and Western (now the Atlantic Coast Line) left Tifton after nightfall late as usual. The bridge across the Little River, three miles west of Tifton, was much longer than it is now. As the train was rolling on to the eastern end of the bridge, the trucks of the combined mail and baggage car jumped the rails, and the first and second-class passenger cars followed. These cars fell nearly thirty feet into the river below and smashed on the logs and stumps of what was once the swamp. The forward cars were in two feet of water while only the rear of the first-class car rested on the bank.

"Why half of the passengers and train crew were not killed is hard to understand. Yet everyone escaped alive and there were only a few minor scratches and bruises. Perhaps this condition was due to the fact that at that time nearly all trains slowed at bridges. The engineer stopped when he found he had no train and backed up near the scene. The conductor and crew crawled out of the baggage cars and went to the assistance of the passengers who were making more noise than a negro revival at the hallelujah stage . . .

"After much hard work, the passengers were all released from the wreck, many of them being pulled through the narrow windows of the upper sides of the overturned cars. A big fire was built of crossties on the river bank, and there the men, women, and children were huddled to dry. There were only two white women on board, an aged grandmother and a young wife with a baby. The comfort of these was given first attention.

"The engine and tender went on to the nearest telegraph office, and the wrecking train was called. At Riverside, a mile east of the wreck, there was a water tank, and help was called from there, as well as with the aid of a pole-car the white passengers were carried across the bridge during the early morning hours, and ultimately got on their way, nearly a day late.

"The wreck was a subject for fireside talks for the country side for many months. People miles away insisted that they heard the crash, and everybody for ten miles around took a holiday next day and visited the scene. It was several days before the track was clean." (John L. Herring, The Tifton Gazette, July 25, 1919.)

Occasionally now old timers chuckle over one incident in the wreck. The engineer peered through one of the windows to get the lay of the land before attempting to bring passengers out. In one corner of the car he saw an old woman apparently doubled up with pain. He called her, but she made no answer. Perhaps the poor old soul was dead, he thought. Since the passenger car lay on its side, it was necessary for the engineer to climb to an open window before he could get into the car. Dropping inside, he rushed to the aged woman. If she were dying he hoped to rescue her before the last breath. If she were still alive perhaps he could save her. Putting his hand on her shoulder he shook her gently. The old lady turned her head and her cold blue eyes pierced his face as she replied, "Leave me be, son, leave me be. Ain't it enough to shake my pipe outer my mouth without trying to keep me from finding it?"

CHAPTER V
WIRE GRASS IN THE EIGHTIES

Boys in jeans and girls in gingham were playing gleefully in the yard that surrounded a little pine-board house. Some of the "scholars" were playing townball; some were dropping the handkerchief; others were riding saplings. From the schoolhouse to the deep woods was but a step; in fact, balls often lodged in the trees of the forest. The clang of a cow bell! Children scattered and rushed to "books," for recess had ended.

This little house was a distinctive and versatile addition to the sawmill village in the eighties, because it was the setting for the Three R's, "taught to the tune of a hickory stick," the scene of trials in the justice of peace court, ice cream festivals, and sermons. This shack, which stood near what is now the Primitive Baptist Church, had meager furnishings: hard military benches with no backs, a rough table for the teacher, and wooden shutters, which threw a gloom over the room in rainy weather. Then the little children, like the lightning bug, had to flash their own light.

During the early part of the eighties there were two other houses that had no connection with the sawmill, a small shack that stood on an acre of ground in the northern part of the village and a widow's home in what is now the southwestern part of Tifton.

There was in the village also stronger moonshine than the kind that entices lovers; a saloon stood on a strip of land that was not for sale. Tifton's father and his brother bitterly opposed the sale of liquor, but could not stop it. Although the flag station was only a rough spot in the woods, the prophetic eye could envison a progressive town.

"In 1880 Georgia exported 570,000 gallons of turpentine and 92,000 barrels of resin and pitch, for the first time threatening to rival North Carolina . . ." (Roswell Earle Smith's unpublished manuscript) Georgia was also filling a very important place in the lumber industry. Tifton in the center of a vast turpentine and lumber section was obliged to grow. A decided improvement during this period was a sidetrack on the Brunswick and Western Railroad. Soon afterwards a post office with W. O. Tift postmaster and a telegraph with W. W. Pace as operator, were established in the commissary.

The growing business in lumber and naval stores meant increased prosperity to the little towns in the wire grass. It, however, meant something else: Southwest Georgia became as rough as the western frontier. Before the advent of the turpentine industry in Georgia, this section was peaceful, and the majority of citizens, honest. It is true that some ruffians were employed at sawmills, but living in towns, they were more or less isolated. The turpentine gangs, on the other hand, spread over a wider territory.

Native South Georgians, therefore, began carrying pistols for protection; in fact, weapons were a part of the costumes. N. L. Turner, who was one of the best informed of the old settlers, said that he could identify his friends by the sound of their pistols as we identify now by the honk of automobile horns. Men carried pistols to town, parties, and to church.

Captain Tift was careful about selecting sober men for mill hands, but not all sawmill and turpentine men were as careful as he. Consequently when the sawmill and turpentine bullies, with their disrespect for law and their money for buying liquor, mingled with the pistol-carrying natives, there was combustion.

Despite the conscientious efforts of H. H. Tift, W. O. Tift, and other reputable citizens, life in Tifton was uncertain. A short time before his death W. O. Tift made the statement that there were a few Saturday nights in the early eighties when a man was not killed in the town. Mrs. Katherine Tift Jones, his daughter who has achieved international fame as an interpreter of negro dialect, when a little girl lived in Tifton. She remembers that her parents would not allow her to leave home on Saturday. The late Enoch Bowen, who owned a store in Tifton fifty-eight years ago, said that four men received fatal blows near his store during his first two years here. Men fought for fun. Bowen, a peaceful gentleman, used his iron safe as a barricade when the shooting began and came out of his hiding place when the excitement ended.

During this period the little school house was the scene of a tragedy. On a sweltering day in 1882 Judge J. J. F. Goodman, justice of peace for the 1314 District, Georgia Militia, called his court together in a session. The building was filled to capacity when court opened: the crowd that chose the court term for business was there and a large group who had come out of curiosity; for rumors of serious trouble had spread.

"Harrell and Guest, Martin Harrell and G. W. Guest, operated a turpentine still about two miles east of Tifton, and a little farther on G. B. Mayo and Company had a loading place on the railroad for their naval stores plant, which was out a mile or so in the woods. Between these two, troubles arose of a source only too common—negro labor—and when it had reached an acute stage, litigation over some timber added fuel to the flame; this growing out of a disputed land line . . . Harrell and Guest took out a possessory warrant for the timber against Mayo and Company. Later a letter written to G. B. Mayo, signed by Harrell, who was the active member of the firm, in which it is said some very abusive language was used. Tradition has it that this letter was written by Jordan, bookkeeper for Harrell, but it was shown by him to Harrell, who signed it. It was what Mayo said when he received the letter that led people to expect trouble." . . . J. L. Herring "The Tifton War." . . . The Tifton Gazette, March 22, 1916.

Trouble did come, for pistol shots broke up the court and wounded or killed several people. "The next week the justice of peace resigned his commission, applied for license to preach, and a short time afterwards organized the Tifton Methodist church in the same pine shack which was once the seat of war" . . . Tifton Gazette.

As the years passed the town knew less of violent crime. No institution probably has contributed so much to the civilization of the Tift County section as the church. Probably the oldest Baptist church in this section is the Zion Hope Baptist church organized in 1877 by the Reverend W. W. Webb. After the organization of this Missionary Baptist church, no churches were organized in the vicinity of Tifton for several years, although visiting ministers occasionally served various settlements. The Methodist Episcopal Church of Tifton was organized by J. J. F. Goodman. The members were J. J. F. and Rhoda Goodman, their son, J. O. Goodman, John B. and Julia A. Greene, Mrs. J. E. Knight, and her mother, Mrs. Anderson. Except for the pastor the church was organized with only two male members.

The shanty in which the church was organized was burned, and in 1884 a larger building was erected near what is now the intersection of Tift Avenue and Fourth Street. The first floor was used for a school and church; and the second floor, as a Masonic hall. In 1887 this building was also burned by an incendiary.

H. H. Tift contributed lots for a church and a parsonage, and in 1888 workmen began building a wooden structure, which was to cost $2,000, on the site of the present Methodist church building and finished it in 1889. Three attempts to burn this building were made during the process of construction; but after this first attempt, church members guarded the building. The incendiary was shot and wounded by one of the guards.

The church at first was a mission of the Alapaha circuit. The first board of trustees was composed of J. E. Knight, J. I. Clements, and Thomas M. Green, the uncle of Miss Leola Greene, now a veteran newspaper writer.

In 1884 the Baptists of this section became active again and organized the New River Baptist Church. The Reverend W. W. Webb and the Revertnd W. F. Cox took a prominent part in the organization. About this time the Tifton Baptists organized a church called Mt. Hermon. This church, the name of which later changed to the First Baptist Church of Tifton, originally had five members. J. K. Graydon was the first clerk. The members of Mt. Hermon met on alternating Sundays in the Methodist Building. There was no regular Baptist preacher until 1890.

Besides the churches, school, and citizens already mentioned, several new people added interest to the town during the eighties. In 1880 John Burwell Greene and his family came from Taylor County to Tifton. Traveling in a covered wagon, drawn by oxen, the Greenes stopped at an old mill in Coffee County and camped one night. Miss Leola Greene, one of Greene's children, though just five years old at that time, remembers the trip. Thomas Mitchell, who was postmaster part of this period had preceded his brother John B., to Tifton. In 1883 J. M. Williford, of Macon County, came to a farm four miles from Tifton and lived here until his death in 1924.

Jack Golden came in 1885; prior to this date he had lived a while at Riverside, a small settlement three miles west of Tifton. When twelve years old he attended school in Tifton, and later when sixteen years old came to work at H. H. Tift's sawmill. After working here a while, Golden owned a drug store with Jake Paulk and Dr. N. Peterson, then with Mr. Pete Strozier. Mr. Golden's work was later in Love and Buck's General Store, then in a machine shop. He entered the hardware business in 1902.

The late Enoch Bowen moved from Brookfield to Tifton in 1887 and bought the store that W. W. Pace had operated. The stock varied from pins and matches to coffins. Bowen was also railroad and express agent. One Christmas during this period one hundred twenty-two jugs of liquor were unloaded at the express office. He began the undertaking business in 1888 and was a licensed embalmer in 1895. This business is the oldest one in Tift County and the only one to bear the Bowen name.

C. C. Guest, who came to Tifton in 1889, clerked in Bowen's store. He boarded with J. I. Clements until the latter became manager of the Sadie Hotel. Guest remembers his first meals at this hotel.

C. W. Fulwood in 1888 moved from Alapaha to Tifton, where he opened the first law office in the town.

In addition to the churches, the building contributions to Tifton were Captain Tift's home in 1885 and the Sadie Hotel in 1889. These buildings allured sightseers far and near. The Tift residence at that time was palatial to the natives of the wire grass and other sections. J. L. Phillips built the Sadie Hotel in 1889; containing fifty rooms it was rare then. This hotel was headquarters for many "drummers," who if in this section would arrange to spend the night in Tifton.

The climax of the eighties for Southwest Georgia was an event on November 25, 1888. The little town in the wildwoods was the gayest it had ever been. Whites, blacks, storekeepers, clerks, sawmill men, turpentine men, "bosses," women, and children feeling the spirit of the day had gathered for the celebration. Since August when the laying of the rails north and south of Tifton had begun, the town had longed to see that engine and hear a new whistle. At last, this engine was puffing an announcement of an introduction of a new era—the arrival of the first passenger train on the Georgia Southern and Florida!

CHAPTER VI
"THE GAY NINETIES"

It was the day of crinoline, leg o'mutton sleeves, psyche knots, tableaux, hops, shadow parties, the first Tifton tobacco, exhibits at the midsummer fair in the Garden Empire City, and chautauquas. It was a day of progress—the "gay nineties." The Georgia-Southern and Florida Railway and the Sadie hotel had significant roles in this drama of social and business progress. In Tift County now are people who remember the first Georgia-Southern and Florida engine that puffed down Tifton rails and the gay events at the Sadie Hotel.

The men who supported the G. S. and F. were primarily interested in the land along their right of way. Knowing the value of the lumber, they advertised that the best pine timber in Georgia was in their territory. Then they said to the sawmill men and manufacturers, "If you will buy the machinery, we will haul it free and will furnish without rental such sidetracks as you need." This liberal policy brought results. "By 1890 Georgia exported 7,251,000 gallons of turpentine and 841,000 barrels of resin and pitch and by 1900, 14,600 gallons of turpentine and 1,409,000 barrels of resin and pitch, completely eclipsing North Carolina and becoming the foremost naval stores state in the union." (Rosewell Earle Smith, op. cit.) The Georgia-Southern and Florida Railroad was partly responsible for the vast increase.

Tifton had a vital reaction to the new railroad; new business men moved to the wiregrass town and a period of building began. E. Gibson, M. W. Gaskins, I. S. Bowen, O. M. Tift, and the Padrick brothers built general stores in Tifton. Dr. J. C. Goodman built the Tifton Drug Store in 1889. In 1890 C. A. Williams erected the town's first brick building for his livery stables. Soon there was a brick drug store, occupied by Peterson and Paulk. With W. A. Henderson's furniture store and H. H. Tift's addition of hardware to his stock, Tifton was becoming versatile.

By 1890 a number of business men had built homes in Tifton and had brought their families here to live. On December 29, 1890, the town was incorporated by act of the legislature. The Tift property lying within the incorporated limits was laid off in blocks, and lots were placed for sale. W. H. Love, claim agent for the Brunswick and Western was elected first mayor. Aldermen H. H. Tift, E. P. Bowen, B. T. Allen, J. C. Goodman, J. A. Alexander, and J. A. McCrea completed the personnel of the first city council.

There appeared in the "Albany Herald" during 1892 an article about Tifton by a correspondent who signed himself Jay Ell Aitch, John L. Herring. Excerpts from the article are: "This little city, which five years

CAMP FIRE GIRLS OF THE NINETIES

Mrs. W. W. Banks, who organized the Camp Fire Girls, is in the center of second row

ago consisted of a still, sawmill, and depot, now has 1,200 inhabitants, eleven business houses, two restaurants, a good market, one of the best hotels in Southwest Georgia, an academy building, costing $3,200, which has about ninety pupils in attendance, a Methodist Church costing $2,200. Added to this it has a mayor and council who are working like beavers to improve their town, and a host of citizens who are ably seconding their efforts . . . When the city was laid out, no real estate was sold unless the purchaser agreed to erect a first class building thereon, and no land in the city is sold to negroes."

The business houses of Tifton depended mainly upon the lumber and naval stores industries for trade during the nineties. There were in or near Tifton seven large mills: Cecil Lumber Company, Oglesby Brothers, Adel Investment Company, Beckwith and Rogers, H. H. Tift, Weston and Gunn, and S. R. Weston and Son. These mills running at full time gave employment to about one hundred hands each, seven hundred in all. Besides, there were a number of smaller mills employing about twenty-five hands each. There were nineteen turpentine farms, employing an average of sixty hands each or a total of one thousand one hundred-forty.

No lumber town exceeded Tifton in progress; this rank was due to the prominence and intelligence of H. H. Tift. Soon after the formation of the Georgia Lumber Exchange, Captain Tift was elected president of the organization, and Tifton made temporary headquarters. "The Northwest Lumberman," a magazine of national prominence, recognized H. H. Tift's ability: "Captain Tift will soon complete a large shingle mill and will ship Georgia yellow pine shingles into Connecticut and other eastern states. Once introduced, they will hold their own against all others." Captain Tift was referred to as "the moving and controlling genius of this region."

Besides the new railroad, the Sadie Hotel was a vital factor in the progress of Tifton. "Drummers" when traveling anywhere near the "gate city to South Georgia and Florida" would arrange to spend a while at this hotel. The train crew and passengers on the Georgia-Southern and Florida train ate lunch every day at the "Sadie."

This hotel was built by Captain J. L. Phillips and named for his daughter, who, according to comments in the Gazette, must have been a lovely character. During the nineties Tifton was very cosmopolitan: people from Indiana, Ohio, Illinois, Pennsylvania, California, Tennessee, and Mississippi lived in the little city. These people with other Tiftonites entertained frequently with whist parties, teas, dances, kimono parties, and suppers. One lady, who lived in the country, would kill two birds with one shot: in evening attire she would bring a load of potatoes in a wagon to sell before attending a party.

The elaborateness of the various entertainments was in harmony with the gay spirit of the charming little town. The Tifton Gazette of 1892 referred to a complimentary hop given by W. H. Love, first mayor of Tifton. Shadow parties were also among the styles of entertainment: gentlemen chose their partners as ladies appeared behind sheet screens. Often the Sadie Hotel parlor vibrated with laughter when belles and beaux learned the various choices.

"The Sadie," although commodious for that time, had only one bathroom, and hotel guests had to pay a quarter for a bath. One time a careless gentleman had allowed his bill to accumulate so much that the proprietor of the hotel after several warnings locked the man in the bath room as security for the debt. The water prisoner was released when a collection was taken for the amount owed.

No phase of life was neglected at "The Sadie," which was not only a social rendezvous, but the scene of literary events. The first history club in Tifton, organized by Mrs. W. W. Banks, met sometimes in the hotel parlor.

The designer for the fashionable gowns worn on these occasions and later was Mrs. Annie Bennet, a needle artist. Many nights the whirr of her machine announced tucks—tucks—ruffles for sunbursts shirtwaists and dresses. Light from her lamps often streamed from her windows at midnight.

Speaking of styles, the Tifton Gazette of 1892 quoted invectics against crinoline and hoopskirts as strong as the protests later against short skirts. A bill was introduced into the legislature prohibiting manufacture and sale of hoopskirts. In the Kentucky legislature there was a bill to prohibit "the manufacture, loan, and wearing of the monstrosities. Fair ones will not be allowed to make balloons of themselves without protests." One of the "hairdos," the psyche, was criticized then as much as bobbed hair later.

The Tifton Gazette of 1892 also gave a quaint description of a leap-year party: "Last night was a conspicuous evening with fair ladies of Tifton, who essayed to give a leap-year party worthy of their rushing little city.

"The events transpired at Park's Hall, and by 9 o'clock the hall was crowded with the youth, beauty, and chivalry of the little city and a number of ladies and gentlemen from abroad. A colored string band from Cordele furnished music. Dancing was indulged in to a late hour, when a recess was taken and dainty refreshments served at the Suwannee Restaurant. After which dancing continued until wee small hours."

The church grounds were often the scene of ice cream festivals—genuine ice cream made of eggs and milk. Churns of custard were frozen and sold with genuine pound cake. Little girls in gay, frilled dresses, carried waiters filled with bouquets for sale. Beaux would buy bouquets for ten cents or a quarter and present to their sweethearts. Expensive corsages were unknown then, and girls enjoyed home-made nosegays as much as girls now enjoy their orchids. Money collected for ice cream and flowers was added to the building fund.

This fund, too, was increased by box suppers, where boxes of delicious food were auctioned with the gusto of modern tobacco auctioneers.

Another attraction, social and educational, was the chautauquas, where there appeared pianists, violinists, singers, and lecturers. The Bowen Opera House, where the artists presented their programs, was the scene of fashionable displays also; for ladies attending wore their best clothes, even decollete gowns.

Bowen's Opera House, which was over what is now Rowe's store had a conspicuous place in the nineties and later. Many celebrities spoke or performed inside those walls: Sam Jones, General John B. Gordon, and Dewey Heywood's New York Stars were among the number.

A crude type of the movie was introduced at the opera house during this period. Two incidents are associated with this movie. One night several boys were watching the picture of a train moving down the track. Suddenly it flashed larger and seemed to be moving toward the audience. The boys reeled back and fell out of their seats. On another occasion a villain was playing the leading part in a picture. A negro sat there watching the fiendish acts, growing more angry every minute, until he shot the villain on the screen.

Besides these programs, Tifton often presented its own talent on the stage. A typical program was given on November 4, 1892:

Vocal quartette—Come Where My Love Lies
Tableau—On the Fence
Vocal solo—Miss Jackson
Tableau—The Stitch of Love
Vocal solo—Mr. Julian Cole
Tableau—The Five Foolish Virgins
Instrumental solo—Mr. H. J. Brinson
Tableau—Coming Through the Rye
Vocal solo—Mrs. H. H. Tift
Tableau—At the Shrine of St. Agnes
Vocal solo—Mr. E. H. Tift

The entire program was concluded with a laughable cantata of the grasshopper.

A good example of the literary club programs of the day was given in February 1895: Reading from Tennyson—Miss Williams; Song—Harriet Goodman; Recitation—J. G. Padrick; Reading. "Essay on Man"—F. G. Boatright; Song—Misses Katie and Harriet Goodman and Catherine Tift; Duet—Misses Baynard; Recitation—Miss Florrie Smith.

Among the favorite sports of the period were bicycle and surrey riding.

Bicycle races were even a feature of the fair. The Tifton Gazette referred to Dr. N. Peterson, J. J. Golden, and F. G. Boatright's bicycle races. Golden took first prize for two minutes and fifty-nine seconds. Peterson came second with a score of three minutes and eleven seconds. Ladies and girls rode bicycles. Mr. J. A. Sibley was very generous with his surrey; he frequently took his friends for a ride.

Tobacco cultivation, destined to reach the throne in Tift County, began in the nineties. In 1892, however, the editor of the Gazette warned farmers not to be too much excited about tobacco. During this year one thousand pounds of tobacco were made to the acre in Tift. The Midsummer Fair exhibited tobacco, vegetables, and fruits.

Although farming was a subordinate industry and in an early state, this section had promoters of agriculture. In 1892 a temporary land association headed by H. H. Tift as president and J. F. Wilson as secretary was formed with 150,000 acres represented. The purpose of the organization was to "Thoroughly and intelligently advertise this section of the state throughout the west and northwest, inviting farmers of that less favored section to come, abide in lower Georgia, and be happy." Real estate agents from other states for example, C. C. S. Baldridge, located in South Georgia and tried to get their friends at home to move to the wiregrass.

Various farmers surrounding Tifton were the scenes of valuable experiments in raising fruit trees and grape vines. At one time it seemed that this section might be recognized as a peach center, for the Tift-Snow farm had developed one of the best small orchards in the state. In 1894 there were in the vicinity of Tifton the following peach orchards: Tift and Snow, 60,000 trees; W. O. Tift, 12,000; H. Holdane, 5,000; A. F. Hoffman, 3,000; W. S. Louther, 3,000; E. H. Tift, 3,000; W. H. Mallory, 10,000; and C. H. Goodman, 2,000. There were 60,000 grape vines on the Tift Brothers' farm. In 1896 Tifton was given recognition as a fruit town when J. A. Sibley and W. O. Tift were elected secretary and treasurer—respectively of the Georgia Fruit Growers' Association. In 1894 Tifton's peach market exceeded that of Fort Valley.

One of the biggest factors in encouraging an interest in farming during the nineties was the Cycloneta farm, established by Willie B. Sparks, in connection with the Georgia, Southern and Florida Railroad. The land, which was donated by H. H. Tift, was used as an experiment station to show the possibilities of the soil. The officials of the G. S. & F. went to the trouble and expense to attract farmers to this section and to improve those who were already here with the importance of diversification. Large parties of Pennsylvanians, Ohioans, and others came to South Georgia to inspect the Cycloneta (now Sunsweet) farm, and it was largely through the efforts of Willis B. Sparks that many outsiders located in Wire Grass Georgia. The settlement known as Little Pennsylvania, located two miles north of Tifton was different; it was the result of the success of two Pennsylvanians in this section, U. S. Louther and A. F. Hoffman.

Four miles southeast of Tifton there was also a Swedish settlement, which included twelve frugal and industrious families of the best class of Swedes. A hundred acres of land were cultivated here by Andy Lundquist, for whom the settlement was named Lumville.

After a trip into South Georgia in 1892, Harry Stillwell Edwards, later a writer of international renown, wrote a letter to the Atlanta Constitution. Excerpt from letter follows: "All admit that the competition of Mississippi, Arkansas, and Texas will eventually destroy the cotton business of Georgia; overproduction has already crippled it. And some day the magnificent pine forests will all be gone and with them the lumber business. If tobacco as a profitable crop and the manufacture of tobacco as a business can take the place of these, the state will grow rich, instead of poorer."

Southwest Georgia did give great promise in tobacco during the nineties. The experiments in the growing and curing of tobacco on the Cycloneta farm—Cycloneta was named for a cyclone that swept that spot—and the donation of tobacco seed by G. S. and F. influenced many farmers to experiment with the bright leaf variety. The only problem was the lack of a suitable market. John Haralson in 1896 introduced home-consumption by establishing a small cigar factory, but his enthusiasm was short lived. Difficulties in marketing caused interest to wane and finally stopped the cultivation.

Despite the Gazette and the Cycloneta farmers' attempts to make the farmers of this section diversify their crops, despite the fact that the Tifton Canning and Manufacturing Company stood in constant need of truck products, King Cotton ruled the farming industry in this section with even a firmer hand than in the present day. Of course, there is much more cotton produced now than there was at that time, for farming has replaced the lumber and naval stores business as the most important industry.

From the beginning, the Tifton Gazette sponsored worthy campaigns; the diversification of farming was only one of them. In April 1891, B. T. Allen established in Sparks a weekly newspaper called the Berrien County Pioneer. In October of that year he moved his paper to Tifton, changing its name to the Tifton Gazette. The earliest copy of the Gazette now available is the issue of January 22, 1892.

For several years after the founding of Tifton, the schools here were very poor—cold and bare log cabins where teachers, not well trained, attempted to drill the fundamentals of reading, writing, and arithmetic into the heads of indifferent "scholars," who learned to the tune of the hickory stick. Teachers received six or seven cents a day for each student.

About 1898 the little building that served as school house and Masonic hall was burned by some enemy of education. After this fire Tifton parents were left without a school. Not many of them could afford to send their children to a boarding school, and most of the town people were eager to give their children the advantages of an education. Fortunately there were two schools near Tifton: one was on the old Union Road where Abraham-Baldwin now stands; the other, on the site of the present County Alms House.

The parents in this growing lumber town, however, were not satisfied until there was a school building near their homes. True to the progressive spirit, the citizens in 1891 came together to form a stock company for the purpose of establishing and supporting a school. The Tifton Institute, a $3,800 building, was the result. The work of the first school began in the early fall of 1891, under direction of Professor L. A. Murphey, with the following monthly tuition rates: primary $2.00; intermediate $2.50; high school, $3.00. H. H. Tift, W. O. Tift, W. W. Timmons, E. P. Bowen, and W. H. Love composed the first board of education.

When J. J. Huggins was principal of the Tifton Institute in 1892, there were just 75 pupils attending. During the summer of 1893, the Tifton Educational Company, through its board of directors, deciding to put their school on a new basis, placed it in the hands of Professor E. J. Williams. Referring to the situation, the Gazette on August 4 said: "He will conduct the school upon its merits under the supervision of a board of trustees to be chosen by the patrons of the school. Really, the building is turned over to the community free of rent, provided the citizens will maintain a first class school in it." The lowering of the tuition that followed probably accounted in a large part for the increase in the size of the student body. Anyway under "Zeke" Williams, the increase from 75 to 150 students made necessary the employment of an assistant, Miss Martha Williams, and a music teacher, Miss Ella C. Bacon.

In 1896 when John O'Quinn became principal an even larger faculty was necessary. Miss Ina Coleman had charge of intermediate work; Miss Edna McQueen, of the primary department; Miss Myrtle Pound taught music; and Miss Sally Perry, art. Among the Tifton Institute pupils at that time were Mrs. Harriet Goodman Harman, Mrs. Edna Cox Shaw, Mrs. Lena Gordon Williams, Mrs. Ella Youmans Coleman, Mrs. Ellie Millie Cox, Mrs. Blanche McLeod Harrell, Guy A. Cox, Lester Youmans, Elbert Youmans, and J. A. Walker.

Fortunately the early teachers in the Tifton Institute were comparatively superior men and women. Even then the school was weak enough.

Like the school and the newspaper, the Tifton churches flourished during the nineties. The growth of the Methodists and Baptist Churches corresponded to the growth of the town.

Early in 1895 the Baptists decided to erect a brick church. This plan could not have been effected had it not been for the enthusiasm of B. T. Allen, the determination of numerous women, and the benevolence of H. H. Tift. The April 8, 1895 issue of the Tifton Gazette was edited by ladies in honor of the laying of the corner stone of the new church. The staff was as follows: editor-in-chief, Mrs. Geo. H. Padrick; associate editors, Mrs. B. T. Cole, and Mrs. W. T. Hargrett; local and society editors, Mrs. J. W. Greene and Mrs. W. N. Cole; business managers, Mrs. F. T. Snell, Mrs. J. K. Carswell, Mrs. W. W. Timmons, and the Reverend F. T. Snell, an Englishman, who succeeded the Reverend O. M. Irwin, the first regular pastor.

The Methodists were progressing too. The first notable growth was in the fall of 1885, when a revival conducted by the regular pastor, G. R. Parker, assisted by the Reverend E. M. Whiting, brought in nearly thirty members.

In 1895 Southwest Georgia was enjoying prosperity and Tifton was in the center of it all. A statement written by the editor of the Worth County Local after a visit to Tifton follows:

"There is not another section of the state that is receiving the same amount of voluntary advertising, which, within itself, speaks volumes for Tifton and adjacent country for twenty miles around.

"It is true, Tifton enjoys advantages, by virtue of her neighboring little towns, and will hold her place as a central point around which fruit and truck growers will gather, but as time comes on apace, all of her nearby territory will be taken up and the ever increasing stream of newcomers will be compelled to reach out into the inviting and almost inexhaustible territory that is to be found reaching far into the surrounding country."

There were four important business developments in Tifton during the middle and last of the nineties: the establishment of two new railroads, the securing of banking facilities, the building of a telephone exchange, and the sale of the Tifton Gazette.

When P. H. Fitzgerald, at that time editor of the American Tribune, the official organ of the Grand Army of the Republic, conceived the idea of establishing a colony of old soldiers in Georgia, where they would be free from the blizzards and freezing cold of the northwest, his dream was not far from realization. In July, 1895, the first payment on the lands was made, and from that time there began an increasing immigration from the North and West. Within a year's time, there were six or seven thousand colonists located in Fitzgerald.

The Georgia and Alabama Railroad, within four miles of the site chosen for the colony city and with the grading completed to the town, was urged to rush its work to an end. Captain H. H. Tift, who had a tram road extending within thirteen miles of Fitzgerald, saw a possibility of opening a shorter route to the colony. Although he began his work six months after the corporation, the Tifton and Northeastern Railroad entered Fitzgerald only ninety days after the Georgia and Alabama. By the latter part of May 1896, the new railroad was doing a substantial business under the following officers: H. H. Tift, president; W. O. Tift, vice-president; F. G. Boatright, traffic manager; E. J. Williams, Jr., cashier.

Another railroad was built during the nineties, the Tifton, Thomasville and Gulf. On August 10, 1899 an immense crowd celebrated with a barbecue the completion of the first fifteen miles of the T. T. & G. railway. The Business Men's League of Tifton with Briggs Carson, chairman, and J. H. Hillhouse, secretary, raised about eight hundred dollars for the celebration. Special trains brought crowds from a distance. They came from the country "horse, foot, and dragoon, in cart, wagon, buggy, and horseback, and their families came with them."[1]

Another sign of progress was the banking business. Late in 1895 Messrs. Julian, Love, and Buck filled an important need by establishing a general banking business in connection with their wholesale grocery house. It was not, however, until the establishment of the Bank of Tifton in 1896 that the banking facilities of the town compared favorably with those of the best towns in Southwest Georgia. Practically all of the prosperous citizens of Tifton contributed toward the new bank. When the building was completed and the bank capitalized at $50,000, the achievement was the result of a community enterprise. W. S. Witham was made president; Captain H. H. Tift, vice-president; C. W. Marsh, cashier.

The Telephone Exchange, too, was organized in 1896 by C. W. Fulwood, who was its first president, Briggs Carson, C. W. E. Marsh, W. O. Tift, and W. O. Padrick. The central office was located in the Tift building. During the same year, long distance telephone connections were established with Ty Ty, Sumner, Poulan, and other points along the Brunswick and Western Railroad. The end of this line was located in the wholesale establishment of Julian, Love, and Buck, to whose enterprise the town was indebted for the line.

In May, 1895, B. T. Allen sold the Tifton Gazette to C. W. Fulwood and C. C. S. Baldridge. On May 17, the new editors came forward with the following statement of their policy: "It will be the earnest and constant care of the new management to place the Gazette among the best country weeklies of the state and to make it a potent factor in the upbuilding and general improvement of the section which is its peculiar territory."

The change in control of the Gazette was obviously a good one. Baldridge and Fulwood were primarily interested in the development of real

---
1. Tifton Gazette.

estate in this section, and it was a time when possibilities of the land needed intensive advertising.

In November, 1895, the paper was sold to a stock company, composed of C. W. Fulwood, J. L. Herring, W. O. Tift, J. A. Phillips, H. H. Tift, W. O. Padrick, and S. G. Slack. The importance of this change was the fact that it brought the man who had the ability to make The Gazette a real and lasting influence, J. L. Herring. On July 10, Editor Herring followed the example of the previous year, and published a trade edition of the paper, to be distributed free to the visitors at the Midsummer Fair. This eighteen-page issue, attractively made up and amply illustrated, gave a thorough discussion of the towns and the possibilities of the land in this section as well as much miscellaneous material.

Excerpts from the paper give pictures of the progress of Tifton:

"Tifton is essentially a railroad town. Here cross the two great systems, the Plant and the Southern. Then add connection with the Georgia and Alabama system, by way of Fitzgerald and Abbeville, and the route graded to Thomasville, and you will see that we are in the midst of a network of rails. Within eight hours of Jacksonville, twenty-four hours of Key West and thirty hours of New York we have mail, express, and railway facilities of the very best . . . Four to six train crews stop over in Tifton each night, and the supervisors, claim agents, attorneys, etc., of this division of the three roads reside there.

"Time only prevents us also giving a picture of the city's foster mother, the big mill, that for over twenty years has daily woke it from its morning slumbers by the long blast of the powerful whistle, echoing over the green hills and sunny slopes, through the cool and balsam-laden air, and at night has bid the city rest in peace. This mill has a capacity of from 50,000 to 60,000 feet of merchantable lumber daily with steam dry kilns, and a large planing mill, with a daily output of 30,000 feet, with acres of sheds, open yards, and sidings. Also, near the mill, is the turpentine distillery, which has been a fixture in Tifton as long as the mammoth sawmill. These two industries give active employment to about 250 men, whose payroll is over $1,000 per week. To serve the mill requires two locomotives on the road and one in reserve.

Our Business Men

"Beginning at the southern limit of the town, we come first to sales stables, built the year past by Perryman Moore . . .

"Facing Fifth street is the well equipped blacksmith and repair shop of Youman and O'Quinn, who do all kinds of repair work and have a wide experience in the business . . .

"Just west of them is the iron finished, two-story building, which Col. John Murrow is having built and which is nearly finished.

"Mr. C. A. Williams was the first man to erect a brick building in Tifton, his livery stables going up in 1890 . . .

"On Railroad Street Mr. J. M. Garrett has located the Tifton City Bakery in a building recently erected by Col. Murrow. The bakery has a capacity of 400 pounds of cakes, seventy-five pounds of rolls, and twenty-five ponds of doughnuts daily.

"For years Tifton felt the need of a wholesale grocery establishment, and early in 1895 Mr. W. H. Love established one in his two-story brick building facing the Georgia Southern Railway. He had associated with him Mr. E. A. Buck, of Douglas, and Dr. G. W. Julian, of Pearson . . . Later in the same year they established a general banking business, which also met with marked success. This year Dr. Julian retired, owing to professional duties, and the firm is now Love & Buck . . . Mr. M. W. Kirkland is bookkeeper.

"Mr. D. W. McLeod, the veteran hotel man from Sumner, is proprietor of Hotel Julian, which he is most successfully conducting . . .

"Dr. J. C. Goodman is the pioneer druggist of Tifton, having built the Tifton Drug Store in 1889. In it he carries a first class line of drugs . . .

"Next door is the post office, with T. M. Greene in charge. During the past year this office has been advanced from the fourth to the third class, and is the distributing point for three star routes—southwest to Obe in Colquitt County, by way of Debbie and Hadley; northwest to Hat, by way of Sutton, and northeast to Irwinville, and thence to Minnie, Abla, Ocilla, Ocala, etc. A daily mail to Fitzgerald, over the T. and N. E., is one of the possibilities of the near future.

"Back of the post office is Mrs. Martin's boarding house, which she has run successfully for a number of years . . .

"The Georgia Southern depot is in charge of the best of agents, W. F. Rudesill, with R. B. Easley assistant and E. O'Quinn night operator.

"On the eminence midway between the two depots is Hotel Sadie, now owned and run by Mr. W. W. Timmons with Mr. Robb as manager.— It has long borne a reputation as the leading hotel in this section, which the present management is fully sustaining, if we may judge by the crowds that throng its corridors.

"In its basement is Tifton's veteran barber, George Davis, who, despite the changes of season and vicissitudes of fortune, has shaved Tifton's citizens for years past.

"On the corner, in the Timmons building, is located J. J. Golden and Company. Tifton's new druggists . . . Here they have $1,100 soda fount . . . Mr. P. J. Strozier . . . is in charge of the prescription department . . .

"Mr. E. B. O'Neal . . . came to Tifton from Lakeland, Florida, in the spring and purchased the Parlor Grocery from Mr. W. H. Love . . .

"In his store is located G. W. Robinson, a first-class watchmaker and jeweler.

"Upstairs is the office of Briggs Carson, who represents all lines of insurance.

"Across Third Street is the Tifton Market and House, Wilson and Company, proprietors.

"Next door is the general store of I. S. and R. L. Bowen, who carry a nice and complete line of goods . . .

"Mr. A. S. Averett carries one of the prettiest little stocks of dry goods in town, and his ice cream parlor is a marvel of cleanly neatness.

"In the same building with him is clever J. G. Dedge, the veteran sewing machine man . . .

"Next door is the first mercantile business in town established by Hebrews. The three Marcus brothers came to Tifton early in the year from Buford, S. C. Since then, one of the brothers has sold his interest to the others . . .

"Over Bowen Bros., Mrs. Turner runs a boarding house . . .

"This history of the Padrick Bros. is interesting, they having started five years ago with one room in the Love Building, and their floor space now covering 1,700 square feet . . . East of their store they have built a bed spring factory.

"Across in front of them are two German families, Robt. Woods and L. Meyers, who run a grocery store and restaurant.

"In the Pitts Building, Mrs. W. F. Ford has established a boarding house . . . In the lower story is a nice line of family groceries, with Mr. W. E. Greene in charge . . .

"Next door is the Suwanee Restaurant, erected by the lamented James I. Clements, and the first hotel built in Tifton. Mr. Jno. B. Greene is in charge.

"The City Restaurant and Grocery, Guest, Kell, and Company, proprietors, under the able management of Mr. H. Fordham, one of the firm, and his charming wife, has a complete line of groceries, and serves a meal that is first-class in every respect.

"Everybody knows Mich Gaskins, yet few know why he has never sought wedded bliss. In his line of goods, he has a complete and varied one, to which he is constantly adding . . .

"Upstairs M. Leo Isaac, of Brunswick, has set up a first-class merchant tailoring establishment . . .

"Mr. Geo. Smith, druggist, is in charge of the Smith Drug Store . . . Master Murrow is employed as clerk.

"Mr. D. A. Fulwood does watch repairing and keeps a full line of stationery, books, and office supplies, as well as fishing tackle and sporting goods.

"L. S. Shepherd & Co. have their large building stocked with an immense line of every kind of goods kept in a general store . . .

"The Bank of Tifton, capitalized at $50,000, occupies a marble front building of its own, with Mr. C. W. E. Marsh as cashier. It is doing a large business . . .

"At the B. & W., Mr. W.. M. Touchton, well and favorably known along the line of road, is in charge, with the Western Union instruments under the fingers of clever F. M. Mangham. They make a good team.

"Mr. E. P. Bowen is one of the best known men in Tifton, and his store, filled with a fine stock of general merchandise, well patronized. He also has an undertaker's establishment, the only one in town.

"Adjoining him is the express office, a paying one, in charge of Mr. W. T. Mangham . . .

"The lower story of the Tift building is occupied by W. O. Tift, merchant, and S. G. Slack, hardware. Mr. Tift is the pioneer merchant of the place . . . His store is a mammoth one, filling a floor space 50 by 90, and a hall 60 by 80 feet to repletion.

"One year ago S. G. Slack first put in a small line of hardware, which a fast increasing trade has caused to grow to colossal proportions. His floor space is 50 by 90, and every inch of this, except bare standing room, is jammed with goods, piled to the ceiling . . .

"Overhead are the offices of Sebley and Company, real estate, recently changed to the Tifton Land and Immigration Company. These hustlers have the topography of the country on their finger-tips, and hold options on thousands of acres of Georgia fruit and farm lands.

"Located in the office with them is James H. Price, general insurance, who represents a large number of companies.

"In the same building is cigar factory No. 164, in charge of J. A. Haralson, who learned his trade in Key West, Florida.

"Just east of the large mill is the Tifton Foundry and Machine Company, R. S. Kell manager, which employs a number of hands. It employs 20 hands and has a full capacity of from 150 to 200 finished barrels daily.

"Another Tifton institution is the dairy farm of Padrick Brothers, under the management of Mr. G. H. Padrick. They have about twenty-five head of fine blooded stock, and find ready sale for more milk and butter than they can produce.

"Mr. R. A. Reese, an experienced cabinet maker, makes a specialty of fine office work.

"Nor must we omit our hustling contractors, S. G. Slack, W. N. Pittman, 'Pony' Smith, and others, together with Mr. Geo. W. Rex, one of the finest sign painters and decorators that has ever come to the state.

"Now go to Sutton & Young, near the Hotel Sadie, who keep some of the nattiest turnouts and fastest teams in town.

"No mention of Tifton is complete without its corps of professional men. As they have located with us, they are, Drs. J. A. McCrea, J. C. Goodman, N. Peterson, and R. T. Kendrick. Of these men one grand truth can be stated. Each has made the study of his profession a life work and has risen to the top. Each is a man of experience and the strictest honor and integrity . . . We doff our hats to you M.D.'s!

"Dr. John A. Peterson, a graduate in dentistry, has handsomely appointed office on Love Avenue.

"Col. John Murrow is one of South Georgia's self-made young men, and by energy, vim and industry is rapidly climbing the ladder . . His office is in the Love building.

"Hall & Hendricks are two Georgia boys just admitted to the bar who are already coming into a good practice and making a reputation. They are plucky and enterprising, and success will be theirs. Office in Paulk building.

"Col. J. B. Murrow has established quarters in the Tift building. This young man, an apt pupil of his brother, is forging to the front ranks of the men of his profession.

"City Clerk Murray, of Fulwood & Murray, is a young man of brains and ability.

"Everybody that knows Tifton knows C. W. Fulwood, and his fight up the rugged hill."

During the period the Tifton Canning and Manufacturing Company and a branch plant of the Columbus Barrel Factory deserve emphasis. This canning plant, with E. B. Warman in charge, had a capacity of 10,000 cans and employed one hundred twenty men. Mr. J. L. Reinschmidt was superintendent of the branch plant of the Columbus Barrel Manufacturing Company.

Another achievement in the nineties was the first Empire Garden Midsummer Fair, July 10-11-12, 1894. About this exhibition the American Farmer, published in Chicago, said, "This fair, which was held early in July, was a magnificent success in every respect, and the display of the products of the soil of Southwestern Georgia was a visible and emphatic proof of all that has been claimed for this section. The display of fruits and vegetables was such a one as has never been excelled on a similar occasion in the South."

Nature contributed snow, a partial eclipse of the moon, and Aurora Borealis to the history of this period. In 1895 children celebrated Washington's birthday by making snow figures; snow fell from three to six inches on that day. The winter of 1894-95 was the coldest that anyone in Tifton remembered at that time. The partial eclipse of the moon occurred on the night of September 14, 1894. In August of the same year between twelve o'clock at night and two in the morning Tifton people had the opportunity of witnessing a colorful spectacle—the Aurora Borealis. Brilliant red clouds with silver linings flashed in the northern sky at twelve, then suddenly faded, but reappeared later and lasted an hour.

Health conditions in Tifton during the nineties were good. People could not begin a cemetery because the death rate was low. There were five deaths in five years: one, an infant; the other, a man killed on a raliroad. Despite this fact a visitor had a different idea. In reference to turpentine stills the Tifton Gazette of 1892 had this paragraph:

"The stripped trees became white with the resinous sap and on a dark night one would take a turpentine farm for a huge cemetery with thousands of tombstones. A newcomer was heard to remark that he always thought South Georgia was unhealthy, but after seeing one of these seemingly large cemeteries he knew it. He packed up and left on the first train."

Although Tifton was more or less healthy and gay during the nineties, gayety did not extend to all parts of the rural district. Some families were living in one-room log houses with stick and clay chimneys and tending small farms. The following excerpt from a visitor's report about rural life near Tifton was published in 1895 in The Tifton Gazette: "The wife goes to church in a springless cart, to which is hitched a single ox, which is guided by ropes tied to each other." Tenants on farms worked for twelve dollars a month.

Despite the epithet, "gay nineties," Tifton had financial strain during 1892; some of the old negroes attributed the trouble to the fact that the year began on Friday.

Rural and town people, however, enjoyed many social events together regardless of financial difficulties. Candy pullings or "candy snatches" were very popular. Boys and girls from different groups mingled during wagon straw-rides to cane grindings. Many matches were effected to the rhythm of squeaks as the old mule went round and round his beaten path, and the mill crushed fresh sweet juice from the long stalks of red Georgia cane. Then couples would separate and exchange word affections, while beaus peeled cane for the town girls and rustic maids.

The grand finale of the cane grinding was the candy pulling. The last boiler of syrup cooked until it reached the candy stage; then partners pulled the candy together until losing its dark color, it turned a golden hue; then the merry party broke and filled the wagons again. On the way home the young people sang popular songs and ballads.

The ballads were often directed by John Sutton, the wire grass minstrel of the nineties. In 1893 he moved to a farm, about six miles from Tifton and led the singing plays at cane grindings and other entertainments. One night he went to a place where some of the guests were playing cards. A card objector, he took a group of young people into a room and led the singing. Lusty voices announced such a good time that the choristers broke up the card game and the card players joined the singing.

Sutton, too, led church songs at Salem Church. Regardless of this contribution, however, the preacher and deacons tried to turn Sutton out of the church because of his belief in open communion; he "outargued" all of them and stayed in the church.

Although Sutton passed the three-score and ten mark several years ago, he still remembers the ballads sung at different parties and vividly describes the singing plays. Many nights during cane grinding season breezes carried such tunes as,

"London Bridge is falling down
Oh, law, my lady is gay!
We'll mend it up with sticks and clay
Oh, law, my lady is gay.
We'll mend it up with sticks and clay."
* * * * * *

"Old Sister Phoebe how merry was she.
The night she sat under the juniper tree.
Put this hat on your head
To keep your head warm.
* * * * * *

"Ten thousand sweet kisses
Will do you no harm
No harm no harm I say
But a great deal of good I know.
* * * * * *

"Arise you up, Phoebe, and
Go choose you a one.
Choose you a fair one
Or else choose none.
* * * * * *

Oh, what a wretched choice you've made!
In your grave you'd better been laid.
Sing him a song and make him gay
Give him a kiss and send him away."

"Come under, come under
My honey, my love
My heart's above.
My love's gone aweeping
A long way from me
I've got you here

I keep you here
My honey, my love,
My heart's above
My love's gone aweeping
A long way from me."

"Old Uncle Johnnie
He had a little mill;
All the wheat and corn he got
He rolled it down the hill.
Hand in the hopper,
Other in the bag;
Every time you turn around
The miller says grab."

"Corn in the crib,
Poultry in the yard,
Meat in the smokehouse,
Tub full of lard.
Milk in the dairy,
Butter on the board,
Coffee in the little sack
Sugar in the gourd."

The conclusion of the gay period—the Spanish-American War—was inconsistent with the epithet, gay. After the insidious sinking of the Maine, the slogan, "Remember the Maine," vibrated from coast to coast. The Spanish government accepted as a declaration of war the President's ultimatum to Spain, on April 16, 1898, giving that nation until Saturday at noon to say whether or not the Spanish troops would vacate Cuba. On April 21, 1898, the United States Fleet at Key West sailed for Cuba.

Among the Tifton sons who volunteered to join the colors were Raleigh Eve, Bill Jones, and Ezekiel Williams. The patriotic women of Tifton sent them a handsome hamper of necessities and luxuries. On top of one of the packages were a linen duster and a palm-leaf fan. These women also organized a Ladies' Relief Society for the purpose of providing refreshments for the troops passing through Tifton.

The gloom of the war period was brightened by the bravery of Tift County boys and by the honor conferred on one of Tifton's daughters— Katherine Tift, daughter of W. O. Tift. On May 16, 1898 she received this telegram:

"Miss Powell, sponsor for Georgia at the unveiling of the monument to signers of the Mecklenberg Declaration of Independence at Charlotte, N. C., May 20, selects you as one of the maids-of-honor. Leave Atlanta Thursday. Hope you accept.

"W. Y. Atkinson."

Miss Tift accepted the honor and was a credit to Tifton and Georgia.

On August 12, 1898 the Spanish-American War, which had lasted three months and twenty-two days, ended at 4:23 o'clock, when Secretary Day for the United States and M. Cambon, for Spain, in the presence of President McKinley, signed a protocol, the basis of a definite treaty of peace.

The United States paid Spain $20,000,000 for the Philippines. For several months after the war the United States had to fight the Filipinos, who declared that our country had no right to govern them and that they would fight as hard for their liberty as they had fought under Spanish misrule. Finally, however, the Filipinos had to accept "Old Glory," which later they learned to love and honor. These people proved their loyalty to America during World War II.

CHAPTER VII

THE EARLY NINETEEN HUNDREDS

In 1900 pine groves near Tifton still had their aesthetic and financial values. Turpentine distilleries, lumber and planing mills still attracted visitors. The Atlanta Georgian, May 8, 1903, carried an interesting article:

"Tifton is situated in the middle of the yellow pine lumber and naval stores belt of South Georgia. It is the home of the Georgia Saw Mill Association, and for each of the six working nights of the week four solid train loads of lumber are transferred in the railroad yards . . . This aggregates nearly 1,300 train loads of twenty cars each during the year, and gives you some idea of the volume of this business."

Despite these facts, the pine was not the absolute monarch that it had been in former years. The tendency toward stressing farming was strong during 1900. The attention to cotton was one of the indications of this interest in farming. In March, 1900, stockholders of the proposed Tifton Cotton Mills met and effected a temporary organization by electing the following officers: H. H. Tift, President; W. S. Witham, financial agent; L. G. Manard, L. S. Shepherd, and W. S. Witham comprised the board of directors of the new company.

In April H. H. Tift, L. G. Manard, and W. S. Witham after spending a week in the inspection of the leading cotton mills in Georgia, made a trip to Charlotte, North Carolina, to meet with the agents of the leading cotton mill machinery manufacturing concerns of the country. The representatives of the Tifton mills found machinery in great demand; however, they finally closed a contract with the agent of an English manufacturer, who had just filled a contract for the machinery of a small firm that had "gone broke." The machinery was left on his hands, and according to the contract, it was to be delivered in Tifton by July 1.

Soon after the return of the Tifton representatives, a permanent organization was effected. H. H. Tift was chosen president; S. M. Clyatt, vice-president; and L. G. Manard, secretary and treasurer. The board of directors was composed of H. H. Tift, L. S. Shepherd, W. W. Banks, E. P. Bowen, S. M. Clyatt, L. G. Manard, and Briggs Carson.

In 1900 the Tifton Ginning Company organized with the following officers: J. L. Ensign, president, and E. P. Bowen, secretary and treasurer. The board of directors was composed of H. H. Tift, J. Lee Ensign, H. Kent, E. P. Bowen, and L. G. Manard.

By 1904 other cotton gins and several cotton warehouses had been established as indispensable to Tifton's economic future. Furthermore the Tifton Cotton Mills were operating at a maximum rate of speed, reaching a weekly amount of 8,000 pounds of Number 30's a ply yarn. During 1903 the cotton mills showed a net earning of $22,000.

As farming interests increased, J. L. Herring envisioned the possibilities of this section. His words later proved a fulfilled prophecy:

"Every year the professions are becoming worse crowded; every year entrance into them made more difficult; and success after entrance is gained, made harder to obtain. In business lines, it is noteworthy that not one man in twenty-five goes through life without a failure.

"Yet, on the millions of acres of farming lands in South Georgia is room for every son of her soil. And under the tillage of an educated, comprehensive husband-man, the return is a thousand fold, and success is assured . . .

"Educate your sons, men of South Georgia, but educate them for the farms; for the calling to which his maker assigned man, and you prepare them for a life of long years, peace, and happiness, and lay up for yourselves the plaudits of your grateful countrymen!"

During the pre-county period there were a number of economic developments. Adequate long distance telephone service was effected in the fall of 1902 when the line of the Southern Bell Telephone Company arrived in Tifton. About this time the Tifton Ice and Power Company was organized. The franchise of the new firm—good for five years and carrying an extra five-year option if the arrangement proved satisfactory—was first bought by B. M. Griffin, who later sold it to L. P. Thurman.

The new power company was organized with the following officers: S. M. Roberts, manager, and L. P. Thurman, secretary and treasurer. The stockholders were: S. M. Roberts, L. P. Thurman, J. G. L. Phillips, H. H. Tift, W. T. Hargrett, and W. W. Banks. A light plant was soon installed and in March, 1903, "The fair hands of Mrs. W. W. Banks and Mrs. S. M. Roberts pushed the lever and instantly, as by a magician's wand, the city sprang from darkness into a light as of day!" (Tifton Gazette).

During this period W. S. Cobb and J. M. Price, of Canton, Georgia, and S. N. Pool and Mr. R. E. Dinsmore, of Tifton, planned the erection of a ten-thousand-dollar guano plant in Tifton. Briggs Carson and C. W. Fulwood gave the town a modern foundry, when they bought and consolidated the plants formerly owned by P. J. Clark Foundry and Machine Company and the Gifford Iron Works Company. Another step in progress was taken by the management of the Tifton Cotton Mills when a twenty-thousand-dollar knitting mill was built. The finished plant had a capacity of from two to three hundred dozen pairs of hose a day of ten hours.

At this time there was a tremendous increase in banking business in Tift County. In December, 1903, a meeting was held at the office of Colonel John Murrow, and the Citizen's Bank of Tifton was organized with the following officers: E. A. Buck, president; C. A. Alford, vice-president; and J. M. Paulk, cashier. The directors were I. H. Myers, W. F. Rudistill, C. E. Fryer. J. B. Murrow, J. M. Paulk, E. A. Buck, C. A. Alford, and G. F. Alford The bank was organized with twenty-five thousand dollars subscribed and paid capital.

In the late summer of 1903 plans were completed for the organization of the First National Bank, number 6542 on the official roster at Washington. By September, capital stock worth twenty-five thousand dollars had been sold. The first officers of the new bank were J. J. L. Phillips, president; I. W. Myers, vice-president; O. D. Gorman, cashier. The directors were H. H. Tift, Briggs Carson, Asa G. Candler, J. J. L. Phillips, W. E. Baker, I. W. Myers, A. B. Hollingsworth, O. D. Gorman, and Perryman Moore.

On October 5, 1905, Tifton's fourth bank was organized, when the stockholders of the Merchants' and Farmers' Bank met and elected the following board of directors: J. L. Brooks, L. O. Benton, W. H. Hendricks, Perryman Moore, E. E. Slack, J. N. Horne, M. L. McMillan, I. W. Bowen, and J. L. Gay. The following officers were elected: L. O. Benton, of Monticello, president; W. H. Hendricks, first vice-president; Perryman Moore, second vice-president; and J. L. Brooks, cashier. The new bank was capitalized at thirty thousand dollars.

Devastating fires swept over many buildings during 1904 and 1905. In January of 1904, the Tifton Supply Company in the H. H. Tift building caught fire. Losses were estimated at twenty thousand dollars, with about fifteen thousand dollars insurance.

Three months later F. J. Clark and Company's Foundry and Machine Shops were damaged to the extent of three thousand dollars.

In February, 1905, the building occupied by Carson Brothers was destroyed by fire. The loss was nine thousand dollars above insurance. Then on February 24, the Tifton Gazette issued a fire extra. Bold headlines announced: "Hotel Sadie Is No More!" Excerpts from the story are:

"What was yesterday the home of hundreds, a hive of life and industry, is now a smoking ruin, and the stranger in Tifton is without a home.

"Four lines of hose were quickly laid to the main from the fire pump at Tift's mill.

"For a while the Williams, Clyatt, Smith, and Boatright buildings, the Bank of Tifton, and Sumner's stables were in imminent danger and but for the fact that it was a calm, still night, and that the fighters fought valiantly, probably the balance of the business part of Tifton would have fallen victim to the ravenous appetite of the God of flames."

In March fire caused about three thousand dollars damage above insurance coverage in the building owned by Mr. John Murrow.

Probably the most disastrous fire in the history of Tifton was on November 4, 1904 when a blaze began in the four-story Slack building, sweeping through it, the two-story Regent Hotel, covering more than a full lot, the two-story Bowen building with the opera house on the second floor, the E. B. O'Neal building, the E. H. Tift building, and all the stores and offices in these buildings. The residences of Mrs. Julia Pope, H. W. Brown, C. B. Holmes, and Mayor W. W. Timmons were also destroyed by fire. Only heroic efforts of Tifton citizens saved the National Bank and the post office. The loss was estimated at between $115,000 and $125,000 with $60,000 insurance.

On Sunday evening November 7, the Tifton Knitting Mills, with all machinery and other equipment, were burned. The mill and machinery, owned by H. H. Tift and valued at twelve thousand dollars, were a total loss.

Disconsolately Tifton citizens viewed a bleak town, but looking into lifeless ashes, and envisioning new structures, soon effected plans for reconstruction.

In connection with these fires Mr. J. L. Williams, editor of the Tifton Free Press, tells a mysterious story. After a traveling group of men and women had preached for several days on the streets of Tifton, causing some disturbance, the city council passed a resolution to request these evangelists to leave town. Infuriated, the band gathered on the northwest corner of Love Avenue and Second Street; weird sounds issued from the spot. Tifton citizens could not understand all of the speeches, but could hear the pronouncing of a curse and the stamping of feet on the spot. The incantation, "In forty-eight hours something terrible will happen in Tifton!" floated from the corner distinctly enough for by-standers to hear; then the group shook Tifton dust off their feet and stalked away.

Exactly forty-eight hours afterward the flame began in the basement of the Slack building, increasing to a conflagration, which swept in all directions from the corner where the incantation sounded. Fire raged, but stopped before reaching Mr. W. T. Hargrett's home. This fire destroyed the buildings on the property of all the councilmen who owned any except those of W. T. Hargrett, who, strange to say, opposed the resolution to make the visiting preachers leave, and H. H. Tift. The latter, however, soon afterwards lost his knitting mills by fire.

Excerpts from the Tifton Gazette:

"March 15, 1901—William Tygart, representing the Standard Oil Company, arrived in Tifton last week and is superintending the erection of an oil reservoir to care for the growing business here.

"March 22—Colonel R. Eve, Mrs. Neville, and Mrs. Maud' Greer, undaunted by the potential wrath of Tifton's first baby show announced winners: to the boy and girl under one year, Malcolm Peterson and Ruth

Harmon; one to three years, Ralston Padrick and Leona Wilcox; three to five years, Ernest Baker and Mary Tift.

"May 3—Tifton Lodge Number 47, Free and Accepted Masons, with the duly constituted ceremonies of the order, laid the cornerstone of Tifton's new $8,000 Methodist Church Wednesday afternon at 3:30.

"June 21—Measurement of the railroad tracks within the corporate limits has elicited the information that Tifton contains over sixteen miles of railway track.

"Nov. 1—It is plain to every citizen, and even to the most casual observer, that the law against selling intoxicants is being violated every day in the city and in the two negro suburbs immediately adjoining. And although they have had several months, both city and county officers appear powerless to either stop the sale or bring the lawbreakers to justice.

"Nov. 15—At the state fair, James Clyatt won the first prize in the grammar class of oratory; Miss Laura Smith won first prize in the elocution contest.

"Jan. 17, 1902—A visitor to Tifton had the following to say of Superintendent Harmon: 'I am sure the people of Tifton realize and appreciate their good fortune in having such a fine preceptor and organizer as Professor Harman since he built up the school from the crude state in which he found it, with only 65 pupils to the present well-ordered, thoroughly-graded school of more than 200 scholars.'

"Jan. 31—An idea of the work that is being done in Tifton now can be gained from the fact that 25 residences have been built and contracted for since the first of January.

"Of these, eight for the knitting mill have been finished; eight for Slack and Phillips are soon to be built; two for H. Kent, two for B. W. Hightower, and five on Tifton Heights will be completed in the near future.

"Feb. 1—The Atlanta papers quote John Temple Graves as saying: 'Tifton is a type of life and progress in all the Southern section of the state . . . Time was, and I recall it, when to spend a summer amid the supposed malaria of South Georgia was deemed equivalent to a written invitation to fever and death. Now the artesian wells flowing crystal and freely through all these southwestern towns have made the wiregrass as healthful as the Piedmont hills and demonstrated to a certainty that it is malaqua, and not malaria that has been the curse of southern climes.'

"Feb. 14—Bishop Nelson, of the Georgia Episcopal Church, says: St. Anne's Church, Tifton, is the outcome of a missionary effort begun under the direction of the Bishop by the Reverend Frank B. Ticknor in 1894.

"April 18—Inclement weather is no handicap to Sam Jones; during less than a week, his revival has brought over a hundred new members to the local churches.

"June 27—Prof. Jason Scarboro, for three years head of the Moultrie public schools, has been elected principal of the Tifton school system.

"September 2—There are thirty-five business houses in Tifton less than two years old.

"October 24—Harry Goodman enjoys the distinction of having brought to Tifton the first "Auto-Bi" or motor-bicycle. The vehicle when steamed up to the right temperature is calculated to make the speed of one mile in one minute and twelve seconds.

"Nov. 7—The Women's Literary Club was organized Wednesday afternoon with the following officers: Mrs. C. D. Fish, president; Mrs. F. S. Harrell, secretary; and Mrs. W. E. Myers, treasurer.

"Jan. 2, 1903—A Tifton German Club was organized last Friday night. Standing chaperons are: Mr. and Mrs. E. H. Tift, Mr. and Mrs. Boatright, Mr. and Mrs. Bond, Mr. and Mrs. Greer, Mr. and Mrs. T. S. Williams, Mr. and Mrs. H. S. Murry, and Mr. and Mrs. Delph.

"Jan. 23—In the first race for judge and solicitor of the city court F. G. Boatright was elected judge and C. C. Hall, solicitor. O. L. Chestnutt, justice of peace for two years, resigned his office to accept the clerkship. T. B. Henderson, a former sheriff of Ware County, was appointed sheriff.

"Feb. 13—Last week, seventeen Tifton carpenters met for the purpose of organizing a union. The following officers were elected: R. W. Terrill, president; J. L. Hamilton, secretary; M. Chance, treasurer; B. W. Harrell, financial secretary; H. Harris, conductor; and Mr. Martin, warden.

"Feb. 20—Following the lead of the carpenters in union consciousness, yesterday the skilled sawmill workers of Tifton met and organized a union, with the following officers: R. E. Hall, president; John Bruce, vice-president; W. W. Cowan, secretary; C. L. Gaulding, sergeant-at-arms. The enrollment of this union has reached sixty names, embracing the best workers in this section. The local organization is under the protection of the National Federation of Labor.

"July 3—The Tifton and Northeastern railroad was sold to the Title Guarantee and Trust Company in Atlanta Saturday last. The money was paid and the stock transferred, President H. H. Tift making the transfer to attorneys representing the trust company. The cash price was $243,750. The stock was transferred in blank.

"July 17—Tax returns for the Tifton district of Berrien County show a big increase over last year, having passed the million dollar mark. In exact figures, they are $1,033,144. Last year, they were $965,090, showing an increase over 1901 of $243,301.

Twenty years ago, the total taxable property of Berrien County reached the sum of $1.000,000.

Wednesday night, Juniper Camp No. 105, W. O. W. was reorganized in Tifton, and the following officers were elected: J. L. Williams, Council Com.; W. T. Mangham, Advisory Lieut.; R. H. Hutchinson, Jr., Banker; C. R. O'Quinn, Clerk, and N. Peterson, Camp Physician.

"July 31—The Tifton Terminal Company has been organized to control the railroad yards formerly belonging to the Tifton and Northeastern Railroad. Mr. H. H. Tift is president and Mr. J. L. Jay, Junior-superintendent.

"Dec. 11—The Tifton Rifles, Company F, Fourth Georgia, received their uniforms and other equipment Monday. There are two uniforms for each man, fatigue and dress. The guns are the Krag Jergensen rifle, with several thousand rounds of ammunition, side arms and accoutrements. R. Eve is captain of the new unit.

"Manager Keith Carson, of the opera house, has arranged with the Van Epp Vaudeville Company to give their high-classed entertainment Saturday afternoon and evening. The very latest and best of moving pictures will be presented—among others, the celebrated Harvard-Yale football game, at Cambridge. 'Still His Trousers Grew' is another new fascinating picture; 'Happy Hooligan,' another.

"Jan. 22, 1904—Since the merger of the Tifton, Thomasville and Gulf, rumor has been rife that the Atlantic and Birmingham would also absorb the Brunswick and Birmingham. This rumor has been confirmed.

"April 1—The pupils of Tifton Public School took the clapper out of the bell, the handle off the pump, scattered the chalk and books and nailed up the door this morning. A sign over the door says: 'Nothing doing at school, and the boys and girls are off to the woods.'

"April 15—The Tuesday Afternoon Whist Club was entertained this week by Mrs. Erminie Scott at the home of her sister, Mrs. F. S. Harrell, on Sixth Street.

"April 22—John Murrow was elected judge of the city court with a majority of 63 votes over Raleigh Eve; the voters named J. J. Murray solicitor.

"May 23—Carrie Fulwood, Charles H. Garrett, and Effie Kent took part in the program for the first commencement exercises of Tifton Public School last week.

"July 1—Effective July 1, Tifton post office will be advanced to the second class, due to the fact that the receipts of the office have averaged over $8,000 per year for fifteen months past.

"July 15—For the past year, the Tifton district showed a gain of $133,113 in tax returns, making a total of $1,166,257 worth of taxable property. The Tifton district has shown a gain in tax returns since 1890.

"July 22—J. L. Johns, of Tifton, caused a near riot early in the week when he carried an automobile to Cordele. He was carrying passengers to the ball diamond, working under a liveryman's license. He was fined a dollar for creating disturbance, despite the fact that Cordele did not have an ordinance to cover automobiles.

"Dec. 30—Washington Camp Number 8, Patriotic Order Sons of America will be instituted in Tifton Jan. 16.

"Jan. 27, 1905—J. L. Johns, the liveryman, who bought Tifton's first automobile last summer, received three handsome, new Rambler machines last week. One of them, an eighteen horse power roadster, speeded to forty miles an hour, was purchased by J. L. Brooks.

"Feb. 10—A meeting was held Saturday afternoon at the home of Mr. and Mrs. E. H. Tift to organize a literary and social club. Mrs. W. O. Tift was elected president; Mrs. W. S. Walker, vice-president; and Mrs. N. Peterson, secretary and treasurer.

"March 3—The Henderson Oil Co. was organized in Tifton this week. The charter members and officers are: W. J. Henderson, president; Dr. O. Daniel, vice-president; J. E. Peeples, secretary; and W. W. Banks, treasurer.

At the meeting it was decided to put fifty shares of stock on the market, at $100 per share. After a canvass of one day by the secretary, thirty-five shares of the stock were sold. The company owns 120 acres of land in Washington County, Florida.

"March 31—Sixty-five lots were sold by the New England Development and Improvement Company, at prices ranging from $136 to $325. The lots were on Park and Ridge Avenues between tenth and Twelfth Streets.

"April 21 (Chipley, Florida, April 20—Special to the Gazette):

"Struck a fine grade of petroleum oil today at Orange Hill, Washington County. Great excitement here. W. J. Henderson.

"Mr. Perryman Moore began work yesterday on a thirty-room hotel building on Main Street, one lot south of Fifth.

"November 3—The bond election held Monday in the city courtroom, to authorize the issuance of $50,000 of thirty-year bonds to purchase a site, erect a school building, and put in a system of waterworks and sewerage system, and the remainder for water works.

"Dec. 1—At the Georgia Baptist Convention held in Macon, President Jackson, of Monroe College, read a note from Mrs. H. H. Tift, stating that her husband would donate $37,000 to complete the Bessie Tift memorial hall at the Forsyth Institution. This is one of the largest gifts in the history of Baptist benevolence.

CHAPTER VIII
TIFT COUNTY

A tremendous crowd had gathered in Tifton for a celebration. It was time for rejoicing—the time for speeches, barbecues, and bonfires! Exactly at 5:20 Wednesday afternoon August 16, 1905, Tift County was born! The Tift County bill passed the senate by a unanimous vote—it had passed the house the previous Friday. On Thursday morning S. M. Clyatt and W. W. Banks, committeemen, carried the county bill—the birth certificate—to Governor Joseph N. Terrell, "who affixed his signature with a handsome gold pen, made for the purpose by Jeweler Cochran, of Tifton, and bearing Tift County on a pearl name piece." (Tifton Gazette.)

Many citizens had worked strenuously for this moment, but no one had excelled J. L. Herring, editor of the Tifton Gazette, in his efforts. According to the Ocilla Star, Mr. Herring cut the pigeon wing in four languages, when the news about the county came. In 1895 John L. Herring began agitating the creation of new counties in South Georgia. He strongly contended for a new county with Tifton as its seat. The only road from Tifton to Nashville, twenty-five miles away, was a three-path trail, made by horses and buggies. The long trips to the county seat were burdensome; it took hours for one to travel this distance.

Many people agreed with the editor, but when his efforts assumed the form of a crusader, few were willing to march with him. The few people with foresight gave the movement its initial impetus. In a few years the cause had gathered more followers. The strongest newspapers and some of the influential citizens of South Georgia had joined forces in the fight for new counties. People of Tifton had had opportunities to observe the benefits of a county seat. The need for new counties had increased as the rural sections became more thickly populated.

On October 7, 1894, complete returns of a state-wide vote showed that amendments for new counties were carried by a large majority. The feeling between Nashville and Tifton became very intense. C. W. Fulwood, of Tifton, and John Knight, of Nashville, ran for the legislature on the new county issue, and Knight was the successful candidate. Tifton's chances seemed slight.

Tifton's leading citizens, however, began to lay their plans with determination to win. A committee on boundaries began work early in 1905. The proposed county was to embrace ninety square miles from Berrien, ninety-five from Irwin, and sixty-eight, from Worth.

In a meeting in February Mr. C. W. Fulwood suggested the name Hansell for the new county, in honor of Judge A. H. Hansell of the Southern

Circuit; Mr. Monk suggested Tift for H. H. Tift. This suggestion was adopted without a vote, and the first motion, withdrawn by C. W. Fulwood. Later at a mass meeting in March the question was discussed, and the motion to name the county Tift was carried. S. M. Clyatt, Briggs Carson, and T. S. Williams were appointed to notify Mr. Tift of the action and escort him to the hall. When he appeared in the door, loud applause greeted him. S. M. Clyatt in an enthusiastic speech presented Mr. Tift.

The editor of the Tifton Gazette commented on the choice of name:

"While naming the new county to be created here Tift aids in perpetuating in the memory of the people of the state the distinguished services of the late Mr. Nelson Tift, yet the people of this section, in choosing a name for their county had in mind their own fellow citizen, the man who founded Tifton, and but for whom there would have been no Tifton and consequently no Tift County. As a factor in the development of South Georgia, he yields place to no man, and the reason for naming the county here for him are ample and sufficient. Tift County was named for H. H. Tift, of Tifton, although we are glad that the name aids in perpetuating the memory of Nelson Tift."

The reason for naming the county for the great benefactor, H. H. Tift, resembled a boy's argument that Columbus deserved more credit for discovering America than Washington for defending it. The podgy boy on Friday afternoon during the nineties arose, went to the stage of the old school house and succinctly argued: "Columbus deserves more credit for discovering America than Washington for defending it. If Columbus hadn't discovered America, where would we have been?" If Tift had not founded Tifton, where would the new county have been?

When August of 1905, a legislative committee decided to name no county for a living man, the honorary beneficiary was changed to the honorable Nelson Tift, who was responsible for much of South Georgia's early progress.

Since there had been trouble between Tifton and Nashville, to effect a conciliation, Mr. Fulwood in a letter requested the Honorable John Knight, Berrien County representative, to help frame the county bill. Mr. Knight granted the request and promised not to oppose the bill.

The Gazette, meantime, was busy. This paper carefully reported every development in the plan. Opinions of prominent citizens here and elsewhere were quoted. To stimulate interest in the movement, Editor Herring wrote a series of front-page attractive editorials, in which he argued every phase of the county question. Some of the subjects were:

"It Originated Here," "The Necessity for It," "In Keeping With Progress," "Territory to Spare," "Crowded Superior Courts," "The Question of Expense," "Tifton's Resources," "Tifton's Accessibility," "Business Growth," and "Unanimously Endorsed."

To carry on the work in Atlanta, the following committee was appointed: S. M. Clyatt, chairman; W. W. Banks, treasurer; Charlie Parker, C. W. Fulwood, and H. H. Tift. Chairman Clyatt scarcely let the capitol out of his sight for sixty days. According to his statement, the other members of the committee usually spent their week-ends in Atlanta, planning for the next week's activities. Charlie Parker, whom Mr. Clyatt considered the most valuable man on the committee, was in Atlanta the most of the session. J. H. Hall, of Macon, chairman of the house committee on new counties, and Clayton Robinson, a capable lobbyist of Milledgeville, deserve special appreciation.

A news story, dated July 15, in the Atlanta Constitution gave a brief account of a problem:

"The proposed new county of Tift, with Tifton as the county seat, had the first innings before the senate and house committees on new counties yesterday.

"The committee room was crowded with members of new county delegations who gathered to hear the proceedings. Senator Crawford Wheatley, of the thirteenth, chairman of the senate committee, and Mr. Hall, of Bibb, chairman of the house committee, presided.

"Tift County occupies the unique position of not only having no opposition to its establishment, but of having members of other people on all sides of it who are anxious to get into the new county, but who have not been included in the territory mapped out. They were represented before the committee and earnestly requested that their territory be included in Tift County. This very fact, however, caused considerable opposition to develop as the hearing progressed. Mr. C. W. Fulwood presented maps showing in detail the lines of the old counties as well as those of the proposed new county.

"J. L. Herring presented the claims of Tift County. The new county of Tift, Mr. Herring said, proposed to take ninety square miles from Berrien, ninety-five square miles from Irwin, and sixty-eight square miles from Worth.

"R. C. Ellis, of Tifton, made an appeal in behalf of the citizens of Enigma and of a strip of territory comprising about forty square miles on the southeastern border of the new county, who wanted to be incorporated in Tift County.

"Mr. Knight, representative from Berrien County, strongly opposed the petition declaring that the people of Berrien County were unwilling to give up any more of her territory than had originally agreed upon.

"M. L. McMillan, of Berrien County, said he lived ten miles from Tifton and seventeen miles from Nashville. He wanted to be incorporated in the new county of Tift so that he could be nearer the courthouse. He owned about 3,500 acres of land.

"W. E. Williams, of Ty Ty, said the people of his town all wanted to go into the new county instead of being divided by the new county line, as is now proposed.

"W. B. Parks, of Ty Ty, appeared and requested that two additional Worth County lots be taken into the new county so that his farm would not be divided.

"Mr. Alford, of Worth, said requests had been made to take in more Worth County lots than had been agreed on, and all his people would like to have a hearing before any action was taken."

Before the bill was finally passed. the question of whether the first county commissioners should be appointed or elected was discussed. H. H. Tift. C. W. Fulwood, and W. W. Banks were the leaders of the faction favoring appointment of the commissioners. In a speech before the senate's committee, Mr. Fulwood stated that the primary need of the new county was a sound business administration and that it would be the height of folly to trust the selection of such important officials to popular vote. S. M. Clyatt, E. A. Buck, and Perryman Moore argued for adherence to democratic principles. When the matter stood at a deadlock and neither faction seemed willing to break it, the investigating committee decided in favor of the appointment of the first county commissioners. The recommendation of W. S. West, state senator from the district in which Tift County was to be included, settled the argument.

In the latter part of August, the voters of Tift County held a mass meeting for the purpose of organizing a democratic club. J. L. Herring was elected permanent chairman; J. H. Price, secretary. The members of the first democratic executive committee were: Omega District, Joab Taylor; Chula District, B. B. Sumner; Ty Ty District, William Gibbs; Harding District, J. L. Gay; Tifton District, C. W. Fulwood, chairman, and C. C. Hall. The voters signed a resolution of thanks to the county committee, to J. H. Hall, and to J. L. Herring for efforts in securing the new county.

The following were nominations of Tift County's first primary:

Ordinary—W. S. Walker
Clerk—J. E. Peoples
Sheriff—J. B. Baker
Collector—J. Henry Hutchinson
Tax Receiver—J. A. Marchant
Treasurer—S. F. Overstreet
Surveyor—J. T. Webb
Coroner—J. E. Johns

First election in Tift County was held October 4, 1905; the first term of Superior Court November 6, 1905 in building on the southwest corner of Love and Second Streets. Robert C. Mitchell was first judge.

The first Grand Jury was:

Dempsey W. Willis, J. N. Brown, Henry Sutton, J. T. Mathis, J. R. Mason, W. B. Parks, J. R. Sutton, J. J. Baker, Geo. Smith, T. E. Fletcher. I. W. Bowen, T. A. Shipp, T. E. Phillips, I. S. Bowen, L. J. Gray, J. J. Hall, G. W. Crum, William Gibbs, G. W. Guest, John A. Branch, C. W. Haistings, J. M. Branch, G. T. Phelps, Briggs Carson, J. R. Moore.

There were seven militia districts: Tifton, Chula, Brighton, Ty Ty, Dosia, Eldorado, Brookfield.

The problem of defraying the cost of the first court was solved in an unusually interesting way. Very secretively some men dropped hints to Judge Mitchell about prominent citizens' gambling. When the sheriff brought them before Judge Mitchell, he fined them enough to pay the cost of the court.

CHAPTER IX
AGRICULTURAL SCHOOL

"From Turrets peak to Donjon keep
The Salvos of glad tidings sweep
Blare the trumpet and roll the drums
The Hallelujah Day has come!" Tiftonites proclaimed in November 1906.

"Tifton's father did it with his little hatchet!" exclaimed J. L. Herring upon receiving the news that the agricultural School for the Second Congressional District would come to Tifton. A zealous committee had been working: J. L. Pickard. H. H. Tift, R. Eve, C. L. Parker, J. H. Scales, J. J. L. Phillips, P. D. Phillips, W. W. Banks, Perryman Moore, T. J. Parker, J. W. Hollis, J. L. Brooks, W. T. Hargrett, E. P. Bowen, J. N. Horne, P. W. Robertson, W. W. Timmons, S. S. Monk, I. W. Myers, C. C. Hall, J. W. Baker, C. A. Williams, C. C. Guest, W. B. Parks, J. T. Mathis, E. L. Vickers, Briggs Carson, W. S. Walker, R. C. Ellis, and O. L. Chestnutt.

In October a mass meeting of Tifton citizens decided to make a bid for an agricultural college. H. H. Tift volunteered to give the necessary two hundred acres of land and offered to increase any sum the county might raise as donation by one-sixth. Late in November, the Tifton committee went to Albany to enter the contest for one of the proposed state institutions. J. L. Herring gave an interesting account of the event.

"The committee went with $32,000 raised by individual subscriptions from the people of Tift County, to secure the location of Agricultural School of the Second Congressional District, to be decided upon by the Board of Trustees.

"Organization of the Board of Trustees was perfected by electing Judge Frank Park, of Worth, chairman, and A. J. Lippitt, of Dougherty, secretary . . .

Soon after the opening of the afternoon session, at 3 o'clock, the bids were submitted, the counties being called in alphabetical order.

"Dougherty came first, with an offer of $20,000, 200 acres of land, an artesian well and free lights and water for ten years.

"Camilla offered to raise $51,000 cash, donate 300 acres of land, buildings, and timber estimated at $4,000, and free lights and water for five years. When called to close figures on the cash proposition, it was admitted that only $10,000 was at hand.

"Pelham offered the choice of several fine tracts of land, free lights and water and a certified check for $19,000.

"Tift County's offer was 315 acres of land lying along the G. S. & F.

right-of-way, one mile north of town, and $30,000 in cash.

"Ashburn's offer was 250 acres of land, lights and water for five years and $45,000 in cash.

"Hon. Jos. S. Davis, a most eloquent gentleman, and fluent speaker, presented Dougherty's claims, fifteen minutes having been allowed each applicant after the bids were opened by the secretary. Judge W. N. Spence and Col. I. A. Bush spoke for Camilla, Hons. H. H. Merry and D. C. Barrow for Pelham, and Col. J. D. Hutchason for Ashburn.

"When he arose to fill five minutes of the time allotted Tift County, Mr. Tift presented an amended bid of $55,000 in cash, free lights, water and telephone service for ten years, a sewerage system, and 315 acres of land worth $50 per acre. Later, learning that the timber on the land was desired for forestry study, he contributed this also, it being valued at $4,500. The raise of $25,000 at a jump caused the audience to catch its breath.

* * * * * *

"After the committee went into executive session, Pelham's bid was raised to $32,500 cash; Camilla's to $58,000. and Ashburn's to $60,500. Mr. Tift added $5,000 to Tifton's offer, making $60,000 in cash. Of this he gave $36,400 cash, the land, $4,500 in timber, and a portion of the lights and water offer. It was estimated in the committee room that Tifton's total offer netted $95,700. Mr. J. J. L. Phillips gave the telephone service.

"After the financial question was settled, it was a tug of war between personal influence of Mr. Tift and J. L. Hand, of Pelham.

"Inside the committee room J. L. Pickard, nobly assisted by J. J. Knight, and after Albany dropped out of the contest, by A. J. Lippitt and other strong friends, was having the fight of his life.

"It was decided, there being eighteen votes in the committee, that ten should decide the winner. On the first ballot, Tifton led with seven, Pelham having six. Camilla started with three, and held them through the contest. Ashburn, although the highest bidder, never stood any show, receiving only three votes.

"Tifton led in every ballot, and in the fifth had nine, while Pelham reached seven, its high-water mark. Finally, in the eighth ballot, Tifton received eleven, one more than necessary to win."

"Here the good news had preceded us, and we were met by the blasts of whistles, boom of fireworks, and an enthusiastic delegation seated Mr. Tift in a wagon and pulled him through town to the courthouse corner, where he and Mr. Pickard made few minutes' talks, and the crowd was told how the fight was won.

In 1907 the first faculty for this school was composed of J. D. Smith, of Griffin, principal; L. O. Freeman, of Sylvester, assistant principal; K. C.

Moore, of Thomasville, agriculturist; Miss Russell, of Milledgeville, home economist; and Mrs. Wilson, of Pike County, matron.

Besides the winning of the school in 1906, there was another important event: the changing of the name Monroe College to Bessie Tift College, in honor of Mrs. H. H. Tift, a graduate of this institution at Forsyth, Georgia. Mr. and Mrs. Tift were benefactors of the college.

The following telegram announced the news to Mr. and Mrs. H. H. Tift:

Cartersville, Georgia
Nov. 21, 1906

"With profound pleasure I announce to you that the Board of Trustees of Monroe College, in regular session last night, by most hearty and unanimous vote, changed the name Monroe College to Bessie Tift College.

"This crown we cheerfully place upon the brow of the unfailing friends of our beloved college.

"J. L. White, Pres.
"Board of Trustees."

The building program expanded during this period. In the spring of 1906, I. W. Myers contracted with Hugger Brothers, of Montgomery, Alabama, for the rebuilding of Hotel Sadie at a contract price of about fifty thousand dollars. After the completion of the building there was a contest to determine a name. Over three hundred names were submitted, and the first prize was won by Judge Eve, who suggested "Hotel Myon," My for Myers and on for Tifton. His prize was a month's free board at the hotel.

During the same year E. E. Slack gave to Mr. Millegan the contract for the erection of a brick building on Second Street. In 1907 S. M. Clyatt let the contract to T. E. Amason for a five-story building, Tifton's first skyscraper, on the corner of Second Street and Love Avenue. Between 1906 and 1910 numerous smaller houses were built in Tifton and Tift County.

Especially important was the erection of public buildings. During three years Tift County schools made more progress than they had ever made before. In 1906 the Omega correspondent of the Gazette reported that a school house was being built. In the same year the citizens of Ty Ty planned to erect a five-thousand dollar building. The next year the Nipper, Fletcher, Brighton, Zion Hope, and Midway school districts planned the construction of school buildings.

A school survey at the time of the creation of Tift valued the school property at seven thousand dollars. In December, 1908, the evaluation of the school property was one hundred fifty-five thousand dollars. The survey showed further that Tift built more school houses in 1907 than any other county in the state. Every school building in the county had been rebuilt

ABRAHAM BALDWIN AGRICULTURAL COLLEGE
Top—Modern auditorium and gymnasium on the campus
Center—Air view of the main college buildings
Bottom—View from the administration building

or remodeled during the previous three-year period. The rise in the valuation of school property was due to agitators led by Superintendent Jason Scarboro and Captain H. H. Tift, who urged that Tifton should have new and adequate school buildings. A bond election authorizing the constructin of a twenty-thousand-dollar school building was voted in the fall of 1905.

The lot chosen as a school site was bought from H. H. Tift for twenty-five hundred dollars. S. N. Adams, of Tifton, was awarded the contract at twenty-three thousand five hundred seventy-five dollars. In July Tifton voted for local taxation for a public school. Then for the first time the school would be town owned and operated.

On August 10, the corner stone was laid with appropriate ceremony; a majority of the business houses in town closed. Chairman W. W. Timmons of the Board of Education was master of ceremonies; J. D. Duncan, chief speaker.

Students headed by Professor Scarboro and teachers marched to the site selected for the building. A scrape was secured to which a hauser with three ropes was attached pulled by boys and girls and guided by Professor Scarboro and Mosley. The first scoop of dirt was pulled by merry children. The building and furniture cost $30,000.

Nineteen-six marked Tift County negroes' first interest in education Sometime before a negro newspaper, the Afro-World, the editorial policy of which was that Southern negroes should be good Democrats or Conservative Republicans, had urged its following to turn to education for salvation. During this year the negroes of Tifton began a school building that was to cost two thousand dollars.

At a meeting of the congregation of the Baptist Church in Tifton early in 1906 the question of building a new church was considered. A committee to solicit pledges to build a twenty-five thousand dollar edifice was appointed. About twelve thousand five hundred dollars was subscribed at the meeting. During the summer a lot was bought from E. P. Bowen and the contract for the new building was given to Wagener and Dobson, of Atlanta and Montgomery, for twenty-six thousand dollars.

On October 31, the cornerstone of Tifton's new church building was laid with appropriate ceremonies. The Reverend Henry Miller, pastor of the Baptist Church, and the Reverend J. W. Domingos, pastor of the Methodist Church, conducted the devotional program. The cornerstone was laid by Amos Tift with the same trowel with which his oldest brother, Henry, laid the cornerstone of Tifton's first brick church building, Monday, April 8. 1895.

The new church building was dedicated in June 1908, with Dr. S. Y. Jameson, president of Mercer University, delivering the dedication sermon. A financial statement from the building committee showed a total cost of forty-two thousand dollars.

Other buildings in the city were the handsome new home of the Bank of Tifton, steam laundry, and McClure's Five and Ten Cent Store, which opened on December 14, 1906.

Another sign of progress during this period was the city waterworks and sewerage system. The same bond issue that assured Tifton of a public school building also provided for a twenty-thousand-dollar waterworks plant. In May 1907, the waterworks system was ready for the city. The cost of a building constructed by the city ran the total cost to twenty-five thousand dollars. A short time afterwards Tifton authorized the issue of thirty thousand dollars in bonds, fifteen thousand dollars for sanitary sewerage. Another improvement in the sanitary division was the street sprinkler, which arrived on July 30, 1909.

Plans for county building also were effected in 1906. Early in the year, Ordinary W. S. Walker purchased from H. H. Tift the vacant lot facing the Tift brick building on Second Street as a site for Tift County's new courthouse. A short time afterwards the ordinary gave the contract for a new jail. The successful bidders were Wagener and Dodson; the contract price was eight hundred and ninety-four dollars. The contract called for the completion by September.

Important organizations which began during this period were the Twentieth Century Library, the Charlotte Carson Chapter of the United Daughters of the Confederacy, and the Tifton History Study Club. The Board of Trade was revived.

Further marks of material progress were the new lumber company, Phillips Pine Company, owned by J. J. L. Phillips, P. D. Phillips, H. H. Tift, and H. H. Scarboro with a capital stock of $25,000, the Tanning and Plumbing Company, with R. W. Terrell, manager, and the half million deposits in the four banks. Tifton in 1906 had a banking capital and a surplus of over $200,000.

There were two important, but widely different, meetings in 1907. The wool growers of Tift and portions of Irwin, Berrien, and Colquitt Counties met in Tifton for the purpose of selling that year's clip. Between 15,000 and 20,000 pounds brought $5,000. The Georgia Federation of Women's Clubs were entertained by the Twentieth Century Library Club of Tifton. Twenty delegates, headed by Mrs. Lipscomb, attended the convention.

Interesting Items from the Tifton Gazette:

1906

"Jan. 26—Keith Carson is the new commander of the Tifton Rifles, replacing R. Eve, who has resigned.

"Judge Eve while expressing an intention to never again take to the sword, acknowledges that the glare of stars and stripes, roll of drum, and voice of bugle will never cease to arouse him and stir his patriotism. He was Captain of Co. F, 4th Infantry National Guard of Ga.

"Population of Tift is 13,000; area of Tift is 308 sq. miles.

"Feb. 2—Wiley Branch remembers when four acres of land, where Hotel Sadie was built, was once traded for a horse, a bridle, and a saddle. This property is now worth, without improvements, $25,000.

"Feb. 16—Brookfield—Two creditable brick blocks have recently been built; one by the McMillan Supply Company, consisting of two store rooms occupied by this company, carries dry goods, groceries, and a full line of farmers' supplies. The second, built by Bowen and McMillan, has two store rooms.

"March 9—Dr. John A. Peterson has a beautiful practice having been here for fourteen years. Dr. Peterson was born in a mighty good county, Coffee; Douglas was his home. He was graduated from Atlanta Dental College in 1890, and later began practicing in Tifton, uses Wilkerson chair, hydraulic engine, and everything modern that can be used in Tifton. He has an elegant suite of rooms.

"Tifton post office receipts will soon enable the post office to be a first class post office. Mr. John M. Duff is postmaster.

"March 30—E. P. Bowen has been elected Tift County's first representative with a majority of 263 votes over S. M. Clyatt.

"April 27—The board of trade was reorganized last week with the following officers: J. L. Herring, president; Briggs Carson, vice-president; H. W. Brown, secretary; J. D. Duncan, treasurer.

"May 11—The Taylor Furniture Company has formed a stock company, embracing many businessmen of this section. It proposes to incorporate with a capital stock of $25,000, and do a general furniture and hardware business under the name of Taylor Furniture and Hardware Company. The stockholders are J. S. Taylor, R. S. Short, J. L. Cochran, J. L. Brooks. G. W. Crum, J. W. Taylor, J. L. Gay, J. N. Horne. W. W. Fender, H. W. Clements, J. D. C. Smith, R. E. Dinsmore, and T. E. Maultsby. Mr. J. S. Taylor is president of the company.

"June 8—Omega—'Our town is small, but young; we have two churches, a nice school building started, five dry goods and grocery stores, one drug store, one livery stable, two blacksmith shops, two cotton gins, plenty of good water, good health, and good people.' Correspondent.

"June 15—Tuesday afternoon, about 1:15, a severe wind, scarcely attaining the force of a cyclone yet far beyond the average whirlwind, struck Tifton, inflicting a damage of $8,000 and injuring three persons. The Presbyterian church was totally demolished and the plant of the Tifton Manufacturing Company was seriously damaged.

"June 22—It was decided last week to reincorporate the Merchants' and Farmers' as a national bank, and to increase the capital stock to $50,000, with a surplus of $10,000.

"July 13—W. J. Henderson is convinced that he has found a good location for an oil well one and one-half miles northeast of Tifton.

"Aug. 3—Tift County's taxable property is estimated at $3,500,000.

"Aug. 25—Contractor W. A. Taylor, who is building the new A. B. & A. depot has the work well under way and the framing up.

"Oct. 5—According to appointment, a representative number from the churches of all denominations in Tift assembled at Zion Hope church on Sunday last, to organize the Tift County singing convention. The convention was organized with the following officers: J. J. Baker, president; W. B. Johns, vice-president; J. L. Jay, Jr., secretary. The following were elected as an executive committee: W. H. Spooner, chairman; Wm. Gibbs, J. L. Jay, J. B. Livingston, and David Whiddon."

1907

"Jan. 18—The formal opening of the new school was held Monday with H. H. Tift, W. W. Timmons, and Jason Scarboro addressing the students and parents.

"Jan. 25—Arrangements have been made by the county board of education for opening a school this week at the Tifton cotton mills.

"April 26—In an expression, declamation, and music contest with Nashville, Valdosta, and Moultrie, Miss Florence Rice, of Tifton, won the music medal.

"May 24—For the first time in five years, Tifton has an elaborate program of commencement exercises for the public school. The students who will take part in the programs are: Amos Tift, Lennon Bowen, Agnes Scarborough, Charles Soule, O'Zelma Crosby, and Edwin Scarborough.

"June 28—In a baby show held in Tifton last week, the following won prizes: 3 months to 1 year old, Lois Sineath; 1 to 3 years old, Harriet Evans; 3 to 5 years old, Banks Carson. Mrs. E. L. Vickers was awarded the prize for the most handsomely decorated cart.

"July 5—This contract and agreement made and entered into this the 1st day of July, 1907, by and between the city of Tifton, acting by and through the mayor and council of the city of Tifton, of the first part, and L. P. Thurman, I. W. Myers, W. W. Banks, O. Daniel, J. E. Cochran, E. F. Bussey and J. J. L. Phillips of said county and state, of the second part, witnesseth:

"1. That the said party of the first part has this day granted to the parties of the second part, their successors or assigns, the exclusive right and privilege for the period of ten years to build, equip, maintain, and operate in and along the streets of the city of Tifton, a street railway . . .

"July 12—Iroquois Tribe, No. 73 Hunting Grounds of Tifton, Reservation of Georgia, Improved Order of Red Men, was organized Friday night of last week with the following officers: J. A. Ryals, C. C. Hall, W. C. Spurling, O. F. Sheppard, Wm. M. Sellars, A. G. Dickard, E. F. Conley, R. G. Coarsey, R. M. Manning, J. A. Peterson, E. O'Quinn, C. M. Boswell, C. R. Dickart, W. S. Smith, S. C. Dorsey, J. M. Jones, R. A. Smith.

"Aug. 1—The Georgia-Florida Sawmill Association has decided that every mill operated by a member of the association will close during the month of August.

"Aug. 23—The mills have decided to stay shut down. Labor conditions have improved, but prices continue entirely too low to warrant cutting timber bought on a high market.

"Sept. 6—Postal receipts for the fiscal year 1907 are $15,000.

"Sept. 20—Ty Ty—Mrs. C. E. Pitt is Ty Ty's pioneer merchant, having been in business for twenty years. W. E. Williams, J. R. Willis, B. F. Crum, and Jehee Whiddon are among Ty Ty's merchants. The farmer's cotton warehouse handles about 3,000 bales of cotton annually.

"Nov. 8—Yesterday officials of the four banks of Tifton met and organized the Tifton Clearing House Association; H. H. Tift was elected president, J. M. Paulk, vice-president, and Frank Scarboro, secretary. Four trustees were elected to take charge of its affairs: J. J. L. Phillips, W. H. Hendricks, E. A. Buck, and E. P. Bowen.

"It was decided that, in order to make the cotton crop move without delay, to maintain the price of the staple and to meet the demands of local business, clearing house certificates to the amount of $50,000 would be issued, and this was done at once, the certificates being in circulation this morning.

"This issue is backed by a deposit of $75,000 in gilt-edged collateral, made necessary only by the fact that local banks have been unable to obtain currency, due to the recent money panic in the North and East.

1908

"Jan. 3—A survey shows that the total property owned by corporations have paid $3,326.73 to the county treasury for general county purposes and $3,584.52 under the special school levy.

"The corporations include: Western Union Telegraph Company, Southern Express Company, Postal Telegraph Company, Southern Bell Telephone Company, A. C. L., G. S. & F., A. B. & C., and the Tifton Ice & Power Company.

"Feb. 20—Tifton made a holiday of Wednesday. Stores, banks, business houses and the public school closed and all joined in celebrating the opening of the Agricultural School.

"April 3—A large crowd of girls left the high school at recess, All Fools' Day, and were immediately followed by Professor Sewell on horseback, and Professor Scarboro in a road cart. The girls were rounded up near the A. B. and A. depot and driven into town like herded cattle.

"May 1—C. L. Parker yesterday took Joe Brown and J. B. Murrow, Hoke Smith for a five-hundred-dollar bet on the governor's race. The stakes were placed in the hands of R. W. Padrick.

"May 8—Tifton Lodge No. 1114, Benevolent and Protective Order of Elks, was organized last night with the following officers: H. H. Coombs, W. T. Smith, R. W. Padrick, C. D. Fish, Geo. E. Simpson, Frank Scarboro, H. H. Tift, Jr., C. C. Guest, W. W. Banks, and S. M. Clyatt.

"May 29—In consolidating the school census of the city of Tifton, there are many items of public interest: there are in the city, 409 white children of school age and 130 colored. There is one white boy over ten years of age who can read but cannot write. There are 21 colored boys who neither read nor write. 304 children attended school over 5 months during 1907. Six have never attended any school. There are no deaf, dumb, blind, or idiotic children in Tifton.

"Sept. 25—'Ty Ty—There are twelve stores, two barber shops, two ginneries, a sawmill, cotton warehouse, and livery stable. An excellent hotel of 14 rooms is conducted by Mrs. Leila Stephens.' Correspondent.

"Chula—'The town has four stores, a cotton gin, and a blacksmith and woodworking shop. The two-teacher school has an enrollment of 70 pupils.' Correspondent.

"Nov. 6—The Tifton Cotton Mills resumed operation Monday morning after being closed down a year.

"Dec. 11—H. H. Tift is in receipt of advice from Secretary Cortelyou, of the Treasury Department, that the lot offered by him on Love Avenue had been accepted by the Department as the site for Tifton's new post office building. The price paid was $7,000.

1909

"Feb. 19—At first, J. C. Britton, who is in charge of the soil survey of Tift County, thought the soil in Tift was of the variety known as the Norfolk series, but since the work has progressed he is convinced that it is superior to the Norfolk, and a grade that he has never yet found in any other county during his survey of Georgia.

"Wednesday, L. E. Lapham, field superintendent and inspector of soil survey, with headquarters, came to Tifton and in company with Mr. Britton and Clarence Wood, spent Thursday going over the survey made. He confirmed the opinion previously formed by them that the soil in Tift County was of a new and distinct series and they have named it the Tifton loam and Tifton Sandy loam, and by that name it will be known in the future.

"Feb. 26—Mrs. N. Peterson went over to Ty Ty Saturday, the 13th, where she organized a club in that little city styled the Ty Ty Improvement Club, with the following officers: Miss Dowd, president; Mrs. Frank Pickett, vice-president; Miss Mary Nelson, recording secretary; and Mrs. R. R. Pickett, treasurer.

"Aug. 6—The old village of Tifton is going some when she gains a hundred thousand dollars in tax values during as bad a year as the past twelve months have been.

"Aug. 27—Twelve names had been sent in up to yesterday to the Tifton Chapter, U. D. C., by Confederate veterans who are entitled to crosses of honor, as follows: D. A. Fulwood, J. J. F. Goodman, T. S. Moore, D. R. Willis, R. H. Hutchinson, Sr., J. A. Dickinson, O. L. Chesnutt, J. M. Eason, Robert Henderson, J. J. Baker, W. A. Patton. and W. H. Partridge.

"Sept. 10—Omega has a population of 300 people, but there are possibly twice this number supplied by her merchants. The Omega Grocery Co. is one of the strong mercantile establishments of this section and enjoys a large patronage. The company has been doing business in Omega five years, and each year has shown a steady and substantial growth over the previous year. Guy A. Cox is manager of the company and is the Omega postmaster.

"Miles Cowart is a pioneer in general merchandise. Joseph Marchant has a meat market. There is a cotton warehouse, two cotton gins, and a grist mill at Omega.

"Sept. 17—W. O. Tift, Tifton's postmaster died Sept. 14 at 3:00 o'clock in Mystic, Conn., of paresis. He was sixty-seven years old. He came to Tifton in 1876, was appointed postmaster and held that position until 1890.

"Sept. 24—The Myers Seed & Plant Company, of Tifton, shipped last week 100,000 strawberry plants. They are shipping about 10,000 daily this week.

"Oct. 15—First Boys' Fair:

"Corn Prizes—First ($10) C. H. Fletcher of Chula School. Second ($5) Paul Bolton, of the Fender School, Third ($2.50) Homer Bolton, of the Fender School.

"Cotton Prizes—First ($10) Paul Bolton, Fender School. Second ($5) Lonnie Exum, Brookfield School. Wilbur Long third ($2.50) Chula School. Those receiving $1 each for cotton exhibits: Houston Overby, Lloyd Crum, Eddie Yen, Lonnie Exum, Paul Bolton, Wilburn Long, and Hughy Johnson.

"Those receiving (?) each for corn exhibits: Ben Jones, R. L. Summers, Emory Logue, Houston Overby, Geo. Shannon, J. H. Lieneberger, Ernest Dauce, Homer Crum, Etheridge Gay, and Clifford Whiddon. C. W. Fulwood also presented each with a pocket knife.

"Oct. 22—The Gazette carries to its Tift County readers this week an announcement that means more for the city of Tifton and Tift County, than any move that has been made since the legislative act creating Tift County. The woodlands belonging to H. H. Tift will be put on the market. Mr. Tift owns 28,736 acres of land in Tift County, nearly all of which is woodland. The woodland lots of 490 acres each, will be cut up into tracts of 100 acres, or in varying sizes to suit the purchasers, the land cleared and fenced and houses built thereon, and sold on comparatively easy terms to those desiring homes."

CHAPTER X
PROGRESS FROM 1910—1917

The year 1910 was ushered in by literary programs in Tifton. The Author's Club dedicated its first program to Ralph Waldo Emerson. Later "Enoch Arden" was interpreted by Mrs. Frederick Herr Jones, with the accompanying music of Richard Strauss by Miss Deborah McRae. The Twentieth Century Library Club celebrated its fifth anniversary with a literary and musical program.

In 1914 this club presented in a grand opera program Signor and Madame Bernia, famous artists of the Metropolitan Grand Opera Company, New York. Signor Bernia alternated in tenor roles with the great Caruso, and Madame Bernia was from the Savage English Opera Company, where she was a leading soprano.

Superior to even grand opera was Nature's distinctive contribution to this period, Halley's Comet in April, 1910. People in Tift County rose early to observe this celestial phenomenon as it was visible to the naked eye in the eastern heavens from a few minutes before 4:00 a.m. until daylight. This morning star, named for Edmund Halley, English astronomer and mathematician, was so brilliant that the early rising moon appeared dull in contrast. It had appeared probably twelve times before 1910: 1373, 1456, 1531, 1607, 1682, 1755, 1835; it is probable that astronomers referred to the comet in 12 B.C. and A.D. 989, 1066, 1145, and 1501.

Many people, white and colored, in Tift County thought the world was coming to an end when they saw this illumination.

In connection with Halley's Comet an interesting coincidence challenges attention. Mark Twain, internationally famous writer, who was born in 1835 during the appearance of the comet, died in 1910, the last year the comet has appeared.

During this period there were celebrations and meetings of different kinds. The great Wire Grass Exposition opened on September 27, 1911. The main building having 24,000 feet of floor space was draped in colorful bunting and brilliantly lighted with electricity. The exposition grounds, within five minutes walk from the center of Tifton, covered a space of five hundred by six hundred feet between the National Highway and the Georgia Southern and Florida and contained eight beautiful buildings.

Over fifty counties participated in the exposition. Cities had special days, Macon, Atlanta, and Savannah. On Governor's Day—also Atlanta day—Governor Hoke Smith and staff, Mayor Winn, President Paxon, and two hundred members of the Atlanta Chamber of Commerce came.

The meetings of different organizations were beneficial. The eighth annual convention of the Masons of the Second Congressional District was held in Tifton in 1911. A Good Roads Association, having as its purpose the building and repairing of roads throughout the county was organized. Chairman H. H. Tift, of the Central Route Association, called for a meeting of the auxiliary committee for the purpose of securing the speedy completion of the National Highway and to form a National Highway Association.

Tift County was represented on Cotton Day at State Federation of Women's Clubs in Albany. This celebration was the first of its kind in South Georgia since the War Between the States. Mrs. Jane Walker, a widow, wove the cloth on an old-fashioned loom.

Spring Day at the District Agricultural School was a success. Prizes in athletics were offered for such achievements as one-hundred-yard dash, one-fourth-mile run, one-half-mile run, one-mile run, running broad jump, running high jump, shot put, society wall scaling, greased pole, greased pig, sack race, and three-legged race.

Versatility of progress was further attested by the addition of another religious organization—the Primitive Baptist Church. Meetings were held in the Presbyterian Church until the Primitives completed their brick church. The membership consisted of twenty-five.

The great era of building which began in 1906 continued vigorously through 1916. In May, 1912, Tift County authorized an issue of sixty thousand dollars in bonds with which to pay for a site previously selected and to build a courthouse. The contract for the erection of the new building was given to Edwards, Jenkins, and Company, of Ocala, Florida, for fifty thousand dollars. On December 10, of the same year, the cornerstone was laid with appropriate ceremonies conducted by the Tifton Masonic Lodge; but it was not until a year later that the Tift County commissioners met with a representative of the contractors to accept the completed building. The cost of the building was fifty-four thousand, seven hundred dollars.

In an oil mill stock canvass of the city early in 1912, a committee from the Chamber of Commerce secured subscriptions amounting to sixteen thousand dollars. Twenty thousand dollars of the capital stock had been pledged previously by several outside oil mills that desired to establish a plant in Tifton. The seventy-five-thousand-dollar cottonseed oil mill, declared by an authority to be the best of its kind in the world, was completed in 1912. The petitioners for charter were, J. D. Little, John Hill, H. H. Tift, W. W. Banks, W. L. Harman, T. E. Stubbs, T. E. and J. J. L. Phillips, L. P. Thurman, H. H. Tift, Jr., and J. D. Cook.

In October of 1912 the International Chemical Company purchased from H. H. Tift fifteen acres of land in the northeastern section of the city. The company erected for about one hundred thousand dollars an acidulating plant, for the purpose of manufacturing commercial fertilizers. The contractor in charge was J. M. Davis.

To Tifton housewives there was an enterprise even more important than this acidulating plant—a broom factory. Many housekeepers pantomimed the saw, "a new broom sweeps clean." The factory was on First Street.

Business men were as interested in Tifton's first cotton compress, for which the Chamber of Commerce was responsible, as the ladies were in the broom factory. This compress pressed the first bale of cotton in 1912.

Farmers had a day of rejoicing in 1913, when contracts between J. H. Bowen, a Missouri owner of the patents for the Common Sense Harrow, and the Tifton Foundry and Machine Company, then recently organized, were signed. The latter company took the exclusive manufacture of Brown's invention for the Southern territory. The contracts required a minimum output of fifty thousand harrows annually, requiring the purchase of twenty thousand dollars worth of new equipment by the foundry.

During the years before the United States entered World War I many people rejoiced over the building program. The following list shows approximate cost of projects in 1916: paving, $50,000; high school building, $30,000; waterworks extension, $25,000; fire department, $6,000; Central Grocery Company, $30,000; Rickerson Grocery Company, $25,000; Tifton Packing Company, $150,000; peanut Oil Mill, $25,000; Southern Utilities Light and Ice Plant improvements, $40,000; T. W. Tift Theater Building, $15,000; and new residences, $50,000.

Another significant mark of progress was the revival of enthusiasm for a new packing plant in Tifton. H. H. Tift, E. P. Bowen, and W. W. Banks agreed to[1] "underwrite sixty thousand dollars worth of the stock if the city would raise forty thousand dollars and the people outside the town, fifty thousand dollars." The fifty thousand dollars to be raised outside the city could be paid in cash, cattle, or hogs, payable on or before October 1, 1917.

Early in 1917 a board of directors was elected for the packing plant: H. H. Tift, E. P. Bowen, W. W. Banks, B. E. Smith, I. C. Touchstone, R. C. Ellis, Briggs Carson, J. D. Cook, W. D. Fountain, J. J. L. Phillips, M E. Hendry, H. H. Tift, Jr., Frank Scarboro, W. L. Harmon, C. W. Fulwood. The officers were: W. W. Banks, president; H. H. Tift and M. E. Hendry, vice-presidents; Frank Scarboro, secretary; and R. W. Goodman, treasurer. A short time afterwards contracts were given for the construction of our one hundred thousand dollars worth of buildings. R. V. LaBarre, of Jacksonville, had charge of most of the work.

In the building program Uncle Sam had a part. The contract for the erection of a post office building was given in 1913 to James Devault, of Canton, Ohio; the Treasury Department approved of his bid April 16. The cost of the building was forty-six thousand five hundred dollars. Three

---

1. Fred Shaw's manuscript about the history of Tift County.

years later the directors of the Bank of Tifton decided to erect an even more imposing edifice than the post office—a fifty thousand dollar bank structure.

Tifton in 1917 authorized bond issue of thirty-seven thousand dollars for addition in the waterworks system, for improvements in the fire department and for the erection of a new school house. The new building was to be used for high school, and the old, for grammar. The contract for high school building was given to V. C. Parker and Company, of Waycross; the plumbing to a local firm, Morgan, Johnston, and Morgan.

During this period there was distinctive progress in education. The Twentieth Century Library Club had a conspicuous part in the development of the rural schools. At that time Mrs. Nicholas Peterson was chairman of the education committee. From the beginning she encouraged the teachers in the poverty-stricken schools of Tift County to confide in her. Mrs. Peterson, a former school teacher herself, was determined to effect a reformation in the rural schools. She struggled for an idea—finally it came. There were twenty-five rural schools in the county and fifty women on her committee. Every two members would adopt a school and inspire it to depart from its antiquated methods.

When the women had been selected for the different schools, they on the first visits were impressed by the fact that there was no money, no interest from parents, no equipment, no school house that had a shred of self respect, no roads that could be worthy of the name for several months in the year, no provision made for housing the teachers; it was one long unvarying tale.

"This survey of the ground was the first step. Mrs. Peterson needed to do more proselyting. Everyone of the fifty women—and the large number she had found necessary to add to that original group—was as interested and enthusiastic as she herself. From then on the Tift County rural schools changed, sometimes by leaps and bounds, sometimes slowly . . . Every magazine, pamphlet, or book that had any bearing on rural schools was eagerly seized upon. The women found out what art companies supplied pictures and casts for school use and learned their catalogs by heart. They wrote to the Bureau of Education, at Washington, D. C., to send its bulletins regularly and for the very complete handbook on athletic games for schools, issued by the Philippine Bureau of Education; and to the Normal School at Kirksville, Missouri, for their plan by which any school could have a complete modern sanitary system for three hundred and fifty dollars.

"The first big step was to get money. Georgia, as the women soon found out by looking up the law, has a regular school tax apportioned out to each county, according to the number of children. In addition, it has the county unit plan whereby a county may ask that the question of levying a local tax be submitted to the vote of its people, a two-thirds majority being required to carry it. Mrs. Peterson immediately saw her opportunity. The women all became politicians and not a person in the county was allowed to go unmolested until he had been convinced by one means or another that a local school tax was the one preeminently desirable thing. As a result, when the measure was brought up, it received an overwhelming majority vote. With that money, new buildings were secured, the term lengthened to seven months, and the teachers' salaries raised to forty dollars, monthly, and in some instances to fifty.

"The first year Mrs. Peterson and her band of workers had many discouragements. They learned that a rural school does not grow up like a beanstalk, and that once adopted it has to stay in the family for a good many years. Although many of the reforms they wanted to institute needed only money, the majority demanded the cooperation of not only the teacher, but of the children and their parents as well."[2]

The attainment of state requirements for a standard country school was the goal of all school mothers; after the struggles of these sponsors for five years, sixteen schools qualified for their diplomas, and six or eight were lacking in only one point.

"Mrs. Peterson has a typical story to tell of the Camp Creek School, which she took into her charge.

" 'The first thing I did was to go to my school. I naturally felt timid about going on a mission of this kind; but I mustered up courage, and one morning I invited some friends to join Dr. Peterson and myself in a little picnic on the river about three miles beyond the school. In my car I carried a delightful reader, one who could entertain children by the hour. I told her what I was going to do and urged her to come to my rescue and do her best. First, I spoke to the children and told them that I wanted to help them make their school the best in the country . . . ; then I had this friend recite, and she completely captured the children. When I asked them if they would like to have me bring her back again, they responded as one.

" 'Next, I sent them "Miss Minerva and William Green Hill" for the teacher to read to them. Very soon I went again, this time taking some pictures I had left from my school work. I carried tacks and hammer and had the children help me group them and put them up. Asking questions about those I knew they were familiar with and telling them about others. This pleased them.

" 'They had their stove set in a box of sand that had never been emptied and in which all expectorated; so I talked to them on sanitary health topics, told them dangers of such things, and asked if they would not take it up and send to town to get a piece of tin. They did this right away. I also

---

2. McCall's Magazine, November 1915.

called their attention to the need of cleanliness and of washing windows and polishing the stove. The very next Saturday, when the teacher came to town, he asked me where to buy polish, as the girls had told him not to come back without it. I also gave him a waste-paper basket and several story books. Then I offered a medal for scholarship, a prize for penmanship, a prize to the neatest and cleanest child in the school, and to the child who used only his own drinking cup.

" 'On one visit I asked the children if they would like to own their own library. Of course, they said "yes." I told them, then, if they would make up enough money to buy a good bookcase that I would give them the library, never dreaming that they would do it that term. This was on Tuesday morning. The teacher came to town on Saturday with twenty dollars the children had sent for me to buy their bookcase. You can imagine my surprise as well as delight. I canvassed every agency I' could think of and in a few days I had it filled. When I carried the books down, I had the teacher dismiss the school and let the children help fix them. I believe they were the happiest children I have ever seen in my life. But I have never been quite so extravagant in my promises since.

" 'Our attendance was increasing so steadily on account of the new things being done for the school that a new room was in sight, and by Christmas we had to add it and employ another teacher. Next, we planned to improve the grounds. I went down and spent the day, and while the men plowed the ground, and put up a fence, the women and children planted the seed and plants that I had brought them. It looked very nice at dark when I left for town. At the same time I had an old piano which the Tifton Board of Education had discarded taken out to them. Since then, we have kept adding improvements, from time to time, until we have beautiful grounds, two rooms filled with good pictures, piano, books, water cooler, tables with nice covers, pretty pot plants in jardinieres, shades and curtains to all windows, cloakrooms, and large clock. The little girls exhibited at our fair whole suits of underwear, luncheon-sets, towels, pillowcases, scarfs, centerpieces, caps, aprons, dresses, in fact, everything that you can think of. They have also been taught canning, preserving, cake-baking, candy-making, and the boys woodwork. We have had our diploma from the State Board of Education for over a year'."[2]

In 1915 Tift County had a signal honor. At an educational meeting in Atlanta, a resolution was passed for the association to try to stamp out illiteracy in Georgia. As a preliminary step there was to be selected a county in which to blot out completely adult illiteracy. After much discussion Tift was selected on account of its progress in rural education.

Closely allied to the progress in education was another improvement, the Tift County Hospital, which opened on May 21, 1915. The equipment

---
2. Ibid.

was among the best in this section of the state. It consisted of nine rooms, including an operating room and maternity ward.

Tift County not only progressed in education during these peaceful days, but discovered itself as an agricultural center. The blast of the long whistle at the H. H. Tift mill on June 23, 1916, announced not only that the employee's work was over for all time, but that a new era had dawned —the era of agriculture. In relation to this last whistle the Tifton Gazette said, "It sounded its own requiem and bid Tifton farewell. All of the timber in this section has been cut.

"H. H. Tift established the mill in 1872. It was burned in 1887 and soon afterwards rebuilt. Except for the interval and a short period from the summer of 1915 until early in the present year, the mill has been in constant operation.

"The mill will be dismantled, the best parts sold and the remainder scrapped. The tram road will be taken up and the rails sold. The planing mill will be retained for a while, the machinery operated by electric motor."

As early as 1912 farsighted lumber brokers left Tifton. During June of that year a farmer's institute was conducted in the courthouse by the State College of Agriculture. At the conclusion of the program the Tift County Agricultural Association was organized with J. W. Hollis, president, and C. V. Martin, secretary.

Two months later Henry Tift announced his intention of building a thirty-six foot boulevard, eight miles in length to encircle the city. It was finished in 1914, and the entire cost, $10,000 was borne by H. H. Tift. Land bordering on the boulevard was placed on sale, inside land being put into city lots and outside land into five-and-ten-acre lots.

The presenting of the second exhibition of the South Georgia Land and Agricultural Exposition was an accomplishment of 1912. The prizes won by Tift County farmers were: cotton, W. H. Willis $50; J. T. Mims, improved corn and cotton planter with plates, valued at $15; hay, W. L. Harman, $25; peanuts, G. R. Denby, $10; cotton, corn, and peanut planter with roller, valued at $13.50; cane, W. H. Ponder, $15.

Early in 1913 the State College of Agriculture offered a two-day course for farmers of Tift County. Experts in every phase of farm work, including soil selection and preparation, seed selection, fertilizing, cultivation, harvesting, and marketing, together with stock and poultry raising and dairying gave free lectures.

At this time there were a number of large farms near Tifton, including the following: the J. D. Cook farm with 702 acres in cultivation; the W. A. Greer farm with 900 acres in cultivation; the J. H. Young plantation with 1,800 acres in cotton alone. The most money, however, was made by small independent farmers. An indication of a modern trend in farming was the organization of a truck growers' society with two hundred acres pledged. In 1914 P. D. Fulwood had on his truck farm twelve acres in cabbage seed which expected to yield ten million plants.

In 1915 Tift County won first prize for the best county exhibit at the Georgia-Florida Fair. The exhibit of the Tifton Farm Tool Manufacturing Company won five blue ribbons. Foremost among Tift County's individual competitors was R. S. Kell, whose cotton exhibit won three prizes. The following Tift County Corn Club boys won trips to Atlanta Harvest Festival: Warren Walker, Mike Tucker, John Barnes, R. A. Griffin, Butler Hollis, Joe Cravey, Jeff Mickle, Hunter Royal, Joseph Blount, Colin Malcolm and George Conger. The following received a scholarship to the Boys' Corn Club short course at Athens: George Conger, Johnnie Conger, Sim Stewart, and Richard Drexel.

A distinct sign of progress was Tift County's donation of $1000 to secure a farm demonstrator; an equal amount was to come from the State College of Agriculture and the National Department of Agriculture. Of Tift County's share, three hundred dollars was to be paid by the A. and M. School, and the remainder secured by private subscription. L. S. Watson was appointed the first farm demonstrator in the county.

The climax of the period was the introduction of a bill in the legislature to provide Tift County with an experiment station. The author of the bill, R. C. Ellis, was also the author of the statewide sanitation bill. His arguments were so convincing that much sentiment was attached to his proposal.

CHAPTER XI

"WORLD EARTHQUAKE"—WORLD WAR I

The Archduke Francis Ferdinand and his wife were assassinated in June 1914 at Sarjavo—then followed on July 28 the first tremors of the "World Earthquake"—Austria declared war on Servia. "The Archduke and his wife were assassinated in Austro-Hungarian territory by an Austro-Hungarian subject."[1] The Servian government had no responsibility in the crime. Austria, however, blamed Servian secret societies and individual Servians who influenced Austro-Hungarian subjects. When the Austrian government demanded that Servia denounce activities that incited such crimes as this assassination, the latter agreed, but refused to allow Austro-Hungarian officials a part in the punishment of the instigators.

Austria used this refusal as a pretended cause for declaring war. The genuine reason, however, was the former's desire for more territory. Austria wanted access to the Aegean Sea and the route through Servia was the most desirable.

These tremors grew into a quake that finally shook the entire world. Germany, Austria-Hungary, and Italy for a while stood together as the Triple Alliance; England, Russia, and France, as the Triple Entente.

The quake shook cotton low and food prices high in Tift County. There was, on the other hand, a favorable effect. September 14, 1914 was another achievement day for Tift County: on that date in order to give quick service with war news, the Tifton Gazette appeared with a new name, the Daily Tifton Gazette. This change made Tifton distinctive; it was the smallest town in the United States with a daily newspaper.

About three years after the establishing of the Daily Tifton Gazette, April 6, 1917, bold headlines in the Gazette told a story: "United States Declares State of War With Germany." Crowds in front of the Tifton Gazette office, waiting for news; cheers of listeners in front of the courthouse as the band played "Over There," "A Long, Long Trail;" moist eyes as the rhythm changed to "Keep the Home Fires Burning," "Till We Meet Again," "Smile the While"; school children knitting sweaters or making candles; liberty loan drives; war sermons from the pulpit; service stars on the window; Red Cross activities; a whole town fasting and praying for the tide of war—these pictures were true to the Tifton of 1917-1918.

The large number of men who enlisted for military service through the Tifton station during the latter part of April and the early part of May attested a high degree of patriotism in Tifton. On May 18, people re-

---
1. Tifton Gazette.

ceived notice of President Wilson's proclamation that all male persons between the ages of twenty and thirty-one years should register on June 5, 1917.

Patriotic citizens continued to volunteer for service from the county after the first registration. During this crisis the county and town were in accord with the nation. There were, of course, a few "slackers," but the blaze of patriotism outshone these sparks of dissension.

A Tift County negro, who was filing his questionnaire with the local board, exhibited a patriotic attitude. Although he had a wife and child, he requested no exemption. When asked if his wife wanted to file an exemption claim, the negro replied, "No, boss, she would if I wanted her to, but I don't. I was born and raised here and want to go along with the rest." In reference to this statement, J. L. Herring, editor of the Tifton Gazette, said, "Had this negro been a gifted orator and spoken an hour, he could not have said more. A hero could not say more."

According to Captain Heidt, Tift County sent to the army more men, in proportion to population than any other county in the state.

Despite the turmoil of war, there were various developments in Tift County. The Tifton Packing Company, Fulwood Park, Heinz Salting Station, and the new passenger station for Atlantic Coast Line and Georgia Southern and Florida, worth twenty-five thousand dollars, were completed during the war period. The Bank of Tifton moved into its new home on March 26, 1917.

During this year, too, the undergrowth on the land given by H. H. Tift for a park was cleared, trees trimmed, the banks of the big ditch, running through the grounds, leveled, and trees, such as magnolias, arbor vitaes, holly, dogwood, crepe myrtle, and weeping willows were set out.

The year 1917 was also important on account of an illustrious visitor to Tifton, William J. Bryan.

An innovation in the Tifton High School that year was the publication of the first annual, the Talisman, which sold for fifty cents. Pat Fulwood was editor-in-chief.

The second issue, which came from the press in 1918, was dedicated to J. L. Herring, editor of the Tifton Gazette. One of its main features was its section honoring the boys in service. Mildred Slack was editor-in-chief.

Another innovation during the period was the introduction of daylight saving. On the first night after this change Tifton people, forgetting that the hands of the clock had moved up, yawned and stretched, when suddenly observing that it was ten o'clock. Then realizing that ten o'clock was just eight by the former time, these citizens laughed at themselves.

Along with daylight saving came fasting according to the following lines:

> "Monday is wheatless.
> Tuesday is meatless.
> Wednesday is wheatless.
> Saturday is porkless.
> Every day one meal wheatless.
> Every day one meal meatless."

This kitchen theme for 1918 was as important as the liberty loan drives. Tift during April of 1918 led all Georgia counties except Fulton in the organization of war savings and thrift stamps. Every school in the county organized for the sale of stamps and for other phases of war aid. Students of the junior high school in Tifton made in two weeks fourteen hundred trench candles for our "Doughboys" and "Sammies," pseudonyms for the United States soldiers. ("Boches" was the nickname for German soldiers. The term was derived from Coboche, French word for head, big thick head.) Tift went over the top with the fourth liberty loan drive.

For women there was in 1918 an amendment to the Constitution that was almost as significant as the liberty loan drives. For the first time women in Tift County, as well as those in the entire nation, had the privilege of voting.

An important literary achievement for Tift County in 1918 was the publication of J. L. Herring's "Saturday Night Sketches," which received enthusiastic applause from all groups of people. Herring was hailed as "the prose laureate of the Wiregrass."

These signs of progress, material and literary, were the rifts in the clouds of war. Every home in Tift County was touched by the horrors of this "storm and stress" period. Then finally one day anxious mothers, wives, and sweethearts welcomed a calm.

On November 11, 1918 there was great rejoicing in the world, and Tifton joined other towns and cities in celebrating peace. In the absence of Mayor Hargrett, Mayor Pro Tem. McLeod issued a proclamation, closing all business houses at 1:30 and declaring the day a holiday.

Whistles screamed for thirty minutes. Cars filled with merry noisemakers paraded the streets all the afternoon and part of the night. Young and old with tin pans, bells, horns, tomato cans, and crackers kept the vibrations going. A long procession marched to the rhythm of Herbert Moor's drum. Over a hundred Packing Plant employees marched into town, carrying large American and British flags. Trucks from the Central Grocery and other companies carried at intervals different loads of people, who were giving joyous yells. The Red Cross Chapter filled one impressive float.

Many cars were attractively decorated. The town band in fantastic costume added to the colorful parade.

The fighting had ceased, but the effects of the upheaval could not cease. The struggle for normal conditions was active for years after the Armistice. During this struggle, however, Tift County again achieved. In 1919 came the announcement that Tifton had secured the experiment station. Long blasts of the fire whistle gave the good news.

At a meeting of the board of trustees of the Coastal Plain Experiment Station in Waycross, Tifton and Tift County's bid for the station was accepted. Tifton's cash offer was raised to $25,000 to meet that of Savannah, her nearest rival. Furthermore, such articles as the following from "Cairo Messenger," no doubt, had a strong influence in the selection of Tifton.

"By all means, and by all that is right and fair, the Experiment Station should be located in Tifton.

"When the bill was passed at the last session of the Georgia Legislature, creating an experiment station for this portion of Georgia, it was intended that it should be placed where it would be of best service to the greatest number of farmers. This being true, then Tifton is the logical and proper place for it."

At the first meeting of the board of trustees in Savannah, they inspected the site offered by Chatham County. A few days before their final decision, they came to Tifton to inspect the site here. Later the trustees inspected the sites offered by Worth, Ware, and Appling Counties. Not until 1922, however, did Spooner and Cauthen receive the contract for erecting the administration building.

Tift County was acquiring the habit of "building, bonding, and booming." (Fred Shaw's manuscript on Tift County History.) In the Spring of 1919 the county floated a $300,000 bond issue for the improvement of the roads. This bond issue was followed by smaller issues in every town in the county.

In the industrial division of Tifton an important change came when Armour and Company of Chicago bought the plant of Tifton Packing Company. Another important phase of industrial progress in 1919 was the establishing at Tifton of the first tobacco market in Tift County.

Along with material progress Tifton did not forget to pause for tributes to some of its citizens. The Twentieth Century Library Club dedicated a program to mothers, Mrs. H. H. Tift and Mrs. J. C. Goodman, and presented J. L. Herring a loving cup. The town expressed its confidence in and appreciation of H. H. Tift by requesting him to serve as mayor of the city, and he responded to the request. The Board of Trade presented a silver loving cup to Mr. J. L. Herring.

CHAPTER XII

THE TURBULENT TWENTIES

The active prosperity in Southwest Georgia lasted only a few years after World War I. Although there was little dire want in the early twenties, prosperity was bidding farewell to this section.

During the war, the thrifty packing plant, the meteoric cotton market, the successful Frank Scarboro Company, the success of all forms of business gave Tifton's business square the air of the nineties. The material progress of churches often gives an index to financial conditions in a community: the Primitive Baptists of Tifton, though few in number, built at this time a seven-thousand-dollar church building.

Nineteen-nineteen was important for two developments, which eventually gave Tifton and Tift County such distinctions as few things had given since the farewell blow of the whistle at the big Tift mill: the revival of interest in tobacco and the establishment of the Coastal Plain Experiment Station in Tifton.

A tobacco warehouse company leased the plant of the Tifton Compress Company, and made additions costing $3,500. A survey of the tobacco acreage within the county revealed that there were one thousand two hundred acres used for cigarette tobacco in Tifton. During that summer 539,735 pounds of tobacco was sold for $111,933.35 or an average of $20.74 a hundred pounds—a remarkable achievement. In 1920 the tobacco stemming and redrying plant of Imperial Tobacco Company began operation.

The following year more than one hundred tobacco barns were built in the county. The greatest evidence, however, of the interest in tobacco was the construction of a $200,000 stemming and redrying plant by the Tifton Investment Company in 1920. The Imperial Tobacco Company immediately took charge of the plant—a transfer that assured Tifton of large payrolls during the summer and fall when the plant was in operation, and of the employment of scores of white men and a hundred negroes. In 1922 the Investment Company sold its interest in the plant to the Imperial people and used the profit to erect a large tobacco warehouse.

Although the financial structure of Tift County was beginning to totter in 1920, Tifton enjoyed for a while the "hang over" from war-time prosperity. Not realizing the financial uncertainty that they would encounter during the transitional period between the saw and the plow—this community then was on the verge of the change to agriculture—Tifton people continued to build. The Imperial Tobacco Plant at $206,000, Southern Bell Telephone office at $35,000, L. E. Bowen building at $18,000, residences and small business houses, $359,402, were constructed. In 1922

E. P. Rose gave the contract for a $5,000 edifice. The South Georgia Power Company built a cold storage plant in connection with local ice plant. Howell and Gibbs built a large refrigerator plant at their market.

Although this building program indicated prosperity, early in 1923 J. L. Herring wrote: "1922 was marked by more than the average of business worries, industrial distress, and financial uncertainty."

There were many proofs of a vital interest in agriculture. Governor Walker spoke at a county-wide rally, stressing cow-hog-hen week. Georgia Duroc Breeders Association was formed with headquarters in Tifton—a result of cow-hog-hen week. A livestock day was sponsored by the Tifton Board of Trade. A stock judging team from our county won first place in the district contest and second in the state contest. Through the agricultural committee of the Tifton Board of Trade, the Boys' Cotton, Corn, Pig and Calf Clubs were formed. About one thousand farmers attended the farm school in cooperation with County Agent Culpepper and Georgia State College for Men. Tift County shipped 2,000,000 tomato plants in 1923, and in 1929 shipped peanuts to Africa.

In addition to the building and agricultural program in the twenties there were other signs of progress: the opening of the Ritz Theater, the establishment of a bakery, printing shop, feed store, South Georgia Advertising Company, peanut shelling plant, a new furniture store, the first dry cleaning plant in the county, and eight new filling stations in one year. Cohen's Store was enlarged. The Tifton Garden Club organized and planted shrubbery near the Bank of Tifton, Board of Trade, courthouse, and high school building. The first new industry in 1927 was an ice cream factory operated by Wilson Brothers, R. C., and I. E.

Conspicuous improvements in 1928 were: the completion of a whiteway described "as the largest and finest of any in any city of equal size in the state;" the presentation of memorial columns at entrance to the Georgia State College campus, erected by members of the class 1928-29; and the receiving of official wave-length designation and broadcasting license from the Federal Radio Commission for Radio Station WRBI, operated by Kent's Furniture and Music Store. After operating for twenty-one years and twenty-one days the city court of Tifton closed in 1928. During the period 4,401 civil and 3,181 criminal cases were tried.

Among the significant improvements in 1929 was the opening of the new bus terminal, which with two waiting rooms and two rest rooms, well heated or cool, according to season, satisfied all requirements of passengers. Complete telegraph service—day, night, and holiday—was effected in 1929 for Tift County citizens.

During the period Tifton was alive with new clubs and other organizations. In 1920 a band, a local organization of the American Cotton Organization, a Sweet Potato Growers' Association, and the Tift County

Post of the American Legion began. In 1921 the Tift County Masons, potato curers, retail food dealers, and watermelon growers organized. In Omega a woman's club was organized.

In 1922 group activity continued. Ty Ty organized a board of trade. The Kiwanis Club, three troops of Boy Scouts, and the Tifton Chapter of the W.C.T.U. were active. The Georgia Cotton Growers, Georgia Association, Berry School alumni, Forestry Club, and Lions Club made their contributions to the progress of Tifton. The Ku Klux Klan made its ghostly entrance and quick exit that year.

Only the American Legion and the peanut growers joined in 1923 the organization unit. In 1925 the Tifton Country Club began with twenty members and subscriptions amounting to $1,500.

The activity of these clubs increased the morale of the town and county and created the appearance of prosperity, even if prosperity was in reality on the wane. In 1921, however, there was one support for the club impression: the first city manager, W. T. Hargrett, gave Tifton one of the best business administrations in its history. A summary of his record follows:

"Tifton came out of 1921 $18,000 to the good. Besides this, $1,175 was spent in betterments; the tax rate on realty was reduced 5 per cent and there will be a substantial reduction of water rates this year."

"According to Mr. Hargrett's report, over $11,000 was paid on outstanding accounts brought over from 1920, including $1,600 for livestock, and $2,500 was paid on the bonded indebtedness of the city. There remains due the city on 1921 taxes $31,580.59. On the same date last year there was due $21,988.25, leaving a balance due this year above last of $9,492.64. Against these total assets there is an outstanding voucher of $2,600 and a difference in the stock on hand this year as compared with last of $1,371.42. This leaves the city $18,271.22 better off financially Jan. 1, 1922, than it stood on Jan. 1, 1921."

His hearers caught their breath when Manager Hargrett asked the commission to reduce his salary from $3,800 to 3,600.

A very interesting point about the commission form of government was that this type was introduced on the thirtieth anniversary of Tifton's organization as a city. On the first of January, 1891, five councilmen were sworn in: H. H. Tift, E. P. Bowen, W. W. Timmons, John Pope, M. A. Sexton, and J. C. Goodman; two of these men, H. H. Tift and E. P. Bowen, were members of the first commission.

Late in October of 1922 Mr. Hargrett tendered his resignation as city manager to accept the position of president and general manager of the Live Oak, Perry and Gulf Railroad in Florida. R. E. Hall succeeded him as city manager.

Another phase of progress during the twenties was education. When M.

L. Duggan, rural school agent, made a survey of the Tift County schools in 1918, there were in the county the following schools: Salem School, Old Ty Ty, Vanceville, Nipper, Pine View, Brighton, Bay, Omega, Excelsior, Oak Ridge, Brookfield, Harding, Ty Ty, Red Oak, Myrtle Camp Creek, El Dorado, Fletcher, Filyah, Hot Creek, Fairview, Chula, Ansley, Pearman, Midway, and Emanuel. In addition there were fourteen schools for negroes.

As the result of the consolidation program we have the following consolidated schools: Brookfield, Chula, El Dorado, Excelsior, Harding, Omega, Ty Ty, Emanuel, and Red Oak. In addition to the Tift County Industrial School there were several one-teacher negro schools in the county.

The school system of Tifton under the management of A. H. Moon progressed rapidly during this time. He raised Tifton High School to group one in the state and Southern Accredited Association lists. In the late twenties the junior high school building was constructed at a cost of $45,000. A capable faculty with Mrs. Nan Clements operated this school. The grammar school under direction of Miss Annie B. Clark advanced rapidly. In 1927 there was new consolidated school in El Dorado.

In July 1924 "the House Committee on the University of Georgia and its branches reported out a recommendation for passage by substitute the bill of Representative R. C. Ellis, of Tift County, to establish a college of agriculture and mechanical arts and normal school as a branch of the University of Georgia, in Tifton, to be known as the South Georgia Agricultural and Mechanical College.

"The bill provides that the new institution be located on a tract of land on which the Second District Agricultural and Mechanical School is located. The measure also provides that tuition shall be free to all residents of Georgia."

Further discussions about education are given in another chapter of the history of Tift County.

The March wind that comes in like a lion goes out like a lamb. Financially speaking, the nineteen-twenties came in with a roar and went out with a slump. Nineteen-twenty-nine is a memorable year, for it marks the beginning of a different era. The entire world changed drastically between the twenties and thirties. The step from the former to the latter was like crossing the line between two states; the step also resembled the few minutes at the altar between the titles, Miss and Mrs.

Few things have been the same since 1929. Instances will support the theory. There was a drastic fall in salaries after that year: people who in the twenties worked for two hundred dollars a month worked in the thirties for seventy-five dollars a month. Jobs were difficult to secure in the latter period, and there were more demands on the applicant: a woman who in 1922 secured an excellent college position without a personal interview could not in 1930 get a minor high school position without a personal interview. Age was stressed more in the latter period than in the former; forty years, for instance, were marked old.

From the files of the Tifton Gazette

1920

"Honor arch to C. W. Fulwood is to be erected by Twentieth Century Library Club . . . The Gazette office has just completed the installation of an Intertype, one of the latest models of typesetting machines . . . Organization of the Georgia Division of the Old Indian Trails Highway Association was perfected at a meeting held in Tifton Friday, at which every county in Georgia traversed by the highway was represented with one exception."

1921

"Eleventh District Press Association for second and third districts met in Tifton . . . Twentieth Century Library Club pays tribute to Mrs. N. Peterson."

1922

"M. A. McMillan was in Tifton Tuesday and called at the Gazette office. He says he taught what was Tifton's first school in 1874. He taught in a log house on east side of New River, between where the present church is located and the river. He had about twenty pupils, four or five from Tifton."

1923

"Thirty thousand dollars will be spent on city improvements."

1924

"On February the fourth Woodrow Wilson died . . . Churchwell will put on a sale in celebration of Churchwell's store anniversary twenty-eight years in Tifton."

1925

"City commissioners and city manager have turned over the park to C. W. Fulwood for beautifying. March 20, plans were laid for a real park in Tifton . . . The State Highway passed a resolution to appropriate $50,000 to start work in Tift County on paving highway, provided Tift would put up $100,000 . . . John Temple Graves was buried Monday, August 10 . . . Tifton Trade Territory Day, Tifton, Georgia. $1,000 in gold free. Shower of gold took place in Tifton on Tifton Trade Territory 'Get-Together-day'."

1926

"Tifton put over a bond election as the result of which $90,000 is made available for paving and other municipal improvements. Plans for $25,000 three-story Sunday School plant at Methodist Church agreed on . . . Susquecentennial Exposition was opened at Philadelphia and will continue until December 1. Celebration of the 150th anniversary of the signing of the Declaration of Independence in observance of 100th anniversary of death of Thomas Jefferson."

1927

"Record breaking receipts at the Tifton post office . . . During December fifty new families moved on rural routes, and population on routes increased 300 . . . Honorable Chase S. Osborn will lecture for the Herring Memorial scholarship fund at A. and M. Twentieth Century Library Club is sponsoring the lecture . . . Tift County was forced to turn away over a hundred prospective settlers because we did not have the farms. We've placed 50 families, among them people from Illinois, Maine, Massachusetts, Carolina, and Florida. These people are our best advertisers . . . The paving of National Highway in Tift and the overpass were finished in 1927."

1928

"There was encouragement of a house building program, ready-to-go-farms, and efforts toward the promotion of the cow-hog-hen-plan . . . In May the Georgia Association, termed the Georgia Board of Trade was guest of the local Board of Trade. As a result, Tifton and Tift County received nation-wide advertising . . . In June we (Board of Trade) sponsored Air-Mail Day. Tifton is one of only 7 points in Georgia to which air mail is accessible . . . In November the Board of Trade sponsored Hospitalization Day. On the highway north of town we entertained out-of-state visitors, who came by, and the form of entertainment was lunches consisting of Tift County products."

1929

"Board of Trade ordered 1,000 plants for highway beautification . . . Postal receipts increased from $36,230.74 to $40,292.31 . . . Red Cross had free courses in life saving and first aid . . . Population of Tifton in 1929, 4,508 . . . Seventeen new residences. W. P. Bryant, of Tift County chosen as master farmer. Twelve general farms selected from a list of ninety-eight nominees will receive the award of the Progressive Farmer and Farm Magazine. . . . Chase Salmon Osborne lectured recently to the Board of Trade about the possibilities of Tifton's becoming a great city."

CHAPTER XIII

THE DEPRESSION

The thirties were the dark spots on the financial maps of every county in our land. Everyone was depression conscious; guests at parties and other social gatherings did not hesitate to discuss finances. Depression plants, depression entertainments, Hoover's depression carts, and depression money, script, were introduced.

The depression plants in shop windows and homes were beautiful and inexpensive; the plants grew from a combination of salt, soda, water, coal, and mercurochrome; the chemical reaction produced the flower. Simplicity characterized the entertainments; refreshments, decorations, and guests' gowns were inexpensive. Some homes had depression shrubbery in the yards; gall berry bushes and other wild plants were effective substitutes. Times were so strenuous that Democrats put automobile wheels on carts, signifying that people had no use for cars. Tifton and other towns issued script to employees.

Jobs were difficult to secure; in fact they were so scarce that even Ph.D. graduates in some of our cities roamed the streets looking for employment, and it was not unusual at all to find taxi drivers with degrees.

In 1931 small hats, small dollar bills, and small high school diplomas were introduced. Probably some of these changes were the results of the depression.

The depression topic, however, dropped for a while in 1936 for the romance of the Prince of Wales, who upon the death of his father had became King Edward VIII of the British Empire, and Mrs. Wallie Warfield Simpson, of America. Since England opposed the marriage, the king had to choose between the throne and Mrs. Simpson. On December 11. 1936 Edward abdicated the crown, and his younger brother, George VI, ascended the throne. Everyone who had a radio in Tifton tuned in for the famous farewell speech of Edward. By some Tifton citizens his words were received with disapproval; by some, with admiration; by others, with tears. His closing words, "I cannot carry on without the woman I love," have become a classic in the list of famous romances. His voice, strong and clear in the beginning, broke on the farewell sentence. This romance may have a place with that of Elizabeth Barrett and Robert Browning.

To return strictly to Tift County, in 1934 Tifton High School began a new type of commencement exercises by choosing a celebrity and centering the program around his achievement. The graduating class that year selected as class honoree Harry Stillwell Edwards, nationally famous author of "Eneas Africanus," "Sons and Fathers," and other stories. Ernest

Tift Theater and Street Scene

Neal, Georgia poet laureate, was selected in 1935; Dr. W. F. Melton, poet, teacher. journalist, and later poet laureate, in 1936; Morgan Blake, journalist. in 1937. William Sutlive, journalist, in 1938; Ralph McGill, journalist. in 1939.

Despite the depression there was progress in Tift County. In 1930 farm schools were operated, and educational pictures presented. Boys received $2,685 for their cotton on September 15, 1930, Annual Cotton Club Day. The county tour was held in July. Cooperative sales were under direction of County Agent Culpepper. Poultry brought $23,350; hogs, $38,356; velvet beans, and sweet potatoes, $375. Truck farming revived and more than fifteen hundred people called for farms in Tift County.

Several new enterprises opened in Tifton during this period. Downing and Company, Auto Supply Company, Loel's Ten-Cent Store, four new grocery stores, Phoenix Mutual Life Insurance Company, and a bureau of markets were among the number. A large pecan shelling plant, with capacity to handle all the pecans the county could purchase in this section, began operation in Tifton November 1, 1937, on second floor of the Coleman and Chandler Building.

In 1933 two lumber markets, a large chicken hatchery, cotton mill, fertilizer plant, peanut mill, and a tobacco stemming plant were additions to Tift County. Kent's furniture store and Kulbersh's new department store were opened. The cornerstone for American Legion Home was laid. The formal opening of the $15,000 basketball shell was significant in the progress of athletics. Tifton Coca-Cola Bottling Company finished a handsome new plant, a modern sanitary, and up-to-date building. A new Nehi plant was constructed. The Columbian Peanut Company finished a large peanut warehouse, an office, and weighing shed.

The Tift Theater with some of the best equipment in South Georgia opened on February 22, 1937. The magic eye, operating doors and fountains, was an innovation in this section of Georgia. The theater received from the Ritz Theater in Marianna, Florida, the largest post card that ever came to Tifton. This card of congratulation, twenty-four by forty-eight inches, required $2.62 postage.

Electrical progress was exhibited in the 110,000 volt electric power substation of the Georgia Power Company; it was practically completed with cutting in of the new Tifton-Valdosta 66,000 volt line. The Tifton station, which cost a half million dollars, was connected with Columbus through Americus. Another phase of this progress was the one hundred miles of rural electrification line.

The Farmer's Bank of Tifton opened for business in February 1937. Joseph Kent, Senior, was president, and J. S. Harris and Dan Fletcher, vice-presidents.

A new water plant was constructed at a cost of $79.000. "Omega installed a hypochlorinator on its municipal water supply. All municipal and industrial water supplies were sterilized in Tift County. This county is the first with more than one city system in the deep-well section to have sterilization equipment on all its supplies."[1]

Among the improvements in buildings were the remodeling of new rooms at the Colonial Inn, the additional equipment of the Tifton Floral Company and the Southern Ornamental Nursery, changes in the Myon Hotel, and Armour's expenditure of $50,000 on the plant, which re-opened on November 1, 1935. It had closed in 1920. The Tifton Board of Trade helped the athletic association with enclosing field and grading ground. The ball field was equipped with metal fence, and flood lights for night games.

Several Tift County people and institutions were honored during this time. Senator Moore was honored at a program dedicating Moore Highway, which connected Abraham Baldwin College and Georgia Coastal Plain with state route seven. She was presented a loving cup. The highway was named for Mrs. Susie T. Moore because she introduced the bill to have paved roads in front of all colleges in the University system. She was

---
1. Tifton Gazette.

also nominated for honorary membership in the International Pilot Club. The Democratic Luncheon Club of Georgia, with Mrs. Dunn as president, gave a dinner at the Atlanta Athletic Club in honor of Senator Moore, vice-chairman of the Georgia Democratic Executive Committee.

A granite marker at Tenth Street entrance to Fulwood Park was unveiled to the memory of J. L. Herring, H. H. Tift, founder of Tifton, and C. W. Fulwood, first chairman of the Park and Tree Commission. Trees were planted in Fulwood Park for Mr. Fulwood and Miss Leola Greene.

Mrs. N. Peterson, Dr. Peterson's wife, was presented a certificate of leadership and later named one of the captains in the Women's Field Army for the control of cancer for the Second District. She received national recognition on account of her pioneer work in rural education.

Mrs. H. H. Tift, benefactor of Bessie Tift College, was honor guest at a reception at Rhodes Memorial Hall, when Miss Ruth Blair, state historian, and the officers of the Bessie Tift Alumnae Association received guests. An exquisite miniature portrait of Mrs. Tift had been presented the state's collection of famous Georgians in Rhodes Memorial Hall. In 1937 the second edition of "American Women's Who's Who" contained names of four Tifton women: the late Mrs. Bessie Willingham Tift, educator; Mrs. Josie Golden Clyatt, organist; Mrs. Nell Britt Tabor, singer; and Mrs. Lillian Britt Hensohn, singer. The name of Mrs. Hensohn was also included in "Who's Who in the East."

Mrs. Clyatt was elected president of the Georgia Federation of Music Clubs, during the meeting of State Federation of Music clubs in Tifton, and Mrs. C. R. Dyer corresponding secretary.

Lillian Britt Heinsohn and Nell Britt Tabor appeared in recitals in and near Philadelphia. A Pennsylvania paper, The Daily Local News, commented:

"Songs from the South by two charming sopranos, who looked as though they had stepped out of a family photograph album of a generation or so ago, formed the entertainment at the opening meeting of the New Century Club, of this place, yesterday. Lillian Britt Heinsohn and Nell Britt Tabor, wearing costumes reminiscent of the middle of the last century, sang negro spirituals, plantation songs, and ballads that were favorites fifty or sixty years ago, in a manner that brought back to the memory of many a hearer, voices long silent and made them realize anew how sweet the old songs were."

Mrs. Heinsohn and Mrs. Tabor broadcast old-time Southern songs over WHAT, the Philadelphia station, which was under the direction of the son of W. W. Atterbury, president of Pennsylvania Railroad. They succeeded so well with their program that they received an invitation to present a group of songs at the spring meeting of the agents of the New York Life

NOTED TIFTON WOMEN

Top—Mrs. Susie T Moore, first woman state senator in Georgia, well known in politics and for charities.

Second row—Mrs. Nichols Peterson, who has made distinctive contributions to education and women's club work in Tifton and Tift County.

Second row, right—Mrs. Paul D. Fulwood, Sr., known over the South as rose gardener and in Tifton for interest in civic improvements, especially in beautifying city and Fulwood Park.

Insurance Company in Washington, D. C., at the New Williard Hotel . . .

Several Tift County boys and girls were honored during the period. Herbert Hall, of Omega, won the Southwest Georgia District prize in the Arcadian Nitrate of Soda Contest by producing 2,655 pounds of cotton on one acre.

Whitfield Scarboro was selected by the commander of his company at Fort Moultrie as the best Four-year man and sent before a board of examiners to compete with the best Blue course trainees from other companies. Having proved to be the best Blue in the C.M.T.C. battalion, he was decorated publicly by Major Shield Warren, camp commander, Eighth Infantry U. S. A.

Fourteen-year-old Willis Dysart, of Omega, Georgia, startled Emory University professors when he exhibited in 1938 such feats as adding in seven seconds a group of seven three-digit figures, adding in twelve seconds a group of eleven three-digit figures and finding the square root of such figures as 138,799,961. He calculated without pen or pencil. Willis said that his mathematical gift came to him in a dream on the night his mother died. He stopped school because he could not get on with teachers or students. A favorite trick was to learn one's bithday and tell immediately the person's age in days, hours, minutes and seconds.

Prof. H. W. Martin, Emory psychologist, and Dean E. H. Johnson, head of business adminitsration pronounced Dysart a prodigy. On July 5, 1938 Willis appeared on Robert L. Ripley's radio program. Another Tift Countian was presented by Ripley. Smoky Joe Cravy, of Chula, appeared with the Ripley show at the New York World Fair. Joe played his harmonica and blew a police siren through his ear.

Miss Pauline Weatherington in 1937 was chosen princess at the Slash Pine Festival. Miss Mildred McLeod was elected Miss Georgia in a state contest. Miss Iona Beverly was queen of 1933 festival of States celebration at St. Petersburg. Miss Christabel Kennedy received an appointment as clerk in capitol branch of the post office in Washington, D. C., and was later appointed secretary to Senator George. Miss Lillian Touchstone's biography with biographies of two other Wesleyan seniors appeared in American College Year Book. Miss Caroline Kelley represented Tifton at a Beach celebration in Jacksonville.

George Sutton, who made the supreme sacrifice in 1945, by a competitive examination, won a scholarship to Emory University during the thirties.

Toby Cook, seven-year-old Tift County boy, who rode on ponies eight hundred-eleven miles from his home in Chula to Washington, D. C., to be in the inaugural parade of 1933, while passing the reviewing stand, received a salute from President Roosevelt. Toby was received by three governors, Blackwood, of South Carolina, Ehringham, of North Carolina, and

Pollard, of Virginia. The boy spoke three times over radio at Richmond, and over the NBC and Columbia networks from Washington, met senators, other public officers, screen notables, and radio stars, including Kate Smith, Tom Mix, Joe E. Brown, Amos 'n' Andy, Buffalo Bill, Jr., and Thelma Todd.

Toby was enthusiastically received at many points on the trip by officials, school children and other citizens. In South Hill, Virginia, A. W. Jeffry directed a reception in honor of Toby. Pictures of the boy, his ponies, and retinue were published in newspapers and magazines over the country. He was guest of the Georgia Congressional delegation in Washington until he rode in the parade.

Accompanied by his father, and two negro servants, John Townsend and Jesse Allen, Toby rode in five-mile relays his ponies, Billy, Jim, and Pet, for fifteen days to Washington; he spent three days getting out of Georgia. The riding time computed in hours was between one-hundred-fifty and one-hundred-sixty. Mr. Cook drove a car, to which he had attached a house van to accommodate ponies and provide feed, food, such as Georgia cane, ham, "taters," et cetera, and camping equipment. The boy had selected Billy for the parade, but the intervention of an accident changed the plan to Jim. Within thirty-five miles of the end of the trip he and his retinue were stopped on a highway, which was being repaired and forced to ride on a shoulder of the road. Cars going in opposite directions tried to pass; one car skidding struck Toby, throwing him thirty-five feet over a fence and down an embankment and killed Billy. Although bruised and stunned, the boy rode on after first aid.

Toby was to lead the fourth section of the parade, heading Georgia delegation, but he accepted an invitation from the chairman of the New Jersey delegation to lead their section, which was third, to show friendship between the two states. He was entertained at lunch by the New Jersey delegation. A noted New York cartoonist, a guest at the luncheon, drew a cartoon of Toby; all the guests, hosts and hostesses autographed it. He secured a number of autographs during the trip.

He and Frances A. Bishop, ninety-two years old, at that time oldest holder of a Congressional Medal for bravery, had their pictures made before CBS.

The Cook party had planned to stay in Washington a while after the inauguration, but on account of the bank holiday they hurried home, driving night and day. The ponies enjoyed a ride home.

For several weeks after his return, Toby had fan mail; as many as thirty-one letters arrived in one day. He answered with post card scenes of Tifton.

None of these rich experiences affected Toby who, the same unassuming, affable little fellow when he returned, continued his school work and later entered Tifton High School. After completing the tenth grade here, he went to Florida, where he later received a diploma. During World War II he volunteered for service in the Marines. On March 26, 1945, Mr. Cook received this message from the Navy Department: "Pfc. James W. (Toby) Cook killed on Iwo Jima, Volcano Islands, of the Marine Corps killed March 1 'in the performance of his duty and in the service of his country'." The message was signed by Lieutenant General A. A. Vandegrift—Commandant of Marine Corps.

E. P. Bowen, Jr., of Tifton, one of the largest farm operators in this section, was appointed by Henry A. Wallace, Secretary of Agriculture, as one of the collaborators on the new soil conservation program, which took the place of Triple A.

Some of the colored people of Tift County were honored during the period. Lilla Deas, wife of J. M. Deas, principal of the Tift County Industrial School, colored, was for her group head of the Georgia W.C.T.U. She was one of the best teachers ever connected with the local negro school. Besides being state president of the colored W.C.T.U., she did efficient work in Tifton after organizing a union.

In 1939 the first novelist of Tift County had a novel, "Leila's Unusual Heritage," published by Pegasus Publishing Company, New York.

Institutions and organizations, as well as individuals were honored. In 1932 the Gazette was the first newspaper in the state to win the award offered by the Georgia Bankers' Association for the newspaper in Georgia doing the most constructive work for the restoration of confidence. In 1936 the Gazette was the first paper in the state to win the award offered by the War Cry, publication of Salvation Army, for the best editorial published during the year 1935 to 1936, on a religious subject.

The Gazette was the first and only paper in the state to win award offered by the Emory School of Journalism for the best editorial on the aims, ideals, and purposes of a newspaper.

During the session of the Georgia Press Association in 1932 the Gazette received the Bankston trophy for carrying the largest percentage of local news of any newspaper in the state, and the cash prize for producing the best job printing.

In the educational department, Tifton High School won first place in a district meet, second in state debating contest, and contributed the most points to the banner which the Second District won in the State contest. The school paper, the Pioneer, won in a contest conducted by Emory University and the Atlanta Journal a certificate of distinction for being among the best high-school mimeographed papers in the Southern states. The Pioneer also won the cup for being the best high-school mimeographed paper in the state.

In 1936 the City of Tifton won second place and a cash award of $750 in the home-town contest conducted by the Georgia Power Company. Mrs. N. Peterson received the prize for Tifton and made an acceptance speech.

Another honor came to Tifton when the first cabinet officer, Henry A. Wallace, Secretary of Agriculture, visited the city.

The Telephone Exchange, first in the Valdosta District to recover from the telephone depression set a new record in the number of telephones in service. The event was celebrated with a barbecue in Fulwood Park.

Chula received congratulations on being the first community in this section to establish a Red Cross first aid.

The American Legion honored Jefferson McLendon Parker in a memorial service and unveiled his picture. Mr. and Mrs. Ed Moore donated two acres in the northern part of Omega to be used as a memorial park to their son, Joe Warren, who lost his life in a gin. The Peterson baby memorial fund—citizens whom Dr. N. Peterson ushered into the world contributed to the fund—grew large enough to furnish a nursery at the Tift County Hospital. Irwin County, the grandmother of Tift County, unveiled in 1936 a monument to Jefferson Davis, president of the Confederacy "at the spot where[1] his arrest lent a touch of drama and a fifty-year argument to the end of the War Between the States."

Mrs. Ralph Johnson, now of Tifton, was master of ceremonies at the unveiling. "Mrs. Johnson, president of the Mary V. Henderson Chapter U. D. C., of Ocilla, and division chairman of the Jefferson Davis Memorial Committee, has worked energetically and persistently for sixteen years to see the dream of the Davis Capture ground converted into a memorial because of standing reality." (Tifton Gazette.) Mrs. Johnson is a charter member of the Tift County Historical Society.

In 1938 the Tifton High School annual, the Talisman, revived for the first time since 1918 and dedicated that volume to Tifton High School graduates who served in World War I; Gerald Herring, Sr., Bob Herring, Jeff Parker, Neil Ryder, Silas O'Quinn, Roy Thrasher, Donald Ryder.

In 1934 the Tifton High School dedicated a program for the U. D. C. to Beverly Patten Leach, the only surviving Confederate soldier in the county.

In 1931, according to the vote of the people, Tifton's most valuable men were: E. P. Bowen, Sr., J. L. Bowen, F. G. Branch, R. E. Freeman, H. F. Freeman, George Gibson, J. G. Herring, C. B. Holmes, Joe Kent, D. C. Rainey and H. D. Webb. The Tifton Gazette sponsored the voting.

During the thirties Tifton was host for several meetings of organizations. Board of Governors met with vocational teachers of South Georgia and visitors from Washington, D. C. The Regional Red Cross, a regional medical association, and a county agent's meeting were held in Tifton. The District Educational Association, which met here, had one thousand

1. Tifton Gazette.

HISTORY OF TIFT COUNTY   105

teachers and the Georgia Agricultural Society had a good attendance. The Kansas F. F. A. was entertained in Tifton. The Tobacco Institute with assistance of our warehouses and the Experiment Station was successful. Attractive quarters where visitors could read or rest were established. The meetings of Georgia Federation of Music Clubs in 1930 and of Georgia Press Association in 1932 were distinctive honors for a small town.

The eleventh convention of the Georgia Federation of Music Clubs opened in Tifton on April the second, 1930. After Mrs. J. D. Downs gave a prelude on the piano, a procession of officers, directors, chairmen, and distinguished guests followed to the rhythm of "God of Our Fathers." Miss Elizabeth Spence read the collect of the National Federation of Music Clubs, and Dr. W. L. Pickard pronounced the invocation.

Mrs. M. E. Hendry, president of the Tifton Music Club, introduced Dr. W. L. Pickard for the main address. She then introduced the state president, Mrs. W. P. Harbin, of Rome, who after giving her response introduced the state officers, district directors, department chairmen, and Mrs. De Los Lemuel Hill, of Atlanta, Georgia, member of the national board. Mrs. Hill introduced the two national officers here for the convention, Mrs. Grace W. McBee and Mrs. Helen Harrison Mills.

The opening session of the forty-sixth annual meeting of the Georgia Press Association at Tifton was mainly a tribute to William G. Sutlive, associate editor of the Savannah Press and best known as "Bill Biffem."

On the last evening of the convention, in recognition of the services of Miss Leola Greene, society editor of the Tifton Gazette, as a veteran newspaper woman, Mr. Bruce Donaldson, in behalf of the Tifton Presidents' Club, presented her with a bouquet of roses.

The Georgia Ice Manufacturers and the Canning Institute, with three hundred delegates, too, had an interesting meeting. Three October days were Tifton Trade Days, which advertised the town and allured crowds here.

Nature made the most spectacular contribution to the events of the period. On the morning of February 15, 1934, children with gleeful yells welcomed a beautiful scene—a phenomenon to South Georgia—snow had fallen 2.2 inches on Tifton soil. On January 24, 1935, the town was covered again with snow.

Another unusual thing about the thirties was the longevity of Tifton people. According to Roland Harper, research specialist, who studied the length of lives recorded on tombs in the Tifton Cemetery, the span of life of Tifton citizens showed an increase from an average of twenty-eight years in 1900 to fifty-five years in 1930. He examined two-hundred-ninety-nine records. Three per cent of the people reached eighty. The average life from 1895 to 1900 was twenty-eight years; from 1900 to 1905, twenty-five years; 1905 to 1910, seventeen years; 1915 to 1920, thirtye-ight years; 1930, average fifty-five years.

Women lived longer than men except from 1920-1925: males lived forty-three years; females, forty.

In connection with longevity of Tifton people in the thirties, the Gazette commented about the number of Tift couples who had been married more than fifty years. Mr. and Mrs. E. E. Youmans celebrated their sixtieth anniversary; the Honorable and Mrs. T. B. Young, their fifty-ninth. Mr. and Mrs. S. N. Adams and Judge and Mrs. J. J. Baker were married more than fifty years. "If you want to be happily married, move to Tifton," was the slogan the Tifton Gazette suggested.

Others who celebrated their golden wedding anniversaries were: Mr. and Mrs. A. L. Bishop, Mr. and Mrs. W. T. Hargrett, Mr. and Mrs. J. N. Horne, Judge and Mrs. S. F. Overstreet, Mr. and Mrs. James M. Varner, Dr. and Mrs. Milton Price, Mr. and Mrs. Edgar Scott Hand, Mr. and Mrs. Walter Pearson, Mr. and Mrs. T. E. Fletcher, Sr., Mr. and Mrs. Davis Whiddon, Mr. and Mrs. J. M. Davis, Mr. and Mrs. W. T. Dean, Mr. and Mrs. J. Z. Paulk. Mr. and Mrs. J. J. Bryant were married fifty-seven years.

Some of the people who reached three score-and-ten or more during this period were: Mrs. Rhoda Goodman, Brookfield, celebrated her seventy-ninth birthday; M. L. Whitfield, seventy-ninth; J. T. Tyron, seventy-first; Mrs. N. A. Bowen, ninetieth; Mrs. Susan T. Partian, seventy-ninth; Mrs. W. A. Doss, seventieth; Aunt Jane Branch, ninetieth; Mrs. Babe Gibbs, eighty-second; Mrs. J. H. Crisp, Fender, celebrated her eighteenth birthday, although she was seventy-two years old—she was born on February 29; Mrs. Matilda Moore, eighty-ninth; Mrs. W. W. Griner, her eighty-eighth; J. W. Taylor, eightieth; Mrs. N. J. Goggans, eightieth; Mrs. A. Conger, seventy-ninth; Mrs. Elizabeth Paul, eighty-first; William Willis, seventy-second; Mrs. M. T. Ford, seventy-seventh birthday; Mrs. Mary D. Jones, eighty-ninth; G. W. Conger, eighty-third; "Grandpa Greer," ninetieth birthday; Jacob Hall, eighty-second; Mrs. J. Rigdon, Sr., seventy-fifth; Mr. Freeman Hall, seventy-ninth; Mrs. Ellen Lankford, ninety-second; Mrs. W. W. Griner, eighty-ninth; William Willis, seventy-third; Mrs. J. T. Pitts, seventy-fifth; Mrs. J. R. Willis, seventieth; Mrs. W. A. Doss, seventieth; Babe Gibbs, eighty-second; Mrs. W. M. Pound, eighty-second; George Seay, ninetieth; Mrs. J. D. Bozeman, seventy-fifth. Mrs. N. A. Bowen, mother of E. P. Bowen, Sr., made the highest score on blows when she blew out ninety candles on an angel food birthday cake. Mrs. N. G. Goggans scored next when she blew out eighty candles on her cake.

The two salient birthday celebrations were the observance, beginning on September 16, 1937, of the one-hundred-fiftieth anniversary of the signing of the Constitution of the United States of America and the celebration of Georgia bicentennial in 1933 by the Tifton High School graduating class.

Proclamation

"Whereas the Constitution of the U. S. was signed on Sept. 17, 1787 and had by June 21, 1788 been ratified by the necessary number of states and

"Whereas George Washington was inaugurated as the first President of the United States on April 30, 1789

"Now, therefore I, Franklin D. Roosevelt, President of the United States of America, hereby designate the period from Sept. 17, 1937, to April 30, 1939, as one of commemoration of the 150 anniversary of the signing and the ratification of the Constitution and of the inauguration of the first President under that Constitution.

"In commemorating this period we shall affirm our debt to those who ordained and established the Constitution in order to form a more perfect union, establish Justice, insure domestic tranquility, provide for the common defense, promote the general welfare, and secure the blessings of Liberty, to ourselves and our posterity.

"We shall recognize that the Constitution is an enduring instrument fit for the governing of a far-flung population of more than one hundred thirty million, engaged in diverse and varied pursuits even as it was fit for the government of a small agrarian nation of less than four million.

"It is therefore appropriate that in the period herein set apart we shall think afresh of the founding of our Government under the Constitution, how it has served us in the past and how in the days to come its principles will guide the Nation forward."

Excerpt from a pamphlet prepared by the Georgia Education Department:

"The period fixed by the President of the United States for the country at large and by the Governor of Georgia for this state for celebrating the sesquicentennial of the Constitution of the United States extends from September 17, 1937, to April, 1939. This period begins with the one-hundred-fiftieth anniversary of the day the Constitution was signed in Philadelphia, September 17, 1787, and ends with the one hundred-fiftieth anniversary of the day George Washington the first President of the United States (which office was first created by the Constitution) was inaugurated in New York, April 30, 1789."

The Constitution was signed by William Few and Abraham Baldwin from Georgia. The latter signer is especially interesting to South Georgians because Abraham Baldwin College near Tifton bears his name.

During the celebration week organizations and schools in Tift County gave appropriate celebrations, commemorating the signing of the Constitution.

Top—Business street scene in Tifton
Second row—Entrance to Fulwood Park. Home of Mr. and Mrs. Paul D. Fulwood, Sr.
Third—Woman's Club and Public Library
Bottom—Tifton street scene during Shriners ceremonial parade

Another pointer to the past, though less significant, was interesting. During the thirties there was a revival of quilting and making quilts. Groups of women and girls in the country and town made quilt squares and quilted. The editor of the Tifton Gazette in 1935 had this article: "It has been a long time since we saw a school girl patching and quilting but little 7-year-old Myrl Marchant is patching a quilt at the home of her parents, Mr. and Mrs. A. L. Marchant. Myrl has a quilt she made when only five years old. Now that is what we call industrious, also unusual for modern times." Skipping from 1935 to 1938 we find another article: "The quilting out at Mrs. E. L. Lott's was of great interest for the ladies for 3 and 4 miles from Enigma. There were only 2 quilts, but they were tedious." During other years in the thirties there was a revival of quilting.

Young and old enjoyed these quiltings, which were a novelty to the former and a reminder of the "good old days" to the latter. Sometimes reminiscences were interrupted by discussions of the New Deal, which was introduced by President Roosevelt.

The first effective change in his administration was the closing of all the banks in the country for several days in 1933 and making depositors safe for the first time in years. There had been so many bank failures that people were afraid to deposit their money in banks. In fact, some people in different sections of the country returned to the old method of banking, socks and bags. There were various kinds of organizations to help the unemployed and relieve the starving. The length of the bread lines was appalling.

The alphabet had its part in the New Deal. Some of the organizations to help relieve the strain were: A.A.A. Agricultural Adjustment Administration; C.C.C., Civilian Conservation Corps; F.E.R.A., Federal Emergency Relief Administration; H.O.L.C., Home Owners' Loan Corporation; N.I.R.A., National Industrial Recovery Act; N.R.A., National Recovery Administration; P.W.A., Public Works Administration.

Before this federal relief came, people were desperate. Newspapers were full of suicides on account of financial strains. There were, however, different reactions to the New Deal: some Tift County people hailed it as the savior of the country and declared that there would have been a revolution had it not been for the election of Roosevelt, for hungry people know no limit to fierceness; others criticized the New Deal as government interference. In a democracy there will always be conflicting opinions about every movement. Nothing can be perfect in a world of imperfections. There will always be people who exemplify the truth of Burke's statement: "And having looked to the government for bread, on the very last scarcity they will turn and bite the hand that fed them." Some people will always take advantage of relief.

The New Deal although magnanimous in its purpose, like all other movements, had its flaws. There were conscientious job seekers who received aid efficaciously and went to work at the first possible moment; there were also indolent people who received undeserved aid. In Tift County there were both classes. An example of the former was a man's returning groceries given by the government after securing a job.

Some people will abuse always privileges of a democracy. Should we abolish our form of government, which is the best, on account of flaws?

CHAPTER XIV

WORLD WAR II—SECOND "WORLD EARTHQUAKE"

Mingled emotions of sadness, fear, and gayety characterized 1940. Germany had blitzed into Poland on September 1, 1939, and started World War II. Our country, though declaring neutrality was tense; for no one knew where the Axis would crash next, and almost everyone feared that Germany's ultimate aim was the United States. Despite premonitions of danger, however, there was prevalent at times gayety—sometimes a desperate form—that expressed itself in different kinds of entertainments. Wedding bells pealed with the speed of war years. There was a large number of birthday celebrations, golden weddings, and more dances than usual. The revival of quilting parties, which began in the thirties, extended through 1940. Some of the weddings were among the most elaborate in the history of Tifton.

Several octogenarians celebrated their birthdays. Mrs. L. D. Taylor, born on February 29, although eighty-four years old, had had only twenty birthdays. Other octogenarians who celebrated their birthdays were Mrs. Sumantha Branch, Mrs. Emily Owens, and Mr. Tommie Walls.

There were improvements, too, in Tifton. The Tift County Department of Public Health was the first county health department in the state to be selected to give field training for public health nurses. Holmes Orgrain, County health engineer, reported that the rat control in the city was progressing. The vent stoppage program was successful.

The bookmobile with a capacity for handling one thousand books in Tift County arrived from Atlanta during this time and began operation immediately. The W.P.A. rented the chassis and the county commissioners, library committee, and county board of education helped buy the body.

The bookmobile covered the entire county every two weeks, and books were available to every person in the county. Two thousand dollars was spent on new reading material.

Tifton's first streamlined train, which made its first trip through Tifton on December 19, was an innovation.

The Young Democratic Club and Sportsman Club were organized. The following officers were elected for the former: John T. Ferguson, president; R. M. Kennon, vice-president; John Henry Davis, secretary-treasurer; for the latter club: J. P. Short, president; L. O. Shaw, vice-president; Willard Gaulding, secretary-treasurer; board of directors. George H. King, J. L. Stephens, Blanton Smith, Oren Ross, E. A. Gibbs; membership committee: W. F. Zimmerman, Chairman Ed Kent, and J. O. Ross; Jake Herring, publicity chairman.

Housewives were particularly interested in the opening of the Tift County Farm Women's Club Market. The Tip-Top Pants Manufacturing Company opened a plant at Omega.

In 1940 preparations for defense began. Judge R. Eve was appointed Tifton District Commander of the Georgia State Defense Corporation. Home Guards experienced strenuous practices, and blackouts gave an idea of civilians' action during a raid.

Tifton citizens, young and old, grabbed newspapers and sat by radios for news about the war in Europe. In perusing papers for war news, readers occasionally took time to read about achievement of Tifton people. The Star, a six-page weekly at Brunswick, began in 1940 with Lutrelle Tift editor, Amos Tift, Jr., business manager, and David Tift, circulation manager. The paper was chockfull of news of the Golden Isles of Georgia. Howard P. Smith, Jr., received a scholarship to the National Institute of Journalism, and recognition in a national magazine for his achievement in astronomy and for the construction of a telescope.

The greatest celebrations of the year were: "I am an American Day," proclaimed by President Roosevelt for those who had attained their majority or become naturalized citizens during the year; the ninety-eighth anniversary of Crawford W. Long's successful use of ether for the first time; National Newspaper Week with the theme that the press constitutes the first line of defense in the battle for democracy. Dr. Crawford W. Long was a great uncle of Mrs. J. D. Cook, of Tifton. Her mother's father was Dr. Long's brother.

The gravest event of 1940 was the teachers' registering men for the army. On a bleak rainy day, October 15, teachers in Tift County—the registration was nation wide—registered 2,584 young men. Among the numerous points of information was the color of eyes. Teachers were surprised to learn that some men did not know the color of their eyes. Later McKinley Bradford, colored, thirty-five years old, of Brookfield, was the first person to have his name drawn for the army. He received serial number one as the Tift County Board began drawing and numbering registration cards of those registered for selective service. Cards were thoroughly shuffled and placed in a zinc tub. Mrs. Peggy Coleman, blind-folded, drew the first card.

People were more war-conscious in 1941 than in 1940. Defense measures advanced. School children bought defense stamps and bonds on every Tuesday and knitted sweaters for soldiers during study halls. First-aid courses and home nursing were taught in schools and in the town. Almost everyone in Tifton bought stamps and bonds.

The first important project of 1941 in Tifton was the completion of thirty mattresses a day. Miss Lucy Ruth Hall, demonstration agent, was in charge of the project.

On passing the former Alms House, about three miles from Tifton, one might have thought that people were enjoying an old-fashioned picnic. These farm families were having a mattress picnic. About thirty families went to the community center for the purpose of "building" mattresses. These families worked congenially together in three shifts of ten each. Only people of low incomes or salaries were eligible.

One woman in each family cut and made a tick while the men cut and fluffed a mattress. After the woman had finished the tick, she joined her family and helped finish the mattress, which consisted of ten yards of heavy grade ticking and fifty pounds of lint cotton. Each mattress when completed was inspected by a government representative.

"Happy were the days spent at the mattress center."[1] Rural families enjoyed the contacts with new and old friends and appreciated the opportunity of getting new mattresses and altering the old ones.

Farm women advanced in other ways. Mrs. E. J. McCrary was president of the executive board of Tift County Farm Women's Market. She was president of Innis Home Demonstration Council in 1940-1941. "The curb market has been our living,." Mrs. McCrary declared, "for the past six months. Practically all our bills are met with the money which I receive from sales at the curb market."

An important achievement for the whole county in 1941 was the completion of the Tift County Hospital. The dedication on February 13, was very impressive. Dr. F. O. Mixon gave the invocation and A. B. Phillips, Tift County Commissioner, was master of ceremonies. The Tifton Gazette described the dedication:

"Mrs. E. L. Evans, president of the Tift County Medal Auxiliary, Colin Malcolm, Tift County Commissioner, and Dr. W. H. Hendricks, dean of medical profession in Tift County were introduced and spoke a few words. Acknowledgment and appreciation for donations and equipment were made to several Tifton citizens.

"Mrs. Beulah Harrell, superintendent of the hospital, introduced Mrs. Jewell White Thrasher, representing the Georgia Association and National Hospital Association.

"Dr. Tom Little, president of Tift County Medical Association, introduced Dr. J. C. Fisher, who spoke on the operation of small hospitals."

An interesting part of the dedication was the assembling at the hospital of all people whom Dr. N. Peterson had ushered into the world. The "Peterson babies" inspected the nursery department, which the hospital committee dedicated to Dr. Peterson.

Rooms were also dedicated to Dr. V. F. Dinsmore, Dr. G. W. Julian, and Dr. J. A. McRae. One member from each family Dr. Dinsmore had attended was extended an invitation to register in his memory book.

The handsome $50,000 one-story brick building, standing on Tift Avenue and facing Fulwood Park, accommodates thirty-nine beds. There are various kinds of rooms: four waiting rooms, rooms for superintendent of nurses, dressing rooms for doctors and nurses, delivery room, diet kitchen, operating room, nurses' stations, emergency rooms, X-ray room, colored ward, laboratory, utility room, kitchen and pantry, lecture and dining rooms, isolation ward, and white patients' rooms. The building has a modern system of lighting, plumbing, and steam heating.

Another dedication ceremony was held at Memorial Chapel in Woodlawn for J. G. Herring.

People walked, rode bicycles, and went in cars to the dedications. The

---
1. Tifton Gazette.

HISTORY OF TIFT COUNTY 115

evolution of transportation was presented on the streets every day. On account of the tire and gas rationing, bicycles and buggies revived. Women, men, boys, and girls rode on wheels. Transportation of the nineties returned in 1941. There were, however, no bicycles built for two, but old Dobbin again had a conspicuous place.

"Gay nineties" returned again in celebrations: Mr. and Mrs. G. L. Blalock observed their golden wedding anniversary; Mrs. Nellie Swift celebrated their golden wedding anniversary; Mrs. J. A. Whaley, her ninetieth birthday; W. M. Baker, eighty-second; Mrs. C. E. Walters, eightieth.

Several civilians were honored in other ways besides celebrations. Jessie Morgan, Route 6, Tifton, was honored on the Home Folks Program, broadcast over WSB. The comment from the announcer was: "Jessie is one of the safe drivers of Georgia. She won her title in a recent state-wide contest and will go to Detroit soon to represent this state in the national safe driving finale." She won honors also in the national contest.

Mrs. N. Peterson was appointed N.Y.A. supervisor for boys and girls in Tift County. Mrs. Rose Hooks, co-author of a novel, attended the authors' colony in Asheville and autographed her book, published at Brown's bookstore in that city.

The following story by Mrs. Elizabeth Pickard Karsten appeared in Macon Telegraph, August 6, 1941:

"Mrs. Rose Corley Hooks, and her daughter, Miss Flora Hooks, both of Tift County, are co-authors of a novel, "Leila Inherits Adventure," published by Dorrance and Company of Philadelphia, and just off the press.

"The book is written as though the authors enjoyed writing it; and certainly people will enjoy reading it, for it is highly entertaining. Without attempting to confine itself to usual events, the authors sustain the illusion of verity and have produced an adventure story with a happy ending.

"Both of the authors are living on a Tift County farm where they have been at work on the book over a period of about five years. The mother wrote the plot of the story and worked it out. The daughter, who is a teacher in the Excelsior School, did much of the editing . . .

"Mrs. Hooks, a widow, has made her home in Tift County since she was thirteen years old. She is a native of South Carolina, born at Lexington, daughter of the late Izell and Emmoline Taylor Corley. Besides her author daughter, Mrs. Hooks has another child, a son, James Hooks, in the air corps, at Key West. Miss Hooks is a native of Tift County."

Dean George P. Donaldson, of Abraham Baldwin Agricultural College, was one of the outstanding Georgians, awarded honorary Georgia Planters degrees at the State Future Farmers of America Convention held in Macon.

In behalf of the family of the late Dr. John Arch McCrea, pioneer citizen and physician, his daughter Mrs. R. C. Balfour, of Thomasville, made a gift of one thousand dollars in equipment to the Tift County Hospital, as a memorial to Dr. McCrea.

Miss Christabel Kennedy, daughter of Mrs. J. C. Kennedy, of Tifton, Senator Walter George's secretary, became the first woman to direct the clerical staff of the Senate staff of the Senate Finance Committee.

County Agent C. B. Culpepper was awarded a certificate of distinguished service by the National Association of County Agriculture Agents for long, efficient services to the agricultural industry. On account of the fact that Mr. Culpepper could not attend the national convention in Chicago, Mr. J. K. Luck, president of the state county agents association, presented the certificate.

Pickett Harris, ten-year-old son of Mr. and Mrs. P. T. Harris, an outstanding patrol boy, won a trip to Washington, District of Columbia.

Nature's distinctive contribution to 1941 in Tifton was the Aurora Borealis or Northern light, which citizens saw in September. Someone inquired about the new neon light.

One of the improvements in the city was the Georgia Power Company's 110,000 volt line from Tifton to Jasper, Florida.

On Sunday, December the seventh, as people sat listening to their radios, the most significant message of years vibrated—the dastardly attack of Japan on Pearl Harbor while her representatives were in the United States pretending to be effecting peace. The days that followed were gloomy. Japan for months was victorious while our country was preparing. True Americans, however, prophesied that one day light would pierce the gloom.

On December eleventh Secretary of War, Henry Stimson, notified Mrs. Jennie Mae Anderson, of Omega, that her son, Garland C. Anderson, was killed in action in defense of his country at Hickman Field, Territory of Hawaii, on December the seventh. Mr. Anderson was the first Tift County casualty. He was with the radio department of the Air Corps and had been in service several months.

Tift County's second casualty was Theodore Wheeler Croft, of Omega. He was the son of Mrs. Henry S. Brooks, wife of the chief of police of Omega.

The chief celebration of 1941 was on December 15, the sesquicentennial of the American Bill of Rights, the first ten amendments to the Constitution of the United States of America. This celebration was especially significant because our war with the Axis nations was to preserve individual liberty.

Blackouts, which began in 1941, were more numerous in 1942. Often the signal directed people in a huddle in one room of a house, where heavy black drapery kept out every speck of light from shining through windows. Here the experience appeared so real that people sometimes whispered while waiting for the all-clear siren. Policemen would call on people who did not cooperate.

Knitting sweaters was as popular as it was during World War I. Students in the different schools continued knitting. Women met regularly in the Red Cross Rooms to make bandages and other things to send to our soldiers.

Practices for air raids were frequent in the schools. School principals or superintendents used police sirens for air raid alarms and the all clear signals. At the grammar school all of the children on the top floor came to the hall on main floor, and children in rooms on main floor hid under desks. At the junior high all children marched into the hallway and sat down. Students at the high school gathered on second floor hall and rooms.

Tifton schools sponsored scrap drives and collected enormous piles of tin cans, iron, and rubber. The Tift Theater had a rubber matinee, which netted six hundred fifty pounds of scrap rubber for Uncle Sam.

Citizens took first aid courses at Red Cross rooms and students received instructions at the high school. Tifton went over the top in bond rallies and Red Cross war relief campaign.

Nineteen-forty-two recorded birthday celebrations: Mr. J. T. Pitts celebrated his eighty-first birthday; Mrs. J. J. Baker, her eightieth; Twentieth Century Library, its thirty-seventh anniversary. Mrs. J. W. (Granny) Poole celebrated her eighty-fourth birthday on December 7, Pearl Harbor Day. Her only son, Ralph Poole, was wounded in World War II. Her two grandsons, Julian Reynolds and Raleigh Smith, and her great-grandson, Henry Bostic, were also in service. Mr. and Mrs. T. U. Slayton, Omega, celebrated their golden anniversary.

Improvements continued in Tifton. The city bought a fire truck of five-hundred-gallons capacity. The body had a capacity of 1,200 feet, two-and-one-half-inch double jacket. Fire hose and panels were made of heavy special body steel. The pump had a capacity of five hundred gallons. The new peanut shelling plant at the Southern Cotton Mill was one of the most modern in the South.

Among the people honored, during 1942 was Mrs. T. C. Tidwell, whose song, "Mother Eagle's Lullaby" was accepted by Five Star Music and played by Lew Tobin's orchestra.

Mary Mason Barkuloo, an accomplished musician, was the first woman from Tifton to be sworn in as a member of the Woman's Army Auxiliary Corps. Miss Grace Bohannon was the second Tift County girl accepted in the W.A.A.C.

Tifton was honored in receiving in 1942 a new citizen, Commander William Woodward Outerbridge, of the United States Navy. He was decorated with the Navy Cross for distinguished service as commander of U. S. S. Ward.

Commander Outerbridge registered at the Tift County courthouse for the first time to vote in the United States. He, the son of Jessie, an American citizen, and William Outerbridge, an Englishman, was born in China, April 14, 1906. Young Outerbridge came to America when eight years old and entered the fourth grade at Middleport, Ohio. Before coming to America he had attended a school in Dover, England. After graduating at the preparatory school in Marion, Alabama, he entered the Naval Academy.

On December 15, 1928, he married Grace Fulwood, of Tifton, at Wilmington, California. Their three sons are Billy, Tommie, and Bob.

Commander Outerbridge was presented the Navy Cross by Admiral Chester W. Nimitz, commander-in-chief of the United Pacific fleet. In connection with the Navy Cross, Commander Outerbridge received a citation signed by Frank Knox, Secretary of the Navy, for the President.

The incident which was responsible for Commander Outerbridge's receiving the Navy Cross was described in the Tifton Gazette:

"The U. S. S. Ward, of which Mr. Outerbridge was commanding officer, was on inshore patrol duty three miles out from the entrance to Pearl Harbor on the morning of December 7, 1941. At about 6:40 o'clock the officer of the deck sighted some object behind the U. S. S. Antares and at first thought it was a buoy, but there were no buoys there and the object was seen to move. Commander Outerbridge, who was in the Captain's emergency cabin, was notified by the officer that he had sighted a strange object that looked like the conning tower of a submarine, and gave the order to go to general quarters, which is to man the battle stations, and the general alarm was sounded.

"Commander Outerbridge then gave the order to fire and the first shot was fired by number 1 gun, but the shell went over the sub. The second shot was fired by number 3 gun from 50 yards or less and the shell struck the sub at the waterline, which was the junction of the hull and conning tower. The damage was seen by several men of the crew and the hit was square and positive, with no evidence that the projectile ricocheted. The projectile was seen to explode and the sub heeled over to the starboard and sank. The Ward then rushed across the course of the sub and dropped depth bombs. The sub, which was of the midget Japanese type, just settled to the bottom and did not explode. The Ward was not fired upon by either the sub it sank or by the two others contacted by the sound device."

The Ward fired at 6:40, in the morning, an hour and ten minutes before the attack on Pearl Harbor. Commander Outerbridge has the distinction of firing the first effective shots in the war between the United

States and Japan. The number 3 gun of the Ward has received an honor plaque.

While Outerbridge was serving on U. S. S. California after his graduation at Annapolis, the boys on the ship presented him with a bronze, miniature light house, sixteen inches tall, thirty-two inches at the base, and eight inches near the tower. Outerbridge treasured the little bronze house as if it had been a talisman, but when the call came for him to go overseas he left the light house with his brother-in-law's wife, Mrs. Paul Fulwood, Sr.

On D Day at three o'clock when the whistle sounded in Tifton Mrs. Fulwood lighted the little house with electricity. Exactly at the moment President Truman was announcing Germany's unconditional surrender the topmost light went out. The lower light, where the watchman should stay, still burning welcomed Captain Outerbridge to his home, Tifton, where he addressed the American Legion on Pearl Harbor Day in 1945.

The Tifton Gazette in 1942 honored couples who had been married the longest. Mr. and Mrs. Funderburke married sixty-one years, won first prize in the longest marriage contest, a year's subscription for the Gazette; Mr. and Mrs. T. A. Hardy, Omega, married fifty-eight years, second prize; Mr. and Mrs. J. M. Davis, Tifton, married fifty-six years, third prize, three months subscription. Mr. and Mrs. J. W. Whiddon, married fifty-four years, Judge and Mrs. J. H. White, fifty years, Mr. and Mrs. J. D. Parkerson, forty-five years, and Mr. and Mrs. W. H. Willis, forty-three years, received honorable mention.

These celebrations, although relieving the strain to a certain extent, could not get people's minds off the war; for there were constant reminders. President Roosevelt set April 27, 1942 for registration day for all men between forty-five and sixty-five years old.

A little humor, however, was sprinkled in the seriousness of the situation, when Irvin S. Cobb, famous humorist, was a visitor to Tifton for a few hours in July, 1942. "He stopped off here en route from a South American trip to Hollywood for the purpose of some work that has just been completed by Mrs. Mary Duff Arnold for Mrs. Clayton Sedgewick Cooper, to be placed in the Museum of Natural History in New York and in some other museums to be selected." (Tifton Gazette.)

By December, 1942, there was so much news about Tift County boys and girls in services that we could not even mention all the facts. Ed Tyson, a former T. H. S. student and star football player, however, had such an unusual experience that a reference is befitting here. He was on the Joseph Hewes transport when the Japanese torpedoed and sank it off the coast of Africa. After floating for hours on a life raft he was rescued. Upon his return to the States in December, he told interesting stories about his experience among the Arabs.

Tift County had three young men on the aircraft Wasp, torpedoed by the Japs: Marvin Lester McGill, son of John McGill; Everett Hammock, Omega; and electrician Talmadge May, son of Mr. and Mrs. J. W. May, Route 2, Tifton. Talmadge was lost, but the other two boys were rescued.

The story of the Wasp according to John Everett Hammock was published in the Tifton Gazette:

"The Wasp with a task force was in the Coral Sea off the Solomon's Islands on September 15, watching for a Jap fleet that was attempting to land forces in the Solomons. The ship's crew had been at general quarters (battle stations) that morning and at 10:30 o'clock were secured from general quarters (called off battle stations). Some planes from the carrier had been in the air and come in and landed at 2:10. It was around 2:30 in the afternoon when the first torpedo struck the Wasp. Just a few minutes before the torpedo struck, seventeen planes took off from the Wasp and were circling the ship when the torpedo struck.

"Hammock was in his compartment when the first torpedo struck. Immediately the men assumed their battle stations. Hammock's station was in the radio room . . . Three torpedoes struck the Wasp . . . Hammock went up on flight deck, which was listing as one side of the carrier was filling with water.

"The explosions from the fuel and ammmunition stores were terrific. Flames were everywhere. Men grabbed water hose and fought like mad to control the fire on the ship . . .

"Men fought hours before receiving orders to abandon ship. Some of the men had life rafts, some jumped into the sea with life jackets on, and some did not have on life jackets. Some were partially dressed, some in underwear, and some with no clothes.

"Hammock, in underwear, jumped overboard and for thirty minutes swam with no life jacket on until a fellow with two jackets gave him one. Hammock with 720 others was picked up by a destroyer. He was on the destroyer two days before reaching New Caledonia."

McGill said the Wasp was one of the cleanest and best ships that ever sailed on the ocean. To him it was just like home. He preferred the aircraft carrier to any in the navy. The first English Spitfire plane that landed on any aircraft deck landed on the flight deck of the Wasp.

McGill was in his living compartment when the Wasp was first hit. Hearing the first two torpedoes hit, he grabbed his shirt and started for his battle station on the signal bridge. When the third earthquake torpedo hit, it knocked down everyone who was standing. When he reached the signal bridge, the explosions were deafening. McGill was almost stiffled and his hair was singed. After leaving the battle station he went to the stern of the flight deck and began pushing off planes that had crashed in the explosion. He witnessed horrible sights before abandoning the ship. McGill shed tears as he saw the ship burn, for it had been his home. He and others in rubber life rafts were desolate as they paddled away from the burning ship.

After three hours on water he was picked up by a motor whale boat. Salt water and oil made him deathly sick. Finally he was transferred from a whale boat to a destroyer and returned to the States on a transport. He landed in San Diego, California.

Nineteen-forty-three began with a time confusion in Tifton. The town changed from eastern war time to central war time, then in a few days returned to eastern war time.

The war theme continued with little hope of a change to peace. During February the Tifton schoo's collected clothes for the unfortunate Russians whom the German army had left desolate.

Mrs. Ellen Forrester Dyal, of Tifton, was commissioned ensign in the United States Naval Reserve and assigned to active duty, May 4. Sara Roan Coan received her commission as second lieutenant in the Women Reserve of the United States Marines. Coan was the first Woman's Auxiliary of the Marines to receive a commission.

Five of the schools of Tift County received jeep citations for participation in the May school-at-war bond campaign: Omega, Harding, Chula, Emanuel, and Ty Ty.

The fighter-plane that the Tift County school superintendents had the pleasure of naming on account of oversubscribing to the war bond quota was named Christabel Tift County for Miss Christabel Kennedy, Senator Walter George's secretary, who helped secure the Tifton air base for her home town, Tifton. The Tift County in the name indicates that Tift Countians oversubscribed the bonds.

Carolyn Barkuloo was the first eighteen-year-old in Georgia to register under the new law, which allowed eighteen-year-old boys and girls to vote.

Nineteen-forty-four was gloomy with war news. Many of Tift County's best young men were killed in action. There were, however, a few gleams that pierced the darkness. Walter B. Leverette, Jr., Route 2, was one of twenty Georgians, Future Farmers of America honored in Atlanta. At the Macon Convention in 1938 he received an award, the Georgia Planters' degree.

A daughter of Tifton, Mrs. Robert Heinsohn, now of Thomasville received an inquiry about her biography to be included in "Who's Who of America."

As a respite from war, Tifton took time to rejoice over the achievements of Major Henry T. Myers, who piloted a C-54 army transport plane on the first non-stop flight from London to Washington (see chapter on pioneers for details), and of Dr. S. A. Martin, who wrote a history of

Florida. In connection with Florida's centennial celebration Dr. Martin's history, "Florida During Territorial Days" was published by the Georgia University Press.

The Tifton Gazette commented about the history: "The thoroughness and attractiveness of Dr. Martin's centennial study have been highly praised by distinguished historians."

Sidney Walter Martin, son of Mr. and Mrs. S. A. Martin, was born in Tift County, Georgia. He attended public schools of Tifton and graduated from high school in 1929. His undergraduate courses were completed at Furman University, Greenville, South Carolina, where he was graduated cum laude in class of 1932. From 1932-1934 he was instructor at Palatka (Florida) High School.

After studying in the graduate school in the University of Georgia, Martin received the master's degree, with history as a major, in 1935. He was then made instructor of history at the University of Georgia; in 1939 he was elected assistant professor, and in 1944, promoted to an assistant professorship. He was granted a leave of absence in 1938-39 and in 1941-42 to do graduate work at the University of North Carolina. Martin received the Ph.D. at this institution in 1942.

Besides his history of Florida he has contributed to the American Historical Review, Journal of Southern History, Georgia Historical Quarterly, and the Florida Historical Quarterly. He is now writing a biography of Henry M. Flagler, associate with John D. Rockefeller in the Standard Oil Company and builder of the Florida East Coast Railroad.

From 1943 to 1945 Martin was acting head of the history department at the University of Georgia, and in 1945 was assistant dean of faculties, a position which he now holds along with his teaching duties.

He is active in civic and religious affairs in Athens, being a member of the Kiwanis Club and the First Methodist Church of that city. He is a member of the Southern Historical Association.

His wife is the former Clare Phillips of Palatka, Florida. Their only child, Ellen Claire Martin, was born in 1942.

The climax of 1944 was D Day on the sixth of June—the invasion of Germany. A long time before this event all the Tifton churches were open for people to visit and pray for peace. At three o'clock in the morning the siren in Tifton brought hundreds of people bounding from their beds to pray.

Nineteen-forty-five, one of the momentous years in the history of the world, gave us V E Day, May 8, Germany's surrender, August 10, Japan's surrender, and V J Day, August 31, the date of the signing of the final surrender document aboard the Battleship Missouri in Tokyo Bay.

Different types of events came swiftly. The Memorial Recreation Committee of the Tift County Chamber of Commerce, J. E. Newton, Mrs.

F. H. Corry, Mrs. J. J. Clyatt, Judge R. Eve, J. G. Jolley, Joseph Kent, and J. E. Waldrop met with Charles M. Groves, recreation representative of the Federal Security Agency to discuss plans for the proposed $150,000 recreation center in memory of veterans of World War I and World War II.

The Tifton Playground and Recreationg Board, named by the Tifton City commission, elected Judge Eve, president; Dr. L. O. Shaw, secretary, and J. E. Newton, treasurer. Other members were A. C. Tift and J. E. Waldrop.

Another bright spot in the war gloom was the experience of Lieutenant Colonel Henry T. Myers, son of Mrs. and the late Mr. I. W. Myers. Lieutenant Colonel Myers flew President Roosevelt from Malta Island, in the Mediterranean, to the Crimea for his conference with Marshal Stalin and Prime Minister Churchill and later flew the President back to Egypt.

Progress continued in Tifton during 1944. The town established itself as a bee center and shipped twenty-five tons of bees to different points. A modern cannery shop was opened. Trucks, wagons, and cars filled with corn and lined up on both sides of the street near the modern plant of Phillips Milling Company on Second Street reminded people of the old days during cotton ginning season.

Another conspicuous sign of progress was the success of the bookmobile, which visited eight county schools once every four weeks, besides visiting homes in rural districts.

Mrs. E. G. Thornhill, librarian, circulated between thirteen hundred and fourteen hundred books over the county. She left Tifton about nine o'clock in the morning. Young and old eagerly awaited the sound of the bookmobile and rushed to get books as soon as it parked. Its success was due to the cooperation of Tift County Board of Education, county commissioners, school superintendents, teachers, children, and the librarian.

The horrors of war continued, but occasionally a gleam of light broke through the dark clouds. On March 25, 1945, Leon Swindell, who had been in a Japanese prison, arrived in Tifton. The Tifton High School and Spence Field bands met him at the train and paraded to the courthouse where the town gave Swindell a welcome.

S. B. Lassiter, chairman of Tift County Red Cross Chapter acted as master of ceremonies, and the Reverend Davis Sanders gave the invocation. After the introduction of Sergeant Swindell to the crowd, the Spence Band played "God Bless America."

Dean G. P. Donaldson welcomed Sergeant Swindell; Mrs. H. B. Durham presented flowers, A. E. Danielson presented to Swindell a chest of silver from Tifton citizens. The meeting closed with "The Star Spangled Banner."

Swindell, who was in the army before the war started, flew to the Pacific when General Douglas MacArthur called for technical men. While sitting in a barracks at Nichols Field, Sergeant Swindell, an experienced radio man, listened on December 7, 1941 to the news about Pearl Harbor disaster. He was taken prisoner the following April.

On January 30, 1945, he was among the Americans rescued by Rangers from the camp at Cabanatum; while at this prison he lost forty pounds on account of the starvation diet and tropical diseases.

The return of Swindell and good news about some of our boys who had been missing in action cheered the hearts of Tifton people. On April 12, however, a cloud of sorrow hung over the nation—President Roosevelt was dead! The White House announced that Franklin Delano Roosevelt suddenly died of a cerebral hemorrhage at Warm Springs. The announcement was made by Commander Howard Bruenn, naval physician, who described the President's last hours: "At one o'clock this afternoon he was sitting in a chair while sketches were being made by an artist. He suddenly complained of a very severe headache. Within a few moments he lost consciousness and died at 4:35 p.m."

Memorial services were held by different organizations in Tifton. The Tifton High School in a special chapel program paid tribute to Roosevelt and later the high school annual, the Talisman, which the staff had already dedicated to the President, published the tribute.

Harry S. Truman, vice-president, was sworn in as President of the United States at 7:09 P.M. eastern war time.

The death of Roosevelt was "like the falling of an empire,"[2] but the nation went forward with plans for victory, and on May 8, President Truman announced the surrender of Germany. Mother's Day was set aside as a day of prayer, and union Thanksgiving services were held at the First Baptist Church in Tifton.

People were thankful for the surrender of Germany, but they knew the war was not over and that our boys had a tremendous task in conquering the Japanese. Before the final surrender of Japan the main celebration was on Flag Day, June 14, 1945, the one hundred-sixty-eighth anniversary of the day on 1777 our American Congress officially adopted the Stars and Stripes as the flag of the United States. President Wilson first proclaimed Flag Day in 1916.

The day of all days was August 14—the event of all secular events—the surrender of Japan! Tifton had its noisest, biggest, and safest celebration after President Truman announced Japan's acceptance of the surrender ultimatum. As soon as the news flashed, people rushed to the streets and screamed. Then they rode, yelled, blew horns and beat tin pans until

---

2. Description of Swift's death in Thackeray's "English Humorists of the Eighteenth Century."

early in the morning.

Other events of 1945, though important, were insignificant in comparison with Japan's surrender. Two hundred German prisoners of war were received at the camp located at the Tifton Air Base. The camp here in command of Major Henry A. Florence was designated as Peanut Camp. Tift County voters favored the revision of the Constitution of Georgia (1877). Tifton High School's selling three thousand dollars worth of victory bonds and stamps entitled it to have a unit in some veterans' hospital in the United States named for the school. Mr. and Mrs. W. G. Woody celebrated their golden wedding. A. E. Amos C. Fennell, who died in February, would have reached the century mark had he lived until May 10, 1945. A. E. Danielson, general manager of Armour and Company at Tifton for nine years, retired after forty-two years of service with the company.

Rationing was cancelled to a certain extent after the surrender of Japan. Gas, tires, kerosene, butter, grease of all kinds, canned goods, fruit juices, and sugar had been rationed. Four ration books had been issued. No one had ever dreamed that lowly grease would one day ascend the ladder of fame, but a wad of grease, during the forties, more precious than a nugget of gold, reached the top round. People watched for trucks bringing groceries to some of the stores and rushed in a stampede to be first in the grease lines. During sales of scarcities clerks and customers were near exapseration. Only the rationing of sugar continued after the surrender.

Within a few months after the surrender of Japan, some of our boys returned. Then eventually other survivors came home. Tift County values the services of its boys from the most humble private to the officers of highest ranks. Since, however, a volume would be necessary for a full account of decorations, achievements, and bravery, we have details about only those who lost their lives.

CHAPTER XV
POST-WAR EVENTS—ATOMIC ERA

Nineteen-forty-six did not record events as important as those of 1945, but a great era—the atomic age—which began during the last days of the war, was in 1946 the theme of discussions among young and old. Radios, newspapers, and magazines debated about whether the United States should give to Russia the secret of the atomic bomb. How to win the peace—how to make atomic energy subserve and not master mankind—were some of the grave problems.

Unconscious of the great era, however, little Charles Randall Clifton, son of Mr. and Mrs. Carlos Clifton, Route 5, was the first baby to appear in Tift County in 1946.

Among the problems for Tifton in 1946 were improvements of schools. Mrs. O. V. Barkuloo was appointed chairman of a fact finding committee to survey the school problems. The investigation resulted in improvements in the grammar school, which especially needed them. The city had already spent $27,000 on the high school auditorium.

As far as we know, Tifton was the first town to ship gladioli bulbs by air. A C-47 twin-engine cargo plane carried them to New York. They were shipped by Byles Brothers, of Valdosta, and the Nick Peete Company, Ty Ty, to two firms in New York.

"The shipment launched the overnight contract freight services out of Tifton to Washington, Baltimore, Philadelphia, New York, and Boston. The freight service is handled by the United States Air Lines, Inc., St. Petersburg." (Tifton Gazette.)

The tomato plant and shipping in Tift County reached a high point in 1946.

The main organization of the year was the Tift County Historical Society. An account of the charter of this society was published in the Tifton Gazette:

"Charter was granted in Tift Superior Court, June 6, to the Tift County Historical Society, Inc., for a period of thirty-five years, the petitioners being a group of Tifton and Tift County citizens and a few others, former citizens of the county, who are interested in the purposes of the county.

"According to the charter provisions the society is to have no capital stock and is not organized for pecuniary gain or profit but for the purpose of publication and distribution of a history of Tifton and Tift County.

"It is the plan and purpose of the society to continue the compilation of historical information and from time to time to publish such volume or volumes as may be necessary to preserve a complete and accurate record of Tifton and Tift County.

"The society has as one of its plans and purposes the ultimate donation of copies of publications to each school and public library in the state. Its purpose and plan of society and its members to originate, plan, and participate in movements for the betterment of the community through the promotion of its educational, cultural, and moral interest. It is an agreed plan and purpose of the society to seek out children with talents, musical, artistic, and inventive.

"In re: The Tift County Historical Socieyt, Inc., Petition to incorporate in Tift Superior Court.

"The foregoing petition of C. A. Baker, Joseph Kent, George W. Branch, J. L. Williams, Robert Herring, B. H. McLeod, E. L. Webb, L. E. Bowen, R. D. Smith, S. F. Mitchell, O. V. Barkuloo, W. Jelks Warren, C. L. Carter, John T. Ferguson, T. W. Tift, E. D. Gibbs, Lott Whiddon, S. A. Youmans, Harry Hornebuckle, A. B. Phillips, Mrs. N. Peterson, Mrs. Susie T. Moore, Mrs. Ruth Vickers Fulwood, Mrs. Briggs Carson, Sr., Mrs. Pearl Willingham Myers, Mrs. Martha Williams, Mrs. Ralph H. Tift Jones, Miss Ida Belle Williams, Mrs. Ralph H. Johnson, Mrs. Elizabeth P. Karsten, Mrs. Robert A. Heinsohn, Mrs. Robert Balfour, Mrs. Hazel B. Mitchell, Mrs. J. E. Newton, and Mrs. Agnew Andrews to be incorporated under the name of Tift County Historical Society, Inc., read and considered. It appearing that said petition is within the purview and intention of the laws applicable thereto, and that all of said laws have been fully complied with, including the presentation of a certificate from the Secretary of State as required by Paragraph 22, 1803 of the Code of Georgia annotated:

"It is hereby ordered, adjudged, and decreed that all the prayers of said petition are granted and said applicants and their associates, successors, and assigns are hereby incorporated and made a body politic under the name and style of Tift County Historical Society, Inc., for and during the period of thirty-five years, with the privilege of renewal at the expiration of that time according to the laws of Georgia and that said corporation is hereby granted and vested with all the rights and privileges mentioned in said petition.

"Granted at Chambers this 6th day of June, 1946.

"R. Eve, Judge
"Tift Superior Court."

Besides this organization, there were other additions to the city in 1946, the new Austin-Weston pick-up and street sweeper and the Dixie airways. The street sweeper the first that Tifton ever had, not only swept the streets and gutters, but picked up the trash. The machine, operated by one man, was gasoline powered.

The Dixie Airways, which opened at the Tifton municipal airport gave to Tifton and the surrounding territory a complete flying service air with the larger trading centers. The organization was composed of H. A. Hornebuckle, S. M. Phillips, and C. A. Randerson. The initial flight service on July 4 was from Tifton to Atlanta within an hour. On the return trip the plane left Atlanta at 5:30 p.m. and arrived in Tifton at 6:30 p.m.

There was a school for students, which is still in operation and airplanes for rental to rated pilots for cross country travel.

G. K. Loftin, owner of Tifton Bus Lines, began operation of bus service in Tifton in June, 1946. The service included Unionville, Phillipsburg, cotton mill, Armour and Company, and the city residential section.

Other material improvements were the loan of $460,000 from the Rural Electrification Administration to the Colquitt Electric Company, which operates in Colquitt and adjoining counties including Tift, and the $25,000 set aside by Governor Arnall for improvements at the Tifton State Farmers' Market. The Tifton Board of Education and the State Department of Education, offered an education course for veterans, who are engaged in the on-the-job training program. During March thirty-two building permits, amounted to $96,000.

During the progress citizens rejoiced to see our boys returning from the battlefield. The boys who lost their lives were not forgotten. Beautiful Fulwood Park was the appropriate setting for memorial services held on Sunday afternoon in June, honoring the forty-one young men of Tift County who made the supreme sacrifice in World War II.

Tift County Post No. 21 American Legion, under command of J. G. Whigham, had charge. T. H. S. band under direction of Lastinger, gave several numbers before the service began and played "The Star Spangled Banner" for the presentation of the Flag. Mr. Ray Shirley gave the invocation.

Commander Whigham and Mrs. E. U. Holder, president of the Legion Auxiliary, told of the purpose of the services and Commander Whigham introduced the speaker, the Reverend R. C. Grisham, pastor of First Baptist Church, Moultrie.

The Gold Star citations, with the American Legion emblem, were delivered by Raymond Brooks to the mothers or the next of kin of the dead heroes. One mother, Mrs. Henry S. Brooks, is twice a Gold Star Mother.

After a three-volley salute by a firing squad, Mr. Len Lastinger, and Dean George P. Donaldson, of Baldwin College, led the people in singing, "God Bless America." Mrs. Gresham pronounced the benediction. As the name of each soldier was called, a flower was placed in his memory on a cross in front of the audience. After the services the decorated cross was placed on the grave of J. P. Adams.

The names of Tift countians who died during the recent war are: Garland C. Anderson, Theodore W. Croft, Silas B. Brooks, Samuel W. Spillers, Durwood Lee Willis, Cletes J. Watson, Tom H. Rooks, Charles W. Matthews, Albert J. Mullis, Wyman D. Martin, Robert B. Powledge, George M. Sutton, Alva McLeon Woodal, Elton J. Aultman, W. A. Kelley, Jr., Ralph Gibbs, Benjamin McIntosh, Frederick E. Sears, Eugene Hobby, Paul Johnson, Cecil H. Willis, George C. Johnson, Clyde F. Lavender, Tilton Belflower, Winford Evans, John Dowdy, Ollie Gibbs, Talmadge May, Horace Goff, Charles E. Patton, Francis A. Cooper, Murren Arrel Barbee, Jesse Penn Adams, Heyward W. Whiddon, Russell Leonard Garner, Edward Carl Cromer, Sidney Neighbors, Curtis Matthews, Reuben Funderburke; colored, Robert Lee Board, Jr., and Joseph Alvan McKinney.

Longevity during 1946 was represented by Mrs. Elizabeth Whaley, who on April 11, celebrated her ninety-fifth birthday. Her hearing is still good, but her eyesight is poor. She is very active for her age. Mrs. Whaley still goes to the table three times a day for her meals, cleans up her room, does other chores, and answers the telephone. She attributes her longevity and good health to hard work, which she began during the War Between the States, and to her regard for the laws of nature.

Mrs. Whaley, a daughter of Madison and Trecia Burch Gaughf of Laurens County, was born on April 11, 1851. Mrs. Whaley, married in 1881 James Whaley, who fought in The War Between the States, under command of Robert E. Lee. Mr. Whaley was wounded when his horse on which he rode was shot and killed. Mr. Whaley died in 1924.

She and her husband moved to Tift County the year they married. Mrs. Whaley when a young girl was a member of the Red Oak Methodist Church and is now a member of the Omega Church. She is also a member of the United Daughters of the Confederacy. One of her sons died in 1924; the other, whom she stays with, lives in Tifton. She has ten grandchildren and four great-grandchildren.

Miscellaneous happenings of 1946 were:

Marian Aultman, daughter of Mr. and Mrs. L. W. Aultman, of Tift County, left for Tokyo, Japan, in July. She was one of the first civilian workers with the United States occupation forces in that country.

The Tifton Lions Club placed new lights and wires in Fulwood Park. Lion Joe Kent at the request of the Tifton Garden Club placed the new lights. An automatic switch turns the lights on every night at seven o'clock, and they remain until eleven.

Order was placed for one hundred white concrete posts, costing six hundred dollars, for street markers in the city.

The new four-room annex to the Annie B. Clark Grammar School was completed in December. Fluorescent lights and a new automatic coal stoker, which heated new and old buildings, added much to the comfort of the faculty and students.

A five-man board was appointed to control the affairs of the Tift County Hospital: C. R. Choate, Ralph Puckett, and A. R. Corry, of Tifton; M. H. Evans, of Ty Ty; and W. R. Ponder, of Omega.

On September 19, 1946 grape production for Tift County was planned. E. L. Love, of Moultrie, was in Tifton for ten days in connection with the South Georgia Grape Growers Association.

Two of the most important events in 1946 were the opening of the Tifton Frozen Food Market and the Shriners' Convention. The market opened on September 23. The handsome building, located at the corner of Second Street and North Central Avenue is one of the best of its kind in this section. The market was erected by Spooner Construction Company of Tifton. H. A. Hornebuckle is president of the $200,000 enterprise; J. G. Chambliss, vice-president and general manager; and W. S. Weeks, secretary-treasurer.

A week after the opening of the Frozen Food Market about two thousand Shriners came riding in jeeps, on horseback, and on trains to Tifton. About three weeks before, Mr. Allen Johnson, Jr., on behalf of the Tifton Lumber Company, had presented a gold plated key to City Manager Frank Smith. The inscription, "Tifton, Georgia" is on one side of the handle, decorated with a wreath; "Compliments of the Tifton Lumber Company," on the other side.

John C. Helmken, illustrious potentate of Alee Temple, Savannah received from City Manager Smith this gold key, which unlocked the hospitable door of Tifton for the Shriners. After the registration of the Nobles at the Hotel Myon and at the high school auditorium the Shrine band in full regalia gave a concert in front of the Tifton Bank. City police and State Patrol cars cleared the way for the parade. Alee Temple band marched, followed by the official cars carrying the potentate and officials of the Tifton Shriners.

The Shriners had their fun playing all kinds of jokes on people, but exhibited in their float, which presented doctors and nurses in their treatment of crippled children, the main project of the Nobles.

Another sign of progress was the report of the third bank in Tifton, the Citizen's Bank, which opened on July 1, 1945, with H. D. Hand as president and H. P. Sanders as cashier. On June 29, 1940 the statements showed deposits of $250,929.48.

In November, 1946, people in Tifton and in other American towns were mentally and physically shivering over the complete shut down of the nation's coal mines. No one could buy coal unless he would sign an affidavit saying he had enough coal for only a few days. After the District Court of the United States made a case against John L. Lewis, he finally sent the miners back to work.

This war period was permeated with terrors and prayers for victory, the master word for the allies. People talked about the letter V, the symbol of the allied nations, thought about it, and saw it in various places. The letter V actually appeared in the formation of clouds. Reliable Tifton people saw it. Mrs. W. I. Lane, of Ty Ty, found a gray and green colored spider with a distinct grayish V on his back. Two ears of corn in B. B. Tyson's corn patch grew in the shape of a V. Cane in an almost perfect V grew in the patch of Henry Folsom, Route 5, Tifton, Georgia. No one can explain such phenomena as these. The V's, however, might have existed before without anyone's observation.

The Holy Grail of War, the symbol V, was found. Only time can tell whether or not the search for the Holy Grail of peace will be in vain.

CHAPTER XVI

SMALL TOWNS

HISTORY OF BRIGHTON

(by Mrs. Dan Sutton)

When Brighton community was first formed, it was a part of Irwin County. In 1905 it became a part of Tift County. Captain H. H. Tift named Brighton for some town near his home at Mystic, Connecticut.

A man known as one-armed Jim Walker was perhaps the first settler. He cleared a rather large tract of land, and today his daughter Jude and her boys still live on this farm. Mr. and Mrs. Jonathan Walker were probably the next settlers to move to this community. Other early settlers were Mr. and Mrs. Elbert Fletcher, Mr. and Mrs. Thomas McMillan, Mr. and Mrs. T. D. Paulk, Mr. and Mrs. Otis Luke, Mr. and Mrs. W. L. Conger, the Barton family, the Reason Gibbs family, the John Arnold family, and the Jordan Baker family. These are the families who really cleared the land and made way for other settlers.

Captain H. H. Tift built a tramroad from Tifton to Brighton, and with Charlie Jenkins as engineer, the train hauled the logs which had been cut from the virgin timber, to Tift's sawmill in Tifton where they were made into fine lumber. Log rolling and quilting parties were the order of the day. Much of the wood was piled together and burned.

About 1890, the first railroad was built from Tifton to Pinetta in Irwin County, the first engineer also being Charlie Jenkins. Wood was used as fuel to run the train, and when fuel gave out, the train was stopped for wood to be gathered. The engineer stopped just anywhere for passengers to board the train.

W. W. Lennon brought a large group of negroes from North Carolina to turpentine the timber and they, together with negroes from Albany, bought lots from Elbert Fletcher and settled what is known as the Brighton Negro Colony. Some of these negroes are buried under the Farmers' warehouse in Tifton. These negroes worked for the white pioneers, hoeing, share-cropping the farms, washing, ironing, scrubbing, and tending the children. They had a great part in the growth and development of both Brighton and Harding. Many of them were held in great respect by the pioneer families.

The church was begun in the first schoolhouse which was built about 1890. J. J. F. Goodman, George Clark, and Joe Mixon were among the first preachers. Then the Mount Olive Primitive Baptist Church was established as an arm of Turner Church, and Elder James Gibbs was the first pastor. Today Elder W. F. Mims is the pastor, and the church is a very progressive, flourishing church made up principally of the children, grandchildren and great-grandchildren of the pioneers. George M. Fletcher donated the land for the church and the school. Jonathan Walker sawed the lumber and Henry Sutton built the first church and donated the organ to the church.

These men also built the first schoolhouse. Miss Edna Cox, who later became Mrs. M. S. Shaw, was the first teacher. Other early teachers were Miss Lummie Mann, Arch Shaw, W. B. Hitchcock, and Mrs. Leona Yarbrough Sutton. These first teachers boarded around with their pupils, and their salaries were meagre. They were real teachers though, and did a great work. Brighton School was finally consolidated with Harding School and is now known as Harding Consolidated School.

Mr. Walker had the first cotton gin in the Brighton community. People hauled the cotton to the ginhouse in wagons, and emptied it into stalls. Then they carried it from the stalls to the gin in large baskets. After the cotton was ginned, it was put into the press by hand. When they got a bale into the press, they pushed a lever until it was pressed. Today farmers from Brighton bring their cotton to Tifton where it is ginned on an electric gin.

The Brighton post office was established about 1900. Henry Sutton was the first postmaster, and Walter Sutton was assistant. Soon after this a rural route was established with Will Clark as the first rural carrier. After this the post office at Brighton was soon abolished.

The first store at Brighton was set up by Henry Sutton in his house. Later he moved it to the station at Brighton. There is no store at Brighton now.

The J. S. Belflower family and the Charlie Jenkins family and others moved to Brighton since the pioneers first settled it and they have helped in the growth and development of it.

Today Brighton and Harding Communities make Brighton Militia District 1550, and Harding Consolidated School District.

MR. AND MRS. ELBERT FLETCHER
BRIGHTON COMMUNITY

by Mrs. Dan Sutton

Elbert Fletcher was born in Irwin County near Fitzgerald. He was a soldier in the War Between the States. He married Katie McMillan of Alapaha and they owned a large plantation in the Brighton community, being some of the very first settlers. Mr. Fletcher died at the age of fifty-two, but Mrs. Fletcher, who was affectionately known as "Aunt Katie," lived to be ninety-one years of age. Their children were Dan, George M., and Sarah.

Mrs. Fletcher was a good financier, a good neighbor and friend. She was a staunch charter member of the Mount Olive Primitive Baptist Church, never missing a service except for illness. At "Big Meeting" time, her home was filled with visiting members during the three days. Her hospitality, as did that of the other pioneers, knew no bounds, especially during these meetings.

She was a famous cook of the old style. She cared nothing for dress, but her character was pure gold. She lived alone for many years. She kept a large herd of cows all the time, and loved them dearly. No matter what time of night one came straggling in, she would get up out of bed and go turn him in the cowpen. Aunt Katie was really a brave pioneer. They rest in the Turner Church cemetery.

MR. AND MRS. HENRY SUTTON
BRIGHTON COMMUNITY

by Mrs. Dan Sutton

Henry Sutton was born in the Zion Hope community in 1861, a son of Joe and Missouri Sumner Sutton. He had one sister, Susie. In 1881 he married Sarah Fletcher, and a little later they purchased a 650-acre farm in Brighton community. Here they reared six children: Walter, Willie, Dan, George, Kate, and Bessie.

Mrs. Sutton was an invalid for many years, but had somewhat recovered during her last years. She had a great sense of humor, and everyone enjoyed her. When one drove up to her gate, she met him there with a friendly smile and one felt welcome at once. Her smile lighted up her whole face and there was a twinkle in her eye. She enjoyed homemaking, and since she had lived in the house so much when she was ill, she particularly liked to walk about the yard and lot, feeding her chickens, etc., spending as much time as possible outdoors. She was exceedingly cheerful for one who had suffered for so many years.

Mr. Sutton liked to minister to the sick, and he spent many a weary night watching at the bedside of those who were ill. When sorrow, illness, or trouble entered a home, he was the first person thought of.

He was a charter member of the Mount Olive Primitive Church, and was a leading member and faithful in fulfilling his church duties as long as he lived. He always worked to maintain the best school possible. He loved and enjoyed his family and, like all other pioneers, they were exceedingly hospitable in their home. The latch string was, in truth, always on the outside.

Just as at the other pioneer homes there were cane grindings and sugar boilings for a month. Mrs. Sutton was an expert at making sugar. Then came hog killing time with "chiltlins" and stuffed sausage.

Mr. Sutton served four years as Tax Receiver of Tift County. He had the first store in Brighton and was postmaster during the time the post office was at Brighton. He died in 1926, Mrs. Sutton having preceded him in death in 1924.

MR. AND MRS. JONATHAN WALKER
BRIGHTON COMMUNITY

by Mrs. Dan Sutton

Jonathan Walker was born near Irwinville. His father died when Jonathan was very young, and he helped his mother rear eight children. For several years Jonathan ran a ferry across the Alapaha River near Crystal Lake. Jonathan carried the mail on horseback from Irwinville to Broxton. He set up camps along the mail route and here he stopped to eat and sleep. He was Tax Collector of Irwin County for one term. He was a great fisherman and spent much of his latter days tramping the woods he loved so well and fishing.

In 1880, he married Margaret Fletcher, better known as "Gallie." After his marriage, he bought two lots of land in the Brighton Community, and here they reared their family: Alice, James (present sheriff of Tift County), Edna, and Kate.

Mr. Walker was a good neighbor, a real friend to the poor and unfortunate, often going out of his way to befriend them, a devoted husband, a good provider for his family, and a civic minded man—always working for the best interests of his community.

He died October 1, 1917. Mrs. Walker survived him several years. She was a faithful, active member of the Mount Olive Primitive Baptist Church, a fine cook, kind to the sick, and even though her health was poor for many years, she went about as long as she lived, giving "A cup of cold water in the Master's name." They rest in the Tifton cemetery.

BROOKFIELD

(Tifton Gazette)

Jan. 5, 1923

(By Nathan L. Turner)

Brookfield started September or October 1870. George W. Bowen, father of Enoch P. and I. W. Bowen, built a little cypress log store, near where the Brookfield Methodist Church now stands, about 14 by 16 feet, about the time stated above, and put canned goods, crackers, and groceries in it.

This was just as the grading crew of the what then was to be the Brunswick and Albany Railroad, moved their camps to what is east Brookfield now; the track-laying crew was somewhere east of Alapaha river then, I think about Willacoochee.

Bowen had to haul his goods by team fifty miles, probably from Valdosta and Albany.

The railroad now belongs to the A. C. L. Railway Co. They were building, but he sold goods and kept on doing business until the road began running trains as far as Brookfield, and it was a station from the first train that reached there until now.

Elisha S. Mallory built the first sawmill there, also in the bounds of Tift County about a year or two after the railroad was finished that far. Brookfield was a town before Tifton or Ty Ty was started. The next station above Brookfield was Riverside, just north of Little River. It had a sidetrack and store before Tifton was started, but Tifton got the store and killed it.

It was in this store of Mr. Bowen's that I spent my first dime. I bought five cents worth of streaked-stick candy, and five cents worth of lemon crackers, and got five of each and that was the best candy and crackers I ever ate, or ever will.

I was six years old and had on my first suit of clothes, made from home sheared, home-spun, home woven and home-made "jeans." It was half of woven wool, and the other half of warps of cotton, home-grown. home hand-seed picked, for I helped to pick it and home-spun. I also had on about my first pair of shoes, and they were made out of home-tanned cowhide, tanned and made by my brother-in-law Dempsey Willis with pegs from maple wood and sewed with home-made thread. (Willis lives at Brookfield now.) They were not very good, but they kept a fellow's feet warm. So as smart as the boys think they are of today, we can boast of things they never saw, even had.

There was one train a day up, and down next day, with fifteen to twenty-five box and flat cars, with a coach with a division through the center, the front end used for baggage, express, and mail car, and the other on hind end, used for colored people and then the last car used for white folks. They looked like street cars used now.

There were no air-brakes then, only hand-brakes, and when they wanted to stop, they blew brakes about a half to three-quarters of a mile before they got to the place where they wanted to stop, and often then, would run past it before they could stop. One short blow of the whistle was to apply brakes and two short blows to release them, and when they blew for brakes you would see the fellows on top of the freight cars in a trot, running from one car to the other twisting on brakes. Wet or cold weather, or even sleet or snow, they had to stay up there.

The engines were wood-burners, and had to stop every few miles to take on wood to fire with and sometimes they could not make it to the next wood rack, and would have to stop and get some wood out of the woods, along side the track to fire up, so they could make the next woodrack. When they got there, the conductor had to get off and go to the engine and punch a ticket made for that purpose, the numbers of quarter cords they took and drop it in a little covered box attached to the woodrack for that purpose. That was what the man who run the rack got his pay from the paymaster with.

There were no depots for several years after the road was built along the line, and the conductors collected freights and fares in cash, except what went to Albany or Brunswick.

Conductors carried a duplex ticket to punch the place the passenger got on and off, the date, and amount collected. He gave you one-half of it, but you had to pay ten cents extra, for this receipt ticket he gave you, but the paymaster would redeem those tickets on the pay car once a month at ten cents. This is the only way he could check up with the conductor on cash fares.

This road ran, this one train one way and next day the other until 1879, when they put on one each way. The first daily train that ran from the east, brought old Uncle Jimmy Gaulding to Tifton in July, 1879.

I am the oldest man from point of occupancy in Tifton, I think. I came and lived here May 9, 1879, just ahead of Uncle Jimmy Gaulding, and Mrs. J. B. Huff, had lived here with her father, Uncle Billy Mathews, just before I came. I think she is the oldest resident in Tifton, from a point of occupancy. Now, don't think I am old.

I was clerking in the store of Turner and Fletcher, composed of my brother, Jack Turner, and James Fletcher, who was killed later by James Gibbs, near Alapaha river (between here and there). This was the only store here then and Tift did not even have a commissary then. It was that year that Mr. Tift bought his first engine to pull his log trucks and the road ran out southeast to the Old Myer Baker place. I rode with him on the engine the first trip he made out with it.

(Editor's Note: There was great difficulty in getting facts about Brookfield because of conflicting opinions. We finally decided to use two articles, which may give some contradictory statements, but we did our best to get accuracy.)

THE HISTORY OF BROOKFIELD
(Eulala Tyson)

Brookfield, a small village seven miles east of Tifton, was founded in the late 1870's. It was settled by a small, compact group of peace-loving citizens; farmers, merchants, and lumber men grouped together to form this small unit they called a community.

The citizens of Brookfield did not make its history. They merely lived there and in living Time and Fate slowly chiseled their age-old story on the faces of these old settlers. Each face is a history in itself—history of peace, love, and harmony, fear, death, and disaster, joy and sorrow. They are all etched on the faces of the survivors. They will tell you that Brookfield has no history. It has no beginning and no ending. It has always been there—a meeting-place of the local boys, shopping center for the enterprising young ladies of the surrounding parts, and gossip-post and hitchrack for all the men and mules.

Brookfield began with Fender's Lumber mill which produced lumber for surrounding territories. This lumber mill was followed by two stores operated by Mr. John Churchwell and Mr. J. M. Brown of Nashville, Georgia.

In Mr. Churchwell's stores one could find an odd assortment of goods. Farmers could purchase their mule shears, plow lines, gear, seed, and chewing tobacco. The good ladies, their wives, could make their purchases of gingham, grits, and white sugar. For the children shopping was quite a problem. The candy counter was there with its attractions. The youngster of yesterday had to rack his brain. Shall we buy peppermint sticks, gumdrops, or licorice?

Mr. Churchwell, a notable character in Brookfield's early history, led a hectic life. Aside from operating the largest merchandise store for miles, he was postmaster, express agent, and depot agent. Mr. Churchwell would gladly oblige one by selling a ticket, but the train-waving was left up to the individual.

When Brookfield's population increased so that Mr. Churchwell could not handle all of its thriving business, Mr. Charles Hardy and Mr. Enoch Bowen opened stores of their own. Brookfield was growing. The virgin timber was being cleared away, and more and larger farms were being cultivated. Mr. Sanders Gibbs operated a long staple cotton gin. Business was humming.

When Mr. Churchwell gave up his store in Brookfield and went to Albany, Georgia, Mr. Henry Webb and Mr. Archer McMillan took over his store. They continued his practice of business.

The landowners of Brookfield were farmers, and merchants and lumber men. They owned all of the territory in and around Brookfield. They made the community what it was then, a proud heritage to leave to their children. They left a responsibility to be shared by all who lived there. Today their children and grandchildren accept that responsibility and listen with pride to the tales of their forefathers.

Out of the haze of the past then comes a reminiscent gleam that makes the shadowy figures of the past a vague reality. Farmers in the village with their high stepping buggy horses, merchants, business to the core, all gathered with one common interest, to live, to build a home, to build part of a county, a state, and a nation, and a world. The children of yester-years may see Mr. Richard Gibbs, pole and can in hand, headed for the Alapaha River. Jolliest of the old settlers was Mr. Will Coursey. His merry laugh and cheery words were the joy of all his friends. Mr. Dempsey Willis was a squirrel hunter while Mr. Mac White liked to hunt birds. Mr. Jim Taylor, farmer, was a very religious man, and he took his religion seriously. Every Sunday one could see him jogging along in his buggy. The Reverend R. A. Lawrence was pastor of a church called "Booges Bottom." Each Sunday this bearded gentleman could be seen coming from his home on the Alapaha, his old mule and road cart putting out small dusty puffs behind him.

A visit to the mill operated by Mr. Charles Hardy was always a delight to the children. Just the words "Hardy's mill" would send the youngsters scrambling for their swimming suits, fish hooks, poles, and the inevitable can of worms.

The merchants, Mr. J. L. Gay and Mr. I. W. Bowen took their business seriously. Through their good works, Brookfield thrived and grew.

Mr. C. H. Patton, son of Mr. Will Patton, one of Brookfield's settlers, was a mere child when the community was formed. Even though he was young, he remembers the tales told by his father of their early life at Brookfield. Their forefathers' pride still lingers. Pride in living well—in living good—in dying revered by all.

Life in early Brookfield was not too dull, so Mr. Patton said. After the farmers' "laying by" time in July, the farmers all took off from one to two weeks to hold their annual "big-meeting." Church services were conducted by half a dozen preachers. Often the Baptists and Methodists would hold their meetings together. The preacher of one denomination would hold his services while the others listened. The next would then take his turn. After services were over, the converted ones would join the church of their choice. Out of these "big meeting" there arose one of the greatest evangelists in our church history, Bishop Arthur J. Moore, Brookfield's presentation to a dark world in bad need of His light.

After two weeks of "big meeting," fodder was ripe and ready to pull. The long staple cotton was ready for picking. Cane was ripe for grinding after cotton was picked.

Cane grinding was always fun for the young and old. A good drink of ice cold cane juice drunk under the light of a mellow harvest moon was headier than champagne drunk in society's glamor and glitter.

While the children played such games as Goosey-goosey-gander, William Trimble Toe, and Club Fist around a lightwood-knot fire, the elders would indulge in the latest gossip, horse-trading news, or a general discussion of the wayward trail taken by the younger generation.

A serenade after a wedding was more fun than a movie, then unknown to Brookfield's younger generation. When any young couple were married, young and old, big and little, joined in the serenading. This procession of merry-makers, making music or noise with big plow sweeps, dish pans, cow bells, and big circle saws would dance around the house two or three times, making as much noise as deemed possible. When everyone was tired of the clamor of dishpans, the jangle of cow bells, and the shrill "twing" produced by the circle saw, they congregated as close to the bride and groom as possible for the final serenading. The banjo, harmonica, and the old grinder's organ made sweet music. Every one sang to the disgruntled newlyweds. When the moon was high and it was time to leave, the songsters sang "Home, Sweet Home." Everyone was gay and happy, but the bride. Her tears flowed like wine.

In 1906, a druggist from Tifton drove the first automobile ever in Brookfield. The ladies marvelled over the great speed while the men tried to hold their panicky horses and mules. This event came close to causing a revolution in Brookfield's mode of transportation. It had been the custom of the young blades to go to Tifton to rent a horse and buggy to take their best girls for a Sunday ride. Two and one-half dollars would rent one of Tifton's highest-stepping buggy horses and classiest buggies worthy of any young lady. Did the first Brookfield-owned car arouse envy in the hearts of our Brookfield's Romeos?

The reminiscent gleam slowly fades and one can hear the soft murmur, "Ah, those were the good old days."

George Levere, one of Brookfield's oldest negro citizens, gave his version of the way Brookfield got its name. He said, "Missey, them white folkses tell you dat Brookfield got hits name from dat stream down yonder 'hind Mr. Harrell's, but old George can tell you better. When us darkies furst come to Brooksfield, us had to go through Mr. Brook's field to git to de sto. Us jist say 'We gwine fru Brooks' field'." Even now one never hears a darky say Brookfield. It's always Brooksfield.

Brookfield grew gradually. Its people lived and died. Only the memory of the days gone by remains. Today Brookfield is still a drowsy country village loved by all its inhabitants.

BISHOP ARTHUR MOORE

by E. Pickard

Arthur James Moore, born at Argile, near Waycross, Georgia, December 26, 1888, was son of John Spencer Moore and Emma Victoria Cason Moore, both of Ware County. When little more than an infant Arthur moved to Brookfield where he made his home with his parents for many years, John Spencer being section foreman with the Atlantic Coast Line Railroad.

On April 26. 1906, Arthur J. Moore married Mattie T. McDonald, of which union were William Harry, Wilbur Wardlaw, Alice Evelyn, Dorothy Emma, Arthur James, Jr.

When the Reverend C. M. Dunnaway, of Atlanta, was preaching at a revival at the First Methodist Church, Waycross, in 1909, Moore was converted. That year he joined the South Georgia Methodist Conference and that fall he became pastor of a group of seven McIntosh County country churches, of which Townsend was his first pastorate. None had a membership exceeding thirty.

Moore attended Emory, 1909-1911. He was ordained in 1914. He became a general evangelist and conducted evangelistic meetings throughout the nation until 1920, when he became pastor of the Travis Park Methodist Church, San Antonio, Texas. He received the Doctor of Divinity degree from Asbury College, Wilmore, Kentucky, 1922, and from Central College, Fayette, Missouri, 1924. Asbury, in 1930, conferred upon him the LL.D. degree.

After the death of Dr. George Barr Stewart, pastor of the First Methodist Church, Birmingham, Dr. Moore succeeded Dr. Stewart as pastor and remained at that charge four years.

During Dr. Moore's ten years as pastor of Travis Park and at Birmingham, more than six thousand members were added to these churches.

In 1930, at the general conference of the Methodist Church, held in Dallas, Texas, Dr. Moore was elected Bishop. His first assignment was to the West Coast of the United States, and it embraced California, Oregon, Arizona, and Washington State.

In 1934 Bishop Moore was assigned the general supervision of mission work of the Southern Methodist Church. Under his direction was work in China, Japan, Korea, Asia, Poland, Belguim, Czechoslovakia, and the Belgian Congo of Africa. All of these places he visited annually. He maintained offices in Shanghai and Brussels, and was wont to travel to Africa by plane.

In 1940 Bishop Moore was again appointed to supervision of Methodist work in the United States. He was assigned Georgia and Florida. Headquarters were in Atlanta. Also, he is head of missions of the entire Methodist Church, carrying on work in fifty nations.

For a year Bishop Moore served as president of Wesleyan College, Macon, the world's oldest chartered female college. He preceded Dr. N. C. McPherson, of Atlanta, who became president in 1942.

In June, 1942 Bishop Moore was preacher at an evangelistic meeting held at his boyhood home, Brookfield. Other preachers having a part in the Brookfield meetings were Dr. Orion Mixon, of Tifton, and Dr. John Sharp, presiding elder of Cordele District of the Methodist Church. Following the Brookfield meeting, Bishop Moore came to Tifton where he spoke at union services held in huge Twin Brick Warehouse and attended by approximately a thousand people at many of the services. Dr. Inman Johnson, professor of music at Southern Baptist Theological Seminary, Louisville, Kentucky, led the singing.

On May 25, 1947, Bishop Moore dedicated the Brookfield Memorial Methodist Church. Among others taking part in the dedicatory services was his son, the Reverend William Harry Moore, pastor of the Broadway Methodist Church, Orlando, Florida.

(See article on Churches, this book, re Brookfield Memorial Church.)

CHULA

by Billy Jean Pearman

The first Chula community, as was typical of South Georgia, was merely mile after mile of pine trees and wiregrass.

Gradually a few pioneer families moved from other sections. Jehu Branch, Sr., was one of the first men to bring his family to this district for settlement.

From its first settlement the chief occupation of this small community has been farming. Few crops were grown in the first year or two. Sheep roamed the open country, and once a year they were driven to market to be sold. With the money received from the sale of livestock were bought various goods not grown on the farms. The women and children received their yearly clothing requirements on this eventful occasion. New farm equipment then in use was purchased for the farms. Until the next annual trip to town, the wives discussed their new gowns and slippers.

Then in the early '80's Jehu Branch, Sr., began the local grading for a railway. Construction of the railway began and 1888, the first train ran over the road. A highway was built through the community, but U. S. No. 41 was not paved until the spring of 1928.

After Branch helped with the grading of the road, he erected a turpentine still and general store. Then a few years later he sold his stock to George W. Fletcher, another early settler in the community.

About the same time Polk Milner erected a sawmill one mile south of Chula near the present site of Rigdon's Camp. For a few years he sawed lumber and when he moved, sold the mill to A. B. Hollingsworth, who continued its operation.

The community's first post office, with George Branch as postmaster, was called Ruby. Upon discovering that another post office in the United States carried the same name, postal authorities changed the name to Chula, probably an Indian name meaning "flowers."

After the name was changed to Chula, the town was incorporated. Three bar rooms were erected and continued to operate until several years later when the charter expired.

Upon completion of the Georgia Southern and Florida Railroad through this section, people began to move into the Chula community. Much of the land bought by the new settlers had been cleared. Today practically all the land is farm land.

Since the coming of the first settlers, no provision had been made to fill the religious wants and needs of the people. In 1905 the people of the community, under the supervision of A. B. Hollingsworth, erected the Chula Methodist Church. A number of years later the Baptist Church, Reverend D. C. Rainey, pastor, was constructed.

An interesting note is the fact that all deaths in the Chula community have been from natural causes with the exception of two.

The first community doctor was Dr. Ellis. Dr. W. H. Hendricks assisted Dr. Ellis for a short time. Today Dr. Hendricks is a well-known Tift County physician. After Dr. Ellis's stay, Dr. W. E. Tyson practiced medicine in Chula. At the time of his death about thirteen years ago, Dr. Tyson was a much-loved citizen of the community. Since that time the community has been without a resident physician except for a year at a time.

In 1925 Berry Rigdon erected a turpentine still at Chula. Rigdon operated the still until it was destroyed by fire about fourteen years later. Since that time naval stores products have been taken directly to Tifton, with the exception of those under the direction of Willis' Still.

The Chula community has always had an excellent school. The first school was near the W. E. Tyson home. The second building was located directly to the rear of the present Fred Pearman home. From there the site of the building was moved to the V. D. Tyson home. Several terms were taught there. In 1925 the Chula Consolidated School, said to be the first in the state, was erected. For a few terms the school was a senior high school; however, it was deemed wise for the upper two grades to be sent to the high school in Tifton.

Since the time the Southern Railroad was first built, the Chula community has grown. Today it is typical of the many small villages that constitute a part of our county, state, and nation.

A LONE SOLDIER IN GRAY
(Ida Belle Williams)

May 3, 1934—Copied from Tifton Gazette.

The following tribute, by Miss Ida Belle Williams, to Tift County's only surviving veteran, was read at the Memorial Day Exercises here last Thursday.

While ploughing a field in old Dixie and listening to soldiers' tramps, a lad of sixteen years dreamed of joining the "Grays." Finally the struggles of the sixties grew so desperate that the call came for Southern youth to join the colors. The morning thrills of young manhood swept over Beverly Patton Leach, as shouldering his gun to the rhythm of a Southern martial air, he stepped up to bid goodbye to loved ones and to the old farm near Griffin, Georgia. Alas, his heart grieved as his old mother clasped her son and wept farewell.

This soldier boy marched directly toward Andersonville, Georgia, where later he met 62,000 prisoners in blue. For several weeks young Leach helped guard the stockade there. During this time the overflow of a stream washing away many of the logs, enabled a few prisoners to escape; but the alert Southern boys caught these prisoners.

Oh, the hardships of this brave Southern lad, who ate fat meat and corn bread and slept under the sky! Such things as coffee and biscuit were foreign to his diet. Many times this soldier boy, while sleeping on a log pillow, dreamed of the yesterdays on the old farm near Griffin. Leach would force back a tear as he awoke to the thundering realization of war.

From Andersonville to Savannah, Leach went with 1,000 prisoners. In this city by the sea he continued guarding and enduring the hardships. Fat meat and corn bread were still the only food contribution to his strength.

Upon leaving Savannah, the young soldier marched to Blackshear where he guarded for weeks Yankee prisoners. His experience there did not differ very much from those at other stockades.

His next change was his departure for Thomasville. From this little town to Albany, young Leach, with his sack and gun, tramped about fifty miles.

Later, while in Thomasville the soldier served as a messenger boy. Soon after his period of message work, Leach returned to his first post at Andersonville to get 1,000 prisoners, whom he and other guards had orders to carry to Ocean Pond, Florida. Upon arriving at Lake City, however, these guards placed the prisoners into Florida official's custody. On April 9, 1865, the end of the war, Leach after receiving an honorable discharge, disconsolately plodded his way toward Griffin.

Upon arriving at the old home place, Leach found, as Grady said, "his house in ruins, his farm devastated, his stock killed, his barns empty, his trade destroyed, his money worthless, his comrades slain, and the burden of others heavy upon his shoulders." What did Leach do? This soldier stepped from the trenches into the furrow, and fields that ran with human blood in April were grown with the harvest in June.

Beverly Patton Leach, Tift County's lone soldier in gray, lives at Chula, Georgia. Although eighty-six years old—he will be that age on May 3—Leach is still active enough to manage a store, in which he sells school supplies and candy to school children. This affable old gentleman's pseudonym is "Granddaddy Leach."

Like many others of the sixties, Mr. Leach had no educational advantages. Being the oldest of eight children, he spent his time behind a stubborn mule instead of at a desk to the tune of a hickory stick. Despite the fact that his school days numbered only seven, Granddaddy Leach rejoices that the youth now has opportunities minus the hickory.

The same indomitable spirit that characterized the brave lad in gray has permeated the life of this Confederate soldier. He has lived through three wars and is still able to smile a greeting to the modern generation. He has fought and won in the battle of life.

May the sun in all its splendor rise many more times for Tift County's lone soldier in gray! When finally at sunset the evening star beckons him on, may he follow with a heart still loyal to the gray, to the immortal white flag that waves over a land of eternal peace!

ELDORADO
by Mrs. A. N. Adcock

Eldorado was named by the Georgia Southern and Florida Railroad soon after its completion in 1888. The name signified the rich growth of pines. Even the wiregrass grew almost high enough to hide a horse and buggy.

Many years ago Enoch Bowen had guano shipped to Eldorado for farmers, and he had to deliver the fertilizer in a wagon. He once said, "The grass was so high and rich looking that I had difficulty finding an open space where I could tie my horse."

Years later the fact that there was another town named Eldorado caused a confusion about names. The post office at Eldorado was changed to Fender, the namesake of Frank Fender, a turpentine operator, who went to the town more than fifty years ago. Fender can boast of being the smallest town in Georgia with two names.

About one mile west of Fender was the Union Road through which Sherman's army passed on their march to the sea.

A. N. Adcock, Sr., owns a farm with an old settlement log house, where Sherman let his men stop to drink from the old well.

The first school was known as the old Mt. Vernon school as it was taught in the Mt. Vernon church and located about two miles north of Eldorado on what is now one of T. E. Phillips's farm.

About the year 1900 Mr. T. E. Phillips and P. D. Phillips came to South Georgia and bought Fender's interest in the turpentine still and also began farming. The Phillipses lived near the station. In 1902 they built a little one-room school building, which the Baptists and Methodists used also for church services. In 1905 each denomination built its own church. Several years later, the new consolidated school was built.

Mr. J. P. Davis and family moved to Eldorado in 1898. His daughter, who was the first child born on the mill ground was named Eldora for the town. As far as we know, she is the only Tift County citizen named for a town. This family moved from Eldorado to Tifton in 1905. His daughter, Maggie, affectionately known as "Miss Maggie" worked with the telephone exchange for years.

HISTORY OF THE EXCELSIOR DISTRICT

When Mr. John Y. Sutton moved into the Excelsior community on January 14, 1893, there was no school nearby. He sent his two children to the Warrenton School located between the Logan Glover and J. J. Warren farms. This building was in no condition to be used for the 1896 school term.

For two years, 1896 and 1897, Mr. W. H. Partridge furnished a tenant house for a school. The next year 1898, Mr. William Gibbs furnished a house. The 1899 term was taught in one of Mr. John Y. Sutton's houses.

Growing tired of these arrangements, Mr. John Y. Sutton, Mr. William Gibbs and Mr. James Gibbs decided to build a school house. During 1900 they built and equipped a school house on the old Pittman place, owned by Mr. Bill Warren at that time. This was called "Willis School." Here the children were happy until 1905 when Mr. W. H. Willis bought the land, and moved a family into the house.

Something had to be done so that the community would never be without a school again. A community meeting was called and plans were made for the erecting of a school house that could not be disposed of.

Both Mrs. William Gibbs, daughter of Mr. W. H. Partridge, and Mr. John Y. Sutton gave two acres of land. The place for the building was chosen where the Omega-Ty Ty road and the Tifton-Pine Forest road meet. The Downing Company gladly gave enough timber that had been blown down by a storm for the building. Mr. William Gibbs gave $125.00, Mr. John Y. Sutton gave $100.00, Mrs. M. P. Young gave $50.00, Mr. M. Tucker $50.00. The remainder of $50.00 needed for erecting and equipping the building was given in small donations. Rev. James Gibbs gave the name "Little Creek" to this school. This building was used as a meeting place for any denomination as long as the services did not interfere with the school activities.

The first teacher was Miss Ida Middleton, of Tennessee. She changed the name to Excelsior, meaning "Yet higher or ever upward." Everyone has learned to love the name even though the name was changed over the protests of those who first furnished the name and the building.

This building was used until 1928. At this time the old Ty Ty, Salem and Excelsior Schools were consolidated into the present Excelsior School. Two-thirds of this school yard was given by Mr. George Ford, Sr. The other one-third was given by Mr. J. S. Taylor. Ten grades were taught at this school for three or four terms; since then the tenth and eleventh grade students have been carried to the Tifton School. During 1929 the old Salem school house was moved over to the Excelsior school yard to be used as a teacherage.

(This sketch was compiled by Mrs. Hazel Whittington Fowler as given to her by Mr. J. Y. Sutton, pioneer of the Excelsior School Community.)

HISTORY OF HARDING

(Mrs. Dan Sutton)

Harding community was begun about sixty years ago with a tramroad built by Captain H. H. Tift. This tramroad was used to haul logs from across the Alapaha river to Tifton. People living at Harding at that time often road on this road. Charlie Jenkins was the engineer. After Fitzgerald was settled, Captain Tift built the tramroad on into Fitzgerald. and the day of all days for the settlers of Harding were those when excursions were run between Tifton and Fitzgerald. The tramroad was sold to the A. B. & C. Railroad and later became the A. B. & C. Railroad. Today the A. C. L. Railroad owns it.

Sixty years ago Captain H. H. Tift bought six lots of land at Harding for $150 per lot. He cut the two lots around Harding Station into forty-acre tracts and named them the Harding Fig Farm. The name Harding was taken from the name of a town on the railroad where Captain Tift lived in Massachusetts, and he hoped that the forty-acre tracts would be developed into fig farms. Instead there was only one fig tree, and it was in Dan Fletcher's yard.

Azor Paulk owned four lots of land around Harding and these were cut up into farms for his children: Charlie, Mack, Hillsman and Jim Paulk, and Effie Paulk Jenkins, Faithy Paulk Hall, and Becky Paulk Gibbs.

Dan Fletcher was one of the very first settlers at Harding, and at his death he was a large land owner there. Other families who have bought homes at Harding or have lived there for several years and have had a great part in the growth and development of the Harding Community are E. L. Vance, L. L. Simmons, J. D. McAllister, Y. E. Matthews, John Goff, Sr., Jacob Hall, Jim Ellis, W. H. Kelley, R. Arnold, C. S. Garner, H. D. McAllister and Harding Vance.

E. L. Vance bought part of the fig farm land and he and Dan Fletcher set up a cotton gin. Later Mr. Vance purchased the gin, and until three years ago, he ginned cotton for the Harding farmers as well as for many others.

John Churchwell from Brookfield built the first store at Harding and sent J. L. Gay over to Harding to run it. Later Mr. Churchwell sold the store to William Matthews who in turn sold it to Dan Fletcher. The store went out of business for a few years and was again opened by Dan Fletcher and E. L. Vance. Today Mr. Vance owns the store and does a good business there.

About forty years ago the Harding post office was opened with Dan Fletcher as postmaster and his wife, Mattie Churchwell Fletcher as his assistant. Dave Branch carried the mail from Waterloo to Harding on horseback. J. R. Fletcher who carried the mail from Tifton to Irwinville picked up the mail at Harding Post Office. The Harding Post Office was a trunk and was kept at either the house or the store. Soon rural routes were opened up and the post office was abolished.

Captain Tift had a large turpentine still at Harding and did a big business turpentining the timber. Turpentine is one of the major enterprises at Harding today.

The first school was taught in Liberty Baptist Church. Two terms of school were held in the Antioch Methodist Church with J. J. F. Goodman as the teacher. Then the first real Harding schoolhouse was built, being a one-room wooden building. Miss Gussie Hines was the first teacher. Soon another room was added and later the school was consolidated with Brighton School and became a three-room school. In 1926 a four-room brick building with an auditorium was built at Harding. Today the Harding school runs nine months. They have nine grades, the tenth and eleventh grades being taken to Tifton on a bus. They have a lunch room where they serve hot lunches to all the children.

There are two churches in the Harding Community—the Liberty Baptist Church, constituted about fifty-five years ago and the Harding Methodist Church, constituted thirty years ago.

Cotton, tobacco, and peanuts are the main crops grown in the community, but plant farming has been begun. Many of the farmers practice soil conservation by terracing, rotating their crops, and planting winter cover crops. Some are dairying on a rather large scale. Most of the farming is done by tractors now. Many of the homes now have electricity and are constantly adding conveniences.

MR. AND MRS. DAN FLETCHER
HARDING COMMUNITY
by Mrs. Dan Sutton

Dan Fletcher was born in Berrien County in 1867, a son of Elbert and Katherine McMillan Fletcher. In 1891 he married Mattie Churchwell of Brookfield, a daughter of John and Fredonia Churchwell. They lived with Mr. Fletcher's parents two years, and then moved to the Fort Place for a short time. Later they purchased a large plantation and settled at Harding where his family still lives. The following children were born to this union: Erris, Melvin, Mrs. Fredonia Simmons, John H. (who is nationally known as Big John Fletcher, the football player), Dan, Jr., Mrs. Edgar Pritchett, Sarah, and Mrs. Virginia Corley, all of whom are living.

Mr. Fletcher was a large land owner and livestock man. He liked better than anything else to ride the woods among his livestock.

Mrs. Fletcher is a charter member of Mount Olive Primitive Baptist Church, Mr. Fletcher becoming a member after the church was organized. They were big-hearted Christian people, always attending faithfully not only their own church services, but also the services of the other churches in the community. They were well-wishers to all with whom they came in contact. They were real friends to teachers and preachers. They were active participants in the civic and religious organizations of the community. They were good neighbors. Hundreds of men, both white and colored, have lived on his farms, and they held him in highest regard. This was proved by the large number of colored people who filed by his bier for the last look.

Mr. Fletcher was a great financier. It has been said of him that even though he was ill, he could make one dollar go further than any one else could make ten dollars. He survived successfully such disasters as years when he expected to gather three hundred bales of cotton and gathered twenty-six.

The Fletchers were a very devoted family, and the children always found help in time of need. The large family of children have always gathered at the old homestead at least once a week if possible.

Mr. Fletcher died early in 1946. He has been sorely missed by his beloved family, his friends, and his neighbors since his death. Mrs. Fletcher still carries on and is greatly beloved by all who know her.

MR. AND MRS. JOHN GOFF
HARDING COMMUNITY

by Mrs. Dan Sutton

John Goff was born in Irwin County near where Liberty Baptist church now stands Oct. 29, 1841. Even though he was not of military age, he served the four years of the War Between the States. He served at first for another person who paid John to serve in his place. Then John enlisted for himself. He was a drummer boy. He saw action in the battles of Gettysburg and Bull Run.

Just after the war, he married Nellie Hall of Irwin County, who was born Nov. 23, 1852. They purchased several hundred acres of land surrounding Liberty Baptist Church and here they reared a large family of children who have been influential in the church and civic life of Harding. The children are: Kano (now deceased), George (better known as Kip), Mrs. Lou Goff Goodman, Jack, Jake, Mrs. Lettie Goff Ellis, Mrs. Malissa Goff Thigpen, Hilburn, Milton, Dan (these three deceased), and John.

Mr. Goff served Irwin and Tift Counties as Road Commissioner for sixteen years. He donated the land on which Liberty Baptist Church was built, and was a charter member of that church. Both were faithful members until their deaths. Their descendants largely make up the church today. Rev. L. B. Allen has been their faithful pastor for many years, and under his leadership, the church is growing and prosperous.

Mr. Goff was trustee of the Harding School for years.

Mr. and Mrs. Goff were fine Christian characters, good neighbors, greatly beloved by those who knew them, hospitable in their home, and good citizens.

Both were good singers and this trait has been handed down to their posterity. One can still hear Mrs. Goff singing treble as they sang the grand old hymns of their day. Today these two rest side by side in the cemetery of Liberty Baptist Church they loved so well.

MR. AND MRS. JACOB HALL
HARDING COMMUNITY
by Mrs. Dan Sutton

Jacob Hall was born in 1856 in Irwin County. His mother died when he was very young, and Jacob lived with Warren Paulk near Ocilla until he was grown. He spent his young manhood working at odd jobs wherever he could find them. In 1880 he married Faithie Paulk, daughter of Azor and Judy Fletcher Paulk. Jacob Young performed the marriage ceremony.

They purchased a farm in the Harding community, on the old Ocilla highway and here they spent all their married life.

Mr. Hall was sheriff of Irwin county for at least one term, was a member of the Tift County Board of Education for 16 years, and was on the building committee which built the modern brick school that Harding now has. Mr. Hall donated the land for the first Harding school.

Mr. and Mrs. Hall were staunch members of the Mount Olive Primitive Baptist church for many years. One can still see Mrs. Hall shaking hands with the people who came to church, for she was a friendly person, and saw to it that no one ever left her church without being spoken to.

Their home was a hospitable one. Large crowds of people, both old and young, often gathered there from church and they were always welcome. Mr. and Mrs. Hall always met visitors at the gate if possible, with a friendly smile, and the visitors knew they were welcome as soon as they arrived. Mrs. Hall was a wonderful cook and was neatness itself. Her house and surroundings were always spotlessly clean and her larder was always full.

In later years Mr. Hall was not able to do hard work and he spent much of his time sitting on the front porch where he could see his neighbors when they passed. One can see him now in his old accustomed place. Both were kind to the unfortunate and the sick.

Their children are Walter who resides at the home place, Albert, Gilbert, and Ada now deceased, Charlie J., Shesley M., and Mrs. Perry Mixon. Those now living own homes and are substantial citizens of the Harding community.

Mrs. Hall died in 1938 and Mr. Hall in 1940. They rest side by side in the cemetery at Turner Church, one of the oldest churches in Tift County.

MR. AND MRS. AZOR PAULK
HARDING COMMUNITY
(Mrs. Dan Sutton)

Azor Paulk who married Judy Fletcher was one of the very first settlers of what is now Harding community. Because the records were burned, much information is unattainable. They had a large family of children. They owned a large section of what is now Harding. Their plantation has now been divided up into many homes. Rigdon's still quarters are on a part of their land.

Mr. Paulk was a big livestock man, owning hundreds of sheep, cattle, and hogs. Sheep-shearing was a great time on their plantation. The men of the community would get up before day and ride for miles to bring in the sheep. As the sheep were brought in, they were penned in barns. The lambs were placed in a pen by themselves. The next morning the hungry lambs would run to their mothers and each lamb would then be marked in the owner's mark. Neighbors came in to help with the shearing. Often the women had a quilting party while the men sheared the sheep. The women prepared and served bountiful dinners at the sheep-shearings, mutton being one of the main dishes. These sheep-shearings took place on all the large plantations.

Mrs. Paulk outlived Mr. Paulk for several years. They are buried near their home.

HISTORY OF OMEGA
(by Mrs. Lois Grimes)

In the year 1889 the Union Lumber Company built a railroad from Tifton to Thomasville. It was called T. T. and G. Tifton, Thomasville and Gulf. Later it was called A. B. & A., and then A. B. & C. About ten miles southwest of Tifton, on this road the little town of Surrey was laid off by a Mr. Hall. It was located on the land of G. W. Ridley and B. L. Smith. It had five avenues: Tennessee, Alabama, Georgia, Mississippi, and Florida. It had six streets: Cedar, Oak, Maple, Chestnut, Cypress, and Pine. The population was fifteen. Later the name was changed to Omega. The 1940 census showed a population of 602, but in 1947 it is at least one thousand.

The first store was built by a Mr. Scarboro, on the south side of the depot. Later a store was built by Joe Marchant, on the north side of the railroad. In 1911 J. W. Lang went into the mercantile business. The drug store was built in 1912. G. W. Ridley, George Robinson, and Miles Cowart built brick stores about 1918.

AIR VIEW OF OMEGA—Enterprising Tift County community and one of the largest shipping points for vegetable plants in the United States.

Omega has been burned out four times, but in 1947 it has an up-to-date drug store, six grocery stores, one general merchandise and grocery store, five meat markets, hardware store, furniture store, ten cent store, two modern cafes, two barber shops, two beauty parlors, five filling stations, four garages, dry cleaning establishment, theater, park, cannery, grist mill, four warehouses, two blacksmith shops, and a feed mill. This mill averages about a car of dairy feed a day for six months of the year. The City Hall, jail and fire truck are all housed in a brick building. A volunteer fire department was organized in 1936, and they have done a good job whenever fire broke out.

In 1936 a deep well was dug and water works installed. Lights are furnished by the Georgia Power Company.

The first cotton gin was built by Joe Marchant, in 1901. W. C. Mobley put in a more modern gin in 1915. Omega now has two electric gins, owned by H. A. Hornbuckle and Omega Plant Farms, Inc.

A Georgia State Bank was organized in 1912 with a capital of $25,000. It closed in 1926, and Omega had no bank until A. G. Jones established a private bank in 1937.

J. W. Taylor was postmaster of the first post office, which was fourth class. Earl Tolbert is postmaster, and the office is now second class. There is one regular clerk and two substitutes, who work regularly during plant season.

The Baptist Church was organized in 1887, with a small membership which has grown to 343. They are giving Christian training to a large number through their Sunbeams for small children, R. A.'s for small boys, G. A.'s for small girls, and training unions for young people and adults. They have a large, active missionary society.

The Methodist Church was organized in 1901, with twenty members, and has grown to 204. They have an active youth's organization, Women's Society of Christian Service, and a Missionary Guild.

A beautiful spirit of Christian cooperation is shown by the way Sunday School and prayer services are conducted. Both churches have half time service and Sunday school is held at the church having preaching. Prayer meeting is held one week at the Baptist and next at the Methodist. The same people attend both churches. Both churches have a building fund and plan to build new churches as soon as it is practical. The Methodists have a nice parsonage and the Baptists plan to build a new pastorium. They rent a very nice place for the pastor.

Omega is very proud of its school. The first school was held in the Baptist Church, with about forty pupils. The first teacher was Miss Beulah Watkins, and her salary was $18.00 a month. The first school building was a two-story wooden structure, and was built on an acre of land given by G. W. Ridley. He also gave an acre for each church. The top story was used as a Masonic Hall; later they sold their part to the school and this building was used until 1923 when a new brick building was erected on the northwest side of town. Since that time two more rooms have been added, a four-room wooden structure built for the primary grades. The old pump house was converted into a class room now used for music.

A ball shell, built several years ago, has recently been remodeled. A nice brick agricultural building has also been added. The school has an enrollment of 451, operates two busses and has twelve teachers. It has a fine Vocational Agriculture and Home Economics Department. The music teacher also has a large class. Instead of one acre the campus now has six acres. The school also has a nice home for the principal.

Omega owes its growth to the fact that it is surrounded by some of the best farm land in Georgia. Peanuts, vegetable plants, and tobacco, are three of the best money crops. In 1946 over a million dollars worth of peanuts were sold in Omega. The first vegetable plants grown for sale in Omega were grown by E. L. Patrick, H. Roberts, and W. M. Ponder, in 1918. To begin with Patrick and Roberts planted about one acre of cabbage and bedded about 2,000 bushels of potatoes. E. L. Powell began his plant business in 1921. He began by planting five pounds of cabbage seed, and last year his son planted about five tons. They began growing tomato plants for sale in 1922. There are now a number of vegetable plant companies shipping cabbage, tomatoes, onions, pepper, lettuce, broccoli. cauliflower, and beets. There are six packing sheds in Omega. Roy Ponder has recently erected a large shed of cement blocks, just inside the city limits, on the Tifton road. Harry Hornbuckle was the first one to ship vegetable plants by plane. It is estimated that three hundred million plants were shipped from Omega in 1946. Recently a number of farmers have planted vineyards. Mrs. T. M. Hornbuckle and Mrs. Colin Malcolm are the first to grow flowers for sale. They have gladioli and chrysanthemums.

Omega's first newspaper was the "Civic Bulletin," edited by Earl Tolbert, in 1936. This was a very small paper. In 1938 W. L. Lang began publishing a weekly, "The Omega News." This is a standard size newspaper.

The civic clubs have been instrumental in the growth of the town. The Lions Club was organized in 1943, and has thirty-six members. They are responsible for the dial telephone system, and for the stop lights. They have played a large part in remodeling the ball shell. Together with the Woman's Club they are erecting a brick club house in the park. Ed Moore of Tifton, formerly of Omega, gave the land for the park and it is called Joe Warren Memorial Park, in honor of his deceased son. The Lions Club had the arch built over the entrance to the park.

The Woman's Club has thirty-six members. They helped in remodeling the ball shell. They sponsor the Youth's Canteen which meets once a week.

The P.-T. A. is a very active organization, which has done much for the school, especially for the lunch room.

Omega is said to have more paved streets to its size than any town in the United States.

(Some information used taken from article written by Louise Fletcher, granddaughter of the late G. W. Ridley.)

ABOUT TY TY

(by Mrs. Maude D. Thompson)

There is nothing unusual about Ty Ty, except its name, which one traveling man said was a town spelled with four letters—two capitals and no vowels. The story of the name is:

When the B. & W. railroad was being built in 1870 and trains began to stop at a sawmill sidetrack, in 1872, a small town was built, consisting of log houses, near a creek called "Ti Ti Creek" (later called "Ty Ty Creek"). The creek had been named for a small evergreen shrub with a white tassel-like flower, which grows profusely on this creek. A name for the town was the subject of much discussion at that time.

[1]A great many people sold hand-hewn cross-ties of pure heart pine to the railroads. So many accumulated that it was called a tie-town, just "ties and ties" all around. When the storekeeper "Daddy Jelks" wrote the post office department for a post office here, he suggested the name "Ty Ty." His spelling was a personal affair, and he liked the looks of big shaded capital letters. The name or spelling has not been changed. "Daddy Jelks" had no children. He was a very public spirited man and wanted a good town and worked for its good. Ty Ty is his only memorial.

[2]The first settlers came from North Carolina and Virginia. Their first enterprise was raising cows on an open range. The timber, then large, tall pines, was some of the best for lumber making, but the first homes were log houses, with "stick-and-dirt" chimneys. The houses were far apart, the markets and even the post office was some distance from home, and the mode of travel was "on horse back," in a horse cart, or an ox cart. When the men went to market they usually went in groups and "camped out," sleeping in the open at night. The trips from Ty Ty to Albany required two days.

[3]The names of the first settlers were Gibbs, Willis, Warren, Hannan, Sumner, Branch, and many others whose descendants remain in the county.

The little town grew rapidly, with a turpentine still, owned and operated by Mr. W. E. Williams and Mr. George Warren, and a large saw-

---

1. As told by W. A. Nipper

mill operated by a Mr. Waters. A great many transient people came just to make money and move on. Small stores sprung up rapidly, and they all sold whiskey, by the drink or any way the buyer wanted it. So, when Saturday and payday came times were exciting with fights and sometimes a murder. Women did not venture down town on the street on Saturday. There were always some good people who wanted a peaceful, law-abiding town, and worked to make that. They began getting a good school. The first school was a three-months school in 1872, and was taught in a log house near where Dr. Pickett's residence now stands. Mrs. Mary Bozeman, of Albany, attended the school. The next year in the middle of the term a frame building, with a "stick-and-dirt" chimney and puncheon seats, was finished. It stood where Mr. E. C. Parks' house now stands.

At this school house preachers began to come and hold meetings. All denominations were welcomed. At this school house the Methodist Church was organized.

[4]Just one mile east there was another town called "Hillsdale." There, Mr. Joel T. Graves was instrumental in organizing the Presbyterian Church and a Sunday School. In these days people began to talk of local option and prohibition of the liquor trade. A number of people began to canvass this district, which was then in Worth County, in the interest of closing the bar-rooms. Dr. J. H. Pickett practiced medicine all over this section, then he talked and plead with people he saw to let's try a dry town. Prohibition carried in 1883, to the utter surprise of many indifferent people.

The town behaved better and built rapidly, soon having three churches and a good school. After the town outgrew the one-room school building a neat school building was built just in front of where the cemetery is. It was called "Mayflower." Then, in 1905, the citizens built a concrete block building, by public subscription, on the present school lot. This building is still being used for a lunchroom and canning plant. The blocks of the upper story were removed recently, and used to make a school house for our colored children.

In 1931 a new, modern school building was put up with money obtained from bonds. Mr. W. E. Williams, father of Mrs. F. B. Pickett, contributed to the building of four school houses in Ty Ty.

When Tifton grew large enough to want to be the county seat of a county and a new county was to be made, some of the most influential people wanted to be in the new county and even made trips to speak before the legislature, asking to be included in Tift County. That is why Ty Ty district is a jagged line into Worth County. We are still glad we are a part of Tift County.

2. As told by Mrs. Mary Bozeman.
3. As told to me by Mrs. Mary Bozeman.
4. As told to me by Miss E. R. Sutton.

Ty Ty is only half as large as it was in 1920. The cotton warehouses all closed when the bank failed in 1926. The turpentine still closed, the gum is carried to another town to be worked. We still have a sawmill and a great many good farms around.

The growing of vegetable plants to be shipped to northern markets is quite an industry. We have some industrious, progressive men who ship plants and gladiolus flowers and bulbs. Among these are M. H. Evans, C. A. Harrell, and E. A. Gibbs.

Two young men, the Sledge Brothers, began a small dairy business near here a few years ago. Now they have a large herd of dairy cows and furnish milk to a firm in Albany. The pecan is only a side industry, but amounts to considerable income each year. The staple crops are corn, peanuts, and tobacco. Very little cotton is grown.

We have a good modern gin, owned and operated by W. H. Vance; a grist mill, automobile repair shop, drug store, and six grocery stores.

Thus the town, begun long ago, is still a small town, with people who love you and are kind and neighborly when you live among them, and our citizens are as content as those in any town I know. Our colored citizens are well behaved, as a rule, and have good churches and schools. Some of our colored people have contributed a great deal to the upbuilding of their own race. G. J. Lane, a colored preacher, has a wonderful influence for good over his people, and often helps keep peace between his people and his white friends.

We are proud of our large oak trees for shade, our small clinic, our good school, our three churches, and some noble citizens.

Many forgotten people were loyal to their community, and were builders for good in the early days. The early families came from North Carolina, Virginia and South Carolina and built homes among the pines, and raised cows on wiregrass.

Among the first who built homes in and near Ty Ty were the Williams family, the children of Ezekiel Williams and Flora McDermit Williams, who came from North Carolina, and settled near Sparks. Three of their sons came to Ty Ty; they were John Williams, William Williams, and Edwin J. Williams. They all contributed to the progress of the community.

The Gibbs family was another very large family reared a few miles of town. The sons who settled near here were Elder James S. Gibbs, who preached forty years at Hickory Springs. Allen Gibbs' son, H. Grady Gibbs, lives here. Johnny E. T. Gibbs has five sons living here—Silas Gibbs, James Ernest, Edgar A., Carl and Clayton.

Mr. T. A. Inman came from South Carolina, married Miss Elizabeth Murrow, and they were some of our people who sacrificed and labored to make life better. Mr. Inman gave the land that the school house is built on, giving the major part of his land. He was a wonderful school trustee, visiting the school every week and always a friend to the teachers.

The Ford brothers came from Oakfield, and were intelligent men and successful business men. They were Robert James and Iverson L. Ford. J. C. Ford, who lives here now, is a son of James Ford, and Mrs. Lola Knight is a daughter.

Green S. Nelson had many friends here, and he built houses and had a mercantile business here. James Nelson, of Tifton, is his son. Mrs. Mary Nelson Woodham, of Fitzgerald, is his daughter.

Mr. and Mrs. W. B. Parks came from South Carolina. They accumulated property and built a nice home and a brick store building. They were generous and loyal to their church and their friends, and left a family of sons and daughters. One son, E. C. Parks, and his family, live here still.

Mr. and Mrs. C. G. Dell came here from Sumter County, when there were no bridges across the streams. They were among the charter members of the first church built here, the Methodist Church. Mr. Dell kept prayer meeting going for thirty years, often walking several miles to be present.

Mr. Chas. W. Graves was a loyal church member, a man above the average in intellect and integrity. He was the first Ordinary of Tift County, the office he held until he died.

W. C. Thompson was a pioneer citizen of this section. He was an active church member, genial, honest, and true, always helping his neighbors and friends; never losing patience with their faults, always seeing good in every one.

W. S. Scott was a Christian gentleman, always at work, whistling as he went. Suffering reverses with courage.

W. H. Davis came here from the West. He had lived in a number of states. He loved young people, and could interest most people with stories and philosophy. He was a watchmaker with personality.

Some of our citizens in business now are:

Dr. F. B. Pickett, who came here soon after he was graduated, to begin practice with his uncle, Dr. J. H. Pickett, the grandfather of Mrs. O. N. Dowd. Dr. F. B. Pickett was reared in Webster County, and began practice here in 1895. He married Miss Martha Williams, daughter of Mr. and Mrs. E. J. Williams, in 1897. Dr. and Mrs. Pickett know by sight the names of more people in this section than any one here. They have both been very active in progressive moves and church affairs, both being officials in the Methodist Church.

The late Dr. R. R. Pickett came from Sumner here, and practiced medicine with his brother, Dr. F. B. Pickett. Dr. R. R. was very interested in progressive farming too. He married Miss Susie Grubbs. They had one daughter, who is now Mrs. C. A. Harrell. Mrs. Harrell was graduated from Wesleyan, and taught for several years before her marriage. She is now president of the Woman's Society of Christian Service. Her love for folks is very generous. Mr. C. A. Harrell was reared in Quitman, Ga. He is genial, pleasant and most industrious. His skill in the plant growing and shipping means much to this section. He even tried to outdo Mrs. Harrell in generosity.

Mr. Marcus H. Evans settled down on his farm after having attended college. He married Miss Maxine Walea. Mr. Evans cultivates and harvests many different crops. He delights in growing gladioluses. He succeeds wonderfully in growing and selling tomato, pepper, and cabbage plants.

Mr. W. F. Sikes and his brother, Wylie J. Sikes, are two of the most accommodating people. W. F. has been rural mail carrier for 39 years.

Mr. Edgar Allen Gibbs married Miss Charlotte Alexander, of Nashville, Ga. Mr. Edgar Gibbs, a son of J. E. T. Gibbs, has a large farming interest, and has shown his neighbors that cattle raising is still profitable. He takes pride in his beautiful herd of cows, but is more proud of his lovely daughter, Miss Charlotte Gibbs, a teacher in Tifton High School. She is a graduate of Huntington, Ala., College.

Mr. Ebenezer J. Cottle and his wife, the former Miss Hudie Knight, have succeeded wonderfully with lumber business and a big farming interest. Mr. Cottle is deacon in Baptist church. Mrs. Cottle teaches adult Sunday School class at the Methodist Church.

Mr. W. H. Swain, a genial merchant, has been in his business longer than any other general mercantile business here.

Samuel H. Lipps, reared near Albany, Ga., came to this section years ago and farmed near here. Now he and his wife, the former Miss Minnie Conger, are the friendly people uptown with their store and business and they find time to investigate the needs of people in trouble and help, too. They are proud of their sons and daughters. Four sons answered their country's call to service.

Mr. W. C. McCormic was reared in North Carolina, moved here from Lenox, and is engaged in naval stores business. Mrs. W. C. McCormic is a teacher of outstanding ability in our public school.

Mr. M. D. Vinson has made the Gulf gasoline station very popular with his pleasant manners and his efficient work.

Mr. C. A. Arnold, who married Miss Ada Adams, is always smiling and accommodating, and very courteous in his business.

Mr. and Mrs. Charles A. Walker live on their own farm, have more good things to eat—produced on this farm—than any one near. Charlie is deacon in the Baptist Church. His wife, Lula Mae DeVane Walker, can smile at her friends and help them in patience always.

Miss Emma Rebecca Sutton, daughter of Green Sutton and Rebecca Welch Sutton, was born in Albany, Ga., in 1848. She was one of our most public spirited women. She went to New York as a newspaper reporter years ago, when women had few fields of labor open to them. She wrote and made many researches for her employer, Mrs. Hallet, who wrote books, but always loved the South and South Georgia, frequently using her talent of wit and wisdom defending and complimenting. She was very loyal to her church, the Episcopal Church. She was a member of St. Anne Church, at Tifton, when she died in 1931. She made her home with her sister, Mrs. Francis Owens, after her parents died. In her last years she lived alone in her cottage on a small plot of land She had two nieces in Waycross: Mrs. R. H. Redding, and Mrs. Mary Watt. She was head of the Red Cross Chapter, at Ty Ty, when we had a chapter here, and was very loyal to it when it was moved to Tifton.

To her family she was always loyal. Though she suffered injustices often, seldom discussed it and never lost confidence in plain people and never thought an honest, Godly, person common.

CHAPTER XVII
TIFTON AND TIFT COUNTY EDUCATION
by Mrs. Nicholas Peterson
EDUCATION

In the early days of Tifton's existence there was no such thing as a public school system with any uniform length of term or any salary schedule for teachers then existing in Georgia. Only those who were able hired private tutors for their children. Occasionally one man or perhaps a group of men would hire someone to teach the children in the community for any length of time they could hire the teacher. The most of such schools ran from six week to three months duration. The buildings used were more often used for storing cotton and housing sheep than for school purposes.

The first official teacher that can be accounted for, who taught the children of this mill village of Tifton was a Mr. William Fish, a friend of the Tifts who came down from Mystic, Connecticut, and helped the Tifts organize a little school. It was taught in a one-room building located somewhere in the vicinity of the present county jail. It was used for all public purposes, church, school, court and any other public meeting. Some of the pupils who attended this school are now living in Tifton and supplied me with this information: Mr. Jack Golden, Miss Leola Green, Mrs. L. C. Spires, and Mrs. Catherine Tift Jones. Capt. H. H. Tift, Col. C. N. Fulwood, E. P. Bowen, S. L. Herring, also gave much information.

After the Georgia Southern Railroad was completed through Tifton in 1888, Captain Tift laid out the city of Tifton. City officials were elected and Tifton began to make progress in earnest. One of the first acts was to call a mass meeting where a corporation was formed, and stock was sold to build Tifton's first real school building.

This building was erected on the corner of Tift Avenue where the Primitive Baptist Church now stands. It was called the Tifton Institute; it was rather a pretentious looking building. It contained two very large class rooms, two cloak rooms, and one small room that was later used for a music room.

Mr. A. L. Murphy was the first teacher to teach in the new building. He was assisted by his daughter, Miss Mary Emma, who is remembered by several of Tifton's first music teachers. He taught from 1890-1892.

Mr. J. R. Hudgens of Mississippi succeeded Mr. Murphy for the next two years.

Mr. E. J. Williams was principal from 1894 to 1895. His sister Miss Martha (Mrs. Frank Pickett of Ty Ty) ably assisted him. Mr. Williams resigned to accept a position as bookkeeper for Capt. Tift, a position he

Top—Tifton Grammar School
Center—Tifton Junior High School
Bottom—Tifton High School

held until called into the Spanish-American War in 1898. He entered with the rank of first lieutenant, being a graduate of Gordon Military Institute. He chose to remain in the service of his country, seeing active duty in World War I. He rose to the rank of Lieutenant Colonel before his death in November 1929. His body was interred with the nation's heroes at Arlington.

Professor John Henry O'Quinn succeeded Mr. Williams and came to Tifton in the fall of 1895. He was assisted by Miss Ina Coleman of Clarksville, Tennessee, during the first term. He was considered quite an educator in this section, and several young men came from surrounding towns to study under his leadership. This move necessitated adding more teachers to his faculty. In the fall of 1896 Miss Edna McQueen of Nashville, Tennessee, was added as teacher of primary grades. Miss Myrtle Pound, of Jackson, Georgia, as music teacher, and Miss Sallie Perry, of Little Rock, Arkansas, as expression, or rather elocution as it was called in those days.

Miss Pound and Miss McQueen met their fate in Tifton during that year. In the summer of '97 Miss Pound married Mr. E. J. Williams, and Miss McQueen married Dr. Nichols Peterson. Mrs. Peterson is still living in Tifton with just as much interest in the schools of Tifton and Tift County as the first day she landed in South Georgia. Mrs. Williams spends most of her time in Jackson, Georgia, with her sisters.

Mr. W. L. Harman was elected to take Mr. O'Quinn's place during the summer of '97. He accepted on condition that he be allowed to bring his entire faculty from Chipley with him. Under his capable leadership the school was properly graded for the first time and competent teachers put in charge of each grade. The school had a phenominal growth during his four years administration. He was a born leader as well as a great educator and endeared himself to all with whom he came in contact. All Tifton rejoiced when he returned after a few years absence to make his home until his death. He served as the very efficient Tift County School Commissioner from 1929-1934.

Emerson says: "History is but the biography of a few great men." Unfortunately he did not tell us who were great. In that instance we shall draw our own conclusions as to whom to term great.

First, I shall choose Arthur J. Moore. This boy grew to manhood and received in a crude building all the schooling he got until after he was married. His schoolmates in the village of Brookfield enthusiastically relate many of his pranks. They say that he was never known to open a book, yet he easily outstripped the most studious members of his class, so alert and active was his mind.

The picture of the school house he first attended proves that it is not at all necessary to have gilded halls and palaces in which to mold and shape human character. Does there exist a county, city, state or nation that would not be proud to claim him as a son? Surely Tift county is bursting with pride to know that it was our happy privilege to give to the world one of its greatest citizens—Bishop Arthur J. Moore.

TIFTON AND TIFT COUNTY EDUCATION
ANNIE BELLE CLARK SCHOOL

by Mrs. N. Peterson

1906-1947

When this school opened its doors for its first term in the fall of 1906 it was known as Tifton High School. Tifton was proud of its first fine brick school building and thought it would serve for all time to come, so commodious did it seem in comparison with the old building, left behind on Tift Avenue. It remained Tifton's only high school until 1917 when the sides began to bulge with children crowded into every conceivable space. Another building was the only solution.

The new high school building was completed and the six higher grades bade farewell to the old school and moved in for the first term in the fall of 1917. The old school then became and was the Tifton Grammar School until 1943 when its name was again changed to the Annie Belle Clark School in honor of its faithful beloved teacher, who remained at its head for thirty-one years.

Miss Clark came to Tifton as teacher of the primary class in 1910. When the school had to have a new principal when the school was divided, the board did not hesitate to promote her to the position. Many changes were made in the building at her suggestion. She had the old basement remodeled and put in such good condition that they were able to have a nice assembly room, a large room for preparing and serving hot lunches daily by the P.-T.A., to the student body, also an extra class room. The P.-T. A. mothers were of great help in all of this improvement.

There was rarely a resignation or vacancy in her school. The teachers, as well as the children, were devoted to her. Miss Annie had only to speak and her request was granted. Several of the present faculty have been with the school almost as long as Miss Clark. In 1943 Miss Clark had a serious illness which was to such extent that it forced her to resign. Mrs. W. H. Walters and Mrs. G. O. Bailey were appointed to take charge until a principal could be secured. Miss Elizabeth Yow, of Martin, Georgia, was elected principal and began with the Annie Clark Grammar School in September, 1943. Many improvements have been made in the past three years. Five new teachers have been added to her staff, making twenty teachers in the school. Public school music is taught to all grades by Mrs. Agnew

Andrews. Two new electric victrolas have been purchased; each teacher is furnished with a pitch pipe for each classroom; art is also taught in each grade. Many new books have been added to the school library including a set of musical appreciation and other reference books for the use of the teachers, a new moving picture machine has been installed. Hundreds of dollars worth of playground equipment has been placed on the campus. Last, but not least, a new annex was added last year to take care of four of the grades. This building cost $26,211.00.

It has been said that a "nation moves forward on the feet of its children." If this statement be true, then surely Tifton school children are on the forward march.

G. O. BAILEY, JR.

(Copied from the Tifton Gazette)

Mr. Bailey came to Tifton in July 1928, as principal of the high school and football coach. In 1931 he was elected superintendent and has held that position for fifteen years. Under his leadership much progress has been made by the schools. During his administration, the high school band, public school music, commercial courses enlarged, vocational agriculture, public school art, boys and girls glee club, physical education for all the students, full time librarian, lunch room program in all three schools in which 1,500 lunches are served daily, have all been added to the school system. Also during his administration the gymnasium, a vocational education building, and a 4-room addition to the grammar school have been erected; the high and grammar schools repainted and modernized; and the high school annual was reinstated, having been discontinued in 1916.

Since he has been in Tifton, the band, glee clubs, and athletic teams have attained an enviable position in South Georgia.

Mr. Bailey also values the audiovisual picture showing machine and program of study that was instituted in the school seven years ago and is proud of the fact that 1,500 students participated in the May Day festival this year.

Professor Bailey, son of Mr. and Mrs. Glen Owen Bailey, Sr., was born at Turin. He is a graduate of Senoia High School, and Mercer University. He is a member of the Kappa Delta Phi, national scholastic fraternity.

He is a member, and past president of the Tifton Lions Club, a member of the Tift County Chamber of Commerce and Baptist Church. He was president of the Second District High School Association and of Tift County Education Association.

His wife is the former Miss Hazel Humber, of Lumpkin, whom he married in 1927, and they have two children, Humber aged 12, and Holly aged 10.

Top—Tifton High School Band broadcasting in 1947
Bottom—Scene from Tifton High School Glee Club program in 1947

MR. W. L. BRYAN

1917-1918

Mr. W. L. Bryan, of Atlanta, served Tifton High School as its first superintendent for one year. Dr. M. L. Brittain, then state superintendent of education, came to Tifton to assist in the dedication exercises. Prof. Scraboro, who had been prevented from opening the school on account of his health, gave the history of the Tifton schools and Dr. Brittain made the principal address.

Mr. Bryan was well liked, but he resigned at the close of his first term to continue his study of law. He is at present practicing law in Atlanta.

MRS. J. E. COCHRAN

Mrs. J. E. Cochran came to Tifton, from Roswell, Georgia, in 1905 as a teacher of the fourth grade in the old Tifton Institute during Prof. Jason Scarboro's administration. She taught one term. During the time she met and married Mr. Cochran, Tifton's first jeweler. She did not teach again for a period of about twenty years. After Mr. Cochran's death in 1924, she applied for the position of seventh grade in Tifton High School. Here she remained until the junior high school was completed; then she was transferred to that building.

In 1942 when Mr. Alton Ellis, who was then principal of the school, was called into the service of his country, Mrs. Cochran was appointed to take his place. This position she filled very acceptably until Mr. Ellis's return last year. She once again took up her grade work where she left off four years before.

Mrs. Cochran has contributed a great deal to the educational, social, and religious life of Tifton during her long residence. She is one of the best teachers Tifton Junior High School has had.

MR. A. H. MOON

by Mrs. N. Peterson

1918-1923

Mr. Moon came to Tifton in 1918 from the Baxley Public Schools, where he had been superintendent for eight years and never once while there was the school defeated in a contest by a competitor.

He was a graduate of Mercer University, University of Georgia, and received his M.A. degree from Northwestern University, Chicago, and was working on his doctor's degree from the same university at the time of his death; he was a Phi Beta Kappa. His refusal of a Yale scholarship was on account of illness in the family.

He exerted every influence towards fitting boys and girls for useful, healthful, and happy living. He felt that if in an atmosphere of culture and an appreciation of social responsibility were maintained on the school grounds, it would be carried over into the daily lives of the young men and women of tomorrow. He believed that personal development and self motivation might be initiated through such avenues as debating teams, essay contests, and other extra-curricular activities. In many of these Tifton boys and girls won state and district recognition.

It was his desire that every student might be more eager to learn when he left high school; therefore he tried to choose faculty members who could not only teach to meet the immediate needs of the students but could also inspire them to go farther in their educational pursuits. He was ever alert to recognize the best possibilities within any student, and encouraged such pupils to avail themselves of every opportunity to help themselves.

He introduced home economics into the high school for the first time. Through the efforts of Miss Nebraska Findley and Miss Mattie Lou Phillips, teachers in this department, the sewing room, kitchen and dining room were fully equipped.

Mr. Moon was very civic-minded. He saw that lights were not only needed on the front of the building but would add greatly to the attractiveness of it.

The South Georgia Methodist Conference was to convene in Tifton in the fall of 1922. Mr. Moon asked the board of education to install lights before they came. The board felt the city could not afford them at this time, so he appealed to the members of the Twentieth Century Library Club as a matter of civic pride. Mrs. John Wesson and Mrs. Carl Kimberly were appointed as a committee to see this project through. The night before the conference was to hold its first session, the beautiful lights, that still light the campus of the building, were turned on in all of their glory and all Tifton was proud.

His one plea to the board of education as long as he remained in Tifton was for better pay for his teachers. He argued that in education as in all other phases of life you got only what you paid for. He said that Tifton could not hope to cope with other surrounding towns unless the salaries of her teachers were in keeping with those of other places. He finally succeeded in getting the salary of Miss Annie Belle Clark, principal of the grammar school, raised from 90 to 100 dollars, and his primary teachers from 65 to 70 dollars per month.

In the spring of 1923 Mr. Moon's health began to fail. He was granted a leave of absence for two months. He went to Atlanta and entered a hospital for treatment. He had waited too late. On the eve of the graduating exercises not only the school but all Tifton was shocked to hear that he had quietly passed away. Both he and his efficient wife, who was also a teacher in the school had endeared themselves to Tifton people, who mourned the loss of these valuable citizens.

MR. R. E. MOSELEY

1927-1930

Mr. R. E. Moseley, who was acting principal of the Tifton High School during Mr. J. C. Sirman's administration was appointed to the place of superintendent following Mr. Sirman's resignation at the close of school in May, 1927. Mr. G. O. Bailey was elected principal at the same time.

The most important event of his administration was letting the contract for the erection of the Tifton Junior High School on January 7, 1928. This had to be done in cooperation with the county board of education.

The school was completed and furnished in time for the fall opening of school. This building served to take care of 225 children in the Tifton consolidated school district. It also helped to ease the strain on the overcrowded grammar school, the fifth grades being transferred to the new school.

Mrs. Nan W. Clements of Montezuma, Georgia was elected as first principal.

PROFESSOR JASON SCARBORO

1901-1908-1912-1917

Professor Jason Scarboro moved to Tifton during the summer of 1901. He came to accept the principalship of the public school from Statesboro, Georgia, where he had been superintendent for several terms.

At the end of his first term in Tifton he had enrolled 272 students, far too many to be crowded into the small space the old Tifton Institute had to offer. By the opening date of his second year he had succeeded in getting an addition of three large rooms built. This took care of the first four grades for several years. There was no auditorium in which to hold graduating exercises, public debates, or meetings of any kind. His next move was to agitate the question of a real high school building adequate for all purposes. He had to hold his first graduating exercises in the courthouse in

1904. The courthouse then was in the third story of the Bowen block on the corner of Love Avenue and Mill Street (now Second Street).

The members of this class were Hains Hargrett, Charlie Garrett, and Effie Kent. The class chose as their valedictorian Charles Garrett, who had become quite a public speaker and debater for the school. He chose for his subject "Good Roads." He predicted that automobiles, then very new in South Georgia, would supplant the horse and buggy. He argued for hard surfaced roads from town to town and from farm to market. He contended that the public convenience and economy would justify our going in debt to meet the heavy expense. His speech was printed in the Gazette and highly publicized as being probably the first plea ever made for good roads in South Georgia.

Charles graduated from Mercer University in 1908 with an A.B. degree, received his M.A. degree in 1909, and his LL.D. degree in 1911. He worked with Judge Park for four years on the Annotated Code of Georgia and practiced law in Macon for a number of years. He has been solicitor General of the circuit (Bibb, Peach, Houston and Crawford counties) since 1919.

Haines Hargrett graduated from the University of North Carolina, Chapel Hill.

He studied law and rose rapidly in his profession; was associated with a corporation of lawyers in Washington, D. C., for a good many years. He moved back to Atlanta and was connected with one of the city's most prominent law firms until his sudden death. He married Miss Maud Timmons, a Tifton girl who with one son, Haines, Jr., still resides in Atlanta.

Effie Kent finished her education at Wesleyan College, Macon, Ga., taught school, married a Mr. Hambleton, of Meigs, Georgia. After his death she had charge of the postoffice for several years. She is now making her home with an only daughter in Thomasville.

Tifton will long hold in affectionate memory the members of its first graduating class, who so highly distinguished themselves and have brought honor to their home town and alma mater.

In 1906 Tifton High School was placed on the accredited list of the Association of High Schools. This was made possible by the school being able to use the Twentieth Century Library Club's books. The club was then housed in the Wade-Corry building in close proximity to the school.

Also in 1906 Tifton's first academy, built by public subscription gave place to its first fine new brick building erected at a cost of $50,000. It was finished in time for the 1906 fall opening of school. This building is now the Annie Belle Grammar School.

All went well until the summer of 1908. Cordele needed a good man to head their schools so in casting about they fell on Tifton and hired Prof.

Scarboro at a much greater salary than Tifton was able to pay; so we had to let him go. Tifton retaliated though in 1912 and brought him back to take over the school.

When Mr. Scarboro returned he found that Tifton population had once more outgrown its school bounds. The auditorium of the nice new school he had left had been cut up into class rooms and still there was not sufficient room to house the children comfortably. Again the graduating classes were forced to seek other quarters for their exercises.

Always a builder, he lost no time in starting the movement for another school building. By 1917 Tifton was the proud possessor of our present handsome high school building. It was erected at a cost of $100,000.

Unfortunately time and hard work had taken its cruel toll of Mr. Scarboro's strength. The doctors advised a leave of absence from his arduous school duties. It grieved him not to be able to christen the dream of his life. It fell to Mr. W. L. Bryan, of Atlanta, to be the first high superintendent of the new high school.

Mr. Scarboro never saw fit to return to the school room, but continued to make Tifton his home as long as he lived.

Tifton will long cherish the memory of Mr. Scarboro and his fine family, who labored so long among us. His work and good deeds will live long in the hearts of his innumerable friends. He will be remembered as one of the greatest educators in our history.

Mr. W. G. Davis and Mr. J. M. Mulloy, who filled in during the interim Mr. Scarboro was in Cordele were fine men and well liked as school men, but neither was strong physically and each had to resign before his terms of office had expired.

Mr. Davis served as superintendent from 1908 to 1910.

Mr. Mulloy served one year in 1911.

MR. JOHN C. SIRMANS
1923-1927

Mr. Sirmans succeeded Mr. A. H. Moon as superintendent of Tifton Public Schools. Anyone following in Mr. Moon's footsteps naturally had a hard job, but Mr. Sirmans proved himself equal to the occasion from every standpoint as was evidenced by his rapid promotions in the educational field.

During his administration a lady was placed on the board of education for the first time. Mrs. W. T. Smith was appointed to this position and made an acceptable member as long as she chose to remain as such. She served for four years and the board members were very reluctant in accepting her resignation. They extended to her a vote of sincere thanks and appreciation for her valuable services as a member of the board.

The women of the Twentieth Century Library Club once more came into the picture. Tifton's schools had never had a P.-T. A. The club women sensed this need. After conferring with Mr. Sirmans a meeting of the high school mothers was called and the first P.-T. A. organized. Mrs. S. A. Youmans was elected as president. It did not take them long to realize that this work was too important to be confined to just one branch of the school, so Mrs. Youmans and her co-workers reorganized and put two strong bodies of interested mothers to work in both of the schools later extending to the Tifton Junior High School upon its completion. This organization is considered by all today as one of the strongest forces in the entire school system.

In the fall of 1929 Mr. Sirmans tendered his resignation as superintendent to become dean of men at the newly created South Georgia College for Men. This position he held as long as the College functioned. When it became the Abraham Baldwin College the Board of Regents at the University of Georgia appointed him as dean of education at Dahlonega, a position he is still holding with distinction.

IDA BELLE WILLIAMS

Principal 1940-1947

(Copied from Tifton Gazette)

Miss Ida Belle Williams, recognized as one of the most outstanding English instructors in the state, has resigned as principal of Tifton High School.

Miss Williams has brought honor to the Tifton High school by her association with the school, her educational background, and her accomplishments. The school has been extremely fortunate to have had her services as English instructor for 15 years and as principal for 6 years. Citizens hope that she will remain as head of the English department.

Since Miss Williams has been teaching English in Tifton the work has been commended by the English Commission of Georgia and individual college teachers. Some of the G.M.C. professors, who have taught in other colleges, state that they can spot her English students. Some of her students have been exempt from freshman English on account of placement tests.

The Tifton High School has received prominent recognition for unique graduation exercises, which Miss Williams introduced in the school. In these exercises, the graduates honor prominent Georgians and Georgia institutions. Last year the graduating class paid tribute to the press of Georgia.

Miss Williams has an M.A. degree from Johns Hopkins University and University of Georgia. She has studied at Columbia University, University of Tennessee, University of Georgia and Bessie Tift College. She has had recent correspondence courses in English and creative writing. She has won a scholarship to the Richard Burton School of Creative Writing; won prizes in the State Parks contest for writing a feature story about Indian Springs; won a letter writing contest sponsored by the Atlanta Constitution; a prize with Scott Foresman for a project about "Silas Marner;" one of her stories was considered for a $1,000 prize by Reader's Digest; and honor in her college studies. Her feature stories have been accepted by the best magazines and newspapers in the country. Her teaching experience includes high schools in Georgia and she was assistant professor of English at Winthrop College, Rock Hill, S. C.

The Talisman, the Tifton High school annual, was dedicated to Miss Williams last year in recognition of her work with the school and the esteem in which she is held by the student body and faculty.

Miss Williams, daughter of the late Robert James and Mary Elizabeth Camp Williams, was born in Swainsboro, Georgia. She was the first woman in Georgia to make a nominating speech for a congressman.

MRS. DAN SUTTON, MISS FOLLIS, MISS SHAW

We have followed with a good deal of interest and pride the careers of a few of the teachers who began their work as pioneer teachers of the newly created Tift County. We shall consider only those who have never deserted the fold for other professions. They are Mrs. Dan Sutton of Tift County, who is librarian at present for the Coastal Plain Experiment Station; Miss Fannie Shaw, of Adel, Georgia, who is now at the head of the department of health and public welfare at the Woman's College, Tallahassee, Florida; and Miss Hattie B. Follis of Nashville, Tennessee, who has been principal of the Baker Street School, Birmingham, Alabama, for over thirty years.

Miss Hattie Bess Follis of Nashville, Tennessee, came to Tift County to begin teaching the first year the county was created. Her first year was at Omega, the second at Ty Ty. The last three years in the county she had charge of the fourth grade in the Tifton Public School. After leaving Tifton she went to the Quitman Public School, where she remained for three years. She next went to Birmingham, Alabama, where she was elected principal of the Baker Street School in Ensley where she is still as active, seemingly, as she was over thirty years ago.

During these thirty odd years of service she has so endeared herself to the Birmingham system that she could have her choice today of any position in their keeping, but she still remains true to the place where she began. Some of the positions of honor she has held are:

President—Delta Kappa Gamma, Honorary Society for Women Teachers.
President—Birmingham Teachers' Association.
President—Alabama Branch of Peabody College Alumni.
President—Of the Elementary Principals' Club.
Co-author of Friendly Hour Readers, published by American Book Company and used in Tift County.

Miss Follis received her A.B. degree from Birmingham-Southern College and M.A. degree from Peabody College, Nashville, Tennessee.

In addition to all these projects, she finds time to teach a class in Ensley Methodist Church. She is also a member of the choir and serves on the board of stewards of the church.

Stella Caudill Sutton (Mrs. Dan Sutton) teacher and librarian, was born at Owenfork, Kentucky. She married Dan T. Sutton of Tift County on June 6, 1913 and came to the Harding Communtiy that year to make her home. She has been an active worker in the civic and church life of Harding and perhaps no one has had a greater influence in the progressive development of her community and county than has Mrs. Sutton. She has always had a class in Sunday School and has been an active member of the board of stewards. She is a charter member of the Harding Methodist Church.

Aside from her home duties, such as rearing a good family, she has never relinquished her hold on her fist love—that of the school room. She taught in the Harding School for thirteen years, at Brighton one year, at Chula eight, and at Omega three, being principal of the Omega High School the last two years, She was one of the best teachers of the county.

Mrs. Sutton organized the first P.-T. A. in Tift County, at first called "School Improvements Club," and was president of the Tift County Council of P. T. A. for several years. She was the first teacher in the county to take students on a trip at the close of school. She was president of the Tift County Teachers' Institute for one year. Mrs. Sutton is now librarian for the Coastal Plain Experiment Station.

She has always been a staunch supporter and builder of libraries and was an active promoter of the bookmobile. She was chairman of the Tift County Purchasing Committee when she became librarian at the Experiment Station.

When Mrs. Sutton began teaching she did not have a degree. As soon as her children, Murris and Mildred, were old enough to take care of themselves she began studying each summer at college summer schools until 1943 when Teachers' College at Statesboro conferred on her the A.B. degree.

All of Mrs. Sutton's accomplishments have been no small job for any one, especially a mother. We congratulate her on her attainments and appreciate her services for Tift County.

Miss Fannie Shaw of Adel, Georgia, a native of South Georgia, of whom we are very proud, taught several years in Tifton and Tift County when the county was young. Since she did not have a degree when she began teaching, Miss Shaw requested a leave of absence and registered at Columbia University where she later received the A.B. and M.A. degrees.

She became so much interested in health education, one of her major subjects, while attending Columbia University that she attracted the attention of some of the faculty. The authorities of the university offered her a position on the staff. While connected with the school she and one of the leading members of the staff were co-authors of a textbook on health education.

She returned to Georgia on account of her parents' health. The State Health Department secured her services as state supervisor of health in schools of North Georgia. Dr. Abercrombie reluctantly released her on two occasions to accept a place as director of public health in two large midwestern universities during summer terms.

At present she holds the chair of health and public welfare in the Woman's College, Tallahassee, Florida.

HISTORY OF ABRAHAM BALDWIN AGRICULTURAL COLLEGE AND PRECEDING INSTITUTIONS
(George King)

A detailed history of the various State educational institutions, from the Second District A. & M. School beginning in 1908 through Abraham Baldwin Agricultural College now enjoying its largest enrollment, would require too much space and would inevitably leave out some facts or persons who should be included. For that reason, only the high points will be touched.

The Second District A. & M. School was established as one of the twelve district schools of the State, which were authorized by an Act of the General Assembly in 1907 during the administration of Governor Terrell. Tifton and Tift County were able to have the school located at Tifton because of the public spiritedness of its citizens. Capt. H. H. Tift donated 315 acres of land and the citizens of Tifton and Tift County, rich and poor, gave generously to raise money to defray one-half of the cost of erecting the three original buildings. It is interesting to note here that during subsequent years, regardless of the name of the institution, this fine spirit and generous attitude have always prevailed among the citizens of the city and county.

The Second District A. & M. School opened its first term on February 19, 1908. Only boys were allowed to board during this first term, although girls in the vicinity attended. Opening day was declared a holiday by Tifton. Stores and the public school were closed. A special train was run from Tifton to the school and some 1,200 people attended.

Mr. W. W. Driskell was president of the school for the term beginning February 19, 1908, and also for the year beginning in September 1908. Judge Frank Park was the first chairman of the Board of Trustees. The institution remained an A. & M. School until June 1924. During this time only high school work was given.

The presidents serving the Second District A. & M. School and their terms were as follows:

W. W. Driskell—February 1908 to June 1909
W. G. Acree—September 1909 to June 1910
S. L. Lewis—September 1910 to June 1912
J. F. Hart, Jr.—September 1912 to June 1914
S. L. Lewis—September 1914 to June 1924

Because of the growth of high schools in the towns over the section, the necessity of maintaining district high schools became less, and the Legislature of 1924 changed the Second District A. & M. School to South Georgia A. & M. College. Mr. S. L. Lewis who was president of the District School became president of the college. Mr. R. C. Ellis was Chairman of the first Board of Trustees. The college offered only Freshman college work the first year and dropped the first year of high school work. Each succeeding year a high school grade was dropped and a college class added, until the institution was giving only college work.

Mr. S. L. Lewis resigned in June 1929 after 16 years of faithful and unselfish service. He was succeeded by Mr. F. G. Branch, who took over the duties of president in September 1929. During the summer of 1929, the Legislature changed the name of the college from South Georgia A. & M. College to Georgia State College for Men. Mr. R. C. Ellis was the first Chairman of this Board of Trustees and served as such until the College was placed under the newly formed Board of Regents of the University System on January 1, 1932.

In 1933, the Board of Regents asked permission of the General Assembly for "power to consolidate, suspend, or discontinue institutions and merge departments." The permission was granted upon the signing of the bill by Governor Talmadge on February 21, 1933.

On April 17, 1933, the Board of Regents announced its consolidation plans, which included the abolishing of many of the State units. The Board directed that the Georgia State College for Men be abolished and that a two-year College of Agriculture, to be known as the Abraham Baldwin Agricultural College, be established in its place. This was somewhat of a shock to the people of Tifton who were justly proud of the four-year college. However, as they had always done, as soon as the objectives of the new college became known, the citizens rallied to its support and have been to a large measure responsible for its success.

Abraham Baldwin Agricultural College started its first term in September 1933. The enrollment for the freshman class that year was 63. The September enrollment 13 years later was 467, including an overflow unit of 150 men students located at Spence Field, Moultrie, Ga.

Dr. J. G. Woodroof was President for the 1933-34 term. He was succeeded by Mr. George H. King, who has been President to the present time, September 1946. In November 1942, Mr. King was also made Director of the Georgia Coastal Plain Experiment Station upon the death of Mr. S. H. Starr, who had been director since the founding of the Station in 1919. At the time Mr. King assumed double duties, Mr. George P. Donaldson, who had been with Abraham Baldwin Agricultural College since its founding and had served for a number of years as Dean of Students, was made Executive Dean. This is the administrative setup at the present time.

ABRAHAM BALDWIN

by E. Pickard Karsten

Abraham Baldwin, for whom Abraham Baldwin Agricultural College, of Abac, near Tifton, is named, is also honored by having named for him Baldwin County, whose county seat, Milledgeville, was once the capital of Georgia.

Like Tifton's founder, Henry Harding Tift, Abraham Baldwin was a native of Connecticut. Born in 1754, he graduated from Yale at the age of eighteen and earned the reputation of being one of the best classical and mathematical scholars of his time. For part of the time during the Revolutionary war he was a professor of Yale, and for part of the war period he was a chaplain in the Continental Army.

At the close of the American Revolution Baldwin studied law. Georgia about that time offered inducements to immigrants and Abraham Baldwin came South, arriving at Savannah in 1784 and was immediately admitted as a councillor at the Georgia bar. He established his residence in Columbia County and so quickly gained the confidence of his fellows that they elected him to represent them in the legislature.

Possessed of a literary and scientific mind, Baldwin had a high regard for learning and he is credited with being the originator of the plan of the University of Georgia, formerly called Franklin College. He drew up its charter and persuaded the legislature to adopt it, and thus was instrumental in establishing in Georgia the first state university in the United States.

In 1786 Abraham Baldwin went to Washington as a member of Congress and thereafter served either in the House or the Senate until his death.

The year after Abraham Baldwin entered congress his father died. Baldwin assumed the care and support of his six orphaned half-brothers and sisters. His father's estate was in debt but he paid off the indebtedness, quit-claimed his share of the inheritance to his brothers and sisters, and educated them, largely at his own expense. He never married.

To the Federal Convention which in 1787 framed the Constitution of the United States, Abraham Baldwin was a delegate from Georgia. He was active in the Convention and to him is credited the influence which resulted in the existence of the United States Senate. Baldwin and William Few were the two Georgia signers of the Constitution.

In 1802 Abraham Baldwin was one of the Georgia commissioners who signed the treaty of session of Georgia's western territory to the United States. That year also he was president pro tempore of the United States Senate from April to December but in 1903 he declined re-election because he preferred the floor to the presiding officer's chair.

Nathaniel Macon in a conversation with Col. Tatnal declared Baldwin's eloquence of a high order and his reasoning powers equal to those of any statesman in Congress.

Of gentle manners but firm character and pure morals, of a high order of mind, well educated and with extraordinary eloquence, Abraham Baldwin was a man of rare personality and lofty attainments.

Faithful to his duties, Baldwin missed but one day from his seat in Congress during twenty-two years. He died suddenly at Washington, March, 1807. By his going a nation was saddened.

TIFT COUNTY INDUSTRIAL SCHOOL

by Mrs. N. Peterson

Prof. E. O. Bynes, Principal

In writing of the growth of the Tift County Industrial School, I should give credit where credit is due. I shall begin with a bred and born colored boy by the name of Johnny Wilson, son of Henry and Maria Wilson, who came to Tifton with Capt. H. H. Tift. Henry helped to build the saw mill and worked as a mill hand as long as he lived. Aunt Maria, his mother, is still living in Phillipsburg. She is very old but her mind is quite alert, and she can relate many interesting facts concerning the early history of Tifton.

Johnny Wilson received what training he could from the ramshackle negro schools of Tifton. He was ambitious for an education; so he went to Booker T. Washington's School in Alabama; finishing there he returned to Tifton, fired with a determination to do something for the colored school children.

He taught for several years in the old Unionville School house, located next door to the first old Shiloh Baptist Church. He appeared time and again before both the county and city boards of education pleading for assistance to build a decent school building. He always received a vote of sympathy and a promise to aid financially as soon as they were able.

He was not easily discouraged. He next solicited the aid of his white friends. Mrs. H. H. Tift and Mrs. N. Peterson helped in every way they could. As was Capt. Tift's custom, he donated six acres of land on which the present school building is located.

Johnny's next move was to appoint a group of his young colored friends to begin raising a building fund. This task he accomplished by giving suppers, dances, and other public forms of entertainment. It was not long before they had enough to enable them to start on their new building. They tore down the old school house and salvaged all material available for the new structure.

When the public and the county and city boards of education realized his determination to succeed they came to his rescue and donated $900.00 in order to complete the building in time for the opening of the fall term in 1917.

Mrs. Tift and Mrs. Peterson were asked to name the school, but we felt that Johnny Wilson deserved that honor; so he gave it the name of Tift County Industrial School. When he had accomplished his mission, he resigned to accept a better job in the Augusta schools, where he remained until his death.

This wooden two-story building took care of all the negro school children in the Tifton school district for ten or twelve years. With its meager equipment and poorly trained teachers the school did not make the progress that it should have made during these years. There are many colored men and women in Tifton who owe their start to one old faithful teacher who mothered the school through all of its trials and tribulations. I am speaking of Lucy McKinnon, who could never qualify for even a third grade certificate. This handicap did not keep her from coming before the board each year to take the examination. The board was finally forced to drop her from their rolls on account of strict laws requiring all teachers to hold higher grade certificates.

Top—The one-room school attended by the beloved Bishop Arthur Moore as a boy.
Center—Omega Consolidated school, typical of the school in each district of the county.
Bottom—The Brookfield Consolidated school, successor to the one attended by Bishop Moore.

In 1928 the county board of education hired Prof. J. M. Deas from Adel as principal of the school. From that day the school has steadily moved forward. Prof. Deas was not only an educator of note but a splendid executive. He was his own truant officer going out and compelling the parents to send the children to school.

He next began working for a larger and better building. It was not until 1931 that the city and county boards with the Rosenwald aid granted the request to build a new brick building—the cost not to exceed $10,000. The negroes agreed to raise $1,500, the city $1,500, the County $2,500, Rosenwald $4,000 and to furnish same. This left a deficit of $500 which the county finally decided to pay.

Aside from his school duties Prof. Deas did much to raise the standard of living among the negroes of Tifton. He reminded them that as a race they had a duty to perform toward society for making a better community in which to live and rear their families. All Tifton joined with the negroes in their sorrow over the sudden death of a true friend of education and humanity. He laid a firm foundation on which his successors found it easier on which to build.

Prof. Emerson O. Bynes was elected principal of the Tift County Industrial School in 1941. He had hardly begun his work when World War II slowed down his activities as it did all other schools in the county. However, with the government aids and other donations from other sources he was able to make progress. In 1941 with Mrs. Hazel Brantley as NYA supervisor and his students doing all of the labor, they were able to complete their vocational building and equip it at the cost of about $4,000.

A large number of his students went into the service of their country, and so far the records prove they rendered valiant service.

During the past three years the school has almost doubled its attendance necessitating enlarging the building. Several of the smaller colored schools in the county were closed and two steel buses were bought to bring their children to Tifton to school. He now has a teaching staff of 23 as against 13 when he took charge. With the assistance of a well organized P-TA he has been able to add $1,200 worth of play-ground equipment to the campus, pay $200 for a new curtain for the stage, pay $1,200 towards buying new chairs for their auditorium; he has $1,000 in the bank for installing new sanitary equipment throughout the buildings. The P-TA serves hot lunches to about 600 pupils daily. They have installed a public address system with a loud speaker. The office is well furnished with the latest cabinets and cases, a typewriting machine, and three mimeograph machines. The library is fairly well equipped.

They have a fine music department, a good glee club of both boys and girls. They publish a school paper twice each year. They are fully accredited in the association of high schools.

TIFT COUNTY'S FIRST SUPERINTENDENT OF EDUCATION

Mr. W. R. Smith

1906-1910

After the establishment of Tift County the Grand Jury met in October and named the following men to constitute the first county board of education: Mr. Briggs Carson, Mr. J. N. Horn, Mr. G. W. Crum, Mr. P. D. Phillips and Dr. F. B. Pickett. Dr. Pickett is the only surviving member of the original five. He served continuously and most effectively until his services on the draft board of World War II became so heavy that he had to resign from the board of education.

On Nov. 3, 1905, the members of this board having received their commissions from the state superintendent of education, Mr. W. B. Merritt, met and were duly installed by Col. H. S. Murray. Mr. Briggs Carson was appointed chairman and Mr. J. N. Horn as acting secretary until the election of a county superintendent. The time for the election was set to take place on Dec. 4, 1905 after being advertised for ten days in the Tifton Gazette.

Mr. W. R. Smith and Prof. Jason Scarboro announced as candidates for this office. They took the required examination and both qualified. A secret ballot was taken and Mr. Smith was declared the nominee having received three of the five votes cast.

After making satisfactory bond, Mr. Smith was sworn into office and assumed the duties as Tift County's first commissioner of education Jan. 1, 1906.

A special meeting of the board of education was called for the purpose of arranging a schedule of teacher salaries. The county had been notified that her apportionment of funds for the year would be $4,619. With his information the following rates were fixed.

White teachers—First grade license____$30.00 per mo. for five months

White teachers—Second grade license___ 25.00 per mo. for five months

White teachers—Third grade license____ 20.00 per mo. for five months

Colored teachers—First grade license____ 25.00 per mo. for five months

Colored teachers—Second grade license__ 18.00 per mo. for five months
Colored teachers—Third grade license___ 15.00 per mo. for five months

Mr. Smith's salary was fixed at $300.00 per year with no maintenance fund or traveling expense. At that time the state did not put any money into the salary of county superintendents. His work was doubly hard on account of the fact that his home was in Eldorado and he did not own any kind of conveyance. This did not deter him in the least in starting out on foot to accomplish all that had to be done. How he ever covered the county and did the work that was done is almost unbelievable. He tells of one occasion on coming into Tifton late one night after walking all day speaking in interest of local tax and did not have enough money to buy a train ticket to Eldorado; so he climbed the three flights of steps to the courtroom in the Bowen Building and slept on one of the hard wooden benches. The next morning he started on the same mission, speaking at three different schools that day.

Before the opening of the schools in the fall the board voted to raise Mr. Smith's salary to $60.00 per month. He assured them that he was being paid all he was worth as he had to learn by experience how to conduct the county's educational affairs. He also stated that as long as the school children had to sit on soap boxes instead of comfortable desks, he should not accept any more pay.

The first real work the board, with Mr. Smith's assistance, had to do was to establish the school districts. This work meant that existing lines had to be changed, some new schools established and a few eliminated. This was not only a hard task but one fraught with many misunderstandings, quarrels and hard feelings, which in the end made Mr. Smith so unpopular that he was not only defeated when election time came again, but suffered indignities of which the county should always feel ashamed.

When the work was completed the following school districts were established: Ansley, Branch Hill, Brighton, Brookfield, Camp Creek, Chula, Eldorado, Emanuel, Excelsior, Fairview, Filyah, Fletcher, Glover, Harding, Hat Creek, Little Creek, Midway, Mt. Zion, Myrtle, Nipper, Oak Ridge, Old Ty Ty, Omega, Pearman, Pine View, Salem, Ty Ty, Vanceville. There were about a dozen colored schools located in the county.

In 1906 the board of education voted to pay $200.00 on the new artificial stone building being erected at Ty Ty, provided they would agree to wait until the end of the year for the money. They also voted to pay Mr. J. F. Ross $20.00 per month to transport the children in the Ty Ty district to the Ty Ty school in a one-horse wagon. Was this transportation the beginning of our fine steel bus system of today? Let's take a little trip back to the Brookfield community. I always enjoyed talking with Mr. E. P. Bowen, Sr., about the school situation as they were when he was a young-

TIFT COUNTY BOARD OF EDUCATION

Top row—E. L. Patrick, Omega District, chairman. R. G. Harrell, Tifton district.

Center row—W. D. Doss, Chula District. M. H. Evans, Ty Ty District.

Bottom—J. C. Branch, Chula District.

ster in school. In one of our early conversations he told of years before there was a railroad anywhere in this section of Georgia how his father used to take his wagon and gather up the few children who lived great distances apart and take them to and from a little log school house just a few miles north of the present day thriving Brookfield community. If I should be asked to choose the first bus line this would be my first choice. Out of this frontier determination to acquire knowledge has come the sturdy Bowen line that has been and still is among Tift County's most successful builders.

In 1907 after seeing the results of having highly trained teachers work in the schools, the board of education ruled that in order to teach in the county, a teacher must hold a first grade certificate, attend normal school, have had three years experience in teaching and must not be addicted to the liquor or tobacco habit.

In February 1908, Mr. Smith asked the board for the privilege of closing all the schools in the county in order that his teachers and pupils might attend the opening of the new Agricultural and Mechanical School and also inspect the first agricultural train to stop in Tifton. Little did we dream at that time that this same little school with only 37 pupils, on opening day, would develop into one of the greatest educational institutions not only in Tifton but the entire state. I proudly refer to Abraham Baldwin College.

In March 1908 Ty Ty was the first school in the county to apply to the board for a seven months term. This petition was granted, the board agreeing to pay one-half of the extra months expense.

Mr. Smith worked hard to secure local tax, longer school term, better paid teachers and greater improvement in every respect for the entire school system. When his four years' work was ended he had remodeled every old school building, painted every one white both inside and out and secured as much up to date equipment as possible with the limited funds he had. The school fund had increased from $4,619 to $16,000; 33 teachers instead of 21 functioning in 28 white schools.

Much ground had been broken, foundations laid, construction begun but hard tasks still lay ahead for those who were to follow and take over the helm.

The picture represents the entire faculty of Tift County's first school year. When we consider that at that time Georgia had no state salary schedule nor any uniform length of term; that it was almost impossible to find anyone willing to board the teachers, especially the women, we feel that this special group should be hailed as the new county's real pioneer teachers and should receive special commendation for their work.

Mr. Smith moved to St. Marys when he left Tift County and has been actively engaged in all movements for the betterment of Camden County

First corps of Tift County Teachers (1907) and Tifton Gazette correspondent Ladies standing in the back row, left to right, Miss Carrie Fulwood, Miss Florence Hill, Miss Maude Burns (Mrs. W. T. Smith, Sr.)

for thirty-five years, having served the county as superintendent of education for several terms. His health failed a few years ago forcing him to retire. His many friends in Tift County were grieved to hear of his death a few days ago.

TIFT COUNTY SUPERINTENDENT OF EDUCATION
Mr. R. F. Kersey
1911-1916

Mr. Kersey's administration as superintendent of Tift County Education was not one to be envied. A good many people in the county had not as yet accepted the changes that had been made during the previous administration. This antagonism combined with other difficulties created a difficult situation for a man of Mr. Kersey's easy-going nature to handle.

The high standard set for teacher qualifications coupled with the fact that it was next to impossible to secure homes for them made the hiring of high-grade teachers almost prohibitive. Employment of local talent became necessary. Many of these were young men and women with little or no experience who could not qualify for more than a third grade certificate. Naturally there began a decline in curricular activities.

Mr. Kersey also inherited part of World War I which did not add anything to the morale of the county. The thinking public soon sensed that the educational status of their county had reached a low ebb and that something must be done to relieve the situation.

An educational department had been set up in the original plan of work in the Twentieth Century Library Club; so the members of this organization volunteered their services whenever or wherever needed. They conferred with Mr. Kersey and the members of the board of education and made some suggestions that both seemed to appreciate and promised to cooperate in every plan that would work for the betterment of the county.

One of the first suggestions acted upon was the holding of a teachers' institute at the end of each month. The club women served a free lunch each month. Some of the members assisted in arranging programs for these meetings that were both helpful to the teachers in their work as well as entertaining. In order to vary the monotony of those teachers living away from home the women would entertain them occasionally over the week-end in their homes. This courtesy the teachers appreciated very much.

I remember on one occasion having two young ladies over the week-end. In the course of conversation I asked them how they entertained themselves in the evenings. One, being rather witty said, "On clear nights we put ourselves to sleep by counting the stars through our roof; on nights when it rains we keep busy moving our bed from place to place trying to keep it dry." Each of these girls walked three miles each morning in opposite directions to their schools. Can you feature even one of the students doing such a thing at the present time?

"Adopting a Rural School" became the slogan for our Educational Program in our club. Two women were assigned to each of the twenty-eight schools. They were told to adopt any method they saw fit to help improve the school and community. Visiting the schools back in those days was almost impossible. Automobiles were very few and the roads so bad that about the only contact was through the teachers and patrons when they would be in town. A great deal of good work was accomplished however. Books were lent to be read to the children. Some small libraries were started in a few of the schools which made provision for taking care of them. I got caught in rather a predicament in the school that had been assigned to me. On one of my visits I told the children if they would make up money and buy a book case I would see that they got enough books to fill it. In less than a week they sent me twenty dollars to buy their book case with the order that the books must accompany it. Maybe I did not have to get busy to carry out my promise. An SOS was sent out to my friends to come to my rescue. I never knew how the news reached a Boston, Massachusetts librarian, of whom I had never heard, but to my utter surprise one morning the expressman unloaded a large box on my porch; and on opening it, I found nearly one hundred good books suitable for school children. It did not take me long to get them out to my little school and Camp Creek School was the proud possessor of the first rural library in the county.

Dr. M. L. Brittain was then state superintendent of education for standardizing all schools in the state. Some of the conditions to be met were: all buildings should be in good condition; there were to be no broken window panes; buildings should be well heated; all wells must be covered; each child should have individual drinking cup; sanitary toilets must be installed; each school must have at least one or two shelves of books toward a start on a library; and must own a good dictionary. All floors must be oiled to allay the dust; a square of tin must supplant the old germ laden sand box under the stove; the schools were urged to put up basketball courts or any other playground equipment possible.

In order to stimulate the schools to quicker action the club women came into the picture again. Some very valuable prizes were offered, including a piano donated by one of the members who had moved away. They assisted the teachers in arranging and holding box suppers to raise funds for much of the equipment they had to buy. They secured nearly all of the books for the library shelves; donated a number of good pictures for each school room, potted plants for windows; most of the schools were supplied with shades and curtains; cut flowers were always in evidence on the teachers' desks. Seven schools entered the contest for the piano and all worked toward obtaining the certificate for the standard school. When the day came for the judges to decide the winner of the piano, all of the schools were in shining readiness. Two people living out of the county were selected to serve with Prof. J. L. Lewis, President of the A. and M. School, and Prof. Jason Scarboro, superintendent of Tifton Schools, as judges. The Excelsior school won the piano with all six of the others as close seconds.

Two school fairs were held in Tifton that would have done credit to most any county fair today. Prizes were given for contests in music, reading, declamation and athletics in addition to those for school work and manual arts. The people of Tifton will long remember the parade of those happy school children through town to converge at the Courthouse where they helped put on an interesting program. A basket dinner was served and a general good time was had by all. In the presence of the happy children neighborhood differences were forgotten and out of it all grew a quickened sense of larger opportunities and responsibilities for the rural school and a better knowledge of the service it could render.

It was during Mr. Kersey's administration that Tift county had her first health officer. This was due to the influence of Col. R. C. Ellis, author of the Ellis Health Law. He got the board of education to accept the services if the Rockefeller Foundation in sending one of their employees to assist the county authorities in ridding the county of hook worm. Dr. T. F. Abercrombie, our very efficient Secretary of State Board of Health, made his debut in health work in Tift County. So new was this idea to our rural folk that had the announcement of the presence of a voodoo doctor in our midst, no greater consternation would have been caused. Many parents ordered their children to come home the minute the strange doctor visited their school. The doctor likes to relate that on one occasion a little ten year old boy was seen to jump from a window and run like a turkey when he drove up in front of the building. So badly did we need this work it was found that out of 1,400 adults and children examined 1,200 active cases of hookworm were found. Most of them were given treatment.

World War I intervened and put an end to most of our forward movement.

Mr. Kersey served but one term. When he left Tifton he moved to Florida where he continued in the ministry until his death a few years ago.

MR. A. J. AMMONS
County Superintendent of Education
1917-1929

During the summer of 1911 there came to Tifton a young man by the name of A. J. Ammons, who had just graduated from Martha Berry's

TIFT COUNTY EDUCATORS
Top row—Mercer H. Mitcham, superintendent of Tift County Schools. C. B. Culpepper, Tift County's veteran farm demonstration agent.
Bottom—Miss Edna Bishop, Tift County home demonstration agent.

School near Rome. Having decided to make teaching his profession he applied to the county board of education for a position as teacher in Tift County. He was accepted and was placed in charge of the Harding school at a salary of $40 per month.

He was elected as principal of the Omega School the next year. They raised his salary to $60 per month. He remained at the head of this school for five years. It was here he met and married Miss Janie Bozeman, of Ty Ty, who was also a teacher in the school.

Mr. Ammons was a young man of unusual intelligence, with a scintillating personality, always vibrating in human interest. He attracted this attention of the public and made many friends throughout the county.

When the time came to elect the next county superintendent his friends announced him as a candidate for the office. He was easily elected.

After receiving his commission and meeting all requirements, he was sworn into office on January 1, 1917. He held this office for twelve years. Many things of vital import in the county occurred during his administration.

In 1918 the board agreed to pay $40 per month towards the salary of the first home economics teacher in the county. They likewise agreed to pay one half of the salary of G. W. Burton (colored), the first vocational agricultural teacher, who was employed by the Tift County Industrial School. On account of lack of space, poor equipment and little interest, this work was done on a very small scale; yet it marked the beginning of a great movement in the schools of the county.

Another great movement was inaugurated during this year—that of planning for the first consolidated school. There were more small schools around Chula than any other school; so a large delegation from that section asked for permission to meet with the county board of education to discuss the merging of some of the smaller schools with Chula. The idea was met with favor, but much planning and hard work lay ahead for all parties concerned. It was not until 1922 that Chula's new brick building was completed. The small schools of Pearman, Fairview, Hat Creek, and part of the Fletcher school closed their doors and moved into the first consolidated school building in the county. From that date forward consolidation became the order of the day. Buses had also replaced the horse and wagon as a means of transportation for the children.

In 1919 the legislature passed a law whereby the state could pay each County Superintendent $50 per month. The Tift County board subsequently raised Mr. Ammons' salary to $75 per month with an additional $25 for expense of operating his own car. This enabled him to hire some office help which gave him more time for visiting the schools and looking after many other details.

In 1922 Mr. J. S. Royal, a representative of the Tifton Gazette, and a great lover of music, met with the board of education and asked that music be installed in all of the schools as a regular branch of study. The board thanked him for his interest, but said that it would have to be left up to the individual schools as there were no public funds available for such.

In 1924 the board agreed to take over from the county commissioners the full payment of the salaries of the farm and home demonstration agents. This made possible by the Acts of 1922 Georgia School Code for same.

By 1926 each of the twenty-eight small schools with the exception of Oak Ridge and Emanuel had been consolidated into seven schools. Each one housed in spacious, comfortable, attractive brick buildings. All were furnished with the most modern equipment. All had basketball courts, Parent-Teacher Associations, and served hot lunches to most of the children. County-wide curricula activities were rapidly taking place.

In 1929 the board of education did their first humanitarian act for the Negro children of the county by electing Prof. J. M. Deas, of Adel, as principal of the Tift County Industrial School. From then on matters began to pick up for that school. (This school will be considered under separate article.)

Mr. Ammons did a great deal of work with both the county and city boards of education in planning for the creation of the big Tifton consolidated district. This meant establishing the lines of full twenty-four lots of land and part of eight others. The carrying out of the plans and the erecting of the Tifton Junior High Building fell to the lot of his successor, Mr. W. L. Harmon.

When Mr. Ammons finished his work as superintendent of education in Tift County there had been as previously stated the consolidation of all but two schools; sixteen transportation routes established transporting one thousand children to and from high school each day. Every phase of educational work had been raised to a higher standard and much other valuable work for the county in general accomplished. The board of education and all with whom Mr. Ammons had to deal expressed themselves as well pleased.

On vacating the office of superintendent he did not sever his relations with the schools. Chula happened to be without a principal at that time so he stepped in and taught two years for them. Omega then called him back to take charge as principal for that school. He remained with them for nine years.

When Alma High School was in need of some one to head its school and offered a better salary Mr. Ammons accepted the position.

Two years ago his retirement was in order, but on account of the teacher shortage Alma prevailed upon him to continue teaching still. He has bought a home in Alma with considerable acreage and says he hopes to spend his later years in quietude.

In a recent letter from Mr. Ammons he says:

"It is a pleasure to know that I had a small part in the constructive work of the Tift County Schools. I want to express my deep appreciation to the various members who composed the board of education. Some have gone home to glory but many are still living. I am greatly indebted to the members of the Twentieth Century Library Club for their assistance in the early days of our consolidation. I remember distinctly how they visited the schools and helped to sponsor various projects.

"In my long association with the county the dream of my life almost came true. If the work with the boys and girls helped to build character, instill higher ideals, stir ambition and aspiration I should be happy. And I am."

MR. W. L. HARMAN
County School Superintendent
1929-1934

It seemed almost that the cruel hand of fate stepped in and took matters in hand when Mr. Harman took over the reins of the county's school system. The country was plunged into the most terrible depression in its history. Instead of being able to make the progress that one of his training, experience and love for the higher things of life, he was forced by circumstances to shorten the school term, lessen the teachers' salaries and curtail every other means of improvement for lack of funds.

Knowing Mr. Harman, as most of us did, we felt that this condition almost broke his heart and no doubt did help to shorten his life.

In order for the county to keep the Rosenwald aid we had to assist in the campaign to remove adult illiteracy. For this work Mr. Harman called for volunteers to teach at night for a period of six weeks. The following white teachers responded: Prof. A. J. Ammons, J. C. Sirmans, Mr. and Mrs. A. D. Dean, Mr. W. C. Bryan, Miss Marian Ragan and Mr. J. C. Adams. Four colored people were taught to read and write.

Mr. Harman had the pleasure of supervising the construction of the splendid junior high school building and almost within the same year witnessing its total destruction by fire. This added another burden of planning and rebuilding in time for the next term of school. This program necessitated so much extra work that the board of education appointed Mr. Charles C. Harman to assist his father in the office.

Mr. Harman was of great assistance to Prof. Deas in building the new Tift County Industrial School which the county finally approved, and donated the sum of $500 toward its erection.

Mr. Harman was re-elected at the close of his four years work and had just finished the first year on his second term when he died.

The resolutions passed by the board of education express the sentiments of the entire county.

"We take this method of expressing our sympathy to his loved ones and we call upon all who loved him to bow in humble submission to God's will in calling him home and to lift hearts of gratitude and rejoicing that we were privileged to know him and work with him in the schools of Tift County.

"We rejoice for his long life, his wonderful school work, his love of children and his fellow man, his undying interest in the education and welfare of the children of this county and state.

"Therefore, be it resolved that a copy of this resolution be spread upon the minutes of this Board of Education, and that a copy be sent to the family of Mr. Harman as a testimonial of our sincere appreciation of his usefulness, not only as superintendent of the Tift County Schools, but also as a citizen of Tift County.

"Tift County Board of Education."

Mr. Charles C. Harman
TIFT SUPERINTENDENT OF EDUCATION
1935-1937

Mr. Charles Harman was appointed by the Tift County Board of Education to fill the unexpired term of his father, Mr. W. L. Harman.

He was a young man of superior intellect and his training under the guidance of his father well qualified him for the duties of the office which he was seemingly filling in an acceptable manner until his tragic death, which occurred on May 5, 1947.

"Whereas, the life of Charles Goodman Harman, our late superintendent has come to an untimely end, and

"Whereas, for a number of years he served the schools of this county both as clerk in the superintendent's office and later as superintendent of schools, we, the members of the Tift County Board of Education, wish to express our genuine sorrow and keen regret caused by his going. It is impossible to understand the mysteries of life and death. We do not attempt to divine the infinite but only recall the warm personality which was so recently among us.

"Therefore, be it resolved that we express our heartfelt sympathies to the loved ones who mourn his passing and pray the light of Heaven to ever guide them during the dark hours of life.

"Tift County Board of Education."

FACULTY MEMBERS TIFT COUNTY SCHOOLS
1946-47 TERM

Brookfield—W. M. Melton, Principal; Margaret Booth, Martha Dean Jenkins, Mamie Moore, Mrs. H. D. Lee. Mrs. W. M. Melton, Norma Touchstone, Mrs. Warren Tucker.

Chula—E. W. May, Principal; Ethelene Pirkle, Mrs. J. Wilbur Tyson, Mrs. Mary Pollette, Marjorie Gibbs, Helen Melton, Mrs. Henry Barfield, Mrs. Mattie Carroll.

Eldorado—F. J. Moon, Principal; Mrs. Morgan Greene, Mrs. Clara Wells, Billie Rowland, Agnes Marchant, Mrs. Geo. Julian, Mrs. B. R. Stocks.

Emanuel—Mrs. R. R. Moore, Principal; Kathleen Page, Eula Daniels, Willord Massey.

Excelsior—Mrs. A. D. Dean, Principal; Murl Rountree, Mrs. D. B. Spinks, Mrs. G. C. Avery, Lois Horne.

Harding—Mrs. J. M. Rooks, Principal; Lena Gordon Williams, Mrs. J. M. Elrod

Omega—G. M. Schlegel, Principal; A. O. Lee, Voc. Ag. Teacher; Emily Thomasen, Homemaking; Mrs. Bertha Rollins, Marjorie Simmons, Mrs. Lois Griner, Ruby Young, Mrs. Estelle McFarland, Mrs. L. Bass, Mrs. Lucy S. Gibbs, Mrs. C. G. Weeks, Annette Shannon.

Ty Ty—Howard Evans, Principal; Mrs. J. L. Monk, Mrs. H. C. Gibbs, Mrs. Hazel Fowler, Reba Arnett, Mrs. Judith Chesnut, Mrs. W. C. McCormic.

Frances Benson, County School Supervisor.

Virginia Quattlebaum, Visiting Teacher.

TIFT COUNTY

Superintendents of Education:
  Mr. W. R. Smith—Jan. 1, 1906—December 31, 1910
  Mr. R. F. Kearsey—Jan. 1, 1911—Dec. 31, 1916
  Mr. A. J. Ammons—Jan. 1, 1917—Dec. 31, 1928
  Mr. W. L. Harman—Jan. 1, 1929—Dec. 31, 1934
  Mr. C. E. Harman—Jan. 1, 1935—May 5, 1937
  Mr. W. T. Bodenhamer—May 12, 1937—Oct. 17, 1939
  Mr. C. F. Hudgins—Oct. 17, 1939—Dec. 31, 1940
  Mr. M. H. Mitcham—Jan. 1, 1941—
First County Board of Elucation:
  Mr. Briggs Carson, chairman, Dec. 9, 1905; Mr. P. D. Phillips, Mr. G. W. Crum, Mrs. J. N. Horne, Dr. F. B. Pickett.

Present County Board of Education:
Mrs. E. L. Patrick, Omega District; Mrs. L. W. Whiddon, Chula District; Mrs. J. C. Branch, Brookfield District; Mr. M. H. Evans, Ty Ty District; Mr. R. W. Harrell, Tifton District.

M. H. MITCHAM

1941-19—

Mr. Mitcham may well be termed the war superintendent of the county, as he had to fight many local battles throughout the length of World War II on account of ever changing conditions and general unrest, which naturally follow such conditions.

To read the minutes of his administration one marvels that he managed to keep his schools intact, with teachers resigning to accept war jobs or to go to some other place where higher salaries were being offered. These conditions did, to a certain extent, lower the standing as many emergency certificates had to be granted to those who were less qualified, but simply offered their services as a patriotic duty.

He and his board are to be congratulated on holding things together and accomplishing as much as they did under the existing circumstances.

In 1941 the county was declared out of debt for the first time in its history. In order to progress you must have funds, so it was not long before we were in debt list again, but many new projects were in the making.

All schools were operated for nine months for the first time in the history of Tift County and without aid from the school district. All buses were county-owned and all steel for the first time.

Lunch rooms in every white school in the county were operated for the first time.

The Bookmobile and County Library Program was greatly expanded, having over 2,500 volumes, which are circulated and read many times during each year.

The Tift County Board of Education has offered more financial assistance to county schools than ever before in the school history.

The Tift County Industrial school with N.Y.A. assistance built its vocational building at a cost of $3,500 to the County.

In 1943 the schools of the county completed 67 courses in woodwork, elementary electricity, care and repair of farm machinery. Six hundred-seventy participated in this program. Several canning plants were installed in which 97,000 cans of fruits and vegetables were processed. The Omega school qualified for Victory School. All schools cooperated in every war request and drive.

On October 30, 1944, the first nursery school in the county was established in connection with War Public Works. In order to secure better teachers the board voted a 25% increase in teacher salaries. A letter was sent to the county representative urging that he work for a 50% teacher increase of salary in the state.

The new state compulsory education law was put into effect.

In 1944 the Tifton Board of Education and the county commissioners met with the County Board of Education to discuss final plans for new vocational building to be erected on the high school campus in Tifton. Each agreed to pay one-third of the cost of building which was to cost $19,570.00.

In 1946 the county suffered a distinct loss in the death of Miss Lucy McKinnon.

The county now owns property at $300,000.00 valuation: $230,000 white schools—$40,000 colored school. Eighteen buses owned and operated daily over 40 routes. A hundred teachers are employed.

The county board is erecting maintenance shops for buses now. This work will make it possible to save the taxpayers of the county many dollars, for repairs have been one of the greatest expenses.

CHARLES LUTHER CARTER

Charles Luther Carter, the first Tift County teacher to retire under Georgia's new retirement law, was born near Jackson, Butts County, Georgia, Jan. 1, 1880. He is a first honor graduate of Jackson High school. In 1903 he received an A.B. degree at Mercer University. He was editor-in chief of the Mercerian in his senior year. In 1930 he received the Master's degree at Mercer.

He has been a teacher for thirty-seven years, thirty-five of which were taught in Georgia. He has served as president of Green and Cook County Teachers' Associations. In thirty-seven years of teaching he has lost only one day on account of illness. He has held the superintendencies at Pelham, Union Point, Ballground, Morven, Ray City, Lenox, Ty Ty, Excelsior, and Enigma.

His residence has been in the vicinity of Tifton for past seventeen years. In 1935 he purchased his present home in Tifton. Perhaps he has visited more Tift County homes than any other individual. In 1940 he took Tift County business and population censuses. Also he registered three school district censuses in this county. Deeply interested in Christian training, he taught six years in church schools and has been director of Baptist Training Union of Mell association for past three years.

CHAS. F. HUDGINS

1939-1941

For the third, and we hope the last, time, the Tift County Board of Education was compelled to appoint some one to fill the unexpired term of their County Superintendent of Education.

In this instance it was not hard to make a selection, as Mr. Chas. F. Hudgins was well and favorably known in educational circles of the county, having been assistant principal of the Chula school for two years previous to this appointment. His scholastic attainments, highly approved Christian character, and his universal social appeal made him acceptable to all concerned.

He took over the reins of the county affairs on October 9, 1939, serving the remainder of Mr. Bodenhamer's term, or until the next election in the fall of 1940.

Mr. Hudgins came into office on the crest of the government wave of alphabetical letters, WPA, CCC, PWA, NYA. He at once set about to avail himself of all that each had to offer the county.

The Twentieth Century Library Club had already been operating under the WPA in extending their library services to the county schools. Mr. Hudgins began to work with the club women and helped to secure the present bookmobile. This was done by the county furnishing the body for the chassis, for which we paid seventy-five cents an hour until paid for.

In dedication of the Bookmobile to the county, a public program was given on the front lawn of the courthouse. Mrs. N. Peterson was given the honor of christening it in the name of Tift County Bookmobile. Participating in these exercises were: Mrs. N. Peterson, originator of Tifton and Tift County's first libraries; Mr. S. A. Youmans, City Manager; Mr. C. F. Hudgins, County Superintendent of Education; Mrs. Estelle Fisher, City Librarian; Mrs. Ruth Thornhill, County Librarian; Mrs. J. J. Clyatt, Chairman Library Commission; Mrs. C. B. Culpepper, Member Library Commission; Mrs. Dan Sutton, teacher in the county (1908) to whom Mrs. Peterson lent the first book to be read to the school children, thus paving the way for the first rural school library.

Mr. Hudgins must have credit for several firsts in the county during his administration.

All schools were operated for eight months at the expense of the county and state boards.

Four schools extended their term to full nine months, with local assistance.

A supervisor for the primary and elementary grades was employed, filling a long felt need.

The WPA and NYA funds enabled the schools to provide additional help, and make it possible to serve milk and hot lunches free to all the children.

An NYA supervisor was employed to visit all schools and assist the local help in preparing and serving nutritious food. The girls were taught to preserve large quantities of vegetables, furnished by patrons, to be used in the next year's lunches.

All schools were required to fly the U. S. flag during the hours school was in session and to give the salute to the flag.

The board of education voted that in order to be eligible all school principals must hold a four years' professional certificate from the state department of education.

Mr. Hudgins has been associate professor of education in charge of guidance and training at the University of Georgia since leaving Tift County.

On April 1, 1947, he was made national chairman of vocational guidance and supervision.

W. T. BODENHAMER

1937-1938

Mr. Bodenhamer was appointed by the Tift County Board of Education to fill the unexpired term of Mr. Chas. C. Harman, whose death occurred on May 5, 1937.

Mr. Bodenhamer possessed all of the attributes of capable leadership and proved himself an executive of ability during the short time he filled the office. His job was very much complicated, but he greatly endeared himself to the board, by the masterly manner in which he solved some of the problems to which he had fallen heir.

He worked unceasingly for everything that would be for the highest and best interest of the county. Every phase of work was raised to a higher standard. He placed the welfare of the school children of the county above all else. He was instrumental in getting all-metal bodies for the school buses, thus better insuring the safety of the lives of the children.

That he was an educator of outstanding worth was proved by the fact that during the summer of 1939 he was appointed to a much higher position by the State Department of Education, that of State Supervisor of Education.

The board was very loath to release him, but in doing so they felt they were relinquishing him for a much greater field of service. They extended a special vote of thanks and appreciation for his work in the county, and wished for him every success in his enlarged service for the enrichment of a greater number of people.

Mr. Bodenhamer is now president of Norman Junior College, at Norman Park, Georgia.

ALTON ELLIS—1947

An excerpt from an article written in the Tifton Gazette when Mr. Ellis was elected principal of the Tifton High School gives a sketch of his life:

"Mr. Ellis is one of the most outstanding young men in the state. He is an honor graduate of Griffin High School; received his bachelor of science degree at Georgia Teachers' College, Statesboro; and is a candidate June, 1947, for his master of education degree at the University of Georgia.

He has had nine years of experience as teacher and principal in Georgia Schools. He came to Tifton in 1941 as principal, stayed one year, and then enlisted in the United States Army. He returned to the Tifton Junior High School in 1946 and has underway an exceptional program for that school . . .

He has Asiatic-Pacific theater ribbon with Bronze Star, American Theater ribbon, and good conduct medal. Mr. Ellis, 32 years old, is married to the former Miss Margaret Hicks Thompson, of Dublin, and they have one son, William West Ellis, seven months old."

MRS. NICHOLAS PETERSON
by Ida Belle Williams

Mrs. N. Peterson (Edna McQueen) was born in Florence, Alabama, but her home until after her marriage was Nashville, Tennessee. In 1896 she came to Tifton to teach, and in 1897 married Dr. Nicholas Peterson. She has one son, Malcolm.

Mrs. Peterson has held every office in the Twentieth Century Library Club, which she organized in 1905. She was president of this club after Mrs. H. H. Tift had held the office for thirty-one years. At present Mrs. Peterson is parliamentarian of the club.

She has received local, state and national recognition for a renaissance in Tift County rural education. Mrs. Peterson conceived the idea of having the Twentieth Century Library Club adopt rural schools in Tift County and improve them. Details of this project are given in Chapter X of this book.

This educator has received many honors for her contributions to education and other worthwhile causes. She is director for life of Georgia Federation of Women's Clubs, the highest honor one can attain. She is now historian for Second District Federation of Women's Clubs. She was NYA director for six counties during the war. The Second District Federation of Women's Clubs gave in Mrs. Peterson's honor the Edna McQueen scholarship for a worthy Second District student who wished to attend Abraham Baldwin College. Mrs. Peterson also received from the Georgia Division Field Army American Cancer Society a citation of honor and a certificate of appreciation. In 1940 she received a medal for the most outstanding club work in Second District. She is a life honorary member of Adel Women's Club. The General Federation of Women's Clubs (national) at Salt Lake City, Utah, presented Mrs. Peterson a pin in recognition of her achievement. The Twentieth Century Library Club presented her a loving cup.

She is a member of Georgia Historical Society of Research, a member of Georgia League of Women Voters, on Board of Public Welfare, a member of U. D. C., and chairman of rural education. Mrs. Peterson was the first Georgia Woman delegate to Democratic Convention in New York. She served four years on Board of Education for Milledgeville School for Boys.

Mrs. Peterson has sung in the Metholist choir in Tifton for forty-five years.

In 1914 she spoke on rural education at the General Federation of Women's Clubs in Chicago; in 1916 she gave a similar address at the same type of meeting in New York.

"First the blade, then the ear, after that the full corn in the ear."

One who has lived amidst and observed the growth and unfolding of a community such as has taken place here on our coastal plain in South Georgia, can but exclaim: "What God hath wrought!" The growth and development here has been truly wonderful. Only a few years ago this was a piney wilderness covered with wire grass. Today it is a land flowing with milk and honey. The pines and wire grass have given way to fertile fields and vineyards, with every road and highway dotted with beautiful homes and contentment, with villages and cities, and a civilization that would do credit to the foremost section of our great country, and withal a citizenry educated, refined and cultured, and prosperity abounding everywhere.

But all this achievement did not just happen. It required long and tiresome days, a strong faith and indomitable courage. The way of the pioneer is always long and hard. Whether it be to pass over unknown seas and discover new worlds; to climb mountains and traverse dark wildernesses; to discover the glory and beauty of freedom to those who have long sat in darkness and been bound in chains of slavery, the pioneer's way is difficult. That which makes his work doubly hard is that he is so often misunderstood and must work alone.

If space would permit I could name a long list of pioneer families of this section out of which came a noble strain worthy to take their place with the mighty who have brought things to pass.

These were the men who struggling against the foes of nature to free themselves from the bonds of illiteracy, saw, had faith and dreamed, and had courage to make their dreams come true. Nothing great has ever been done that was not some time a dream. Along with these were the splendid native people who caught inspiration from these men of vision and joined with them and worked for the things which we now have and enjoy.

Simultaneous with the dawn of civilization was the art of teaching; in fact, had there never been a school teacher, there would not have been civilization. Whatever has been accomplished here and everywhere has been done through education. Education is both the foundation and the means by which all noble and worthy things have been built.

There could have been no school without teachers. These faithful evangels of light came early to our section. They began their work in log cabins far back among the pines with the children of the humble. Part of their mission was to plead for the cause of education, plead for better houses and equipment, and last, for a little better pay for the arduous work they were doing. These beginnings back in the little one-room school houses were torches flashing their gleams out in the wilderness of illiteracy; they were lighthouses on the beach of time, throwing out light to warn and guide the mind to better things. All hail to the pioneer school teacher who toiled and labored, many times without straw for their bricks, to build the noble and beautiful walls and temples of knowledge here in our Southland.

I believe Poor Richard said: "Great oaks from little acorns grow; great streams from little fountains flow."

In our half century of progress we have come a long way, but even though the scope and character of our educational work has become broader and more inclusive we are still studying the needs for better homes, better citizenship, better library advantages, more money spent for education—thus the cycle comes back to a new beginning in an atomic age. We are pioneers still!

> "So I speak not for myself, but for the age unknown.
> I caught the fire from those who went before,
> The bearers of the torch who could not see
> The goal for which they strained, I caught their fire,
> And carried it only a little beyond;
> But there are those that wait for it,
> I know, those who will carry it on to victory
> I dare not fail them, Looking back,
> I see those others—with their arms outstretched,
> Pointing to the future."

CHAPTER XVIII

CHURCHES

THE BROOKFIELD BAPTIST CHURCH

The Brookfield Baptist Church was organized on May 10, 1896. The charter members are: Mr. and Mrs. I. S. Bowen, Mr. and Mrs. I. W. Bowen, Sr., Mrs. N. A. Bowen, Mrs. J. L. Gay, Mrs. Mary J. Gibbs, Mrs. W. E. Gibbs, Mrs. Mattie Henderson, Mrs. Melissa McCrea, Mr. and Mrs. W. A. Patten, Mrs. Willie S. Patterson, Mr. A. J. Pope, Jr., and Mrs. Dollie Reynolds. Mrs. J. L. Gay and Mrs. Mattie Henderson are the only living members of the charter group.

The Reverend J. A. Cox and the Reverend W. I. Patrick organized the church. The other ministers were: The Reverend C. M. Crowe, the Reverend T. J. Harring, the Reverend J. C. Moore, the Reverend D. C. Rainey, the Reverend L. L. Batts, who was instrumental in adding Sunday School rooms to the present building; the Reverend W. M. Taylor, the Reverend C. W. Willis, and the Reverend Rex Whiddon. The Reverend Albert Crowe is the present pastor.

The first church, a one-room building used for religious services and for school, is still standing. The present church, which has eight Sunday School rooms, was built in 1900.

I. W. Bowen, Jr., the only minister from the membership of this church, was ordained in 1946. He received the call to the ministry in 1943 and began last fall his courses at the Southern Baptist Theological Seminary, Louisville, Kentucky.

BRIEF HISTORY OF THE FIRST BAPTIST CHURCH OF TIFTON

In the early days of Tifton, a little village which grew up around a large saw mill operated by H. H. Tift, brave pioneers began to plan for a Baptist Church. In cooperation with the State Mission Board, work was begun, and by 1889 a Baptist church was established with a small membership but a triumphant faith.

The first pastor, C. M. Irwin, who served about a year and J. L. Underwood, 1892-1894, were supported jointly by the Mission Board and the infant church. The first building was destroyed by fire about 1894.

In 1895, a brick building was erected during the pastorate of F. T. Snell, 1895-1896. Mr. Snell, an Englishman, was a protege of Spurgeon. It was at this time that the church became self-supporting. For five years P. A. Jessup, a distinguished gentleman with goatee, led the growing congregation. In 1903-1904, C. G. Dilworth was the pastor and was described as "an interesting and wide-awake minister."

The coming of Henry Miller, 1904-1908, marked the second phase in the development of Titton Baptists. In his pastorate the commodious building now in use was erected in 1906. It was of the latest architectural plan containing rooms for the Sunday School. In 1909-1910, A. J. Reamy, a highly educated and splendid preacher, served the church.

The longest pastorate was that of C. W. Durden, 1911-1922. The church grew rapidly and expanded its program. Friendly and forceful, Dr. Durden was greatly beloved and was given up reluctantly. In 1921, the budget was $6,000, and the membership had reached the 500 mark.

F. C. McConnel began his ministry in 1923. His youthful vigor and splendid personality added zest to the program of the church, and his pastorate which ended in 1927, was especially fruitful. Succeeding Dr. McConley in 1928 was George C. Gibson, who served effectively until 1934. In spite of the depression years in this agricultural area, the church continued to move forward under the guidance of Dr. Gibson, and the evangelistic fires continued to burn brightly. During this pastorate the membership crossed the 900 mark.

The pastorate of F. O. Mixon, 1934-1943, marked the third stage in our history. His splendid leadership and church-wide support resulted in a great advance. An educational building was erected in 1938 to house the greatly enlarged Sunday School which had for the first time been departmentized. This modern plant increased the effectiveness of the Sunday School and Training Union.

The present pastor, Davis M. Sanders, succeeded Dr. Mixon in the summer of 1943. Property has been purchased for the building of an additional educational plant, and $31,000 has been raised for this project. At the last meeting of Mell Association, the church reported a membership of 1,409, total receipts for the year of $44,546.35, and property valued at $100,000.

An outstanding characteristic of the church has been the spirit of harmony and good will. Never has there been an experience of discord which has characterized many churches. Marked confidence in the leaders has been a significant factor in our progress. Complete harmony exists.

Outstanding individuals have given full support. From the earliest days consecrated manpower explains the uniform strength of the church. Such leaders as W. W. Timmons, B. T. Allen, B. T. Cole, W. H. Love, E. P. Bowen, J. D. Duncan, W. S. Cobb, Jason Scarboro, W. H. Spooner; such Sunday School Superintendents as J. K. Carswell, Briggs Carson, I. D. Morgan, 1918-1937; E. P. Bowen, Jr., 1937 to date; and many other workers recall to our people the vital part played in the cause of Christ.

From the beginning until her death in 1936, Mrs. H. H. Tift was a moving spirit whose powerful influence only God can properly evaluate. Although not a member, her husband fully cooperated in Mrs. Tift's desires for the church, and their large gifts through the years made possible many

TIFTON HOUSES OF WORSHIP

Top row—First Presbyterian Church. Bessie Tift Chapel (Cotton Mill). The first church built in Tifton.

Center row—Brookfield Memorial Methodist Church. First Baptist Church.

Bottom row—First Methodist Church. St. Anne's Episcopal Church.

accomplishments. From the first, there has been a Missionary Society, and until her death, Mrs. Tift was its honored president. Her memory will ever be a motivating power in the church. Beyond the community her influence was felt, for Bessie Tift College was named for her.

The church has sent forth four young men to serve as pastors: R. Davis Carrin, James M. Windham, Willis Hollingsworth, Robert H. Culpepper, and two young ladies for full time Christian service, Miss Eula Heard Windham and Miss Frances Allen.

In addition to Davis M. Sanders, the church officers are E. P. Bowen, Jr., S. S. Superintendent; H. G. Petty, Training Union Director; Fred Bell, Chairman of Deacons; Mrs. H. G. Petty, W. M. U. President; Miss Dora E. Solomon, Educational Director, and Mrs. Sewell C. Holland, church secretary.

—Church Historian

CHULA BAPTIST CHURCH
by H. D. Webb

Chula Baptist Church was organized on October 8, 1922 by the Reverend G. C. Rainey. The names of pastors who have served the church since its organization are W. T. Bodenhamer, Rex Whiddon, J. A. Skelton, Ashbery Burrell. The value of the church property was $5,000. Services are held semi-monthly. The present pastor is Ashbury Burrell, and church clerk is George W. Pearman.

TY TY BAPTIST CHURCH
by H. D. Webb

Ty Ty Baptist Church was organized in 1890 by the Reverend Blitch. The value of the church property now is $2,500. Services are held on the first and third Sundays. Pastors who have served the church since its organization are G. J. West, J. S. Sauls, George F. Clark, C. E. Walters, V. F. Johnson, A. W. Thompson, D. C. Rainey, Jeffry W. Jones, W. T. Bodenhamer, Hamilton Daniels and T. H. Matthews, who is now pastor. Grady Jones is church clerk, and Mrs. Grady Jones, assistant church clerk. The Reverend D. C. Rainey served the Ty Ty church seventeen years in succession.

ZION HOPE BAPTIST CHURCH
by H. D. Webb

Zion Hope Baptist Church was organized in 1877 by the Reverend W. W. Webb and Isaac Hobby. The pastors who have served since the organi-

THE OLD-TIME RELIGION
Three scenes from a baptizing following a revival at one of Tift County's rural churches.

zation are Wiley Pipkins, S. E. Blitch, George F. Clark, Frank Cox, P. A. Jessup, Floyd Hobby, D. C. Rainey, J. C. Cochran, George C. Gibson, and F. F. Barbre. The present pastor is D. C. Rainey and church clerk, Mrs. Seth Kelley. The value of the church property was $1,800. Church services are held monthly.

BESSIE TIFT CHAPEL

Bessie Tift Chapel, erected by the Methodists in 1889 and sold to H. H. Tift in 1901 when they built a new church, is the oldest house of worship in Tifton. Mr. Tift moved the building to the cotton mill, named it for Mrs. Bessie Tift, his wife, and invited all denominations to use it for worship.

Later deciding this plan was not best, Mr. Tift in 1902 deeded the land and building to the First Baptist Church of Tifton. For some unknown reason the deed was not recorded until 1924.

There is no record of preachers until 1911 when the Reverend Dave Rainey, who preached there for fourteen years, was pastor; the Reverend Banks Allen preached from 1925-1929; the Reverend Tom Matthews. from 1929-1931; the Reverend Banks Allen from 1931-1935; the Reverend Willis Hollingsworth, 1935-1939; the Reverend Banks Allen, from 1939-1941; the Reverend T. W. Snider, 1941-1942; the Reverend C. W. Willis, 1945-1947; the Reverend T. W. Branch is the present pastor.

THE HISTORY OF EVENTS LEADING UP TO THE CONSTITUTION OF THE TIFTON PRIMITIVE BAPTIST CHURCH

(Dr. L. A. Baker)

The beginning of the history of the Tifton Primitive Baptist Church has a rather wide geographical distribution; which in order to give, it will be necessary to set forth part of the history of two other churches, namely, Old China Grove, located about a mile and a half southwest across Warrior Creek from Poland, Georgia, and Corrinth Church at Ty Ty, Georgia.

In the 1870's there moved to Ty Ty Station two brothers, William W. and W. Edwin Williams with their wives—sons of Elder Ezekiel J. Williams who was a very famous Primitive Baptist preacher living on a farm on the site of what is now the town of Sparks, Georgia. These two sons and their wives brought letters from churches in that section. Some time during the 1880's, these four, together with Elder I. P. Porter, his wife, and others, revived the church which had gone dead at Old China Grove.

For several years, they prospered there as a church during which time Joseph J. Baker joined and was baptized.

A few years later, by mutual consent, the China Grove Church dissolved and moved to Ty Ty, where they had themselves constituted into a new church called Corrinth. W. Edwin Williams gave the land on which the church now stands. William W. Williams gave and cut the timber off his farm into lumber to build the church. Much of this lumber was hauled to Poland to the planing mills to be remilled for the construction of the building.

This church prospered for many years. Sometime along about 1900, Mrs. Joseph J. Baker joined and was baptized into the fellowship of this church.

About this time, there was a heavy movement of settlers from middle Georgia to this section; from among whom, Corrinth Church received the following splendid members: Mr. and Mrs. J. M. Davis from Newton County—Mr. Davis bringing a letter from Shoal Creek Church and Mrs. Davis from Harris Springs Church—Mrs. J. W. Hollis from Newton County with a letter from Harris Springs Church. Mr. and Mrs. J. M. W. Lyons and Mr. and Mrs. F. Z. Dumas from Upson County bringing letters from Sharon Church. Mr. and Mrs. J. T. Davis from Morgan County in 1904, uniting with Corrinth Church in 1905 by baptism. Also in 1904, Mr. and Mrs. S. N. Poole came from Fulton County with letters from Mars Hill Church in Forsyth County.

In October 1905, Dr. L. A. Baker, then a medical student at the beginning of his second year in college, joined Corrinth Church and was baptized. Mr. and Mrs. S. D. Spillers came to Corrinth Church with letters about this same time.

Most of these middle Georgia people settled in and around Tifton. In 1911, Dr. Baker moved from Ty Ty, where he settled after coming out of college, to Tifton to practice medicine. A few years later, Elder J. T. McArthur of Cordele, Georgia, began to hold services off and on in Tifton. Finally in 1916, the following members asked for letters of dismissal from Corrinth Church in order to form a church at Tifton: W. E. Williams, Mrs. W. E. (Katie) Williams, J. J. Baker, Mrs. J. J. (Sarah) Baker, Dr. L. A. Baker, Mr. and Mrs. J. M. Davis, Mr. and Mrs. J. T. Davis, Mr. and Mrs. S. D. Spillers, Minnie Spillers, Mr. and Mrs. F. Z. Dumas, Roy, Alene, and Gladys Dumas, Mr. and Mrs. J. M. W. Lyons, Mrs. Fannie C. Long, Mrs. Annie M. Hollis, Carolyn Hollis, and Mrs. S. N. Poole.

This left Corrinth Church with an active membership and they are carrying on to this day. Elder J. T. McArthur of Cordele, Georgia, is the present pastor.

CONSTITUTION OF THE TIFTON PRIMITIVE BAPTIST CHURCH

On November 30th, 1916, Elders J. T. McArthur, J. M. Thomas, J. E. Spillers, W. H. Crouse, and A. V. Sims met with the constituting brothers and sisters for the purpose of constituting them into a church of Christ. The above mentioned ministers organized into a presbytery—electing J. T. McArthur as moderator and Elder A. V. Sims, clerk. They examined letters from Corinth Primitive Baptist Church at Ty Ty, Georgia, and found letters duly in order. They proceeded to constitute the above mentioned members into a church of Christ, located in Tifton, Georgia. Elder W. H. Crouse delivered the charge to the church, and there were talks by Elders Thomas and Sims.

After the constitution of the church, they had no church home. The Presbyterian Pastor and Elders were approached for the use of their church house until such time as the young church could procure a place and build a church. This request was very graciously granted on the part of the Presbyterian Church and a very nominal fee was charged to cover only incidental expenses. For this Brotherly gesture of the Presbyterian Church of Tifton, the Tifton Primitive Baptist Church will ever be grateful.

On January 7th, 1917, the church met in conference, and by unanimous vote called Elder W. H. Crouse to serve them for the year 1917. Elder Crouse accepted and served the church for sixteen consecutive years—during which time the church had a phenomenal growth, baptizing many members among whom were many of the prominent people of this section of the state.

After looking around, the church members found two lots on the corner of Tift Avenue and Fourth Street, which belonged to the City of Tifton, on which stood the Old Tifton Academy. These lots were purchased from the city of Tifton for $1,500—the city removed the old academy building.

Each member subscribed generously of his or her means toward the building fund for a church. With that subscription as the basis, they went to the business people of Tifton for subscriptions and met a most generous response.

Mr. Charles Fulwood, architect, was employed to draw plans for the church. Mr. Spooner, a well known builder in Tifton at that time, contracted to build the church which was done as speedily as possible. The building, with the furnishings and piano plus the lot, cost $13,500.00.

On April 7th, 1918, with a very impressive program, the dedicatory service was held in the new church. Dr. Baker gave a history of the membership of the church and the reasons for organizing a church in Tifton. Elder Crouse read the church covenant and articles of Faith, with appropriate remarks, and then gave opportunity for remarks by others of the church and congregation. Appropriate talks were made by W. E. Williams, Dr. L. A. Baker, Elder J. T. McArthur, Professor J. C. Scarboro, principal of Tifton Schools, Reverend Warren Watson, pastor of the Wesleyan Methodist Church, Dr. J. M. Price and Professor J. M. Thrash, principal of the Agricultural School. At this meeting, upon the opening of the doors of the church, Mrs. N. E. Lawrence, wife of Elder R. A. Lawrence who lived on the Brookfield road, and Mr. W. Jelks Warren were received by letters—Sister Lawrence from Turner Church and Brother Warren from Hickory Springs Church. Sister Ethel Warren joined by experience and baptism. So, the new church was well launched on its way; the minutes and proceedings of which are on record.

It is desired by the narrator that this history be put on the minutes of the church, if agreeable to the church, and that, from time to time, his history be read to the members of the church down through the ages.

The original members of this church gave of their time, and means, and prayers, and tears, that this church might stand, by the will of the Lord, through many years; that those in this community who love the story of salvation by grace and of the atonement of Jesus on the Cross, might have a place to worship. The only reward sought by them was that this doctrine and this order might be kept pure and unsullied, and that this house and grounds might be held sacred, as dedicated by them, to the worship of God. It was their hope that those of future generations who cast their lot here would appreciate and love this church as they did; always keeping it in good repair and thanking the Lord for those who went before and built this home for them.

May the blessings of God and the direction of the Holy Spirit ever be with those who follow to guide them in the ways of sound doctrine and truth and righteousness.

October 12th, 1946　　　　　　　　　　　　　　　　Dr. L. A. Baker, Narrator.

ST. ANNE'S EPISCOPAL CHURCH

Second Oldest Church Building in Tifton

by Latrelle Tift Rankin

Simple beauty greets a visitor, always welcome, as he enters St. Anne's. Many exclaim and compare this lovely little church, whose doors are always open, to the similarly simple but far more famed "Little Church Around the Corner" in New York City, and the "Wee Kirk of the Heather" or "Little Church of the Flowers" in Los Angeles.

Perfect design and craftsmanship that contribute so much to the interior beauty of the building was the handiwork of local builders who com-

menced work on the church on March 20, 1898. Mr. Edmund Harding Tift, assuming responsibility for providing required material and payments, supervised the construction with untiring zeal.

At the time this work began, C. K. Nelson was Bishop of Georgia, having been consecrated Bishop in 1893. After his consecration, he immediately began locating isolated members of the Episcopal Church, and found three or four communicants in Tifton which, by that time, had grown from merely a saw-mill site to a progressive little town. He sent the Rev. J. W. Turner to conduct monthly services, necessarily on week days as they were held in the Methodist Church building.

Gradual increase in the town's population brought additional Episcopalians, and eventually it became evident that they ought to have a church building. Bishop Nelson heartily approved the project and in a letter to Mr. E. H. Tift, dated February 7, 1898, pledged $300 toward the building.

As work progressed in the building, friends, even though not Episcopalians, showed much interest by cooperating in many ways. Soon the building, second oldest church building in Tifton, was completed and on January 1, 1902, was consecrated by Bishop Nelson.

Since that time many illustrious and fine men have served as ministers at St. Anne's including:

1898—The Rev. J. W. Turner (also served Jekyl Island and Leighton Chapels) organized the Mission.
1899—The Rev. Allard Barnwell
1900—The Rev. T. C. Tupper
1901—The Rev. L. C. Birch
1903—The Rev. Harry Thomas Walden (Cordele)
1905—The Rev. Samuel Denman Day (Dundarf, Pa.)
1909—The Rev. W. L. Mellichampe (Douglas)
1912—The Rev. Gerald A. Cornell
1915—The Rev. John Moore Walker, Jr.
1918—The Rev. William Bee Sams
1922—The Rev. J. Harry Chesley (Diocese of Easton)
1927—The Rev. A. D. Caslor
1929—The Rev. H. S. Cobey (Rector at St. Paul's, Albany)
1932—The Rev. J. F. Wilson
1932—The Rev. John R. Bentley (Augusta)
1942—The Rev. Henry T. Egger (Tifton)
1943—The Rev. Charles E. Crusoe
1946—The Rev. T. E. Mundy.

In September 1940, it became apparent that facilities were needed for a Church Sunday School. The people of St. Anne's met on the evening of September 27 and planned a building to contain an apartment for the rector, a large meeting hall, a kitchen, and storage room. This Parish House, built soon thereafter, serves not only the Woman's Auxiliary and Wardens and Church School, but has been used by the Boy Scouts, the Girl Scouts, the Junior Women's Club, the Tifton Garden Club, and other community groups.

HICKORY SPRINGS CHURCH

by George Branch

Hickory Springs Primitive Baptist Church was organized at Little River Meeting House in 1872. Elder Jacob Young was the first pastor. Charter members are: James Gibbs, Sr., Mrs. Mahala Gibbs, Frances Mayes, J. W. Whiddon, Lucy Whiddon, Frances Whiddon, James Gibbs, Jr., Allen Gibbs, B. G. Willis, Mary Willis, A. E. Clements, James Luke, Matilda Luke, Louisa Jane Branch, James I. Clements, Lott Whiddon, Juda Whiddon, Green Keen, Mathew Bishop, Elizabeth Porter, W. M. Register, Ann Young.

Elder Jacob Young served as pastor from 1872 to 1886; Elder James Gibbs, from 1886 to 1921; Elder J. A. Sutton, 1921 to 1923; Elder Gilford Baker, from 1923 to 1927; Elder W. C. Kicklighter, from 1927 to

1935; Elder A. R. Crumpton, from 1935 to 1943; Elder H. C. Stubbs, from 1943 to 1946; Elder A. H. Garner, 1947 —

The name of the church was officially changed to Hickory Springs in 1902. Ten acres of land were donated to church by James Gibbs, Sr., whose son, James Gibbs, Jr., served as pastor for a long time. The lumber for the present church, which was built in 1886, was sawed from the best timber at a sawmill at Whiddon's Mill Pond, owned by J. N. Whiddon. All labor for building the church was donated by members and friends of the church.

HISTORY OF THE METHODIST CHURCH IN BROOKFIELD
by the Reverend J. H. Bridges

To have lived for nearly three-quarters of a century is an achievement for either a person or an organization. To have lived so long as the center of Christian faith and unselfish service is an honor indeed.

In the year 1878 the Reverend J. J. F. Goodman, one of the pioneer Methodist preachers of this section with Christlike purpose to extend the kingdom, went five miles east of Tifton and organized a new church. The church was named Bethesda and built on land donated by a Mr. Matthews. The building was not only used for worship but served for a time as a public school. Among the charter members were J. B. Coarsey, Ryan Kinard, Sim Harrell, Mr. and Mrs. Tom Baker, and members of the Marchant and Lamp families. On the land adjoining the church was developed one of the best known cemeteries in the county and in whose sacred soil rests today the earthly remains of many of the pioneers of this lovely community.

It is to be regretted that a complete list of the godly ministers who have served this congregation is not available for this record. In that honored list would be found the names of J. J. F. Goodman, P. H. Crumpler, John Taylor, E. E. Rose, M. B. Ferrell, E. L. Padrick, S. S. Kemp, N. H. Olmstead, W. K. Dennis, J. S. Jordan, E. A. Sanders, T. A. Moseley, L. E. Pierce, J. D. Snyder, J. E. Buchannan and others of equal devotion.

In 1903, under the ministry of the Reverend S. S. Kemp, it was decided to move the church building three miles into the village of Brookfield. J. L. Gay, J. N. Brown and J. N. Horne were leaders in this movement. The name was then changed to the Brookfield Methodist Church. It was here that Bishop Arthur J. Moore worshipped as a growing boy and at these altars found the ideals which have led him to a ministry covering the entire world.

One of the striking stories associated with this church is that of the coming of two boy preachers in 1912. Their names were "Arthur Moore" and "John Sharp." Their first act after arrival and before the first service was to remove the doors and windows from the church so as to accommodate the large crowds which they were sure would be coming. Their faith was justified and congregations far beyond the capacity of the building were in attendance. Many were converted and an active Sunday School was organized with Mr. C. V. Taylor as superintendent, a position he filled with fidelity for thirty-six years.

It has been apparent for some years that the old building had served its day. Bishop Moore, John Churchwell, Gus Churchwell, and Nath Coarsey took the lead. The present lot was donated by Nath Coarsey, Sr. The following were named as the Building Committee: A. F. Churchwell, J. H. Churchwell, N. L. Coarsey, Sr., C. B. Coarsey, C. V. Taylor, E. R. Gibbs, J. L. Akins, W. E. Beasley and the Rev. Joe H. Bridges Nathan L. Coarsey, Jr., was named to succeed his father. The plans were drawn and donated by Rev. C. M. Lipham and the construction was under the supervision of Mr. Joe B. Adams. To name those who by love, prayers and gifts have made this beautiful building possible would include the entire membership of the church, a host of friends in Tifton and from over the entire state. Their names are known to God and He will reward them.

HISTORY OF CHULA METHODIST CHURCH
by Mrs. Dan Sutton

Captain H. H. Tift gave the land on which Chula Methodist Church was built about 1913. A. D. Hollingsworth sawed the lumber with which it is built and the people of the community built the church.

Rev. F. A. Ratcliffe organized the church. Some of the charter members are Mr. and Mrs. Albert Whiddon, Mr. and Mrs. Mack Lesueur, and Mr. and Mrs. A. B. Hollingsworth.

The parsonage for the Chula Charge was built several years ago. It burned recently and a beautiful parsonage has been built in its stead.

A long line of preachers has served the church and all have done some good.

Rev. J. H. Bridges is the last pastor serving here for five years. Under his pastorate the church has been painted inside and out and Sunday School rooms have been built.

The church is now heated by gas.

Approximately 50 people were added to the church under Brother Bridges' preaching. The attendance at church and Sunday School more than doubled during the five years. His work with the young people was also outstanding. The church is in good condition in every way and ready to go forward under the guidance of the new preacher—Rev. C. M. Infinger.

THE HARDING METHODIST CHURCH
by Mrs. Dan Sutton

In May 1915, Rev. F. A. Ratcliffe, evangelist, set up his big tent at Harding and began preaching the Word of God. At first not so many people came to hear him, for few people living in the community at that time knew much about the Methodist Church. As the days passed by though the gospel as preached by this grand old man of God and the wonderful singing as led by the Lovett brothers and their sister, Rhoda, began to stir men's souls. The tent was soon crowded to the limit each night for about three weeks. Then came the last night—a night long to be remembered in the Harding Community. The large tent was running over and there seemed to be as many people on the outside as were on the inside.

Forty-four people joined the church during this tent meeting and the Harding Methodist Church was organized. Some who are charter members still worship there regularly as Mr. and Mrs. E. L. Vance, C. J. Hall, and Mrs. Dan T. Sutton. At first they worshipped in a building at Paulk's Crossing. In 1916 the church was built at Harding on two acres of land donated by Captain H. H. Tift. Since then Sunday School rooms have been added, and a vestibule with a steeple.

The first years were trying years. The church had many obstacles from every side, but one by one these were met and surmounted. They lost several of the forty-four members during those years.

Rev. R. W. Cannon was the first preacher. Perhaps our list of pastors is too long for this article but each has come, has done what he could for the church, and has gone on his way, some to very high places as ministers. Our first real revival was accomplished when Rev. H. E. Wells and Rev. Walter Churchwell held a series of services in 1921. Many were added to the church at this time and the church was greatly strengthened.

The Sunday School was organized in June 1915 and has been an integral part of the church ever since. Mr. George W. Blizzard was the first superintendent. Other superintendents who have served several years each are Mr. Henry Mathis, Mrs. Dan T. Sutton and Clarence Sutton.

The Sunday School has never been closed down since it was organized. In the early 1930's it was rated as the outstanding small Sunday School in the South Georgia Conference. Mr. W. S. Kelley was largely responsible for this rating.

The most faithful member of the Sunday School has been and is at the present time, Mr. E. L. Vance.

After the revival in 1921, for many years the Church and Sunday School climbed. Then there was a decline in their services until five years ago when Rev. Joe Bridges was sent to the church as pastor. He, with the cooperation of his flock, has been instrumental in building a strong membership, many of whom are leaders in church work. At present there is a fine progressive Sunday School at Harding, which is doing a great work. They have plans made for the beautification of their church and grounds and hope one day to be an outstanding church of the community both physically and spiritually.

HISTORY OF MT. CALVARY METHODIST CHURCH
by Mrs. Dan Sutton

Mt. Calvary Methodist Church was organized in 1915 by Rev. F. A. Ratcliffe. One hundred and forty-six members constituted the church in its infancy. This church has been on the Chula Charge since its organization and is today perhaps in many ways the strongest church on the charge.

Mt. Calvary Church has had several pastors. Some were faithful and some let the church go downward. The church feels that Rev. J. H. Bridges is due much credit for its present status. He preached in the church and out. He visited everybody and talked and prayed with them. As a result of his hard work around this church, they today have an outstanding Sunday School. In 1942 the average attendance was 25. Today it is 122. Rev. Bridges has baptized a large number of people, both young and old, and has received 93 into the church during his stay there. He helped the church plan a building program which includes adding Sunday School rooms. The church today hopes, with its large cooperative membership, to make great strides forward under the leadership of their new preacher—Reverend C. M. Infinger.

OAK RIDGE METHODIST CHURCH

Oak Ridge church was organized in 1913 by Rev. E. L. Padrick. Services were held under a bush arbor for a year. Then the building was erected. The pastors who served the church were: Rev. E. L. Padrick, Rev. Aaron Kelly, Rev. Salter, Rev. J. P. Chatfield, Rev. C. G. B. Johnson, Rev. J. F. McTier who served the church six years, Rev. W. B. Raburn who served the church at two different times, Rev. C. C. Smoke, Rev. J. N. Snell, Rev. J. W. Williams, Rev. J. B. Roberts, Rev. Ralph Brown, Rev. H. E. Wells, Rev. Charles Britton, Rev. Tom Mosely, Rev. J. L. Peck, Rev. Dewit Shippy, Rev. Gordon King, Rev. Ellkis Miller, Rev. Sam Mayo, Rev. J. H. Bridges, retiring pastor, served the charge for five years. Under his leadership the church buildings were renewed, membersip revived and attendance greatly increased.

Rev. C. M. Infinger is incoming pastor.

At one time the church was very active with every member except one tithing.

W. K. Overby was superintendent of the Sunday School for more than twenty years. Mr. H. J. Vernon followed him as superintendent for twenty-three years.

All other denominations were made welcome and cordially invited to take part in the services. It was the aim of the church to uplift every one and make all feel that they were welcome in God's house. The members felt that this was a spiritual home where comfort, courage, and inspiration could be gotten. Oak Ridge church opened its arms to every hungry soul.

The Baptists of that community were warm-hearted and added greatly to the sweet spirit and well going of the church. They helped in every possible way that they could.

There were no denominational lines to be found. Even those who searched for them could not get a glimpse of one. Cordiality, love, and helpfulness was the goal of the early days of the old church and she did not miss her mark.

HISTORY OF THE TIFTON METHODIST CHURCH

Written by Mr. J. L. Herring and his son, Mr. J. G. Herring

In writing the history of the Tifton Methodist Church, the history of Tifton is also written.

When this church was organized it had five members, the village being made up of saw mill shanties and bar rooms. The bar rooms have been gone for many years. The church helped to close them.

As the settlement grew to the village, the village to the town and the town to the city, the church progressed to the Mission, then to the Circuit, then to the Station and now it counts its membership compared to its organization as more than one hundred to one.

Previous to the organization of the church, the Methodists in Tifton were occasionally served by servants of the Master, notable among them being that earnest, consecrated man, J. J. F. Goodman; also that giant in the forum of debate, Rev. W. S. Armistead. Mr. Goodman was Justice of the Peace at this time. He resigned his office and asked for a license to preach as a local Methodist preacher. This was granted him and he served the church in this capacity as long as he lived.

The church proper was organized by J. J. F. Goodman on the first Sunday in March, 1882. The members at that time were Mr. J. J. F. Goodman, Mrs. Rhoda Goodman, their little son, J. O. Goodman, John B. Greene, Mrs. Julia A. Greene, Mrs. J. E. Knight and her mother, Mrs.

Anderson. It will be seen that except for the pastor the church was organized with only one male member who filled the double duty of class leader and steward. Previous to organization, services where held in a small shanty east of Tift's lumber yard but the Methodist church was officially organized in a small building used as a school house and precinct justice courthouse, within fifty yards of where the present edifice stands. This shanty, insignificant as it was, was burned by an incendiary and in 1884 a larger and better building was erected near what is now the southwest corner of Tift Avenue and Fourth Street. The first floor was used for school and church purposes, the second floor as a Masonic hall. This building was also burned by an incendiary in 1887.

Mr. H. H. Tift gave lots for a church and also a parsonage and a neat wooden building costing about $2,000 begun on the site of the present building. The work was begun in 1888 and finished in 1889. Remarkable to say, three attempts were made to destroy this building by fire while it was in process of erection. As it neared completion, some of the members guarded it nightly. It was while they were doing this that the incendiary was shot and wounded by one of the guards.

When the church was first organized it was a mission of the Alapaha circuit and was served by Rev. W. B. Babcock. In 1885 it was made a part of the Alapaha circuit and the church was served in 1885-86 by Rev. G. R. Parker. It was during the fall of 1885 that a notable revival was held by the pastor, assisted by Rev. E. M. Whiting, in which more than thirty members were added to the church. Rev. J. M. Foster was pastor in 1887-88 while it was still on the Alapaha circuit. In 1896 the Tifton Methodist Church was made a Station with a resident-pastor.

The present church edifice was erected in 1900 and 1901. The Educational Building adjoining the church was built in the late 20's.

No attempt will be made to comment upon the influence for good that the Methodist Church has exerted upon the town and community since its organization. Its good work speaks for itself.

These are the names of the ministers who have served the church: Reverends W. B. Babcock, G. R. Parker, J. M. Foster, J. G. Ahern, L. A. Snow, P. M. Crumples, W. F. Hixon, C. E. Crawley, J. W. Domingos, E. M. Whiting, J. M. Glenn, T. H. Thomson, J. F. Ryder, G. W. Matthews, W. H. Budd, C. A. Jackson, Robert Kerr, J. H. House, W. E. Toroson, H. T. Freeman, N. H. Williams, Reese Griffin, M. P. Webb, J. H. Wilson, W. A. Kelley and L. E. Williams.

THE CHURCH OF NAZARENE

In 1939 the Reverend Byron LeJune, pastor of Nazarene Church in Fitzgerald, held a tent meeting on corner of Fifth and South Park Avenue in Tifton. Seven Tifton people joined this church. There are only two of the charter members who are active now, Mrs. J. P. M. Wadkins and Mrs. H. C. Carmichael. The Reverend LeJune held regular services on Sunday afternoon and prayer meeting on Wednesday night until the accidental burning of the tent. After the tent was burned, meetings were held in the Mrs. H. C. Carmichael's living room until a church was built.

Mr. H. C. Carmichael built the church and leased it for one dollar a year. The Reverend Figgie was the first pastor in the new church building on South Ridge Avenue and Eleventh Street. He was followed by the Reverends Homer Naybors and Aubrey Ponce.

The Reverend W. Lee Gann is pastor now of the Nazarene Church, which has forty-four members. Sunday School, which meets in the new parsonage, has eighty-eight members.

NEW RIVER CHURCH
by H. D. Webb

New River Church was organized in 1887. The first house of worship was built of logs, which Mr. Ryan Kinard, Mr. John Kinard, Mr. George Guest, and the Reverend W. W. Webb cut from young timber near the church environs. These men not only cut the logs but shouldered them to the site where a carpenter was constructing the building. It was used twelve years for a school house as well as a place of worship. About 1889 a frame building was constructed and later used for educational as well as religious purposes until 1893, when a school house was built at Vanceville. A cyclone destroyed the church building in 1913, but the persistent members erected another room afterwards. The church grew until December 22, 1946 when fire destroyed the building. The members are now using the cotton mill church for services until they can erect a new brick building.

The church was organized with twenty members but, its membership has grown continually to one hundred eighty-seven. "New River" has the distinction of leading all other country churches.

HISTORY OF TIFTON PRESBYTERIAN CHURCH
written by
Mrs Frank Corry, Sr., Tifton, Ga.
Mrs R. A. Heinslow, Thomasville, Ga.

Prior to 1899 the small group of Presbyterians living in and near Tifton had no organized church but faithfully held Sunday School in the homes of the members of like faith on Sunday afternoons. On May 7, 1899 the school had met at the home of Mr. M. S. Harrison and after dismissal the adult members remained for conference, at which a petition was written asking Savannah Presbytery to organize a church in Tifton. The petition was signed by Owen L. Chesnutt, Mary A. Chesnutt, Mary M. Chesnutt, Thomas M. Chesnutt, Sallie S. Harrison, Louise T. Harris, Lydia A. Fulwood, Isaac A. Fulwood, Miss Catharine S. Tift, Mrs. Clifford Harris, Abram M. Chesnutt, O. Lee Chesnutt, Moses S. Harrison, Mary E. Harrison, James M. Harris, Mrs. E. C. Tift, W. H. Harris.

This petition was forwarded to Savannah Presbytery and on June 14, 1899 the church was organized with Mr. D. L. Chesnutt as ruling elder and Mr. W. H. Harris as deacon. This organization proceeded with the work of the church and a committee was appointed to secure a suitable location for a building. In November, 1900, the congregation had built and paid for a neat frame building located at the site which is now 210 North Central Avenue. Rev. J. B. Cochran was the first pastor, and services were held the third and fifth Sundays each month.

In the summer of 1906 the building was completely destroyed by a cyclone. For a time services were held in the school building and in neighbor churches; however the membership was so small the burden of support so heavy that all formal services were finally discontinued. The spirit of Presbyterians was not lost, for the few children of the congregation met continuously at the home of Mr. Henry H. Britt and were taught the catechisms and the fundamental doctrines of the church and the love and appreciation of it as an organization.

In the spring of 1911 Rev. Tollett of Macon made three trips to Tifton in an effort to revive interest in the church. His efforts were blessed and through representations made to Savannah Presbytery (by Mr. H. H. Britt and Mr. B. Y. Wallace) at their spring meeting in Blackshear, Rev. George L. Bitzer was commissioned to reorganize the church, and on April 23, 1911 the reorganization meeting was held at the home of Mr. and Mrs. Bennett Y. Wallace. The congregation numbering twenty-one members.

It then became necessary for the new organization to secure a church building, and the building formerly owned by the Missionary Baptist Church was bought, remodeled, and made into an attractive church home. The last of the indebtedness on the building was paid in the spring of 1914. The dedication service was held at the evening service April 26, 1914.

Ministers serving the church are as follows: Rev. W. S. Milner, Rev. Daniel Iverson, Rev. R. M. Man, Rev. H. B. Fraser, Rev. E. S. Winn, Rev. Freeman Parker, and Rev. D. C. Landrum. The present pastor, Rev. John R. Howard came to the church Feb. 1, 1946. Under his able leadership the congregation has grown from 105 to 172 in one church year. On

April 1, 1945 the church went on a self-supporting basis, financial aid having been received from the Presbytery up to this time.

A bronze plaque placed in the church commemorates the long and useful service of Mr. Henry H. Britt and attests the affection in which he was held by members of the church.

As a tribute to their parents, the children of Mr. and Mrs. Britt placed a beautiful Baptismal Font in the building in March, 1947.

SALEM CHURCH

(Copied from Tifton Gazette)

Miss Catherine Tucker gave the following history of Salem church which was told to her by John Y. Sutton, pioneer of Tift county:

Salem Baptist church is the second oldest Baptist church in Tift county. In the latter part of the 19th century a small group of humble hardworking people met in an old log school house for Sunday school and church services. A brush harbor had to be made on one side of the log cabin in order to accommodate the increasing number of people. The church community was very large at that time covering miles around.

Those honest Christians walked to service, rode in buggies, ox carts, and wagons. No matter the type of transportation, they came and all the family with them.

In this little log cabin in the year 1890, Salem Baptist church was organized with only 12 charter members. Wheeler Norman saw the need of a larger and more adequate building and he met with the board of Christian workers and laid his plans before them. He generously contributed the lumber for building and $100 to pay on the construction. The men more than gladly gave their time in hauling the lumber to the place of construction. John Y. Sutton and Henry Willis, assisted by Shabe Conger, Ben Hall, and John Castleberry, gave the boards to be used as the covering. J. B. Arlington agreed to construct the building for $100. In June, 1894, John Y. Sutton contributed benches, some of which are still in use today.

Sunday School was organized with Miss Nora Finsley and Mrs. Charlie Thompson as the first teachers. The first pastor was Rev. J. S. Sauls, of Ty Ty. The church now is a member of the Mell association and has been for years.

HISTORY OF TURNER CHURCH

by Mrs. Dan Sutton

Turner Church has the distinction of being the oldest church in Tift

County. It was establishel July 13, 1866. John McMillan and Ryan Kinard built the church out of logs. Later it was covered with boards and changed a little. In 1929 it was repaired and made more attractive as it stands today. It is a very large building and is always kept as neat and clean as can be.

The first pastors were Richard Tucker and Andrew Connell, both serving the first year. Other pastors before 1914 were Jacob Young, John Churchwell, James Gibbs, John McMillan, Joseph Mixon, and Frank Smith.

One lady who has been attending the Annual Meeting at Turner Church for the past sixty years tells of the thrill the young people would always get when on the Sabbath morning Jacob Young would appear on the opposite side of the river on a big fine white horse and someone would row the flat across to get the preacher and his horse. That must have been beautiful in the sight of God on those Annual Meeting days, particularly, as well as on other meeting days, when people for miles around would arise early, prepare big baskets of food, gather their families together and go marching to Turner Church, there to take part in the singing of grand old gospel songs, and listening to the ministers of God expound the Gospel at great length. Then would come the lunch hour. A great feast was spread under the trees and southern hospitality reigned supreme. When singing was heard in the church the members returned for the communion and footwashing just as they still do today. People were sincere in their religion and they believed in an all-wise, all-powerful God to the uttermost. After the footwashing they "sang a hymn and went out" with enrapt faces because they had worshipped God in spirit and truth.

In those days people came from all directions in road carts, in two-wheeled carts drawn by oxen, on mule back, in wagons, on foot, and in buggies. A woman now living tells how they never missed a service though they had to walk several miles. They carried their shoes until they reached the stream near the church. Here they rested, bathed their feet in the water and pulled on their shoes, and entered the church with uplifted faces.

James Albert Sutton served the church in 1914, R. Allen Lawrence 1915-1917, John Thomas Tyson 1918-1919, James Gibbs 1920-1921, Edd Gilbert Baker 1925-1932, Algier Bishop 1933 and 1934, when he died, and James Albert Sutton finished out 1934. Elder Leonard McMillan has been pastor since 1935 until the present, except two years when Elder Jesse J. Johnston served.

The first four members of the church in 1866 were Mr. and Mrs. Malcolm McMillan and Mr. and Mrs. Daniel Griffin. Outstanding old members were Mr. and Mrs. M. L. McMillan, Mr. and Mrs. Richard Gibbs, and Mr. and Mrs. James McMillan.

Some of the most active members now are Mr. and Mrs. R. L. Mc-

Millan, Mr. and Mrs. Thomas McMillan, Mr. and Mrs. Willie D. Alexander, Mr. and Mrs. Lonnie J. Lawhorn, and Mrs. Lovie Camaron.

There is a large cemetery beside the church where many of these fine God-fearing, God-loving Saints lie at rest.

It is hard to conjecture just the great religious influence this fine old church has had upon the people of Tift County and surrounding counties. Tift County is proud that Turner Church is within her bounds and that the influence from this Church is still felt by many people all over the County.

CHAPTER XIX

CLUBS

BOY SCOUTS
by L. E. Bowen, Sr.

Tift County has had one or more Boy Scuot troops intermittently since about 1915. Until recent years the work has been directed by interested adults and with little or no direct assistance from the national organization, Boy Scouts of America. Mr. A. B. Phillips and Dr. L. O. Shaw were active during most of these years directing the entire activities even to the point of serving as troop scoutmasters. For several years prior to 1940 the Lions Club of Tifton sponsored a troop.

During 1940 representatives from the National Council Boy Scouts of America succeeded in interesting a group of Tifton men in scouting and this resulted in the organization of the Tift District of the Chehaw Council. Ralph Puckett was the first president of the Tift District and served in that capacity until 1946, when L. E. Bowen, Sr., became district president. Since 1940 scouting has made excellent strides in Tifton and Tift County.

There are now five active troops in Tifton, including one negro troop. Chula and Omega also have troops. Cub Scouting is now also on a sound basis with two Cub packs operating. Cub Scouts almost always develop into excellent boy scouts.

Citizens generally are very enthusiastic about scouting, recognizing in this work one of the two or three very best mediums of character building and future good citizens.

GUN LAKE COUNTRY CLUB

Below are the minutes of the first meeting of ths stockholders of the Country Club at Gun Lake on the Alapaha River:

"The Country Club met in regular session, January 5, 1912; the following members present: C. W. Fulwood, acting chairman; J. S. Ridgdill, acting secretary; H. D. Webb, W. W. Timmons, Charlie Mathis. Henry Sutton, L. L. Simmons, Johnathan Walker, W. H. Hendricks, N. Peterson, J. E. Cochran, B. H. McLeod, R. C. Ellis, and W. E. Farmer, by proxy.

"Charter read and accepted by the club. C. W. Fulwood, elected President; B. H. McLeod was elected Secretary-Treasurer.

"Moved and seconded that President appoint three members of the Club to draft Rules and By-Laws for the government of the club. The following draft Rules and By-Laws for the government of the club. The following were appointed: C. W. Fulwood, Charlie Mathis, and H. D. Webb.

"The following members, W. W. Timmons, R. C. Ellis, and L. L. Simmons were appointed to go out and look over the 150 acres of land adjoining the lands belonging to the club with full power to purchase the same if they think it to the interest of the club.

"It was ordered that C. W. Fulwood be paid $40.00 to cover all expenses of getting the club together, with all expenses including advertising cost, etc., and each member was assessed $2.00 to cover same.

"Meeting adjourned to meet when called by President. C. W. Fulwood President; B. H. McLeod, Sec.-Treas."

"(Note. In addition to the members above named, the following were the other Charter members of the club, to wit: H. H. Coombs, W. L. Harman, J. W. Hollis, Jno. Marchant, W. H. Bennett, and J. H. Hutchinson)."

The Country Club, whose membership is limited to twenty members, has had four presidents as follows: C. W. Fulwood, began office, January 5, 1912; 2. R. C. Ellis, began office, January 2, 1915; 3. Raleigh Eve, began office in 1922; 4. Otis J. Woodward, began office March 21, 1941.

Ben McLeod acted as secretary at the first meeting. At the second meeting Henry D. Webb was elected secretary and so continued until fall of 1923. In 1936 he was again elected secretary and has continuously served in that capacity.

The club has numbered among its members through the years many prominent men. George W. Coleman and W. L. Pickard were ardent Ike Waltons.

BRIEF HISTORY OF TIFTON LIONS CLUB
LIONS INTERNATIONAL

As early as 1914, Melvin Jones, the founder of Lions International, endeavored to unite on the basis of unselfish service the business men's clubs in the United States, which were not affiliated with any other national association. This was a distinct departure from the existing practice of forming business men's clubs primarily for business exchange purposes.

On June 7, 1917, many of the clubs with which Melvin Jones had been corresponding were represented at a special meeting called in Chicago, Illinois. The name "LIONS" was adopted and charters were granted. A call was issued, however, for a meeting to be held in Dallas, Texas, October 9-11, 1917, to ratify the action taken at the meeting in Chicago. Approximately 25 clubs were represented at the Dallas meeting, which formally approved the name "Lions" and the granting of charters. The meeting in Dallas, therefore, is known as the first annual meeting of Lions International.

At the close of the fiscal year, June 30, 1944, or 27 years from the time of the organization meeting in Chicago, the International Associations of Lions Clubs was composed of 4,477 clubs with 177,579 members. Lions clubs now total over 4,740 with approximately 210,000 members. Lions now are at work in 15 nations of the world.

The Tifton Lions Club was first organized in November, 1922, with 30 members. On May 6, 1925 this club disbanded with 12 members. On April 15, 1935, the club reorganized with 30 members and has progressed until at present we think we have the best club in Georgia with 35 members. The following Lions have served since reorganization:

Presidents	Year		Secretaries
Herman H. Hill	5-1935 to	1-1936	Charles Harman
Herman H. Hill	5-1936 to	1-1937	Charles Harman
Joe Kent, Jr.	1-1937 to	7-1937	Dr. L. O. Shaw
Herman H. Hill	7-1937 to	11-1937	Joe Kent, Jr.
Ross H. Pittman	11-1937 to	7-1938	Joe Kent, Jr.
Riss H. Pittman	7-1938 to	7-1939	Joe Kent, Jr.
Roy Thrasher	7-1939 to	7-1940	Joe Kent, Jr.
Geo. H. King	7-1940 to	7-1941	Joe Kent, Jr.
G. O. Bailey, Jr.	7-1941 to	7-1942	Joe Kent, Jr.
B. L. Southwell	7-1942 to	7-1943	Joe Kent, Jr.
L. L. Kennedy	7-1943 to	7-1944	T. P. Poole
E. L. Rollins	7-1944 to	7-1945	Turner Rountree

When the club was reorganized in 1935 the meetings were held at Mrs. Walker's boarding house; later, when Mrs. Walker moved away, we moved into the "Lions Den," which was located over Kent's Furniture Store. The meals were brought over from the Kopper Kettle. (This was the worst year of the club, as a matter of fact the club would have gone under if it had not been for a few hard working members who fought valiantly to keep the club alive. Membership dropped as low as 9 to 10. In order to pull the club out of this hole they decided to move from the "Den" to the Myon Hotel (this was in 1937) at which time the progress started that brought the membership up to 25 within a very few months.)

The Tifton Lions club is the oldest civic club in Tifton and has been responsible for a great many improvements in and around Tifton. The Tift County Health Department was promoted by the Lions, Railroad safety crossing signs were suggested. Highway signs installed, glasses and aid to the blind. The Lions take a big portion of the credit for the present airbase, if it had not been for the Lions, Carson Chalk would never have located here, and this is what grew into our present airport. The Lions have donated their time and money to assist the Red Cross, Boy Scouts, and all other worthy organizations. The Lions have cooperated with the Tift

County Chamber of Commerce, the Rotary Club, the Kiwanis Club, the Pilots Club, City and County Commissioners and other civic organizations in Tifton. The Lions are now sponsoring the Boy Scouts of America, Troop 61, which is no doubt the best troop in Tifton. The Lions have helped in the waste paper campaign, in collecting and baling for shipment. The Lions have assisted the schools in numerous ways. The Lions have participated in the scrap iron salvage campaign, war bond sales and all other patriotic movements. We also sponsored the Omega Lions Club of which we are very proud. We have furnished Lions International, District 18B, the following officers:

Zone Chairman (1938-1939) ----------------------------Dr. L. O. Shaw
Deputy District Governor (1939-1940) --------------Dr. L. O. Shaw
Deputy District Governor (1940-1941) --------------Ross H. Pittman
District Governor (1941-1942) ----------------------Ross H. Pittman
Cabinet Secretary-Treasurer (1941-1942) ----------Truman P. Poole

Liberty
Intelligence
Our
Nation's
Safety

PRIMROSE GARDEN CLUB

Primrose Garden Club was organized in 1937 by Mrs. Hull Atwater at the Coca-Cola plant with eight ladies present. Mrs. Atwater was elected the first president. She and Mrs. W. F. Zimmerman are the charter members now in the club.

Among the projects sponsored by the club are:
Members planted the first cut-flower garden at the Tift County Hospital.

Club was hostess to the divisional conference at Abraham Baldwin College.

Mrs. Dwight Knight organized the Forget-me-not Club.

Beautified grounds around vocational buildings at high school, and grounds at grammar school.

Beautified park between Ridge and College Avenues.

Adopted a constructive conservative program.

Established a circulating library within the club.

Still working on highway committee to have objectionable bill boards removed from the entrances to Tifton.

Sending special holiday remembrances to patients at the hospital.

Sending books and magazines to the hospital.

Sponsored several adult flower clubs.

Sponsored a field trip under the direction of Dr. Eugene Heath, president of the Georgia Botanical Society to study native plants.

Entertained Second District Council of Flower Clubs in 1939.

Requested to assist in beautifying grounds of new recreational center.

Hold annual flower shows.

Participated in the Labor Day Parade.

Specialized in Christmas decoration.

Furnished material for the Boy Scouts to build bird houses for city park and private homes.

During the war the club bought and sold war bonds, planted and sponsored victory gardens, and helped with home canning. The members studied home nursing, first aid, nurses' aid and nutrition. The club responded to all other patriotic calls. It furnished flowers for the local airport and local hospital, folded bandages for the Red Cross and local hospital, filled Christmas stockings, worked at the U.S.O. and helped buy a Red Cross Ambulance.

The club is helping develop the Blue Star Highway as a memorial to World War veterans. The purpose of the club is to continue always to try to enhance the beauty of Tifton and Tift County and promote more and better gardens among the members.

The following have served as presidents: Mrs. Hull Atwater, Mrs. Blanton Smith, Mrs Emory Owens, Mrs. Jack Rigdon, Mrs. Malcolm Tyson, Mrs. H. S. Bolton.

The present officers are: Mrs. R. W. Patrick, president; Mrs. Louise Stamps, vice-president; Mrs. J. L. Peacock, Jr., recording secretary; Mrs. Walter Spurlin, treasurer; Mrs. Bruce Donaldson, corresponding secretary; Mrs. Dwight, parliamentarian.

TIFTON'S FIRST KIWANIS CLUB

On April 11, 1922, the first Kiwanis Club of Tifton, Georgia, was organized with 62 members. Mr. Holmes S. Murray was elected president, Mr. Mose Hendry, vice-president, and Mr. Frank NeSmith, secretary-treasurer.

The Presidents of the club for the 12 years of its existence were: Holmes S. Murray, 1922; John L. Herring, 1923; Jason Scarboro, 1924; S. L. Lewis, 1925; H. B. Felder, 1926; H. H. Tift, 1927; J. C. Sirmons, 1928; Charles M. Saunders, 1929; John T. Ferguson, 1930; O. J. Woodard, 1931; W. Bruce Donaldson, 1932; C. W. King, 1933.

The Club was particularly active in Underprivileged Child Welfare, giving Minstrel Shows and operating a swimming pool, the proceeds of which were used in this work. The club worked with the children in the public schools, and was active in Boy Scout, 4-H, Hi-Y and Tri-Hi-Y work. Considerable attention was also given to Town-County relationship. Donations were made to the Georgia Hall Fund at Warm Springs. The Club also operated a Student Loan Scholarship Fund. It cooperated with the Board of Trade in movements for the betterment of the city and projects of public interest.

The charter of this first Kiwanis Club was revoked by the International Board of Trustees on November 8, 1935.

Through the efforts of this club more than 2,000 volumes of books were added to the Library of the Georgia State College for Men, now called Abraham Baldwin Agricultural College.

TIFTON'S SECOND KIWANIS CLUB

The present Kiwanis Club of Tifton was organized on February 15, 1940, with 28 members. Dr. John R. Bentley was elected president, Dr. G. O. Wheless, vice-president, and Mr. Horace P. Morgan, secretary-treasurer.

The Presidents of the club for the seven years of its existence are as follows. Dr. John R. Bentley, 1940; Dr. E. L. Evans, 1941; Dr. A. G. LeRoy (term finished by Orin Mitchell), 1942; Dr. G. O. Wheless, 1943; G. N. Herring, 1944; J. C. Parker, 1945; J. W. Pehler, 1946.

The School Lunch program was started in 1940 with equipment furnished by this Kiwanis Club. This work is one of the main projects of the club at the present time. It is primarily interested in work with Underprivileged Children. The club donated sweaters for underprivileged boys and girls, paid hospital bills for indigent patients, helped to furnish the New County Hospital in 1940, and is active in 4-H Club work, sponsoring various contests, in Boy Scout work, and was identified largely with all Bond Selling campaigns during the war, with Clothing and Food Drives, Red Cross work and War Relief. At Christmas time, baskets are prepared for the needy.

In 1941 Tom Cordell, one of our most active members was elected to the position of Lieutenant Governor of the 3rd Division, Georgia District, Kiwanis International.

THE TIFT COUNTY CHAMBER OF COMMERCE

The Tift County Chamber of Commerce, which marked its 50th anniversary March 10, 1947, was organized in the law offices of Fulwood & Murry, March 10, 1897. It was then called the Tifton Board of Trade and Transportation. J. W. Greer was elected temporary chairman with J. H. Price, permanent secretary, and W. H. Love later elected permanent chairman. A large membership joined at the initial meeting.

The name of this organization, which has been the hub around which the other organizations in the community have worked for fifty years, was changed three times. On May 13, 1910, 67 business men met and organized the Chamber of Commerce from the old Board of Trade, which at that time was headed by John L. Herring. Judge R. Eve gave as a motto for the organization "If it's a good thing, get it for Tifton" and this was adopted unanimously. Officers elected were: C. W. Fulwood, president; E. A. Buck, 1st vice-president; W. W. Banks, 2nd vice-president. The directors included H. H. Tift, W. H. Hendricks, C. L. Parker, J. J. L. Phillips, J. L. Herring, L. P. Skeen, C. C. Guest, Briggs Carson, J. J. Golden, B. W. Mills, W. S. Cobb, John W. Greer, and I. W. Myers.

Some time during the passing years the name was changed back to the Board of Trade. January 9, 1936 the name was changed again to Tift County Chamber of Commerce and has remained that since that time. That year Heber Kent was elected president; E. P. Bowen, Jr., and S. B. Lassiter, vice-presidents; B. H. McLeod, treasurer.

Presidents of the organization during the years include Mrs. P. D. Fulwood (only woman president), I. W. Myers, R. Eve, H. L. Moor, J. S. Taylor, L. E. Bowen, George W. Coleman, Joseph Kent, B. Y. Wallace, H. H. Hargrett, S. B. Lassiter, G. N. Herring, E. J. Bowers, Jr., E. L. Rollins, W. H. Underwood.

Branches of the Tift Chamber of Commerce were the Presidents' Club. organized by Mrs. Fulwood in 1931, and the Ty Ty Board of Trade, organized in 1922 with R. R. Pickett, president.

In 1922 the Tift Chamber of Commerce brought suit before the State Railroad Commission and Interstate Commerce Commission against the railway lines entering Tifton and more just rates were the result. In 1910, the organization campaigned for an auditorium and opera house. In 1912 the project was a better roads campaign. In 1931 the privilege of living in Tifton and in Georgia was stressed. The Chamber worked with the Twentieth Century Library club in 1910 to secure a park site; in 1912 it stressed a 10,000 population for Tifton; in 1920 it helped secure the tobacco stemmery and re-drying plant for Tifton. In 1935 the slogan was "Keep Tifton Trade in Tifton."

The Chamber of Commerce has sponsored many projects for the good of the community. The Retail Merchants committee and the Tobacco Board of Trade have been very active. The Tifton Chamber sponsored the organization of the 319 Highway Association in 1947. Secretaries have included Mrs. Fannie Kate Hill, Mrs. Lillian T. Jones, and S. A. Spivey.

HISTORY OF THE TIFTON GARDEN CLUB

The Tifton Garden Club was organized July 30, 1927 in the offices of the Board of Trade. Fifteen of Tifton's garden-minded ladies were present at the meeting. The following officers were elected: Mrs. J. S. Taylor, president; Miss Fannie Kate Hollingsworth (now Mrs. T. U. Hill), secretary; and Mrs. V. F. Dinsmore, treasurer. A membership committee of five was named with Mrs. W. H. McCartney, chairman; Mrs. J. W. Gaulding, Mrs. C. A. Christian, and Mrs. Rebecca Martin.

The Tifton Garden Club became a member of the Federal Garden Club of Georgia, in the year 1930.

The club cherishes as its prize possession its fraternal relationship with all local organizations. The club has established for itself a reputation for service, cooperation and good-will, which is, after all, the highest goal to be reached by organized civic endeavor.

During the twenty years of activity of the Tifton Garden Club a remarkable change has taken place in the general appearance of the city. In every quarter may be seen the results of the club's example and precept. Green lawns, foundation plantings, flowering trees, evergreen shrubs, and back yard gardens have appeared instead of yard swept premises and disorganized flower plantings.

Space limits a detail record of all of the accomplishments of the Tifton Garden Club.

Major facts in a brief form follow with presiding officers and the club's outstanding achievements.

Mrs. J. S. Taylor—1927-1929

Pioneer work in school and church grounds beautification program. Thousands of roses and shrubs planted in Tifton.

Mrs. W. H. Walters—1930-1931

Promoted plan of outdoor Christmas decorations. First public flower show. Became member of Federated Garden Clubs.

Mrs. Fred Bell—1931-1933

Seven miles of highway No. 41, planted in seedling pines in cooperation with highway department. Fire and vandalism have destroyed all but small percentage.

Mrs. Warren Baker—1933-1934

Handsome granite arch erected in Fulwood Park, at approximate cost of $1,000.00, in honor of Columbus Wesley Fulwood, beloved citizen, who was father and founder of the park.

Mrs. P. D. Fulwood—1934-1935

Granite memorial marker erected in Fulwood Park, approximate cost $500.00, in honor of John Lewis Herring, editor of the Daily Tifton Gazette.

Mrs. J. L. Bowen—1935-1936

Cooperated with the city and W.P.A. in laying water mains and installing general watering systems in the Tifton Cemetery. This project cost more than $1,000.00, made possible the transformation of barren land into a veritable garden of grass, trees and shrubs.

Mrs. E. P. Bowen, Jr.—1936-1938

Municipal rose garden of formal design planted with 300 choice rose bushes in Fulwood Park. Hundreds of azaleas and native shrubs also planted in Fulwood Park. Unsightly snipe signs removed from highway No. 41, through the best residential section of Tifton.

Mrs. T. U. Hill—1938-1940

Planted drive in front of cemetery and alley-ways throughout the Tifton Cemetery with thousands of dogwood and redbud trees. Added numbers of dogwood and redbud trees, and also replanted lost trees of the same nature in Fulwood Park. Dogwood and redbud trees added beauty to the City of Tifton during this period.

Mrs. John Fulwood—1940-1942

Landscaped and beautified the city Water Works with azaleas, camellias, rose bushes and evergreen shrubs. Truck loads of dirt were used to level the lots at the cemetery before re-sodding with Bermuda grass. Approximately 500 seedling pines planted on the lots throughout the Tifton Cemetery.

Mrs. R. S. Dormiey—1942-1944

Attention centered almost entirely on war work. Cooperated with American Red Cross in local departments, such as Production, Surgical Bandages, U.S.O., Citizen's Defense Committees, and War Savings Council. Tift County Hospital grounds landscaped and planted to harmonize with the picturesque beauty of Fulwood Park, which the hospital faces.

Mrs. F. H. Corry—1944-1946

Continued to assist with all local civilian war work. Sponsored the planting of 550 dogwood trees as memorials to the men and women from Tifton and Tift County who were in service for their country. An improvement program for the Tift County Hospital grounds and Fulwood Park included the purchase of new benches and a better lighting system.

Mrs. W. A. Hodges—1946-1948

At the end of one half of the Club's fiscal year a rose garden at the Tift County Hospital was completed. The sole purpose of the garden is to keep fresh roses in the rooms of all patients during rose blooming season.

THE COUNTRY CLUB

In 1927 when J. S. Taylor was president of the Tifton Board of Trade, among the achievements of the year was the Cabin Country Club, now called the Country Club. After the members selected a location, J. L. Hoffman, a landscape gardener who had just completed Radium Springs, Albany, Georgia, laid out an eight-hole golf course. The site is its present location, two and a half miles southwest, just off the paved Tifton-Moultrie highway.

The tract of land acquired by thirty progressive Tifton citizens contained one hundred acres and a lake. This body of water, effected by engineers closing the old McInnis millrace, and the border of stately long leaf pines on the south banks of the lake make a beautiful setting for the clubhouse and golf course. This spot is one of the prettiest outings in South Georgia. Professional golf players assert that this location is ideal for golf. Old settlers say that the fishing there is the best in the county.

For the early settlement of this section pioneers used the water bordering this site for a grist mill, which ground meal for the early settlers. According to tradition, the owner threw up with an ox and spades dirt for one-eighth of a mile. Strenuous labor for several years was necessary in the completion of the millrace. One of the speakers at the initial club banquet facetiously commented: "It is a dam by a mill site; but not a mill by a dam site."

The present membership of this club has grown to about two hundred members. The club house is modern. The original building of logs is used for the caretaker, golf equipment, and lockers.

This location, one-half mile from paved route 50 and one mile from paved highway 41 is accessible to Tifton people.

This project started with an investment of $5,500, but the improvement on grounds, club house, and deep wells have increased investment to $20,000. Jim J. Clyatt was on the grounds committee in the beginning and is still serving in many official capacities.

Mr. J. S. Taylor was the first president of the Country Club, and Mr. L. L. Kennedy is the president now. Mr. Warren Baker, Norman Park, Georgia, served as president and in many official capacities as well as being one of the original stockholders. The late Dr. W. T. Smith, Dr. W. H. Hendricks, Dr. Pittman, the late I. W. Myers, C. A. Fulwood, and the late H. H. Tift, Jr., Cliff Parker, R. S. Short, C. R. Choat, L. E. Bowen, Sr., Ben Bowen, Paul Fulwood, Steve Mitchell, Sr., C. O. England, Sr., J. S. Taylor, Sam Lassiter, Ralph Puckett, and Billie Barlow were original stockholders. The late I. W. Myers, C. W. Fulwood, and H. H. Tift, Jr., helped to organize the club. L. E. Bowen, Sr., the second president, was one of the organizers. Fannie Kate Hollingsworth, former secretary of Board of Trade, rendered valuable assistance to the club.

GARDEN CENTER ESTABLISHED IN TIFTON

Through a generous offer made by the Tift County Chamber of Commerce, the Tifton Garden Club and the Primrose Garden Club have been able to establish a Garden Center in the Chamber of Commerce Building.

The purpose of the Garden Center is to create interest in gardening and flower growing in Tifton and Tift County, and to create or provide a centralized source of information for interested gardeners.

The plan of the clubs is to have attractive furnishings of pictures "in color" of Tifton gardens, comfortable chairs and tables, seasonal flower arrangements at all times and bookshelves for the Garden library.

The clubs hope that Tifton and Tift County gardeners will enjoy and benefit by this public Garden Center. Visitors to our city are cordially invited to visit our gardens and enjoy the Center with us during their stay in Tifton.

TIFTON PARENT-TEACHER'S ASSOCIATIONS

The Tifton Parent-Teacher's Associaitons were organized in the fall of 1928. Mrs. T. A. Mitchell, Sr., Mrs. G. H. Clark, Mrs. J. L. Cochran, and a few ladies from Douglas helped with the organization of the association. At that time a City Council was organized, which functioned until 1936. There was also at one time a City Council. The County Council reorganized in 1945 with Mrs. Earl Olson as president. The three Tifton associations are members of the County Council. The other associations making up the council are Omega, Brookfield and Chula.

No club in Tifton has done more effective work than the Parent-Teacher's Associations, which have sponsored lunch room programs, equipment for playgrounds and lunch rooms, for the high school an eighteen hundred dollar grand piano, which probably now would cost twice as much, furnishing of rest rooms, and suppers to make money for the schools. This year the High School P.-T. A. with Mrs. E. U. Holder president, helped to remove a large debt on the high school lunch room equipment.

Presidents of Tifton Parent-Teacher Associations:

1937-1938—Grammar School, Mrs. E. U. Holder; Junior High School, Mrs. O. M. Sanders; High School, Mrs. W. J. Boyette.

1938-1939—Grammar School, Mrs. J. M. Carr; Junior High School, Mrs. Bob Herring; High School, Mrs. W. A. Rowan.

1939-1940—Grammar School, Mrs. J. M. Carr; Junior High School, Mrs. Bob Herring.

1940-1941—Grammar School, Mrs. Joseph Morton; Junior High School, Mrs. T. C. Tidwell.

1941-1942—Grammar School, Mrs. Joseph Morton; Junior High School, Mrs. Baldwin Davis.

1942-1943—Grammar School, Mrs. Joe Kent, Jr.; Junior High School, Mrs. Baldwin Davis.

1943-1944—Grammar School, Mrs. Joe Kent, Jr.; Junior High School, Mrs. L. O. Shaw. Mrs. Earl Olson was elected to serve the unexpired term of Mrs. Joe Kent, Jr., and Mrs. J. E. Newton was elected to serve the unexpired term of Mrs. L. O. Shaw.

1944-1945—Grammar School, Mrs. Earl Olson; Junior High School, Mrs. J. E. Newton.

1945-1946—Grammar School, Mrs. Earl Olson; Junior High School, Mrs. O. J. Woodward. The County Council was reorganized with Mrs. Earl Olson, president.

1946-1947—County Council, Mrs. Earl Olson; Grammar School, Mrs. J. P. Short; Junior High School, Mrs. R. E. Martin. The High School P.-T. A. was reorganized with Mrs. E. U. Holder president.

1947-1948—City Council, Mrs. J. B. Chapman, Chula; Grammar School, Mrs. J. P. Short; Junior High School, Mrs. R. E. Martin; High School, Mrs. E. U. Holder.

Presidents of Tifton Parent-Teacher Associations:

1928-1929—Council, Mrs. S. A. Youmans; Grammar School, Mrs. A. B. Phillips; Junior High School, Mrs. Lynn Brannen; High School, Mrs. C. A. Christian.

1929-1930—Council, Mrs. P. D. Fulwood; Grammar School, Mrs. Frank Corry; Junior High School, Mrs. A. D. Daniel; High School, Mrs. Ralph Walton

1930-1931—Council, Mrs P. D. Fulwood; Grammar School, Mrs. Frank Corry; Junior High School, Mrs. Joe Kent, Sr.; High School. Mrs. Ralph Walton.

1931-1932—Council, Mrs. A. C. Tift; Grammar School, Mrs. S. R. Bowen; Junior High School, Mrs. G. O. Wheless; High School, Mrs. I. C. Touchstone, Sr.

1932-1933—Council, Mrs. H. S. Garrison; Grammar School, Mrs. S. R. Bowen; Junior High School, Mrs. G. O. Wheless; High School, Mrs. A. J. Whitehurst.

1933-1934—Council, Mrs. I. C. Touchstone, Sr.; Grammar School, Mrs. W. H. Walters; Junior High School, Mrs. G. N. Herring; High School, Mrs. A. J. Whitehurst.

1934-1935—Council, Mrs. C. S. Pittman, Sr.; Grammar School, Mrs. W. H. Walters; Junior High School, Mrs. G. N. Herring; High School, Mrs. J. A. Johnson.

1935-1936—Council, Mrs. Geo. Webb; Grammar School, Mrs. R. C. Bowen; Junior High School, Mrs. C. S. Pittman, Sr.; High School, Mrs. W. A. Rowan.

1936-1937—Grammar School, Mrs. E. U. Holder; Junior High School, Mrs. C. S. Pittman, Sr.; High School, Mrs. W. J. Boyette.

UNITED DAUGHTERS OF THE CONFEDERACY

by Ella Pate Carson

*(Historian of Charlotte Carson Chapter
United Daughters of the Confederacy)*

In March 1908 Judge and Mrs. T. J. Latham of Memphis, Tennessee, en route to their home from Florida stopped in Tifton for a brief stay. Mrs. Latham being Vice-President General of the U.D.C., began looking for material with which to organize a chapter in Tifton. Leading women were contacted and meetings were called at the Myon Hotel. After a few meetings in which plans and purposes were discussed the organization came into being. It was decided to name it the Charlotte Carson Chapter in honor of the widow of the hero of Fort Steadman, Captain Joseph Carson. The following officers were elected:

President—Mrs. Charlotte Briggs Carson
First Vice-President—Mrs. Susie Tillman Moore
Second Vice-President—Mrs. Lelia DeLaughtre Gatchell
Registrar—Mrs. Bessie Willingham Tift
Recording Secretary—Mrs. Mary Williams Giddens
Corresponding Secretary—Mrs. Virginia Cunningham Pinkston
Historian—Mrs. Ella Pate Carson
Treasurer—

Twenty-four members applied for charter. Immediately plans were made to make charter night a public occasion. On April 10, 1908 at eight-thirty, in the evening a program was presented in the school auditorium, now the

Grammar School. Mr. W. L. Harman was master of ceremonies. George E. Simpson made the address of welcome. Rev. Wiley Pipkin, a veteran, gave the invocation. Mrs. Latham presented the charter and also a gavel made of wood from a Tennessee battlefield. Mrs. Carson received the charter and the gavel with words of appreciation. Dixie was sung by thirteen little girls. Little Bula Bivins, granddaughter of Mrs. Carson, sang a popular song. An account of the capture of Fort Steadman was read by Mrs. Susie T. Moore. Estora Timmons read "The Conquered Banner." Lillian Britt sang The Homespun Dress. Nine veterans occupied the stage and gave reminiscences of the War Between the States. The Tifton Band played selections throughout the evening. A color scheme of red and white made the decorations, with a Confederate flag, brought from the battlefield by Veteran M. Dinsmore, occupying a conspicuous place on the stage. Plans were made to observe Memorial Day, April 26. Dr. W. L. Pickard, pastor of the First Baptist Church, Savannah, was chosen speaker. During the thirty-eight years of the chapter's existence Memorial Day has been observed each year. Governor Hoke Smith and Senator Walter F. George are among the eminent statesmen to deliver addresses. Distinguished citizens of Tifton have also served in this capacity.

The next project of the chapter was to plan for a monument. Contributions were solicited from County Commissioners and citizens of Tifton and the county. These generous contributions were encouraging and in April 1909 an order was placed with the McNeal Marble Company. The monument was constructed of Georgia and Italian marble at a cost of $2,000.00. Various methods of raising money to meet the payments were employed such as rummage sales, sales of home-made cakes and candies, ice cream festivals, oyster suppers, theatricals by home talent, and sponsoring of picture shows.

On Tuesday, April 26, 1910, the First Baptist Church was the scene for the program preceding the unveiling of the monument which was located at the intersection of Fourth Street and Love Avenue. The U.D.C. colors, red and white, were used to decorate the church. Briggs and Keith Carson, E. P. Bowen, John Greer and O. Lee Chesnutt were ushers. There was an escort of sixty-two veterans; there were also many visitors from adjoining counties. The officers of the chapter occupied the rostrum:

President—Mrs. Charlotte Briggs Carson
First Vice-President—Mrs. Donnie Traylor Hudson
Second Vice-President—Mrs. Rowena McClendon Parker (Mrs. T. J.)
Treasurer—Mrs. Ida Mae McCormick Johnson
Secretary—Mrs. E. L. Overby
Historian—Mrs. Ella Pate Carson
Mrs. Oren Gatchell and Miss Carrie Fulwood
A choir composed of Mrs. J. J. Golden, Mrs. L. P. Greer, Mrs. Scar-

borough, and Messrs. Davis, Beasley and Myers sang "All Hail the Power of Jesus' Name." Mrs. C. B. Carson presided. W. W. Banks, son of a veteran and the mayor of Tifton, spoke in appreciation of the occasion. The orator of the day, Judge George Hillyer of Atlanta, was introduced by George E. Simpson. After the address, Mrs. Susie T. Moore delivered bronze crosses to eighteen veterans, paying a beautiful tribute to the Confederate soldiers. The following veterans received crosses: O. L. Chesnutt, G. M. Cannon, G. W. Guest, D. A. Fulwood, J. G. McRae, J. C. Sumner, W. A. Patton, W. H. Oliver, D. R. Willis, R. H. Swain, W. W. Webb, C. A. Williams, R. E. Wheeliss, R. H. Hutchinson, M. Dinsmore, B. C. Hutchinson, S. J. Glover, Robert Henderson, and crosses ordered for twelve others had failed to arrive. Exercises were continued at the monument. A chorus of thirteen girls sang "The Sunny South" written by Julia Spalding of Atlanta. Each girl represented a seceding state: Gertrude Robinson, Arkansas; Nellie Timmons, South Carolina; Blanch Britt, North Carolina; Clara Bell Duff, Tennessee; Jacie Webb, Maryland; Nellie Guest, Virginia; Melona Scarborough, Alabama; Ada Padrick, Georgia; Margurite O'Neal, Florida; Augusta Skeen, Missouri; Jennie Soul, Texas; Amelia Hargrett, Mississippi; Estelle Morgan, Louisiana. As Miss Carrie Fulwood pulled the cord that unveiled the monument music played by the band wafted to the breezes. Thus ended a momentous occasion in the history of the Charlotte Carson Chapter U.D.C.

The Charlotte Carson Chapter was the inspiration to the Confederate veterans of the county to organize a camp with the following officers:

Commander—C. A. Williams

First Lieutenant—S. A. Lipps

Secretary—C. F. Miller

Chaplain—W. W. Webb

Editor J. L. Herring was made an honorary member. There were about forty members of the camp which functioned for several years.

No opportunity is lost by the chapter to interest the youth in Southern history. In the spring of 1911 Captain E. V. White of Norfolk, Va., was visiting his niece, Mrs. Joseph Kent; the chapter arranged for him to appear before the school and give an account of the battle between the Monitor and the Merrimac. He having been captain of the Merrimac gave a graphic and authentic description.

In the autumn of 1916 Miss Millie Rutherford gave her famous address on the Old South to a Tifton audience.

Almost every year the Tifton schools have entered the essay contest sponsored by the chapter. In 1909 the chapter furnished a scholarship to a Tift County girl. Liberal contributions have been made each year to the educational fund and to all other causes sponsored by the Georgia Division U.D.C.

In 1930 the graves of thirty veterans were marked. Mrs. Ella Pate Carson was in charge of this project. Markers were placed for: J. B. Arrington, William D. Brady, J. J. Baker, J. T. Beverly, Sr., Solomon Mills Cottle, B. N. Bowen, James Harrison Ford, J. J. Fillyaw, Goodman Bryant, S. J. Glover, J. J. Goodman, F. L. Hall, Robert H. Hutchinson, Luda P. Jones, Benjamin F. Kennedy, Jack Lindsey, J. W. Mitchell, W. A. Nipper, William H. G. Oliver, Anthony Oliver, J. R. Patterson, W. A. Patton, J. F. Paul, Joseph Shirley, Robert H. Swain, G. W. Willis, Barney Willis, James J. Willis, Chesley A. Williams, J. G. Young. Later a marker was placed on the grave of B. P. Leach.

In 1937 Mr. B. P. Leach, the only surviving veteran of Tift County, invited the forty-fourth annual convention of the United Confederate Veterans to meet in Tifton October 13, 14, 15. The Charlotte Carson Chapter sponsored this event. The local staff consisted of Mrs. E. U. Holder, president; Mrs. C. B. Holmes, Mrs. O. J. Woodard, Mrs. A. L. Bowden, Mrs. J. N. Mitchell, Mrs. Joseph Kent, and Mrs. W. L. Gaulding. The Civic Clubs and other organizations contributed toward making this one of the most delightful occasions ever brought to Tifton.

The following have served as presidents throughout the years: Mrs. Charlotte Briggs Carson, five years; Mrs. Ethel McCormick Hendry, (M. E.) four years; Mrs. Rosalie Marshall Mitchell (J. N.), sixteen years; Mrs. Elsberry Dana Kent (Joseph), six years; Mrs Sankie Chiles Holder (E. U.), seven years.

The officers recently elected are:

President—Mrs. J. N. Mitchell
Vice-President—Mrs. E. U. Holder
Secretary-Treasurer—Mrs. S. A. Martin
Corresponding Secretary—Mrs. Joseph Kent
Historian—Mrs. Ella Pate Carson
Program Chairman—Mrs. W. L. Harman
Registrar—Miss Verna Parker.

Active members Charlotte Carson Chapter U.D.C. 1946 and 1947: Mrs. J. N. Mitchell, Mrs. E. U. Holder, Mrs. S. A. Martin, Mrs. Ralph Johnson, Mrs. C. B. Holmes, Mrs. Briggs Carson, Mrs. T. E. Jolley, Mrs. John G. Padrick, Miss Lizzie Fulwood, Mrs. O. J. Woodward, Mrs. W. H. Underwood, Mrs. J. D. Cofer, Mrs. Willard Gaulding, Mrs. J. W. Miller, Mrs. Joseph Kent, Miss Verna Parker, Mrs. Harriet Goodman Harman, Mrs. Marietta Goodman Vickers, Mrs. R. W. Goodman, Mrs. A. L. Bowden, Mrs. Marion Holmes.

Deceased—Mrs. Charlotte Briggs Carson, Mrs. Leila De Laughter

Gatchell (Oren), Mrs. Fannie Lee Thrasher Goggans, Mrs. Ethel Johnson Puckett (W. A.), Mrs. Rowena McLendon Parker (T. J.), Mrs. Leila Estill Hargrett (A. M.), Mrs. Eliza Chestnutt Britt (H. H.), Mrs. Meta Deering Fulwood (C. W.), Mrs. Abbie Clements Rousseau (J. L.), Miss Ava Virginia Baker, Mrs. Ethel McCormick Hendry (M. E.), Mrs. Elizabeth Turner Bowen (E. P.), Mrs. Bessie Willingham Tift (H. H.), Mrs. Belle Willingham Lawrence, Mrs. Grady Cunningham Short (T. H.), Mrs. Virginia Cunningham Pinkston (N. D.), Mrs. Beatrice Hunter Thurman (L. P.), Mrs. Willie Wade Spooner (W. H.), Mrs. Mae Dell Hendricks (W. H.), Mrs. Cora Tyson Hollingsworth.

Confederate Veterans of Tift County, May, 1910—William H. Oliver, M. McIntosh, M. Dinsmore, G. J. Glover, J. G. McRae, A. Johnson, W. W. Webb, B. H. Hutchinson, J. J. Baker, R. H. Swain, W. C. Price, W. A. Patten, T. C. Moore, J. S. Gaulding, W. B. Johns, G. A. Goff, G. W. Guest, S. P. Dubose, J. A. Whaley, J. B. McNeal, A. J. Pope, J. J. Tucker, B. N. Bowen, S. O'Quinn, D. R. Willis, T. M. Green, W. H. Oliver, N. C. Greer, Joel Corley, G. W. Willis, W. H. Partridge.

TIFT COUNTY WELFARE DEPARTMENT
Cassie E. Goff

During the year 1932, there was wide-spread unemployment in Tift County as well as over all of the country. Surpluses were stacked up in warehouses and stock piles while the people who helped to produce them suffered because they had nothing with which to get back these products. It was a problem of national scope.

The County Commissioners, headed by N. L. Coarsey, chairman, and the City Manager George Coleman, accepted a plan to borrow funds from the Reconstruction Finance Corporation through the Georgia Relief Commission for the purpose of employing those in need of work. They appointed a county administrator and a projects engineer. The plan proved totally inadequate. At this point the Federal Government came into the picture. Work relief passed over to Civil Works Administration.

Cassie Goff, the same administrator, was appointed and she became the executive head of operations for the Civil Works Administration in the county. The administrator, a board of five men serving in an advisory capacity, and a staff of from fifteen to twenty assistants, comprised the county department.

Within three months after the work program was instituted, over one thousand unemployed had registered, but the peak of the load of those working at one time was close to five hundred.

Under the Civil Works Administration, those accepted for work relief were paid a minimum of forty cents per hour. The men worked on projects which were beneficial to the general public. In Tift County, drainage for the prevention of malaria was carried on under the supervision of a health engineer. Stumping and clearing land on property of the Georgia Coastal Plain Experiment Station and Abraham Baldwin College were done on an extensive scale.

The work program changed over to the Georgia Emergency Relief Administration in 1934, under which administration it was possible to pay for relief in almost every field of human need Conditions were such that emergency measures were justified and the administrator was authorized to meet drastic needs.

Under this program work was allocated up to the number of hours required by a man to earn his budgetary needs.

In 1935 the activity passed to the Works Progress Administration, with the emphasis again on work relief throughout the Works Projects Administration, which ended in 1937.

Under the Federal Surplus Commodity Corporation, surpluses were taken off a glutted market and turned over to the welfare department to be distributed to those whose need had been established. Thus, they did not compete with private markets, relieved an overload, and enabled the person without sufficient funds to have better food. This program was carried over into the County Welfare Department as was the Civilian Conservation Corps, where unemployed young men were enlisted in work camps for training and conservation of natural resources.

The Tift County Department of Public Welfare, in its present form, was established under the Reorganization Act of 1937, a Georgia law which set up a welfare department under the jurisdiction of the State Department of Public Welfare in each county. Under this law, a county welfare board of five members, headed by Chairman, Sam Lassiter, was appointed by the State Director of Public Welfare. The executive head of the county department was known as the county director. Cassie E. Goff, who had administrated all of the previous assistance programs, was appointed by the county board, approved by the State Director.

The plan of operations for the County Welfare Department was designed to meet approval of the Social Security Board, and the provisions of the act enabled state residents to receive benefits provided under certain State and Federal laws.

When the State Welfare Department was set up in 1937, relief giving was segregated into categories. The Tift County Department of Public Welfare was conscious of the variety of its community problems. Every effort was sustained to keep the administration well rounded and develop all resources to meet varying needs.

The number applying for assistance far exceeded the expectancy. County offices were deluged with old age assistance applications. In Tift County, a sole director was provided on the staff by the state plan, and often she spent the entire day taking applications, with still at night a waiting line which she had been unable to interview. Before the applications could be approved, a field investigation had to be completed. A brief, recording all documentary evidence used in setting up eligibility, was filed and the case given to the Board for its decision. With registration reaching one hundred per month, the office was almost deadlocked at first. After the director's day was taken up with applications, there was little time left for completing claims. Soon the Tift County authorities saw the wisdom of employing additions to the staff.

Probably the major activity of the Welfare Department during its first years was to administer old age assistance. Because it required a minimum age limit in order to qualify, many people over sixty-five confused it with an old age pension. Disappointment was expressed when people of sixty-five years of age learned that the plan was not designed for those whose living needs were met from some other source. Indeed, many people refused to accept the grant when they learned that liens were taken on their property. This practice was early discontinued and the interpretation of need has grown more liberal as the years have passed.

The Tift County Department granted full need based on a minimum standard, from the beginning of the program in 1937 until May 1939 when lack of funds forced a cut. In 1946, it was again possible to raise grants to 85% of the standard, but limit of funds allocated to the county held down the total number of those receiving assistance.

Aid to dependent children provided a plan for those under sixteen who were deprived of parental support. Among its major aims were to enable a widowed mother to keep her children with her, to hold families together, to strengthen the home situation of those groups deprived of a bread winner.

It was hoped that under this plan the orphaned child might have the same health, education, and welfare advantages as other children. The program has met such a definite need, one wonders why the country was so long making a place for it.

A plan of assistance for the blind was also inaugurated when the Department was set up in 1937.

When the welfare office was established in 1937, it was again a county organization, although it administered benefits drawn from Federal and State sources. Upon the advice of the State Welfare Department, the local alms house was closed and general relief passed over from the County Commissioners office to the Welfare Department This change threw the welfare doors wide open, for General Relief is assistance to the needy without category. Every person in this group who could qualify was shifted to some other plan.

Previous to 1937, a goodly proportion of the county welfare funds had been spent for medical care and this factor influenced the demand made upon the Welfare Department.

Crippled Children's service was available through the Welfare Department. Crippled children referred by doctors were invited to clinics set up by a staff of doctors and nurses in various sections of the State. After examination and diagnosis, orthopedic cases were treated by the State Crippled Children's Service. In Tift County, however, treatment had already broadened out beyond this scope through the use of other funds. The Georgia Crippled Children's League became an important factor in the treatment of children. It was their policy to accept any handicapped child and they cooperated with the Welfare Department in a willing way. They were of tremendous value. The National Foundation for Infantile Paralysis was another coordinating service. They accepted welfare cases for treatment and in turn the Department did investigations for them. Local churches and civic clubs have had an important share of the activity in this field for when called upon, they never failed to respond.

As the years passed, the programs that were no longer needed were closed. The surplus commodity plan and the work programs were ended in 1937. The Welfare Department's functions have changed to meet changing needs.

During the Second World War, the Director served as medical field agent to the Selective Service Board and was available for special reports to other Government departments. This plan was followed by another service added in behalf of the State Hospital at Milledgeville. The case workers are doing psychological case histories for the use of the psychiatrist in diagnosis and treatment of patients.

TIFTON MASONIC LODGE, NO. 47

Chartered November 1, 1883, at Tifton, in Berrien County. First officers named on charter: J. S. Goulding, Worshipful Master; J. L. Matthews, Senior Warden; J. G. Graydon, Junior Warden.

Grand Lodge Officers: John S. Davidson, Grand Master; James M. Rushin, Deputy Grand Master; Reuben Jones, Senior Grand Warden; J. H. Estill, Junior Grand Warden; Joseph E. Wells, Grand Treasurer; J. E. Blackshear, Grand Secretary.

First return of officers and members made to the Grand Lodge Office, in 1884; J. S. Goulding, Worshipful Master; J. L. Matthews, Senior Warden; J. G. Graydon, Junior Warden; J. W. Overstreet, Treasurer;

L. J. Riggins, Secretary; J. D. Calhoun, Senior Deacon; H. C. Overstreet, Junior Deacon; D. McInis, Senior Steward; J. Pope, Junior Steward; B. J. Holland, Tyler; S. N. Adams, W. S. Bussey, H. C. Baker, Zachariah Bass, J. L. Bass, F. M. Coker, R. V. Douglas, J. J. F. Goodman, J. B. Huff, R. T. Kendrick, J. E. McRae, John Murrow, J. W. Morrison.

Following are the names of Worshipful Masters, Secretaries and Treasurers who have served the Lodge:

Master   Secretary   Treasurer

1885—J. S. Gaulding, J. G. Graydon, J. W. Overstreet.
1886—J. S. Gaulding, L. J. Riggins, J. G. Graydon.
1887—J. S. Gaulding, J. A. McCrea, J. G. Graydon.
1888—J. S. Gaulding, J. E. Knight, J. G. Graydon.
1889—J. S. Gaulding, J. E. Knight, J. G. Graydon.
1890—J. S. Gaulding, M. A. Sexton, J. G. Graydon.
1891—J. B. Hannon, W. H. Love, J. G. Graydon.
1892—C. A. Williams, E. E. Youmans, J. G. Graydon.
1893—F. G. Boatright, W. H. Love, J. G. Graydon.
1894—John Pope, W. H. Love, J. G. Graydon.
1895—W. H. Love, J. A. McCrea, J. G. Graydon.
1896—J. S. Gaulding, B. T. Cole, J. G. Graydon.
1897—W. H. Love, O. L. Chesnutt, E. P. Bowen.
1898—John G. Graydon, O. L. Chesnutt, E. P. Bowen.
1899—W. F. Rudisill, O. L. Chesnutt, E. P. Bowen.
1900—J. S. Gaulding, O. L. Chesnuttt, E. P. Bowen.
1901—J. S. Gaulding, O. L. Chesnutt, E. P. Bowen.
1902—J. S. Gaulding. O. L. Chesnutt, E. P. Bowen.
1903—G. L. Blalock, O. L. Chesnutt, E. P. Bowen.
1904—T. C. Gray, O. L. Chesnutt, E. P. Bowen.
1905—M. M. Haygood, O. L. Chesnutt, E. P. Bowen.
1906—M. M. Haygood, O. L. Chesnutt, E. P. Bowen.
1907—T. A. Shipp, Jr., G. L. Blalock, E. P. Bowen.
1908—J. S. Gaulding, G. L. Blalock, E. P. Bowen.
1909—J. S. Hutchinson, G. L. Blalock, E. P. Bowen.
1910—J. S. Hutchinson, G. L. Blalock, E. P. Bowen.
1911—M. Tucker, G. L. Blalock, T. D. Smith.
1912—M. Tucker, G. L. Blalock, T. D. Smith.
1913—Alex Kemp, G. L. Blalock, E. P. Bowen.
1914—W. W. Banks, G. L. Blalock, E. P. Bowen.
1915—S. F. Overstreet, G. L. Blalock, E. P. Bowen.
1916—Alex Kemp, G. L. Blalock, E. P. Bowen
1917—Alex Kemp, G. L. Blalock, E. P. Bowen.
1918—Alex Kemp, Frank NeSmith, E. P. Bowen.

1919—S. A. Matthews, G. L. Blalock, E. P. Bowen.
1920—A. J. Hutchinson, R. M. Lankford, E. P. Bowen.
1921—C. W. Durden, R. L. Little, E. P. Bowen.
1922—E. Lloyd Knight, R. H. Little, E. P. Bowen.
1923—George P. McCranie, R. H. Little, E. P. Bowen, Sr.
1924—Linwood Pickard, R. H. Little, E. P. Bowen, Sr.
1925—J. H. Hutchinson, E. O'Quinn, Jr., E. P. Bowen, Sr.
1926—B. K. Hardison, E. O'Quin, Jr., E. P. Bowen, Sr.
1927—B. K. Hardison, E. O'Quin, Jr.-I. Y. Conger, E. P. Bowen, Sr.
1928—C. C. Stripling, I. Y. Conger, E. P. Bowen, Sr.
1929—W. A. Ross, I. Y. Conger, E. P. Bowen, Sr.
1930—W. T. Roughton, I. Y. Conger, E. P. Bowen, Sr.
1931—I. Y. Conger, J. B. Hollingsworth, E. P. Bowen, Sr.
1932—S. L. Marr, W. T. Roughton, E. P. Bowen, Sr.
1933—Jas. R. Belflower, W. T. Roughton, E. P. Bowen, Sr.
1934—B. K. Hardison, W. T. Roughton, E. P. Bowen, Sr.
1935—J. M. Tyson, J. B. Hollingsworth, E. P. Bowen, Sr.
1936—E. W. Spooner, J. B. Hollingsworth, E. P. Bowen, Sr.
1937—F. B. Wilson, J. B. Hollingsworth, E. P. Bowen, Sr.
1938—B. K. Hardison, J. B. Hollingsworth-Jas. R. Belflower, E. P. Bowen, Sr.
1939—J. M. Malloy, Jas. R. Belflower, E. P. Bowen, Sr.
1940—J. M. Malloy, Jas. R. Belflower, E. P. Bowen, Sr.
1941—Ira D. Hutchinson, Jas. R. Belflower, E. P. Bowen, Sr.
1942—Joel Hubbard, Jas. R. Belflower, E. P. Bowen, Sr.
1943—Rev. F. O. Mixon-J. P. Culpepper, Jas. R. Belflower, I. L. Conger.
1944—Joel Hubbard, Jas. R. Belflower, I. Y. Conger.
1945—Joel Hubbard, Jas. R. Belflower, I. Y. Conger.
1946—Moss G. Dozier, Jas. R. Belflower, I. Y. Conger.
1947—Joel Hubbard, Jas. R. Belflower, I. Y. Conger.

There are three hundred-fifty members of the Tifton Lodge and this organization owns its three-story building.

TIFTON SHRINE CLUB
by J. W. Pehler

The Tifton Shrine Club was organized in December 1945. Formal acceptance of charter took place at a dinner dance held at the Myon Hotel on May 8, 1946. The charter was presented by the Illustrious Potentate John C. Hebmken of Alee Temple, Savannah, Georgia.

Club officers are: John W. Pehler, president; Eben W. Spooner, vice-president; B. L. Hinson, secretary; C. C. Robinson, treasurer; Frank H. Smith, director; James R. Belflower, director; E. S. Grant, director; W. T. Hawkins, director.

This club consists of members from an area including a radius of thirty miles surrounding Tifton. The purpose of the club is to help with all civic affairs in the community.

VETERANS OF FOREIGN WARS

The Veterans of Foreign Wars of the United States traces its origin to a group of thirteen Spanish-American War Veterans which was formed in 1899. In the forty-seven years intervening, the Veterans of Foreign Wars has grown to a membership of about 2,000,000 members, and every member a veteran of Overseas Service. The Veterans of Foreign Wars is today one of the largest if not the largest Veterans organization in the United States. Our commander-in-chief today is Joseph M. Stack.

The local Veterans of Foreign Wars post, named in honor of the first Tift County boy killed in action, Garland Anderson of Omega, was organized in 1946. He was killed at Pearl Harbor in the beginning of the war. Until April 1946 all men who joined were charter members.

The following officers were in command in 1946: Dan Moor, commander; Oria Powers, senior vice-commander; L. U. Payne, junior vice-commander; Bobby J. Mixon, quartermaster. Trustees: George Slager, Harris Walker, Fred Durden.

WOODMEN OF THE WORLD
PRESENT OFFICERS OF CAMPS IN GOOD STANDING
AS OF APRIL 15, 1947
144 GEORGIA

Financial Secretary ___A. L. Bowden _____P. O. Box 143, Tifton, Ga.
Banker _____._____ _____102 W. 7th St., Tifton, Ga.
Consul Commander___Joseph K. Branch _____215 13th St., Tifton, Ga.
Adviser Lieutenant __M. M. Fletcher _____R.F.D. Tifton, Ga.
Escort _____R. B. Hughes _____Tifton, Ga.
Watchman _____J. D. Hayes _____Prince Ave., Tifton, Ga.
Sentry _____I. D. Peters _____316 S. Ridge Ave., Tifton, Ga.
Chairman of Auditors.J. M. Bailey _____801 Murray Ave., Tifton, Ga.
Auditor _____W. G. Massey _____110 W. 8th St., Tifton, Ga.
Auditor _____M. C. Holmes __409 N. Central Ave., Tifton, Ga.
Dist. Field Mgr. ____A. L. Bowden _____110 W. 8th St., Tifton, Ga.

317 GEORGIA

Financial Secretary ___M. D. Vinson _____P. O. Box 29, Ty Ty, Ga.
Banker _____Nas Gibbs _____R.F.D. 2, Ty Ty, Ga.
Consul Commander ___Chas. Walker _____R.F.D. 2, Ty Ty, Ga.
Chairman of Auditors_W. S. Gibbs _____R.F.D. 2, Ty Ty, Ga.
Auditor _____L. B. Lyons _____R.F.D. 1, Tifton, Ga.
Auditor _____J. W. M. Tomberlin _____R.F.D. 3, Ty Ty, Ga.

OMEGA CAMP 1404

Financial Secretary ___John B. Mallory _____Omega, Ga.

Camps organized in towns located in Tift County, Georgia.

Camp No.	Location	Organized	Charter	Status	
144	Chula	8- 1-03	3-11-04		
144	Tifton	8- 1-03	3-11-04	Good standing	4- 1-47
317	Ty Ty	5- 8-08	6- 9-08	Good standing	4- 1-47
324	Omega	6-24-08	8-25-10	Defunct	6-21-20
347	Eldorado	10-29-08	9-16-09	Defunct	5-19-20
581	Unionville	6-18-12	9-17-13	Defunct	6-30-14
727	Brookfield	1-28-14	no charter	Defunct	2- 9-16
1088	Abba	6- 5-19	no charter	Defunct	4-16-20

We are only able to furnish the names of the charter officers of one Camp, same being Omega, Georgia, No. 324:

Consul Commander _____Guy A. Cox
Adviser Lieutenant _____W. C. Woodall
Banker _____W. M. Logan
Financial Secretary _____W. H. Young
Escort _____W. T. Deane
Watchman _____J. S. Johnson
Sentry _____S. S. Bass
Manager _____S. M. Hall
Manager _____V. L. Horne
Manager _____W. B. Woodall
Physician _____Irwin Willis

The present membership of Camp at Tifton is 527; Camp at Ty Ty is 51, Camp at Omega is 31.

PURPOSE OF THE WOODMEN OF THE WORLD LIFE INSURANCE SOCIETY

The objects of this Society shall be to combine white persons of sound bodily health, exemplary habits and gool moral character, under the age of sixty years, into a secret, fraternal beneficiary and benevolent Society; provide funds for their relief; comfort the sick and cheer the unfortunate by attentive ministrations in times of sorrow and distress; promote fraternal love and unity; to issue to its members, either with or without medical examination, benefit certificates providing for death benefits and/or endowments, annuities, retirement income, disability, monument, accidental injury and death, sickness and hospitalization benefits, and may provide for cash surrender and loan values, extended and paid-up insurance, and other withdrawal equities and non-forfeiture options.

THE TIFTON JUNIOR WOMAN'S CLUB

The Tifton Junior Woman's Club was organized in April, 1940, by Mrs. N. Peterson, state officer of the Woman's Federation. Members included young women residents not passed the age of 35, who in cooperation with Mrs. Peterson organized to foster interest among its members in social, economical, educational, and cultural conditions of the community, and to support civic and charitable enterprises by volunteer service and other available means.

Mrs. E. L. Rollins was the first president, and charter members included: Mrs. Johnson Goodman, Mrs. H. E. Huff, Mrs. R. E. Jones, Mrs. Ray Shirley, Mrs. E. L. Rollins, Mrs. Ross Pittman, Mrs. P. D. Fulwood, Jr., Mrs. Ido Touchstone, Jr., Mrs. C. S. Pittman, Jr., Mrs. J. P. Short, Mrs. George Wright, Mrs. Jack Rigdon.

HISTORY OF TIFTON MUSIC CLUB
by Mrs. M. D. Braswell

In 1905 the Tifton Music Club was merely a small group of women whose duty was to provide all musical programs for the Twentieth Century Library Club, a club which was the oldest civic organization in Tifton. It soon became evident that all of Tifton's musical talent was not being reached, and, as the Georgia Federation of Women's Clubs was urging the organization of music clubs throughout the state, a committee was appointed to organize a separate music club and to federate as such. In September 1920, under the splendid leadership of Mrs. Nichols Peterson, a call was made to all who were interested. The meeting was inspiring and full of enthusiasm, and Mrs. T. J. Durrett, of Cordele, Georgia, assisted in perfecting the plans for this new organization. The charter members were Mesdames J. J. Golden, W. B. Bennett, Julian Peeples, Nichols Peterson, and Miss Josie Golden. The officers selected were Mrs. J. M. Paulk, president; Miss Elizabeth Lawrence, vice-president; Mrs. W. B. Bennett, recording secretary: Miss Josie Golden, corresponding secretary; and Mrs. Julian Peeples, treasurer.

The first meeting was held in October 1920, and it was decided to call the club Tifton Symphony Club, but at the December meeting the name was changed to The Tifton Music Club, with a limited membership of forty. During the next two years the club was quite active in the work with the General Federation of Women's Clubs, and Miss Leila Julian (now Mrs. Allen Garden, of Fitzgerald) was chosen as the first delegate to go to the State Federation of Clubs at Savannah, Georgia.

In 1922 it was decided to withdraw from the General Federation of Women's Clubs and became a member of the State and National Federation of Music Clubs.

With this limited number of members, the Tifton Music Club became one of the strongest, most active, and interesting organizations in Tifton. Officers were elected annually for four years, but beginning in 1924 they were allowed two years in office. Meetings were held twice during the month and the programs presented were very outstanding in the selections of classics, and compositions of our own composers, whose melodies and arrangements will never be equalled nor surpassed. Among the presidents who served so efficiently were Mrs. J. M. Paulk, a musician of rare ability, and who for years held the highest place in music in the Tifton Schools. Other presidents were, Mesdames J. J. Golden, Julian Peeples, W. L. Harman, John Waters, W. B. Bennett, W. A. Puckett, M. E. Hendry, I. C. Touchstone, John Ferguson, K. S. Trowbridge, C. W. King, B. L. Southwell, J. N. Mitchell, C. J. Woodard, J. J. Clyatt, Agnew Andrews, Frank Youmans, John Corry (formerly Miss Elizabeth Whiddon), and Mrs. John Turner, who now occupies the president's chair until June 1948.

Many efficient co-workers have served during these years and a number of artists of note and Glee Clubs of national fame aided in the development and interest of the club. Out of the Tifton Music Club many musicians, singers and leaders now occupy enviable places in the musical world.

Among the members whose name is outstanding is Mrs. W. A. Puckett, a composer of note, though her quiet modesty and retiring disposition kept her from being known nationally. For her closest friends she often played many of her countless compositions, which possessed a wealth of pure unrivalled music, ever lingering in the hearts and minds of those who had the rare privilege of hearing her. She was an organist for the Tifton Methodist Church for many years, and many people came just to hear her play, for she was a genius—a soul embedded in music of inexpressible charm.

Another member of the club whose fame became national was Nell Howze, a most gifted vocalist. She was known in the radio world and also in the movies, and her most outstanding work was with Schuberts Company, of New York, which brought her deserved popularity.

Another member of whom the music club is justly proud is Mrs. J. J. Clyatt, formerly Miss Josie Golden, who was a charter member while a college student. She received her degree in piano and organ at Shorter College, in Rome, Ga., and her post-graduate work was with the American Institute of Applied Music, in New York. Mrs. Clyatt held office of District Director of Music for six years. In 1930 she was elected president of the Georgia State Federation of Music Clubs, which place she held for four years. It was due to her untiring efforts that the Tifton Music Club was hostess to the Georgia State Federation of Music Clubs in 1930. (Mrs. M. E. Hendry, who was president of the club at this time, with her most efficient assistants, made this meeting one of the greatest events in the history of the club.) Mrs. Clyatt is a member of the National Board of Directors and is a director for life for the Georgia State Federation of Music Clubs. Her motto is, "Today's preparation is the basis of tomorrow's progress."

As a member and president of the Tifton Music Club, Mrs. Agnew Andrews, who came to Tifton in the past few years, has been a very outstanding asset to the musical circles. She had a very successful two years as president. Then she accepted the work as director of music in the Tifton Schools, which work deserves much praise and appreciation. Each year her excellent programs presented have been worthy of note, for they not only brought music to the children, but found hidden talent in many of the children who came under her supervision. Mrs. Andrews part of the time contributed her services as director of Tifton High School Glee Club.

Among the great artists of the club are the names of Hugh Hodgson, composer of note and director of music at the University of Georgia at Athens, Ga.; Minna Hecker, Professor Maerz, Macon, Ga.; Franceska Lawson, vocalist from New York, and Miss Irene Leftwich, well known pianist, and many others. The Emory University Glee Club, who sang before crowned heads of Europe, was guest of the club on several occasions; also, the University of Georgia Glee Club.

The Tifton Music Club is not only recognized at home for its splendid worth and talent, but is recognized by the state for its valued leaders and outstanding musical programs given during the years past.

Cooperation and music of high quality has always been the club's goal. "Music, 'Tis the cradle of God's love."

TWENTIETH CENTURY LIBRARY CLUB
by Mrs. N. Peterson

From its pinnacle of forty-two years of public service the Twentieth Century Library Club has every reason to look back on its progress with joy and satisfaction.

On February 3, 1905 nine women responded to the call made by Mrs. N. Peterson to meet at the home of Mrs. E. H. Tift (now Frank Corry home) on Love Avenue for the purpose of organizing a club that would be interested in promoting a public library for Tifton as well as self culture. These women were Mesdames W. O. Tift, J. A. Peterson, H. S. Murray, I. L. Ford, R. W. Goodman, E. H. Tift, W. S. Walker, Mrs. N. Peterson and Miss Mary Carlton (Mrs. R. D. Smith). They constituted the charter members of the club. Mrs. W. O. Tift was elected the first president; Mrs. N. Peterson, secretary-treasurer. The dues were $1.00 per year.

The fact that the membership was limited to twenty-five was due to meeting in the homes, but the growing interest in the library and the need for a larger membership forced us to seek larger quarters at the end of the first year.

Our first move was to the Bowen building corner of Love Avenue anl Second Street. We moved next to the Tift building where Capt. Tift had donated four large rooms upstairs. After Wade-Corry rented the building they needed more storage space so we moved down on Main Street over Roberts Dry Goods store where we remained until we had sufficient funds to buy the J. J. L. Phillips home on the corner of Central Avenue and Twelfth Street. This building we remodeled into one of the most beautiful club houses in the state. When it was completed and furnished we had spent about $15,000.00, but felt amply repaid for we not only had ample space for the library, lovely club rooms, but also a splendid auditorium to be used by the public for all kinds of public functions. It is rented to the Catholics each Sunday morning for eight o'clock mass. The Karn Kindergarten is also taught there.

The club hose is free of debt and the club members are enjoying their first freedom after twenty-five years moving from one building to another.

The City and County have contributed to the upkeep of the library for the past several years, giving the women more time for other duties. Being just a little older than the County, the Womar's Club has been a vital factor in promoting, from the creation of the county, every movement for both the city's and county's advancement, especially in matters pertaining to civics, health, and education.

Although we could not vote for about fifteen years, we were active in seeing that those who could do so went to the polls and voted for local tax, bonds, and any other matters necessary to put Tifton and Tift County to the front with their fine school system. This program was particularly true concerning Abraham Baldwin Agricultural College from the time it began as the old Eleventh District Agricultural and Mechanical School.

We rendered valiant service to this struggling institution for a period of years. We paid every expense, even to graduating flowers, for a Tift County girl who could not have gone to school without this assistance. Later she was able to assume the support of her widowed mother and several brothers and sisters. Small gifts and loans were made to other boys and girls needing help for their education.

When Mr. J. L. Herring died the club women raised $500.00 for a scholarship fund to be used by the A. & M. School for boys or girls whom the faculty thought worthy.

We were unwise in turning the entire sum over to the school without better guarantee, as poor management resulted in the fund doing but little good. We blame the terrible depression more than any thing else for its loss.

The work that really put the club women in the eye of the public was with the rural schools of the county. "Adopting a Rural School" became their slogan. So unique in plan and execution was this program that Tift County gained state and national fame for rural work. The work was featured in the November, 1915 issue of McCalls Magazine, Woman's World, and many state papers. Franklin K. Lane, when Secretary of the Interior, asked that 5,000 copies of plan be put in the department for rural education. We know that had it not been for the timely assistance of the club women in helping to mold public opinion our consolidated schools would not have existed as early as they did.

Being the first and only civic club in Tifton, we are proud to be the mother of the Tifton Music Club, the Parent-Teacher Association, the Junior Woman's Club, and Garden Club, which functioned at first as Tifton's Better Homes and Gardens. Later both the music and garden clubs withdrew from the mother club and went into their own state federations.

All of the federated clubs in South Georgia give the club women of Tifton a vote of thanks for starting the movement for organized club work by inviting the Georgia Federation of Women's Clubs to meet in Tifton in the fall of 1907. There were only two federated clubs south of Macon until that time.

The Club is now functioning under the following committees: Fine Arts, Conservation of Natural Resources, Education, Citizenship, Public Welfare, and International Relations, American Home.

No club women anywhere rendered greater War Service in every de-

partment than the women of Tifton.
The following have served as presidents:

*Mrs. W. O. Tift—1905-1906
*Mrs. H. H. Tift—1906-1937
Mrs. J. C. Parker—Feb. 1937-May 1937 (unexpired term)
Mrs. N. Peterson—1937-1939
Mrs. J. J. Clyatt—1939-1941
Mrs. G. O. Wheless—1941-1944
Mrs. J. J. Clyatt—1944-1945
Mrs. W. H. Underwood—1945-1947
Mrs. I. C. Touchstone, Sr.—1947—

The club has furnished the following State Federation Officers:
Corresponding Secretary—Mrs. G. O. Wheless _____1944-1946
State Treasurer—Mrs. G. O. Wheless _____1946-
Director for Life, Georgia Federation Women's Clubs—Mrs. N. Peterson
—*Mrs. H. H. Tift

The club has had a unique history in that it had the same president for thirty-one years. It was due to her wonderful executive ability, and lovely, sweet, Christian character that Mrs. H. H. Tift was able to hold the love and respect of the women so long.

ROTARY CLUB OF TIFTON

The Rotary Club of Tifton received its chapter April 9, 1937. The club began with the following twenty-six charter members: E. P. Bowen, Jr., J. L. Bowen, L. E. Bowen, J. L. Brooks, C. R. Choate, Cecil Clark, J. J. Clyatt, Frank H. Corry, W. Bruce Donaldson, Jr., Geo. P. Donaldson, P. D. Fulwood, James A. Harvey, John G. Herring, E. U. Holder, Joseph Kent, S. B. Lassiter, J. C. McNeese, I. W. Myers, Carl S. Pittman, Ralph Puckett, Albert Rowe, R. D. Smith, J. S. Taylor, Wheeler Willis, S. H. Starr, A. E. Danielson.

Officers for the year 1937-38: S. B. Lassiter, president; L. E. Bowen. vice-president; W. Bruce Donaldson, Jr., secretary and treasurer; Ralph Puckett, sergeant-at-arms.

The club organization was sponsored by the Rotary Club of Macon, Georgia, with the assistance of L. E. Bowen, Sr., of Tifton. This club has the distinction of being the only one ever organized over a telephone. Mr. Bowen selected a list of twenty-six business men, contacted each one by telephone and enlisted them as members. This procedure was conclusive evidence of the reputation of Rotary and of the desirability of membership.

*Deceased.

The Tifton Club has been always interested in the community and has rendered effective service in all community projects.

At the end of ten years the Tifton Club still has twenty-one active members of the original charter members. Three charter members are dead. I. W. Myers, J. G. Herring, and S. H. Starr; two have moved from Tifton: James Harvey and Cecil Clark.

1937-1938 S. B. Lassiter, President; W. Bruce Donaldson, Jr., Secretary and Treasurer.
1938-1939 L. E. Bowen, President; W. Bruce Donaldson, Jr., Secretary and Treasurer.
1939-1940 Rev. F. O. Mixon, President; W. Bruce Donaldson, Jr., Secretary and Treasurer.
1940-1941 J. S. Taylor, President; W. Bruce Donaldson, Jr., Secretary and Treasurer
1941-1942 J. L. Bowen, President; W. Bruce Donaldson, Jr., Secretary and Treasurer.
1942-1943 C. C. Perry, President; W. G. Windham, Secretary and Treasurer.
1943-1944 Dr. W. T. Smith, President; Henry D. Collier, Secretary and Treasurer.
1944-1945 Ralph Puckett, President; Henry D. Collier, Secretary and Treasurer.
1945-1946 Geo. P. Donaldson, President; Henry D. Collier, Secretary and Treasurer.
1946-1947 W. Bruce Donaldson, Jr., President; Henry D. Collier, Secretary and Treasurer.
1947-1948 Rev. D. M. Sanders, President; Henry D. Collins, Secretary and Treasurer.

BRIEF SUMMARY OF THE FOUNDING AND HISTORY OF TIFT COUNTY POST NUMBER 21 THE AMERICAN LEGION

by Major Steve Mitchell

Tift County, Georgia, since its creation by Act of the Georgia General Assembly August 17, 1905, has progressively grown, as well as its towns and City of Tifton, and City of Omega, and many civic and welfare groups have largely contributed to its astounding growth, and perhaps no one of them has contributed more to such progressive growth and civic pride than Tift County Post Number 21, and its Legion Auxiliary, since its founding about September 1, 1919.

Immediately after Congressional founding of The American Legion, and The Department of Georgia, and at a time when most of the World War I veterans had returned to their homes, as few as fifteen honorably discharged veterans could petition for a charter. Following named veterans appeared as charter members, namely: M. Earl Phillips, Steve F. Mitchell, Roy Thrasher, N. Russell Overstreet, J. Albert Pope, Harry Kulbersh, Robert S. Herring, Benjamin K. Hardison, J. Ferrell Jolley, Reid Corry, Jeff Parker, Dr. Willie H. Hendricks, H. G. Short, J. G. Whigham, C. A. Harrell, Charles Y. Workman, Dr. Wm. T. Smith, Osmont V. Barkuloo, S. T. Kidder, Jr., W. B. Bennet, Ethridge Gay, Gerald N. Herring, Henry C. Overstreet, Francis N. Goggins, Roy E. Lytle, Cornelius R. Ryder, S. F. Overstreet, Jr., M. C. Owen, Alfred J. Goggins and W. L. Royal. The post by its number was the 21st post to be established in Georgia, meeting at Chamber of Commerce rooms, until later establishing its meeting room in Hall Building, which later became Woodman Hall, until its commodious home was erected on Moore highway, near home of Mr. P. D. Fulwood. Steve F. Mitchell was elected first Commander of the Post and Roy Thrasher, as Adjutant on 9 Sept. 1919, and later upon legal authority the post was properly chartered by order of Tift County Superior Court. Space forbids the naming of the many able Commanders and Adjutants to follow, though it must be mentioned that it was during the very able leadership of Post Commander M. L. Webb, and his staff that the present Legion Home was erected in 1937.

Only a few months after its founding, the Post felt the need of an Auxiliary, and by no mean efforts has contributed more to its growth and respect, charter members being: Mrs. W. H. Hendricks, Miss Margaret Hendricks, Miss Louise Hendricks, Mrs. W. B. Bennet, Miss Clara Bell Duff, Miss Carrie Fulwood, Mrs. Emerson Mitchell, Mrs. J. C. Hargraves, Mrs. D. D. Dixon, Mrs. W. Roy Lytle, Mrs. A. J. Whitehurst, Mrs. J. C. Algee, Mrs. Robert Herring, Mrs. Wm. T. Smith, Mrs. Harry Kulbersh, Miss Louise Algee, Mrs. John S. Waters, Mrs. G. N. Herring, Mrs. J. L. Herring, Miss Billie Hendricks, Mrs. Frank NeSmith, Mrs. Steve F. Mitchell, Mrs. T. A. Mitchell, Mrs. D. D. McCaskill, Mrs. J. P. Short II, Mrs. M. C. Owen, Mrs. Frank Goggins, Mrs. Jack Barkuloo, Mrs. Hattie Gibbs and Miss Leila Hargrett, and the Auxiliary has had a fine record, as proved by one of its members later becoming State President, namely, Mrs. D. D. Dixon, after she had moved to Thomasville, Ga.

Forever faithful to the principles set forth in its preamble,—"For God and Country," etc., the Post and its auxiliary have worked as a team, and its leavening influence has always been felt in any worthy move for the betterment of the Veterans position, and certainly for Tift County, and Georgia. Its home has become a meeting ground for most every worthy cause, and for recreation for both Youth and Age, and now, as in the words of

Col. John McCrea in his beautiful poem, "Flanders Field" we are ready to, and have already drawn to our membership, World War Veterans 'II from Saipan to Remergen, and to them and their Auxiliary we throw the torch of the Four Freedoms.

CHAPTER XX

WHO'S WHO IN TIFT COUNTY

There are many Tift County people who deserve a place in the Who's Who of the county, but we could include only a few. The following names were selected by popular vote and two committees of Tifton citizens:

S. J. Akers
L. S. Alfriend
G. O. Bailey, Jr. (See Education chapter for sketch)
L. E. Bowen, Sr.
Elias Branch (See Pioneer chapter)
W. P. Bryan
Annie Bell Clark (See Education chapter)
Ethel Clements
Josie Clyatt (Mrs. Jim Clyatt)
Nathan Coarsey
Peggy Herring Coleman
George P. Donaldson
Judge R. Eve (See Pioneer chapter)
Paul Dearing Fulwood Sr. (See Agriculture chapter)
Ruth Vickers Fulwood (Mrs. P. D. Fulwood, Sr.) (See Agriculture chapter)
Mrs. J. J. Golden
Leola Judson Greene (See Pioneer chapter)
Mrs. W. S. Harman
Dr. W. H. Hendricks (See Pioneer chapter)
Joseph Kent
George Harris King
Harry Kulbresh
Arthur Moore (See Small-Town chapter)
Susie T. Moore (See Pioneer chapter)
R. C. Patrick (Sketch unavailable)
Mrs. John A. Peterson, Sr.
Mrs. Nicholas Peterson (See Education chapter)
T. E. Phillips, Sr. (See Pioneer chapter)
Dr. Franklin Pickett
Mrs. J. W. Poole
D. C. Rainey

Mrs. W. T. Smith
Mrs. Dan Sutton (See Education chapter)
John Y. Sutton
Amos Tift (See Pioneer chapter)
E. L. Webb
Ida Belle Williams (See Education chapter)
J. L. Williams (See chapter Wire Grass Journalism).

LINTON STEPHENS ALFRIEND, JR.

Linton Stephens Alfriend, Jr., son of Linton Stephens and Nancy Gilbert Alfriend, was born on March 2, 1881, in Albany, Georgia. He attended school in Albany and in 1889 during vacation began work with the Atlantic Coast Line Railroad. In 1901 he came to Tifton to work with the railroad; later he worked in other places, but returned to Tifton in 1911 as freight agent, in which capacity he has served efficiently and faithfully. When offered a promotion to Jacksonville, he said, "I'd rather be a policeman in Tifton than mayor of Jacksonville."

He is a member of the Tifton Baptist Church, has served on Board of Directors of Atlantic Coast Line Y.M.C.A. fifteen years, on Board of Directors of Tifton Chamber of Commerce, and is a member of the Tifton Rotary Club.

He married Josephine Meara. Their children are Rosalie (Mrs. R. B. Bevan) and Nannette (Mrs. R. L. Hargrett). His second wife was Mabel Day Meara.

During the flood of 1925 when transportation was difficult, Alfriend rendered valuable service by borrowing extra locomotives from Waycross and by putting nineteen hundred sacks of rock on the Alapaha River bridge.

He is a direct descendant of Pocahontas. His ancestor, Dr. Shadrach Alfriend, married Elizabeth Woodlief, seventh in line from Pocahontas.

SAMUEL JASPER AKERS

Samuel Jasper Akers was born in Carroll County, Georgia, on February 24, 1886. His father and his grandfather were Baptist preachers and he was ordained to the full work of the ministry in February of 1920 by the Terrell Missionary Baptist Church. During the past twenty-seven years he has served as pastor of thirteen Baptist churches in Georgia and Florida.

On April 21, 1907, he married Miss Dora Elizabeth Bradley of Bremen, Georgia. They have five children, four sons and one daughter.

For fifteen years he taught school, mostly in Turner County, Georgia.

He moved to Tift County in 1931, and he has been serving as pastor of the Eldorado Baptist Church since 1929. He is at present engaged in full-time pastoral work. He is also editor of the *Baptist Anchor,* a paper devoted to the interests of Baptist churches in Georgia, Florida, and Alabama.

LENNON ELIAS BOWEN

Lennon Elias Bowen, Sr., son of Enoch and Elizabeth Turner Bowen, was born and reared in Tifton. Young Bowen graduated from the Tifton High School in 1907, and received his A.B. degree from Mercer University in 1912. For several years he was his father's associate in the automobile business.

Mr. Bowen was Tift County representative in Georgia Legislature in 1919-1922. He was a member of the Tifton City Council and later of the city commission, 1916-1920. He was president of the Rotary Club and of the Chamber of Commerce. During his service of fifteen years on the Tifton Board of Education Mr. Bowen fostered the progress of the schools.

He is president of the Bank of Tifton, secretary-treasurer and general manager of Tifton Cotton Mills, president of Georgia Baptist Foundation, president of Baptist Men's Bible Class, president of Boy Scouts of America, and a member of the Tifton Recreation Board. He is a Mason, Knight Templar, a Shriner, and a member of the Tifton Baptist Church.

He married Margaret Austin Bailey. They have two sons, Calhoun and Lennon, Jr.

WILLIAM PERDUE BRYAN

William Perdue Bryan, son of William Robert and Salina Sanders Bryan, was born in Pike County, Alabama on August 3, 1892. William Perdue attended schools in Pike before coming with his parents in 1909 to Tift County; here he studied at the A. and M. School.

When twenty-one, Mr. Bryan went to Calhoun County, Georgia, as manager of some farms. In 1915 he married Elizabeth Mansfield. Their children are Grace and William. Mr. Bryan returned to Tift County in 1918 and settled on Fair View Farm. In 1928 he was one of the youngest persons in the United States to receive the honor of being selected Master Farmer. The University of Georgia presented him a certificate of merit; the Progressive Farmer, a medal.

He is a member of and elder in the Presbyterian Church.

In 1934 Mr. Bryan was appointed supervisor for the Farm Security Administration project in Irwin County, later changed to Farmers' Home Administration. He is the only person in the United States to supervise one of these projects continuously until completion. Mr. Bryan is still with this project, one of the biggest of its kind in Georgia, and his work has high government rating.

Mr. Bryan helped to organize the Sowega Melon Growers at Adel and Irwinville Cooperative Association.

ETHEL CLEMENTS

Ethel Clements, daughter of Mr. and Mrs. G. E. Clements, was born on a farm at Brighton, Tift County, July 25, 1911. When three months old she had polio, which seemed to leave her a hopeless cripple. Finally, however, she learned to walk on her knees and for thirty-five years could not change her mode of walking.

Her family taught her for a while at home and she attended Harding School as many days as possible until she finished grammar school. With a brilliant mind, however, she educated herself beyond the seventh grade. Her versatility is attested by her drawing, painting, cooking, understanding poety, and reading in public. She organized a class in speech and read at secular and religious meetings.

Ethel has believed always in being self-supporting. At one time she owned a herd of cows. She stood on her knees, spaded the ground, and planted flowers to sell. For the past few years she has earned money by designing and making a distinctive type of doll, which she has sold in all parts of the country. These dolls attracted the attention of the counselor of Vocation Rehabilitation to her. He arranged for her to see an orthopedic surgeon and enter a hospital. After an operation she now can walk with the help of braces and a cane.

Her indomitable courage has directed her progress despite handicaps. From every standpoint Ethel is an excellent citizen.

MRS. JOSEPH JAMES CLYATT

Mrs. Joseph James Clyatt (Miss Josie Golden) daughter of Joseph Jackson Golden and Mary McLeod Golden, was born October 1, 1898. Josie Golden married Joseph James Clyatt, June 30, 1925. They have one daughter, Betty Jean Clyatt.

Miss Golden graduated at the Tifton High School and received her B.M. in organ and piano at Shorter College in 1919. She had special work in organ at Institute of Applied Music and Wurlitzer Organ Company, New York City.

Mrs. Clyatt was president of Georgia Federation of Music Clubs 1930-1934; honorary first vice-president and director for life, Georgia Federation of Music Clubs; director of National Federation of Music Clubs, 1933-1937; trustee Shorter College, 1939-1941; president of Shorter College Alumnae Association; president of Tifton Music Club, 1937-1939; president Twentieth Century Library Club, 1939-1941 and 1944-1945; state chairman of music, Georgia Federation of Women's clubs, 1940-1942, second vice-president, Second District Federation of Women's Clubs.

Her biography is in "Who's Who in the South and Southwest" and "American Women."

She was sponsor for the Junior Woman's Club 1940-1942 and will be sponsor through 1947.

Mrs. Clyatt has been organist for years at the Tifton Baptist Church, where she is a member.

NATHAN COARSEY

Nathan Coarsey, son of W. H. Coarsey and Ardelia M. Turner Coarsey, was born on June 13, 1888, one mile from Brookfield and lived in this town all his life. Mr. Nathan Coarsey married the first time Mary Vicey Cox; their three children are N. L. Jr., Jack and Wiley, all now of Brookfield. Their daughter, Myrtle, died in 1915.

In 1919 Mr. Coarsey married Nora Lee Partin, of Berrien County; their children are Raleigh, Grace, Audrey, Austin, Dorothy, Mrs. J. T. Tyson, and Mrs. Marvin Goodman; the last two are from Brookfield.

Mr. Coarsey served as member of the Board of Commissioners of Roads and Revenue for Tift County from 1923 to 1943. He was elected chairman of the county commissioners in August 1927, and served until 1943, with the exception of two years. During these years of his service Mr. Coarsey established a good record. According to the Tifton Gazette, he was noted for the standard of roads, bridges, public works of the county, and the many improvements to county property. During his administration the County Hospital was erected, and the Tifton airbase and the Tift County curb market established.

PEGGY HERRING COLEMAN

Peggy Herring Coleman, daughter of Editor John Lewis Herring and Martha Susan Greene Herring, was born in Tifton, Georgia, April 30, 1910. She was third honor graduate in class of 1927 at Tifton High School. Peggy won Second District ready writers medal and Lincoln Memorial national essay medal. She graduated from the business department of Georgia State College for Men in Tifton. Peggy was president of the N.L.N., a high school club, for three years.

In 1927 she began work with the Tifton Gazette. She is associate editor, sports editor, feature editor, roving reporter, and columnist for "Romain' Round" for the Gazette. Peggy is a member of American Legion Auxiliary, Woman's Club, Charter member of Pilot Club, and a member of First Methodist Church. She was state publicity director of Georgia Department American Auxiliary, publicity director of American Red Cross, reporter for Lions and Kiwanis Clubs, district air-raid warden for Civilian Defense during the late war and secretary-treasurer of Tift County Farm Bureau for four years.

Peggy is correspondent for United Press Association, Associated Press, Atlanta Constitution, and the Macon Telegraph. She has written sparkling feature stories for these papers and for the Atlanta Journal Magazine.

On October 31, 1936 Peggy married Amiel Walsey Coleman.

GEORGE PETER DONALDSON

George Peter Donaldson, son of Leona Mercer and Robert Franklin Donaldson, was born on October 21, 1893 in Statesboro, Georgia. He graduated from Statesboro High School, Gordon Military College, the University of Georgia with a B.S. degree in 1916, and from Ohio State University with a M.S. degree in 1933.

In 1918 he married Holly Twitty, of Pelham, Georgia. They have two sons, Major George B. Donaldson, Jr., veteran of Pacific campaign of World War II, and William Twitty, veteran of United States Navy of World War II.

While in Statesboro, Mr. Donaldson was a member of the Cowart-Donaldson firm, deacon in the Baptist Church, secretary-treasurer, and president of the Chamber of Commerce. He served two terms as representative from Bulloch County in the Georgia Legislature.

A veteran teacher, Donaldson has taught in several Georgia high schools, at the Georgia Military College, South Georgia Teachers' College, and Abraham Baldwin Agricultural College.

Since his first connection with Abraham Baldwin College in 1933 Donaldson has fostered the interest of 4-H clubs, Future Farmers of America and Future Home Makers of America. He is probably the only person in the United States whom all three groups have honored with life membership.

He is a member of the Tifton Baptist Church, Tift County Chamber of Commerce, and member and former president of Tifton Rotary Club.

For several years Mr. Donaldson has been dean at Abraham Baldwin, but this year he accepted the position of president.

MRS. JOSEPH JACKSON GOLDEN

Mrs. Joseph Jackson Golden (Mary McLeod), daughter of Daniel Washington Golden and Katherine Parker McLeod, was born in North Carolina, but in early childhood moved to Sumner, Georgia. On January 1, 1896, Mary McLeod moved to Tifton, and on August 11, 1897 married Joseph Jackson Golden. They have one daughter, Josie Golden Clyatt.

Mrs. Golden was chairman of the fine arts committee of Twentieth Century Library Club from 1916 to 1947, director of choir of Tifton First Baptist Church from 1920 to 1946, president of the Music Club from 1921 to 1922. She is a charter member of the Tifton Music Club and a member of the Tifton Baptist Church.

HARRIET GOODMAN HARMAN

Harriet Goodman Harman, musician and church woman, daughter of Dr. Charles Goodman and Henrietta Ann Goodman, was born in Somerton, Nansemond County, Virginia, February 5, 1875. The Goodmans moved in 1890 to Tifton. After her public school work, Miss Goodman entered Wesleyan College, Macon, Georgia, where she studied piano, voice, and literary subjects. After leaving Wesleyan, she taught music in the Tifton schools.

In 1901 she married George S. Evans. To this union was born a daughter, Harriet Goodman Evans. After Mr. Evans' death Mrs. Evans returned to Tifton, and in 1908 married Willard Inther Harman. To this marriage was born three sons, Charles, Eugene, and Allen. The first two are dead.

Mrs. Harman since childhood has served her church, the Methodist. She has been assistant director of and soloist in the choir, organist and teacher in Sunday School, and president of Missionary society.

Mrs. Harman has held offices in the Twentieth Century Library Club, of which she is a charter member. She is a member of the Tifton Music Club, the U.D.C., the W.C.T.U., and the Tifton Wesleyan Club.

JOSEPH KENT, SR.

Joseph Kent, Sr., son of Mr. and Mrs. Harry Kent, was born March 3, 1881, at Staffordshire, England.

At the age of thirteen months he, with his parents, sailed for America and later landed in Wilkinsburg, Pennsylvania, where he spent his boyhood.

When fourteen years old Kent came with his parents to a farm three miles from Tifton. Four years later he and his father began the warehouse business. Afterwards this father and son operated a furniture store for twenty-five years.

After retiring from the furniture business, Mr Kent successfully devoted much of his time to civic affairs in Tifton. He was president of the Board of Trade for two consecutive years and postmaster from 1929 to 1935. While postmaster he sold shares and formed the Tifton Building and Loan Association. It later changed to the Tifton Federal Savings and Loan Association, of which Kent is secretary and treasurer. He helped organize and became president of the Farmer's Bank of Tifton.

Mr. Joseph Kent, Sr., married Ellsberry White Dana. They have five children: Alice Elizabeth Kent Hodges, Joseph Kent, Jr., Edward Dana Kent, Ellsberry White Kent, and Doris Mae Kent Blanton.

Probably his greatest contribution to his country was his untiring efforts and accomplishments as chairman of the Bond Drive in Tift County and in the entire Second District.

GEORGE HARRIS KING

George Harris King, son of William Peter King and Mary Harris King, was born on November 14, 1900, in West Plains, Missouri. He graduated from Griffin High School in 1916, received his B.S.A. at the University of Georgia in 1924 and his M.S. at the University of Georgia in 1932, and did graduate work at Cornell University in 1932-1933.

Mr. King taught in Marion County at Brantley School, in the agriculture department in Barrow County, was master-teacher of vocational agriculture in 1929, and was teacher trainer in College of Agriculture, University of Georgia. He was professor of farm management and dean of instruction at Abraham Baldwin College in 1933-1934 and president of Baldwin College in 1934-1947. He retired in 1947 to devote all his time to the Georgia Coastal Experiment Station, where he has been director since 1942.

In 1923 Mr. King married Marguerite Benson; they have two daughters, Betty E. and Margaret. Dorothy died several years ago.

Mr. King is a member of the Lions Club, Masons, and Tifton Methodist Church.

HARRY KULBERSH

Harry Kulbersh was born in Poland in 1889. When a young, inexperienced lad of sixteen years, he traveled to the United States to make his home. In September, 1908 Mr. Kulbersh left Atlanta to live in Tifton and to start his present dry goods business on a "shoe-string."

Mr. Kulbersh is definitely a self-made man: his educational advantages were few, and his struggle for success, long and difficult.

During World War I "Mr. Harry," as the most of Tift Countians call him, served in the United States Army. After returning from overseas, he married in 1920 Irene Jolton of New York City. Both Kulbersh and his wife have contributed to everythnig that would better Tift County.

Mr. Kulbersh is charitable; during his life in Tifton he has never refused financial or other material donations to a social, civic, or religious cause. His interest in all affairs of Tifton is vital. He is a member of the Chamber of Commerce, the Masons, the Fitzgerald Hebrew Congregation, and a charter member of the American Legion.

During World War II "Mr. Harry" did his part on the home front, buying war bonds, supporting drives, and contributing to Red Cross and U.S.O.

The small business which he began in 1908 has grown like a sturdy oak from a little acorn, and is now the oldest drygoods store in Tifton.

MABEL HAULBROOK PETERSON

In the plantation home at Homer, Georgia, near Athens, Mabel Haulbrook Peterson, daughter of William Coleman and Susanna Mason Haulbrook, was born. When six years old Mabel moved to Calhoun and attended the public school, later, graduating from the high school. She then attended the Woman's College at Athens.

In 1901 the family moved to South Georgia and for a year and a half she taught in the Tifton County Schools. A year later she married Dr. John A. Peterson, prominent dentist of this county. To this union were born three children, two of whom died in infancy. John Haulbrook, the oldest son, is one of the best dentists in this section.

Mrs. Peterson is a charter member and an honorary life member of the Woman's Club of Tifton, a member of the Methodist Church and Bible teacher in a circle of WSCS. She has been superintendent of juniors in Church School, efficient counselor of young people of the Epworth League, and Sunday School teacher of college girls.

In her home she gave spiritual and mental training to other children, besides her own, who have gone out to bless the world.

FRANKLIN BROWN PICKETT

Dr. Franklin Brown Pickett, son of Jeptha B. Pickett, Sr., and Kathryn Raines Pickett, was born in Webster County. In high school he received special instruction to enter the medical department of the University of Georgia at Augusta, Georgia. After receiving his degree in 1897, he went to Ty Ty to practice medicine. Dr. Pickett later did post-graduate work at the Polyclinic, New York City.

Dr. Pickett came from a family of physicians, whose combined service extended over a period of one hundred-fifty years in Worth and Tift Counties. He helped to establish a progressive school system in Ty Ty and Tift County, serving as chairman of the local and county Board of Education during a long period, and served as mayor of Ty Ty for many years.

He volunteered for services in World War I and later received a captain's commission. Dr. Pickett was chairman of the local Selective Draft Board during World War II, and received a congressional medal.

Dr. Pickett married Miss Martha Williams, daughter of W. E. and Kathryn Gibbs Williams. The Pickett children are Theodore Franklin, Mary Kathleen, and Frankie Evelyn.

After many years of heavy service Dr. Pickett is still active.

MRS. J. W. POOLE

Mrs. J. W. Poole (Carrie Ayers) daughter of Sam and Emily Dennard Ayres, married J. W. Poole on June 11, 1878, and they moved to a place in Berrien County (now in Tift) fifty-two years ago. Their children are Mrs. Nan Musselwhite, Mrs. W. W. Reynolds, Mrs. J. C. Smith, Mrs. Fred Cody, Miss Ellie Poole, and Ralph Poole, who served in the World Wars I and II. Her two grandsons and one great-grandson fought in the last war.

This star mother and grandmother has two affectionate titles, conferred by her admirers: "Granny Poole" and "Sweetheart of the American Legion of Tift County Post Number 211." Each year she leads in selling poppies. Besides her contribution to patriotic and religious organizations, she helps the underprivileged, white and colored.

She has been a member of the Tifton Baptist Church for fifty-two years.

DAVID CROCKETT RAINEY

David Crockett Rainey was born at Amboy, Turner County, Georgia on August 22, 1884, the son of Daniel L. and Mary Evelyn Rainey. His early years were spent on the farm. In 1903 he attended Georgia Normal School at Abbeville, Georgia.

In 1910 he answered the call to the gospel ministry and was liberated and ordained by the Rebecca Baptist Church. In the fall of 1910 he entered Norman Institute at Norman Park, where he was active in the debating societies, and made all the athletic teams, playing right end on the football team, guard on the basketball team and left field on the baseball team.

In the spring of 1911 he became pastor of Bessie Tift Chapel, in Tifton, Georgia. Since that time he has served the following churches in the Mell Association: Zion Hope, Ty Ty, Mt. Zion, Eldorado, Lake View, Lenox, Pine Grove, Omega, Brookfield, and Brushy Creek, and Pine Forest Church in the Mallory Association. He was active in the building of the Chula Church and served there as pastor. At the present he is serving Zion Hope, Mount Olive, in the Ben Hill Association, and Antioch, in Colquitt Association.

In 1913 he married Miss Cammie Starling and to this union was born five children: David Carl, Henry Grady, Mary Claire, Myrtle Grace (deceased) and Donald Dinsmore Rainey.

In 1930 he became probation officer and Welfare Worker for Tift County. During these years he has married over five hundred couples, and conducted a large number of funerals.

MRS. W. T. SMITH

Maud Burns Smith, the daughter of a prominent farmer and livestock dealer, was born in Columbia, Tennessee. She attended Belmont College at Nashville, Tennessee, and after graduating came to Tift County to teach. Here she met and married Dr. Smith, a beloved Tifton physician, who later became an oculist.

She early became an ardent worker and teacher in the Tifton Methodist Church, and was an influential member in the Tifton school system. Mrs. Smith served one time on the city board of education and was very active in various social and educational circles.

She has received recognition for her outstanding work in the Twentieth Century Library Club, the American Legion Auxiliary, the Tift County Medical Auxiliary, and the Tifton Garden Club.

Her children are: Mrs. Ed Killian, of Anniston, Alabama; Mrs. David B. Howard, of Atlanta, and Dr. William T. Smith, Jr., of Tifton.

JOHN YOUNG SUTTON

(by Murl Rountree)

John Young Sutton, son of Jacob Young Sutton and Elizabeth Welch Turner Sutton, was born February 14, 1862, in Dooly County. His father died during the War Between the States, and his mother, later. He received his schooling by a lightwood fire in the kitchen. Later, Sutton wore a three-dollar suit, a dollar pair of boots, and a fifty-cent hat upon leaving his guardian. During the next few years he worked for sixty or seventy dollars a year.

In 1884 he married Martha A. Smith, of Irwin County. Only two of their nine children are living: Mrs. Ida Daniels and Mrs. Nancy Elizabeth Ingram. He has four grandchildren and five great-grandchildren.

In 1893 he moved to a farm, six miles from Tifton, where he still lives. Four years later, his wife died. In 1901 he married Margie Johnson, of Stewart County. They have no children. He is a member of the Ty Ty Baptist Church and is probably the first Baptist in Georgia to declare a belief in open communion.

He is still a loyal Tift Countian who can attribute his longevity to his living by the Book of Books.

ELIAS WEBB

Elias Webb, son of the Reverend W. W. Webb, was born and reared on a farm near Tifton. He attended the Tifton High School and Georgia-Alabama College. Elias helped his father with farm work before going to business college.

Mr. Webb is a member and director of the Rotary Club, a member of the Baptist Church and Baptist Training Union. He has taught a class of boys at the Baptist Sunday School for twenty-five years. Mr. Webb is one of the two advisers from Tift County for the Chehaw Council of Boy Scouts. He was one of the directors of Tifton Board of Trade. In fact, Mr. Webb has been active in all civic affairs.

Fishing, athletics, and children are his hobbies.

He has educated two worthy students who were financially unable to attend college and is now helping support a foreign missionary.

CHAPTER XXI

SOME OF THE TIFT COUNTY BOYS WHO MADE THE SUPREME SACRIFICE IN WORLD WAR II

(Not all Tift County soldiers who made the supreme sacrifice in World War II are included here. The editor of the book announced several times in the Tifton Gazette that she would use only sketches sent by the families of these soldiers.)

GARLAND C. ANDERSON

Garland C. Anderson was born May 16, 1917 at Crandall, Georgia. In 1920 he moved with his family to Omega, where he attended high school and graduated in 1935. Afterwards he attended the Coynes Radio and Electric School in Chicago, Illinois.

On March 10, 1941 he answered the call to colors and enlisted in the United States Army Air Corps; his assignment was in the radio department. Upon completion of his training here in the States, Garland was sent to Hickman Field, where he met his death during the Japanese sneak attack at Pearl Harbor, December 7, 1941.

Garland C. Anderson, an only child, is survived by his mother, Mrs. Jennie Mae Anderson, who lives in Omega. Early in 1946 his name was selected by the V.F.W. of Tifton, Georgia as the first Tift County boy to lose his life in World War II. The Tifton Post, therefore, was named in his honor the Garland C. Anderson Post Number 5250.

TILTON EDWARD BELFLOWER

Tilton Edward Belflower, son of the late Willie Jesse and Carrie McCook Belflower, was born in Tift County April 18, 1919. He attended the Brookfield and Tifton schools and was a farmer even while studying. He was single and had one sister, Mrs. Billy Pierce, and several half-brothers and sisters.

On September, 1939 he joined the army at Fort Benning, Georgia, and was in the Tank Division. Prior to going overseas, he went to Fort Bragg. He went over the last of November and landed at Oran, N. Africa. Belflower fought in Sicily and Italy before being sent to England for a rest period. After serving in the Normandy Invasion, he received his fatal wound in France, August 24, 1944.

Sergeant Belflower is buried in an army cemetery at St. Andre-de-l-Eure, France, forty-eight miles from Paris, France.

WINFORD ELIJAH EVANS

Winford Elijah Evans, son of Elijah F. Evans and Essie Campbell Evans, was born at Daviston, Alabama. Later Winford lived at Brookfield, Omega, and near Tifton. While attending the Brookfield school he assisted his father on the farm.

In November, 1942, he entered service. He had his training in Camp Walters, Texas. During this time Winford won two medals in rifle contests. His overseas service was first in Africa, where Winford was a guard for several months. His company finally moved to Italy. Evans was killed on May 9, 1944 in battle on the Anzio Beachhead in Italy.

His musical gift was a source of much pleasure to his comrades and him between battles.

REUBEN G. FUNDERBURK

Private First Class Reuben G. Funderburk was born in Pinehurst, Georgia, Dec. 20, 1915, a son of Mr. and Mrs. James Anderson Funderburk. He attended schools in Pinehurst, Georgia, Oakridge, and Tifton.

When war was declared in December, 1941, Reuben G. Funderburk volunteered for active duty with the U. S. Army. Immediately after taking Basic Training at Fort Jackson, South Carolina, he was transferred to the 117th Infantry 30th Division. The 30th Division moved from Fort Jackson to Camp Blanding, Florida, for a six weeks training course. After six weeks of hard intensive training, the Old Hickory Division moved to Fort Benning, Ga., for more advanced training. When the training was completed the Division went on maneuvers in Tennessee. From Tennessee they went to Camp Atterbury, Indiana. For six more long weeks of hard training, the Division was shipped to New York where they sailed for England. In June 1944 the Old Hickory Division landed in France, where the fighting had begun.

Private First Class Reuben G. Funderburk was killed in action near La Cambre, France, July 15, 1944.

RUSSELL LEONARD GARNER

Russell Leonard Garner was born October 23, 1908 at Harding.

When Russell was five years of age he had typhoid-pneumonia, which resulted in an operation.

He received his entire schooling, other than what he received in the Navy, at Harding School.

He joined the U. S. Navy July 2, 1927. He attended school for several months at the Great Lakes Naval Training School at Chicago.

Russell was in service for fourteen and one-half years. On November 27, 1941, he was killed at San Diego, California. He was test pilot and took the plane up for testing when something went wrong about it and he was killed.

Russell was a good boy, was well-liked by everyone, especially his boyhood friends. Although he was killed before war was actually declared, he was one of the first of our fine young men to give his life in service for his country.

OLLIE E. GIBBS

Lieutenant Ollie Gibbs, Jr., son of Mr. and Mrs. Ollie Gibbs, Sr., was born February 24, 1917 in Tift County. He graduated from Tifton High School in 1936. Later Gibbs graduated from an electrical college in Chicago and became an expert electrician.

In 1942 he volunteered for services in the Army Air Forces and afterwards received training in California, Arizona, and Louisiana. In 1944 he had to choose between being an instructor at Harding Field, Louisiana, and going overseas. Choosing the latter to be with his "buddies," Gibbs went to Duxford, England. From this base he sometimes flew two missions daily. On June 22, 1944, the P-47 plane, of which Gibbs was pilot, developing propeller trouble, crashed. Gibbs's temporary resting place is near Cambridge, England.

RALPH GIBBS

Ralph Gibbs, son of Mr. and Mrs. H. F. Gibbs, was born August 4, 1917, in Tifton. While a student at Tifton High School, where he was graduated in 1934, Ralph won first place in music at a district meet.

At Emory University he was soloist and accompanist for the glee club. While a freshman at Eastman School of Music, New York, Ralph had the honor of playing in Kilbourn Hall.

He entered service July 12, 1941, in the Army Air Corps. Ralph went overseas June 5, 1943, and was with the ground forces of the Seventh Army Air Forces in England.

He married Miss Margaret Matheson, Rickmonsworth Herts, England, in 1944. Sergeant Gibbs was killed April 23, 1945, at North Barrules, Isle of Man, in an airplane crash while on a non-operational cross-country flight. He was buried in the American cemetery at Cambridge. His wife and little daughter Rozanne, survive him.

While in service Ralph gave several musical programs in England and was organist for post chapels.

CURTIS MATHEWS

Curtis Mathews, aviation ordnanceman third class U. S. N. R., was born April 13, 1925. His parents are Mr. and Mrs. Y. E. Mathews. Route 4, Tifton, Georgia.

He attended school at Harding and Tifton, graduating with the 1942 class of Tifton High. Until entering service he was employed in the grocery business.

He received his Navy training at Bainbridge, Maryland and Jacksonville, Florida, and saw service at Sanford, New Smyrna, and Titusville, Florida, Atlantic City, New Jersey, and Manteo, North Carolina.

Ordnanceman Mathews died July 23, 1945 at a naval hospital in Norfolk, Virginia, as the result of second degree burns received when a rocket was discharged accidentally.

CHARLES WILLIAM MATHEWS

Charles William Mathews was born in north-east Tift County January 3, 1920. He attended the Harding School.

After entering the navy in March, 1940, he was stationed on the cruiser Helena, which was damaged in the attack on Pearl Harbor, December 7, 1941.

At the time of his death Charles was a coxswain. He was awarded posthumously the American Defense Service medal, World War II Victory medal, and the Purple Heart.

He was listed as missing on July 6, 1943 in the battle off New Georgia Island and declared dead August 10, 1945.

ALVIN McKINNEY*

Pfc. Joseph Alvin McKinney, son of Aaron Alvin and Beulah Powers McKinney, was born at Tifton, Georgia, August 27, 1918. He graduated from the Tift County Industrial School May, 1937. For one year McKinney attended tht Georgia State College at Savannah, Georgia. He entered service May 26, 1941. During the summer of 1942 McKinney went overseas and later on April 27, 1944, died at Bougainville, while defending his country.

SIDNEY NEIGHBORS

Sidney Neighbors, son of Mr. and Mrs. W. R. Neighbors, was born in Tifton, December 19, 1921. He attended the Tifton schools. On No-

---

*McKinney creditably represented his race in the great conflict. Tift County appreciates every good citizen.

vember 7, 1942, he enlisted in United States Navy. Neighbors received boot training at Great Lakes, Illinois. He attended the Arm Guard School in Gulfport, Mississippi. On March 25, 1943 Neighbors left New York in a convoy attached to a merchant ship, which a submarine attacked later in the North Atlantic.

Sidney was missing in action on April 16, 1943. A year later officials presumed that he was dead.

CHARLES EDWIN PATTON

Charles Edwin Patton was born in Tift County, Ga., April 1, 1909, son of Mr. and Mrs. J. D. Patton. He received his education in the Tifton Public Schools. Afterwards, he was employed in the Tifton Post Office for twelve years as city mail carrier. On May 22, 1942 he was called into the services of the U. S. Army. He received his training at Fort McClellan, Ala., Miami, Fla., and Camp Gordon, Johnston, Fla., near Carrabelle. He was then shipped overseas, being stationed in England for some time. He was shipped to LeHarve, France, where he died of coronary thrombosis on Dec. 25, 1944, only a short time after he arrived there. He now lies at rest in United States Military Cemetery St. Andre, France.

ROBERT B. POWLEDGE

Robert B. Powledge was a boy of fourteen when he came to live with his aunt and uncle, Mr. and Mrs. C. B. Culpepper. He was a shy boy who soon entered into all the school activities under the guidance of his teachers and made many lasting friends. He will be remembered for his athletic ability in all sports and especially in football.

Robert voluntarily entered the National Guard in 1941, joining the 101st, Anti-aircraft Battalion in Atlanta. After being at Camp Stewart a year, Robert transferred to the Air Corps as an aviation cadet. After nine months of many trials and hardships, he won his "silver wings." That day was the happiest in his short life.

In March 1943, Robert left the States, a second Lieutenant in command of his own B-17. He was stationed in England. On July 17, 1943, he left on his ninth combat mission to go over Germany, from which he failed to return. His ship was last seen going down over the North Sea.

Though the details of his death are not known, all who knew him are sure he died a hero's death.

FREDERICK E. (BILL) SEARS

Frederick E. Sears, son of Mr. and Mrs. C. A. Sears, was born September 16, 1917. After graduating from Tifton High School in 1937, he worked with Wade-Corry Company until 1940 when he enlisted in peacetime army. Before going to the Aleutian Islands, he was stationed at Camp Stewart, Georgia, and at Fort Monroe, Virginia. After his transfer to the Army Air Forces, Bill returned to the States for training and later was ill of rheumatic fever in a hospital.

Soon after his dismissal from the hospital, he was sent overseas to Germany. He was with General Patton's Third Army. Corporal Sears was killed in March, 1945, after crossing the Mozelle river, trying to capture a small town. He is buried in the American cemetery at Luxemburg, where General Patton is buried. Sears was awarded two stars, the Bronze Star and the Purple Heart.

GEORGE SUTTON

George Sutton, son of Mr. and Mrs. George M. Sutton, Sr., was born March 10, 1918, in Tifton. He was an honor graduate of Tifton High School in 1935 and was one of the best students ever to attend this institution. He won a competitive scholarship to Emory University and a scholarship to Louisiana State University.

While studying at Tech to be an electrical engineer, George was a member of the Kappa Eta Kappa, honorary electrical engineering society, Coop Club, member of track team, and Y.M.C.A. Cabinet, a lieutenant in the ROTC, and a member of an honorary scholastic society.

After his graduation at Tech and his work with the Babcox-Wilcox Boiler Company in Ohio, George entered the armed forces in 1941 with the Army Signal Corps. Later, he transferred to the Army Air Forces and received training as a navigator. Assigned to a B-24 Liberator Bomber, Lieutenant Sutton was sent overseas in 1943 and was killed in England, February 3, 1944.

PFC. DURWARD LEE WILLIS

Pfc. Durward Lee Willis was born in Tift County, June 18, 1922, a son of Mrs. Ollie Lastings Willis, of Tifton, and Lee Franklin Willis, formerly of Tifton. His brother and sister are Lee Franklin Willis, Jr., of Tifton, and Mrs. Pauline Willis Creech, of Brunswick, Georgia.

Durward attended the Brookfield and Tifton Schools. He was a member of the Brookfield Baptist Church.

In 1939, he joined the U. S. Army Air Corps at Fort McPherson, Ga.

From there he was sent to Barksdale Field, Shreveport, La. He trained there as a gunner on a B-17 and was later transferred to the Savannah Air Base, Savannah, Ga. Later his squadron was sent on maneuvers in Louisiana.

Upon completion of these maneuvers he was assigned to overseas duty in the Philippine Islands. He left San Francisco, California, in October of 1941 and arrived in Manila the middle of November. From Manila he was sent to the Island of Leyete. Upon the fall of the Philippine Islands in May, 1942, he was taken prisoner by the Japanese and died of dysentery while still a prisoner November 7, 1942.

TIFT COUNTY BOYS KILLED IN ACTION IN WORLD WAR II

	Name	Branch	Date	Place	Next of Kin
1.	Anderson, Garland C.—Army		Dec. 7, 1941	Hawaii	Mrs. Jennie Mae Anderson, Mother, Omega
2.	Croft, Theodore W.—Navy		Dec. 7, 1941	Hawaii	Mrs. Henry S. Brooks, Mother, Omega
3.	Brooks, Silas B.—Army		July 14,	China	Mrs. Henry S. Brooks, Mother, Omega
4.	Spillers, Samuel W.—Merchant Marine			Tanker "Liebert"	Mr. James Spillers, Father, Rt 1, Ty Ty
5.	Willis, Durwood Lee—Army		July 1, 1943	Philippine Is.	Mrs. Ollie L. Willis, Mother, Tifton
6.	Watson, Cletes J.—Navy		March 9, 1943	N. Atlantic	Mr. L. M. Watson, Father, Tifton
7.	Rooks, Tom H.—Army		May 10, 1943	N. Africa	Mrs. Etta G. Rooks, Mother, Rt. 3, Tifton
8.	Matthews, Charles W.—Navy		July 6, 1942	"Helena"	Mrs. A. O. Matthews, Mother, Tifton
9.	Mullis, Albert J.—Navy				Mrs. Virginia Mullis, Wife, Tifton
10.	Martin, Wyman D.—Army			England	Mrs. W. P. Brown, Sister, Tifton
11.	Powledge, Robert M.—Army		July 14, 1943	Over Europe	Mr. and Mrs. C. B. Culpepper, Aunt and Uncle, Tifton
12.	Sutton, George M.—Army		Feb. 3, 1944	England	Mrs. George M. Sutton, Mother, Tifton
13.	Woodall, Alva McLean—Army			Over Germany	Mrs. Luna Woodall, Mother, Orlando, Fla.
14.	Aultman, Elton L.—Army		May 28, 1944	Over China	Mrs. E. L. Aultman, Wife, Fitzgerald Mrs. L. W. Aultman, Mother, Tifton
15.	Kelley, W. A., Jr.—Army		June 6, 1945	Kwajalein	Mrs. W. A. Kelley, Mother, Tifton
16.	Gibbs, Ralph—Army		April 23, 1945	England	Mrs. Ralph Gibbs, Wife, England Mrs. H. F. Gibbs, Mother, Tifton
17.	McIntosh, Benjamin—Army		April 16, 1945	Italy	Mrs. J. H. McIntosh, Mother, Enigma
18.	Sears, Frederick E.—Army		March 16, 1945	Germany	Mrs. C A. Sears, Mother, Tifton
19.	Hobby, Eugene—Army		Jan. 23, 1945	Luzon	Pauline Hobby, Sister, Tifton Mr. W. W. Hobby, Father, Tifton
20.	Johnson, Paul—Army		Jan. 3, 1943	France	Mrs. Paul Johnson, Wife, Tifton
21.	Willis, Cecil H.—Army			Germany	Mrs. Cecil H. Willis, Wife, Tifton
22.	Johnson, George C.—Army		Oct. 4, 1944	Germany	Mrs. Sol K. Johnson, Mother, Omega
23.	Lavender, Clyde F.—Army		May 24, 1944	Italy	Mrs. Attie E. Lavender, Mother, Tifton
24.	Belflower, Tilton—Army		Aug. 24, 1944	France	Mrs. Billy Pierce, Sister, Tifton
25.	Evans, Winford—Army		May 9, 1944	Italy	Mrs. E. F. Evans, Mother, Tifton, Rt. 5
26.	Dowdy, John—Army		June 27, 1944	France	Mr. Prescott Dowdy, Brother, Tifton
27.	Gibbs, Ollie—Army		June 22, 1944	England	Mrs. O. E. Gibbs, Mother, Tifton
28.	May, Talmadge—Navy		Sept. 15, 1942	"Wasp"	Mr. G. W. May, Father, Tifton
29.	Goff, Horace—Army		Aug. 24, 1944	France	Mrs. Hattie Goff, Mother, Tifton

Name	Branch	Date	Place	Next of Kin
30. Patton, Charles E.—Army		Dec. 25, 1944	France	Mrs. J. D Patton, Mother, Tifton
31. Cooper, Francis A.—Army		June 1, 1944	N. Burma	Mr. and Mrs. W. A. Cooper, Mother and Father, Tifton
32. Barbee, Murren Arrel—Navy		Feb. 12, 1942	Australia	Mrs. John Gladney, Sister, Tifton
33. Adams, Jesse Penn—Army		Nov. 16, 1943	San Diego, Cal.	Mr. and Mrs. P. P. Adams, Mother and Father, Tifton
34. Whiddon, Heyward W.—Army		Jan. 28, 1945	Luzon	Mr. and Mrs. M. E. Whiddon, Mother and Father, Tifton
35. Garner, Russell Leonard—Navy		Nov. 27, 1941	San Diego, Cal.	Mrs. C. S. Gerner, Mother, Rt. 4, Tifton
36. Cromer, Edward Carl—Army		May 25, 1945	Okinawa	Mrs. C. C. Cromer, Mother, Rt. 1, Tifton
37. Neighbors, Sidney—Navy		April 16, 1943	N. Atlantic	Mrs. W. R. Neighbors, Mother, Fitzgerald
38. Matthews, Curtis—Navy		July 23, 1945	Norfolk, Va.	Mr. and Mrs. Y. E. Matthews, Mother and Father, Tifton
39. Funderburke, Reubin—Army		July 15, 1944	France	Mother, Mrs. Ceody Funderburk

COLORED

Name	Branch	Date	Place	Next of Kin
1. Board, Robert Lee, Jr.—Army		Aug. 6, 1943	Brentwood L. I.	Robert L. Board, Father, Tifton
2. McKinney, Joseph Alvan—Army		April 27, 1944	Bougainville	Beulah G. & Aaron A. McKinney, Tifton

CHAPTER XXII

WIRE GRASS JOURNALISM

J. T. Maund, of Dawson, together with J. F. Thompson, of Valdosta, in 1881 established in Ty Ty the first newspaper in what is now Tift County. The Ty Ty Echo was a three-column folio, printed on a job press. The Echo suspended publication in 1882.

Ty Ty business men, pleased with their paper, regretted its suspension so much that they offered inducements to an outstanding wire grass journalist, Hanlon, of the Isabella Star, to move his paper to Ty Ty. He accepted the terms and moved the Star in February 1883 to Ty Ty. Late in the year Hanlon moved to Albany.

Mr. H. D. Webb's father, W. W. Webb, a few years ago had a copy of The Echo, published December 23, 1881. This paper was edited by J. T. Maud and C. A. McDonald. The price of subscription was a dollar a year in advance. The motto was: "The good and bad will be returned by *The Echo*."

Included in this issue are: "How to Tell," which explains the difference in news items and advertisements; "Queer," an article about a dog fight; "Ty Ty's School," of which John Murrows was principal; quotations on cotton, hides, bacon, and turpentine; notice by J. J. Williams, J. P. and J. W. Overstreet, N.P., ex-officio, J. P., that justice court would be held the first Thursday in each month instead of the first Saturday; a dance at the home of Mr. and Mrs. J. T. Hale; the death of Marion Dampier, son of Mr. and Mrs. John Dampier; singing school of twenty-five students, taught by Prof. Nolen; the marriage of Miss C. A. Lawson to W. J. B. Wadkins.

Advertisements included the following: Dr. G. E. White, physician and surgeon, Ty Ty; Morgan and Corbett, attorneys at-law—Morgan, Albany; Corbett, Ty Ty—C. A. McDonald, attorney at-law, Ty Ty; T. K. Mashow's barroom and family grocery, located four miles south of Ty Ty at Pine Forest, Georgia; T. K. Mashow, dealer in naval stores, Ty Ty; the tonsorial saloon of R. G. W. Brooks, who offered to cut hair as smooth as a face, and shampoo heads; livery stable, W. W. Crockett, owner, Ty Ty; Spencer Graves, dealer in fancy articles, notions, patent medicine, patented safety single trees, soap, wagons, newspapers, magazines; J. B. Cannon, agent for New Home sewing machines, also contractor and builder; I. L. Ford and Company, north side of railroad; Ty Ty dealers in furniture, dry goods, groceries, fancy goods, confectionaries, boots and shoes, hardware, tinware, and turpentine tools; J. A. Payne, north side of railroad, dry goods, groceries, gents furnishings and buyer of wool and country produce; W. F. Harrell, dealer in fancy and family groceries, south side of railroad, Ty Ty.

Maund, son of Mr. and Mrs. T. M. Maund, was born in Dawson, Terrell County, September 30, 1863. When very young he learned in the office of the Dawson Journal the printing trade, which he followed for thirty-five years. He edited The Fledging in Dawson, and when about eighteen years old published Ty Ty's first newspaper, The Echo. Later he worked with the Worth County Local at Sumner, and for sometime was editor of the Irwin County News at Sycamore.

On May 3, 1882 he married Electra Kendrick, of Ty Ty. They had two children, a son, Leon, who was with The Times in Valdosta, and a little daughter.

Maund came to Tifton in 1894 and worked with The Gazette for eleven years, then went to Valdosta, where he worked for five years. In 1911 he returned to Tifton and his old job, foreman of mechanical department, and worked until his death, three months later. Maund was a member of the Methodist Church.

The Tifton Gazette, not the daily paper, was established as the Berrien Pioneer in 1889 by B. T. Allen, at Sparks, Georgia. In 1890 it was moved to Tifton and named The Tifton Gazette. The earliest copy of the Gazette now available is January 22, 1892. It is a four-page paper, with six thirteen-inch columns to the page. The outfit consisted of a small assortment of type, a Washington hand press, a job press and a small hand-lever paper cutter. The type was set by hand and the presses were operated by manpower.

[1]"The news items in Allen's paper were much more casual than they are in the Gazette of today; the headlines were smaller; and there was little attempt to separate the important news from the unimportant. Advertisements were segregated from the news, and they were for the most part less effectively written than they are in the present era. Some of the firms, however, notably E. P. Bowen, Tifton Drug Store, and the Padrick Brothers, were modern in their advertising.

"Like other newspapers of the nineties, the early Gazette had a charm that is foreign to modern journalism. Occasional Latin headlines, riming advertisements that carried the rich flavor of old English novels are for the most part a thing of the past.

"B. T. Allen was a man of no mean newspaper ability; his nose for news pointed toward the affairs of his neighbors, in which he realized his subscribers were primarily interested. If a baby boy was born to the Roscoe Hermans, Mr. Herman was made to 'bask in the sunlight of the sweet smile' of a handsome baby boy, newly arrived. An epidemic of measles was an event; and if a dog bit a man, to B. T. Allen, at least, it was news. Though chockfull of news from the town and surrounding territory, Allen's paper neglected state and national news except in editorial discussion.

---

1. Fred Shaw's manuscript about Tift County.

"Like other Gazette editors, Allen was intensely ambitious for his town and section. This ambition found partial expression in a wise thoughtfulness regarding the needs of the town. For instance, soon after the establishment of the paper, Editor Allen began agitation for a bank, a railroad to Thomasville, a better passenger depot, and the clearing of farm lands —all of which things were eminently desirable."

The following is an example of Allen's editorial comments:

"A Third Partyite has had the gall to try to buy our political opinions for a dollar. He agreed to take the Gazette another year if we would let up on our fight against his party—with its dangerous heresies known as the twelfth plank, female suffrage plank, etc. His subscription was declined with thanks. Sorry so thoughtless a citizen lives in Berrien County."

In 1895 Allen sold the newspaper and job printing to Baldridge and Fulwood, real estate firm. J. L. Herring, father of the present editor of the Gazette, accepted a position with the paper, which he later purchased; he served as manager and editor until his death in 1923. Then his son, John Greene Herring, was editor until his death in 1938, at which time Mr. Bob assumed the duties of editor.

During these years of progress the Gazette, paralleling the growth of its town, has sponsored many worthwhile movements in Tifton, and survived three wars, Spanish-American, World War I, and World War II. Since the date of its birth, September 14, 1914, the daily has won distinction. These honors have been recorded in a previous chapter.

The quaint type of wedding "write-ups" was illustrated in the Gazette of 1899:

"Our handsome young friend, Dr. J. A. Gaskins, of Willacoochee, has at last surrendered to the God of Love and was united in marriage Wednesday of last week to Miss Estelle Moate, at the residence of the bride's parents."

Another example is:

"It was on February 3, that Florida's most brilliant son and Georgia's most beautiful and loving daughter made the fatal leap which Lycurges calls the cardinal point in everybody's life. J. K. Fitzgerald to Miss Grace McMillan.

"After a series of congratulations from the lips of the multitude who witnessed the scene, they were seated to a most beautiful table, containing all the delicacies of life." A complete list of wedding presents was given.

Marriages were referred to in the old issues as Hymen's altar.

These were quaint rimes about styles:

> "What are the wild waves saying
> Brother, the whole day long?
> They're saying: Your bathing suit, sister,
> Will certainly shake the throng."

> "Mary had a hobble skirt
> From Paris it was sent
> And wheresoe'er she starts to go,
> She never seems to 'went'."

Some of the clever examples of advertisements are:
"An honest pill is the noblest work of the apothecary"—Dewitt's Early Risers.

"Honest John Liver Pills. A friend in need is a friend indeed. Not less than a million have found just such a friend in Dr. King's New Discovery."

"Noah advertised the flood. He lived through it, and the fellows who laughed at him were drowned. Ever since then the advertiser has been getting strong, and those who do not advertise, getting left."

> "Late to bed and early to rise
> Will shorten the road to
> Your home in the skies
> But early to bed and
> A Little Early Riser
> The pill that makes life
> Longer, and better, and wiser."

Entertainments were written up in a flowery style during the nineties:
"Wednesday evening Mrs. Boatright gave an entertainment in honor of the visiting young ladies and a gathering of youth and beauty did honor to the occasion. The game of Pillow Dex afforded much amusement and the recitation by Miss Belle Willingham of 'Prince Eric's Christ Maid' was superb. Miss Katherine Tift [now Mrs. Katherine Tift Jones, noted radio artist] rendered 'Aux Italiens' in the charming and inimitable style that is peculiarly her own and which so delights and entertains her listeners. Exquisite piano and guitar music was rendered by Miss Bertha and Mr. Ray Larkin, and with delicious refreshments, a feast of reason and a flow of soul, the evening was delightfully spent."

References to politics were interesting:

> "Rockaby, baby, your mamma has gone.
>   She's out at a caucus
> And will be till dawn.
>   She wore papa's trousers
> And in them looked queer
>   So hushaby, baby
> Your papa is here."

One advertisement suggested that Cleveland or Harrison would be elected President, according to the one who took Dewitt's Early Risers.

"The Gazette is for democracy pure and simple, first, last, and all the time . . . These are political times when Democrats cannot afford to compromise their faith in the slightest degree. Those who are not for democracy are enemies and should be treated as such."

"The conspiracy in which Tom Watson is engaged is damnable enough to make the departed spirit of Aaron Burr turn green with envy."

A negro said about the Third Party:
"Well, now lemme tell you, boss, you know dat de white folks is de fust party; de niggers am de second; now if you thinks I's gwine ter jine a party neaf a nigger, you is badly fooled, for I be dadsnatched if I do, dey is low down enough for me.—Fort Valley Leader."

Miscellaneous quotations from the old files are also interesting:

> " 'Come Eve,' said Adam sadly
>   From this place we must repair
> Because you ate that apple dear,
>   We must quit this garden fair;
> Then Eve looked meekly up at him
>   And sprang this gaglet rare,
> Which all her sisters since have used
>   'I've not a thing to wear'!"

"As a rule, man's a fool either accidentally or intentionally."

> " 'The man that speaks a dozen tongues
>   Is wise,' says Pat, 'but then
> He's wiser still if he has learned
>   To keep his mouth shut in'."

"Dr. Nick Peterson had a narrow escape last Friday while speeding his horse on Love Avenue. One tire of his road cart burst and the wheel spread out to such large dimensions that it overturned the cart, throwing the Doctor out on his head. He crawled out of the ditch somewhat disfigured about the forehead, but not seriously hurt."

"Prof. Gray of Alabama will preside over the destinies of McPherson. Academy, Nashville."

Modern reducing is suggested in the following:
"Oh, who would not a mermaid be?
She never moans or wails,
For even though she takes on flesh
She's not afraid of scales."

John Greene Herring, who was born on December 8, 1891, became editor of the Tifton Gazette after the death of his father, J. L. Herring, in 1923. He was graduated from the Tifton High School in 1909. He held every position on the paper from carrier boy to editor. During his connection with the Gazette it won the trophy given by the Georgia Bankers' Association for the Georgia newspaper doing the most constructive work for the restoration of confidence, the award offered by the War Cry, publication of Salvation Army, for best editorial on a religious subject, and a prize offered by the Emory School of Journalism for best editorial on the aims, ideals, and purposes of a newspaper.

For a while Mr. Herring was city editor of the Albany Herald and later a reporter for the Dublin Courier, but he returned to the Gazette and worked until his death in 1938.

He married Miss Ruby Hewitt. There are seven children in this family: Paul, Jack, Reuben, Tim, Lois, Sue, and Eunice.

Bob Herring, son of J. L. Herring, has been editor of the Gazette since 1938, when his brother died. "Mr. Bob," as many people call him, has lived in Tifton since his birth on July 28, 1899. He graduated from the Tifton High School in 1916 and went overseas in 1918. In 1919 Herring returned to the States.

Mr. Herring married Ida Mae Broadwell. They have two girls, Barbara and Jean (Mrs. John Matthews).

He is a member of the Tifton Chamber of Commerce, the American Legion, and the Methodist Church.

His connection with Gazette began as carrier when he was a little boy; press feeder was the next step; linotypist next; editor, last. Under his leadership the paper has progressed and as usual has paralleled the growth of Tifton. The paper has been honored and is considered one of the best small-town papers in the state. The last addition to the paper is an Associated Press teletype.

Miss Leola Judson Greene, Mr. Bob's maternal Aunt, who in 1947 celebrated her fiftieth anniversary of work with the Gazette, is another prominent Wire Grass journalist. She has done all kinds of work, from setting type to writing feature stories and editorials. She has written during three wars: Spanish-American War, World War I and World War II. A veteran newspaper woman and citizen of the highest type, Miss Leola though true to the ideals of the Old South is still progressive.

Miss Emma Rebecca Sutton, who wrote many interesting articles for the Tifton Gazette was a noted Wire Grass journalist. Years ago she went to New York as a newspaper reporter and stayed several years, but returned to her home in Ty Ty, where she was a benefactor to her community.

Gus Pat Adams, who selected Smada for his penname, wrote for the Tifton Gazette many interesting articles about Tift County people. The following article gives a sketch of his life:

GUS PAT ADAMS

(Copied from the Tifton Gazette)

"Nov. 24, 1933—Gus Pat Adams, 76 years old, one of the best known residents of this section of the state, died Friday morning at 2:20 at his home 3½ miles northeast of Chula. Adams was taken ill last summer while on a visit at Harrisburg, Va. He hurried to Tifton and was taken to the Coastal Plain Hospital, later being carried to his home near Chula, where he died. He was not married and made his home with D. H. Hogan and family who lived on Adams place.

"Adams was born in Brooklyn, N. Y. He was a painter and decorator and came to this section 35 years ago. He followed his profession many years and traveled about over this section, from town to town and went from home to home. He knew all the old residents of this section and visited with them. He made headquarters around Chula and it was at the home of William Branch near Chula 30 years ago that he was given the nickname, 'Pat.'

"Adams worked for the Gazette for several years as country circulator and became a regular contributor under the name Smada. Visiting around over the country he came to know all the old families and wrote up all of them in an interesting manner. He attended family reunions, annual meetings, and celebrations, and his writings of these gatherings were an interesting feature in the Gazette for many years.

"Pat Adams was an institution in this section. He was best known in Tift, Turner, and Irwin counties, but also known in a dozen other counties. He was an interesting talker as well as writer. He was well read, kept posted on politics, and could converse intelligently with learned or ignorant on any subject. Pat was a man of generous, jovial nature, and unfortunate was the man who didn't claim him as a friend. He had no relations in this section, but a host of friends, who will regret to learn of his death. Three sisters survive: Mrs. Francis Hale, Brooklyn, N. Y.; Mrs. Anna Gluckley, of Hackensack, N. Y., and Mrs. Emma Bailey, of Coscob, Conn. Buried at Hickory Springs by request.

The Tifton Free Press was established in September, 1940, by J. L. Williams, a pioneer of Tift County. For years while traveling in different parts of the United States he wrote for the Tifton Gazette several interesting articles. The Free Press is distributed in three groups, each group receiving papers every three weeks: five rural routes in one direction; six in another; and all directions in the city. These papers go into thirty-four different homes. Some are sent as far as Texas and Pennsylvania.

The Press is an unusual paper, which combines the journalism of a newspaper and magazine. Subjects range from humor to pathos; they are reminiscent, informal, thought-provoking, entertaining, and informational. The editor gives the reader the benefit of his observation and keen memory. Instead of publishing sensational articles, Williams gives historical, secular, and sacred sketches, biography, treatises on political and geographical subjects, discussions of ornithology, animals, diseases, economic problems, stories of human interest, and humorous informal essays.

Some of his best articles are "Koreshans at Estero, Florida," "The Humming Bird," "Cancer," "Monkeys," "Moses," "The Wise Men and Star of Bethlehem," "Reading and the Human Mind," "Short Skirts," "The Last Supper and Resurrection," and "Egypt."

Often Williams intersperses an interesting chapter of his own life and refers to many incidents connected with Tift County pioneers. During the last war he wrote articles about the different countries in the conflict.

The Omega News, a weekly newspaper, was established by J. W. Lang and his son, W. L. Lang, in 1938 at Omega, Tift County, Georgia. At that time the paper was three columns wide and ten inches in length. The type was set by hand and the paper printed on a hand operated press.

In 1940 some additional equipment was purchased including a cylinder press, driven by electric power. The size of the paper was increased to four pages and six columns. The type was still set by hand. In 1946 a linotype was purchased and the paper increased to six pages, still six columns in width.

The largest edition ever published by the Omega News was the Christmas 1946 special edition which included 22 pages. The News has been operated by the Langs ever since its establishment. J. W. Lang is co-owner and W. L. (Bub) Lang is managing editor. Bub took time out during World War II, when he served four years in the U. S. Navy holding the rank of lieutenant senior grade.

The Omega News has marched along with the progress of its community, which has doubled in population during the time the news has been serving its people.

Lucy Maude Dowd Thompson, daughter of William Richard Dowd and Mary Ann Overby Dowd, was born on October 8, 1876, in Stewart County, Georgia. She attended high school at a country community, then called Pleasant Valley, and later attended the State Normal School, first in 1898-1901.

Miss Dowd taught school from January 1, 1895 until June 1912. Seven years teaching was in one-teacher schools; the last teaching in 1912 was in Statesboro High School. She taught in Ty Ty from 1907 to 1910.

She married William Charles Thompson, of Ty Ty, Tift County, on August 8, 1912.

Mrs. Thompson was postmaster at Ty Ty from January 1, 1915 to July 1, 1930, and counts among her mementoes the commission signed by her admired President Woodrow Wilson.

She has been a member of the Methodist Church since a small child, and is now general superintendent of the Church School at Ty Ty Methodist Church, which appointment came seven years ago.

She is a life charter member of the Woman's Society of Christian Service; a charter member of the Woodman Circle, and financial secretary since 1920; a member of the D.A.R., and is eligible for membership in Colonial Dames.

Her hobbies are folks and flowers. She still feels a deep personal interest in each person she taught in school or Church School.

Some of her feature stories have been published in the Tifton Gazette and other newspapers of the state. Her articles and other contributions have meant much to the development of Ty Ty.

The life and distinctive contributions of J. L. Herring, former editor of Tifton Gazette, are presented in the pioneer chapter. Mr. Herring as an editor and author of "Saturday Night Sketches" deserves a distinctive place in Georgia. He was the prose Robert Burns of the Wire Grass. The following is one of the "Saturday Night Sketches":

A WIRE GRASS EASTER

We walked to church—we had no other way of going. The path led over the gently undulating hills, through swishing wire grass, verdant with the return of spring. Overhead the sighing pines also had taken on a brighter tinge with the life of the new year. The poplars and blackgums in the branch to the right were in leaf; the dark green of the bay was relieved, as by a snowy shower, by the dogwood in full bloom. Out on the edge of the bushes the gallberries formed a greenish saffron background for clumps of honeysuckle in full pink flower. The air was heavy with perfume, redolent with the lassitude of spring.

The little log church stood in a small grove of oaks on top of the hill. Between the cracks of the logs the spring breeze came unobstructed; the tiny shutterless windows on either side were useless The broad door in one end marked a dividing aisle, on either side of which the rough benches were ranged. On one side sat the women and girls; on the other the men and boys. In the pine-board pulpit stood the preacher, a patriarch with white, flowing beard, deep voice and a knowledge of the Bible gained through many years of study at noon rest time, or by the light of a tallow candle, or a lightwood-knot fire.

The Boy lounged lazily on a bench underneath the small window and watched the door. For a while vainly, and then She came! And with her a breath Elysian, a sense of completeness; all in the world worth while was there!

Not even a small part of the large sum required now for Easter toggery went toward her adornment, but to the eye nothing was lacking. Her dress of delicately figured calico had been fashioned by her own skilled fingers; with tight-fitting basque and flowing skirt her figure was faultless; just the tips of her shoes showed as she stepped, a rustle of many skirts betraying the efficiency of the home laundry. A ribbon at her waist, another at her collar, a tiny bunch of violets pinned at her breast.

No Easter bonnet of fabulous price upon her head, but a real bonnet of pink calico, corded and quilted until it stood out stiffly as board (aided by thin strips of pine inserted), enshrined her face, as a priceless living picture in its frame.

A wonderful thing, that bonnet. Its front came down as her chin retired, just at the time to tease; it went up as her head was raised, in a manner most alluring. Back in its depths her cheeks glowed with the blush of the rose in springtime; her eyes sparkled with the light of the stars in summer; her hair rippled as the nut-brown throat of the thrush, catching the light from the sunbeams dancing outside; her fluttering breath came and went as the perfume of the summer pinks beside the walk at home.

Then, the bonnet was laid aside to catch the summer air, and all the wonderful glories it had half concealed came with amazing suddenness to the youth who gazed, entranced. Only one brief glance did she vouchsafe him, when she turned reverently to where the preacher, who had opened his Bible, was searching in his hymn book for the Easter anthem to line to the waiting congregation.

A sermon of power it was, of the risen Jesus, and the fearful price he had paid, but of a Jesus triumphant, because He had conquered by love;

of the promise and the invitation; of the wonderful brotherhood of Man and the certainty of immortality through Him who went down into the grave and rose again to live and conquer, giving life everlasting through death of agony.

When the sermon was over, the Boy was waiting outside. She came hesitatingly, laughing with girl companions, and pretending not to see. But, although he blushed and stammered, he was resolute, and when the direct question came she could not ignore. So they walked to her home through the springtime and the sunshine; the life of one, and the warmth of the other in their hearts.

JAMES LUTHER WILLIAMS
Who Started the Florida Boom
by Elizabeth Pickard Karsten

James Luther Willliams was born in what formerly was called the Talokas District, in Brooks County, Georgia, February 1, 1880, son of Dr. Greene Berry Williams (born Wilkinson County, Georgia, April 19, 1836) and Martha Brice Williams (born Brooks County, Talokas District, April 21, 1843).

Almost from infancy Luther Williams loved horses. Early he learned to ride. His uncle, Mitchell Brice, of Brooks County, owned large farms and Mitchell and his son had a long string of race horses. They raised them and young Luther rode them, at the smaller towns in Georgia, and in Savannah and at Orlando, Florida. Among the most famous animals owned by Mitchell were Jennie B., Maude, Baltic, Little Baltic. Jennie B. equaled the world's record for a quarter of a mile, at Rome, Georgia, in 1890. One vacation Luther had an unusually happy holiday period; then came his bitterest disappointment: he could ride in the races no more, because he had grown too big to be a jockey.

Luther remained at home until he was twelve. Thereafter he attended school a year and worked a year. For several years this was his wont. He went to the Quitman public schools.

When not yet sixteen Williams went into the telephone business, first at Quitman, then in Valdosta, then in Quitman again, and, in 1898, in Tifton, where he came to overhaul the telephone exchange. He remained here from January to July, 1989. From Tifton he went to Newbern, North Carolina, where he was manager of the telephone company of which Nathan Strauss, of New York, was president. He was at Newbern until December, 1898. Thence he went to Waycross. Thence he returned to Tifton, in March 1899.

October 2, 1900, James Luther Williams was married to Lelia Linton

Goff, of Cochran, daughter of Charles Gordon Goff and Missouri Salome Thompson, of Houston County. Dr. Charles Dilworth performed the ceremony at the Tifton Baptist parsonage, later the B. B. Grantham home.

At Valdosta in 1898 Mr. Williams experienced his first wireless achievement. He was talking in broken conversation from Valdosta to Waycross with a quarter of a mile of line out. Next day he told of the extraordinary experience and people were skeptical. Since no one believed him he stopped telling the incident. The line was a high powered cable and the atmospheric conditions were excellent for reception.

During World War I when the United States was experiencing a sugar shortage Mr. Williams invented a new kind of plow which revolutionized the method of cultivation of sugar cane in the vast cane growing fields of Cuba.

Cuban cane fields had been oxen-plowed. Tractor cultivation had failed. Williams, then with a large harvester company, designed and had built at Chattanooga a model which successfully did the difficult work. He narrowed the furrow from ten to five inches, doubled the weight of the plow, and made the frame twice as high. This was used successfully in Egypt and elsewhere. At that time Williams had succeeded better than any other known man, perhaps, in designing, building, and operating tractor plows.

A horse could not work in the Everglades. In 1916 Mr. Williams traveled through the Everglades with the idea of plowing them with a tractor plow. Traveling, he did not plow until 1918, when he made a tractor plowing demonstration before 238 people, gathered fifteen miles up the Miami Canal. Most of those present were real estate men. Williams was asked to make a speech. He did, and told what it would mean to Florida if the five million acre Everglades were brought under cultivation. He was requested to make the same speech before the Miami real estate firm of Tatem Brothers, next morning at 9:00 o'clock. He did. He spoke to a large gathering of Miami real estate men. After the talk Tatem Brothers raised the price of land ten dollars per acre. They owned 190,000 acres. Other realtors followed. Two-thirds of the Everglades were brought under cultivation. Land prices rose. The speech was carried in the Miami paper, Savannah, Tampa, Atlanta, Baltimore papers, and elsewhere. Florida land prices rose. The boom was on.

Mr. Williams put in telephone exchanges at Ashburn, Adel, Boston, Marianna, Florida, and remodelled many elsewhere.

In his wide travels Williams saw many interesting things. Of some of these he wrote and his articles were printed in the Tifton Gazette, whose editor, Mr. J. L. Herring, was a close friend of Mr. Williams. Williams never at any time had a position with the Gazette either as writer or as printer.

About 1930 Mr. Williams decided to have a printing shop of his own.

In 1936 he began printing the Tifton Free Press, for which he wrote the articles. It appeared occasionally. In 1940 he began printing the paper regularly as a weekly and this he continues to do.

After going out of the telephone business Mr. Williams for a time manufactured cross arms, the first manufactured in Georgia. Prior to this, manufacture had been in Chattanooga.

James Luther Williams and Lelia Goff Williams have five children: Ralph James, Frederick Claude, Martha Blanch (Mrs. Ashley McLeod), J. L. Williams, Jr., Lena Gordon Williams.

Mrs. Elizabeth Pickard Karsten, author of the pioneers' biographies in this volume, has made distinct contributions to the journalism of this section and other places. Her feature stories have appeared in New Rochelle News (New York), the New York Herald, New Haven Register, Boston Transcript, and several Georgia papers. While staff correspondent for the Macon Telegraph, she rendered valuable services to Tift County. Her work on the pioneers' chapters of the History of Tift County is another contribution to the county and Tifton.

Mrs. Karsten did her first historical writing for the Macon Centennial Pageant. She has written a biography of Mrs. H. H. Tift and many historical sketches of different places in the United States. She is the author of genealogical publications, dramatization, and miscellaneous articles.

Her advanced training includes courses at Wesleyan College, Abraham Baldwin College, Mercer University, and Yale University. She is a member of the Macon Writers' Club (of which she was secretary, treasurer, historian, vice-president, and president), and Gun Lake Country Club, New Haven Point and Clay, and New Haven Brush and Palette. Mrs. Karsten is also a member of the R.A.R. and Phi Mu.

The daughter of William Lowndes Pickard (clergyman and former president of Mercer University) and Florence Willingham Pickard (artist and painter) Elizabeth Pickard Karsten was born in Louisville, Kentucky. In 1914 she married Paul Daggett Karsten of Macon, Georgia. Their children are Paul Daggett, Jr., (married Elizabeth La Field), Florence Willingham Karsten (married Robert Clements Carson), and Mikell Baynard Karsten. Their son, Billy Karsten died in 1941.

"Who's Who in Georgia" and "The Standard Biographical Dictionary of Notable Women" have sketches of Mrs. Elizabeth Karsten.

CHAPTER XXIII

TIFT COUNTY AGRICULTURE

by George Harris King

Different counties are prosperous for various reasons. Tift County is prosperous because of its agricultural interests. A progressive group of some 1,600 farmers produce a number of varied farm products. Within the towns of the county are markets and processing plants for these products. The industry of Tift County, to a large extent, is based on its agriculture. The result is an agricultural market reaching beyond the borders of the county and bringing in the products of a large area. The farm products sold in Tift County yearly amounts to twice or three times the value of the products produced within Tift County.

The history of agriculture in Tift County is a story of change and progress. Originally the area now known as Tift County was settled for its wealth of lumber and naval stores, and until about 1910 those industries absorbed the attention of the inhabitants. The change from a timber economy to one of agriculture occurred about the same time as the formation of Tift County in 1905.

Fortunately for the inhabitants of Tift County the removal of the timber disclosed a responsive agricultural soil adapted to a number of agricultural enterprises. As the adaptability of the soil became known, there was a migration of farmers from other sections of Georgia seeking fresh agricultural lands. This brief history must of necessity deal with trends rather than personalities. Few names and few concerns will be mentioned. It is sufficient to emphasize the fact that the progress of Tift County was due not only to the adaptability of its soil, but also to the initiative and courage of its pioneer farmers.

A Bureau of Soils bulletin written in 1909 saw at this early period the possibilities of the Tifton Sandy Loam Soil which makes up the greater part of the county "Cotton, corn, sweet potatoes, Irish potatoes, peanuts, sugar cane, tree and small fruits, pecans, vegetables, and, in fact, all of the crops grown in the county do well on this soil."

Changes which have taken place over the years may be noted by quoting from this report made in 1909:

"Good farming land 5 miles from town selling for $15.00 to $30.00 per acre."

"Corn and cotton are the principal crops."

"The favorable soil and climate, the splendid markets and the ease with which pests and diseases can be controlled ... are abundant reasons why the peach growing industry should be given a thorough trial."

"Livestock raising in this area is profitable and should be given more attention. At present, practically all of the livestock run loose in the swamps and pine woods and get their living as best they can."

"The use of improved machinery is strongly advised. The character of the soils and the smooth topography are both suited to it."

Some changes not even predicted in 1909 have taken place over the years. Flue-cured tobacco was first grown on a commercial scale in Tift by Irvine Myers in 1917 although Captain H. H. Tift had tried some tobacco along with his other agricultural experiments at an earlier date. By 1919 there were 615 acres of tobacco grown in the county. Twenty years later the golden weed was being grown on 4,696 acres. Tifton had developed into one of the leading markets of the State and held first place for a number of years.

The first vegetable plants grown for commercial shipment were produced by Myers Brothers about 1907 when they shipped small amounts of cabbage and sweet potato plants. P. D. Fulwood, Sr., started growing cabbage plants in 1909 and tomato plants in 1912. He is regarded as the first to grow plants on a real commercial scale in this area. From this beginning has grown an industry involving thousands of acres and hundreds of thousands of dollars.

In 1909 the peanut was looked upon as good hog feed although "one concern is preparing to grow peanuts on a commercial scale." In 1923, only 670 acres were dug. In 1940 peanuts were harvested from 8,000 acres. During World War II, the Government stimulated the production of peanuts and in 1946 peanuts were dug from 18,000 acres.

The preceding three enterprises (tobacco, plants, and peanuts), have possibly brought the greatest changes in land use in Tift County, and, yet, these crops were hardly recognized 40 years ago. With these new enterprises in mind, let us contrast the agriculture of 1947 with that pictured in 1909.

Where good farm land 5 miles from town sold for $15.00 to $30.00, today it sells from $75.00 to $150.00 per acre.

In 1909 corn and cotton were the principal crops. In 1940 only 9,629 acres of cotton were grown and by 1944 this dropped to a low of 3,000 acres which had increased some by 1947. This may be contrasted with an acreage of 27,000 acres in 1923. This change to a large measure was brought about by the advent of the boll weevil which hit Tift County in the middle teens and reached the climax of its damage in 1923, when only 3,753 bales of cotton were produced on the 27,000 acres planted. This forced the producers of cotton to other enterprises, mainly peanuts, tobacco and livestock.

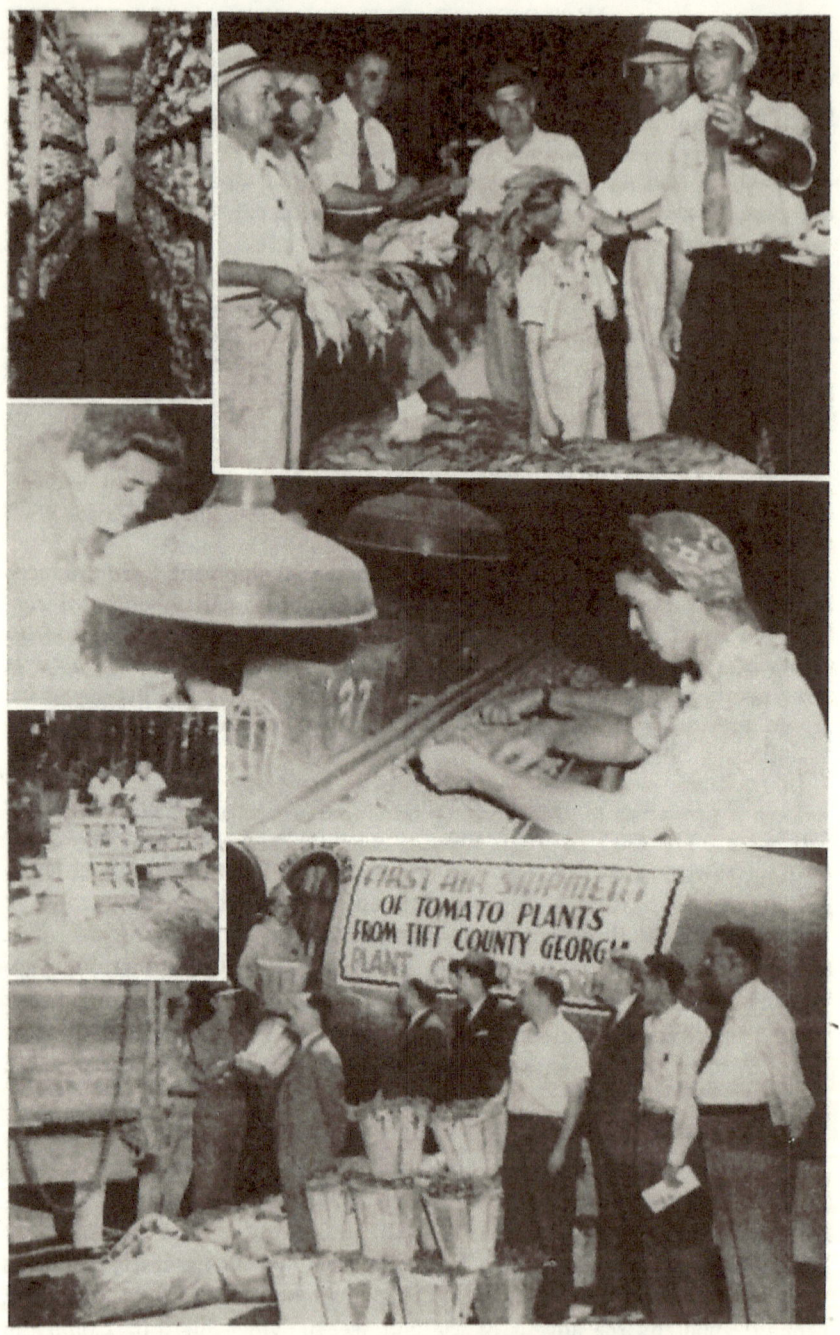

TIFT COUNTY'S DIVERSIFIED AGRICULTURE

Top row—Interior of one of several meat curing and storage plants at Tifton. The chant of the auctioneer in one of Tifton's tobacco sales warehouses.
Center—Grading and sorting peanuts at a Tifton mill
Bottom row—Preparing honey for shipment in Tift County piney woods. The modern in agriculture—Tift County's first shipment of vegetable plants by air.

There has been little change in corn acreage. The smaller amount needed for diminishing numbers of workstock is offset by the needs of increased numbers of hogs and cattle.

In 1909 peaches were looked upon as a promising crop but the prevalence of the rootknot nematode in the soil brought the realization that this section was not an ideal one for this susceptible fruit. At present, there is hope that peaches may again be grown on a commercial scale due to newly developed chemicals and rotations which check the ravages of the nematode.

When the 1909 report cited the inferior livestock and the lack of fencing, we find that by 1940 the livestock situation has shown marked improvement. The no-fence law was passed in 1921. Better breeds of livestock have been introduced, better managerial practices are followed, pastures have been improved, and feed crops have increased in acreage. So promising was the livestock industry that Armour and Company took over the packing plant in Tifton in 1919. This plant had been constructed in 1917. This was closed in about a year on account of lack of livestock, but reopened in November, 1935, and has been in constant operation since that time.

The number of beef cattle on the farms at the first of the year more than doubled from 1920 to 1940. The number of swine on the farms at the same time has increased by 30 per cent. The total value of all livestock and livestock products sold in Tift County in 1945 was $549,249.00.

The increased use of machinery has been almost phenomenal. In 1910 the value of machinery and implements on Tift County farms was $93,735.00. In 1920 this value had risen to $368,819.00, while in 1945 the farm implements and machinery of Tift County farmers were valued at $988,690.00. 266 Tift County farmers operated 315 tractors in 1945 and 368 farmers were operating 453 trucks. Less than 100 tractors were in operation as recently as 1940.

A glance at the 1945 farm income figures tells the story of farm prosperity:

Crop Sales	$3,075,832
Fruits and Nuts Sales	79,899
Vegetable Sales	44,270
Horticultural Specialties	303,461
All Livestock & Livestock Products	549,294
Forest Products	42,439
Farm Products Used on Farm	701,632
Total	$4,796,827
Average value per farm	$ 2,872

The above figures are taken from the 1945 census and possibly do not include the full value received from the sale of vegetable plants.

The farm population of Tift County is stable. For the most part, the farming is done by white farmers. Of the 1,683 farms in the County, 1,345 are operated by white families. The number of farms in the County has varied some with the economic conditions. The following table shows the number of farms for census years:

Year	Number of Farms
1910	1142
1920	1360
1930	1398
1940	1344
1945	1683

Over half of the farm operators are tenants. The following table shows the percentage of tenants for census years:

Year	Per Cent of Tenants
1910	57%
1920	60%
1930	70%
1940	56%
1945	59%

The work of professionals in agriculture has always been sponsored by Tift County. Two years after its organization, Tift County secured the Second District A. and M. School by donation of land and public subscription. This school, after some changes, is now Abraham Baldwin Agricultural College. In 1919, through the same method, Tift County was selected as the site of the Georgia Coastal Plain Experiment Station. The Smith-Lever Bill providing for county agents was passed, and Tift County secured its first county agent and its first home demonstration agent shortly after this time. Tifton High School has a teacher of Vocational Agriculture and two teachers of Home Economics under the Smith-Hughes Law. These are agencies requiring expense on the part of the County. Those agencies, purely Federal, have received the support of the farmers of the County and the County has benefited through its cooperation with the Soil Conservation Service, Farm Home Administration and the Production Marketing Administration.

Tift County, because of its soil and climate, is agriculturally blessed. From a land of timber it has developed into an agricultural section, growing enterprises of enough diversity to insure a prosperous agriculture. Its people have proved themselves progressive by adapting themselves to a changing agriculture. Its agricultural history is something of which we may all be proud; its agricultural future is something to which we may look with confidence.

TOBACCO IN TIFT COUNTY

by E. Pickard

Georgia's earliest tobacco-growing project was during her colonial days. Near the coast a small town built around the culture and sale of tobacco became a flourishing little trade center. Tobacco was its life; but the town, which had little other than tobacco, died and became one of Georgia's ghost towns. Few people know that it ever existed.

It appears that after the above mentioned project, what is now Tift County was the next place where tobacco was grown for market, though many old gardens contained a few plants for the personal supply of their owners. In 1892, H. H. Tift grew tobacco in what was then Berrien but is now Tift County. He was interested in seeing what crops could be successfully grown in this section of the state, and he grew the tobacco experimentally. The Tifton Gazette in 1892 carried in one of its issues the following item: "Growing tobacco bids to become an important industry in this section."

The Tifton Gazette of February 12, 1892 stated: "The officers of the Snow Modern Tobacco Company, President D. A. Walters, of Philadelphia, Secretary, D. G. Bevenish, of Oxford, North Carolina, and W. H. Snow, general manager, spent several days in Tifton prospecting for a location for a Georgia branch of their company. All expressed themselves as delighted with the possibilities of tobacco growing here."

Burwell Greene was in charge of H. H. Tift's several farms and was in charge of that early tobacco experiment. Men came down from North Carolina to do the curing. It was flue-cured and the old tobacco barns used at that time stood on the Experiment Station land, then owned by H. H. Tift, until a few years ago. Satisfied that tobacco could be successfully grown here, Captain Tift abandoned the project in favor of others in which he was more interested.

In 1893 Tift City Council placed a high tax on the sale of cigarettes in Tifton, but repealed the ordinance on February 5, 1894.

A preacher came from North Carolina to Douglas and there began cultivating tobacco.

About 1915 the A. B. and A. railroad began promoting the culture of tobacco. W. W. Croxton, general passenger agent for the road, was in charge of the movement, and the tobacco was sold at Timmonsville, South Carolina.

About the same time, the Central of Georgia hired Jim Winslow to promote the tobacco growing industry in Alabama and Georgia. The Southern also had a similar program.

The production of bright leaf in Georgia in 1917 was less than half a million pounds. It was not until the boll weevil infested the Sea Island

Scenes in Tift County

cotton area of this section that Tift County again turned to the growing of tobacco. Tobacco production in Georgia exceeded three million pounds, in 1918. Tobacco was grown in Tift County in 1918. That year I. W. Myers had fourteen acres in tobacco which brought him about $5,000.00. Others grew it here that year, also. In 1918 there was only a part time tobacco market in Tifton. In December, 1918 J. J. Taylor and N. C. Taylor, brothers, tobacco experts were in this vicinity promoting tobacco growing.

In 1918 tobacco was sold at Ashburn in the morning and at Tifton in the afternoon, or it was sold at Ashburn one day and at Tifton the next. At Tifton it was marketed at the old Cotton compress, by Fenner. In 1919 the warehouse was renovated to become a regular tobacco warehouse and to 1922 it continued to be operated as Fenner's Warehouse. In 1922 it was operated by W. E. Fenner.

In 1922 the first brick warehouse was built, the south building of what is now Twin Brick. In 1923 Fenner's name changed to Banner Warehouse and operated under its present management. In 1925 the New Brick Warehouse—the north half of what is now Twin Brick—was built. In 1928 the Banner and New Brick's names were changed to Twin Brick, which was built by the Tifton Investment Company.

In 1920 the Imperial Tobacco Company of Great Britain began operation in Tifton, where Sam Lassiter was in charge of the company. He has been its only resident manager from then until now. Not only has he handled the affairs of the company capably but he has also taken a prominent part in other affairs of the community. For a number of years he headed the Tifton City Council; he was head of the Tifton Board of Trade; was president of the Tifton Rotary Club; is a steward of the Tifton Methodist Church; during World War II he was Tift County Chairman of the American Red Cross.

In 1921, Dr. Silas Starr, head of the Georgia Coastal Plain Experiment Station, announced that the Station had been chosen as the location of the United States office of tobacco investigation.

On Thursday, August 2, 1923, Tifton and Tift County Tobacco Boosters, 140 strong, in 30 cars, toured the tobacco growing section making an 190-mile trip to boost Tifton as a tobacco market. First stop was Lenox. Thence the motorcade went to Adel, Cecil, Hahira, and to Valdosta.

At the Experiment Station the most complete experiments made were in tobacco. Work in this began just about the time the crop began to be grown in this section and the work of the station was of inestimable value to the growers. J. C. Hart was in charge of tobacco work at the station until 1925, when he went to Brazil. Next came J. M. Carr, from Virginia. R. C. Thomas experimented at the Station with diseases of tobacco.

J. G. Gaines later made valuable discoveries for control of blue mold and root knot.

Tifton-sold tobacco is not tied. Once there was a great stir about the necessity of tying. It was tied for a few days. The practice was not popular with the growers, and the matter was dropped. It continues to be sold untied.

In 1926 Tifton ranked fourth in the state in tobacco sales. First place was held by Douglas; Blackshear was second; Nashville was third. That year Tifton's first hand sales were 3,987,598 pounds, at $22.66 average, for $903,759.75.

That year was organized the Tifton Tobacco Board of Trade, on Monday night, August 2. Sam Lassiter was chosen president, J. L. Bowen (treasurer of the Tifton Investment Company), was chosen vice-president; J. P. Culpepper was secretary and treasurer.

The September 3, 1926 issue of the Tifton Gazette was a Tobacco Edition. In it appeared an article on tobacco by H. H. Tift, Jr.

In 1927 Tifton leaped into rank of a million dollar sales market.

In 1928 Farmer's Warehouse was built.

In 1931 Tifton sold 8,280,076 pounds. Valdosta came next with 7,114,453. Moultrie had third place. However, that year the leaf brought the lowest price brought by Georgia tobacco since the establishment of the Georgia market. Nevertheless that year Tifton took the lead among the markets of the state, and with brief exception has continued to hold first place

In 1932 Tifton headed the state with 2,168,386 pounds sold. Valdosta was second; Moultrie third. However, Tifton's average that year was in third place, at $11.23. Nevertheless, the state average that year was even lower: $10.41. Adel led in average.

In 1933 Tifton sold 9,178,398 pounds, which brought $1,115,000.00, at average $12.16 per 100 pounds. It led in average as well as in poundage.

That year, 1933, Tifton had the two Georgia warehouses leading in total tobacco sales for the 1933 season—the only Georgia warehouses selling more than three million pounds each that season. Farmers' Warehouse, managed by A. W. Jeffreys, led the state, with total of 3,235,016 pounds, averaging $12.76. Twin Brick, managed by W. H. Winstead, was second, in the state, with 3,192,338 pounds, at $11.80 average. Fenners, managed by C. G. Weathersby, was fourth in the state.

In September, 1933, at the Georgia Coastal Plain Experiment Station, county agents and growers met to plan a reduction of tobacco acreage.

Blue mold first appeared in the flue-cured tobacco belt in 1931. In 1932 and 1937 the disease was severe.

The Triple A program for tobacco began in 1933. Excepting 1937, this has continued. That same year Washington placed a processing tax on tobacco, thus placing it with cotton and wheat as to this measure.

In the spring of 1934 the Georgia Flue-cured Tobacco Growers Association was formed, at Tifton. Judge J. F. McCrackin, of Valdosta, was president. J. C. Lanier spoke. The second meeting was held in Tifton May 2, 1935. E. P. Bowen, Jr., was invited to address the meeting.

In 1935 United States sale of tobacco was cut by the largeness of the Chinese tobacco sales of that year.

In 1936 Tifton sales exceeded that of 1935. In 1937, despite unfavorable weather conditions, sales were good but did not reach 1935's record; for blue mold took its toll.

In 1935 the new Banner warehouse was built South of the A. B. and C. depot. In 1936 Fenners' No. 2 was built. It was destroyed by fire that fall but was rebuilt in 1937. This brought the number of Tifton tobacco warehouses to six.

1935 and 1936 were high years for the Tifton market.

With brief exception Tifton has led the state in poundage and in price since 1931. However, in 1945 she dropped from first place. Perhaps it was because her volume in other agricultural crops is constantly increasing, and the big warehouses are often filled with other plants that are shipped in vast quantities and over a wide area.

The result of the 1947 season is not yet known. The market opened July 24, and the big warehouses, as usual, were crowded with tobacco and with people, and the leaf today brought a high price. The huge warehouses have long rows of neatly stacked fragrant leaf, placed in flat baskets. The crowd of country people are picturesque and colorful in their bright colored clothing, a contrast to the saneness of the tan of the leaf. The melodious chant, or the unintelligible jargon of the auctioneer, drawing after him, like iron to magnet, the long line of buyers, and lookers-on, draws and holds the attention of all. It is almost as though one were under a spell—the spell of the fragrance of the tobacco, the humming drone of the voice—the sultriness of the air. It is the spell of the tobacco season.

The town will be flooded with out-of-town buyers, whose money will support the town for many months. The town also will be flooded with crooks and thieves, come to steal or swindle from the unwary; and in the hottest time of the year it is necessary to be constantly vigilant against prowlers. Young and old will dance at the tobacco ball, the Tobacco Queen will be crowned, the Chamber of Commerce will give away valuable prizes.

The town will be gay, and happy and tired, and thankful for the money earned; but it will really have earned it, and in the hard way.

MRS. PAUL FULWOOD, SR.

Ida Belle Williams

Mrs. Paul Dearing Fulwood, Sr., daughter of Mr. E. L. and Mary Etta Goodman Vickers was born in Tifton, Georgia, on March 3, 1892. She received her education at Tifton High School and Wesleyan College.

In 1910 she married Paul Dearing Fulwood, Sr., who the year before had begun experimenting in raising plants near what is now the airport in Tifton. For a while Mr. and Mrs. Fulwood lived in Tifton, but later they and the children, Paul and Ruth, moved to a crude little house in the woods, where the plants were growing.

It was not long, however, before Mrs. Fulwood with her artistic taste transformed the shack into an attractive home. She made curtains of seed bags, had the walls and exterior of the house painted, and planted radiance roses and other flowers in the well-kept yard. (Some of the same rose bushes are now growing in her garden in Tifton.) Morning-glories shaded her front porch, and two enormous cabbage plants growing in kegs on either side of her front steps attracted much attention. Since there was not enough room for the company bed and there were no day beds then, Mrs. Fulwood cleverly improvised a drawer in the loft, where the extra bed stayed when not in use.

From this humble beginning of planting roses to beautifying a rustic cottage, Mrs. Fulwood has achieved national distinction as an authority in rose culture. She accepted invitations to speak about roses at the convention of the American Rose Society, at the Potomac Rose Society, Washington, District of Columbia, at the American Rose Society in Knoxville, Tennessee, and in Columbus, Ohio. Mrs. Fulwood has written magazine articles about roses. She is a member of the advisory board of the American Rose Society, representing the Southeastern section. Besides being president of the Tifton Garden Club, she served for two terms as president of the Georgia Rose Society.

Her home with its attractive gardens on Twelfth Street in Tifton is one of the beauty spots of South Georgia. Mrs. Fulwood has thousands of rare specimens of roses. Among the number are exotic rose trees. Her talent for beautifying does not end at her home; her floral contributions are obvious on the hospital grounds, at Fulwood Park, and at the cemetery.

Mrs. Fulwood has contributed to the progress of Tifton in many other ways besides beautification. She was the first woman in Georgia to be president of a board of trade and probably the first one in the world. She was elected president of the Tifton Board of Trade in 1931. Mrs. Fulwood organized the first presidents' club in Georgia and the first P.-T. A. Council in Tifton. She directed at Abraham Baldwin College a rose school, which others in different sections of the county copied. During the time she was president of the Board of Trade, Mrs. Fulwood directed a spectacular pageant, to help cotton industry and made other effective contributions to the development of Tifton.

Governor Richard B. Russell, Junior, appointed Mrs. Fulwod a member of the Georgia Committee to advertise the state and arrange for an exhibit at the World's Fair in Chicago. She was also appointed on a similar committee for the World's Fair in New York.

In addition to her material contributions she is a vital force in the spiritual welfare of her native town. For many years Mrs. Fulwood has taught a Sunday School class at the Tifton Methodist Church and served in other religious organizations.

PAUL DEARING FULWOOD, SR.
Ida Belle Williams

The name, Paul Dearing Fulwood, Sr., connotes plant development in Tifton. When a boy Paul ran away from home to escape being a machinist, the choice of his father, C. A. Fulwood. At Fort Myers, Florida, young Fulwood worked with a man in the tomato plant industry. Deciding to become a planter himself, the boy returned to Tifton in 1909 and began raising plants near what is now the airport. The first year he planted thirty-five pounds of cabbage, nine pounds of tomatoes and bedded three-hundred-fifty pounds of potatoes.

After experimenting a while, young Fulwood went to the University of Georgia to study agriculture.

In 1910 he married Miss Ruth Vickers, and they lived in Tifton for a while, but later moved to the farm. There were few conveniences in the rustic cottage, but determined to have a telephone, he and his wife while standing in a wagon put up the wires.

The evolution of sales is interesting. During the first year people came to Mr. Fulwood to buy plants. His advertisements were placards on trees. The next step was to deposit his plants in stores, where sales would be easier. Then people living in different directions ordered tomato, cabbage, sweet potato, and onion plants. The idea of shipping dawned and Fulwood was the first person in this section to ship plants. His next progress was his connection with Massingale Advertising Agency. From the modest leaflet and pamphlet to the artistic pictorial calendar, the advertising program has grown. Now beet, onion, cabbage, potato, pepper, broccoli, tomato, lettuce and brussel sprout seedlings are shipped.

Although one of the busiest men in the state, Mr. Fulwood observes vacation time by enjoying his hobbies, boating and swimming.

His versatility is further shown in his religious work. For twelve years Mr. Fulwood was superintendent of the Tifton Methodist Sunday School. He is also one of the county commissioners.

Scenes on Farms in Tift County

Tomato plants used to lead the sales; however, in 1946 the Fulwood Company shipped 120,000,000 plants which grew from five thousand pounds of bedded potatoes, twelve thousand pounds of cabbage seed, twenty-seven-five hundred pounds of onion seed, and three thousand pounds of tomato seed. These plants are shipped in wet moss to practically every state in the country and to Hawaii. Such companies as Campbell Soup and Stokeley-Van Camp learned that Fulwood's seedlings grown in a field were stronger than those grown under glass. Campbell Company buys 80,000,000 tomato plants a year.

Mr. Fulwood's son, Paul Dearing, Junior, general manager of the company, and ex-student of plant pathology at the University of Georgia, Howard Davis, and Baldwin Davis, Sr. (deceased), contributed much to the plant industry in Tift County. The Davises were the machinists of the company. Paul while studying at the University of Georgia proved in his thesis that plant diseases come through the seed. He is responsible for certified seed in this section.

Hail and freezes used to cause Mr. Fulwood to lose thousands of dollars until he learned to replant soon after a loss.

The Fulwood farms cover about eighteen hundred acres of land, eight hundred of which have irrigation. The packing plant containing 45,000 square feet of floor space, is probably the largest packing house for vegetables in the world. This industry, one of the largest in the country, pays plant pullers as much as twenty-eight dollars a day; the first year this labor brought seventy-five cents a day.

CHAPTER XXIV
INDUSTRIES
THE SOUTHERN COTTON OIL COMPANY

The Southern Cotton Oil Company was organized in 1912 as the Planters' Cotton Oil Company. H. H. Tift was the first president; J. H. White, first manager. At first it was operated by local stockholders—among the number were W. W. Banks, E. P. Bowen, Sr., and H. H. Tift. The mill was sold in 1930 to the International Oil Company, which also operated mills in the Philippine Islands. At this time the mill was partly financed by a Boston Bank.

In 1936 the organization was sold to the Southern Cotton Oil Company. This mill has one of the largest cotton seed crushers in the country. From 1936 to 1941 the mill was operated only as an oil mill; in 1941 the company put in a peanut shelling plant.

The Southern Cotton Oil Company is owned and controlled by Southerners from New Orleans, Louisiana. R. A. Kelly has been manager of the company since 1930.

ARMOUR ENTERS TIFTON TERRITORY

Co-incident with the first world war and the food and commodity problems which accompanied it, Southern farmers adopted a program of diversification in which livestock naturally played an important role. Noting the considerable increase in the number of cattle and hogs being raised on Southern lands, Armour and Company looked about for a way to assist in the diversification movement by improving the marketing outlets for southern livestock growers. When a packing plant at Tifton was offered to the company at a reasonable price Armour bought it and thus became identified with the livestock business in the southeast.

The Tifton Packing Company, financed largely by South Georgia farmers, had been in operation a year or two before Armour came into the territory. It seems probable that the promoters had under-estimated the importance of experienced management and established outlets to the retail trade, and in consequence the plant was not doing well financially despite satisfactory supplies of livestock in the Tifton territory.

Immediately following purchase of the plant, Armour took possession and on June 30, 1919 began operating it. The plant is equipped to handle the slaughter of cattle, hogs, sheep and calves and to process those cuts which require curing, smoking, rendering or other processing. The plant also operates a sausage kitchen.

Full operation of the Tifton plant calls for the employment of about 250 people. When livestock receipts are heavy, employment runs a little higher and in times of scarcity employment drops somewhat.

In the depression period which followed several years after the ending of the first world war the livestock movement in the south suffered temporary relapse and in 1923 the plant had to be closed, primarily for lack of raw materials. By 1935 the pendulum had swung in the opposite direction and November 4, 1935 the plant was reopened and has been in operation continuously since.

The plant draws its raw material supplies largely from Southern Georgia though it occasionally gets livestock from Northern Florida and from Alabama. Most of the products from the plant are sold in Armour and Company's branch houses located throughout the southeastern part of the country.

HISTORY OF TIFTON COTTON MILLS

by L. E. Bowen

The Tifton Cotton Mill is by far the oldest manufacturing establishment in Tifton. The Corporation was formed in March, 1900, and began operation in early 1901. It has manufactured carded cotton yarns throughout its entire history.

The first Board of Directors was composed of the following members: H. H. Tift, E. P. Bowen, W. S. Whitham, S. M. Clyatt, C. W. Fulwood and L. G. Manard. Capt. H. H. Tift was the first president and served in that capacity until his death in 1922. Among other Tift County pioneers whose names have appeared in the records as Directors are: J. H. Hillhouse, W. W. Bank, Briggs Carson, A. B. Hollingsworth, T. A. Shipp, Jr., T. B. Puckett, N. P. Pinkston, C. R. Choate, R. W. Goodman. The offices of Secretary and Treasurer were filled during the first twenty-five years by L. G. Manard, T. B. Puckett, N. D. Pinkston and R. W. Goodman; those filling the position of Plant Superintendent during the same years were: T. A. Shipp, Jr., W. R. Reed. and W. R. Neighbors.

The plant has been enlarged in three separate expansions from 3,584 spindles to the present 10,000 spindles. The mill buildings have been enlarged each time. The Village has increased over the years from twenty-five houses, originally, to eighty-one.

The name of Tift was closely identified with the corporation from its beginning to 1928, at which time it was purchased outright by E. P. Bowen, Sr., and his sons, E. P. Bowen, Jr., and L. E. Bowen. The Bowen interests are now its operators. Immediately following the death of H. H. Tift, Sr., his son became president and he was succeeded as president in 1924 by H. H. Tift, Jr., who served until the Bowen interest took over. E. P. Bowen, Sr., was a member of the Board of Directors from the beginning in 1900 until his retirement in 1934. He was president at the time of his retirement. Today E. P. Bowen, Jr., is President, L. E. Bowen is Secretary and Treasurer and General Manager, L. E. Bowen, Jr., Assistant Manager, J. H. Wideman, Jr., assistant secretary, and T. B. Reynolds, superintendent.

The Tifton Cotton Mill, through its payroll, has contributed materially to the growth and progress of Tifton and Tift County throughout its entire existence of forty-six years. Today it regularly employs 350 to 400 people, operates three 40-hour shifts, has one of the largest payrolls in this section of the state, and consumes about 10,000 bales of cotton annually.

TIFTON COCA-COLA BOTTLING COMPANY
(Copied from Tifton Gazette)

In March 1900, Mr. Holmes became connected with the Tifton Bottling works, which then was located in the John Murrow building on Railroad Street. The company later moved to Main Street between Third and Fifth Streets, and in June, 1906, moved to the corner of Third and Railroad Streets. Here the bottling works remained until the new building of the Tifton Coca-Cola Bottling Company was constructed at the corner of Love Avenue and Tenth Street, and the company occupied the new building in April 1937. When Coca-Cola first came out, the Tifton Bottling Works manufactured the beverage and was one of the first to do so in this section.

Mr. Holmes was a pioneer in the soft drink business in this section and the progress of that business advanced under his leadership. He was engaged in the business from the time the old Hutchinson, or rubber, bottle stopper was used until this day of modern machinery and bottle caps. In 1903 he originated the famous Red Race Ginger-Ale and had the drink copyrighted in 1905. Mr. Holmes was also agent for the Standard Oil Company in this section for twenty years. He retired from active business in 1943 because of ill health.

CHAPTER XXV

MISCELLANEOUS PART I

FACTS COMPILED BY THE CHAMBER OF COMMERCE

Tifton, the county seat of Tift County, is located in the central portion of South Georgia and is about 195 miles South of Atlanta and 150 miles northwest of Jacksonville. Tift county is in the heart of the Coastal Plain area of South Georgia. Tifton is now the center of a thriving agricultural and trade area.

The city of Tifton has an area of 2.75 square miles or 1,776 acres. Tift County has an area of 243 square miles or 165,057 acres. The altitude is 350 feet above sea level. Annual mean temperature average 67 degrees. The average yearly rainfall is 48 inches.

The 1946 population of Tifton, including suburbs, is estimated at 10,000. Tift County 1946 estimated population 20,000. The form of government is commission-manager.

The city tax rate is 2.3 mills, based on fifty per cent valuation; total assessment 1946, $4,952,744. Public utilities—valuation, $1,200,000 approximate. The county tax rate is forty mills based on 40 per cent valuation. Total assessment 1946, listing homestead exemptions, $4,586,277.

Tifton has three schools—grammar, junior high and high school—with competent corps of 53 instructors, practically all of whom have degrees and some with the master's degree. The full enrollment reached 2,000 students. This overflow of pupils has made necessary a four-room addition at the grammar school. The system ranks high among the school systems of Georgia and has won the district and state banners in educational contest. Many Tifton High graduates have been at the top in college work and have achieved distinction in different professions and trades. Music, speech, vocational work, including commercial courses, and physical training supplement the regular literary courses. Tifton High School Band and Blue Devils (football team) have won state-wide acclaim.

Tift county schools include eight modern school plants, conveniently located on public highways and railroads, provided with modern physical equipment and served by eighteen modern school busses. Tift County has seventy-seven white teachers with an enrollment in excess of 2,200 pupils, of whom about one-third attend the city schools. There are thirty-five colored teachers with an enrollment of over 1,100 pupils. Students completing grade school in the county are brought to Tifton to complete their high school education.

The Tift County Board of Education employs and offers the following services in addition to regular class room instruction: one librarian and bookmobile; one home demonstration agent; three teachers of vocational agriculture; three homemaking teachers; two instructors for veterans farm training program; one visiting teacher; one white supervisor and one colored supervisor.

Tifton has the following: one golf course; four hotels, Myon, Lankford Manor, Wilton, and Colonial; four tourist courts; five schools; one kindergarten; one business school; two nursery schools; one college; one library; one bookmobile for rural area; three theaters, two white and one colored; one band, Tifton High School Band.

The water comes from deep wells.

Tift County—Tift County is in many respects a banner Georgia county. Among the thriving and progressing towns in the county are: Omega, Ty Ty, Chula, Eldorado, Brookfield, Harding and Dosia.

Tift County soil is generally of the Tifton sand loam type, productive, well drained and adapted to the cultivation of a wide variety of farm commodities, together with dairy, swine and beef production. There is a State Farmers' Market located at Tifton which handles produce for this area and there are cotton gins, cotton warehouses, tobacco warehouses, peanut shelling plants, cotton seed and peanut oil plants and frozen food lockers.

An illustrated pamphlet represents a modest effort to briefly portray some of the advantages and assets of the Tifton area. Much of importance —and pictures of interest—could not be included. A visit will mean more to you.

Occupations—The main occupations of Tifton and Tift County people, in the order of their importance, are: diversified agriculture, merchandising, manufacturing and producing forestry products, including turpentine, lumber, rosin and pulp wood.

Agriculture—Because of soil advantages, Tift County claims to be the most diversified farming section of the South and the plant producing center of the United States.

The principal crops are: Plants, tobacco, peanuts, cotton, pecans, corn, potatoes, hay, sugar cane, livestock, poultry, bees and milk products. Truck crops produced include: watermelons, cantaloupes, tomatoes and other vegetables.

The following are the figures for produce handled at Tifton in 1945:

Peanuts	$ 3,292,000.00
Naval Stores	867,547.29
Pecans	330,158.50
Cotton and Cotton Seed	223,750.00
Plants	4,750,000.00
Bees and Honey	50,000.00
Tobacco	3,915,530.91
Livestock	3,750,000.00

Produce (including watermelons, cantaloupes and potatoes)   1,000,000.00

$18,178,986.70

Tifton is famous for its tobacco sales through its five large warehouses. The figures for the 1946 sale are as follows: 10,817,178 pounds sold with a return of $4,331,419.82.

Armour and Company operates a packing plant in Tifton with several hundred employees. This provides a good local market for livestock and hogs and the packing plant cooperates with the farmers in their production problems.

Tifton is famous for its shipments of tomato, potato, cabbage, pepper and other plants and its bee industry. Plants are frequently transported by airplane to northern states. Queen bees and hives are shipped all over the United States. The growing of gladioli bulbs and flowers is becoming an important industry.

Recreation—In the Tifton area one can enjoy golfing, swimming, fishing, hunting, dancing, ball games and motoring. Fulwood Park, area of 35 acres, is equipped for picnicking, concerts, etc., and has a wading pool for children. Located just a short distance from town is the Tifton Country Club and Golf Course. There are three theatres—two white and one colored.

A $150,000.00 Recreation Center has been planned and construction of a swimming pool at a cost of $50,000.00 has been authorized. This Recreation Center, when completed, will have baseball and football fields, tennis courts, bowling alleys, swimming pool with bath houses, pavilion, game rooms. Construction will begin as soon as building restrictions will permit.

Tourists—Tifton's location on U. S. Highway No. 41 and U. S. Highway No. 319 is the cause of a large tourist trade that has been built up during a number of years. This is particularly true of tourists who are traveling between Florida and points in the north and west. Four hotels, four tourist courts, two theatres, numerous cafes and tourist homes assist in supplying the needs of tourists.

Transportation—Tifton is served by two trunk line railway systems; namely, the Atlantic Coast Line Railroad and Southern Railway. The Atlantic Coast Line now owns and operates the Atlanta, Birmingham and Coast Railroad which also serves Tifton. Twenty passenger trains are operated in and out of Tifton daily. The average number of freight trains is fourteen. Greyhound Bus lines and National Trailways both serve Tifton. Tifton Bus Lines operate buses in Tifton and vicinity. Several freight truck lines serve Tifton. Tifton's municipal airport, located one and one-half miles from business section of Tifton, has three paved runways, each 5,000 feet in length. Dixie Airways supply a complete flying service from Tifton.

Highways: Six paved highways radiate from Tifton, including U. S. Highway 41 and U. S. Highway 319. These supply Tift County with good roads in all directions.

Airport: Tifton's airport, in addition to having a flying service to Atlanta and by contract to distant points, is also expecting to be placed on the route between Atlanta and Jacksonville, via Macon, for a feeder line service.

Facilities—Electric Power: The Georgia Power Company supplies Tifton with abundant electric power. Included in local power facilities are two 110,000 volt lines, one 66,000 volt line, and three 44,000 volt lines, drawing energy from hydro-electric plants and steam plants in north and middle Georgia and upper Florida. In addition, a contract has been let for another plant and power line which will connect with Tifton's through state wide net work of lines. The Georgia Power Company also serves some rural areas of Tift County.

Two REA lines furnish electricity to parts of Tift County.

Gas: Butane and other forms of stored gas are available.

Communication—The Southern Bell Telephone and the Western Union Telegraph Companies both give continuous service to Tifton residents and business places. The telephone company extends rural lines over much of the County and it is planned to expand this service. Omega, one of Tift County's smaller cities, has its own independent telephone service, which is connected, however, with the Southern Bell system.

Mail Service—Tifton enjoys excellent mail facilities through regular mail trains and by Star Route to and from Thomasville. Over night mail service is available to and from Atlanta and Jacksonville via through trains. Air mail posted in Tifton in the early afternoon arrives in Washington, New York and Chicago the following morning.

Commerce—Tifton has the usual number of retail and wholesale houses, service shops, professional offices, etc. Three wholesale grocers and one wholesale dry goods company are located in Tifton. All of the leading oil distributing companies have agencies here.

Labor—The Tifton area has available labor, both white and colored, skilled and unskilled, male and female. The type of labor in this section is quite satisfactory.

Banking—Tifton and Tift County have four banks, namely: The Bank of Tifton, The Farmers Bank and the Citizens Bank (all in Tifton), and the Citizens Service Bank in Omega, with combined resources, as of June 1st, 1946, of $8,958,086.71. Tifton Federal Savings & Loan Association,

Tifton Production Credit Association, and other concerns supply capital for building and other purposes.

Manufacturing—Among the successfully operated industries located at Tifton are: Armour and Company (packing house), Tifton Cotton Mill, Southern Cotton Oil Company, International Minerals & Chemical Corp., Columbia Naval Stores, Builders Supply Company, Imperial Tobacco Company, Tifton Brick Company, Tifton Peanut Company, Quality Concrete Products Company, Phillips Milling Company, Short & Paulk Supply Company, Tifton Seed Shellers, Tifton Chenille Rug Company, Tifton Feed Mill, Cotton Gins, Dairy Products Plants, Bottling Plants, Ice Manufacturers, Lumber Yards, Frozen Food Locker Plants, Bee Industry, Bulb Industry.

Good sites, with or without railroad sidings, are available at reasonable rates for new industries.

THE BENCH AND BAR OF TIFT COUNTY

by Major Steve Mitchell

It is by no means intended that this outline will give a detailed history of the Bench and Bar of Tift County but the author will touch upon such high spots as he considers of interest from a historical standpoint, and the early recitals of facts will be from hearsay since the author has only a personal knowledge from the time of his residence in 1913.

After the establishment of the town of Tifton by Legislative Act of 1890 when Tifton was a thriving town in the old County of Berrien, there soon became by its growing pains a demand for a local tribunal; and in 1902, there was established a City Court of Tifton in such Berrien County with Judge John Murrow as the presiding Judge. At that time, the Bar of Tifton consisted of the late C. W. Fulwood, Sr., F. G. Boatwright, C. C. "Pomp" Hall, J. J. Murray, J. B. Murrow, James H. Pate and H. S. Murray. Shortly thereafter, into the active practice came Robley D. Smith, James H. Price, R. E. Dinsmore, J. S. Ridgdill, O. C. Griner and L. P. Skeen. The firms of lawyers at that time consisted of Murrow & Pate, Fulwood & Murray, and Ridgdill & Griner, and associated with the late C. C. "Pomp" Hall, R. Eve. Other early practitioners at Tifton were F. S. Harrell; W. J. Wallace, the first Solicitor of the City Court of Tifton; Leon Hargraves, a practitioner and also a Clerk of the City of Tifton; J. C. Smith, brother of the present William R. Smith, Judge of the Alapaha Judicial Circuit; and R. S. Foy, who practiced here before moving to Sylvester.

The growth of the practice of the Bench and Bar was approximately that of the thriving village of Tifton as evidenced by the creation of a separate

County of Tift by act of the Legislature approved August 17, 1905. It was about such time that Judge John Murrow withdrew as Judge of the City Court of Tifton and Judge R. Eve was appointed his successor which office he held continuously from that date until he became Judge of the Superior Court of the Tifton Judicial Circuit created in the year 1916, when James H. Price became Judge of City Court of Tifton which office he held until his death, when in 1922, W. B. Bennett, who had moved to Tifton after the 1st World War became Judge by appointment of Governor Clifford Walker and was elected to succeed himself until his death about 1925 when Britt W. Davis became Judge of said City Court of Tifton and which Court was abolished in the year 1927.

Steve F. Mitchell came to the Bar in 1913, and for some years was associated with Mr. J. S. Ridgdill under firm name of Ridgdill & Mitchell, and later with Robert C. Ellis, who had been in practice since about the year 1903 under firm name of Ellis, Mitchell & Ellis, engaged principally in farm loans general practice and commercial law. L. P. Skeen, along about 1910 came to Tifton and was associated in the practice of the late C. W. Fulwood until that partnership dissolved and Haines H. Hargett, a young graduate of law of the University of North Carolina, became associated with the late C. W. Fulwood and who later moved to Atlanta and was associated with the firm of King and Spaulding, who later as a tax expert with Miller and Chevalier of Washington, D. C., later moved back to Atlanta where he became associated with the firm of Spaulding, Sibley & McDougal; and it was there while engaged in that practice that he died. At which time, Rob't. R. Forrester moved to the County and became associated with Mr. C. W. Fulwood.

At the time of the creation of Tift County, it was in the old Southern Circuit and Judges of the Court successively were Augustus H. Hansell, Robert G. Mitchell, and shortly after the famous Carter Rawlings Case, the Solicitor-General, William E. Thomas, became the Judge of such circuit by election. Other young attorneys engaged in the practice of Tifton were R. L. LeSeur, who for a while was associated with R. D. Smith before moving to Americus and Sid Toler, W. T. Hargrett, Jr., were at times associated with the firm of Fulwood & Fulwood, also Martin McGhee was associated with Fulwood & Fulwood.

For a short term associated with Mr. Robley D. Smith was Stewart Griggs, son of the Congressman, James Griggs of the Second District. Then later, C. A. Christian from the Nashville Bar moved to Tifton and became associated two or three years with R. D. Smith; and later, Earl Smith, a recent graduate of Emory became associated with R. D. Smith until he moved away and became affiliated with the F.B.I. After the dissolution of the partnership of Fulwood & Forrester, John G. Fulwood, a graduate of Emory University, became associated with his father and was with him until the death of his father about the year 1928. At the dissolution of the firm of Smith & Christian, Mr. John T. Ferguson, recently graduated from Mercer University, became associated with R. D. Smith for a year or two; and about that time, Briggs Carson, Jr., after standing the Bar Examination entered the practice of Tifton. It is by no means amiss that John Henry Poole after practicing some years at Albany, Georgia, has been a member of the Bar of Tift County for some 25 or 26 years. Judge R. Eve is the present Judge of the Tifton Judicial Circuit since its creation and the membership of the Bar now consists in the order of their length of residence the following members: Robley D. Smith, Steve F. Mitchell, John Henry Poole, C. A. Christian, Rob't R. Forrester, John G. Fulwood, John T. Ferguson, Briggs Carson, Jr., Britt W. Davis, and A. L. Kelly, Jr., who has recently since the second World War moved to Tifton where he was for a short time associated with R. D. Smith.

At all times, both Bench and Bar of Tift County have kept high the canons of ethics and generally have brought credit upon the profession out of the common knowledge among the Bar, not only of this County but the Tifton Judicial Circuit that of adjoining circuits, and that the Tift County Bar have in the practice of their profession handling the many matters pertaining to the profession; and many times by oral agreement and thereby have facilitated the administration of justice to an able and high degree, and have played no mean part in the material and economic growth of this highly developed agricultural and thriving County.

TIFT COUNTY (Created Aug. 17, 1905)

TIFT COUNTY REPRESENTATIVES

E. P. Bowen, 1907-08-08
William H. Hendricks, 1909-10
Robert C. Ellis, 1911-12 Ex.-12
Robert C. Ellis, 1913-14
J. H. Young, 1915-15 Ex.-16-17 Ex.
Robert C. Ellis, 1917-18
Lennon E. Bowen, 1919-20
Lennon E. Bowen, 1921-22
Robert C. Ellis, 1923-23 Ex.-24
Dr. N. Peterson, 1925
Thurston Ellis Phillips, 1927
Thurston Ellis Phillips, 1929-31 Ex.
Thurston E. Phillips, 1931
Marcus S. Patten, 1933
Marcus S. Patten, 1935
John Madison Goff, 1937-37-38 Ex.

George W. Branch, 1939
George W. Branch, 1941
George W. Branch, 1943-43 Ex.-44
Ross H. Pittman, 1945
I. Y. Conger, 1947

Ex. means an extra session of the Legislature.

TIFT COUNTY

Created Aug. 17, 1905 (Constitutional Amendment)

TIFT COUNTY SENATORIAL DISTRICTS

Tift County was in the Sixth District, Aug. 18, 1906-Nov. 5, 1918 (See Acts 1906, p. 80)

Tift County in Forty-Seventh District, No. 5, 1918 (Created Aug. 17, 1918; Constitutional Amendment). See Acts 1918, p. 84.

List of counties comprising the 47th Senatorial Districts are: Colquitt, Tift, Turner.

List of Senators from Tift County:

6th District

William S. West, 1905-06
Jonathan P. Knight, 1907-08-08 Extra
E. P. Bowen, 1909-10
T. C. Culbreath, 1911-12 Extra-12
W. L. Converse, 1913-14
George A. Paulk, 1915-15 Extra, 16-17 Extra
William Hartridge Hendricks, M.D., 1917-18

47th District

T. H. Parker (died), 1919
M. M. Kendall, 1920
Robert Cothran Ellis, 1921-22
John Henry Adams, 1923-23 Extra, 24
Robert L. Norman, 1925-26 Extra, 26 2d Extra
E. P. Bowen, 1927
Reason Paulk, 1929-31 Extra
L. L. Moore, 1931
Mrs. Susie Tillman Moore, 1933
C. Z. Harden, 1935
W. A. Sutton, 1937

Mrs. Susie Tillman Moore, 1939
E. W. Garner, 1941
G. W. Newton, 1943-43 Extra-44 Extra
George W. Branch, 1945-45 Extra-46
Walter W. Branch, 1947

Extra means an extra session of the Legislature.

MAYORS OF TIFTON

W. H. Love—1891

C. W. Fulwood—1893

F. G. Boatright—1896

C. W. Fulwood—

W. W. Timmons—1904

S. M. Clyatt—1907

W. W. Banks—1908

W. H. Hendricks—1913

H. H. Hargrett—1916

CITY MANAGERS

W. T. Hargrett

R. E. Hall, Sr.

George Coleman

S. A. Youmans

Frank Smith

Top—Scene in Mrs. Pauline Kent's yard. Amos Tift, son of the founder of Tifton

Center—Home of Mrs. Elizabeth Pickard Karsten, old home of her father; where part of the History of Tift County was written.

Bottom row—The Tift sawmill, built in 1872. Mary Carmichael, granddaughter of Patrick Thomas Carmichael

AIRPORT

by A. B. Phillips

In February 1941, president of the Tift County Chamber of Commerce announced through the secretary, Mr. J. E. Rogers, the following airport improvement committee: L. E. Bowen, chairman, E. L. Webb, J. C. McNeese, J. E. Newton, Carson Chalk, and A. B. Phillips. At this time he urged this committee to break ground for negotiations and seek Federal aid for further improvement of the airport.

Mr. F. H. Brown, vice-president of the G. S. and F. Railway Division of Southern Railway was secured for a meeting through the efforts of his local representative, Mr. Bob Hargrett. He met with us and outlined a procedure for us to follow. This contact proved valuable as Mr. Brown made frequent trips to Washington in our behalf.

Bob Choate, J. L. Bowen, and C. A. Christian made a trip to Washington in an effort to find out to whom we should apply for other necessary details. These men discussed the matter with Congressman E. E. Cox and Senator Walter F. George and their report was not encouraging.

Mr. B. H. Campbell, assistant airport engineer, CAA, Regional office, Atlanta, visited Tifton and suggested that the securing of at least a square mile of land be looked into, as runways would have to be at least 4,200 feet long.

On June 21 telegrams were received from Senator George and Congressman Cox, advising that Tifton was listed for a survey. Then $8,500 for airport was raised at a mass meeting.

The battle raged until December 30, 1941 when the telegram came giving instructions to get options for survey of proposed sites.

On January 5, 1942, a telegram from Senator George announced that Civil Aeronautic Authority had approved Tifton airport project to the amount of $336,039.00. Miss Christine Belle Kennedy rendered valuable assistance in getting project for her home town.

TIFTON CITY MANAGERS

Thus far there have been only five Tifton City Managers. They are:

1. Wesley Thomas Hargrett, began office January, 1921; resigned October, 1922.

2. Robert Edward Hall, began office October, 1922; served through 1932.

3. George Washington Coleman, began office, January, 1933; resigned August 3, 1936.

4. Stephen Alexander Youmans, began office, August 3, 1936; served through 1944.

5. Frank Henry Smith, began office January, 1945, and is still in office.
Mr. Ben Golden is treasurer of the City of Tifton.
For biographical sketch of W. T. Hargrett, see Tift County Pioneers.
For biographical sketch of R. E. Hall, see Tift County Pioneers.
Sketches of other City Managers follow:

Stephen Alexander Youmans—by E. Pickard

Stephen Alexander Youmans, eldest of twelve children of Elbert Edmund Youmans and Mary Elizabeth O'Quinn Youmans, was born in Pierce County, Georgia. When about eighteen he moved to Tifton where he finished his schooling. Thereafter he attended Georgia-Alabama Business College, in Macon.

In 1903 S. A. Youmans married Miss Mary Young, daughter of Mr. and Mrs. T. B. Young, of Irwin County. Of this union are a number of children.

For a number of years Mr. Youmnas was in partnership with his brother-in-law, J. T. Mathis, (Q.V.) in a musical instrument house, Mathis and Youmans, in Valdosta. For a while he was at Hahira. In 1919 he purchased the T. J. Parker home on Love Avenue, and the following January he and his family took residence therein. He engaged in the mercantile business in Tifton for many years. He was elected to serve on the board of Tifton City Commissioners, and at a meeting of the commissioners, August 3, 1936 he was elected to fill the unexpired term of his brother-in-law, George Coleman, who had resigned as City Manager. Mr. Coleman was elected to fill Youman's place on the Commission. Mr. Youmans served as Tifton City Manager until 1945, when Frank Smith became City Manager.

During Mr. Youmans' term of office during one period of about two years $250,000.00 project was inaugurated and completed by means of bonds and W.P.A. This included paving, extension of water and sewerage, a $100,000.00 disposal plant, and a new electric system for the water works, at a cost of about $25,000.00.

At present, Mr. and Mrs. Youmans are enjoying a prolonged period of travel and are seeing the western part of the United States. Greetings to friends at home indicate a delightful time.

TIFTON CITY MANAGER
FRANK HENRY SMITH
by E. Pickard Karsten

Tifton's fifth City Manager was Frank Henry Smith, still in office in 1947.

Frank Henry Smith, born January 31, 1889, at Sayre, Pennsylvania, is son of Charles Walter Smith and Emma Jacoby Smith.

Frank with his parents left Sayre in 1898 and moved to a place in the country near Nashville, Tennessee. Thence the family moved to near Waycross where they remained for about a year and where Frank's mother died.

In 1900 Frank Smith came with his father to Tifton where the elder Smith engaged in the iron molding business.

About 1902 the Smith family moved to Birmingham, Ala., where young Smith was graduated from the Birmingham High School and from the Birmingham Business College.

In 1907 the Smiths moved back to Tifton and Charles Walter Smith opened up a shoe repair business which he conducted until his death, about August 1, 1931.

Frank Smith, after returning to Tifton, worked as an automobile mechanic for H. H. Tift, Jr., and for Amos C. Tift until about 1919, when he entered into a partnership with J. W. Thrasher and W. D. King and formed the City Garage, with which he continued until January 1, 1945, at which time he became Tifton's fifth city manager. He followed S. A. Youmans, resigned. Mr. Smith had served on the city commission continuously from January, 1937, until he was elected city manage. In December of 1936 he had been elected to fill the unexpired term of S. A. Youmans who resigned to become city manager, which term of office he began January, 1937.

High lights of civic progress during Mr. Smith's administration are: Construction of vocational school building at Tifton High School, 1945; remodeling of Tifton High School, 1946; extending of water mains and sewerage to the section of city annexed in 1940.

Frank Henry Smith, on September 15, 1915, married Nora Goggins, daughter of N. J. Goggins, deceased, and Sarah Ann Gibson Goggins. Children of this union are Mae (Mrs. Charles W. Hahn), of Iowa; Frank H. Jr. (married Pauline Arnold), of Perry, Florida; Robert Emerson, of Tifton.

GEORGE WASHINGTON COLEMAN
THIRD CITY MANAGER OF TIFTON

by E. Pickard Karsten

George Washington Coleman was born July 30, 1875, at Pitts, Georgia, where also he received his schooling. He was son of Stephen and Cynthia Elizabeth Fitzgerald Coleman.

When nearly through high school young Coleman left Pitts and went to clerk in a store at Henderson, Georgia.

In 1903 Mr. Coleman came to Tifton and was manager of Churchwell's Tifton store; here he continued until 1907 when he went to Valdosta to open a musical instrument store, Mathis and Coleman.

While in Tifton, G. W. Coleman married Ella Callie Youmans, daughter of Elbert Edmund Youmans and Mary O'Quinn Youmans. The ceremony was performed on June 15, 1905, at the country home of the bride's parents.

After conducting the Valdosta firm, Mathis and Coleman, for two years, Mr. Coleman sold his interest to his brother-in-law, S. A. Youmans, and returned to Tifton, where he engaged in the plant business. Also he was Tifton's third city manager. He began office January, 1933, and served until August 1936, when, because of failing health, he resigned the managership and was succeeded by his brother-in-law, S. A. Youmans. Mr. Coleman, however, took the place vacated by Youmans on the city commission. He continued to conduct his plant business until his death.

Mr. Coleman was a member of the Gun Lake Country Club and he and Mrs. Coleman were hosts at numerous delightful parties at their Gun Lake cabin; for the Colemans, genial, hospitable and friendly, had a host of friends.

Mr. Coleman died at his Tifton home on Love Avenue, November 22, 1937. Burial was in Tifton cemetery.

Mrs. Coleman continues to live in Tifton.

The Colemans had no children.

TIFTON POST OFFICE

Records indicate that the first post office in Tifton was in Captain Tift's commissary, and W. O. Tift was the first postmaster from June 1, 1887 to 1890. The exact location of the office from 1890 to 1900 is not clear. At one time it was located on Third Street in Dr. Goodman's drug store. During these ten years it probably moved to different places. Just when the post office was moved to Love Avenue in the building occupied at present by Western Auto Associate Store is not definite; however, the office was there in 1900. The government building was completed in June 1914, and occupied on July 1, 1914.

Rural delivery was established in 1898. City delivery of mail was authorized July 1, 1907. From 1885 to about 1907, the following offices were adjacent to Tifton: Sutton, Georgia; Harding, Georgia; Goodman, Georgia; Vanceville, Georgia; Brighton, Georgia; Waterloo, Georgia;

Urbana, Georgia; Ansley, Georgia; and Dosia, Georgia. All of these post offices were discontinued with the advent of rural delivery service from the Tifton office.

The following is a complete list of postmasters with dates of service:
W. O. Tift from 1887 to 1890
J. H. Duff, from 1890 to 1895
T. M. Greene, from 1895 to 1898
J. M. Duff, from 1898 to 1907 when he died.

David Comfort was acting postmaster from July 1, 1907 to February 14, 1908. W. O. Tift from February 15, 1908 to September 15, 1909, when he died. J. L. Pickard was acting postmaster from September 16, 1909 to November 25, 1910. Mrs. E. C. Tift (W. O.) postmaster from November 26, 1910 to January 22, 1915. W. H. Bennett, postmaster from January 23, 1915 to June 30, 1930. Jason Scarboro was postmaster from July 1, 1920 to December 31, 1925. E. E. Slack was postmaster from January 1, 1925 to September 30, 1928. Harris Massey was acting postmaster from October 1, 1928 to October 15, 1929. Joseph Kent, Sr., was postmaster from October 16, 1929 to March 27, 1934. Roy Thrasher was postmaster from March 28, 1934 to December 31, 1944. I. Y. Conger was postmaster from January 1, 1945 to January 31, 1946. Harris Massey was acting postmaster from February 1, 1946.

The present postmaster entered the service at Tifton, on April 1, 1907, under the administration of J. M. Duff, when the office was third class. Postal receipts in 1907 were $8,000 a year; postal receipts in 1947 are about $67,000 a year. Massey succeeded Mr. Walter Harrell, a clerk whom the roaches ran away because they ate the stamps. Since postal authorities held Harrell responsible for the roaches' conduct, he resigned. Massey was plowing a field when someone offered him the job. He reluctantly left the plow and mule and conquered the roaches during his novitiate training. At that time clerks made $500 a year; now the salary is $2,100.

In 1900 the Tifton post office changed from fourth to third class; on July 1, 1907, to second class; to first class July 1, 1929; back to second class July 1, 1930; again to first class on July 1, 1944 where we hope it will remain.

UNION ROAD

(The Tifton Gazette)

When the Indians journeyed, they followed the route as the crow flies. Indian trails were later used as guides for the white man's roads because they were the most direct, offered fewer natural obstacles and were the easiest established and maintained.

From Macon south, there runs the great watershed between the Ocmulgee River on the east and the Thronateeska on the west, later between the Alapaha and the Willacoochee on the east and the Thronateeska (which empties into the Apalachicola) until tributaries of the Suwanee are touched.

Along this mighty shed an Indian trail ran, and along this trail the white man built his towns, which grew to be cities, and from town to town ran a road, and because it united the counties and their county seats, it was called "The Union Road."

From Macon, through Perry, the county seat of Houston, through Vienna, the county seat of Dooly, it followed the watershed beneath the whispering pines by where Ashburn, Tifton, and Adel now stand to Troupsville in Lowndes and then on South through Florida.

The Union Road was a tribute to the woodcraft of the Indian. Later the most modern inventions of the white man, the steam locomotive and the motor car brought to the ability of the Aborigines more testimonials.

When the route for the Georgia Southern and Florida railway from Macon to Florida was sought, the surveyors followed the Union Road. Within twenty miles north of Tifton the railway crossed this road seventeen times. (Of course those crossings were eliminated.) The railway civil engineers paid another tribute to the Indian.

Still later, when the National Highway was being mapped out south of Macon, it also followed this Union Road, because it was proved by competitive test that the route was best. Another tribute to the Indian.

This is the route proposed for the Dixie Highway. It is the easiest route, the most direct route, the route proved by test to be the best.

CHASE SALMON OSBORN

Eighteen miles west-northwest of Tifton on Route 55, pleasantly set off from the town of Poulan by an arch of piney woods, is Possum Poke in Possum Lane, for more than fifty years the home of Chase Salmon Osborn, outstanding Governor of Michigan during the first half of the twentieth century in that state, and one of the most famous and best-loved winter residents of Georgia.

In more than one way Governor Osborn is an integral part of the life and history of Tift County. His friendships rooted in this region have been a vital force without diminishment of warmth through the third and fourth generations. His personal interest in every advance attempted and achieved in Tifton and Tift County has been instantaneous, eloquent, and concretely helpful. The words he has spoken at countless gatherings private and public, in Tifton and surrounding rural communities, have instilled a lasting inspiration forever to be associated with his name. One of Tifton's leading citizens has thus defined his influence:

"Speakers come to Tifton who sweep you off your feet for the moment but after they go this mood is followed by a sense of unreality, dissatisfaction and futility—a depression one has to fight against for a while. But when Governor Osborn talks and lifts you into the clouds, somehow he always gives you something solid under your feet, so that you go on forever afterwards with a keen, new appreciation of the blessings and opportunities that are right here in Tifton, under God, and a burning desire and enduring courage to begin at once to carve out of them what Governor Osborn has envisioned."

For years, until the fracture of a hip made other transportation routes more practicable, Governor Osborn stopped at the Hotel Myon always on his way north and south. The friendships that he found at Tifton he counted among the rarest treasures that came to him in all his explorations of the earth.

One day a delegation of civic leaders attended on the Governor to ask the gift of extensive springs on property he owned in Worth County, for the Cheehaw Council of the Boy Scouts, which includes the Scouts of fifteen Georgia counties. He shocked them by inquiring why they had not asked for his entire holdings there, and then proceeded to give them, out of hand, over eight hundred acres of uncut and unturpentined forest. That is how South Georgia's Chase Osborn Boy Scout Camp began.

In many articles, pamphlets and books Governor Osborn has been described as pioneer, statesman, philanthropist, iron hunter, scientist, philosopher, public speaker, author, publisher, and world traveler. What he has been and is surpasses all that he has done. Daniel Willard, great railroad president, once said that of all Chase Osborn's brilliant facets, his chief genius was for friendship. Ernie Pyle wrote that of all the persons he had met in a year's selective roving, Chase Osborn was the most interesting character; and he came a second time to Possum Poke to bring his wife to see the Governor.

Huntington County, Indiana, has put a permanent marker on the site of the log cabin where Governor Osborn was born. Possum Poke in Possum Lane is mentioned often as one of the literary shrines of Georgia. Of the numerous books produced by the Governor, and those in which his adopted daughter, Stellanova Osborn, shares authorship, a great proportion has come into being at this unique Southern homeplace. Miss Osborn's *A Tale of Possum Poke in Possum Lane*—which has a number of appealing references to Tifton and Tift County citizens—preserves the fascinations of the Governor's miniature realm and his winsome reign there; also it bids fair to become a classic picture of the South Georgia countryside of which Tifton is a fast-growing center.

CHRISTIE BELL KENNEDY (Mrs. Russell Scott)

(Copied from "Talisman," Tifton High School Annual of 1945)

Of the Georgia women prominent in Washington, D. C., is Tifton's own Christie Bell Kennedy, now Mrs. Scott Russell.

Mrs. Russell, daughter of Mrs. J. C. Kennedy, was born and reared in Tifton, and graduated from the Tifton High School in 1928. She was employed by the South Georgia Power Company as cashier in the Cordele District office and was later made local manager for the Power Company office in Vienna.

After attending the Clara Bell Smith Business College, Columbus, Georgia, she was employed by Senator Walter F. George in 1932. She was named secretary to Senator George in 1935 and was made clerk of Foreign Relations Committee in 1941, the second woman to hold this position.

When Senator George was named chairman of the Finance Committee, Mrs. Russell was made clerk. She is the first woman to serve in this capacity.

During the latter part of 1944 "Christie" became the bride of Colonel Scott Russell, who is now practicing law in Washington, D. C.

FLORENCE KARSTEN CARSON

In the fall of 1946 "Pearl Songs," a book of very impressive poems by a citizen of Tifton, Florence Karsten Carson, was off the press. Many copies were presented to her friends as Christmas presents; the beautiful sentiment and appropriate expression made them especially valuable as the season's greetings. Florence Karsten Carson is an artist from different angles; she paints as well as she writes. A few years ago Florence held an exhibition of oil paintings at Abraham Baldwin Agricultural College and at the Twentieth Century Library Club. There was also an exhibition of her miniatures at Washington Memorial Library, Macon.

Her paintings have won prizes at the Georgia State Fair Department of Fine Arts and have been included in exhibitions at the Corcoran in Washington, D. C., and at the Telfair in Savannah and elsewhere.

Florence Karsten Carson, daughter of Paul Daggett Karsten and Elizabeth Pickard Karsten, was born in Macon, Georgia in the president's apartments at the time her grandfather, Dr. William Lowndes Pickard was president of Mercer University. On her father's side Florence is a granddaughter of Dr. Gustav Karsten, educator and editor, and Eleanor Daggett Karsten, writer, a direct descendant of Dr. N. Daggett, Revolutionary president of Yale University.

When nine years old she began the study of art with Miss Mollie Mason of Macon. Florence later studied in New York, New Haven, and in Boston. Before entering Bessie Tift College, where she later received her A.B. degree, she graduated from the Cambridge Preparatory School for Girls. At Bessie Tift she also received her diploma in speech.

On July 26, 1942 she married Robert Clements Carson, son of Ella Pate Carson and the late Briggs Carson, of Tifton. On April 8, 1947 in Tifton, Ella Pate Carson was born to Robert Clements Carson and Florence Karsten Carson.

AN APPRECIATION OF TIFTON
Ida Belle Williams

Had I not gone to Tifton, I should have missed some of the richest experiences of my life. Although the compiling of the "Tift County History" has been strenuous, I appreciate the opportunity of writing about the spot where some of my dearest friends live. Had I not gone to Tifton, I should not have known Mrs. H. H. Tift, a great woman, and other valuable people. Browning's lines about Italy express my sentiment:

> "Open my heart
> And you will see
> Engraved inside it"—Tifton!

TIFT COUNTY OFFICERS
by E. Pickard Karsten

TIFT COUNTY COMMISSIONERS

(List furnished by Mrs. Vinson Goff, Clerk of Tift County Commissioners.)

From the organization of Tift County in 1905, until September, 1907, W. S. Walker, Ordinary, was in charge of the County affairs.

Commissioners appointed by Ordinary W. S. Walker to lay out County of Tift into Militia Districts.

Brighton District: John Goff, Dan Fletcher, Henry Sutton.
Brookfield District: John A. Cox, W. A. Patten, R. G. Coarsey.
Chula District: J. Y. Fletcher, John Rigdon, J. W. Branch.
Docia District: Silas O'Quinn, M. Tucker, Jr., J. W. Taylor.
El Dorado District: T. E. Phillips, P. D. Phillips, J. F. Williams.
Omega District: G. W. Ridley, J. W. Carr, A. Conger.
Tifton District: G. W. Guest, G. W. Conger, J. T. Mathis.
Ty Ty District: J. A. Warren, W. E. Williams, William Gibbs.
Tift County Commissioners.
(The first named in each group acted as chairman.)

September, 1907: Thurston E. Phillips, Wm. Gibbs, H. H. Tift, I. W. Bowen, John Goff.

January, 1909: M. Tucker, I. W. Bowen, John Goff.

January, 1911: J. W. Baker, I. W. Bowen, J. F. Summers.

328 HISTORY OF TIFT COUNTY

January, 1913: M. Tucker, M. L. Whitfield, I. W. Bowen.
January, 1915: T. E. Phillips, G. W. Ford, L. L. Simmons.
January, 1916: J. J. Golden, sole Commissioner.
September, 1917: R. E. Hall, M. Tucker, Jehu Branch.
January, 1921: T. E. Phillips, Jehu Branch, W. C. Mobley.
January, 1923: T. M. Chesnutt, N. L. Coarsey, W. C. Mobley. (Each served as chairman at some time.)
March, 1928: N. L. Coarsey, H. F. Gibbs, W. C. Mobley.
January, 1929: N. L. Coarsey, J. W. Taylor, Henry F. Gibbs. (Mr. Gibbs served as chairman for one term.)
January, 1941: N. L. Coarsey, A. B. Phillips, Colin Malcolm.
January, 1943: C. A. Baker, Colin Malcolm, A. B. Phillips.
January, 1945: C. A. Baker, W. C. McCormic, A. B. Phillips.
January, 1947: W. C. McCormic, C. A. Baker, A. B. Phillips.
The last named three are still in office in this August, 1947.

OFFICERS OF TIFT COUNTY

(From the formation of the county in 1905 until the present time, 1947.)

By E. Pickard

Copied from official record books in Tift County Courthouse; recorded by Henry D. Webb and Earl Gibbs.

Clerks of Superior Court and their terms of office:

1. J. Edwin Peeples, took office October 5, 1905, served through December 31, 1908.

2. Henry D. Webb, took office January 1, 1909, served through December 31, 1940.

3. Earl D. Gibbs, took office January 1, 1941, still in office in 1947.

Ordinaries of Tift County.

1. W. S. Walker, took office October 5, 1905, served through December 31, 1908.

2. C. W. Graves, took office January 1, 1909, served to date of death, August 18, 1919.

Henry D. Webb, clerk of Superior Court acted as ordinary from August 18, 1919, to September 30, 1919. Also, he acted as ordinary from August 26, 1936 to September 23, 1936.

3. J. J. Baker, took office September 30, 1919, served till death, August 26, 1936.

4. Mrs. J. J. Baker, took office September 23, 1936, served through December 31, 1936, being the unexpired term of her husband, J. J. Baker.

5. Mrs. Mary E. Rigdon, took office January 1, 1937, served through December 31, 1944.

HISTORY OF TIFT COUNTY 329

6. Phillip C. Kelley, took office January 1, 1945; served to July 24, 1947.

Earl Gibbs, Clerk of the Superior Court, acted as ordinary, beginning July 24, 1947, and still serves on this August 21, 1947.

7. Leon Clements was elected ordinary, in a special election, August 18, 1947, but has not yet entered upon the duties of his office, on this August 21, 1947.

Sheriffs of Tift County from beginning of the County, 1905, until the present time, 1947.

1. John W. Baker, took office October 5, 1905, served through December 31, 1908.

2. E. D. Branch, took office January 1, 1909, served through December 31, 1912.

3. J. M. Shaw, took office January 1, 1913, served through December 31, 1924.

4. J. O. Thrasher, took office January 1, 1925, served to May 22, 1932, date of death of J. O. Thrasher.

5. S. C. Thrasher, took office May 22, 1932 (by appointment); served to September 14, 1932, when he was elected to serve as ordinary for the unexpired term of J. O. Thrasher, through December 31, 1932.

6. J. M. Walker, took office January 1, 1933; still in office, on this August 21, 1947.

Coroners of Tift County, from the beginning of the County, 1905, until the present time, August 21, 1947.

1. J. E. Johns, took office October 5, 1905, served through December 31, 1908.

2. G. W. Walker, took office January 1, 1909, served through December 31, 1912.

3. Charles F. Miller, took office, January 1, 1913, served to date of death, 1918.

4. W. H. Young, took office January 7, 1919, served through December 31, 1920.

5. T. M. Brown, took office January 1, 1921, to date of death, September 11, 1933.

M. S. Patten, Jr., was appointed by Ordinary J. J. Baker, and acted as coroner, beginning October 2, 1933, through December 31, 1936.

6. M. S. Patten, Jr., took office January 1, 1937, served through December 31, 1940.

7. J. M. Simpson, took office January 1, 1940. (Still in office.)

Superintendents of Education and their terms of office, from the beginning of the County until the present time, August 21, 1947.

The Board of Education appointed W. R. Smith.

TIFT COUNTY OFFICIALS
Top—Sheriff J. M. Walker (deceased). Ordinary Leon Clements
Bottom—Clerk of Court Earl D. Gibbs. Tax Commissioner W. Jelks Warren

HISTORY OF TIFT COUNTY

1. W. R. Smith, began office January 1, 1906; served through December 31, 1910.

2. R. F. Kersey, began office January 1, 1911, served through December 31, 1916.

3. A. J. Ammons, began office January 1, 1917, served through December 31, 1928.

4. W. L. Harman, began office January 1, 1929; served to December 28, 1934, date of his death.

Charles Harman was appointed by the Board of Education for the unexpired term of his father, W. L. Harmon, and served from January 1, 1935, through December 31, 1936.

5. Charles Harman, was elected superintendent and began office January 1, 1937 and served until date of his death, May 6, 1937.

W. H. Caudill acted for 6 days.

W. T. Bodenhamer, began office May 12, 1937, served to October 17, 1939, when he resigned to accept position as District State School Supervisor.

C. F. Hudgins was appointed by the Tift County Board of Education to fill the unexpired term of W. T. Bodenhamer, resigned.

C. F. Hudgins began office October 16, 1939; served through December 31, 1940.

Mercer H. Mitcham, began office January 1, 1941, (still in office, this August 21, 1947).

Tax Collectors of Tift County, from creation of county until the present.

1. J. H. Hutchinson, began office October 5, 1905, served through December 31, 1916.

2. T. S. Rigdon, began office January 1, 1917, served through December 31, 1924.

3. R. H. Hutchinson, began office January 1, 1925, served through December 31, 1926 (by appointment).

4. C. A. Baker, began office January 1, 1927, served through December 31, 1928.

The Legislature, in 1927, abolished the office of Tax Collector and that of Tax Receiver and created the office of Tax Commissioner, effective January 1, 1929.

Tax Commissioner of Tift County.

1. W. J. Warren, began office January 1, 1929, still in office (in 1947).

Tax Receivers of Tift County, from the creation of the county until the abolition of the office.

1. J. A. Marchant, began office October 5, 1905, served through December 31, 1908.

2. Henry Sutton, began office January 1, 1909, served through December 31, 1912.

3. George W. Fletcher, began office January 1, 1913, served through December 31, 1914.

4. O. F. Shepherd, began office January 1, 1915, served through December 31, 1916.

5. George Sutton, began office January 1, 1917, served through December 31, 1924.

6. W. J. Warren, began office January 1, 1925; served through December 31, 1928.

The Legislature, in 1927, abolished the office of Tax Receiver, and that of Tax Collector, and created that of Tax Commissioner (see above).

Tift County Treasurers, from the creation of the county until the abolition of the office.

1. S. F. Overstreet, began office October 5, served through December 31, 1912.

2. J. A. Marchant, began office January 1, 1913; served through December 31, 1914.

3. J. S. Royal, began office January 1, 1915, served through December 31, 1916.

The Legislature, in 1916, abolished the office of County Treasurer, and placed the duties of Treasurer in the hands of the Board of County Commissioners, effective January 1, 1917.

Tift County Surveyors, since the creation of the county.

1. Joseph T. Webb, began office October 5, 1905, served through December 31, 1908.

2. M. R. Lindsey, began office January 1, 1909, served through December 31, 1912.

3. A. D. Ross, began office January 1, 1913, served through December 31, 1920.

4. Milton D. Jones, began office January 1, 1921, served through December 31, 1924.

5. Charles R. Pittman, began office May 6, 1925, served through February 10, 1927.

6. T. W. Johnson, began office February 11, 1927, served through December 31, 1928.

7. A. D. Ross, began office December 17, 1929, served to September 4, 1933 (see appointment by J. J. Baker, Ordinary Minute Book A, page 123, Ordinary's Office).

8. M. R. Lindsey, was appointed by J. J. Baker, Ordinary (see Ordinary Minute Book A, page 383, Ordinary's Office). Began office September 4, 1933; served through December 31, 1936.

9. M. R. Lindsey, began office January 1, 1937.

Members of Tift County Board of Health.

(Recommended or appointed by the Grand Jury.)

Dr. C. S. Pittman, February 23, 1931-February 23, 1935.
W. T. Bodenhamer, Supt. of Tift County Schools.
N. L. Coarsey, Chairman of Board of County Commissioners.

W. T. Bodenhamer resigned as Superintendent of Schools, October 16, 1939, and was succeeded by C. F. Hudgins, as Superintendent of Schools, Mr. Hudgins served through December 31, 1940 and was succeeded, January 1, 1941, by Mercer H. Mitcham.

Dr. C. S. Pittman, Chairman of Tift County Board of Health, December, 1943 (see Minute Book 5, page 325).

M. H. Mitcham, January 1, 1941.
Chester A. Baker, January 1, 1943 through December 31, 1946.
Dr. C. S. Pittman, January 1, 1944.
W. C. McCormic, January 1, 1947.
(See Minute Book 6:60.)
Registrars of Tift County.
(Appointed by Judge of the Superior Court.)

I. W. Bowen appointed February 10, 1920, term expired January 1, 1921.

Harry Kent appointed February 10, 1920, term expired, January 1, 1921 (died July, 1927).

William Whiddon appointed February 10, 1920, term expired, January 1, 1921.

I. W. Bowen appointed January 28, 1928, term expired January 1, 1930.
E. E. Slack appointed January 28, 1928, term expired January 1, 1930.
William Whiddon appointed January 28, 1928, term expired January 1, 1930.

R. C. Postell appointed June 27, 1929, term expired January 1, 1930.
(For unexpired term of E. E. Slack, deceased.)

I. W. Bowen appointed January 1, 1930, term expired December 31, 1931.

W. M. Whiddon appointed January 1, 1930, term expired December 31, 1931.

R. C. Postell appointed January 1, 1930, term expired December 31, 1931.

I. W. Bowen appointed January 1, 1932, term expired December 31, 1933.

W. M. Whiddon appointed January 1, 1932, term expired December 31, 1933.

R. C. Postell appointed January 1, 1932, term expired December 31, 1933.

I. W. Bowen appointed January 1, 1934, term expired December 31, 1934.

G. E. Clements appointed January 1, 1934, term expired December 31,

TIFT COUNTY COMMISSIONERS
Top row—W. C. McCormic, chairman of the board. A. B. Phillips, commissioner. Bottom, Chester A. Baker, commissioner.

1934.

Joseph Kent appointed January 1, 1934, term expired December 31, 1934.

(All three of the above held over until December 31, 1936.)

I. W. Bowen, Jr., appointed January 1, 1937, term expired December 31, 1938.

G. E. Clements appointed January 1, 1937, term expired December 31, 1938.

Joseph Kent appointed January 1, 1937, term expired December 31, 1938.

I. W. Bowen, Jr., appointed January 1, 1940, term expired December 31, 1941.

G. E. Clements appointed January 1, 1940, term expired December 31, 1941.

Joseph Kent appointed January 1, 1937, term expired December 31, 1941.

I. W. Bowen, Jr., appointed January 1, 1942, term expired December 31, 1944. Resigned.

G. E. Clements appointed January 1, 1942, term expired December 31, 1944.

Joseph Kent appointed January 1, 1942, term expired December 31, 1944. Resigned.

Harry Hornbuckle appointed May 20, 1943, term expired December 31, 1944.

Wheeler Willis appointed April 1, 1946, term expires March 31, 1948.

John T. Ferguson appointed April 1, 1946, term expires March 31, 1948.

J. C. Williams appointed April 1, 1946, term expires March 31, 1948.

Henry D. Webb appointed April 1, 1946, term expires March 31, 1948.

M. E. Hendry appointed June 22, 1946.

Wheeler Willis refused appointment and Henry D. Webb was appointed, April 17, 1946.

Land Processioners of Tift County

(Appointed by County Commissioners May 2, 1932, for term of four years or until successors are appointed.)

Brighton District: J. S. Belflower, I. L. Simmons, Dan Fletcher.
Brookfield District: I. W. Bowen, Sr., E. F. Harrel, J. L. Gay.
Chula District: L. W. Whiddon, E. D. Branch, J. O. Ross.
Docia District: G. W. Ford, Sr., R. J. Spinks, John R. Willis.
El Dorado District: A. N. Adcock, L. M. Owens, R. G. Harrell.
Omega District: C. R. Patrick, John R. Butler, W. W. Baker.
Ty Ty District: W. W. Willis, Jacob Gibbs, L. M. Whitfield.
Tifton District: J. H. Hutchinson, W. H. Willis, T. E. Mitchell.

Land Processioners of Tift County

PUBLIC BUILDINGS IN TIFTON
Top row—The United States Post Office. Tift County Courthouse
Center—The Bank of Tifton. Confederate Monument in Fulwood Park
Bottom—Tift County Hospital

HISTORY OF TIFT COUNTY   337

(Appointed by the County Commissioners, Monday, May 6, 1940, for term of four years, or until successors appointed.) See Commissioners' Minute Book B, page 110.

Brighton District: Dan Goff, Will Sutton, G. E. Clements.
Brookfield District: J. L. Gay, C. B. Clements, Reason Gibbs.
Chula District: Lott Whiddon, Dempsey Whiddon, Jehu Branch.
Docia District: Warren Tucker, F. W. Massey, R. J. Spinks.
El Dorado District: Lemmie J. Lindsey, A. N. Adcock, R. G. Harrell.
Omega District: C. L. Keith, W. T. Patrick, J. R. Butler.
Ty Ty District: J. H. Glover, Jacob Gibbs, J. S. Gibbs.
Tifton District: J. H. Hutchinson, J. W. Moore, J. J. Golden.

Tift County Tax Assessors.

(Appointed by County Commissioners. Term of office, six years.)

Jacob Hall appointed May 31, 1926, term expired May 31, 1928.

J. W. Hardy, Jacob Gibbs appointed May 31, 1926, term expired May 31, 1928.

George F. Paulk appointed May 31, 1926, term expired May 31, 1928.

Briggs Carson appointed January 6, 1930, term expired December 31, 1935.

J. W. Hardy appointed January 6, 1930, term expired December 31, 1935.

Walter Sutton appointed January 6, 1930, term expired December 31 1935.

Term of office of Briggs Carson, J. W. Hardy, Walter Sutton, vacated in 1933.

S. G. Dodson appointed June 5, 1933, term expired December 31, 1934.
E. F. Preston appointed June 5, 1933, term expired December 31, 1936.
C. V. Taylor appointed June 5, 1933, term expired December 31, 1938.
W. C. Mobley appointed January 7, 1935.

D. B. Spinks was appointed to fill the unexpired term of W. C. Mobley, his term running from April 18, 1938 and expiring December 31, 1940. (County Commissioners' Book 2, page 101.)

By order of County Commissioners, E. F. Preston held over from December 31, 1936 to January 4, 1940, and was re-elected to hold office from January 4, 1940 to December 31, 1942.

By order of County Commissioners, C. V. Taylor held over from December 31, 1938 to January 4, 1940, and was re-appointed to hold office from January 4, 1940 to December 31, 1944. See Commissioners' Minute Book 2, page 101.

TIFTON CITY COMMISSION
Top row—C. A. Sears, commission chairman. Frank H. Smith, city manager
Center row—P. D. Fulwood, Sr., commissioner. R. M. Kennon, commissioner
Bottom row—J. F. Newton, commissioner. A. C. Tift, commissioner

HISTORY OF GEORGIA COASTAL PLAIN EXPERIMENT STATION

(George King)

The Georgia Coastal Plain Experiment Station was established by an Act of the General Assembly of Georgia approved August 19, 1918. The general control of the station was placed in the hands of a Board of Trustees consisting of the Governor of the State, the Commissioner of Agriculture, and seven other men appointed by the Governor from the Coastal Plain section of the State. The personnel of this Board was as follows:

Hugh Dorsey, Governor of Georgia
J. J. Brown, Commissioner of Agriculture
H. H. Tift, Tifton, Ga., Chairman of the Board
A. J. Bird, Metter, Ga.
H. W. Hopkins, Thomasville, Ga.
Newton Watkins, Fitzgerald, Ga.
D. M. Parker, Waycross, Ga.
J. W. Slade. Sandersville, Ga.
H. H. Elders, Reidsville, Ga.

The Board of Trustees was authorized to select a location for the Station. Several sites were considered. Tifton was selected because it was typical of the Coastal Plain and because of a gift of 206.22 acres of land from Capt. H. H. Tift and the raising of a handsome sum of money by the people of Tifton and Tift County.

The Station was governed by the Board of Trustees until January 1, 1932, when the Reorganization Act of August 28, 1931, placed the Station in the University System of Georgia under the control of the Board of Regents, to which the Director of the Station is directly responsible.

The original Station farm consisted of 206.22 acres. This land was practically all cut-over and swamp land with only 36 acres in cultivation. The only building was a four-room cottage.

It has been wisely said that an institution is but the shadow of a man. This was true in the growth of the Station. The first director of the Station, Mr. S. H. Starr, was appointed by the Board of Trustees on October 17, 1919, and assumed his duties on November 15, 1919. Mr. Starr served continuously from this time until the time of his death in November 1942. During his service, the Station made tremendous strides. From 206 acres, the land holdings of the Station increased to approximately 4,000 acres, and from the four-room cottage to buildings valued at a half-million dollars. Two thousand acres were located north of Tifton. In an effort to reach other soil types and farming conditions, land was acquired in Cook County, Berrien County, and Decatur County. In 1920, the Station staff consisted of the Director, farm superintendent, and two research specialists. In 1942, the staff had grown to the Director, the farm superintendent, and 25 specialists.

Two members of the original staff are now at the Station—Mr. Fred Bell, Farm Superintendent, and Mr. Otis Wooward, Horticulturist. Lack of space forbids the naming of all specialists employed during the years. These are available in the Station library.

In November 1942, Mr. George H. King, who had been President of Abraham Baldwin Agricultural College for eight years, was elected Director to succeed the late S. H. Starr. Since this time some 1,200 acres of land have been added, giving the station possession of over 5,000 acres of land. Several new departments have been established, so that the Station now consists of the Director and 32 specialists.

SILAS STARR
by E. Pickard Karsten

Born in Starrsville, Newton County, Georgia, April 3, 1888, son of Joe A. and Mattie Elliott Starr, Silas Starr attended the public schools of Mansfield and prepared for college at the University School for Boys. He was graduated from the Georgia State College of Agriculture at Athens, in 1910. Thence he went to Bolton College, Brunswick, Tennessee, where he was assistant principal and then principal, and also taught agriculture.

From Bolton Starr returned to his alma mater and taught agronomy and became professor of farm management. These positions he held until 1917.

On December 27, 1917 Silas Starr enlisted in the United States Army during World War I. He served as lieutenant in the Field Artillery and was for seven months with the American forces in France. After the close of the war he returned to America and was mustered out January 22, 1919.

Starr after his army service returned to the Georgia State College of Agriculture where he remained until he was appointed Director of the Georgia Coastal Plain Experiment Station at Tifton, November 10, 1919. His work from then until his death in a Thomasville, Georgia, hospital following a leg amputation, was the work which, together with that of the other men at the station, has contributed greatly to the agriculural success of his community. His biography after coming to the station is the history of the station, for he devoted himself wholeheartedly to the interests of the station, and during the time when he headed the institution numerous important experiments were made and much knowledge useful to the farmers of the country was gained. He headed the station from the time of its establishment, January 1920, until his death, November 6, 1942.

In manner one of Tifton's most unassuming citizens, Dr. Silas Starr was one of the community's most eminent men. Governors, senators, and scholarly educators were his close friends, yet he spoke with friendly kindliness to the tiller of the soil to better whose position was his life work.

CHAPTER XXVI
MISCELLANEOUS PART II
NEGRO PIONEERS
by E. Pickard Karsten

No history of Tift County would be adequate did it omit mention of those high-type Negroes whose faithful and efficient service and upright character made a large contribution to the building of Tifton.

Too numerous to mention by name are the faithful and strong mill hands whose service at the Tift Mill helped build the town.

Memory's tribute of appreciation goes to Herbert, long gardener to H. H. Tift, and in charge of fire building in the Tift home. How brightly burned those fires, and how fragrant was the sweet pine lightwood, and the fragrance of the burning rosin chips! How bright the tall brass andirons! How memory goes back to when my mother asked Uncle Herbert what he wished as a gift, and her surprise at his answer "A dictionary!" She gave him one. He was a preacher.

In the Tift home as maid, and nurse to me when I came down to Tifton, winters, was sweet Bertha Copeland. She taught me much of what I learned in those early days, and I remember her always as kind and cheerful and a gentlewoman in her ways. Also, I recall how good tasted the sweet potatoes she would bake for me in the ashes of the fireplace. In after years I tried to bake some thus, but mine never tasted like hers! The last time I saw her was the day when she came to see me after my aunt, Bessie Tift, died. Bertha had come to the funeral and when she learned I was here she came to see me. I cried on her shoulder as I had, when hurt, in my childhood, and, as then, I found solace in her large kindliness, healing to the soul.

There was Flora, for forty years laundress to Mrs. Tift; and no laundry could excel Flora's beautiful work. Her daughter, Lillian Forrester, was a power for good among the people of her own race, and the last time I saw her, her face shone with so much sweetness and goodness that I felt humble in her presence. I was not surprised when, soon afterward, I learned that she had gone from this world. It was evident that she was ready to go.

Jane, whose meals were prepared with great skill, Julia, Jerry, all skilled cooks in the H. H. Tift household; Jeff Mathis, in the service of H. H. Tift, Jr., for many, many years, from childhood until Mr. Tift's death; Sally Ivory, nurse to my own children and later cook to my mother, and again, after my mother's death, cook in my home again, in all a period of thirty years; Matilda Grant, nurse in my mother's household for thirteen years—these, many of them long passed from this world, are yet with me in memory, and I recall with gratitude the part they had in making life much richer and sweeter than it would have been without them.

WITH TIFT COLORED FOLKS

Top left—The day's pick in one of Tift's cotton fields. Top right—Young Dennard, who has celebrated his 101st birthday.
Center, left—Pulling tomato plants in one of the many fields in Tift County.
Bottom—Group singing in the colored school at Tifton

In more recent years, yet now for a long time, have been here Lelia Brooks, and William Brooks. Lelia's patience and kindness with children is such as made her charge eagerly await her hour to come each day, and reluctant to have her leave. Brooks, who for many years has been the one to thorough-clean the library with its many shelves of books, is also efficient at parties, and at any thing he undertakes.

In addition to these there is another whom I wish to mention but whose name I do not know. When I attended the funeral of Sallie Ivory, the woman I refer to sang, and I think I shall never forget the sweetness of her voice, as she sang "Nothing Between Myself and My Savior." Such music is a gift of God.

NEGRO CITIZENS

by Mrs. N. Peterson

A great many of the older colored citizens of Tifton and Tift County came to Tifton with Capt. Tift and worked with him in his mill in the woods felling and hauling logs to the mill or else working in the turpentine forests.

Most of the wives of these men were maids, nurses, cooks, and washer women for many of the housewives of Tifton.

Space will only permit the naming a few who are still living in Tifton where they reared their families, who in turn are doing their bit toward making Tifton and Tift county a better place in which to live.

The first family I shall name will be Charlie and Flora Forester, who came from Albany with Captain Tift. Charlie helped to build the first mill and worked as block setter in the mill until his death. His wife Flora was laundress for Mrs. H. H. Tift for forty-one years—having the laundry in her home at the time of her death. Their daughter Janie married Fred Rutherford, who helped Johnny Wilson to raise funds to build the first Tift County Industrial School. He also served in World War I.

Henry and Maria Wilson were the parents of Johnny Wilson to whom credit is given in the chapter on Tift County Industrial school. Henry worked as a mill hand during his life time. Aunt Maria is still living in Phillipsburg—a unique character in that her mind is still so clear for one her age. She was cook and laundress for Tifton white folk for years.

Doan and Joanna Winters came to Tifton with Capt. John A. Phillips who built the old Sadie Hotel. Doan was general cook and porter for the hotel—his wife was general maid. Clark Winters, their son, now a faithful employee of the local Georgia Power Company, was one of Johnny Wilson's committee to raise funds for the Industrial school.

Jim and Ida May Manuel were early citizens. Jim worked on Capt. Tift's log train while Ida May's hobby was cleaning and taking care of the young men's offices down town.

Tom and Lucy Mathis were faithful employees of Captain Tift. Their son Jeff, when a very young boy started working on the tram engine for the mill.

The story goes that Captain Tift would often run the engine himself to the woods to haul the log train into the mill. On these trips he would take Jeff to stand on the front of the engine to run the stock off the track to keep from being hit by the engine. Jeff drove for the Captain during horse and buggy days and also his automobile as long as Captain Tift lived. He then took over as general house boy for Mrs. Tift until her death. Jeff did fine service in 1929, driving Mrs. Tift's car for six weeks to take some pupils to a night school for adult illiterates taught by Miss Marian Ragan. Jeff now owns and operates a good dry cleaning establishment on Seventh Street.

Wesley and Cherry Holt were old timers. Wesley was a farmer, but worked in turpentine when Captain Tift needed him. Cherry was one of the first mid-wives in this section. She practiced for both white and colored as long as she was physically able. She is still living in Unionville, but is very feeble.

Ned and Lula Manning were good colored farmers of the Chula section of the county for a number of years. This fact is evidenced by their son, Nathan Manning, who has been the faithful janitor at the Tifton post office since July 1921. He owns his own home and has given his children a good education. His oldest daughter has a college education.

Lewis King was an old mill hand. His wife died when his daughter Clara was quite young. She grew to womanhood and married Gus Small, who is a butcher by trade. Clara has been janitress at the Tifton Post Office since 1918.

Jerry Copeland was fireman and blacksmith at Tift's Mill. He passed his trade on to his son, Bill, who is considered one of the best blacksmiths and mechanics in Tifton. His work rated so high that the government took him as a mechanical trainer for colored boys during World War II. He also assisted Johnny Wilson in raising funds for the Tift County Industrial School.

There are several colored pastors that should be given a place in the annals of Tifton's history. I refer to Brother Dan Mosely, pastor of old Shiloh Baptist Church. Another pastor is Cam Whitterker, pastor of Springfield church.

There are a few individual characters who stand out with the older citizens of Tifton. Who does not remember old Uncle Herbert Nichols, who was always soliciting funds with which to build a new church; old Aunt Dina Jones, mid-wife and baby nurse for all who could secure her services when there was a new baby in the home?

There are many others who have left their imprint for good on the lives of both white and black. Could we have done without them?

NEGRO CHURCHES

by B. L. Powers

Shiloh Baptist Missionary Church, which is the First Baptist Church in Tifton (colored)—organized 1882 near Tift Quarter in a small building. It was later built between Tift Quarter and Unionville, a larger building. In 1922 we moved into the present building which is a brick structure.

The first pastor was Rev. Anderson Whitaker; second pastor, Rev. Ben Jones; third pastor, Rev. D. A. Mosley. He served nearly 40 years. Fourth pastor, Rev. H. T. Tarver, served 13 years; fifth pastor, Rev. W. A. Tucker. This year is his seventh. Present location, south of Tifton near the National highway. Present value of church about $15,000. Name of present pastor, Rev. W. A. Tucker; name of present clerk, Mrs. B. L. Powers. Membership, 196. Preaching days, second and fourth Sundays.

Mt. Zion Missionary Baptist Church was organized in the Everett Chapel C. M. E. Church, May 1912, with 18 members under Rev. A. J. Rucker. He served nine months. Second pastor, Rev. D. J. Jackson; third pastor, Rev. G. W. Marlon; fourth pastor, Rev. J. C. Carter; fifth pastor, Rev. B. J. Drummer. Present location, S. Park Avenue, Phillipsburg. Present value of church, about $8,000. Membership 300. Wooden structure. Rev. B. J. Drummer, pastor; Mrs. Julia Folley, clerk.

I Hope Church of God Apostolic. Organized 1941 with 8 members. First pastor, Rev. Louie Odoms. Location, Collins Quarter in Tifton, Ga. Present location, Ind. Drive. Present value of church $4,000. Name of pastor and only pastor of this church, Rev. Louie Odoms. Membership, 83. Number of churches in this town, one. Type of church, wooden structure. Rev. Louie Odoms, pastor; Mrs. L. M. Odoms, clerk.

Primitive Baptist Church was organized ten years ago under the Rev. L. Carter, south of Unionville on Peachtree Street. First and only pastor, Rev. L. Carter. Present value of church about $500.00. Membership 50. Present pastor, Rev. L. Carter.

Friendship Missionary Baptist Church, organized 1900. First pastor's name was Rev. Guss Mingo. Location of church, on the Hill in Phillipsburg, near Mrs. Eloise McCloud's home. Second pastor, Rev. W. D.

Watson; third pastor, Rev. G. B. Moseley; fourth pastor, Rev. N. A. Miller; fifth pastor, Rev. J. S. Murray; sixth pastor, Rev. Jake Parson; seventh pastor, Rev. Henry Strong; eighth pastor, Rev. W. F. Flamman. Present location, Park Avenue, Phillipsburg. Present value of church about $12,000. Membership, 150. Pastor, Rev. W. F. Flamman; clerk, Mr. A. McCrae.

Beulah Hill Missionary Baptist Church, organized, 1900. First pastor, Rev. L. M. Mathis, served 29 years. Location in bottom back of Phillipsburg, near Mr. Jeff Mathis's present home. Second pastor, Rev. R. D. Arline; third pastor, Rev. E. D. King; fourth pastor, Rev. R. H. Williams; figth pastor, Rev. B. J. Jordan; sixth pastor, Rev. Picket; seventh pastor, Rev. E. G. Kirk; eighth pastor, Rev. H. W. Wilburn; ninth pastor, Rev. L. T. Sanders. Present location about the center of Phillipsburg. Present value of church, about $7,000. Membership —? Present pastor, Rev. L. T. Sanders. Present clerk, Mrs. Fannie King.

Springfield Missionary Baptist Church, organized April 8, 1886 at Vanceville, Ga., under Rev. Boss Williams. First pastor, Rev. Bill Mitchell; second pastor, Rev. Sam Jordon; third pastor, Rev Nesbia Johnson; fourth pastor, Rev. Dick Jackson; fifth pastor, Rev. C. W. Whitaker; sixth pastor, Rev. J. H. Sanders. Present location, Ind. Drive. First Deacon of this church Mr. Aaron Thomas; first mother of this church, Mrs. Sarah Thomas. Membership, 188. Present value of the church which is a brick structure, about $10,000. Rev. J. H. Sanders, pastor; Mrs. Lula Tyrus, clerk.

The First A. M. E. Church in Tifton called Isabella Chapel was founded by the Rev. I. G. Glass who served as its first pastor. The church was located south of what is now the A. B. and C. Railroad. Other pastors: Rev. Edwards, Rev. C. O. Mitchell, Rev. Davis, Rev. E. B. Brown, Rev. S. E. Crews.

Allen Temple located on Allen Street was purchased by Mrs. Patsy Lassiter. Rev. Hightower served as its first pastor. After Isabella Chapel burned the members moved to Allen Temple.

Other pastors: Rev. A. T. Tompkins, Rev. R. B. Sheffield, Rev. G. W. Robinson, Rev. J. W. Hall, Rev. C. P. Hobbs, Rev. S. M. Gilliard, Rev. I. N. Middleton, Rev. Lawrence, Rev. Randall, Rev. E. L. Miller, Rev. A. W. White, Rev. Cox, Rev. Gordon, Rev. Cole, Rev. R. W. Williams, Rev. Woods, Rev. Purcell, Rev. Grant, Rev. Lissimore, Rev. Gissentanne, Rev. N. F. Fedd.

Allen Temple was moved to its present location on South Park Avenue by the Rev. R. W. Williams. The value of church $7,000. The present pastor, Rev. James Debro. Membership, 150. Number of churches in town of this denomination, one. Type of church, brick veneered.

Everett Temple Church was organized in 1908 at Phillipsburg with 12 members. First pastor, Rev. N. T. Everett of Albany, Ga. Several pastors followed. Some are as follows: Rev. W. H. Pettigrue, Rev. C. W. Lawson, Rev. H. W. Armestor, Rev. N. T. Patterson, Rev. J. N. Davis, Rev. W. E. Brown, Rev. R. C. Magee, Rev. W. R. Smith, Rev. L. Barton, Rev. A. Bell, Rev. S. A. Thomas, Rev. N. T. Tenseley, Rev. M. C. Pettigrue. Present pastor is Rev. M. D. Davis with membership 148. Present value of church about $6,000.

JOE REEVES

Joe Reeves, janitor at the Tifton High School, is one of the best janitors in the state. He has worked at the Tifton High School for about a quarter of a century. During the war Joe worked in a chemical laboratory in New Orleans and received certificates of distinction for meritorious labor.

There was rejoicing among students and teachers at the Tifton High School when Joe returned last year. He is efficient and honorable in performing his tasks.

CHAPTER XXVII

TRUE TALES OF WIRE GRASS GEORGIA
by J. L. Williams

TIFTON'S FIRST TORNADO
AND WHAT BROUGHT IT ABOUT

In April, 1906, I manufactured building material in Tifton. I had in my employ as a cabinet maker a Baptist preacher, J. S. Weathers. He was a little past middle age and a much better looking man than the average. He was of fair personality and had better than a fair vocabulary. He lived in one of what we called at that time the knitting mill houses. The location was right where the big power station is now, just past the swimming pool.

Weathers was a regular preacher at the Tifton Cotton Mill church. Many times he and I talked of his ministry at the mill. He told me the people were not responding to his preaching as he thought they should. He worried about it considerably. His answers to my questions lead me to believe that he was afraid to really speak out to his flock.

At that time I had heard Sam Jones and the other leading evangelists of the country. With a view of helping Brother Weathers and his congregation I suggested that he let me write a sermon for him, and I suggestel that he study it and deliver it in the way I suggested. He readily agreed. Going into further details I wanted to know exactly what response came from it. The word used now is: the congregation's reaction. He and I began to work out the details which were these: The sermon was to be delivered on Sunday night. I was to be on the outside of the church and just before beginning I was to enter. Then, the brother seeing me enter the church, and on account of my being his employer, he was to invite me up on the rostrum so I could look the congregation in the face for the reaction.

Well, we were quite busy, time passed and the work was put off from day to day.

During that time one day while sawing with a handsaw the saw jumped out of the wood and scratched the knuckle of my thumb. It was a minor scratch and went unnoticed until a couple of days when blood poison set in; it began to look very dangerous. The entire arm was swollen to double normal size. It was wrapped in cotton and kept wet with a liquid solution to counteract the poison. I had to hold that arm up with the other arm.

At that time we had three small children. The youngest was less than a year old and the others just a little older. The middle one was down with typhoid fever at the time I got my hand hurt. He was growing worse day by day and the swelling in my arm had reached into the shoulder. I was spending about half time at the shop and the other at the house helping with the sick and treating my hand. Weathers was working at the shop at the time.

One day at the noon hour I was at home, which was on N. Central Avenue, the next block from the ice house. I was in great pain. The weather looked threatening. The sick child was pale and motionless. While I was walking the floor in the hall holding the poisoned arm with the other, I saw the blackest cloud I thought I had ever seen coming from the east. Suddenly there was a heavy downpour of rain, and more suddenly I heard something sound like a half dozen fast trains running; it was over in the direction of the Post Office. Getting to the front door I saw it was a tornado. I saw lumber, shingles and limbs flying through the air. I felt a great pressure against the house. The Presbyterian church then was located where the Touchstone family lives now. I saw the church go down. I rushed to the bed and took the sick child up with one hand and went to the door, telling the wife and another woman that was living in the house to get the others and get out. They had not seen what was going on outside. They were alarmed only at me. They thought I had suddenly gone crazy. When I got to the door I saw the wind tearing up the barns on the alley behind the Julian and Paulk houses. Thinking it had passed I put the sick child back on the bed. The wind was in a great circle in the air, rolling over and over. Sweeping the ground and then rolling up about 200 feet. There was a sash and door factory where Newton's plumbing shop stands now. It had a metal roof. The roof was torn off. The smokestack was blown down across the steam pipe from the boiler to the engine. The escaping steam made the strangest and most distressing sound I had ever heard. On my looking out the second time I saw all that roofing, brickbats, wood shingles and wagon wheels away up in the air and rolling back towards me. I ran for the sick child and told the women that it was coming back and to get ready and get out with the other children.

When I got to the door that time I saw the four knitting mill houses blowing away. One was the preacher's house. One man in one of the houses was pinned under and hurt badly but not killed. A calf was blown up and killed against the trees. The furniture and bed clothing of Preacher Weathers' house as well as the others was in the top of the trees as far as Little River.

During all that time Weathers was working at the shop, but left and went to the place where his house was, finding his wife unhurt he returned to the shop. When I got to the shop I found him packing his tools in his box. I asked what he intended to do. He said he was quitting, that he was going to the picture gallery and get the man there to go and make a picture of the wreckage; he said further that he thought he could take the picture and start on an evangelistic tour and make some money.

The next day he brought the picture and told me, with that in a revival he thought he could get such collections as was really due him.

It was several months before I saw Weathers again. I asked, what luck? "Mighty poor, Brother William, mighty poor," was his answer .He said it had been a good season for tornadoes, but on account of the time of year that the farmers were busy the attendance was off.

Now fellers, don't ever fool with a preacher by way of helping with a sermon, lest you start a big blow.

TRIBUTE TO J. L. HERRING AT A MEMORIAL MEETING AT THE LIONS CLUB IN 1923

Tifton Lions set aside all business and entertainment at the regular meeting Thursday and held an interesting memorial exercise in honor of the late J. L. Herring.

Good talks were made by Dr. F. C. McConnell, Jr., W. B. Bennet, Roy Thrasher, M. C. Owen, John Etheredge, C. W. Fulwood. Mrs. H. H. Tift, and J. L. Williams.

Tift County's Greatest Man

In his talk to the Lions, Mr. Williams said:

"To my mind the greatest man in any community is the man that does the most good for the most people and does it in an unselfish way. That man in Tifton and Tift county was undoubtedly John L. Herring.

"I had known Mr. Herring since 1898, and every year and day that I knew him he was the same big-hearted, genial gentleman that he was the last week of his life. I never saw him even begin to lose his head on any matter, and I knew him through times of peace and through two wars in which our country was engaged.

"The time I saw him happiest was, perhaps, at the time of the last election of Woodrow Wilson to the presidency. He had worked and toiled for three or four days and nights, giving every detail of news as fast as the wires brought it. That night everybody was gathered about the corner at Brooks drugstore celebrating. For some reason I felt that everybody wanted to express some appreciation for the good work Mr. Herring had done for us; so I got on a soap box and stated that I would receive dollar bills, no more no less, from anybody that wanted to make up a purse to buy Mr. Herring a suit of clothes. The idea went like wild fire. I was swamped with bills. I asked the people to wait until I could get a man to make a list of the people that were giving. I got one man, then another, then another. All three failed to keep up with the inflow of money. So we do not know exactly who it was that contributed to this fund. Little did I think that the same suit would be saved for his burial.

"I always knew that he was a genius, but could not think just wherein his mind was different until he wrote the 'Saturday Night Sketches' of Wire Grass Georgia forty years ago. After analyzing those stories, I came to the conclusion that he was a man with a photographic mind. I was convinced that he held in his mind's gallery every picture of the impressive scenery and customs of the people of his boyhood days. He had one of those peculiar minds and memories that enabled him to close his eyes and review the scenes of 1880; where he could see and hear bleating calves and lambs on the rye. He could recall the scenery and doings of the little log school houses of his country in that day. He could see the line up at the old country church in every detail. He could see the long haired maiden and hear the strong voice of the horny handed preacher at the baptizing down in the old mill stream.

"He died, it seems, at an untimely hour. But since thinking we find that a man can't die at a time that is good for him and good for the people he leaves behind. God took him at a time that was best for him, for he will be remembered only as the powerful, genial, kind Editor, and not as an old, tottering man in the afternoon of life with his good works half forgotten. Mr. Herring recorded with kind words, perhaps more births and deaths than any other man of his age. If there were a single rose petal laid upon his grave for every kind word he said, and for every good deed he did, he would rest today beneath a mountain of roses."

TIFTON'S FIRST RADIO STATION

This, as well as the first filling station was started by Mr. J. L. Brooks, the corner druggist.

It was in 1922 he raised the highest pole ever put up in the county. It stood right where the back part of Bowen's Undertaking shop is now. It was the aerial. The radio was behind the prescription case of the same drugstore he now occupies. The aerial wire went from the back door of the store to the top of the pole.

The loud speaker or amplifier had not arrived then. It was just a receiving station. A private one, but the people made it public.

Mr. Brooks was the announcer. When big news was expected many went to the drugstore. Mr. Brooks did the receiving by way of a double head phone from which a long cord went to a black box, one that looked like a big battery, that was the radio.

Mr. Brooks sat in a chair and told us what was going on in distant places that we had heard was on the map.

When the Dempsey-Firpo fight came on all that were of a sporting mind, crowded in behind the prescription case to hear the fight announced, round by round.

Mr. Brooks being an admirer and follower of Dempsey went to work with great enthusiasm. Everything started off fine. We couldn't hear what the radio said but Mr. Brooks could with the head phones, so he was announcing it blow by blow. The fight was going just about as he could talk. He announced a knock down by Dempsey and in the same second he said, "Firpo is up. He's down again. Again up and again down." Then the announcer looked like he had been struck by lightning. He called out loud, "Dempsey is knocked out of the ring; friends are throwing him back in the ring. Firpo's down, he's up, he's down. By that time the fight was going so fast and reckless he couldn't tell it fast enough, so he jumped up from the chair and began to show us what was going on by swinging both right and left in every direction. We were terribly crowded in there but everybody gave the announcer and actor every bit of room they could spare; so as not to interrupt the proceedings. Had Firpo not gone down to stay when he did, several of us, would have probably gone down.

One time all stations were notified to listen for a certain program to come from London at a certain time. Then, Mr. Brooks pepped up and tuned in at the appointed time. The program could be heard well enough to understand it was from London but no better. That, we believe to be the first radio communication received in Tifton from across the Atlantic.

The radio cost $50.00. Later when amplifiers came out one was bought at $75.00 to attach to the $50.00 radio.

TIFTON'S FIRST AUTOMOBILE
TIFTON'S FIRST FILLING STATION

The first automobile owned by a Tifton citizen was brought in to the town the first part of 1902 or 40 years ago. Its owner was J. E. Johns (livery stable man). It was a one-cylinder Cadillac. Inside room for driver and four passengers. It was painted red; well upholstered and looked good. Didn't have any cover of any kind above the seats. Entrance to the front seat was from the side; no doors. The entrance to the back seats was through a door at the back of the car.

It was used to carry people pleasure riding about town at a rate of 25c or 35c per hour. That auto met the trains and carried people to any part of town for 25c per person. The car cost $1,100.

About a year after this first car our well known druggist, Dr. J. L. Brooks, brought to town a Rambler roadster, 2 passengers. It was a little lighter and more streamlined than the Cadillac. It cost $1,000. Prior to that a well known firm, Gorman and Jefferies, made bicycles called the Rambler. They changed to making autos but held the name Rambler. The Rambler factory and name was bought by a Mr. Nash.

The car Mr. Brooks had would have been fine on the roads and streets we have now. It looked about as well as the present cars. Road conditions were bad, which subjected a car to sudden and unusual strains. All cars were chain driven then. One chain beginning at the motor which was under the center of the body of the car. The chain went to the rear axle.

When Dr. Brooks got into the country in heavy sand and hot weather his chain usually broke. The ruts in the sand were real deep and this put the car close to the ground. There was nothing to do but to crawl under the car and fix the chain. The Doctor weighed 230 and from the fact of the motor being hot and greasy and the sand hot, which together made him hot, he could never find as much room as he needed under there to make the repairs.

There were no garages then; cars were stored in the livery stables. The Doctor put up with all these inconveniences for two years and then sold the struggle buggy to a medical doctor in Fitzgerald for $800.00.

In those first days of the cars there were inconveniences about buying gas and oil. At first only the drugstores sold gasoline, and that was in very small quantities. It was sold only for clothes cleaning.

Dr. Brooks was never a fellow to put up with inconveniences. So, he put up a pump on a vacant lot near his store and ordered gas. By that time some other cars had come in the town, so that pump was Tifton's first filling station. There were lots of horse racks on the lot and many times when gas was wanted it was not unusual to find a horse or team of mules hitched to the gas pump.

I almost forgot to tell the price of gas. Wholesale price was 3c per gallon; retail price from the pump was 5c per gallon, no tax.

I might say here that one of those single cylinder cars on our paved roads at 25 miles an hour would take next to no gas at all.

WHEN TIFTON WAS DRY

Back in the fall of 1898 the women of the Tifton Baptist Church thought they should by all means have a missionary to represent their church—which was new and young at that time—in the foreign fields.

They lit upon what they believed to be a very apt young gentleman. One that had been an enthusiastic attendant at all the various kinds of meetings held at the church. One that saw eye to eye with the entire feminine membership.

This young fellow was sent to Boston, Mass., for special training in a school there that trained workers for the foreign fields. But, the night before the day of his going a merry, get-to-gether festival was held to celebrate his departure. No, there was no drinking at the meeting, not even coffee. Tifton was dry then. It was oyster stew night.

The young man left and arrived in Boston on schedule. He reported at intervals regarding progress, which statements were true and satisfactory. The training course was finished in late December of that year, 1898.

He arrived back in Tifton on Christmas Eve. The plans were to start him foreign, about ten days later. On Christmas morning, the day after his arrival, he was invited out by his friends and former associates to their home. With a desire to give him a royal welcome they had egg-nog in abundance. He joined in wholeheartedly and did his bit. No one took too much. The people were of fine character and members of the Baptist Church; some of them are here now.

By the next day this young fellow had heard so much unfavorable news about himself that he didn't feel able to face the women that had sent him to Boston. He hung his head and strode away.

That fellow was a Western Union telegraph operator at that time. He gave up a good position to make that venture.

THE KEY MAN OF TIFTON IN 1899

One bright morning in 1899 we found in Tifton a strange nice looking tall, slender young man arranging to put on a one-man show the following night in Bowen's Opera House.

In order to advertise some of his unusual abilities, he proposed to find the key to any post office box hidden in any place in town. He proposed further to allow anyone selected to blindfold him as securely as they saw fit, and while thus blindfolded he would drive a team of horses from a livery stable in search of the key and when found drive directly to the post office while blindfolded and unlock the box that the key was made to fit, the first time without trying the key on any box other than the one it was made for. His proposition was promptly accepted. News went out over the town that the drive would begin at 3:00 p.m.

J. E. Johns was the livery stable man and the stable was located on the lot now occupied by Buck Blalock's pool room on Main street. The post office was in the store room now occupied by Mr. Pittman's Firestone store. J. M. Duff was the postmaster.

At 3:00 p.m. Mr. Johns had two horses hitched to a buggy—the key man was there. He was blindfolded with a big black cloth. Mr. Johns went along to hold the horses while the man was hunting the key. The key man did the driving. Mr. Johns did not help him in any way. The people of the town were lined up along the sidewalks waiting for the drive. In a few minutes the blindfolded man came driving the two-horse buggy team up Main street at top speed. Holding his hands high so the people could see that he was doing the driving. He continued out Love Avenue and in front of the home of Senator Susie T. Moore he stopped the horses suddenly and while Mr. Johns held the horses the man hurried through the yard and back in the garden where a board fence was being rebuilt; he turned over two or three boards while blindfolded, picked up the key and hurried back to the buggy—took up the lines—turned the team around and drove at top speed to the post office—got out—hurried in and unlocked the box the key was made for—hurried out and took Mr. Johns and the team back to the livery stable.

It won't be any use to ask me how he did it.

THE PROGRESSIVE MINISTER
THE MODEL YOUNG MAN AND BILLY

This was in Tifton in 1900. The minister was the Reverend C. G. Dilworth of the First Baptist church. I have forgotten the model young man's name. He was of nice size—slightly of the strawberry blond type—medium personality. He worked in the corner drugstore. He had lived in Tifton only a few weeks. He was the right-hand man of the minister. Rev. Dilworth had built two or three very small church buildings on the outskirts of town. One was in Edgewood. It was called the Edgewood Mission. Some kinds of services were held at these outposts every Sunday as well as at the regular church. Both the preacher and the model young man were busy all day every Sunday. The model young man got into the good graces of the preacher early after he arrived here by volunteering his service in any way the preacher might need him, so he was used to supply two or more of the outposts every Sunday. He was undenominational. He stopped and offered his services to other churches; sometimes accepted. Altogether he was a real handy fellow, as there was more of that kind of work here at that time than there were workers.

The young man was very popular with all the people of the town, except the other young men about his age. Outside of his church activities he did quite a bit of courting. Another young fellow here at that time said the girls were plum fools about him. That accounted for his unpopularity with the young gentry of the town. Another reason why he was, his association almost altogether with the elderly gentlemen and of his hi-hatting the younger ones. Also, it was these elderly gentlemen of the town that had most of the world's goods. They were the ones he liked best. After the young man had become quite efficient in his line, the minister, Rev. Dilworth, wrote a rather lengthy article for the local paper telling of the young man's good qualifications and the value he was to the town, and especially of how much help he was to him in the work of the church. He finished the article by calling him a model young man, and that he, the minister, sincerely hoped to see the other young men of the town follow after him.

The second Saturday night after the article in the paper, the model young man went among those elderly gentlemen of the town that had most of the wealth and had each one cash a check for him. I never learned the amounts but none were real large, but they were numerous, for he always liked a large congregation. Needless to say that he didn't have enough money in the bank to cash the first one. The south end of the A. B. & C. Railroad was then the Tifton, Thomasville & Gulf. A passenger train left every morning at 7:00 o'clock for Thomasville. Sunday morning after that Saturday night the young man left on that train. He connected with another train at Thomasville for the west. The first thing we younger fellows thought about was the preacher's wish that many others would follow after him. We checked up on who was here and who was not here. We found that the pracher's article was not entirely without results, for one young man, named Billy, followed after the model. Billy was born and reared in Tifton. He had always worked at the Tifton Planing mill. He was rather short of stature with black hair and blue eyes. Billy went away in a brand new spring suit for it was early in the spring of the year. He wore a new black derby hat. The two traveled due west from Thomasville to the Pacific coast as fast as the trains could run and connect. Arriving at the coast the model turned abruptly to the north. The turn was too quick for Billy. He got knocked loose at that point. We younger fellows had no regret of the model's leaving, but we were worried about Billy. He had been popular with all the people, old and young, especially with the older men that worked at the Tift mill. They had more hope of Billy getting back than we younger fellows had. Just in front and at the edge of the sidewalk of the first house east of the home now occupied by Amos Tift and family, there was a big open well, the first to be dug in Tifton. It had real good water. Capt. Tift always said: "If they ever drink water a few weeks at that old well and go away, they will come back." That was our only hope of ever seeing Billy again. We remembered how nice he looked in that new suit and derby. We went through the long summer months holding that picture in our minds.

So in the late fall of that year when the days were short and cooler, one afternoon when the sun was down below the tops of the trees, we saw something coming in the road from the west. Several went out to look and with shaded eyes we discovered it was Billy. The word quickly went around the block. All came out to the edge of the street and waited. Billy walked up slowly and leaned against a telephone pole. His suit was faded and tattered; he looked five years older; the soles of his shoes were gone; the uppers were none too good; the derby that went away so crisp and new was dented in here and there, it had turned green from the weather and was frazzled on the edge. Billy was really tired. A gentleman, Mr. John Pope who had worked at the mill and known Billy from infancy, said: "Billy, my boy, in your depressed condition, what is the first thing you will have us do for you?" Billy answered and said: "Give me a drink of water from the old well and go and tell that preacher that I followed his advice as long as I could."

Now off the story I wish to remind the readers of an article in the Free Press last year where I wrote about Uncle Josh when he told us 50 years ago. He said, "Boys, don't ever swap horses with the fellow that gets to church on Sunday ahead of all the others and shakes hands with all that come."

THE HORNED NEGRO OF TIFTON

A citizen of Tifton that lived here in the year 1897 and part of the years immediately after 1897 traveled over the country showing a young negro man with horns. The horns were about four inches long. The Tifton showman claimed the young horned negro was right out of the wilds of Africa. Two or three other white men went along with the show. The band of showmen went into the St. Louis World's Fair at its beginning in 1904. They kept their show going almost to the end of the fair, at which time all parties connected with the show while drinking got into an argument over the division of funds and in a free for all fight knocked the horns off the negro and that broke up the show and organization.

The origin of the horns was this way: The Tifton citizen had taken the horns off a calf. He split the skin on the negro's head in two places and attached the horns to the skull in the hair above the forehead in proper or natural position. The hair after that was never cut. With the hair growing around the horns the appearance was perfectly natural which made the subject look extremely wild.

CANDIDATES RUNNING FOR OFFICE

In the first election in Tift county a business man of Tifton ran for one of the county offices on what he called a sensible business-like plan. He said there was no use for continuous hand shaking and lobbying around with the voters. He copied all the names of the registered voters in a little book and began to call on the voters by that list. Everyone that he interviewed that promised to vote for him he checked o.k. in the book. When he had the promises of a substantial majority of the registered voters marked o.k. he quit the drive and returned to his place of business. There were 21 registered voters at the precinct of Brookfield; 20 promised to vote for him; one voter being out of the county that day of the canvass, he did not see that one.

After the election the candidate counted the number of votes promised and the number received. Brookfield gave him one vote and 20 against. Needless to say the candidate lost by a substantial majority.

HOW THE FIRST SESSION OF SUPERIOR COURT OF TIFT COUNTY WAS PAID FOR

The county was created in 1905 in mid-summer. The people had given in taxes in the other counties and had to pay in the other counties.

In the fall of that year a term of superior court was held. Judge Mitchell of Thomasville and Solicitor W. E. Thomas of Valdosta were the high officers. As the session was coming to a close the jury had to be paid as well as other expenses. There was not as much as a dime in the treasury. A way had to be found to pay off. Some one or more gentlemen reported about eight of the high lights of the town for gaming. They were mostly members of the bar in the courtroom. Charges were brought quickly and one by one was called to stand up. They pled guilty and received fines from $50.00 to $100.00 each. In a few minutes there was money in the treasury.

CITY ELECTION FOR MAYOR

In an election in the early days of Tifton for Mayor there were two candidates, one a livery stable man, the other a former mayor, lawyer and smooth politician. The livery stable man had never run for office before. He didn't canvass for votes; he depended upon his announcement only. On the morning of the day of the election before the voting began the former mayor told the livery stable man that it had long been the custom that when two gentlemen were running for the same office the polite way was for each one to vote for the other and not vote for themselves. The livery stable man readily agreed to abide by the long established custom and voted for the other candidate. In the vote counting there was not a singlt vote in the box for the livery stable man.

WHEN TIFTON HAD 17 LAWYERS AND ONE PREACHER

It was about the year 1910 the town council bought a road roller, entirely on credit. It was a gasoline tractor with two real heavy wide rollers for smoothing the streets. It didn't work very well; so the population soon began to call the machine the "dummy." Criticism of the council for buying the dummy was running high. Public sentiment was about to declare the dummy a nuisance. The council were anxious to get it back where it came from without paying. A way had to be found. The 17 lawyers in a meeting found that the city council did not have legal authority to buy anything except necessary supplies for running the town; so the dummy had to go back home.

The lone preacher was a frail Methodist minister named Whiting.

BIG HOG DAN WALKER

There was a citizen of Tift County that raised the largest hogs so far as is known in the world. It was Dan Walker that lived two miles north of Tifton. It was during the years of 1900 to 1910. The hogs weighed from 1,250 to 1,683 pounds. Several weighed 1,600 and 1,683. They were exhibited at the state fairs in Macon. At one time two were driven from the Walker farm drawing a two horse wagon into Tifton and back to the farm. In color the hogs were a pale red, nearly yellow. The hair was extremely coarse. They reached top weight at seven years old.

The writer was on the farm at one time when Mr. Walker was feeding the hogs. To show me the strength of their backs he and a half grown son sat on the back of one of the hogs while he walked around and ate corn. Mr. Walker weigher 165 pounds and the son half that much. There was no difference in the way the hog walked with or without the load.

Mr. Walker was very conservative in his claims for his hogs. I was in his tent on the fair grounds at Macon and found that he represented the hog as weighing 1,600 pounds while that one weighed 1,683.

No one knew of the hogs being of any special breed. Mr. Walker claimed that he grew them to the enormous size with some kind of tonic of his own formula. Mr. Walker died about 1925.

GRAMMAR SCHOOL BLOCK
WHEN THE CIRCUS CAME TO TOWN

The greatest of all shows that ever came to Tifton was about the year 1904 when the John Robinson Shows came and opened up with the great drama of The Queen of Sheba arriving at Jerusalem riding in her chariot drawn by four snow white horses with all her servants and attendants. She was met first by one hundred of Solomon's wives with their maids and attendants; everyone of the wives was nice looking, slender, and taller than the average of women. Everyone walked unusually erect and dressed in the best Oriental style. All appeared to be Syrians; no real blonds or brunettes.

Then at the meeting the leading man of Ethiopia introduced the Queen to the leading lady of Solomon's wives; she in turn introduced the other ninety-nine wives collectively to the Queen. Next the leading lady of Solomon's wives introduced the Queen's leading man of Ethiopia to King Solomon, he in turn introduced the Queen of Ethiopia to the King. Then there was a great march around the four show rings, which carried the great parade around in front of every seat in the tent. The King and the visiting Queen together wearing their crowns with all gold and silver braid and other decorations that could be had in the time of 700 years B.C. The hundred of Solomon's wives marched about six abreast following the chariot of the King and Queen drawn by the four snow white horses.

Altogether it was the greatest of all the shows visiting Tifton from its founding through 1947.

JOHN H. SPARKS, OLD VIRGINIA

Railroad shows came about 1902; it was before the days of electric lights in Tifton. The tent was pitched on the first block east of Fifth Street and South of Main.

There was nothing so unusual about the circus except a baby elephant born two weeks before at Quitman, Georgia. The baby's skin looked as tough as its thirty-year-old mother. The weight of the little one was 200 pounds. It was just small enough to walk under the mother.

The Tifton people leaving the show was the unusual part of it. The show had some sort of lighting system of its own. Just as the show was over and a few of the people had gotten outside the tent in the dark, the lights from some poor connection went out. Someone asked "What's the matter?" The answer was "The lights are out." That was misunderstood to be "The lions are out." Everyone made a wild scramble to get away and towards their homes as fast as possible. Those that did not hear the first report asked what the wild scramble was about. The answer was, "The lions are out." They joined in the race. Down on the next block where Tift Avenue crosses Fifth Street was a swampy branch. There were lots of people at the circus that lived over past the big Tift sawmills. The location now is the Tifton Laundry. The nearest way home for those people was across that swampy branch. When the crowd of runners got in that branch the thought came to their minds that a swamp was where the lions would go when they were out. Everything went into a higher gear which soon put them north of Second Street in what they thought was the safety zone.

THE VANAMBERG SHOWS

The Vanamberg shows came to Tifton only one time. It was about the year 1905. On the lot now stands the grammar school building and grounds. It was at that time the athletic field and show grounds. Rain fell all day long, so much there was no show. The show people succeeded in getting up the main tent and in it they spent the day. The horses were of the very finest. All animals and equipment were in excellent condition.

The only unusual thing with the circus was the lamb and the lion in the same cage. It was an ordinary yew sheep and a female lion. Both appeared contented and pleased with surroundings. Read Isaiah, 11-6.

WHEN LIFE BEGAN FOR ME
SOME PEOPLE I HAVE MET

Maisy Fields

I have heard a lot about a book on the subject: "Life Begins at Forty." I have never read it. An old man once manager of a Philadelphia Ball Club, in a magazine article after he was 73, said life began for him at 70 years old. So it seems that it can begin at most any age.

I started to school I think a year younger than children are started here at this time. I remember going a few times with the older ones as a visitor. I had nothing to do there and I thought it would always be that way; so I insisted on going regular, and they let me go. Soon I was given lessons and told to study. I didn't know how to study because I had forgotten what the names of the letters were and all I could do was sit there and try to remember the names she called them. I was very much displeased for the rest of the term.

I base the younger age on the fact that I was youngest in the school that first term, and at the beninning of the next term several beginners came in of my same age.

One that came in of my age from the other end of the road was a little girl named Maisy Fields. She had brown eyes the same as mine and black curly hair the same as mine except hers hung down her back in curls. We were exactly the same size and the same age. She was very timid and in that respect I was next to her. The first day she attended school she put her arms down on the desk and with her face on her arms she cried all day.

I spent half my time looking at her in hopes that she might get over it. The next day she came and did the same way all day and I did very little except look at her in great sympathy. I was worried, there was gloom and discouragement on every side. On the third morning she came in and took up where she left off the afternoon before. No one in the school room seemed to pay any attention. I looked at her and out the window. There were clouds everywhere. One time she looked up and I noticed her eyes were red, her hair all tangled. She gave me a sad look and buried her face in her arms again on the desk. I looked out the window and it seemed that I would never see the sun shine again. At last at the end of the day she looked up and around over the room. No one saw her except me. She seemed to know, of the many, there was one soul in sympathy.

The fourth day was much like the third except she looked up and over the room two or three times more. Every time, she found me looking in great sympathy. To me the world was growing darker and filling up with gloom and sorrow. At the end of that day on leaving she took a good look at me. She looked tired and worried. On the fifth day she began to look around more. Always in my direction. Meanwhile for me the whole world had grown very tired but at last she looked up and found no one looking but me. That time I saw the sweetest smile I thought I had ever seen. Her face went right down on the desk in her arms; but it seemed to me I heard the gates of heaven swing ajar. I thought I heard the angels come out and with their great white wings paint the clouds with sunshine. All the world seemed bright and cherry. The birds came out and sang better than I had ever heard before. My heart in a few hours grew to enormous size.

I was six and she the same. I cannot recall that I had ever heard the word sweetheart. I had never had a sister. I had never been about girls. They were, or she was a wonderful thing to me. As the days went by smiles continued in school and out. No words were spoken. In playing outside, when the bell rang I looked over to see where she was and always in running in I happened to be going up the steps at the same time with her.

One day when there were few around we happened to stop and look square into each other's eyes. No eyes ever looked deeper. Not a word was spoken, but she seemed to say: "How am I ever to repay you for your sympathy when I was in so much trouble?" From my heart without speaking came these words: "That is all right, I see how you feel. Now, henceforth and forever, we will travel the road together and when I pull a great play on life's stage, your part shall ever be to smile a smile for me."

She was as kind and sweet as the roses she loved. After that in walking the road in spring time as the sun rose I could see the sparkling dew brighten the honeysuckle and dogwood blooms. All the birds seemed to sing the song of real love. So it was, when Maisy Fields smiled a smile for me and I learned that it was for beauty and love that the world was made; it was then that life began for me.

CHAPTER XXVIII
PIONEERS
APPRECIATION

Thanks be to God who has strengthened me to write. It is my hope and prayer that what is written may be acceptable to Him, and to His glory.

Thanks also are expressed to many who were helpful to me. Some are living, some are dead. I am grateful to each. Among these are:

The Tifton Gazette; Smada, Lucian Lamar Knight, Walter G. Cooper, White, Hugh Jones, William Fleming, William Henderson, Mrs. W. P. Cobb, Mary Jones and Lily Reynolds, J. V. Chapman; my late grandmother, Cecilia Matilda Baynard Willingham; my late parents, Dr. and Mrs. W. L. Pickard; my late aunt, Bessie W. Tift; my kinswoman, Mrs. Julia Bacon Osborne; Senator Susie Tillman Moore, Katherine Tift Jones, Cassie Tift Bacon, Mrs. J. J. Golden, Miss Laura Guest, Mrs. J. G. Padrick, Miss Florence Padrick, Miss Lizzie Fulwood, Mrs. Holmes Murray, Mrs. Albert Foster, Mrs. W. W. Banks, Mrs. Briggs Carson, Sr., Mrs. N. Peterson, Mrs. John Peterson, Mrs. Peggy Martin, Mrs. B. F. Pickett, Mrs. Luna Warren Pitts, Mrs. George Washington Peters.

Mrs. Annie Bennett, Mrs. Willingham Tift, Mrs. Amos Tift, Miss Eugenia Allen; my aunt, Mrs. Pearl Myers; the late Mrs. E. P. Bowen, Sr.; the late Mrs. W. T. Hargrett, Miss Leola Greene, Mrs. J. M. Paulk, Mrs. C. B. Holmes, Mrs. Sarah Willingham Griffin, Mrs. Ralph Johnson, Miss Rosa Corry, Mrs. W. T. Smith; my sisters, Mrs. Ralph Edward Bailey and Mrs. Roland Harrison; Mrs. George W. Coleman, Mrs. Minnie Youmans Spires, Mrs. P. D. Fulwood, Mrs. Arch McCrea, Mrs. R. M. Kennon, Mrs. J. E. Cochran, Mrs. Raleigh Eve, Mrs. Arjane Fletcher, Mrs. Lou Greene. Mrs. R. H. McMillan, Mrs. R. H. Hall, Sr., Mrs. W. L. Harman; the late Mrs. W. H. Hendricks, Mrs. J. T. Mathis, Mrs. Lois Carter Smith; the late Miss Verna Parker, Mrs. Mary Belle Scarboro Scott, Mrs. Eugene Slack, Miss Helen Spurlin, Mrs. Homer Meade Rankin, Mrs. Luna Rigdon, Mr. and Mrs. Jack Gaulding, Mrs. W. B. Hitchcock, Miss Eloise Roughton, Mr. and Mrs. J. L. Williams.

Mr. and Mrs. Henry D. Webb, Miss Ida Belle Williams; the late Lilla Forrester; Judge Raleigh Eve, Homer Carmichael, T. E. Phillips, Sr.; the late E. P. Bowen, Sr.; Lennon Bowen, Jim Bowen; the late H. H. Tift, Jr.; Willingham Tift, Amos Tift; the late Dr. Silas Starr; Dr. George King, Boozer Culpepper; my kinsman, Lenwood Pickard; my late kinsman, Dr. James T. Ross, of Macon; my kinsman, Thomas Ellis; Ben Golden, Frank Smith, C. C. Guest, J. J. Golden; Judge Phillip Kelly and his secretaries; W. J. Warren, Sheriff James Walker, Robert Choate, Sam Lassiter, Dr. W. H. Hendricks, S. A. Youmans, J. D. Padrick, L. C. Hall, Ben McLeod, Clem Carson, Elias Webb, Henry Love, Professor S. L. Lewis, F. O. Bullington, J. B. Davis, Jeff Mathis, E. P. Bowers, T. W. Tift, City of Tifton, County of Tift, Mrs. Pearl Myers, Mrs. Robert A. Balfour, Harry Hornbuckle, and G. B. Phillips.

(Signed) E. PICKARD,
Author of Tift County Pioneers.

PIONEERS

by Elizabeth Pickard Karsten

BENJAMIN THOMAS ALLEN

Founder of the Tifton Gazette

Benjamin Thomas Allen, born February 23, 1852, in Thomas County on the Georgia-Florida line, was one of five children of James Allen and Martha G. Whitaker Allen, both of whom died at Valdosta. Benjamin's brothers were Sam, Walter and George. His sister was Mary Elizabeth.

Admitted to the bar when young, Allen early became more interested in newspaper work and wrote for the Valdosta Times. Next he wrote for the Savannah Morning News when it was owned by Col. J. H. Estill. Later Allen wrote for Florida newspapers in Madison, in Crescent City and in St. Augustine.

While living in Crescent City Allen, on Wednesday, December 29, 1886, married Susan, daughter of Captain and Mrs. Amon De Laughter, of Madison, Florida, the ceremony taking place at Mosley Hall, Florida.

Mrs. Oren Gatchell, of Tifton, was Lelia De Laughter (or De Laughtre).

In 1888 B. T. Allen became owner and editor of the Berrien County Pioneer, at Sparks, Georgia. About this time Mr. Allen and his wife were among the approximate dozen charter members of the Tifton Baptist Church. In October, 1891, Allen moved to Tifton and here established the Tifton Gazette, which he owned and edited until 1895, when he sold the paper.

Allen was active in Tifton municipal affairs. June 1, 1891, upon resignation of J. I. Clements, B. T. Allen was elected to succeed Mr. Clements on city council. On September 7, 1891, Allen, H. H. Tift, and J. C. Goodman were named to serve as a committee to suggest method of naming Tifton streets. He served faithfully on numerous committees until he left Tifton.

The last issue of the Gazette published by Mr. Allen and edited by him was on Friday, May 10, 1895. The firm of Baldridge and Fulwood later organized the Gazette Publishing Company. On February 1, 1895 John Lewis Herring came to the Gazette as advertising and collection man. In January, 1898 a controlling interest in the Gazette was sold to W. H. Park, of Macon, and John W. Geer, who operated the paper a few months. Park later sold his interest to J. L. Herring and Briggs Carson, Sr. Mr. Carson sold to J. L. Herring who, many years afterward, on September 14, 1914 issued the first copy of the Daily Tifton Gazette, the first daily paper in Georgia to be published in a town the size of Tifton.

After selling the Gazette, Mr. Allen for a time operated his job printing establishment in Tifton but in 1897, after having been here six years, moved to Pearson where he practiced law.

In 1915 Mr. Allen resumed his writing. He bought and became editor of the Pearson Tribune which he owned and edited until three years prior to his death at the age of eighty. He died on July 2, 1932, at his home in Pearson. Mrs. Allen had died soon after the Allens left Tifton.

He gave about fifty years of his life to newspaper work and was widely known in South Georgia and Florida.

"Bee Tree Allen" was the name by which Benjamin Allen was called by his Tifton friends, because his initials were "B. T." and he had a habit of walking with his head thrown back as if looking for a bee tree. He was greatly beloved and highly esteemed by a wide circle of friends.

Mr. and Mrs. Allen had one daughter, Eugenia De Laughter Allen. Miss Allen is a music teacher of ability and also is society editress of the Pearson Tribune.

JOSEPH JACKSON BAKER
Tift County Ordinary, 1919-1936

Joseph Jackson Baker, son of T. Allen Baker and Nancy Griner Baker, was born near Sparks, Georgia, October 27, 1856. At twenty-one, he left Berrien, now Cook and went to Ty Ty where he worked in W. E. Williams's store for seven years and was assistant postmaster and express agent.

On March 13, 1881, Joseph J. Baker married Sarah Jane Taylor, eighteen-year-old daughter of Mrs. Nancy Taylor, whose husband had been killed in the War Between the States.

Mr. Baker bought and lived at a farm one mile east of Ty Ty for several years. He then bought and for nineteen years lived at the Luke place, west of Little River. Next he lived for about ten years at the W. W. Williams place, which he owned, a mile north of Ty Ty. He was living there when he was elected to fill the unexpired term of Tift County's first ordinary, C .W. Graves, who died while in office, in 1919.

Mr. Baker was a member of the Ty Ty Primitive Baptist Church, and for eight years was a member of the Tift County Board of Education, which position he resigned in order to make the race as ordinary. He served as ordinary of Tift County continuously from 1919 until his death, August 27, 1936, at his home where he had been living for several years.

Joseph Jackson Baker was a charter member of the Tifton Primitive Baptist Church, and his funeral was held there, August 28, his pastor, Elder W. C. Kicklighter conducting the service, and Dr. F. Orion Mixon, pastor of the Tifton First Baptist Church asssiting. Burial was in the Tifton cemetery.

Mrs. Baker, J. J.s widow, was elected to serve out his unexpired term as ordinary, and thus served. She was succeeded by Mrs. Mary Emma Rigdon, who defeated ten men opponents and preceded Judge Phillip Kelley, now in office.

WILLIAM WALTER BANKS
and
MARY EVELYN TOWNS BANKS

William Walter Banks, born in Griffin, Georgia, February 24, 1874, son of John Thomas Banks, planter, born in Forsyth, Georgia, and Mary Ann Rooks

Banks, born in Griffin, moved when two years old, with his parents to Senoia, Coweta County, Georgia, where he grew up. There he was for eight years with a farmers' supply house, M. H. Couch & Co.

At Senoia, on June 10, 1896 William Walter Banks married Mary Evelyn Towns, winsome and beautiful daughter of Jarrell Oliver Towns and Sarah Elizabeth Barnes Towns, daughter of William C. Barnes, merchant, of Vermont, one of the founders of Senoia, and Elizabeth Pope Barnes, of Washington, Wilkes County, Georgia.

Winsome Mary, who had graduated at a Jacksonville, Florida, college of music where she was under Madam Armelini, was possessed of a rich and sweet voice. Her gift of song, her beauty and her charm and W. W.'s business ability and likeable personality combined to make them unusually well liked from the beginning of their residence in Tifton where they came in March of 1897, three years after the founding of the Bank of Tifton, of which Mr. Banks was at first a bookkeeper, then cashier, and then vice-president. The vice-presidency he continued to hold until 1917, when he left Tifton to become vice-president of the Third National Bank, now the Citizens and Southern, of Atlanta. During the time that Banks was vice-president of the Bank of Tifton, H. H. Tift, the founder of Tifton, was president of the bank, and they were warm personal friends. The Bank of Tifton at that time had the largest surplus in proportion to its capital stock of any bank in Georgia and the stock was worth over $1,000 per share.

In 1905 the Banks built the house which is now the Tifton First Baptist Church parsonage, W. H. Spooner, of Tifton, being contractor. Here the Banks lived for many years, and this home was the scene of many beautiful and delightful parties. Here was ever a gracious hospitality.

The Banks were loyal Baptists. It is said that, next to H. H. Tift, Mr. Banks was the church's most generous giver. Mrs. Banks taught a Sunday School class, and she sang in the choir.

Mrs. Banks also engaged in club work. She organized the Tifton Campfire Girls, and the Tifton History Club, Also, she and a friend, Mrs. William Walker, were largely responsible for the organization of the Tifton Twentieth Century Library Club, whose initial meeting was scheduled to be held at Mrs. Banks' home. Mrs Banks was taken ill and persuaded Mrs. Eddie Tift to open her home to the invited group, which Mrs. Tift graciously did.

From October 5, 1908 to 1914 William Walter Banks was mayor of Tifton, succeeding Mayor Sam M. Clyatt, resigned. During Banks's term of office the town steadily grew and its affairs prospered. He was followed by Dr. W. H. Hendricks as mayor of Tifton.

After years of residence elsewhere, Mr. and Mrs. Banks in 1936 returned to Tifton, where Mr. Banks organized the Farmers' Bank of Tifton. However, many beloved friends of former days had passed from the scene, W. W. Banks's strength was impaired, health was failing. Death occurred on January 28, 1938. Burial was in his boyhood home, Senoia, which also was the scene of his marriage to winsome Mary. She still makes her home in Tifton where she is greatly beloved and where she blesses many by her gift of song, especially when there is sorrow.

ANNIE FOGLER BENNETT

Joseph Sayles Havener was born at Belfast, Limerick County, Ireland, of English parents, his mother being daughter of the English Lord Sayles. At Oxford University, England, Joseph was educated to become an Episcopal minister. Before beginning to preach he came to America for a period of travel. In America Havener became associated with Alexander Campbell, the founder of the Campbellites, and with him preached in Virginia.

Later, the Reverend Havener came to South Carolina where he met and married an orphan, Mary Elizabeth Evans, reared by her aunt, Mrs. George Hahnbaum, nee Ruberry, of Charleston, but daughter of James and Elizabeth Ruberry Evans, of the Evans family whose records are to be found in the old Scotch Presbyterian Church of Charleston, South Carolina. Mary and her brother Benjamin, of Athens, were related to Miss Lula Whidden, a Baptist missionary, of Charleston.

The Reverend Havener and his wife lived at Boiling Springs, South Carolina, which at that time had another and older name. He would go to preach at Augusta and other places. Also he prepared many young men for college; for he spoke fluently three languages and was a county school commissioner.

The Reverend and Mrs. Havener had a daughter, Julia, born at Old Allendale, South Carolina. Julia was musically gifted and taught piano. She married John Daniel Fogler, son of Senator John Fogler of Beaufort, South Carolina and his wife, Annie Johnson Fogler. Senator Folger was a native of North Carolina. His wife and son were born at Beaufort.

To Julia Havener Fogler and John Daniel Fogler were born several children, among them a daughter who married R. T. Waldrep and lived in Tifton, and another daughter, little Annie, who would come to Tifton to visit her sister, Mrs. Waldrep.

Annie Fogler was born at Boiling Springs, but, with her parents, she lived at several places where her father engaged in buying and selling land. Five years were spent in Texas, some of the time at Austin and some of the time at Milligan. Several years were spent at Brunswick.

While still very young, little Annie Fogler at Brunswick married a lawyer, James Bennett, an Englishman, born in London. Mr. and Mrs. Bennett spent a year in European travel, visiting London, France, Belgium and Holland. Returning to America they lived for a while in New York and then went to Chicago, where their only daughter, Olive Bennett, was born.

While Olive was still a little girl Mrs. Bennett, bringing Olive with her, moved to Tifton. Mrs. Bennett was very young and inexperienced in business responsibilities, but she had great artistry and skill, and soon built up the reputation of being the most skilled modiste of the vicinity. Gowns which she fashioned were remarked upon for their beauty wherever they were seen, in Savannah, in Atlanta, in Saratoga, in New York. Tifton became known as a place of well-dressed women, and it was "Miss Annie's" skill that made this so.

Mrs. Bennett educated Oliver, whom she sent to Columbia University, and Olive married Robert Lankford, of Tifton. Mr. and Mrs. Lankford own Lankford Manor, in Tifton, and with them Mrs. Bennett makes her home. There also are Mrs. Bennett's grandson, Billy Lankford, and his bride, whom he married soon after his safe return from European service in World War II.

FREDERICK GRANT BOATRIGHT

Frederick Grant Boatright was born in Palestine, Illinois, May 17, 1864. When four years old he moved with his parents to Sullivan County, Indiana, where he was reared on a farm and followed the plow for several years. He later clerked in a store. He learned the printer's trade in the office of the "True Democrat," in Sullivan. His parents were staunch Democrats, and the community in which he lived was a Democratic community. Although Boatright had not gone to college, he loved good books and was well read, and well informed and he taught school for six years. In 1886 he studied telegraphy and began his career in railroading.

On May 12, 1889, F. G. Boatright came to Georgia where he worked for nearly a month in the Brunswick and Western Railroad office in Brunswick. On June 6, of that same year he came to Tifton and at once went to work for Henry Tift as Tifton agent of the Brunswick and Western, which position he held for seven years.

In 1891 Fred Boatright returned to Indiana, where at Terre Haute, his sweetheart, Martha Dechard, lived. She was descended from the Revolutionary soldier, Jacob Dechard. She and Fred were married and Fred brought his bride to Tifton.

At first Fred and Mattie Boatright boarded with Mrs. Barnes on Love Avenue, but later they bought a home on Central Avenue, where they were next-door neighbors to the Holmes Murrays. For five years they were there and then they moved to a place they bought at 406 North Park Avenue. There Mr. Boatright's mother, Ellen, visited them in 1904.

After coming to Tifton Mr. Boatright in 1893 read law. In March, 1894, in Berrien County he was admitted to the bar. He became a member of the firm of Fulwood, Boatright and Murray, Col. C. W. Fulwood and Holmes Murray being the other members of the firm with which he was associated for about ten years. Boatright was elected Tifton city attorney in 1895.

In 1895 F. G. Boatright was elected Mayor of Tifton and served in 1896, succeeding C. W. Fulwood. Holmes Murray was clerk of Council. Councilmen were H. H. Tift, E. P. Bowen, W. W. Timmons, J. A. Phillips, L. G. Manard, and W. O. Padrick.

Mr. Boatright served as mayor through 1899. In 1900 he was succeeded by C. W. Fulwood, but in 1902 he again followed Fulwood as mayor. Also, he was in January, 1903, elected judge of the newly created Tifton City Court, of which the solicitor was Christopher Columbus Hall (born Sumter County, October 3, 1866; moved to Worth County in early youth; taught school; engaged in mercantile business; was railway contractor on Georgia Southern and on the Tifton, Thomasville and Gulf; admitted to bar in 1895; solicitor of County court of Berrien, 1901-1902). O. L. Chesnutt was first clerk of the Tifton City Court. First City Court sheriff was Thomas Berry Henderson.

Boatright drew up and secured passage of the new city charter. In 1904 Mr. Boatright was succeeded by W. W. Timmons as mayor of Tifton.

After the sale of the Tifton and Northeastern, Mr. Boatright went on June 15, 1904, to Moody, Florida to be general manager of the Natural Bridge Railroad, a short line.

Later, the Boatrights moved to Cordele, Georgia, where Mr. Boatright was for four years United States Postmaster. Also, at Cordele he practiced law, until his death there, about 1935. Mrs. Boatright also died in Cordele.

Frederick and Martha Boatright had two children, a son, Bernard Dechard Boatright, who married Mildred Ward, of Cordele, and died in 1920, in Cordele, where also he is buried; and a daughter, Fredericka Boatright, named for her father. She married Emmett Hines, son of the late Judge Hines and Nellie Womack Hines, musician and writer, of Milledgeville. Fredericka and her husband live at Buffalo, New York.

GEORGE WASHINGTON BOWEN

George Washington Bowen, born August 19, 1834, married Nancy A. Pope, born June 18, 1840. They made their home in Pulaski County where were born to them four sons, E. P., I. W., Isaac Stephen, and Lee Bowen, who died unmarried.

George Washington Bowen, expecting that a railroad would be built through Brookfield, moved his family there and purchased more than four hundred acres of land. The railroad went through Tifton instead of Brookfield, but G. W. continued at Brookfield, where he prospered. When his sons grew up they had business interests in both Brookfield and Tifton.

George Washington Bowen died September 4, 1912. Nancy lived to celebrate her 90th birthday with a family reunion and dinner, and she blew out the ninety candles on her cake at one whiff. She died January 21, 1933, aged 92½ years. G. W. and Nancy are buried at Tifton cemetery.

ENOCH PIERCEL BOWEN, SR.

Enoch Piercel Bowen, son of George Washington Bowen and Nancy Pope Bowen, was born in Pulaski County, near Hawkinsville, Georgia, December 21, 1857. When nine, he moved with his parents from Pulaski to Lowndes County. Three years later he came with his parents to Brookfield.

On April 28, 1871, Enoch Bowen married Elizabeth Turner then of Lakeland, Florida, but previously of Wilcox County, Georgia, which county was named for her maternal family.

Mr. Bowen moved to Tifton in July of 1887, and in 1890 built a house at the corner of Love Avenue and Sixth Street, where the Baptist Church now is. Here his children Lennon E., Sarah, Reba, E. P. Jr., Bennie, and Sue were born. After the site of this home was sold to the Baptist Church, the Bowens lived temporarily, during 1906 and 1907, in a small house across the alley from the church, on Fourth Street. Here Elizabeth was born. In 1907 Mr. Bowen built the large and handsome Georgian dwelling at southwest corner of Love Avenue and Sixth Street, and here Edna was born. This continued to be the Bowen homestead so long as Mr. Bowen lived. Nancy Pope Bowen died there February 12, 1942.

Mr. Bowen was an early member of the First Baptist Church of Tifton and was a life member of its Board of Deacons. With exception of one year he was treasurer of the Tifton Masonic Lodge from its founding, about 1890, until his death.

With brief exception Mr. Bowen served as alderman of Tifton from the time of the first meeting of the board after the town's incorporation, in 1890, until the town changed its form of government. Thereafter he served as a city commissioner continuously until his death. After the death of H. H. Tift, in 1922, Mr. Bowen was made chairman of the commission and except for a short time so continued throughout the rest of his life.

Mr. Bowen was a director of the Bank of Tifton from its founding, in 1896, until his death. From 1922 until his death he was president of the Bank of Tifton. He was president of the Tifton Investment Co., from 1922 to 1934; president of the Tifton Cotton Mill from 1928 to 1934. He owned the Bowen Funeral Home and is said to have selected the site for the Tifton cemetery.

Enoch Bowen was Tift County's first representative to the Georgia Legislature; also he was first senator from this senatorial district.

As Uncle Enoch advanced in years he would leave the execution of the bank's business to others, but every day he would go to the bank and when he had attended to such matters as he wished to direct he would go and sit on the wide long stone that flanked the entrance to the bank and there observed all who passed in or out of the bank.

Mr. Bowen felt very lonely after Mrs. Bowen's death; and all his money could not suffice to keep him from feeling bereft, nor all the times he had ministered to others in the hour of bereavement prevent his feeling sorrowful when his own circle was broken. He stood the loneliness a while and then on December 31, 1942, ten days after his eighty-fifth birthday, he married a widow, Mrs. Betty Fletcher Wilcox, of Ocilla, the Reverend L. N. Hartsfield performing the ceremony at Ocilla.

June 26, 1943 was a sultry day in Tifton. The sun was blazing. Neighbors of Mr. Bowen were sitting on their porch seeking a breath of cool air. They saw Uncle Enoch working in his rose garden, hoeing at a great rate as though in a great hurry to finish.

"Uncle Enoch doesn't need to be doing that!" remarked one. "It's too hot for him to be working so hard!"

Not ten minutes later a passer-by came and said to one of the neighbors: "Do you know when a person is dead? It looks like Uncle Enoch is dead!"

Mr. Bowen had finished his work, and had sat down in the door to rest. It was his last long rest . . . Burial was in Tifton cemetery.

Children of Enoch and Nancy Pope Bowen and those whom the children married, are as follows:

Lennon E., married Margaret Bailey. Lennon is now president of the Bank of Tifton.
Sarah Stella married Mc Isaacs.
Mary Rebecca married Robert Hall, Jr.
Enoch Piercel, Jr., married Ilene Adams.
Charles Bennie married Margaret Toney.
Susie Moore married John Fulwood.
Elizabeth married L. M. Polhill.
Edna Smith married Adrian Colquitt.

IRWIN WASHINGTON BOWEN

Irwin Washington Bowen (born Pulaski County, February, 1862; died at his home four miles north of Brookfield, December 4, 1937), son of George Washington Bowen and Nancy Pope Bowen, married Sarah Georgia Turner (born February 26, 1869; died September 20, 1940). The marriage was in March, 1888.

I. W. Bowen came to this section of the state in 1870 and continued here until his death. For several years he was in Tifton in the home now the Rackley House, but most of his boyhood and adult years were spent at Brookfield where he was a farmer and a merchant. He was for many years treasurer of the Mell Baptist Association. He was for thirty-seven years affiliated with the Brookfield Baptist Church of which he was a charter member and where his funeral was held. He and his wife are buried in the Tifton cemetery.

Issue of this union: Piercel (deceased, aged two years); S. R., J. L., I. W., Jr., R. C., S. T., of Tift County; Mrs. Baynard Seckinger, of Glennville; Sibbie (Mrs. Bessie Bowen Williford), born August 25, 1898; died September 1, 1936.

Birthdate on tombstone is February 11, 1862;
Birthdate in obituary is February 12, 1862.

ISAAC STEPHEN BOWEN

Isaac Stephen Bowen, son of George Washington Bowen and Nancy Pope Bowen, was born November 16, 1870, and came when very young with his parents from Pulaski County to what is now Brookfield. At Fort Valley, May 14, 1893, he marreid Sallie Miller, of Fort Valley, daughter of Osburn H. and Mary Brice Miller, both of Fort Valley.

I. S. Bowen, W. W. Simmons and W. J. Goulding were tax assessors for City of Tifton for 1908.

Isaac Bowen died at Brookfield in 1912. Mrs. Bowen died in Tifton, March 20, 1933. Both are buried in Tifton cemetery. To them were born six daughters, Willie Mae, Anne, Stella (Mrs. Earl Gibbs), Mittie (Mrs. B. J. Reeves), all of Tifton; Blanch (Mrs. J. E. Saxon), of Thomasville; Lee (Mrs. F. M. Reeves, Jr.), of Clarkesville, Georgia.

The above dates are furnished by Mr. Bowen's daughter. His obituary in the Gazette gives Lowndes County, near Valdosta, as birthplace and date of birth 1868; it gives date of marriage as 1892.

THE BRANCH FAMILY

Elias Branch, Senior, born in Robinson County, North Carolina, moved to Laurens County, Georgia, sometime prior to 1811; David Branch, his son, was born there. The latter, his brother, James Branch, and his sister, Nancy, moved to Irwin County about 1830. In 1832 David Branch married Millie Fletcher and settled in the place now known as Waterloo. Later he served as one of the judges of the inferior court for several years. His son, William Branch, married Jane Whiddon in 1859 and moved one mile north of Chula, where he reared a large family.

William served Irwin County in the Georgia Legislature 1880-1881. He was one of Tifton's first merchants, and he owned the first mule-power cotton gin in Tifton. He helped the needy, especially the orphans of the War Between the States. His wife, very charitable, administered home-made remedies to the sick and often responded to calls to the bedsides when doctors were not available. He enlisted in the War Between the States in 1862. In 1863 after being promoted to first sergeant, William Branch was wounded in Wilderness, Virginia; he was also wounded at Gettysburg, Virginia in 1865. He had three grandsons to serve in World War I and six great-grandsons and four grandsons in World War II.

Nine children were born to the union of William and Jane Whiddon Branch: Eli, who was born in 1860; W. W. D., in 1862; Juda, in 1865; D. J., in 1867; Rachel, in 1870; Leacy, in 1872; Jehu, 1874; E. D., 1877; Millie, 1882.

Eli Branch, son of William and Jane Whiddon Branch, married Elizabeth Easters in 1881. Their children were: Martha Jane, who married H. Fletcher; W. D. Branch, who married Cora Dorminy, and Betty Paulk; Millie, Josie, Clemmie, Leachy, Rachel, who married Julian Fletcher, and Albert Branch.

W. W. D. Branch, son of William and Jane Whiddon Branch, married Nancy Young in 1881, settled in Irwin County, and served as tax collector for twelve years. His children are George W. Branch, William Branch, and Una Branch. George W. Branch, born June 10, 1885, married Maude Thompson, May 13, 1906. He represented Tift County in the Georgia Legislature in 1939-40-41-42-43-44 and Forty-Seventh Senatorial District in 1945-1946. His son, W. F. Branch, served three years in the United States Navy. W. F. Branch married Sibyl Blitch in 1936; their daughter, Sibyl Frances, was born on January 29, 1940.

William Branch married Ora Cravey in 1905 and moved to the place where he now lives. Their children are Vernon, Willie, George, Harry, Vernelle, and Dorothy.

Una Branch married Eddie Paulk in November, 1904. To this union were born Vercola, John B., Robert C., Eunice Louise, William, Eddie, and Mary.

Juda Ross, daughter of William and Jane Whiddon Branch, was born on October 8, 1865. She married J. F. Ross, December 19, 1883. Their children,

W. A., A. L., J. O., Cora Ellen, A. A., Nora Jane, Dotie Ann, L. F., B. L., and Dollie, are good Tift County citizens with large families.

D. J. Branch, son of William and Jane Whiddon Branch, was born November 25, 1867. He married Clemmie Taylor on December 21, 1890, moved to Turner County, and served two terms in the Georgia Legislature, 1921-1922-1923-1924. His son, Walter Branch, now lives in Turner County and serves as senator from the Forty-Seventh Senatorial District.

Rachel E. Branch, daughter of William and Jane Branch, was born on June 29, 1870. On November 25, 1886 she married Walter Young, later settled in Worth County, and reared a large, useful family.

Leacy Branch, daughter of William and Louisa J. Branch, was born October 2, 1872 and married in October, 1887, J. R. Paulk. They settled in Irwin County, where they reared a large, useful family of ten children.

Jehu Branch, Junior, son of William and Jane Whiddon Branch, married Maggie Young on January 26, 1899. Their children are E. C. and Maggie. Sometime after the death of his first wife Jehu married Minnie Phelps. Their children are: Gussie, Odie, Horace C., Virgil F., Athenn, and Susie, all of whom are citizens of Tift County. Jehu Branch served one term as county commissioner of Tift County, and his son, Virgil, served for three years in United States Navy of World War II.

E. D. Branch, son of William and Jane Whiddon Branch, was born February 3, 1877 and on December 1, 1909 married Daisy Brown. To this union were born J. M., F. I., O. N., and Inez. Ed Branch served the county two terms as sheriff. His son, O. N., served for two years in World War II.

Jehu Branch, Senior, son of David and Millie Fletcher Branch, settled at what is now Chula before Southern Railroad was built. Not having married, he left his property to his brothers and sisters.

John A. Branch, son of David and Millie Fletcher Branch, married Dotie Ann Clements February 28, 1867. To this union were born W. W., Wiley, Mary, Millie, Jane, and Duncan. John Branch served in the War Between the States and also served his county as treasurer for three terms.

Wiley Branch, son of David and Millie Fletcher Branch, married on June 23, 1878, Sarah Young, the only one of the old Branch family of David and Millie now living. Sarah Young Branch is about ninety-six years old. She and her husband reared a large, useful family.

J. M. Branch, son of David and Millie Fletcher Branch, married Martha Tucker, and settled near Chula, where they reared a large family of good citizens. All of these Branches have moved away except Mack Branch, of Chula, and one grandson, Curtis Branch, who lives at Brookfield.

ELIAS BRANCH

Elias Branch, son of Mr. William and Mrs. Louise Jane Whiddon Branch, was born February 3, 1877, in a log house which was built in 1868 on lot number 108 of Sixth District of Irwin County, now in Tift County. Elias was deputy sheriff of Irwin County 1903-1904-1905. In 1908 he was elected sheriff of Tift County and was reelected in 1910-1912; each term was two years. His home is near his birthplace, the old log house.

On December 1, 1904 Elias married Daisy Brown. Their four children are Marvin, Irvine, Nathaniel and Opal Inez, who married G. E. Fletcher.

Branch has been justice of peace here for fifteen years. Although he has reached the three-score and ten mark, he still takes a vital interest in the welfare of Tift.

His father, William Branch, was a Confederate soldier in Company F-49 Georgia Regiment. He was wounded and given a leave of absence in 1864. His maternal grandparents were Mr. Lott and Judie Dorminey Whiddon. In what is now Sycamore she planted from a sycamore tree a riding whip, which grew to be an enormous tree. The town, Sycamore, according to tradition, is a namesake of the tree.

THE BRITT FAMILY

The measure of success of any life can be determined only after ascertaining what was the governing purpose of that life, what its motivation, what ideals and aspirations controlled it, and toward what goal was it striving. This, in spite of the fact that success or failure is generally accounted a matter of wealth or poverty. It is altogether possible for man to live an exceedingly purposeful life in which the acquisition of wealth, or the attainment of public position plays an altogether negligible part.

Such a man was Henry Hardy Britt. Son of Hardy Gregory Britt and Louisa Boyette Britt, he was born in Sampson County, N. C., March 8th, 1860. The Britt family had earlier lived in Nottaway County, Virginia, coming there from the British Isles. Mr. Britt's spiritual inheritance was one of the highest quality from sturdy, substantial English and Scotch ancestors—Gregory, Boyette and Sewell as well as Britt—: an unusually fine, clean mind; a culture and a dignity that were instructive and in no way superficial; uncompromising fidelity to truth and righteousness; a love of learning in all its branches; and a passion for music. These were his spiritual inheritance, his material one was the same sort of poverty that was the heritage of most Southern families as an aftermath of the War Between the States. He was graduated from Warsaw Academy, in North Carolina, in 1880—(and was the featured speaker of the occasion on the subject, "Shall Chinese Immigration Be Restricted?")—He had selected medicine as his profession, but the death of his father necessitated his going back to the family plantation and assuming its management instead.

On December 9th, 1886, Henry Hardy Britt was married to Eliza Laetitia Chesnutt, daughter of Capt. Owen Lemuel Chesnutt and Mary Ann Newkirk Matthis (see Chesnutt Family). She too was born in Sampson County, on Oct. 1st, 1866. On her paternal side she was descended from the Chesnutts, Hayes and Owen families, English and Welsh. On her maternal side, the Matthews, Kunst, Van Bruntshroten, from Gerritt Cornelissen Van Nieukircken (Newkirk) born in Holland 1635, coming to America 1659, and

A GROUP OF TIFTON PIONEERS

Top row—Captain Owen Lemuel Chesnutt, for whom Chesnutt Avenue in Tifton was named. G. W. Crum, member of Board of Education in Tifton.
Center—P. D. Phillips, member of Tift County Board of Education.
Bottom row—Patrick Thomas Carmichael when ninety years old. Henry Hardy Britt, benefactor of Tifton.

from Cornelius Barentsen Slegt, who was one of the first judges to be appointed in the Colony of New Amsterdam, the appointment having been made by Governor Peter Stuyvesant on May 16, 1660. Among the direct ancestors of both Mr. and Mrs. Britt were Revolutionary soldiers.

Mr. and Mrs. Britt lost their first child, Ellis Lemuel, in North Carolina; and they moved to Tifton in the winter of 1899 where their seven daughters and one son were reared. They were among the organizers and founders of the Presbyterian church in Tifton, and served it with utmost loyalty and devotion until their death, Mr. Britt in the capacity of a Ruling Elder. A bronze tablet commemorating this service was unveiled in his memory at the church on August 26, 1928.

Mrs. Britt was gentle in disposition, completely devoted and loyal to family and friends. A keen sense of humor and an inherent gaiety gave her cheerfulness and poise under all circumstances; and those who knew her best knew that she was a poet at heart. In addition to the demands of her growing family, Mrs. Britt found time for a few outside activities, except those of her church and her U.D.C. chapter, both of which claimed her devotion to the end.

A deep student of religion, philosophy and history, Mr. Britt preferred the stimulating conversation and fellowship of a few congenial friends around his own fireside to wider contacts with casual acquaintances. He spent little time in the market places but countless hours with his books; and his philosophy of life was at once grave and mirthful, stalwart and severe, but kind and generous. He considered learning, education, culture, an end in itself, and not a means of finding a niche in the world. He believed that every material success should be achieved unostentatiously and carried lightly. He was deeply interested in every phase of music, in which he had a discriminating taste; and it was his purpose that his family should share that love and cultivate it to the limit of their abilities. He had no happier hours than when there was music and singing in his own home.

In business Mr. Britt was associated with Gress Manufacturing Company from the time of its forming in Tifton, continuing this connection after the firm moved to Jacksonville, Fla., but preferring to maintain his residence in Tifton. While his material business in life was lumber, his chief interests in life were his church, the education of his family, and the stimulus that comes from intellectual pursuits. To that end he and Mrs. Britt bent every effort, nor counted any cost too great. In pursuit of this aim their material substance was spent.

Mr. Britt died February 1st, 1926; Mrs. Britt, September 26, 1929. Their children:

Mary Lou—Bachelor of Arts degree, Flora MacDonald College, Red Springs, N. C. Master of Arts, Emory University, Atlanta. Special study: Peabody College, Nashville, Tenn., State Teacher's College, Greeley Colo.; Columbia University, New York. Traveled extensively in U. S., Canada, and Europe. Head of Science Department, Albany High School, Albany, Ga.; Teacher of Chemistry at Abraham-Baldwin Agricultural College, Tifton.

Lillian Ann—Bachelor of Music degree, Flora McDonald College. Continued vocal study with Margaret Hecht, Atlanta, Ga., and Guiseppe Agostini, Philadelphia. Married Robert A. Heinsohn of Sylvester, Ga., Muncie, Ind., and Cleveland, Ohio. For sixteen years lived in Philadelphia where Mr. Heinsohn was Agency Director, New York Life Insurance Company. Through her singing was active Artist Member Philadelphia Art Alliance; with sister, Nell, in joint recitals, were recognized concert artists. Traveled U. S., Canada, extensively in South America. Home, Labrah Plantation, Thomasville, Ga.

Blanche Birthlotte—Educated in piano and voice at Flora MacDonald College, and Cincinnati, Ohio, Conservatory. Head of Music Department, A. and M. College, Statesboro, Ga., and at Catawba College, Newton, N. C. Married J. Carroll Bell of Anderson, S. C., Entomologist, Plant Board of Florida State Department of Agriculture. At home Eustis, Fla. Children:

1. Lillian Carolyn, married Sidney Phillips, Lt. U. S. Air Force; two children, Lillian Britt, and Sidney Norris.

2. Barbara Blanche, Bachelor of Arts, majoring in Journalism, Florida State College for Women, Tallahassee.

Ruth Patterson—Bachelor of Arts degree Flora MacDonald College; Master of Arts, Emory University, Atlanta. Special study: State Teacher's College, Greeley, Colorado; University of California, Berkeley; Columbia University, New York. Teacher of History, Palmer College, Fla.; Social Sciences High School, Thomasville, Ga.

Esther Lee—Bachelor of Literature degree, Flora MacDonald College; Master of Arts, Emory University. Special study: University of North Carolina; State Teacher's College, Greeley, Colo.; Sorbonne University, Paris, France. Taught French, Brunswick, Ga., and Winnsboro, S. C. Married William R. Anderson, Supt. of Schools, Clinton, S. C., (who has one daughter, Helen, by his first wife, deceased).

Nell Gray—Educated piano and voice Flora MacDonald College, and Cincinnati, O., Conservatory of Music. Continued study: Margaret Hecht, Atlanta; Emory University; Guiseppe Agostini, Philadelphia. Head of Vocal Department Palmer College and at Piedmont College, Demorest, Ga. Married Roy D. Tabor, Toccoa, Ga., with New York Life Insurance Company, Philadelphia. For number of years soprano soloist St. Paul's Episcopal Church, Philadelphia; has active music studio; in joint recitals with Lillian appeared extensively in concert. Two children: Owen Britt and Nell Britt.

Eliza Owen—Educated at Anderson College, S. C., and at Presbyterian Training School, Richmond, Va. Special study in music: Loyola School of Music, New Orleans, La., and Sorbonne University, Paris, France. Director Young People's Work, Presbyterian Churches in Greenville, S. C., and Vicksburg, Miss.; member of Department Religious Education and Home Mission Synod of Mississippi. Written many songs and a number of poems which have been published. Married Rev. Archibald Cole Ray of North Carolina, pastor Claiborne Avenue Presbyterian Church, New Orleans, and

Memorial Presbyterian, West Palm Beach, Fla. Children Richard Archibald and Timothy Britt.

Henry Chesnutt—Abraham Baldwin College; The Citadel, Charleston, S. C.; graduated United States Military Academy, West Point, N. Y., June 1933. Military service, Fort Benning, Ga.; Fort Knox, Ky.; Fort Huachua, Ariz.; May 1939 to September 1941 on Staff of General Parker, 31st Infantry, Manila, P. I.; Lieutenant Colonel, 365 Infantry, with Fifth Army in Italy, World War II; married Doris Pope of Alabama; children, Henry M., Pope Patterson, Sally Leatitia. Lt. Col. Henry C. Britt's present assignment is G.4 of the 6th Infantry Division in Korea.

EDWARD ALLEN BUCK

Edward Allen Buck, born Greenville, North Carolina, November 17, 1848, came in his youth from North Carolina to South Georgia and engaged in the turpentine business on a large scale in Georgia and Florida. Also, he was a member of the Brunswick, Georgia, firm of Buck and Downing.

E. A. Buck married Lillian Lipsey, of Lee County. They at first lived at Douglas, Georgia, but in the 1890's moved to Tifton where he organized the wholesale grocery, grain, and feed house of Julian, Love, and Buck, his partners being Dr. George Julian and Mayor W. H. Love, Tifton's first mayor. In connection with his firm Buck helped establish Tifton's first bank, a private banking house founded in 1895, the year prior to the founding of the Bank of Tifton. Mr. Buck was president of the Citizens' Bank of Tifton and was an officer of the National Bank of Tifton.

In Tifton the Bucks at first lived at Hotel Sadie, but they soon built a large, handsome, brick, Georgian residence on the southwest corner of Love Avenue at Sixth Street. It was the scene of many happy entertainings.

Mr. and Mrs. Buck had two children, Ethel, who attended Lucy Cobb, and E. A., Jr., who was born at Tifton, September 14, 1903 and attended Sparks Collegiate Institute, Sparks, Georgia. At Sparks, E. A., Jr., fell in a large well, but was rescued. E. A., Jr., was killed in an automobile wreck near Tifton, on Christmas night, 1921. Two months later, on February 27, 1922, E. A. Buck, Sr., died at his Love Avenue home. There, on what is said to have been the coldest February weather in the history of the weather bureau, Mrs. Buck died, February 10, 1934.

Ethel Buck, who, after her marriage to Winston McKey, lived in Valdosta, died at St. Joseph's, Atlanta, Thursday, April 4, 1935. Funeral services were held Saturday afternoon at five o'clock at the Buck home in Tifton, where they were conducted by her father's former pastor, Reverend T. H. Thompson, of Bainbridge Methodist Church, but formerly of Brunswick, who, assisted by Dr. C. W. Durden, had conducted her father's funeral services. Before they laid her to rest with the other members of her family in the Buck mausoleum in the Tifton cemetery, friends sang, "Good-night, Beloved."

PATRICK THOMAS CARMICHAEL

Perhaps there has been no more interesting figure in Tift County annals than Patrick Thomas Carmichael who moved from Coweta County, Georgia to Berrien County, now Tift, December 10, 1902, and continued to make this vicinity his home until his death on March 30, 1942, at the age of ninety-one years, lacking eighteen days.

Born in Coweta County, April 17, 1851, son of Lieut. Patrick Carmichael, C. S. A., and Mary Anne Washington Speer Carmichael, Patrick Thomas was a great-grandson of Patrick Carmichael, who was born in Brand, Ireland, in 1754 and came to America in 1773, settling at Newberry District, South Carolina. Patrick Thomas's forebear, had gone to the ship to say farewell to his sweetheart, Elizabeth Thompson (born in Ireland, 1749), who, with her family, was sailing for America. The sweethearts could not bear to separate and Patrick determined to make the journey to America even though doing so would obligate him to a period of servitude in order to pay for his passage. The young people were married on shipboard, in 1773, and the long and hazardous journey across the ocean became for them a honeymoon. Arrived in this country, Patrick faithfully fulfilled his obligation and then became one of the prominent and useful men of the community where he settled. He and Elizabeth became the forebears of a large family of Carmichaels who people South Carolina, Coweta County, Georgia, and now Tift. Members of the family moved to Coweta County in 1851.

Patrick Thomas early felt and heroically discharged the responsibilities of life. When but a lad, the oldest boy left at home when his father and three brothers entered the Confederate Army, he looked after his father's farm. Two of his brothers, Joseph William (born May 22, 1840; killed at Seven Day Battle, in Virginia, June 26, 1862), and Robert M., (born May 7, 1844; killed August 19, 1864, at Petersburg, Virginia), made the supreme sacrifice for the Confederacy.

Patrick and Elizabeth Carmichael had been members of the Associate Reform Presbyterian Church, but Patrick Thomas was a Methodist. He joined the church under the ministry of the Reverend Pierce, at Coke's Chapel, Coweta County, 1866. He became Sunday School teacher, Sunday School superintendent, was a steward, and he helped build several churches. His father was a member of Tranquil Church, out from Turin, but later moved to Turin. He furnished the timber for the Turin Church and his son-in-law hauled the logs to the mill to be cut, hauled the lumber to Carol County to be dressed, then back to Turin for the church, which is still in use, and where Patrick II's funeral sermon was preached. Burial was at Tranquil cemetery. In those days before modern funeral arrangements, the leather driving reins from the buggies were used for lowering the casket into the grave.

On December 16, 1875 Patrick Thomas Carmichael married Elizabeth Tignor Fambrough (born March 11, 1859, Coweta County; died Tifton, October 6, 1929). They lived until 1902 upon their Coweta County farm. After moving thence to Berrien County, now Tift, Mr. Carmichael continued to farm until 1914, at which time he retired and moved to Lenox. Coming to this vicinity, he bought land from Captain John A. Phillips and from J. G. Adcock. On the Adcock land he had bought he built his home. The land he purchased from Phillips he gave to his children, each receiving one hundred acres. From Lenox Mr. Carmichael moved to Woodbury and thence to Tifton in 1925.

On the occasion of Patrick Thomas's 90th birthay, his son, Homer Carmichael, of Tifton, honored him with a celebration unique. Mr. Homer Carmichael owns a lake, formerly called Tift's Pond, now called Lake Mary, for his late daughter, Mary Carmichael, a comely young woman whom death claimed early. Homer Carmichael planned to drain this lake, clear it of stumps and then refill it. He awaited the near approach of his father's ninetieth birthday, timed the draining at a few days before, and for the occasion had seven hundred pounds of delicious fresh water fish of choice varieties. He invited as guests the Carmichael clan who, coming from five states, assembled to pay homage to the revered head of the family, Patrick Thomas, who, though at so great an age, appeared to be in excellent health, and personally greeted each of the several hundred guests present. Receiving with him and Mr. and Mrs. Homer Carmichael was Thomas Patrick's sister, Mrs. Ella C. Christopher (born in Coweta County, February, 15, 1853; died February 9, 1944, at Turin). Her funeral was held in the Methodist Church built with the logs her husband had hauled to make the building possible. Mrs. Christopher, at the time of her brother's birthday celebration was upward of eighty-five, as also was their brother, John Carmichael, who also received with them.

To Patrick Thomas Carmichael and Elizabeth Tignor Fambrough Carmichael were born seven children, Jipsie Mae, Francis Albert, Lula Belle, Harvey Lee, Homer C., Thomas Arthur, Paul Douglas. Of these and their children a full account may be found in the book on the Carmichael Family, now in preparation.

Patrick Thomas Carmichael's wife, Elizabeth. was daughter of the Reverend Dr. William N. Fambrough, Methodist minister and physician, of Coweta County.

BRIGGS CARSON

Briggs Carson, the first of the Carsons to live in Tifton, came here from Cordele about 1896 and continued to make this home until his death, May 27, 1937, at his home at the northeast corner of West Sixth Street and College Avenue.

Briggs Carson was born December 13, 1870, in Macon County, Georgia. He was one of seven children born to Captain Joseph P. Carson, C. S. A., (born June 1, 1839, at Carsonville, Crawford County, Georgia), and Charlotte Briggs Carson (born February 7, 1842, Lincoln County, Missouri), daughter of the Reverend William S. Briggs and O. H. Briggs. Briggs Carson's father, Joseph P. Carson, was a first cousin of General John Brown Gordon, in command of one wing of Lee's army in Northern Virginia. Later Gordon was governor of Georgia. In the War Between the States, Captain

Joseph P. Carson was in command of Company I, in the Fourth Georgia Regiment, C. S. A., and he was commanding officer at the successful attack on Fort Steadman, near Petersburg, Virginia, the capture of Fort Steadman being the last Confederate victory of Lee's army of Northern Virginia. (See account of "Carson at Fort Steadman," this volume.)

Briggs Carson was educated in the schools of Butler, Georgia, and at Marshallville, Georgia. When he was ready for college his father died and it became necessary to go to work instead of going to college. He, his mother, and his younger brothers, Keith and Joseph, moved to Cordele, where Briggs remained for about five years. While there he was bookkeeper for a Cordele firm, and he travelled for another firm.

While living in Cordele Briggs Carson met and became engaged to Ella Pate (born at Pateville, Dooly County, now Crisp, March, ...; attended Dooly County schools; attended Andrews College, Cuthbert, Georgia, and Wesleyan), daughter of John Smith Pate (born June 27, 1847, Dooly County, died August, 1930, at Cordele, Georgia) and Jimmie Clements (married June 27, 1872). Ella's father, John Smith Pate, was prominent in the annals of Dooly County. For an account of his achievements see William Fleming's "Crisp County, Georgia Historical Sketches." At the Methodist Church in Cordele, on April 27, 1898, the Reverend J. T. Stewart, pastor of the church performing the ceremony, Briggs Carson and Ella Pate were wed. Ella Jane wore a white brocaded satin wedding dress with a long train, and a veil. The evening wedding was followed by a brilliant reception at the bride's parents' home. Immediately afterward the young people left Cordele for Tifton.

In Tifton Briggs and Ella Carson at first occupied a house which they owned next door to where the Misses Mattie and Rosa Corry lived on Central Avenue. After two years there they moved to a house which they bought on Ridge Avenue, now the G. N. Mitchell home, where they lived for about ten years, after which they bought and moved into the Vickers house, the large home which after thirty-seven years, is still the Carson home.

Briggs Carson founded the first insurance agency in Tifton. His mother and his brothers, Keith and Joseph, moved to Tifton, and the Carson Brothers for many years owned and conducted a men's and women's ready-to-wear clothing store. Also, with Henry H. Tift, Tifton's founder, and C. W. Fulwood, Briggs Carson owned the Tifton Foundry and Machine Shop. At one time Briggs owned interest in the Tifton Gazette Publishing Company, W. H. Park of Macon, and John W. Greer having bought controlling interest in the Gazette in January, 1898, and Mr. Park after several months, having sold his interest to Briggs Carson and J. L. Herring. Carson later sold his interest to J. L. Herring. Briggs also owned a large farm north of Tifton.

Briggs Carson was chairman of Tift County's first Board of Education. Other members were: Dr. F. B. Pickett, W. S. Smith, G. W. Crum, J. N. Horne, P. D. Phillips.

In 1897, during the pastorate of Dr. P. A. Jessup, one of the early pastors of the First Baptist Church of Tifton, Briggs Carson became superintendent of the Baptist Sunday School, and so continued throughout the pastorates

PIONEER TIFTON BUILDERS

Top row, left—C. W. Fulwood, Sr., Lawyer, (deceased) whose interest in City Beautiful brought Fulwood Park. Top row, right—Briggs Carson, Sr., educator and business man (deceased). Center row, left—Dr. Jasper Brooks, veteran druggist. Center row, right—John L. Herring, beloved editor of Tifton Gazette 1897-1923 (deceased). Bottom row, left—Dr. N. Peterson, beloved physician (deceased). Bottom row, right—John Henry Hutchinson, first tax collector of Tift County.

HISTORY OF TIFT COUNTY 383

of Dr. Charles Dilworth, Reverend Miller, Mr. Reamey, and during the pastorate of Dr. C. W. Durden. Briggs preceded I. D. Morgan. When Briggs became superintendent of the Sunday School, the church was housed in the Park Avenue structure now housing the Presbyterians. He continued until some time after the congregation moved into the edifice at corner of Love Avenue and Fourth Street.

Children of Briggs and Ella Pate Carson were:

Charlotte, aged about six months when she died; an unnamed infant son, who died in infancy;

Pate, a lawyer; lives in New York City; his wife is Georgiann;

Briggs, a lawyer; lives in Tifton; Married Perry Lee Moore Webb, a widow, daughter of Perryman and Senator Susie Tillman Moore. Issue: Charlotte Carson.

Banks, married; lives in Atlanta.

Robert Clements, of Tifton; married Florence Willingham Karsten, artist, granddaughter of Dr. W. L. and Florence Willingham Pickard. Issue: Ella Jane Pate Carson.

James, clerk of the House of Representatives, Washington. D. C.

Joseph, of Tifton; married Edith Wilkes, daughter of a Methodist minister. Issue, Joseph Carson.

Ella Pate Carson has been active in the women's work of the Tifton Methodist Church. She is a charter member, a former president, and long time historian of the Charlotte Carson Chapter, United Daughters of the Confederacy.

Ella Pate Carson continues to live at the Carson home on Sixth Street, and there with her are her sons, Clements and Joseph, and their wives and children, and her son James, when not in Washington.

CHARLOTTE CARSON

Charlotte Ashmore Keith Briggs was born February 7, 1842, at Lincoln County, Missouri, daughter of a Methodist minister, the Reverend William S. Briggs and his wife, O. H. Briggs. Charlotte was a grand-niece of Chief Justice Marshall, of the United States Supreme Court. Reverend William S. Briggs was eldest son of James McDonald Briggs and Charlotte Ashmore Keith. James McDonald Briggs was youngest son of David Briggs and Jane Lansdown Briggs. David, first progenitor of the Briggs family in America, came to Virginia in 1752 and settled in Stafford County, twelve miles from Fredericksburg, near the Rappahannock River. David is said to have been "a gentleman of unusual natural ability, liberally educated, and soon took high rank in the new country." He amassed a considerable fortune, and his original home in this country was bought of Lord Fairfax.

Through one line Charlotte is said to have been descended from Pocahuntas, famous Indian princess.

Upon outbreak of the War Between the States the men of Charlotte's family joined the Confederate Army and the women of the family were sent to Georgia, where it was then deemed safe. Among those appointed to escort the Briggs party was Captain Joseph P. Carson, of Carsonville (born June 1, 1839, at Carsonville, Crawford County, Georgia), son of Joseph J. Carson and M. G. Carson. Carsonville was named for Joseph J. Carson and the large plantation home in which Joseph P. was born is still standing. J. H. Carson and W. H. Robinson were the Macon County delegates to the Secession Convention which met at Milledgeville, January 21, 1861. Both voted to secede.

Soon after the outbreak of the war Joseph P. Carson, on April 27, 1861, enlisted in the Fourth Georgia Regiment, as a private. He was elected to command Company I, in the above regiment and remained in service until the close of the war.

Pretty eighteen-year-old Charlotte Briggs had married Joseph P. Carson before he returned to his duties in Virginia.

Joseph P. Carson received wounds at Sharpsburg, at the Wilderness, at Winchester, and was twice wounded at Petersburg. For two years prior to the close of the war he was in command of General John B. Gordon's sharpshooters, and Carson was in command of the successful assault on Fort Steadman, March 25, 1865, the last Confederate victory of Lee's army of Northern Virginia.

The Confederate army was so greatly outnumbered that it was impossible to follow up the victory of Fort Steadman and the end of the contest came at Appomattox, April 9, 1865.

When the war was over Joseph P. Carson and his distinguished cousin, General John B. Gordon, who later became governor of Georgia, returned to their homes in Georgia and for many years they were in business together in a large farming and cattle-raising project in Macon County, not far from Reynolds, Georgia.

To Joseph P. and Charlotte Briggs Carson were born seven children:
Ophelia G. (born April 9, 1865, Macon County, Georgia, near Reynolds);
Rains (born July 22, 1867, Macon County);
Beulah R. (born August 5, 1869, Macon County);
Briggs (born December 13, 1870, Macon County);
Holmes (born September 17, 1872, Macon County);
Keith (born October 2, 1876, at Reynolds, Taylor County);
Joseph (born March 9, 1879, at Reynolds).

After Joseph P. Carson and John Brown Gordon had been in business for many years, Carson bought out Gordon's interest; but soon afterward Carson died, and his widow, Charlotte, was left with the responsibility of rearing the surviving children, not yet grown. She moved to Cordele and was there for several years. When Briggs, her eldest surviving son, was grown he moved to Tifton, and later Charlotte and the younger sons, Keith and Joseph, also moved there.

Briggs married Ella Pate; Keith married Laura Smith; Joseph married Isadore Timmons, daughter of Mayor W. W. Timmons, of Tifton. After Isadore's death. Charlotte lived with Joseph in the house now owned by Judge Eve. After his second marriage, Charlotte made her home with her son Briggs, and his wife, Ella Pate, at the Carson home on West Sixth Street, where she died November 11, 1913. She is buried in the Tifton cemetery.

Charlotte Carson was organizer and first president of the Charlotte Carson Chapter of the United Daughters of the Confederacy, which chapter was named for her as the widow of Captain Joseph P. Carson, intrepid and valiant hero of Fort Steadman. The chapter was organized in the parlors of the Myon Hotel in the winter of 1908, and received its charter on April 14, 1908, in the auditorium of the Tifton Grammar School. For a history of the chapter, see article by Ella Pate Carson, in this volume.

CAPTAIN OWEN LEMUEL CHESNUTT AND FAMILY

Among the obvious, but none-the-less tragic aftermaths of the War Between the States were the destroyed homes, wrecked plantations, blasted hopes, and interrupted careers. No war that America has ever fought resulted in such sickening devastation to homelands, nor left so deep a hurt. The returning Southern soldier had no G.I. Bill of Rights, no organized and concerted efforts to re-establish him in civilian life, no friendly, grateful government to breach the gap between war and peace. Instead, the young Confederate officer, demobilized from war, began a battle for which he was ill-equipped, and for which his physical and emotional depletion weighed heavily against him. That this circumstance was repeated over and over and over in no way lessened its poignancy; on the contrary it increased it, for the effect on the South of its tragic accumulative weight is incalculable.

Among these returning Confederate officers was Captain Owen Lemuel Chesnutt, age not yet 24 years. Son of Thomas Jefferson Chesnutt and his first wife, Laetitia Owen, he was born in Sampson County, N. C., Sept. 22, 1840. His father, born in 1802 of Welsh and English descent, was an outstanding man in eastern North Carolina, well-to-do, cultured and influential. His mother was Welsh, of distinguished ancestry, being a member of that Owen family whose recorded history dates to 880, (the Owens were Kings of Wales until conquered by Edward 1st in 1282).

Owen L. Chesnutt was graduated from Franklin Military Academy in May, 1860 and entered the war immediately. He served with distinction the entire four years, in North Carolina, in West Virginia, in Tennessee, and in Virginia, and was at Appomattox at the surrender. He was Captain of Company "C", 38th North Carolina, in Scales Brigade, Col. John Ashford commanding the regiment.

In 1865 Capt. Chesnutt was married to Mary Ann Newkirk Matthis. She was a daughter of Abram Newkirk Matthis and Eliza Jane Dollar whose home was "Pleasant Hill" in Sampson County, N. C., and she was the granddaughter of Mary Ann Newkirk and Major James Matthis (also spelled

Matthews) of "White Oaks" in Sampson County. Major Matthis represented Sampson County in the House of Commons, General Assembly of N. C., from 1802 to 1818. This family had come to North Carolina from Virginia, Matthews County, Va., having been named for one branch of the family. Mary Ann Newkirk's family had come from Kingston and Albany, N. Y., where they were among the first settlers from Holland to the New Netherland Colony, in April 1659. They were related to and intermarried with many of the most distinguished Dutch families in New York.

The Matthises were large slave holders, and "White Oaks" and "Pleasant Hill" were scenes of gracious and comfortable living. In this atmosphere Mary Ann had grown up, and she had grace and stamina to face, with her beloved Captain, her world torn and shattered and demanding from them the full measure of strength and courage and faith.

Capt. and Mrs. Chesnutt lived for some years on the depleted old plantation, but his battle wounds had taken their toll (he had been wounded seven times) and he was not physically equal to the battle of farm restoration. In 1887 they left North Carolina to make their home in the little sawmill village of Tifton. Beautifully educated, Capt. Chesnutt turned to teaching school which he did for several years; and later served as Clerk of the City Court and Justice of the Peace. Never a robust man, he retired from active life at an early age. He was one of the organizers of the Presbyterian Church, was one of its first Elders, and served it with love and devotion until his death in June, 1910. (See Presbyterian Church History.) Mrs. Chesnutt followed her husband in death ten days later.

By nature Capt. Chesnutt was unusually genial and affable, of fine bearing and address, hospitable, sincere in friendship, forthright in character, and devout in his Christian life. Unusually gifted as a public speaker, with cultured mind and a beautiful flow of language, he was always in demand as toastmaster and featured speaker on gala occasions. Many of his speeches have been preserved in manuscript and show a breadth of vision and an eloquence comparable to many of the best speakers of his day. These speeches show him to have been particularly advanced in his ideas of the New South; and to have been without rancor or bitterness toward his late adversaries. At the time of his death he probably had as many friends as any man in the country. Chesnutt Avenue was named in his honor.

To Capt. and Mrs. Chesnutt were born the following children:

Eliza Laetitia, married Henry Hardy Britt, died 1929. (See Britt Family.)

Thomas McIntosh, married Janie Williams, daughter of Charles and Flora MacDonald Williams of Fayetteville, N. C. Died 1933. Children: Thomas Williams Chesnutt, Catherine MacDonald, married Roy Benton Allen, children: Mary Catherine and Roy Benton, Jr.

Abram Matthis, married Eunice Brown of Atlanta, Died 1940. Children: Louise, Henry, Mildred, Irene and Edwin (died 1945 in Italian campaign).

Owen Lee, married Mary Carmichael (Ethridge) of Jackson, Ga. Captain in Dental Corps with American Army in France in World War I. Died 1942.

Lillian Gray, died in girlhood.

Mary Marable, married Paul Wingard, Rome, Ga. Died 1944.

SAMUEL M. CLYATT

The Tifton Gazette of May 13, 1904 carried the story that Sam Clyatt and J. M. Gaulding had been appointed by the newly formed Sam Cylatt Fishing Club to select a site for purchase by the club for the location of a club house. Fishing clubs were popular with Tifton men of that day. The Tom Welch Fishing club had been organized by Brunswick and Western Railroad men in 1892, and had headquarters on the Satilla River. The Homosassa Fishing club was another fishing club with many Tifton members.

Not only was Sam Clyatt popular among his fishing friends, but every one who knew him liked him and he was elected Mayor of Tifton, to succeed Mayor W. W. Timmons, who was mayor in 1904 and 1905.

Mayor Clyatt began his term of office as mayor in January, 1906. The event was celebrated by a 'possum supper. "A fine fat 'possum had been baked to an epicure's taste by Jack Garrett and was served in handsome style by Host Brigham, with oysters and accessories. The occasion was a most pleasant one to all attending."

Mayor Clyatt had married Miss Emma Stump, and they had two children, beautiful and beloved Marguerite, and James J. Clyatt, possessed of an excellent voice. Mrs. Clyatt was daughter of valliant James Stump, who, at fifteen, fought in the Mexican War and during the War Between the States was a blockade runner between New York and Richmond. Three of his vessels were captured by the United States. Later, during the administration of President Grover Cleveland, he was sergeant-at-arms at the Capitol at Washington. James Stump died in his seventy-sixth year, in 1905, at Valdosta.

Elected to serve as councilmen with Mayor Clyatt were H. H. Tift, E. P. Bowen, and S. G. Slack. John T. Mathis was mayor pro tem., and Leon Hargraves was clerk of council and city treasurer.

Mayor Clyatt's term of office was a period of much progress in Tifton. S. G. Slack, J. J. Golden and N. Peterson were appointed to draft a sanitary code for the city; and an ordinance was passed providing receptacles for trash and garbage. Raleigh Eve was appointed in June, 1906, to examine the city charter and later was appointed to draft a code of laws for the city; and these were adopted. In June, 1906 the citizens of Tifton voted for public schools and the new school, corner stone of which was laid in 1906, was opened January 14, 1907.

In June, 1906, Council signed a petition of Postmaster J. M. Duff requesting free mail delivery in Tifton.

In 1907, Cylatt was mayor and Tifton councilmen were H. H. Tift, W. T. Hargrett, E. P. Bowen, J. J. Golden, S G. Slack, W. H. Hendricks. Mayor pro tem. was E. P. Bowen. City clerk and treasurer was Leon A. Hargreaves. Dr. N. Peterson was city physician. Chief of police was R. G. Coarsey

In 1907 the "Code of Tifton, 1907," compiled by Raleigh Eve from the Charter of 1902 and the Code of 1895 and adopted by council in 1906, was printed by the Gazette Publishing Company.

In October of 1907, Tifton's first fire department was organized. S. G. Slack was chief and the volunteers who composed it were among Tifton's most prominent citizens.

Mr. Clyatt was elected to serve as mayor of Tifton during 1908 and 1909, and councilmen elected with him were H. H. Tift, S. G. Slack and W. H. Spooner. Dr. W. H. Hendricks was elected mayor pro tem. for 1908, and clerk and treasurer was W. W. Bryan. Mayor Cylatt resigned October 5, 1908, and was succeeded by W. W. Banks.

Mr. Clyatt moved away from Tifton and lived elsewhere for a number of years; but he later returned to Tifton and he and Mrs. Clyatt, the beloved Emma, who had a host of friends in Tifton, spent their tranquil declining years in Tifton. She preceded him in death and both of them now rest in the Tifton cemetery.

Marguerite Clyatt married, and she died at childbirth; but the infant lived and was for a number of years with Mrs. Clyatt, until the child's father married again and took the child to live with him.

James Clyatt married Josie Golden, daughter of his father's good friend, J. J. Golden. For more than thirty years she was organist of the First Baptist Church of Tifton, of which her mother, Mamie McLeod Golden was choir director for the same period.

For a record of Mrs. Clyatt's achievements and honors see "Who's Who in Georgia," published by Larkin, Roosevelt and Larkin, Chicago; also, "American Women," (Vol. III, p. 173). published in Los Angeles, by American Publications, Inc.

THE CHURCHWELLS

John Churchwell, prosperous merchant of Brookfield, died April 29, 1904, aged 71, at the home of his son, A. F. Churchwell, in Albany, Georgia. He was buried in the Churchwell family burial ground near Brookfield, where his wife had been buried a few years previously.

John Churchwell was survived by six children, as follows: John H., of Cordele; A. F., of Albany; Walter, of Hawkinsville; Mrs. J. C. Hind, of Columbus, Georgia; Mrs. Dan Fletcher, of Harding. Georgia; Mrs. M. D. Calhoun, of Bainbridge.

A. F., John H., and Mrs. Dan Fletcher, all of whom grew up at Brookfield, remained for many years in close touch with what is now Tift County.

John H. Churchwell began his business career in McRae in 1895 with a cash capital of one hundred dollars. He so greatly prospered that he sought a larger field for his activities and located at Cordele where he soon had one of the most successful mercantile establishments of the state.

Soon after John entered into business, A. F., in 1897, at Abbeville, opened a store with a starting capital of $250.00. He, likewise, prospered and in 1900, on February 7, he opened a store in Albany, on Broad Street. He later moved to the Davis Exchange Bank Building there.

The Churchwell brothers opened a store in Tifton, and George Washington Coleman was its manager from 1903 to 1907. The store outgrew its old quarters and in 1909 moved into larger quarters, its opening being on March 19. Managers of the store at that time were "Messrs. Padrick and Abbott. Clerks were Messrs. Robert and Abbott."

In March of 1911 the Churchwells were conducting six retail stores in the following towns: Albany, Cordele, Waycross, Fitzgerald, Tifton, Sylvester. Of these the Albany store was owned solely by A. F., and the Cordele store was owned solely by John H. The others were owned jointly. On March 17, announcement was made that a co-partnership had been formed and the retail stores would be conducted under the firm name of Churchwell's, and a wholesale establishment would be opened by them in Cordele. The retail business of the stores in 1910 was four hundred thousand dollars.

Although business took the Churchwells away from Tift County in later years, their hearts and minds returned to the scene of their boyhood at well-loved Brookfield, and they were among those generous donors who have recently made possible the building of the beautiful Memorial Methodist Church at Brookfield. This church, organized in 1878 by Rev. J. J. F. Goodman, was called then Bethesda, and was built on land donated by a Mr. Matthews. In 1903 the church was moved into Brookfield. The name was changed to the Brookfield Methodist Church. The newest building is the Memorial Church, dedicated on Sunday, May 25, 1947. For further details see chapter about churches.

The dedicatory prayer was in part: "God, make the door of this house we have raised to Thee wide enough to receive all who need human love and fellowship and a Father's care; and narrow enough to shut out all envy, pride and hate ... God, make the door of this house the gateway to Thy Eternal Kingdom."

JAMES ELLISON COCHRAN

James Ellison Cochran, born Meriwether County, Georgia, January 24, 1875, was son of Rufus Cochran and Amanda Plant Cochran, both of Meriwether, Amanda being of that Plant family who moved from Georgia to Florida and there founded Plant City.

In Tifton, where James moved in 1899, J. E. Cochran was nicknamed "John E." although his name was not John and he had a brother whose name was John. "John E." set up a watch repair and jewelry shop in the corner of Dr. George Smith's drug store on the site now occupied by Wright's Main Street Store, Tifton. Here he continued until fall of 1906, at which time he moved to the location of what is now the Nifty. He was Tifton's first, and, for many years, the town's only jeweler.

At Marietta, on March 18, 1908 James E. Cochran was married to Sallie Morris, the ceremony being performed at the bride's home by Dr. Patton, for more than forty years the pastor of the Marietta Presbyterian Church. Miss Morris had come to Tifton to teach, in 1905. She was daughter of Marion Pitchford Morris (born October 14, 1844, Cobb County, Georgia: died June 17, 1903, at Roswell; buried at Marietta) and Arkansas Mayes, called

Cantie Mayes, born July 14, 1846, Cobb County; married June 30, soon after close of War Between the States (died November 16, 1927, at Marietta; buried at Marietta).

Mr. Cochran was a Baptist, and he was a Mason.

Continuing in the jewelry business until March 1, 1915, Mr. Cochran then sold his business to Herbert Luther Moor, who came to Tifton from Newport, Vermont.

On January 24, 1926 James Ellison Cochran was killed by a dynamite explosion on his farm near Tifton. Burial was in Tifton cemetery.

Sallie Morris Cochran in 1926 began teaching in the Tifton Junior High School, of which she was principal from September, 1942 until June, 1946.

Mr. and Mrs. J. E. Cochran had an only child, Sarah, who married Hull Atwater, of Tifton.

When Governor Joseph Terrell, on Thursday, August 17, 1905, signed the bill whereby Tift County was created, he used a gold pen made expressly for that purpose, by J. E. Cochran, Tifton jeweler. The pen bore the words, "Tift County," on a pearl name-plate.

ABRAHAM BENJAMIN CONGER

Among the early settlers of Berrien County (presently Tift) was Abraham Benjamin Conger. He came from the state of New York in 1836 to Lowndes County, Georgia, and there married Ann Willis. Shortly after their marriage, they moved to Berrien County, and there acquired considerable landed interest and engaged in farming. Although not born in the South, he believed the cause of the Southern people to be just, and enlisted in the War Between the States on the side of the South. To the union of Abraham Benjamin Conger and Ann Willis were born five sons, George, Abraham, Jr., Barney, Joseph and Jackson. All of these sons settled on nearby farms and reared large families. Added to their interests in farming were stock raising, naval stores, logging and saw mill businesses. During the early young manhood of these sons, there was considerable trouble with the Creek Indians, and all of them engaged in the Indian wars of that period. Near the old homestead of George Conger are the remains of a log fort which housed the womenfolk during the periods of trouble with the Indians. Living conditions were very difficult during this period, and in order to carry produce to market it was necessary to travel by covered wagons either to Albany or Columbus. All of these young men married young women from Berrien and Worth Counties.

Abraham Benjamin Conger, Jr., married Elizabeth Young, whose father and mother were both born in Berrien County, and they also engaged in farming and naval stores operations. Elizabeth Young Conger came of a long line of ministers of the gospel. Her great-grandfather, Rev. William Pate, was a contemporary of Jesse Mercer and founded more than a hundred churches through the central portion of Georgia. He was also a Revolutionary hero, was born in Gloucester County, Virginia, in 1750, and was the grandson of Major Thomas Pate, of Pettsworth Parish, Virginia, at whose home Nathaniel Bacon, the patriotic rebel leader, died in 1676, who in turn was a direct descendant of Lord Edward Pate, Chief Mint Master of King Henry VIII. His ancestral line goes back, also to Lord John Ragland, of England, whose wife was Ann Beaufort. Another ancestor, the Reverend Parkerson, came to America from Sweden just prior to the Revolutionary War and served as a captain in that war. A boulder was unveiled to the memory of Reverend William Pate by the Daughters of the American Revolution at Amboy, Georgia, in 1929. To the union of Abraham Benjamin Conger, Jr., and Elizabeth Young were born eleven children, Barney, Jackson, Nelson, Isaac Young, James, Minnie, Abraham Benjamin III, twin daughters, Sarah and Mary, Green and Dolly. Abraham Benjamin Conger II, died in 1909, and Elizabeth Young Conger died in 1940.

Among the children of Abraham Benjamin II and Elizabeth Conger Isaac Young Conger became postmaster at Tifton. He had two sons in World War II, Captain Preston DeWitt Conger, Medical Corps, in the European theater, who is now practicing medicine at Moultrie, Georgia, and Henry Jackson Conger, Lieutenant Commander, United States Navy, graduate of Annapolis, and one daughter, Elizabeth Conger Harris, whose husband, David P. Harris, served with the Marines in the Pacific theater.

Abraham II's and Elizabeth Conger's daughter Minnie, married Samuel Lipps. They had four sons in the service in World War II, and one grandson; Sergeant Frank Lipps served in the Pacific area and received five battle stars, the Bronze and Silver stars, and the Purple Heart.

Among the sons of Abraham Benjamin Conger II and Elizabeth Young Conger, Abraham Benjamin Conger III has attained a position of prominence in Bainbridge, Georgia, of which he was mayor in 1920-21, succeeding J. W. Callohan. Abraham Benjamin Conger III also represented his district in the Georgia Legislature in 1915, 1916. He was born in Worth County, July 14, 1888, received his early education in the public schools and in Norman Institute, received his A.B. degree from Mercer University in 1911 and his Bachelor of Laws degree from Mercer in 1912. Soon after graduation in law, Mr. Conger began the practice of law in Bainbridge, where for four years he was associated with R. G. Hartsfield. Thereafter he continued his practice of law in Bainbridge.

In 1915, A. B. Conger III married Onys M. Willis, who became president of the Georgia Federation of Women's Clubs, and also was active in the United Daughters of the Confederacy, Daughters of the American Revolution, Society of Colonial Dames, Daughters of 1812.

Abraham Benjamin Conger III is a former president of the Decatur Bar Association and of the Albany Circuit Bar Association. He is a Mason, a member of Rotary Club, of Phi Delta Theta Fraternity. He is a deacon in the Bainbridge Baptist Church.

Benjamin Conger and Onys Willis Conger have the following children, three of whom were engaged in World War II. Captain Abraham Benjamin Conger IV, Medical Corps, European theater; Lieutenant James Willis Conger, Base Legal Officer, Hickan Field, Hawaii; Private First Class Leonard Hodges Conger, who participated in the B-5 Program as a student in electrical engineering, and Margaret Conger Varner, whose husband, Edwin Surles Varner, served in the European theater.

J. D. Conger was born in Irwin County, Georgia, October 25, 1897. Martha Ross was born in 1823 in Irwin County. Her daughter, Nancy Ross, married John Smith. John Smith's daughter, Martha Smith, was born on June 22, 1845, and married John Drew Roberts, Junior, who was born in Irwin County in September, 1847. His father, John Drew Roberts, Senior, was born in Irwin County in 1820. Martha Smith married John Drew Roberts, Junior, and October 6, 1875 Missouri Caroline Roberts was born. Missouri Roberts married in 1896 Bristole Ero Conger, who was born on December 21, 1874. Her son, George Drew Conger was born on October 25, 1897. He Married Annie Laurie Thomas, who was born on April 2, 1898 in Flovilla, Georgia. Their daughter, Dorothy Helen Conger, was born December 6, 1921.

Jesse Wilson (Billy) Lipps, son of Mr. and Mrs. Sam Lipps of Ty Ty, Georgia, entered service February 22, 1941, receiving his basic training at Camp Stewart, Savannah, Georgia, was shipped overseas January 7, 1942, going to the European theater of war and participated in the following campaigns: North Africa, Sicily, Italy—receiving 5 Battle Stars. His Division was the 5th army serving 30 months overseas, arriving back in the States September 17, 1945 and receiving his Honorable Discharge at Camp Gordon, Augusta, Georgia, October 28, 1945, his rating being Corporal.

Joseph M. Lipps, son of Mr. and Mrs. Sam Lipps of Ty Ty, Georgia, entered service of the U. S. Army February 27, 1942 in Columbus, Georgia. He first served in the Coast Artillery and later joined the Paratroop Division and received his training at the A. G. F. Parachute School, Fort Benning, Georgia. He went to the Pacific theater of war June 5, 1945 and was at Luzon, Okinawa and different parts of Japan, returning to the states on December 13, 1945 and received his Honorable Discharge at Fort McPherson, Atlanta, Georgia, December 20, 1945, his rating being a Sergeant.

James R. Lipps, son of Mr. and Mrs. Sam Lipps of Ty Ty, Georgia, entered service of the U. S. Navy September 1, 1944. Received his Boot Training at Bainbridge, Md., later being transferred to Miami, Fla., and from there to New Orleans and on to Pacific. Name of ship Chewancan (Indian name), was in South Pacific when peace was declared.

VIRGIL FRANCIS DINSMORE

Virgil Francis Dinsmore, born in Milton County, Georgia, November 22, 1875, was son of M. Dinsmore and Mary Grogan Dinsmore. He spent his boyhood at Alpharetta, Georgia.

Reared by four different step-mothers, young Virgil worked hard and supported himself, saved his money and accumulated several thousand dollars. By his own effort he put himself through the Atlanta Medical School and through the Bennett College of Medicine and Surgery, Chicago, where he graduated, in 1900.

After graduation young Dinsmore went to Kentucky where he worked among the coal miners in the vicinity of Owensboro, where he remained until his coming to Tifton in 1912 or 1914.

In Kentucky, Dr. Dinsmore met Miss Fannie Belle Kerrick, whom he married in 1901. Of this union are the following children: Wilton Dinsmore, of Atlanta; Mrs. H. B. McCrea, of Thomasville; Mrs. R. M. Kennon, of Tifton.

The late Col. R. E. Dinsmore of Tifton was a brother to Dr. Dinsmore. Half-sisters were Mrs. Lena Overstreet, of Lake City, Florida, and Mrs. Savannah Cochran, of Fulton County.

Dr. Dinsmore had a large practice in and near Tifton. For 21 years he was physician to the Tifton Cotton Mills. For twelve or more years he served on the Tifton City Council, of which he was for a long time vice-chairman and from which, because of ill health, he retired early in 1937.

Virgil Francis Dinsmore died at his Tifton home, corner of Ridge and Sixth Streets August 22, 1937. Funeral services were at the First Baptist Church, Tifton, of which he had for many years been a deacon. The services were conducted by his pastor, Dr. F. O. Mixon, and by the Reverend M. P. Webb, pastor of the Tifton Methodist Church. Funeral was in Tifton cemetery. Tifton druggists were pallbearers. Doctors, dentists, and nurses were an honorary escort.

Dr. Dinsmore was a Mason and was a Woodman of the World.

JOHN M. DUFF

John M. Duff, born on the Duff Place, Irwin County, October 14, 1846, moved to Berrien County. For three years he served with gallantry in the Confederate Army. He was in Company H, 47 Georgia Cavalry.

At Albany, in 1877 John M. Duff married Blanche Catherine Ransome. Of the union were eight children.

Mr. Duff was in the hardware business for a time. He served as postmaster at Alapaha from 1882 until he came to Tifton in 1890 and became postmaster at Tifton where he served for two years. In 1895 he taught school at Zion Hope, near Tifton. On February 1, 1897 he was again appointed Tifton postmaster and so continued until his death early in 1907.

At a meeting of Tifton City Council July 2, 1906, Councilman E. P. Bowen presiding Council signed Mr. Duff's petition to the First Assistant Postmaster General asking for free delivery of mail in Tifton. Council voted thanks to Mr. Duff for his effort to secure establishment of free delivery of mail in Tifton.

John M. Duff and Blanch Catherine Ransome Duff are buried at Albany. One of their sons was Barney Duff. Another son died as a result of a mule kick. Children who survive Mr. Duff were: Mayme Banner (aged twenty-one at the time of her father's death married a Mr. Arnald; lived in Miami; died about 1944; buried in Albany); Rawlins (aged eighteen at time of his father's death); Clara Belle (aged eleven at the time of her father's death; when grown, worked at Tifton post office; later was transferred to Miami).

RALEIGH EVE

Raleigh Eve was born on August 7, more than seventy years ago at Asheville, North Carolina. His father, Charles W. Eve was editor of "The Asheville Pioneer" and his mother, Kate Emerson Reese Eve was daughter of Dr. Jefferson B. M. Reese and was a niece of Judge William B. Reese, Chief Justice of the Supreme Court of Tennessee.

After completing his public school education in Washington, D. C., Raleigh Eve came to Adairsville, Georgia, where he worked for the Western and Atlantic Railroad, which had been leased by Governor Joseph E. Brown, a kinsman of Raleigh's mother. Working as agent and working in telegraphy at Adairsville, in Chattanooga, Tennessee, and at Trion, Georgia, he continued with the railroad seven years.

In the fall of 1896 Raleigh came to South Georgia, going first to Fitzgerald, where he remained for only several months before coming to Tifton. In Tifton he worked for Henry Harding Tift until April, 1898, at which time Eve left for service in the Spanish-American War, in which he served as a non-commissioned officer.

Raleigh Eve had long been interested in law, and when he returned from the war he began to study law. He was one of the first to take a written examination after the passing of the law requiring that type of examination. He took his Georgia Bar examination in Thomasville in 1901, under Judge Augustin Hansell, Judge of the old Southern Circuit of which Berrien, now Tift, was then a part.

After being admitted to the bar, Mr. Eve practiced law in Tifton until 1907, when he became judge. He served as judge of the Tifton City Court for ten years and thereafter became judge of the newly created Tifton Circuit in which capacity he has served from the creation of the circuit in 1916 until the present time. Also he is the senior trial judge in Georgia.

On October 15, 1910 there had arrived in Tifton a young woman, Miss Jewell Vivian Strickland. She had been working in Atlanta but had expressed to her friend, Miss Lizzie O. Thomas, executive secretary of the Atlanta Y. W. C. A., her desire to change her position. Miss Thomas, a retired missionary to Japan, was a woman of much charm and was the original of the character, Miss Dixon, in Frances Little's book, "The Lady of The Decoration." Miss Little told Vivian that a friend of hers had been requested by Henry Tift, of Tifton, to be on the lookout for a good secretary for him. An appointment was arranged for Miss Strickland and Henry Tift in the office of an Atlanta lumber company. Before the interview Vivian, Henry Tift, and the friend watched from the office windows a parade staged in honor of President Theodore Roosevelt, whom she saw from the window. There was wild enthusiasm; for President Roosevelt was son of a Georgian, beautiful Mittie Bullock of nearby Roswell, where Mittie and Theodore Roosevelt, Sr., had been married at stately Bullock Hall, built by Major James S. Bullock in 1840, of great oak timbers to obtain which he had sent all the way to Augusta.

When the excitement of the parade was over Vivian had the interview with Mr. Tift and he engaged her to be his secretary. She was an excellent secretary. Judge Eve met her and liked her and she liked him. Judge Eve found her charming and he paid her court. They were married on the evening of Wednesday, December 16, 1914. After the ceremony Dr. and Mrs. Nichols Peterson were hosts at supper honoring the bride and groom. Among those present were Mrs. H. H. Tift, Rev. Durden, and Miss Nan Wicker, later Nan Clements, who became principal of Tifton Junior High School.

After the wedding supper the Eves went to an apartment which Judge Eve had furnished for his bride at the home of Mr. and Mrs. Perryman Moores where they lived for six months after their marriage.

Jewell Vivian Strickland was born in Meriwether County. She was daughter of Solomon Pace Strickland of Whitesberg, Georgia, and Mary Frances Key, of Harris County, near Warm Springs. Jewel, as a child, used to love to visit her grandmother whose plantation was land now embraced in the famous Pine Mountain Valley Farm Project, dear to the heart of Franklin Delano Roosevelt.

To Judge Eve and Jewell Vivian was born a son, Robert Worth Eve, so named in compliance with a recommendation of the Worth County Grand Jury; for Judge Eve was holding court in Worth County when he received word of the birth of his son on November 26, 1917, and the Grand Jury recommended that he name the child Worth, which the parents did. Robert Worth Eve graduated from Tifton High School in 1934; graduated from Abraham Baldwin Agricultural College in 1936; graduated from the University of Georgia in 1938; took further work at Cornell. Since completing his studies Robert Eve has been with the United States Farm Security Administration at Vienna, and at Camilla.

Judge Eve has through the years of his Tifton residence been identified prominently with practically every civic enterprise that has been for progress. He codified the laws of the city of Tifton in 1907; he served for many years as chairman of the Board of Education of Tifton. He has served as president of the Board of Trade. He is a former chairman of the Board of Stewards of the Tifton Methodist Church. In 1941 he was appointed chairman of the advisory commission of the Jefferson Davis Memorial, near Irwinville. He was for many years president of the Country Club at Gun Lake. He was organizer and is president of the Tift County Audubon Society. He was organizer and is president of the Tift County Historical Society, and is official Tift County Historian, appointed by the Grand Jury to arrange for the compiling of the history of Tift County. Carrying out this request resulted in the founding of the Historical Society which appointed writers to compile and write the history, which is incorporated in this volume.

Judge Eve early in his career as judge appointed probation officers and he has availed himself of their services, often taking care of youthful or first offenders by use of suspended sentences.

Judge Eve has served in three wars. Besides serving in the Spanish-American War, he was commissioned as captain of Georgia state troops in World

War I, and in World War II he was commissioned Major in the 25 Georgia Defense Corps.

However, he is a peace-loving, home body, and when his work is over he walks home and enjoys the good food that Jewell has with her own hands prepared for him, and he is welcomed not only by her but by a long-eared Spaniel who barks a joyous welcome.

THE FLETCHERS

Joseph Fletcher, the pioneer of the Fletcher family, married Mary Henly. They came from Telfair County and settled west of Irwinville, on what in 1912 was called the Smith place. Their children were: William, Jehu, Horton, John, Sandy, Jim, Wiley, Elbert, Sophie, Millie, Polly, Van, Dora, Jennie or Jinsey, and Martha. From these are a host of descendants many of whom are citizens of Tift County. They are a sturdy, God-fearing, industrious people who have been a constructive element in the community.

For further information of the Fletchers see article by Smada, Tifton Gazette of Jan. 5, 1912; also, see William Henderson's book "Henderson and Whiddon Families," pp. 137-141; also Ibid., 282-288.

Jim, called "Black Jim" Fletcher, was tax receiver, treasurer, and representative of Irwin County. He was a son of William Fletcher, and was grandson of pioneer Joseph Fletcher. Black Jim married Melissa Paulk and had four children, one of whom, Margaret, (born January 6, 1862), married Jonathan Walker on February 23, 1881, and became the mother of James Walker, born February 7, 1886, long time sheriff of Tift County.

Another Fletcher who achieved outstanding success in Tift County was Daniel Fletcher, born in Berrien County, September 18, 1867, son of Elbert and Catherine (Katy) McMillan Fletcher. Daniel was reared at Alapaha. On November 22, 1891 he married Mattie Churchwell, daughter of Mr. and Mrs. John Churchwell, Sr., and sister to John H. and A. F. Churchwell. Dan Fletcher and Mattie established a home on Route 4, near Tifton, and there remained for more than half a century, until Daniel's death on Thursday, March 28, 1946. Daniel Fletcher was buried in Tifton cemetery.

By occupation a farmer, Daniel Fletcher was one of the most extensive land owners of the community at the time of his death, and was deeply revered as to his character. He was a Mason and was a member of Mount Olive Primitive Baptist Church, where his funeral was held.

Daniel Fletcher's mother died November 4, 1930, aged ninety-one years, six months. His father died more than fifty years prior to Daniel's death.

Daniel was survived by his widow and eight children, Erris, John H., Daniel, Jr., Mrs. Virginia Corley, of Tifton; Melvin, of Fitzgerald; Mrs. Fredonia Simmons, Mrs. Edgar Pritchett, Miss Sara Fletcher, of Albany.

DANIEL ARCHIBALD FULWOOD

Daniel Archibald Fulwood, born at Fort Valley, February 3, 1833, was son of Jonathan and Mary Fulwood who died when he was a child. He was reared by his grandfather Fulwood, a Methodist minister who had come from North Carolina to Georgia and was one of the pioneers of Houston County. Daniel's uncle, Charles Fulwood, of his grandfather's household, was like a brother to him.

On October 28, 1855 Daniel Fulwood married Caroline Elizabeth Murray (1832-June 15, 1906) and to them were born nine children, three of whom died in infancy. Daniel entered the Confederate Army and fought under General Longstreet. In the battle of Sharpsburg, Virginia, Fulwood lost his left leg.

After the war Daniel, though crippled, valiantly assumed his responsibilities toward his young and dependent family whom he reared to be useful, God-fearing citizens.

In 1882 Mr. Fulwood moved his family to near Alapaha in Berrien County. After a year in the country he moved into Alapaha where the Fulwood family lived until 1898 when he moved to Tifton, where he continued to live for the rest of his life.

Daniel Fulwood's uncle, Charles Fulwood, became an eminent Methodist minister. Charles was a trustee of Emory College, was a member of the old Georgia Conference and later was a member of the old Florida Conference. He served in the ministry for sixty years and died while making his report as Presiding Elder to the Florida Conference.

Daniel lived to see his son C. W. Fulwood mayor of Tifton, and also lived to see gathered about him four generations of boys and girls of his family. He died at the home of his son, C. W. Fulwood, at Tifton, January 24, 1921. Daniel and his wife are buried at Tifton cemetery. A daughter, Emma Smith, (Mrs. F. O. Baker), of Alapaha, died in November, 1917. The children who survived Daniel were: I. A., and C. W. Fulwood, Willie Lee (Mrs. John G. Padrick), of Tifton; E. J. Fulwood, of Adel: Miss Lizzie Fulwood, then of Macon but now of Tifton.

Birth date: Feb. 3, 1833.
Death date: Jan. 24, 1921.

COLUMBUS WESLEY FULWOOD

Columbus Wesley Fulwood was born May 12, 1865, near Fort Valley, in Houston, now Peach County, Georgia. He was son of the Confederate soldier Daniel Archibald Fulwood (q.v.) and Carolyn Elizabeth Murray Fulwood.

Columbus received his schooling in Fort Valley. He did not go to college, but he was a lover of good books and was a great reader. As a youth he came to Berrien County where for two years he boarded with the family of a Dr. Foegal of Alapaha, while he worked part of the time at a sawmill, and some of the time at a drug store.

Daniel then desired that Columbus select for him a farm in the vicinity of Alapaha, which Columbus did. He chose a place about seven miles from Alapaha and the entire Fulwood family, excepting the oldest son, Isaac Archibald Fulwood, moved to the farm. Isaac remained in Fort Valley. Columbus, however, was of the plantation household.

After two years on the farm the Fulwoods moved into Alapaha, and there Columbus Wesley Fulwood began reading law with Colonel William I. Lastinger. Fulwood stood his bar examination at Nashville and he began practicing law in Alapaha where he and Colonel C. I. Stacey formed a partnership.

Some time prior to this there had been living in Savannah a young woman by the name of Meta Dearing. Her father had died and her mother had married again and Meta came to Alapaha to make her home with her married sister, Mrs. Ib Giddings. Columbus met, wooed and won Meta, and they were married at the Alapaha Methodist Church, the only church in town then, the pastor, the Reverend J. M. Foster, performing the ceremony.

To Columbus and Meta was born in Alapaha a daughter whom they named Carolyn Lee Fulwood, for Mr. Fulwood's mother and one of his sisters. Before the baby was two years old Columbus, Meta and little Carrie moved to Tifton where C. W. Fulwood practiced law until his death. In Tifton were born to Columbus and Meta Fulwood seven other children.

When C. W. Fulwood came to Tifton the place was a small sawmill village. Mr. Fulwood and Tifton's founder, Henry Tift, became close and staunch friends and Fulwood was for many years Mr. Tift's legal adviser. Mr. Tift held Mr. Fulwood in high esteem and when Henry Tift gave to the City of Tifton for a park a large tract of land heavily wooded in virgin growth long leaf yellow pines he named the park Fulwood Park in honor of his friend, Columbus Wesley Fulwood, who helped him draw up the papers of conveyance to the city.

In 1934 the Tifton Garden Club, by popular subscription, erected at one entrance to the park a stone gateway on which is inscribed: "This arch erected as a token of appreciation to C. W. Fulwood whose tireless and unceasing efforts have made this park possible and to H. H. Tift, who donated the original park site." The inscription at the right reads: "Erected 1934 by the Tifton Garden Club, by popular subscription. Officers, Mrs. Warren Baker, president; Mrs. Fred Bell, 1st vice-president; Mrs. R. R. Forrester, 2nd vice-president; Mrs. H. E. Herring, treasurer; Miss F. K. Hollinsworth, secretary; C. W. Fulwood, Jr., architect; W. P. Brown, contractor." Th dedicatory address was made by Lennon Bowen.

In 1893 when Mayor W. H. Love resigned his office as mayor of Tifton, Columbus W. Fulwood was elected Tifton's second mayor and began the duties of his office on May 1, 1893 at a meeting held at the office of H. H. Tift, the oath of office having been subscribed before W. W. Rutherford on April 11, 1893. At the first meeting of his mayorality it was ordered that a committee be appointed to confer with the Brunswick and Western railroad relative to street crossings and furnishing better depot facilities at Tifton. Councilmen H. H. Tift and E. P. Bowen were appointed on this committee. A Board of Health was appointed as follows: Dr. J. C. Goodman, Dr. J. A. McCrea, Messrs. E. P. Bowen, J. H. Knight and C. A. Williams. J. H. Goodman was Tifton Council clerk. Mr. Williams asked to be released from serving on the board and at the next meeting John C. Hind was appointed in his

HISTORY OF TIFT COUNTY 399

place. Mr. Hind, a Canadian, was Tifton's earliest contractor, who, in February, 1891, requested that Council set a fee for a contractor's license, which was done.

Prior to Mr. Fulwood's becoming mayor, Tifton Council meetings were held at the office of H. H. Tift. On August 22, 1893 Council met in Mr. Fulwood's office, and thereafter they sometimes met in Tift's office and sometimes in Fulwood's.

At the August 22, 1893 meeting of Council steps were taken to try to prevent the importation of the dread yellow fever peril. A quarantine was ordered and extra police employed to enforce it. Council voted thanks to W. O. Tift for his offer of use of a vacant house on the Tifton and Northeastern Railroad for use as a pest house, if needed. Later, Dame Rumor had her say, and Tifton business men, fearful that their profits would be imperiled were dismayed. Council passed an ordinance whereby it became a punishable offense to "originate a false rumor" relative to yellow fever or to "repeat one whether true or false." Punishment was set at not less than five dollars and not more than fifty dollars, in default of which a culprit was to work upon the public works for a term of not less than ten or more than a hundred days. The quarantine was raised at a meeting in Mayor Fulwood's office, September 13, 1893. Present were Mayor Fulwood, Councilmen B. T. Allen, E. P. Bowen, W. T. Hargrett, J. C. Goodman. Allen was clerk pro tem.

C. W. Fulwood served as mayor of Tifton during 1894 also. That year city officers were elected as follows: Dr. J. A. McCrea, mayor pro tem.; J. H. Goodman, clerk and treasurer; W. T. McGuirt, marshal. Dr. J. A. McCrea was elected city physician.

At a meeting of council on April 2, 1894, at office of H. H. Tift, the fire limits of the city of Tifton were established. Also the matter of city lights was taken up. It was ordered that two street lamps, one north of the Brunswick and Western Railway tracks and one south of them be placed at the B. and W. crossing; also one west side of Georgia, Southern and Florida Railway crossing, and same to be kept filled and lighted by the marshal.

Mayor Fulwood held office in 1895 also, but in 1896 he was succeeded by F. G. Boatright who became Tifton's third mayor.

During the long period that C. W. Fulwood practiced law in Tifton he had a number of men associated with him. His first law partner was Colonel J. A. Alexander, who later moved to Nashville. Others were Holmes Murray, Colonel Skeen of Atlanta, and in later years Mr. Fulwood's youngest son, John Goodman Fulwood.

In 1895 J. A. Alexander, Colonel C. W. Fulwood and C. C. S. Baldridge bought the Tifton Gazette from B. T. Allen (see article on B. T. Allen, this volume), and Baldridge and Fulwood later organized the Gazette Publishing Company.

C. W. Fulwood was the first president of the Country Club at Gun Lake, organized 1912.

The Fulwood home for many years was the house at the southwest corner of Ridge at Sixth Street. Here Miss Carrie Fulwood and her brother, Charlie Fulwood, still make their home.

Meta Dearing Fulwood, born October 23, 1868, died April 11, 1930. Columbus Wesley Fulwood died May 5, 1936. Both are buried in Tifton cemetery.

Children of Columbus Wesley and Meta Dearing Fulwood are:

1. Carolyn Lee Fulwood, of Tifton; at Tifton Post Office.

2. Paul Dearing Fulwood, of Tifton, married Ruth Vickers; is in plant business.

3. Charles Wesley Fulwood, of Tifton; architect.

4. Helen Fulwood (born August 26, 1895—died August 1, 1942) married Jene Whitaker, of Valdosta.

5. Martha Fulwood, a trained nurse, stationed at Fort McPherson.

6. Mary Fulwood (died in infancy); twin to Martha.

7. Grace Fulwood; married Colonel W. W. Outerbridge, credited with having ordered fired the first shot fired by the United States in World War II, at Pearl Harbor.

8. John Goodman Fulwood, Tifton lawyer; married Susie Moore Bowen.

JAMES SMITH GAULDING

James Smith Gaulding was second son of Archibald Alexander Gaulding whom Lucian Lamar Knight in his "Georgia Landmarks, Memorials and Legends," Vol. I, p. 929, lists as among the thirty original settlers of Spalding County, which was carved out of Pike and Henry Counties in December 1851. Griffin is the county seat. Archibald Alexander married Sarah Horton, of Griffin, and to them were born six children: Joe, James, Smith, Charlie, Willie, Fannie, and Mamie. Archibald moved from Griffin to Atlanta where he was a newspaper editor prior to the War Between the States. He died in Atlanta when between sixty and seventy years of age and Sarah soon followed him in death.

1. Joe Gaulding and his wife, Mary, were the parents of Willard Gaulding, Sr., whose son, Willard Gaulding, Jr., is in the Bank of Tifton.

3. Charlie married in Texas and there died. Issue: one daughter.

4. Willie died, aged about seventeen, unmarried.

5. Fannie married Dr. Charles Boyd. No issue. She died in Macon; he in Savannah.

6. Mamie married George Bowen. They moved to Pelham. Issue: Walter, Charlie, Mamie, Pearl.

2. James Smith Gaulding, second son of A. A. and Sarah Horton Gaulding, was born in Griffin. He, when a small boy, moved with his parents to Atlanta and there attended school. In 1861, when eighteen years old, he joined the Confederate Army in which he was one of the Nelson Rangers, made up of young men from Atlanta under command of Captain Nelson. Gaulding was in the cavalry and served for the four years of the war, but came through unhurt.

Soon after the close of the war James Smith visited his brother, Joe, in

Levy County, Florida. There he met and, in 1866, married Juliet Elizabeth McCall, daughter of Lewis McCall and Mary Knight McCall. After their marriage James Smith Gaulding and his wife came to Joshlyn, Georgia, a small sawmill village between Jacksonville and Waycross. After about a year there they came to Tifton, where James Smith arrived on June 3, 1879.

James spent his first night in Tifton in the uppermost room of the tall house that was H. H. Tift's and Bessie Tift's first home after Henry brought Bess to Tifton after their honeymoon. James went to work at the Tift Sawmill and worked there as a sawyer for fourteen years, at which time failing health necessitated his stopping. He owned a farm on the Ocilla Road not far from Tifton and after leaving the mill he spent his time either at the farm or in Tifton until his death, which occurred on the 3rd of June, 1930, on the anniversary of his arrival in Tifton, and in the home of his son, Jack Gaulding, on Second Street, within a hundred yards of the place where he had spent his first night in Tifton fifty-one years earlier. Dr. Nichols Peterson said that he died of old age—"Just wore out." He was eighty-five.

To James Smith Gaulding and Juliet Elizabeth McCall Gaulding were born ten children: Sallie, Charlie, Mary, Parker, Joe, Henry, Jack, Alice, Doney, Bob.

Jack Gaulding, son of James Smith Gaulding, was born November 10, 1881, at Tifton, in a four-room house which formerly stood where the Hotel Myon now is but which stood there prior to the building of the old Hotel Sadie. Jack Gaulding was said to be in 1946, the oldest living citizen of Tifton, that is, had been a citizen of Tifton longer than any other person living in Tifton in 1946. On March 27, 1900, in Irwin County, Jack Gaulding married Miss Mary Jane Branch, daughter of Wiley Branch, Sr., and Sarah Young Branch. Issue: Alda, James, Camilla, Joe, Dan.

The following article about Mr. J. W. Gaulding was copied from the Tifton Gazette:

Mr. Gaulding was born in Pike County, Georgia, March 23, 1867, being sixty-one on his last birthday. He was a son of J. H. and Mary Jane Gaulding, his father dying when he was a boy . . . He came to Tifton in 1893 and was associated in the mercantile business with Shepherd and Manard. When this business was reorganized under the name of L. S. Shepherd and Company, Mr. Gaulding became a member of the firm, and continued his connection with this business until his death. Mr. Gaulding had been a cotton buyer practically ever since he came to Tifton and was for many years cotton buyer for the Tifton Cotton Mills, in which he owned stock.

Mr. Gaulding served several terms as a member of the Tifton City Council and also as mayor pro tem. He had been prominently associated with the business life of Tifton for more than a third of a century. He was a member of the Methodist Church . . . He was an excellent business man, a good neighbor, kind, loving and devoted father, and a true friend

June 3, 1903, Mr. Gaulding was married to Miss Vonnie Summer, of Senoia, Georgia, at Blue Springs, Florida. Their two children are a son, L. W. Gaulding and a daughter, Elizabeth Gaulding.

JAMES LAWRENCE GREENE
JOHN BURWELL GREENE
LEOLA JUDSON GREENE

James Lawrence Greene and Martha Randolph Hannon Greene were living in Taylor County, Georgia, when their son, John Burwell Greene, was born November 5, 1843. James was a descendant of the Greene family of which General Nathaneal Greene, of Revolutionary fame, was a member, and Martha was of the family of which was John Hancock, of Virginia. John Burwell Greene was a descendant of Burwell Greene, Revolutionary soldier whose grave is in the Forsyth, Georgia cemetery. Burwell married a widow, Mrs. Nancy King.

When nineteen, John Burwell Greene enlisted in the Confederate Army. He was under Captain Dunlap, Company B, 36 Georgia Regiment. After serving through the Vicksburg campaign he spent several months at Lauderdale Springs Hospital, at first as a patient, later as a nurse.

Greene's company was sent to aid General Bragg in defense of Chickamauga. On the afternoon of the last day of the battle he was wounded in the side by a shell fragment. Captured, he was carried to Camp Douglas prison, Chicago, where he remained twenty-one months. Then came peace and blessed release. On May 20, 1865, he reached home.

In 1866 in Taylor County John joined the Methodist Church at Turner's Chapel. On November 17 of next year he married Miss Margaret Emerline Boothe. Children of this union were Caroline, Burton, Martha, Catherine, Leola, Joseph, and Burwell. Burwell died in infancy; the other children throve. In 1880, John Burwell, Margaret, and the children, riding through country in a covered wagon, journeyed to Berrien County, after having stayed about six months near a mill in Coffee County. They came to Tifton where Mr. Greene worked for a while before beginning work for H. H. Tift, Tifton's founder. Mr. Tift had numerous farms and John Burwell Greene became superintendent of eight of Tift's large farms, and on horseback would ride from one farm to another overseeing the work. He carried on for Mr. Tift what amounted to a private experiment station, for Tift wished to ascertain what crops would best thrive in this section.

In 1892 Greene grew the first tobacco grown in what is now Tift County; and until a few years ago, the old tobacco barn used by John Burwell Greene for curing, still stood on the property now owned by the Georgia Coastal Plain Experiment Station. Also, he had forty acres in blue Concord grapes and the grapes were shipped by the carload from Tifton. Also he grew various vegetables. Later he worked for W. O. Tift, H. H.'s brother.

Before John Burwell Greene had been in Tifton a year, his beloved Margaret, who had made the long ride here with him, died, in September. When nearly a year and a half had dragged by and it was spring again, he wed Margaret's sister, Julia, whom he married in May of 1882. Julia, born in Taylor County, June 16, 1846, was kind and loving to Margaret's children and was as nearly as possible like an own mother to them. The children

HISTORY OF TIFT COUNTY 403

were taught by their grandfather, James Lawrence Greene, who had attended the oldest college in Georgia. He taught in a one-room log cabin about one and a half miles north of the farm on which John lived, and gradually other children than his grandchildren came to him to be taught, long before Tifton Institute was founded.

John Burwell Greene and his wife, Julia, were among the six organizers of the Tifton Methodist Church, and John's name is the first name on the church roll. For many years he was the only steward of the church, of which he was a loyal member all his life.

The Greenes lived for many years in the country in a house built for them by H. H. Tift upon one of the Tift farms. It was the same now owned by Willingham Tift, of Atlanta, and used by him as a country home. In this house three of Mr. Greene's children were married: The eldest married John L. Herring; Caroline Neisler Greene married Oscar F. Sheppard; Catherine married James W. Hannon.

John Burwell Greene died Tifton, November 29, 1908. Julia died in Tifton, January 2, 1914. Both are buried in Tifton Cemetery.

When John L. Herring bought the controlling interest in the Gazette from Briggs Carson, Leola Greene, who had been born in Macon County, 1875, began work at the Gazette. She wrote; she set type. At one time or another she did everything that was to be done. For fifty years she has written up Tifton's weddings, births and deaths, and Miss Leola's wedding stories are famous. Hers is the gift of descriptive writing, and her travel stories which have appeared in the Gazette are vivid and interesting. Notably so are those on the Okefenokee and those on Duck Island. Every one admires and loves Miss Leola, and her fiftieth anniversary of writing for the Gazette was a time of many congratulations.

THE GIBBS FAMILY

The Gibbs family has many members in Tift County and surrounding territory. The large size of the Gibbs family precludes the setting forth of a comprehensive genealogy in the limited space of this volume. Such however, is to be found on pp. 91-101 in the valuable genealogy, "Family Record of the Henderson and Whiddon Families and their Descendants," written by William Henderson of Ocilla and printed by the Byrd Printing Company, Atlanta, in 1926. Also, that genealogist "Smada," whose real name was Patrick Adams, to whom Tifton is deeply indebted because of his many valuable articles on "Old Families of Irwin," has an article on the Gibbs family in the Tifton Gazette of March 22, 1912.

James Gibbs, born February 28, 1818, married September 19, 1841, Mahala Henderson Paulk, born August 24, 1824, daughter of Nancy Henderson Paulk. James and Mahala settled near Little River four miles from where Ty Ty now is. They reared a family and then moved to the old Jake Clements place where both died. Both are buried at Hickory Springs cemetery.

To James and Mahala Gibbs were born eight children: Ellen (born May

16, 1844; married, first, Lott Ross; second Jacob C. Clements). 2. Martha (born July 28, 1846; married John Warmack). 3. Jacob (born July 18, 1847; died 1870). 4. Catherine (born July 29, 1850; married W. E. Williams). 5. Allen (born March 5, 1853; married Sallie Warren). 6. John (born November 13, 1865; married Sallie Willis). 7. James (born July 29, 1848; married, first Polly Warren; second, Mrs. Mary Paulk, widow of Hon. George Paulk). 7. Frankie.

Of the above children James Gibbs, Jr., became Elder James Gibbs, a Primitive Baptist minister who was an influence for good in the community over a long period of years and was greatly beloved. Among his charges was Hickory Springs Primitive Baptist Church. Elder Gibbs was called "Uncle Babe Gibbs." The book on the Henderson and Whiddon families gives Elder James's wife as Mary Warren, whereas Smada says that he was twice married; first, to Polly Warren; second, to Mary Paulk, widow of George Paulk.

To Elder James Gibbs and Polly Warren were born nine children. One of these, H. F. Gibbs, married Ruby Lee Partridge. Of this union were a number of children of whom one, Ralph Laverne Gibbs, born August 4, 1917, became a pianist of exceptional ability. His promising career was cut short by his death in World War II (see sketch of Ralph Gibbs, chapter of World War soldiers, this volume).

To John and Sallie Willis Gibbs were born six children: Silas, Lonnie. Ernest, Earl, Carl, Clayton. Of these, Earl Gibbs, born April 1, 1897, has since January 1, 1941, been clerk of court of Tift County, succeeding Henry D. Webb, who succeeded Mr. Peeples, first clerk of court of Tift County. Earl Gibbs on March 20, 1918 married Stella Bowen, daughter of Isaac Stephen Bowen. They have one daughter, Sarah Bowen Gibbs, born November 24, 1920.

JOSEPH JACKSON GOLDEN

Joseph Jackson Golden was born September 18, 1868, son of Arch Golden and Abigail McClellan Golden, of near Sparks, Berrien County, Georgia. After receiving his schooling in Tifton, J. J. Golden went to Sibley where he was a planing mill foreman. In April, 1893 he returned to Tifton and became planing mill foreman at the H. H. Tift lumber mill. With him from Sibley came R. E. Hall and they shared a room at old Sadie Hotel, and continued to room together until Hall married. Hall was at the mill as sawyer at the time that Golden was foreman. (See article on R. E. H.) In Tifton, on August 11, 1897, J. J. Golden married Mamie McLeod, daughter of Daniel Washington McLeod and Katherine Parker McLeod, formerly of North Carolina. Mamie was a sister of Ben McLeod, and of Mrs. D. B. Harrell. About 1903, Mr. Golden went into the hardware business and in this continued for many years. Also he and R. E. Hall bought adjoining farms. Later Mr. Golden's farm and part of that of Mr. Hall went into the area comprised in the Tifton Airport.

On November 28, 1903 W. W. Timmons, councilman of Tifton resigned in order to be eligible to accept the nomination as mayor. J. J. Golden at the same meeting was elected to fill Mr. Timmons's unexpired term. He served on Tifton City Council in 1904 and 1905 when Timmons was mayor in 1906, 1907, and 1908 when S. M. Clyatt was mayor, from October 5, throughout 1908 when W. W. Banks succeeded Mayor Clyatt resigned. Golden was on the Tifton school board in 1904, 5 and 6. He served on the standing committee on accounts for several years, beginning in 1904, and was on various other important committees. In 1909 he was elected for a term of two years on the Tifton Sinking Fund Committee.

Few men have had so great a part in the public affairs of the city of Tifton as has Mr. Golden. A quiet, unassuming man as to manner, he has been a powerful influence for accomplishment of nearly every project for the growth and betterment of the town. In 1921 he was a member of Tifton's first city commission.

Many years ago Mr. Golden gave up the hardware business in favor of farming, in which he continues

Mrs. Golden is a gifted singer and for more than thirty years was choir director of the First Baptist Church of Tifton.

Mr. and Mrs. Golden have an only child, Josie, a skilled pianist and organist who has been organist at the Tifton Baptist Church for many years and so continues. She married J. J. Clyatt. (See sketch of Mrs. Clyatt in Who's Who, this volume.)

DR. JOHN CHARLES GOODMAN

By a Tifton Pioneer

John Charles Goodman was of English descent, his grandfather having come to the United States from England the latter part of the eighteenth century. He located in Nansemond County, Virginia, and it was there that he met and later married Miss Parthenia Barnes. He was a member of the Church of England and was a good and useful citizen. Such was the goodly heritage of this Tifton pioneer in both grandfather and father.

John Charles, the son of Barnes Goodman and Harriet Benton Goodman, was born in Gates County, North Carolina. His early education was under Martin Kellogg, an outstanding teacher of his time. Young Goodman received his Bachelor of Arts degree from the University of North Carolina, and his degree in medicine from the University of Virginia. His medical education was completed at Bellevue Hospital, New York City.

He married Miss Henrietta Ann Goodman, a distant cousin. She, too, had splendid educational advantages. After graduation from the Woman's College in Warrenton, North Carolina, she was for several years a member of the faculty of her Alma Mater.

When war between the States was declared, Dr. Goodman offered his services and served the four years as surgeon in Lee's division of the Confederate Army, the hospital base being at Richmond, Virginia. At the close of the war he returned home to resume the practice of medicine, but not in Gates County, North Carolina. He, his wife and little son, Charles Hutchins, moved across the county and state to Somerton, Nansemond County, Virginia, where they lived until they moved to Georgia in 1881. It was in Somerton the other children were born, John Hawkins, Marietta (Mrs. E. L. Vickers), Catherine Williams (Mrs. W. Marvin Thurman), James Henry (Harry), and Harriet Benton (Mrs. W. L. Harman).

When Dr. Goodman came to Georgia he and his eldest son Charles, who had just finished business school, entered the naval stores business near Alapaha in Berrien county, which business they operated for a number of years, Dr. Goodman continuing his practice of medicine.

When the Georgia Southern and Florida railroad was built, it crossed the Atlantic Coast Line at Tifton. The building of this railroad opened up a new territory in South Georgia and gave Tifton the prospect of becoming a real town instead of remaining a saw mill village as it was at that time. Dr. Goodman was far-sighted enough to see this, so in 1890 he left the turpentine farm in care of his son and moved his family to Tifton. He rented a small house next to Captain H. H. Tift's home and there the Goodmans lived the first year in Tifton.

Dr. Goodman opened an office and was soon busily engaged with his practice. In a few months he began the erection of a dwelling on the corner of what was later Second Street and Central Avenue. It was burned a few years ago, thus removing one of Tifton's earliest landmarks. During the same year the Goodman house was built, Dr. Goodman built a store on the corner of Railroad and Third Streets and in this building he opened Tifton's first drug store. Later the business was moved to the Bowen building on the corner of Second Street and Lose Avenue, this being a more suitable location for a drug store.

Dr. Goodman's two sons, Hawkins and Harry, were graduate pharmacists; the former was associated with his father until he went to Fitzgerald and there opened the first drug store in the "Colony City." Harry remained with his father.

Dr. Goodman was city physician for a number of years.

The school facilities were very limited and primitive. That part of Tifton's development was not overlooked and Dr. and Mrs. Goodman, as good pioneers, were interested in everything that meant for Tifton's good and took an active part in its civic, social and religious life. They lent their aid and cooperation in building a school system that would be a credit and a drawing card for a growing, thriving town and community. They made it a point to know the teachers, to make them feel welcome in their new surrroundings, and often entertained them in their home. Mrs. Goodman taught her daughters and prepared them for college, which was a credit to her as an educator and teacher. The three daughters completed their education at Wesleyan College, Macon, Georgia.

In the early days when Tifton was only a saw mill village, the religious need was not overlooked. In the early 80's Mr. J. J. F. Goodman, a native of this section and a local Methodist preacher organized the Tifton Methodist Church. (This Mr. Goodman was not related to Dr. Goodman.) Later a very nice little church was built on the sight of the present First Methodist Church. The pioneers were glad to find a church already functioning and this building served the other denominations for a number of years.

Dr. and Mrs. Goodman, also their sons and daughters were devout members of the Methodist Church and carried in their hearts a deep, abiding love for the church, taking an active part in its every department of work.

Mrs. Goodman was instrumental in the organization of the Woman's Missionary Society and served as president for several years. Dr. Goodman was an official in the church as long as he lived.

No finer tribute could be paid him than to say he was a friend to man and that those who loved him best were the children of the community. He believed in Tifton's future and with other splendid men that had a similar faith and vision, laid a strong and sure foundation for a town of which today's citizens are justly proud.

Dr. Goodman died January 17, 1903. He with the other pioneers can look down from the skies and say, "We did not build in vain."

CHARLES COLUMBUS GUEST

(Ida Belle Williams)

A man with a keen sense of humor, consideration for inferiors as well as equals, the hospitality of the Old South, and honesty—Charles Columbus Guest! Even in the thirties, the years of depression, the Guest home had an air of the nineties, for the C. C. genial spirit could dispel the thickest gloom.

Mr. Guest and his wife were delightful host and hostess on many occasions in Tifton. Guest pranks often added spice to the menus. One November day the dining table was loaded with the usual delicacies and substantials with proper vitamins. George Rastus, a servant in the home, grinned as he passed around luscious sweet potatoes, dripping with their natural candy and seemed to smack mentally his thick lips.

When the family and guests had finished dinner, George came in to clear the table. Alas, his grin changed to a forlorn droop of the mouth, and his step to a drag. No potatoes left! Everyone observed the dramatic disappointment. Mr. Guest finally reached his hand far enough to open a drawer of the buffet; his eyes twinkled with humor as he pulled out the hidden treasures—potatoes—and presented them to Rastus, who grinned his thanks.

Although Mr. Guest has lived longer in Tifton than anywhere else, he was born in Lowndes County, six miles from Valdosta, near Cherry Creek, April 26, 1873. When six years old, he and the rest of the family moved to Berrien County. He attended New River School, near Vanceville, three or four miles from Tifton. His father, George W. Guest, was born in Montgomery County, which is now Wheeler. His mother was Lucretia Pope. Mr. G. W. Guest, postmaster at Vanceville for several years, had a turpentine still and a store. After leaving the turpentine business, he farmed.

When six years old, little Charles Columbus felt his importance, as he tiptoed to hang up mail bags for the train that passed Vanceville. After a few years he assisted on the farm until 1890, the year of his arrival in Tifton, when he began clerking for Mr. Enoch Bowen, the merchant who sold everything from tacks to caskets.

Swift changes followed. Guest went to Americus and traveled for a furniture company, then to Tampa. In 1895 he traveled for a tobacco company. While on this job, he received from W. O. Tift and his son, Ortie, a telegram offering a position in their general store. After working with the Tifts three years, Guest accepted a position with Loree and Buck; when the latter bought the entire business, he made Guest manager of the retail store. At this time the Oakley Boarding House, where he took his meals, was a jolly spot. Judge Eve and Mr. J. L. Williams were among the boarders. One of their favorite pastimes was holding Oakley Court to try violators of the eating laws, such as the number of biscuits. Mr. Eve, who had his first experience as a judge in this court, imposed for biscuit misdemeanors a sentence of fasting. An interesting point here is the fact that Mr. Guest now lives in the house which was once the Oakley Boarding House.

Business activities ceased on November 8, 1899—ceased for the wedding bells of Guest and Minnie Maud Nicholson, of South Charleston, Ohio. Their three children are Laura, of Tifton, Nicholson, of Brunswick, and John, of Tifton. Clifford died when a baby. With his usual sense of humor, Guest frequently tossed this question to Mrs. Guest, "Do you remember that you are a pearl of great price—fifty cents?" He had bought the marriage license for fifty cents. Mrs. Guest would retort, "Remember you went a long way to spend fifty cents."

After his marriage, Mr. Guest was vice-president and general manager of the Tifton Grocery Company. While with this company he was selected as a member of the Advisory Board for Georgia of the Southern Wholesale Grocers Association, which is an organization of the wholesale grocers of thirteen Southern states. Later Tifton Grocery Company became the Central Grocery Company when Downing in Brunswick bought it. Mr. Guest traveled for this Central establishment after his experience in turpentine for the next few years. Then for eighteen years he was deputy commissioner for State Revenue Department. During this time he had the confidence and praise of the department and the people whom he contacted.

During these years Mr. and Mrs. Guest lived harmoniously until her death in 1937. Years have come and gone; Mr. Guest now is one of the oldest citizens of Tifton; adverses and sorrows have had their usual places; but nothing has effaced the Guest geniality and courage.

ROBERT EDWARD HALL

Robert Edward Hall, son of William Oscar Hall and Mary Stuckey Hall, both of Wilkinson County, Georgia, was born November 23, 1864, in Wilkinson County, where he grew up. He was of a large family of brothers and sisters: W. O. Hall, Jr., Gordon Hall, D. O., M. A., I. B., Donnie (married Floyd), Annie (married Knight), Emma (married Collins).

In April of 1893 Robert E. Hall and his friend, J. J. Golden, left Sibley,

Georgia, where Golden was planing mill foreman and Hall a sawyer and came to Tifton. They took a room together at the Hotel Sadie and next day both of them went to work at the H. H. Tift lumber mill, Golden as planing-mill foreman and Hall as sawyer. Both bought farms, and the land adjoined. They continued to room together until Hall married, December 29, 1895. His bride was Miss Claudia McDuffie (born Marion County, South Carolina, February 3, 1878) daughter of William Preston McDuffie and Mary Catherine Jones McDuffie. Mary Catherine's father was a railroad man with the S. F. and W., now the Coast Line, in the days before the Southern was built. Mary had gone with her family from South Carolina to Waycross, and after two years there had lived in Savannah for a year before coming to Tifton when she was about ten years old and before the section houses had been built at Tifton.

When Henry Tift, Tifton's founder, bought the lumber mill at Adel, Robert Hall became mill foreman of both the Tift mill at Adel and the one at Tifton. In the later capacity he continued until the Tifton mill closed in 1916.

Thereafter, Mr. Hall bought from Eddie Tift the Tift Dry Goods Store which for years had been conducted in the building now occupied by Wade-Corry Company. After operating the store for two years Hall sold to W. A. Darnell, and Mr. Hall then devoted his time to his farming interests. About this time he was chairman of the Tift County Commissioners.

In October of 1922 when W. T. Hargrett resigned as Tifton City Manager in order to accept a position with a Florida short-line railroad, R. E. Hall was elected to succeed Mr. Hargrett as city manager, and in this capacity served for many years. He was followed by George Washington Coleman.

In 1918 Mr. Hall bought from J. J. Golden the house known as the Will James home, at 215 West Sixth Street. Mr. and Mrs. Hall joyously celebrated their twenty-fifth wedding anniversary, their children and grandchildren being present at the happy occasion. Years rolled, and R. E. and Claudia looked forward to celebrating their fiftieth wedding anniversary. They often spoke of it, and the time was nearly at hand, when one day R. E., then eighty years old, said to Claudia: "I don't think I'll hold out that long. I don't feel sick, but I just haven't any strength!" Only a few weeks later, on August 2, 1945, he died, at Tifton County Hospital. The funeral was at the Hall residence, and Mr. Hall's pastor, the Reverend W. A. Kelley, pastor of the First Methodist Church of Tifton, conducted the services. Burial was in Tifton cemetery.

Mrs. Hall still makes her home in the Hall home on Sixth Street, where a son and his wife and children are with her.

To R. E. and Claudia McDuffie Hall were born the following children: R. E. Hall, Jr., of Atlanta; L. C. Hall, Donald Hall, Mrs. Henry Davis Collier, Jr., of Tifton; Mrs. Fred W. Mitchell, Columbus; John Hall, deceased, 1945.

Part of the farm which R. E. Hall bought years ago, and the adjoining farm owned by his friend, J. J. Golden, became a part of Tifton's Municipal Airport.

WESLEY THOMAS HARGRETT

Wesley Thomas Hargrett was born in Worth County, Georgia, spent his boyhood in Brooks County, and on May first, 1883 set out to learn the railroad business. Working on the old Savannah, Florida and Western, he started as a section hand drawing fifty-five cents a day. After two weeks came promotion. It was continuous.

In 1867, in Liberty County, Georgia, was born to W. J. and Louisa Edwards Warnell, a daughter, Lelia, who was baptized in 1886 by the Reverend J. G. Norris, the blind pastor of the Ludowici Baptist Church. At that church Mr. Norris on November 16, 1887, performed the marriage ceremony uniting W. T. Hargrett and Lelia Warnell.

The young couple lived at Alapaha, and before they had been married long Mr. Hargrett was made roadmaster of the division between Albany and Waycross of what is now the Coast Line. This position he took on February 22, 1888 and held for twenty-one years.

When the Hargretts had been married but three years they came from Alapaha to Tifton where W. T. purchased from H. H. Tift, Tifton's founder, Lot No. 1. Block 5, the first lot sold after the plat for the town of Tifton was drawn and lots were put on the market. The house which he built on that lot in 1890 and occupied for many years is still standing next to Doolittle's filling station to which position it was moved from its original site, that now occupied by the Doolittle Station. It was in a grove of virgin growth pines, and between it and the Tift home were only three other buildings: the church, which stood where the post office now is; the C. W. Fulwood residence, which was where the Peterson home now is; and, where the other filling station is, across from Lankford Manor, a house occupied by the young widower physician, Dr. Arch McRae. Leila's sister, Pauline, came over from Ludowici to visit Lelia. She and Dr. McCrea met, and later they were wed and Pauline moved into the house across the road from her sister.

Mrs. Hargrett was the first treasurer of the Woman's Missionary Society, organized in 1891, in February, in Bessie Tift's parlor where Dr. C. M. Irwin, the Baptist supply pastor, met with the ladies and helped with the organization.

After being roadmaster, Mr. Hargrett became superintendent of the Gulf Line Railroad between Hawkinsville and Camilla.

Mr. Hargrett on March 2, 1891, was appointed a tax assessor of Tifton, the other assessors serving with him being W. O. Tift and I. W. Bowen. On January 2, 1893 Hargrett entered upon his duties as newly elected alderman, J. C. Goodman and J. A. McCrea being elected at the same time for two years. W. H. Love was mayor. Thereafter Mr. Hargrett served on many committees and in various capacities on City Council for many years. In January, 1921, he became Tifton's first City Manager which office he held until October, 1922, when he resigned to go to Live Oak, Florida, from which place he operated the Ocilla-Southern Railroad, of which he had been appointed receiver the previous spring. Later the Hargretts returned to Tifton.

After the death of John H. Powell, of Jacksonville, president of the Live

Oak, Perry and Gulf Railroad, W. T. Hargrett was made president of that road. In January, 1929, the road changed hands and he became vice-president, which position he held until he retired about two years prior to his death.

Mr. Hargrett attained the remarkable record of not losing a day's salary in fifty-three years, and of not losing but twelve days in fifty-eight years.

The Hargretts moved from the Love Avenue house and lived for many years on Ridge Avenue in Tifton, where they celebrated their golden wedding anniversary with a large and brilliant reception, and also lived to celebrate happily, though more quietly, several other anniversaries, before Mrs. Hargrett died in 1944. Mr. Hargrett missed her greatly and did not stay on much longer. He died in 1945. Both are buried in Tifton cemetery.

Children of W. T. and Lelia Warnell Hargrett are: Mrs. J. C. Rousseau, of Macon; Mrs. Joe Medford, of Jacksonville, Florida; Clyde W., of Atlanta; Wesley, of Miami; Felix, of New York City; Lester, of Washington, D. C.; Robert, of Tifton; Charles, of Norfolk, Virginia.

WILLARD LUTHER HARMAN

Willard Luther Harman was born in Meriwether County, Georgia, August 23, 1863. He was one of eight children of Luther M. and Martha Williams Harman, his brothers and sisters being: James H. Harman of Odessadale; R. Mr. Harman, of Unadilla; D. W. Harman, of Odessadale; Mrs. Mattie Harman Wisdom, of Chipley; Mrs. Katherine Watson, Mrs. Mollie Watson, and Mrs. Emma Watson, all of Odessadale. Of these, only one, D. W. Harman, survived W. L. Harman who died at his Tifton home, formerly the Goodman home on the southeast corner of West Sixth Street and College Avenue, on Friday morning at 7:45, December 28, 1934. His funeral was at the Tifton Methodist Church and burial was in Tifton Cemetery.

W. L. Harman graduated with the A.B. degree from Emory College, Oxford, and thereafter taught school at Washington, Georgia, and at Chipley, Georgia, where he married Miss Irene Floyd, of Chipley, in June 1892. Of this union were two children both of whom died in infancy.

In 1898 Professor Harman came from Chipley to Tifton where he headed the Tifton Academy. He returned to Chipley but later again came to Tifton, in 1907. For a time he was connected with the office of H. H. Tift and later engaged in farming and other business.

On June 10, 1908 Professor Harman married a widow, Mrs. Harriet Goodman Evans, daughter of Tifton's pioneer physician, Dr. Charles Goodman (q.v. this book). Of this union were three sons, Charles Goodman, Eugene, who died in infancy, and Allen.

Professor Harman was a popular and highly esteemed educator and he was elected superintendent of Tift County Schools. He was reelected but his health began to fail and about 1933 he was injured in an automobile accident. Later he became ill and developed pneumonia which was fatal.

It was said that if all the school books which Professor Harman had bought for those who could not afford them for themselves could be placed in a pile they would have made a huge and fitting monument to his memory. The Tifton Gazette editorially paid to him high tribute.

Of a Christian family W. L. Harman joined the Methodist Church early in life, and served in nearly all the official capacities of the church. For many years he was a steward of the Tifton Methodist Church, and he was a Valdosta District Steward. He was for a time superintendent of the First Methodist Sunday School of Tifton. He was a Mason and a Shriner.

WILLIAM HARTRIDGE HENDRICKS

William Hartridge Hendricks, son of Robert and Nancy Parrish Hendricks, was born at Bloys, Bulloch County, Georgia, August 17, 1873. The Hendricks family, of English descent, had come to South Carolina soon after the Revolution and thence one member came to Bulloch County, Georgia where Robert was born and became a farmer of substantial means.

Young William Hartridge spent his early years on his father's Bulloch County farm, and attended the Bulloch county schools. Even as a lad he was interested in biology and chemistry, and in 1894 he entered the School of Physicians and Surgeons, at St. Louis, from which he graduated with honors in 1897.

Immediately after graduation from medical school, Dr. Hendricks began practicing medicine at Lenox, Georgia, whence, he came to Tifton, about 1900; because even before moving to Tifton he had business interests here.

On December 21, 1898, at Ty Ty, Dr. Hendricks was married to Lelia May Dell, daughter of Caple Glenn Dell and Margaret Thompson Dell. The marriage was at the home of the bride's grandmother, Mrs. Mary Speer Thompson. The bride had been born near Americus, in Sumter County, May 20, 1875.

In Tifton Dr. Hendricks soon established a large practice and he was highly esteemed by a wide circle of friends. Dr. Nichols Peterson, Dr. Hendricks established Tifton's first hospital. This was first housed on the second floor of a building which formerly stood where Brooks Drug Store now is. Later the hospital was moved to a house on Central Avenue next door to the old Dr. George Smith residence. Still later the hospital was moved to the old Shepherd home, sometimes called the Johns home, on Tifton Heights. The operating room in the Tift County Hospital is dedicated to Dr. Hendricks and he is, in 1946, chief of staff of Tift County Hospital.

In addition to his medical profession, Dr. Hendricks had various business interests. He engaged in naval stores and agriculture, and he was a director and vice-president of the National Bank of Tifton.

Also, Dr. Hendricks has engaged in politics and he has never been defeated for any office for which he has run. On December 5, 1906 he was elected to serve on Tifton City Council and served one term. Later he served for one term on the Board of Education. In 1907 and 1908 he was in the General Assembly of the Georgia Legislature and in 1914 he was mayor of Tifton, following W. W. Banks. 1915 to 1917 he was in the Georgia Senate, immediately prior to leaving for army service in World War I.

The Hendricks lived formerly on North Park Avenue in the house now the Sam Lassiter residence, but later purchased and moved into the Love Avenue house built by W. O. Tift. There Mrs. Hendricks died March 19, 1946. There Dr. Hendricks and his daughter, Mrs. Louise Stamps, and his pretty granddaughter continue to make their home.

Mrs. Hendricks was a woman of Christian character and was possessed of much sweetness of personality. To her and Dr. Hendricks were born five children; a son, who died in infancy; a daughter, Vera, also deceased; a daughter, Margaret Glenn (Mrs. Thomas Nelson Ricks, of Mount Olive, North Carolina); a daughter, Louise (Mrs. James Allen Stamps, of Tifton); a daughter, named for her father, "Billie," Willie Hartridge (Mrs. Albert Horton Ellis, of Rossville, Ga.).

JOHN LEWIS HERRING

John Lewis Herring, son of William Jasper and Rebecca Paul Herring, was born December 8, 1866, at Albany, Georgia, and moved with his parents to Isabella, in Worth County, when he was about one year old.

At Isabella William farmed and kept a store and John Lewis attended school and grew up in the hard days of Reconstruction. Early he loved books and read all he could procure. Grown, he secured work in newspaper offices at Ty Ty and at Isabella, and intermittently engaged in the mercantile business with his father.

When twenty years old, John Lewis Herring, on December 22, 1886, married Martha Susan Greene, daughter of John Burwell Greene of near Tifton. John took his bride to his parents' home in Isabella, and there they began housekeeping. John continued in the mercantile business with his father in Isabella for eight years.

About 1894 John Lewis Herring came to Tifton where Benjamin T. Allen had started a newspaper, The Tifton Gazette. After being with The Tifton Gazette for several years Herring was with Stovall on the Tampa Morning News for a few months, but thereafter accepted an offer of a position again on the Tifton Gazette. A few years later he purchased from Briggs Carson a controlling interest in the Gazette.

In 1912 Mr. Herring while continuing to operate the Gazette established a connection with the Savannah Morning News. He at this time began writing and sending back to the Gazette his highly interesting and valuable "Saturday Night Sketches," which were published in book form in 1918.

On September 14, 1914 John Lewis established the Daily Tifton Gazette, the only daily paper in the state in a town the size of Tifton. This daily has successfully continued.

John Herring, when young, joined the Methodist Church and he was a faithful member of the Tifton Methodist Church.

Mr. Herring was untiring in his efforts to secure the formation of Tift County from territory carved out of portions of Worth and Berrien, and to have Tifton as the county seat. This was accomplished on August 17, 1905.

In his professional field many honors came to John L. Herring. (See article on "Wire Grass Journalism," this book.)

After the Wilson election the citizens of Tifton presented John L. with a suit of clothes, in appreciation of his handling of election returns. He was deeply touched, and said that when came his time to die he wished to be buried in the suit.

About the close of World War I the men of Tifton, and the women of the Twentieth Century Library Club, separately and unknown to each other, presented him with loving cups.

Mr. Herring was secretary or president of numerous Tifton organizations. He loved and, in 1922, was president of the Kiwanis Club. On Friday, October 5, 1923 the Kiwanis Club was holding a Ladies' Night entertainment at the college. Mr. Herring, having ascertained that all arrangements were satisfactorily carried out, was in happy mood and was heading the receiving line when he was suddenly stricken with paralysis. Death followed, on Saturday night.

Mr. Herring's request about the well loved old suit was remembered and carried out. A hundred and fifty cars followed his body from the Methodist Church, where his funeral was held, to the Tifton cemetery, where he rests beneath a lone pine tree.

In the same issue of the Tifton Daily Gazette which carried its founder's obituary was printed on the editorial page: "The Boys Will Carry On." They have carried on, and well; and ably and valiantly have marched with them dear Miss Leola Greene, and Peggy Herring Coleman, and of late, Mrs. Bob Herring.

The worker, in God's time, finds rest; but the good work goes on.

At the southwest entrance of beautiful Fulwood Park, Tifton, stands a granite memorial erected in token of the love and esteem in which John L. Herring was held by his fellow citizens.

CHARLTON BEACHAM HOLMES

Charlton Beacham Holmes, son of James Russell Holmes and Allie Hester Holmes, of the Dublin community, was born about five miles from Dublin, Georgia, on May 24, 1878. He received his early education in the schools near Dublin and later attended the Valdosta High School while living in Valdosta with his brother, J. F. Holmes.

Upon arrival in Tifton in 1900 the youthful C. B. Holmes at once began a drink bottling business. At first he bottled soda water, and later, when Coca-Cola was on the market, he began bottling Coca-Cola. In this business he continued until his death in Tifton in April. 1947.

On June 17, 1903, Charlton Beacham Holmes married Cora Dickert, daughter of Charles Paschal Dickert and Lucy Suber Dickert, then of Tifton, but previously of Newberry, South Carolina. Miss Dickert had come to Tifton from Dawson, in 1901.

To Mr. and Mrs. Holmes were born five children.

During World War II C. B. Holmes donated to the Red Cross use of an upper room in the Coca-Cola building and this was used as a Red Cross Sewing Room during the war period.

BAILUS CHAMPION HUTCHINSON

Bailus Champion Hutchinson, born September 12, 1846, in Gwinnett County, Georgia, near Stone Mountain, was son of Mr. and Mrs. Henry G. Hutchinson, with whom he, when a lad of twelve years, came down an old trail from Atlanta, following the route now known as the National Highway, and, in 1848, settled in a place in the pine forest with no near neighbors, in the River Bend section about four miles west of what is now Adel.

When not yet twenty Bailus volunteered for service in the Confederate Army, in April, 1864, at Nashville. He served in the army for a year and five days, and was under General Johnston at Greensboro, North Carolina at the close of the war. He drew one dollar and twenty-five cents and walked from North Carolina to Val d' Osta, now called Valdosta.

On June 28, 1868 Bailus C. Hutchinson married seventeen-year-old Nancy Glenny McKinney (born November 5, 1851, in Berrien County), daughter of Isom McKinney. Bailus and Nancy lived for seven years in the River Bend section of Berrien County and they then moved to that part of Irwin County which is now Tift County to a place four miles northwest of Tifton where they continued to make their home throughout the lifetime of Bailus who died however, at the home of his daughter, Mrs. Will Sutton, Monday, september 22, 1930, two weeks after suffering a stroke of paralysis.

For forty years Bailus Hutchinson had been a member of Zion Hope Church and there his funeral was held September 23, 1930. Burial was in Zion Hope cemetery. Nancy died in 1932.

To Bailus C. and Nancy McKinney Hutchinson were born seven children, all of whom survived both parents. They were: A. A., Lenora (Mrs. J. P. Fletcher), John Henry, William B., Arthur, James (May 12, 1878-June 13, 1946), P. L., Mrs. Will Sutton, all of whom, except Mrs. Fletcher, lived in Tift County at the time of their father's death. Mrs. Fletcher lived then in Miami, but later moved to Mystic, Georgia.

John Henry Hutchinson was Tift County's first tax collector and in that capacity served for many years.

Arthur James was called "Uncle Hutch" and was loved and revered because of his honest and upright character and his cheerful disposition. "Uncle Hutch" was a farmer and later for a number of years operated a small store where the Corner Grocery now is. The Masons were in charge of graveside rites in Zion Hope cemetery where he was buried following services in Zion Hope Church.

JOHN HENRY HUTCHINSON
First Tift County Tax Collector

Tift County's first tax collector was John Henry Hutchinson. He announced as a candidate for office on September 8, 1905, soon after the new county was created by act of Legislature, August 16, 1905.

J. H. Hutchinson was a charter member of the Country Club at Gun Lake. Also, he was prominent in the activities of the Tift County Singing Convention, organized about 1913. Often he would lead the singing. Mr. Hutchinson still makes his home in Tift County, not far from Tifton, and, in this 1947, comes frequently to Tifton on business, or to see his friends. He is a Mason, a member of the Tifton lodge, and the only living officer of the original Tift County group.

J. L. JAY, JR.

J. L. Jay was a contractor here in the early days of the twentieth century.

He and his son, J. L., Jr., and another son went first to Fitzgerald from Arlington, and then the two J. L.'s came from Fitzgerald to Tifton. J. L., Sr., did not remain here long.

J. L. Jay, Jr., and his wife, who was an excellent pianist, moved to Tifton and bought and lived in the house a 413 North Park Avenue, now occupied by Miss Maude Bryant. The Jays had two small sons, Wibbie and Wister.

J. L. Jay, Jr., was cashier of the Tifton and Northeastern Railroad until the road was sold, and thereafter he operated Jay's Cotton Warehouse. Also he conducted a mercantile business and his ads in the Gazette of May, 1904 pictured a large Blue Jay, and advertised J. L. Jay believes in oats and hay, and sells plano, the best, lightest, and simplest harvesting machine made— especially adapted for use of the Southern farmer. He also was interested in wool, and the wool growers of the community brought their wool to his warehouse, where buyers from Savannah and as far away as Philadelphia came to bid for the wool in July of 1904.

Mrs. Jay composed "The Tifton March," dedicated to H. H. Tift, and played it at the Tifton fair. It occasioned a pleasureable and gratifying stir in the community.

Mrs. Badger Murrow, who lived in the large house across the street from the Jays, was organist at the Tifton First Baptist Church, but if she had to be absent, Mrs. Jay would play. Mr. Jay sang in the Baptist choir. Also, he was active in the work of the schurch and especially of the Sunday School. In those days the Sunday School picnics were annual affairs participated in by Sunday Schools of all denominations, and looked forward to eagerly as one of the joyous occasions of the year. In 1906 the picnic was held at Red Bluff on the Ocmulgee. "The picnic crowd went as scheduled. The weather was ideal. There was lemonade and baskets aplenty. The water was so clear fish could be seen fifteen feet below the surface but would not be caught." A special train carried the crowd from Tifton at eight in the morning and brought them back at seven in the evening. The Tifton Band, under F. C. Dynes furnished music. The public was warned by an announcement in the Gazette, by R. H. Kelley, Chairman General Committee: "I wish to state that no whiskey, beer, or disorderly persons are wanted. We want a sober crowd and a good day." The various committees in charge were composed of many of the town's most prominent citizens, and on the Basket Committee, "to receive and take charge of the baskets at train, en route, and at grounds" were J. H. Hillhouse, Briggs Carson, Harry Kent, J. L. Jay, Jr.

The Jays moved from Tifton to Arlington where one of the Jays inherited a hotel.

KATHERINE TIFT JONES

Katherine Stark Tift, daughter of William Orville Tift and Eliza Catherine Mallory Tift, was reared in Tifton, and attended the Lucy Cobb Institute, Athens. She married Frederick H. Jones and moved to Pittsburgh, Pennsylvania. Of this union are three children, F. H., Jr., Elizabeth Mallory Jones Traska, and Sarah Jones Gridley.

As a reader Mrs. Jones has won renown, and she also is well known as a radio speaker. She was for many years with the National Broadcasting Company, and with the Mutual Network. In 1933 she was sent to Europe by R. H. Macy and Company to make the first Trans-Atlantic broadcast ever made by a commercial house from London, Paris and Berlin. She has given recitals in London, Paris, and across the continent of America.

Several years ago Mrs. Jones moved back to Tifton where she lives next door to her childhood home.

GEORGE WASHINGTON JULIAN

George Washington Julian, born in Forsyth County, Georgia, near Cummings, December 10, 1857, graduated from the Southern Medical College at Atlanta in 1887, practiced first at Pearson, Georgia, where he remained ten years, and, in 1897, came to Tifton where he practiced medicine until his death.

Dr. Julian, in addition to being a physician, was a member of the firm of Julian, Love and Buck, a wholesale grocery and feed business, of Tifton. His partners in this were E. A. Buck and Tifton's first mayor, W. H. Love, whose wife was a relative of Dr. Julian's wife, both of them having been Kirklands before marriage.

Dr. Julian married a widow, Mrs. Laura E. Kirkland Hargraves, and of this union were three children, Stella, Lelia, and George W., Jr.

Stella married Clinton Shingler, of Ashburn, of that Shingler family which with John S. Betts, were the founders of Ashburn. Stella's daughter, Betty, married Herman, only son of Eugene Talmadge, Governor of Georgia.

Lelia Julian married Allen Garden of Fitzgerald. George Julian, Jr., married and lives in Tifton at the Julian home at the northwest corner of Central Avenue at Second Street. This home was bought by Dr. Julian from Captain John A. Phillips who built it and lived in it after he moved from the Hotel Sadie which he built and owned. At this home Dr. Julian lived until his death there on Tuesday morning, May 29, 1928, at 10:30 o'clock. The funeral, from the home, was conducted by Dr. W. L. Pickard, who had been Dr. Julian's friend for more than thirty years; the

Reverend George C. Gibson, who was pastor of the Tifton First Baptist Church, of which Dr. Julian was a member; and the Reverend J. H. House, pastor of the Tifton Methodist Church. Burial was in Tifton cemetery. Numerous members of the Shingler and Kirkland families were present. Dr. Julian had no living relatives other than his immediate family.

Mrs. Julian, who was born February 1, 1864, died November 13, 1934. She is buried in the Tifton cemetery.

Mrs. Julian had, by her first marriage, a son, Colonel L. A. Hargraves, of Pearson.

THE KENT FAMILY

The Kent family moved into this section of Georgia now known as Tift County in 1894, coming from Pittsburgh, Pennsylvania. Judge Harry Kent, the head of the family, was born in Staffordshire, England, July 27, 1856. In early manhood he married Miss Mary Morris of the same city and remained there, following the occupation of coal mining, until 1881 when they came to America. In 1893 he became interested in some literature advertising this section. In 1894 Mr. and Mrs. Kent and seven children, William, Heber, Joseph, Morris, Frances, Effie and Milton, moved to Tifton where Mr. Kent engaged in fruit farming. Their eighth child, Charles Almer, was born in Tifton.

In 1895 Mr. Kent and son, Joseph Kent, opened a cotton and fertilizer warehouse where the Owens Grocery Company now stands. In 1897 they bought the J. M. Paulk Furniture Store and established a furniture business under the name of H. Kent and Son. This business now under the name of Kent's Furniture and Music Store, lays claim to being the oldest retail business in Tifton, being in 1946 forty-nine years old.

In 1921 the business was bought by Milton U. Kent and Charles Almer Kent, the two younger sons. It is operated today by Milton U. Kent and Mrs. C. A. Kent, widow of the late C. A. Kent who died October 11, 1944. In future years Charles A. Kent, Jr., and Thomas Milton Kent intend to carry on the business as successfully as their forefathers in continuing growth.

During Mr. Kent's residence here he was active in civic and business affairs until his death on May 25th, 1927. He was interested in a number of business enterprises and under his direction in the early days of Tifton, with the able assistance of his oldest son, Will, the Kents became famous throughout this section as draymen. Kent's dray and their fine horses were conspicuous on the streets of Tifton in the city's early days. Later they operated the first long distance truck hauling line in the state. Mr. Kent was for many years Justice of the Peace and ex-officio Justice of the Peace for this district, from which office he obtained the title of Judge. He took an active interest in civic, religious, and political affairs. He became a booster for Tifton and this section soon after moving here, and was prominently identified with every forward movement of the city and section.

Joining the Methodist Church during their youth in England, Mr. and Mrs. Kent remained staunch, faithful and true members until death. They were moving spirits in erection of the present Methodist Church building in Tifton, giving liberally of their time and means. Mr. Kent served as an official, either steward or trustee, for many years. The Harry Kent Bible Class was so called in his memory.

Mr. Kent, as head of the Kent family in this section, made the name Kent stand for something that his boys and his boys' boys will have to rise early and work late to live up to. Because of the characteristics for which he was noted, the name of Kent became a household word in this section which stands for energy, economy and success.

Joseph Kent, the third son is prominently known throughout the state in business circles, being an outstanding business man. He assisted in organizing The Farmers Bank of Tifton and served as its first president. As director of the War Bond sales during World War II he carried the County far over the top in all drives. He is prominently known for his civic and patriotic spirit.

Judge Kent's children still living in Tifton are William, Heber, Joseph and Milton.

BELLE WILLINGHAM LAWRENCE

Belle's story is brief; and only those who knew her can conceive of her sweetness, her radiance, her charm. Belle captivated all—young, middle-aged, and old, but especially the children—and the men. It is said that she had over a hundred offers of marriage.

Belle Willingham, daughter of Thomas Henry Willingham and Cecilia Baynard Willingham, was born at the Yancey Place, near Albany, July 18, 1871. She entered Monroe Female College, Forsyth, Georgia, and there she was first honor graduate, and was chosen valedictorian; but on the day before graduation she went driving, the horses ran away, she was thrown from the vehicle, her foot caught in the reins, and she was dragged. She was seriously injured internally so that she was never robust again though her beauty was unimpaired.

After graduation Belle, whose father had died, became a member of the H. H. Tift household in Tifton, Belle being a younger sister of Bessie, Mrs. H. H. Tift. Belle was active in the social life of the town's early days. She was a leader among the young people of the First Baptist Church, and, for a time, she taught elocution; for brown-eyed, music-voiced Belle was a gifted elocutionist. She and her pupils would stage delightful programs in Tifton's opera hall, a large hall over what is now Corry's store but then was the Tift Dry Goods Store.

Belle visited widely—in New York, Pennsylvania, Connecticut, Virginia, and in many places in Georgia. Wherever she went she was immediately a favorite; and her wardrobe was fit for a princess. Many of her most beautiful gowns were not those New York-bought, but were the ones skilfully fashioned by Mrs. Annie Bennett's deft fingers.

On July 17, 1904, Belle Willingham married William Lawrence, a gifted violinist of New York City, the ceremony being performed in Stonington, Connecticut. After a honeymoon spent in a fashionable New York hotel, the Lawrences came to Tifton where they made their home at 606 Love Avenue, which was freshly painted inside and out, and was beautifully furnished. The matter of furnishing the house and moving in occasioned much pleasurable excitement, not only to Belle and Will, but also to all of Belle's numerous Tifton relatives.

To William and Belle Lawrence were born two children, Cecilia, and William Lawrence, Jr. Belle loved them dearly, but her health was utterly broken and shortly after little Will's birth, Belle died of cancer on April 5, 1912, at the Piedmont Hospital, Atlanta. Burial was on the Pickard lot, Albany, Georgia.

Belle's young children were reared by her sister, Bessie Tift. Will Lawrence lived many years. He died in Orlando, Florida, where he is buried.

WILLARD HERSCHEL LOVE

Love Avenue, Tifton, was named for Tifton's first mayor, Willard Herschel Love. Born October 23, 1856, at Eden, Effingham County, Georgia, near Savannah, he was son of Dr. Love whose forebears had come from England to North Carolina. Dr. Love spent his latter years in Folkston and is buried at Fort Valley.

Willard as a youth went to Kirkland, Georgia, where he was a telegrapher. There he met pretty, dainty, blond Absey Jane Kirkland, daughter of Mathew Henry Kirkland and Mary Jane Bailey Kirkland, and of the Kirkland family for which the town was named. The robust young giant with the bluest of eyes and the fragile, blue-eyed Absey fell very much in love. On December 5, 1878 they were wed at the Kirkland home of Absey's father.

The youthful Loves made their home in Kirkland and there were born to them three children, Henry, named for his grandfather Kirkland; Claude, and Mary.

In 1887 the Loves moved to Tifton. Mr. Love owned two brick buildings on Central Avenue Extension, now Railroad Street, between Third and Fifth Streets. While their beautiful, large dwelling on Love Avenue, at the northwest corner of Second Street was being completed, the Love family occupied quarters over the Love's grain and feed store. When the new home was finished, they moved in. It was a handsome house and one of the first large homes built on Love Avenue. Mr. Love later sold it and it became the Regent Hotel.

After Tifton was incorporated, December 29, 1890, W. H. Love became the town's first mayor. The first Council meeting was held January 9, 1891, and Mr. Love continued in office from then until March 6, 1893 (at which time his resignation was accepted. He was followed by Columbus Wesley Fulwood who took office May 1, 1893).

Mrs. Love was a near kinswoman of Dr. George Julian's wife, both of them being Kirklands. Dr. Julian, W. H. Love and E. A. Buck formed in Tifton a business company known as Julian, Love and Buck, a wholesale grocery and feed firm. Later Julian was not connected with the firm but it continued as Love and Buck, which, in 1895, opened in connection with the business a private banking house, Tifton's first bank. Julian, Love and Buck was the firm which now is the Downing Company.

After selling the large Love Avenue home, Mr. Love built for his family a pleasant residence on the Heights where they continued to live until his death, which occurred in Waycross, where he had gone on business for the Atlantic Coast Line Railroad, with which he was at that time connected as claim agent. He died in May, 1904. Burial was in Fort Valley.

Both Mr. and Mrs. Love were members of the Tifton Methodist Church. Mrs. Love later joined the Wesleyan Methodist Church, and after this became deeply devout. A kindly woman, sweet tempered and cheerful, dainty and pretty, Absey was skilled in the household arts of cookery and sewing.

Soon after Mayor Love's death, Absey moved from Tifton to Waycross to be with her son, Henry (who there had a position with the A. C. L.). Later she moved to Douglas, Georgia, where she died of pneumonia, December 26, 1929. She was survived by all three of her children.

Henry Love married, March 23, 1913, Lucile Ponder, born in Wadley, Jefferson County, Georgia, May 19, 1892. Issue: Ruth (Mrs. James A. Duke), Willard Henry, Eva (Mrs. W. R. Brown), Arthur, Olin.

Claude Love, in 1912, married Alice Alexander, of Nashville, Georgia. Issue: Claude, Jr., and Morris.

Mary Love married Thomas Tucker (died 1918) of Ocilla. No issue. She lives at Valdosta.

JOHN THOMAS MATHIS

John Thomas Mathis, son of John Sidney Mathis and Matilda Raymond Mathis, was born December 16, 1875, in Moultrie, Georgia, where he spent his early life. Thence he moved to Smithville and thence to Sumner.

When a young man Mathis came to Tifton where, in 1901, he conducted a business for the firm of Carter and Dorough, dealers in buggies and fine musical instruments, organs and pianos. Mr. Mathis loved music and took more pleasure in the musical instruments than in the vehicles. However, in 1904, he became manager of the Henderson-Cranford Buggy Company which opened a repository in the Carter and Dorough warehouse.

J. T. Mathis, in July of 1904, in company with E. E. Youmans and S. A. Youmans, both of Tifton, attended the St. Louis Exposition. Mathis married Sarah Lee Youmans, daughter of E. E., and sister of S. A. Youmans.

In 1904, after the W. W. Timmons residence burned, Mr. Timmons cut up his 100 by 200 foot lot into eight lots which sold for a total of $10,000.00. Mathis bought one of them.

That same year Mathis became interested in city politics and on December 17, was elected to serve on the Tifton City council, beginning his term of office on January 2, 1905, when W. W. Timmons was mayor. In 1905 he was on the standing committees on Books and Accounts, and on Finance, H. H. Tift and E. P. Bowen being the other members of the latter committee. Mathis was mayor pro tem. during 1905 and 1906. Also, Mathis was interested in fraternal orders. During the third week in May, 1905, he represented the Tifton Lodge of the Knights of Pythias at the State Grand Lodge meetiny in Macon, and the following week he was representative of Tifton Lodge No. 122, Independent Order of Odd Fellows, at the State Grand Lodge which met in Savannah.

Mr. Mathis was chairman of the building committee for the new edifice which the Tifton First Baptist Church erected on Love Avenue at Fourth Street.

In September, 1906, J. T. Mathis, W. T. Hargrett and Leon A. Hargreaves were appointed a committee to report to City Council respecting a plan for numbering houses and erecting street signs preparatory to establishment of free mail delivery in Tifton. As mayor pro tem. he presided over the meeting, September 21, at which this report was adopted. George Campbell was granted the permit to do the house numbering. In 1906 J. T. Mathis, J. J. Golden and S. G. Slack composed the Tifton City Council's standing committee on accounts.

In 1907 John Mathis moved from Tifton to Valdosta where he and his brother-in-law, S. A. Youmans, opened their own musical instrument house. Later Mathis bought out Youmans, who returned to Tifton, and Mathis continued to conduct the firm, Mathis and Youmans, of which he was president, until his death.

After his death, in 1943, Mr. Mathis's widow, Sarah Lee Youmans Mathis, gave, in his memory, his books to the Valdosta Carnegie Library; and to the Valdosta First Baptist Church she presented Cathedral and organ chimes in memory of him who all his life loved music.

John A. and Sarah Lee Youmans Mathis had two daughters, Edith (Mrs. J. R. Wiggins) and Neva Ella (Mrs. H. Y. Tillman, Jr.), both of Valdosta. Edith plays the piano. Neva won first place in a four-state violin contest.

DR. JOHN ARCH McCREA 1849-1926—Contributed

On New Year's morning 1881 Little River was swollen and ice crackled along its banks. Two young men swam their horses through the torrent to receive Berrien County's welcome of morning sunlight on nature's display of icicles in a wild, rugged forest. They were John Arch McCrea and his brother Andrew Jackson McCrea. This same day they reached Brookfield where they rented a room at the home of the elder Bowens, paying $18.00 per month. They had spent the night of New Year's Eve in the "shed" room of the Gibbs family, about three miles east of Ty Ty, traveling all the way from Sumter County, their former home, on horseback, to settle down and begin a new life in Brookfield, Berrien County.

John Arch McCrea was born at Plains, Georgia, near Americus in 1849 and came from a line of distinguished Scottish forebears, some of whom sailing from Edinburgh, landed at Wilmington, North Carolina, between 1763 and 1775, while others settled in Ontario, Canada.

As one with a vision this young John McCrea, originally spelled "Mac-Crea" by his Scottish ancestors, worked alternately among the pioneer folk and attended the Atlanta Medical College (now Emory University) until in 1885 he received a degree of Doctor of Medicine. Fittingly its salutation read, "To the Friends and Maintainers of the Arts, Literature and the Sciences be it therefore known that—". Later he was made a member of the Georgia Eclectic Medical College of Physicians and Surgeons.

Dr. McCrea's first patient lay in the deep woods. A turpentiner's axe had bounced from a tree trunk and chipped out a section of the skull. The young doctor adroitly shaved the hair from the fragment, cleansed the wound, replaced the dislocated piece, and sewed the wound neatly. The patient recovered to bear witness to the new doctor's skill.

In 1887 Dr. McCrea married Miss Katherine Rhodes, eldest daughter of Mr. and Mrs. Aaron Rhodes of Brookfield, prominent pioneers of that section, and to them was born a daughter. The lovely young mother lived for only a short while and was buried in the old family cemetery, Bethesda, between Tifton and Brookfield.

After leaving Brookfield, Dr. McCrea moved up to the promising saw mill community of Tifton. The Theory of Lister (antisepsis) startled the medical world about this time, and though many doctors refused to accept it, Dr. McCrea eagerly accepted and championed it with amazing results.

Life was tough for this pioneer physician. No bridges spanned the streams, few roads existed, and much of his travel was through trackless forest and wild streams. His medicine and surgical instruments were carried in saddle bags. By night, by day, he moved among the hardy folk where, amidst death, there was life.

In March 1892 he married Miss Pauline Warnell, daughter of Jordan Warnell (of J. E. B. Stuart's Cavalry) and Louisa Edwards Warnerr, of Ludowici in Liberty County. To them were born two daughters and five sons. The second daughter Pearl died in infancy. When he first came to Tifton, Dr. McCrea lived over a store about where Brooks's Drug Store is now located, but the family home built later was on the corner of Love Avenue and 4th Street. It was the first ceiled residence in Tifton and was looked upon at that time as the "showplace" of the little community.

From saddle bags to a red wheeled buggy drawn by a beautiful white Arabian horse, Dr. McCrea progressed as Tifton grew in size and importance. The countryside knew to hail the physician when they saw him approaching.

The doctor became well known in the field of sports, for this was his favorite diversion. He was one of the best quail shots in the county and possessed one of the finest collections of antlers. He established and organized the Ferry Lake Fishing Club, becoming its first president. He was the first president of the Homasassa Fishing Club which annually visited the club in Florida by special train. On one such trip some members wired ahead that the president was coming, whereupon he was forced to speak from the rear platform of the train to the good-natured crowd. Although he was a man of strong character and quiet manner he would at times display quite a sense of humor when talking to his friends of his hunting and fishing experiences along the Alapaha River.

As the buggy replaced the saddle bags, so the automobile replaced the horse and the doctor advanced with the march of progress, inspiring many young men in their quest for knowledge. Dr. McCrea was a member and regular attendant of the Tifton Methodist Church, and he was a Mason in good standing.

While working beyond the strength and endurance of his age to meet the influenza epidemic of the first World War, he was himself mortally stricken. The news of his death March 24, 1926 brought sorrow to hundreds of homes of the older residents throughout this section. After forty-five years of service to his community as its beloved first physician his hands were stilled. Dr. McCrea of Tifton was buried at Oak Ride Cemetery on the beautiful hill overlooking the town. The doctors and Masons of the city formed an honorary escort to the grave.

On the battlefield of Flanders in 1918 another Dr. John A. McCrea wrote, ". . . To you, from failing hands we throw the torch. Be yours to hold it high. If you break faith with us who die, we shall not sleep, . . . "

We quote in part from the following tribute to him which appeared in the Tifton Gazette of March 25, 1926: "He was in truth a family physician of the old school; and he was ever at the call of those in pain or suffering, never thinking if the bill would be paid, but ever willing to place his skill and knowledge at the command of those who required his services. Tifton loses not only its oldest resident and first physician, but one of its most highly esteemed, loved, and respected citizens in the death of Dr. McCrea."

At the Tift County Hospital there is a room dedicated to Dr. McCrea's memory which contains several valuable instruments presented to the hospital by members of the doctor's family.

Mrs. McCrea, at the age of 77 resides at her home on Love Avenue. She is a woman of keen intellect and great force of character.

Dr. McCrea lost not a patient during the influenza epidemic of 1918-19.

In answer to an inquiry as to his success in this field of medicine he replied that he treated his patients as though they had malaria, giving them quinine, being at the same time extremely careful that they had no relapses.

This treatment appears to have been further justified in later years by the Journal of Infectious Diseases of the University of Chicago Press in their article October 1946 "Effect of Quinine on Influenza Virus Infections in Mice."

Children

I. Deborah Greene: Born December 8th, 1888. Married Robert Constantine Balfour, Jr., Thomasville, Georgia. Attended Tifton Public Schools. Graduated Brenau College. Teacher of piano and organ at Brenau. Regent of Daughters of American Revolution Willoughby Barton D.A.R., ancestor; State Chairman Division of Music, Women's Federated Clubs of Georgia; Past president of Thomasville Garden Club, choir director and organist in Thomasville.

Constance Elizabeth Balfour: Born January 29th, 1919. Graduated Thomasville High School; attended Mary Baldwin, Staunton, Virginia; scholarship Brenau College; graduate of University of Georgia and Draughn's Business School. Married Bolling Jones III, Atlanta; Lieutenant U. S. Army Air Force. Constance Balfour Jones born July 26th, 1945.

Robert Charles Balfour III: Born September 9th, 1927. Attended Thomasville Public Schools; graduated Marion Institute, Marion, Alabama; Midshipman U. S. Naval Academy, Annapolis, Maryland.

II. Mary Louise: Born December 12th, 1893. Married Wyatt Rainey Pierce, Culloden, Georgia. Educated Tifton Public Schools and University of Georgia.

James McCrea Pierce: Born May 13th, 1920. Educated Palmetto, Florida Public Schools; Abraham Baldwin Agriculture College, Tifton. Enlisted U. S. Army prior to World War II. Assigned to duty with famous "Hell on Wheels" Second Armored Division. Engaged in active combat in Africa, Sicily and Italy.

Jackson Edwards Pierce: Born December 20th, 1921. Graduate of Palmetto, Florida Public Schools and Middle Georgia College. Flight Officer U. S. Army Transport Command. Pilot of C-46 Transport in China, Burma, India theatre of World War II.

III. Woodbury Warnell: Born April 24th, 1897. Married Colleen Coe, Macon, Georgia. Educated Tifton Public Schools and Georgia Tech. Lieutenant U. S. Army World War I. Engineering Department of Southern Bell Telephone, Atlanta.

Colleen Virginia McCrea: Born July 16th, 1921. Graduate of Atlanta Public Schools. Married Leon Frederick Parr of Washington State.

IV. Joubert Stein: Born March 2nd, 1900. Married Etta Fitzpatrick, Culloden, Georgia. Educated Tifton Public Schools. Served U. S. Navy on U. S. S. Florida during World War I. Based in Scottish waters on the Firth of Forth.

Joubert S. McCrea, Jr.: Born June 21st, 1924. Married Delle Kinsey Love, Charleston, S. C. Graduate of Jacksonville, Florida High School. Lieutenant U. S. Army Air Corps; stationed in Philippines as Pilot of B-24 Liberator.

Henry Fitzpatrick McCrea: Born September 9th, 1926. Graduated Jacksonville, Florida High School. U. S. Navy in World War II. Attended University of Georgia after war.

Mary Louisa McCrea: Born March 29th, 1932. Attending Jacksonville, Florida Public Schools.

V. Thomas Russell: Born July 21st, 1901. Married Lennie Brown, Richlands, North Carolina. Educated Tifton Public Schools, Georgia Tech and North Carolina State University. (B.S. Chemistry), Senior Research Analyst Weyth Institute of Applied Biochemistry, Philadelphia.

VI. Henry Banks: Born February 7th, 1905. Married Pauline Kerrick Dinsmore, Tifton, Georgia. Graduated Tifton High School. Office manager, Balfour lumber interests.

Joan McCrea: Born October 16th, 1929. Graduate of Thomasville High School. Enrolled Wesleyan College.

VII. Everette Edwards: Born June 30th, 1907. Attended Tifton Public Schools and Georgia Military Academy, College Park, Ga.

PERRYMAN MOORE

Perryman Moore, born December 15, 1864, in Valdosta, Georgia, was son of John Moore (born in Ireland), of Moore's District, North Carolina, and Barbara Roberts Moore (born in Coffee County, Georgia). Perryman came from Valdosta to Tifton in Tifton's early days. He married Susie Tillman (q.v.) May 11, 1888, at Quitman.

Mr. Moore was a planter, lumberman and merchant. He also owned a livery stable and a hotel in Tifton during the town's early days. By real estate purchases which increased in value he attained considerable wealth. He died at Piedmont Sanitarium, Atlanta, December 2, 1918, and is buried at Tifton. Surviving are his widow, former Senator and Regent Susie Tillman Moore, and one daughter, Perry Lee (born July 22, 1907); married, first Charles J. Webb; second, Briggs Carson, Jr.

SENATOR AND REGENT SUSIE TILLMAN MOORE

Susie Tillman, born at beautiful Cherry Lake, a five-thousand-acre plantation in Madison County, Florida, was daughter of Judge Joseph Tillman (born in 1823, Edgefield, South Carolina) and Susan Lane Tillman (born Lowndes County, Georgia) of Valdosta. Susie spent her childhood at Cherry Lake where she received instruction under tutors. She attended Mary Baldwin, at Staunton, Virginia, and afterward studied piano under de Graffin, New York City. May 11, at the home of her parents in Quitman where they were then living, she married Perryman Moore (q.v.).

Mrs. Moore took an active interest in her husband's business and thus developed and displayed business acumen. However, she took no part in politics until the Joe Brown-Hoke Smith campaign. At that time Mr. Moore and H. H. Tift, Tifton's founder, were organizing Joe Brown clubs throughout the District. Mrs. Moore favored Smith. She had been appointed by the United Daughters of the Confederacy, of which she was a charter member and at that time president, to select and invite here a speaker. She invited Hoke Smith, and instructed the man who blew the mill whistle to blow the whistle repeatedly and long when he heard the train blow at the crossing, because on the train would be the next governor of Georgia. The whistle blower did as requested and soon all Tifton knew that Hoke Smith was in town. Mr. Tift showed him courtesy, but Mr. Moore ignored him. Smith won the governorship. Thus began Susie T.'s colorful venture in politics. However, it was not until 1932 that Mrs. Moore became active in the state Democratic party and was recognized as a leader. In 1933 she was appointed a member of the State Democratic Committee and that year she became state Senator, the first woman state senator elected by popular vote. Later, while Senator, Mrs. Moore served as vice-chairman of the Democratic Executive Committee. She was a member of the State Democratic Executive Committee under three governors: Clifford Walker, Lemartine Griffin Hardman, and Eugene Talmadge.

In the Senate, Mrs. Moore sponsored numerous measures of benefit to Georgia, and she is credited with breaking the deadlock which tied up both branches of the legislature in 1933. In referring to this Governor Talmadge said: "She stuck to her guns; and she'll stick to her guns in the National Convention." Soon after this Mrs. Moore was elected Democratic National Committeewoman from Georgia.

Mrs. Moore served during three presidential campaigns as finance chairman of the Second Congressional District.

When Mrs. Moore was first elected to the Georgia Senate, the Abraham-Baldwin Agricultural College was among those scheduled to be closed. Mrs. Moore fought valiantly to keep it open. Others closed, but Abraham-Baldwin remained open.

Other projects secured by Mrs. Moore include: stumping of the land north of the college. This, done by the C. C. Camps, was worth between five and ten thousand dollars to the Experiment Station, declared Silas Starr, station director at that time. Mrs. Moore filed and secured passage of a bill whereby it became law that the state of Georgia could pave state property free. The first strip of paving paved under this law was that leading from Tifton to the Abraham-Baldwin Agricultural College. In her honor, it was named the Moore Highway. The formal dedication was on June 21, 1934, and at the exercises Tifton City Manager, George W. Coleman, presented to Mrs. Moore on behalf of the citizens of Tifton a silver loving cup in recognition of her achievement. Numerous distinguished guests were present on this festive occasion, which was followed by a barbecue dinner in the college dining room.

In 1932 notification had been given the college that no more diplomas could be issued because the library was not up to standard. Mrs. Moore succeeded in securing the requisite number of books, and built the library from 1,700 volumes to 8,500 volumes, and the college continued to graduate students.

When the college needed a gymnasium, Mrs. Moore and the Kiwanis Club gave the needed building, the club donating the cost of walls and the roof being Mrs. Moore's gift. Later this building burned but was replaced in 1939 by a building costing $80,000.00.

When Mrs. Moore served under Governor Ed Rivers during her second term of office she was appointed chairman of the University System of Georgia. Largely through her influence the state at this time appropriated $30,-000.00 for purchase of land north of the college for experimental work with animals.

Also, Senator Moore succeeded in securing from the government an appropriation of $25,000.00 per annum, for the Coastal Plain Experiment Station provided Georgia would raise $20,000.00 for purchase of land. At a Board of Regents meeting in Tifton this was done, thus securing the government funds annually. The amount was increased in 1945 to $33,000.00 annually.

HOLMES SYLVESTER MURRAY

Holmes Sylvester Murray (born Irwin County, March 10, 1872—died Tifton, February 24, 1925; buried at Tifton), was son of Joseph Daniel Murray (born Fort Valley, Georgia—died, Sparks, January 7, 1906) and Alice Nance Murray (born South Carolina—died October, 1896). A school teacher, Joseph taught in Fort Valley, Houston County, in Irwin County, and at Alapaha, where he went when little Holmes was a lad of eight years.

In 1891 Holmes Murray came to Tifton where he studied law under his cousin, Columbus W. Fulwood, and after Holmes stood his bar examination at Nashville, in 1897, he practiced law in partnership with Mr. Fulwood, the firm being Fulwood and Murray, for twenty-five years.

At Tifton Holmes met Miss Nelta Dean, daughter of Joel Eldridge Dean and Allie Virginia Dean, of Tifton, but formerly of Eastman. Mr. Dean was with the Tift Lumber Mill in Tifton. Miss Dean finished the junior course in music at Brenau in 1893 and thereafter taught music in Columbia, Florida, where she and Holmes Murray were married on June 30, 1895, the Reverend Dr. Inman, pastor of the Columbia Methodist Church, performing the ceremony. Of this union is one daughter, Nelta, of Columbia, South Carolina.

Holmes Murray in 1893 had become attorney for the Georgia, Southern and Florida Railroad, now the Southern. He continued for about fifteen years. In 1922 he became Tifton City attorney.

In 1905, the year in which Tift County came into existence, Holmes Murray was clerk of Tifton City Council. That year, also, on the Wednesday prior to May 5, the Murrays moved from Central Avenue to a house which they had built on Love Avenue, between Eight and Sixth Streets. Mrs. Murray still makes this her home.

Mr. Murray was a member of the Tifton Methodist Church.

Holmes Murray was keenly interested in politics, and he greatly enjoyed his friends. He was a member of Gun Lake Country Club, and for five years or longer he was president of Ferry Lake, of which he was a charter member, also an enthusiastic charter member of the Tifton Kiwanis Club, he was second president of that organization.

TILLOU BACON MURROW

Tillou Bacon, daughter of Dr. Edwin Henry Bacon (born Walthourville, Georgia, August 28, 1839, graduated Medical College, Augusta; died November 30, 1915, Eastman, Georgia; buried at Eastman) and (Sallie) Sarah Jane Willingham Bacon (born Allendale, South Carolina, March 28, 1849; first honor graduate, Monroe Female College, Forsyth; married in Macon; died, August 11, 1917, at Eastman, and is there buried), was born June 6 1871, at Albany, Georgia, which was the home of her mother's parents, Thomas Henry Willingham and Cecilia Baynard Willingham.

Tillou grew up at her parents' home in Eastman. She graduated from Monroe Female College, Forsyth. After her marriage to J. Badger Murrow, Tifton lawyer, a member of a prominent pioneer family of the community, she made her home in Tifton until her death.

Tillou was niece of Bessie Tift, wife of Henry, the founder of Tifton, Mrs. Bacon being Bessie's eldest sister; and Tillou received as a wedding gift from Bessie and Henry the lot at what is now 414 Park Avenue, North, and the lumber with which to build the large and handsome house thereon, which for many years was the Murrow home, later was the Levy home, and now is the Shaw Apartments.

Like her parents, Tillou was musical. She had an unusually fine voice, and was skilled as an organist and as a pianist. She was a devoted and loyal wife, mother and friend; and she was noted for her delightful hospitality. She was particularly kind to children. She was organist of the Tifton First Baptist Church of which she was a member.

Mrs. Murrow had one brother, Edward Henry Bacon, who married Catherine Harding Tift (Cassie), daughter of Mr. and Mrs. Edwin H. Tift (q.v.) and niece of Henry Harding Tift. Mrs. Murrow's sisters were Sallie (Mrs. Reppard Colcord) and Nelia (Mrs. Roy Abernathy), both of Atlanta, and both frequent Tifton visitors.

Mr. and Mrs. Murrow had an only child, Elizabeth Tift Murrow (Bess), who possesses musical ability. She graduated from Bessie Tift College, studied further at Columbia University, New York, and also studied music in New York City where she lived for many years, after her mother's death, at Tifton, May, 1922. Mrs. Murrow is buried at Tifton.

Bess Murrow married McCalmy Belknap and they lived in Toledo, Ohio. They have a child, John Willingham Belknap.

Badger Murrow, after Tillou's death, moved to Florida, where he married again and now lives in Orlando.

IRVINE WALKER MYERS

Few have been possessed of a personality which so endeared them to a host of friends as was Irvine W. Myers. Exceptionally handsome, possessed of a rich and sonorous voice, and with a kind friendliness, he numbered his friends by those who knew him. When he died a community wept.

Born in Pamplico, South Carolina, June 1, 1876, Irvine Walker Myers was one of eight sons born to A. A. Myers (died 1934, aged 92) and Elizabeth Harrell Myers (died, 1904). After Elizabeth Myers died, A. A. Myers married Lottie Gray. Irvine's seven brothers died before Irvine did, but his stepmother and a half-brother, Monroe Myers, of Pamplico, survived him. Among Irvine's brothers were Carl Myers, of Savannah, and Joe Myers and Will Myers, all of whom were in Tifton at some time.

Irvine W. Myers on December 22, 1899, in Atlanta, married Pearl Willingham, handsome youngest daughter of Cecilia Baynard Willingham and the late Thomas Henry Willingham, formerly of Albany, Georgia, and prior to the War Between the States, of "Smyrna," near Old Allendale, South Carolina. Pearl had grown up in Albany, and, after her father's death, had lived in College Park, where she made her home with her brother, Benjamin Willingham, and his family, and where she attended Cox College. Pearl was youngest sister of Bessie, wife of Henry Tift, founder of Tifton.

Irvine had come to Tifton when eighteen. Immediately upon arrival he became clerk at Hotel Sadie. Later he became proprietor and part owner. After the Sadie burned he operated the Hotel Myon which replaced the Sadie. Also, he owned and operated a large farm, and he had interests in the Fenner Tobacco Warehouse in Tifton. He was an officer in a Tifton bank, and he had various other business interests. He was a charter member of the Tifton Rotary Club, was a member of Tift County Board of Trade and later of the Tift County Chamber of Commerce.

To Irvine and Pearl Willingham Myers were born two children, Marguerite, an exceptionally pretty girl, graduated from Washington Seminary, Atlanta, married Le Roy Miller, and lives in Washington. Henry Tift Myers, born in Tifton, attended Culver Military Institute; graduated from Georgia School of Technology. As early as 1931 Bessie Tift wrote in a letter to a niece. "Brother Myers is here (in Tifton) for Christmas and he has won the highest honors in his aviation class in everything . . . "

By 1937 Henry Myers was a pilot with the Eastern Air lines with headquarters in Texas. In October of that year, Irvine went from Tifton to Tennessee to meet his son and fly with him. He did so and had a glorious experience. To Pearl he wrote that it was a thrill of a lifetime to ride at an altitude of eleven thousand feet, and at more than two hundred miles per hour! The letter reached Pearl on Thursday afternoon, and at six of that same afternoon Irvine died of a heart attack suffered in a Nashville, Tennessee hotel. His body was brought back to Tifton and buried here where all mourned his passing.

After Irvine's death, Pearl bought the other heir's interest in the Myon Hotel, and she operated it until recently when she leased it to a hotel company which operates a chain of hotels.

Henry Myers continued his aviation and in World War II entered the United States Aviation Corps in which he is Lieutenant Colonel. He piloted the famous "Sacred Cow," used by President Truman. During President Franklin D. Roosevelt's administration, Myers often piloted the plane used by Mrs. Roosevelt. He now pilots President Truman's new plane. During the War Col. Myers was pilot of the plane which took the five senators on their famous inspection flight around the world. It was on this flight that he made the hazardous and long flight of four thousand miles above water, the first time that so great a distance above water had been attempted. For this he had made innumerable long flights over land in order to assure himself and his superior officers that the long flight was possible.

In Texas Henry Myers had met Miss Maidee Calaway Williams, daughter of Mrs. Henry Washington Williams and the late Mr. Williams. Miss Williams and Colonel Myers were wed on Saturday, December 1, 1944 at a ceremony performed at Bethesda, Maryland. Of this union is a son, born Washington, D. C., Monday, April 28, 1947.

BENJAMIN HILL McLEOD

Benjamin Hill McLeod, son of Daniel W. McLeod and Catherine Parker

McLeod, from North Carolina, was born at Sumner, Georgia, September 14, 1885. He attended the public schools at Sumner and at Tifton where his parents moved during his boyhood.

On January 1, 1900, when a lad of only fifteen, Ben began work at the Bank of Tifton. After six years he was made assistant cashier; he became cashier in 1912; in 1922 he became vice-president, and, in 1945, executive vice-president, his present position.

In January, 1912, B. H. McLeod was elected the first secretary-treasurer of the Country Club at Gun Lake.

On June 18, 1912 Benjamin Hill McLeod and Hortense Mulloy were united in marriage. Mrs. McLeod, a young woman of exceptional beauty, was daughter of Professor Mulloy, superintendent of schools, first at Eastman and later at Tifton. Of this union were two children, Mildred Floyd McLeod (McLanahan), born January 13, 1914, and Ben Hill McLeod, Jr., born October 23, 1919.

Mr. McLeod, Sr., has two sisters, Mrs. J. J. Golden and Mrs. D. B. Harrell, both prominent in the woman's work of the Tifton First Baptist Church. Mrs. Golden has been choir director at that church for thirty-five years; Mrs. Golden has since the death of Bessie Tift, been teacher of the Bessie Tift Bible Class of the First Baptist Sunday School. Also she was for several years president of the Woman's Missionary union of that church; and Mrs. Golden is treasurer.

The McLeods, during the childhood of B. T. McLeod, Mrs. Golden and Mrs. Harrell, lived in the large house which formerly stood at the northwest corner of Park Avenue, at Fourth Street.

THE McMILLAN FAMILY

Daniel McMillan and his wife, Margaret, were married in Scotland and had six children, of whom the sons were John, Malcolm, and Archie. Prior to 1812 the family emigrated to America and settled in Virginia. Thence they moved to North Carolina; thence to South Carolina, and thence to Georgia, where they settled in Irwin County on the place where in 1912 lived Joe Fletcher, near Alapaha station. John, Malcolm and Archie were among the pioneers of Irwin County.

John McMillan married Sally, eldest daughter of Jacob Paulk, son of Micajah Paulk, and had thirteen children, Dan, John, Jim, Malcolm, Jacob, Archie, George, Margaret, Mary, Sarah, Betsy, Malissa, Kate.

Malcolm McMillan, son of Daniel and Margaret, married Rachel Sumner, daughter of Jesse Sumner. They had fifteen children: Archie, John, Jesse, Jim, Malcolm, Ashley, Randall, William, Burrell, Alexander, Mary, Margaret, Nancy, Jane, Viney.

Archie McMillan, son of Daniel and Margaret, married Margaret Young, daughter of Thomas Young, first. Children of Archie and Margaret Young McMillan were: Red, whose real name was Malcolm McMillan; John, Mary, Jane, Margaret, Thomas, Kate, Becky, Jacob (Jake).

Red Malcolm McMillan, above mentioned, was born October 24, 1853. On November 21, 1873, he married Narcissa Henderson (born November 3, 1858) daughter of Elizabeth Paulk Henderson (born March 26, 1841, daughter of John Jaulk) and Robert Henderson (born February 12, 1831; married March 12, 1857), son of Rhoda Whitley Henderson (born June 5, 1804; married September 19, 1820) and John Henderson (born October 15, 1789, son of Daniel Henderson who married Sallie McBride in North Carolina, probably prior to 1810, and settled in Irwin County about nine miles S. E. of Ocilla at a place later known as the Wyatt Tucker place but then a wilderness still inhabited by Indians and full of wolves and deer. Daniel and Salie had nine chidren and members of their families became well known throughout Turner and Irwin Counties. They produced fifteen members of the House of Representatives of the Georgia Legislature and six state senators, through the year 1926.

Red Malcolm McMillan and Narcissa Henderson McMillan had nine children: Sarah, Elizabeth, Archibald, Margaret, Catherine, Robert H., John H., Edwin, Viola. Of these seven lived to maturity. To each of the girls who lived to maturity Red gave half a land lot, that is, 250 acres or its equivalent in money. To each of the boys who lived to maturity he gave one land lot, that is, 490 acres. Archibald's portion fell in what is now Tift County and there he settled. Robert H. settled at Brookfield.

Archiebald McMillan of what is now Tift County, married Mittie F. Carter, July 9, 1903. To them were born: Aubrey, Lucile, L. D., Julian, Archibald.

Robert H., who settled at Brookfield, married Mattie Irene Connell. To them were born: Mabel, Inez, R. H. II, Edwin W., Emory D.

Of the above, R. H. McMillan II married Gladys Greene, of Tifton, daughter of Mrs. Louise Greene, daughter of Mrs. Arjane Fletcher, daughter of James W. Overstreet, son of Moses Overstreet, Mrs. Fletcher being the oldest living member of the Overstreet family, pioneer residents of what is now Tift County.

Children of R. H. McMillan II and Gladys Greene McMillan are Martha Louise, R. H. III (Tim), Patricia, Christopher Paul. This family now lives at 419 Park Avenue, Tifton.

For further information regarding the McMillan family, see the book, "Henderson and Whiddon Families" by William Henderson.

SILAS AND DUNCAN O'QUINN

At a huge O'Quinn reunion held some years ago near Odum, Appling County, Georgia, more than fifteen hundred persons were present.

The first O'Quinn to come to America came from County Cork, Ireland, to Charleston, South Carolina. There also came from Ireland to South Carolina many years ago Elias Branch and his wife, Mary DeVaughn Branch. Elias and Mary had six children: Dave, Jim, and Nancy, who settled in Irwin County; Mike and Elias, who settled in Appling County; and Rachel, who married Duncan O'Quinn and settled in Berrien County after the War

Between the States. Duncan was judge of the Inferior Court of Berrien County.

Children of Judge Duncan O'Quinn and Rachel Branch O'Quinn were Silas, Elias, Dave, Martha, and Susan.

Of the above children, the sons married as follows:

Silas married, first, Maggie Robinson, of Wayne County; second, Tina Rowland. Elias married Charity Herring. Dave married Sally Edge.

Children of Silas and Maggie Robinson O'Quinn were John, who married Leah Bennett; Ida, who married J. B. Wallace; Marcus; Robinson, who married Minnie McClellan, in 1898.

Children of Silas O'Quinn and Tina Rowland were Gus, Lamar, who married Fannie Morris; Elias, who married Lucy B. Mitchell; Unie, who married J. M. McSwain; Florie, who married G. H. Mitchell; Silas; Donie.

Elias and Charity Herring O'Quinn had the following children: Mattie (Mrs. L. G. Rutland); T. H.; Elias, who married Mattie Whiddon; Charles, who married Maggie Paulk; Estelle, who married M. B. McClellan; Cathleen, who married Ed Willis (of Willis Dairy).

Chidren of Dave and Sally Edge O'Quinn were Daisy, H. M., Varney, Arzula.

The sisters, Martha and Susan, daughters of Duncan and Rachel Branch O'Quinn, married, respectively, Red Bennett and John Bennett.

Children of Red and Martha were Rachel, Viola, Becky, Roxie, Ralphael.

Children of John and Susan were Ruby, Pearl, Gordy, Britt, Essie.

Silas O'Quinn, the elder, and his brother, Elias O'Quinn, were farmers and both lived on farms, which they owned, near Tifton. Silas came to Tifton about sixty years ago and was a blacksmith working for H. H. Tift at the Tift Mill. Silas died in 1933.

Of Silas, the editor of the Tifton Gazette wrote, in July, 1895: "Mr. Silas O'Quinn came around early in the week to make peace with the devil with a lot of peaches . . . the finest specimens ever brought to this office. The devil is full of peaches and gratitude."

THE OVERSTREETS

The Colonial Records of Georgia, Vol. XXII, page 245 quote from a letter of General James Oglethorpe to accountant in which he mentions "a loan in cattle to one Overstreet, an industrious man with a wife and six children in Augusta." This was in 1739.

In 1743 a document in London set forth that the township of Augusta outside of the garrison embraced only a few white people, traders with Indians. Among the list of sixteen names of settlers at the fort was Henry Overstreet.

In 1762 at a meeting of Council in Savannah, on May 4, was read a petition of Henry Overstreet, lately come into the province of Georgia with his wife and six children in order to settle. He was granted 150 acres of land about three miles above the mouth of Briar Creek, famous in history as the stream believed by Georgia's early historian, Jones, to be that which De Soto and his men swam in their march through Georgia. Also it was the stream near which was captured the valiant Colonel John McIntosh, American patriot of the Scotch colony of New Inverness, later called Darien. Near this stream Overstreet was granted additional acreage and this became the Georgia home of the Overstreets. Thence one crossed over into South Carolina and wed. This was James Overstreet who, in 1771, married Sarah Booth (born Dec. 10, 1756, died December 24, 1818). Sarah was daughter of Mary and John Booth, who wed in 1753. John Booth served with the upper Granville County regiment of the South Carolina Militia and was killed in action at Hutson's Ferry 1779 (see Memoir of Tarleton Brown, reprint of 1894, pp. 5 and 6). For this Revolutionary patriot the John Booth Chapter of the Sons of the American Revolution, Columbia, South Carolina, is named.

To James Overstreet and Sarah Booth Overstreet was born a son, James Overstreet, Jr., born in Barnwell District, South Carolina, February 11, 1773; married, in 1795, Eliza Holcombe Brown (born April 13, 1773; died September 6, 1817) whose mother, nee Holcombe, was a daughter of the widow Holcombe who married Bartlett Brown, Sr., uncle of Tarleton Brown, a captain in the Revolutionary War. James Overstreet, Jr., was a lawyer, was justice of the peace at Barnwell, in 1807, and was representative from South Carolina to the 16th and 17th congresses. He died at China Grove, North Carolina, May 24, 18? , while returning from Washington, and Congress adjourned in respect to his memory and a sketch of him was printed in the Congressional Record.

Sarah Booth Overstreet, wife of James, Sr., received 125 acres of land from her mother, and the deed was recorded April 9, 1801. By her will, recorded November 29, 1818, Sarah left property to her son, James Overstreet, and others. Sarah is buried in the Brown graveyard, Barnwell, South Carolina. Sarah Booth Overstreet and James Overstreet, Sr., had six children: James, John, Henry, a daughter (Mrs. Brown), Mary, Samuel.

Of the above family of Overstreets, Moses Overstreet (born about 1798, died March 1, 1852; buried at Royal's Church, Coffee County, Georgia), married in March, 1819 Elizabeth Carter. Of this union were ten children: 1. Henry Josiah (born Sept. 25, 1820; never married); 2. James W. 3. Sarah Ann (born Feb. 25, 1825; died May 5, 1898; married William Royal). 4. Jane Elizabeth (born December 5, 1827; died July 20, 1828); 5. Mary A. (born July 11, 1829; died Sept. 27, 1829); 6 Moses William (born March 10, 1832; died Jan. 9, 1852 never married); 7. Martha Amanda (born Oct. 21, 1835; married Griffis Richatson); 8. Seaborn Franklin (born July 28, 1838; killed in War Between the States, May 26, 1865); 9. Benjamin Jacob (born May 13, 1841; killed in War Between the States, June 29, 1862); 10. Mary Catherine (born July 25, 1843; married John Spell.

Of these children of Moses and Elizabeth Carter Overstreet, James W. Overstreet was the only son to survive the War Between the States and leave descendants. He was born in Burke County, Georgia, October 27, 1822. On February 3, 1852 he married Susan Ann Solomon (born in Coffee County, May 16, 1836; died May 30, 1925; buried at Ty Ty Church), daughter of Godwin Solomon. James was reared in Screven County; later went to Worth County; apparently he or one of his name went from Screven County over into South Carolina but later moved back to Georgia. James was among the pioneer residents of what is now Tift County. He lived on a large farm which he owned near Little River, on the Omega Road, and he had built the Overstreet Bridge which formerly stood near his plantation. This old bridge has been replaced by a concrete structure. James was a Godly man, interested in charity work and is said by some, "to have done more of this personally than any other man of this section in his day." He was interested also in building schools and roads. James and Susan had a large family of children and James died March 6, 1900, and is buried at old Ty Ty Church.

Children of James and Susan Ann Solomon Overstreet were: 1. Delilah: 2. Henry Clay; 3. Elizabeth; 4. Mary Jane; 5. Martha Ann; 6. Seaborn Franklin; 7. Arjane; 8. Susan Clayton; 9. Moses Oscar; 10. James W., Jr.; 11. Josiah; 12. David; 13. Lilla; 14. Lula; 15. Benjamin Jacob.

Of the above fifteen children fourteen lived to maturity. Of these several lived in Tift County. Of these was Judge Seaborn Franklin Overstreet, born August 18, 1864, Coffee County, near Durham's Mill, died Sept. 17, 1941; buried Tifton; married Mary Ann Eason Wills (born May 30, 1872, Worth County) daughter of Dempsey R. Willis and Mary Ann Baker. Issue were: Bessie, C. Crandall, Henry C., N. Russell, Seaborn Franklin, Jr., Julian (Dock), Flora Kate, Lillian. Flora Kate Overstreet (Mrs. Emerson Mitchell) is possessed of an extraordinarily sweet soprano voice, and for many years sang in the choir of the Tifton First Baptist Church.

Arjane Overstreet, born March 17, 1866, Coffee County, married, June 24, 1880, in Irwin County, George Washington Fletcher (born Nov. 11, 1858; died Feb. 17, 1920) son of Jehu Fletcher and Matilda Sumner Fletcher. To Arjane and G. W. Fletcher were born Susie, Leonard and Louise. Early left a widow, Mrs. Fletcher reared her orphaned children and also her orphaned grandchildren. At more than eighty, she is still a beautiful woman; and her piety and shrewd common sense are of exceptional order. Of her grandchildren, Martha Louise Greene was Miss T. H. S. the year of her graduation from Tifton High School. She is a young woman of great beauty. Another granddaughter, Mary Catherine Driskell, is an unusually beautiful blond. Another granddaughter, Gladys Greene, a talented writer, married R. H. McMillan (see article on McMillans).

Lilla Overstreet, born Dec. 13, 1876, Worth County (now Tift); died Jan. 18, 1930; buried Ty Ty Church, Tift County; married Feb. 23, 1893, in Worth, now Tift, George Washington Crum (born Feb. 25, 1869; died Feb. 11, 1913; buried Ty Ty Church). Issue: Jewel, Homer P. (married Ted Wallace); Elder Lloyd, Jim, Robert, William Paul.

For several years prior to World War II the Overstreet Family held a reunion at Abraham-Baldwin Agricultural College, Tifton. Several hundred members of the Overstreet family were in attendance. Mrs. Arjane Overstreet Fletcher, of 419 Park Avenue, Tifton, is the oldest living member of the Overstreet family (in 1947).

A more comprehensive genealogy of the Overstreet family is contained in the book, "The James W. Overstreet, Sr., and Allied Families," by J. V. Chapman.

PADRICK BROTHERS, MERCHANTS

In 1890 W. O. Padrick, a native of Bainbridge, Ga., came to Tifton and opened a dry goods store in the Julian building on Railroad Street. One year later he was joined by his brothers, Geo. H. and Jno G. Padrick, and the business was moved to a large store which they had erected on Main Street in Block No. 12, about where Dismuke's store now stands. This was a department store, carrying dry goods, millinery, groceries, furniture, hardware and all kinds of farm implements. They enjoyed a large trade from the surrounding counties.

In 1896 Padrick Brothers erected the large brick store just across from the Myon Hotel, then the Sadie Hotel. It is now known as the Boatright building.

After conducting a business there for several years they sold to Mr. J. R. Cole, of Newnan, Ga. W. O. Padrick then went to New York where he lived for some years, and Geo. H. moved to Lakeland, Fla., where he still resides. Jno. G. remained in Tifton until his death two years ago last November.

All three of the brothers were active in civic and church work, being stewards in the Methodist church for many years. A younger brother, J. L. Padrick, now lives in Tifton and is connected with the city office; he also is a steward in the Methodist church.

Geo. H. Padrick was a director in the Bank of Tifton when it was first organized. W. O. Padrick was one of the first stockholders in the Tifton Gazette.

THOMAS JEFFERSON PARKER

Thomas Jefferson Parker was the name given to the son born to Joshua Browning Parker and Serena Wright Parker in Henry County, Georgia, December 27, 1850. In his youth he joined the Philadelphia Church (Presbyterian), in Clayton County.

On December 12, 1872, at Forest Park, Georgia, Parker married pretty Martha Rowena McLendon (born Pike County, June 6, 1850), daughter of Preston and Missouri Rucker McLendon. The bride was of the Forsyth Ruckers, and her grandmother Rucker had attended Monroe Female College. Rowena was well educated and had taught school and also was a newspaper correspondent. During her childhood she had joined the Baptist Church.

Not long after marriage the T. J. Parkers moved to Roswell, Georgia. Both of them loved the place. Roswell was picturesque and its historic homes, Mimosa Hall, Bullock Hall, girlhood home of Mittie Bullock, mother of President Theodore Roosevelt, Barrington Hall, which bore the family name of Catherine Barrington, wife of Roswell King, founder of the town, were among the most stately and beautiful in the state. There, also, was

Colonial Place, the home of Dr. Francis Robert Goulding, author of "Young Marooners" and other books for children, and also the inventor of the sewing machine, some time prior to Elias Howe's invention. At Roswell, too, were the great Roswell Mills, established so long ago by Roswell King, that they were in operation at the time of the War Between the States and made some uniforms for the Confederate Army. All of these things interested the Parkers and they took pride in Roswell's history, and they and the Parker children, who grew up there, loved the town. The children were Verna, an only beloved daughter, and her brothers: J. Cliff, G. R., W. H., Harry E., and Charlie. Everything would have been wonderful had not Jefferson Parker had asthma; but asthma he had.

In 1886 Jeff and two of his Roswell neighbors, Bill Gunter and Charles Talley decided to take a trip. They decided they would go to Gainesville, Florida, and see if they saw any land which they would like to buy. The three of them set out. They traveled in a wagon drawn by four mules, and the men would camp out nearly every night.

At Arabi the travellers sojourned for two days with a Mr. Pitts. There Pitts offered to sell Parker a thousand acres of good land for a thousand dollars; but they did not trade. Instead the party proceeded south, passing through Tifton and on to Florida. In Florida Talley remained until his death, but Parker returned to Roswell.

However, Mr. Parker could not get Tifton out of his mind. In 1889 he returned there and stayed for a while with John T. Hightower, who built the Tifton, Thomasville and Gulf Railroad. While in Tifton Mr. Parker was free of asthma, and enjoyed everything as he had not for years. He decided the thing to do was to move to Tifton.

Back he went to well loved Roswell to get his family and his possessions. He left his family at Roswell until he could make ready for them in Berrien. In 1900 he sent his stock and sixteen mules and horses through country in charge of fourteen men. He went by train. When he arrived in Tifton the first man he saw was John B. Greene, whom he asked if he had seen a number of men from North Georgia. They had dined at his restaurant the night before, Greene told him.

Mr. Parker bought land at Omega, set up a sawmill there, and there built a house for his family and several houses for the mill hands. He sent for his family, and the Parkers lived at Omega for one year then went to Docia where he had a sawmill and where he and his family remained for another year. There they were neighbors of the George W. Warrens. Mr. Parker owned eight sawmills near Tifton.

In 1902, Thomas Jefferson Parker and his family moved to Tifton. Here Mr. Parker built fifty-two houses. The first home here was one of nine houses which he built. From this he moved to the Love Avenue house now occupied by S. A. Youmans. This Parker built, and his son, Charlie, built the house next door, now the C. B. Holmes residence. After three years in the Love Avenue house T. J. Parker built and moved into the home which now for many years has been called "Parker House," on Central Avenue, next to the corner of Twelfth Street.

Mr. Parker farmed also; he owned eight large farms, and of his farming venture made a tremendous success. He became famous in the community because he cleared $3,000.00 one year on a two-horse farm. He was a believer in wheat growing and said he longed to see Tifton have a flour mill.

Parker's eldest grandson was Tift County's first volunteer in World War I.

In 1920, when Mr. Parker was past seventy he and a friend made a journey up into the mountains of North Georgia. They became lost in the great woods of the mountains above Ellijay, and for forty hours they wandered without food. Afterward he wrote of his experience:

"Finally we reached the Connesauga River and our means of escape was practically assured . . . after five hours of hard riding we had to cross the stream on the bottoms of solid rock . . . This was about eighteen miles from any place where a vehicle could go . . . After a while we came to a trail . . . we came to the abode of an old mountain preacher, a Mr. Hall . . . a two room house built of the timber which grew all around. His wife and little daughter lifted the hearth stone and brought up eggs and bacon . . . This was the best meal I have ever eaten!"

Mr. and Mrs. Parker celebrated their golden anniversary. There was a brilliant reception at Parker house and Rowena and Jeff got married all over again, with a double ring ceremony, and with their children for attendants, and with many friends present, and numerous handsome gifts.

After the golden wedding the Parkers enjoyed ten more happy years together before Mrs. Parker died, December 29, 1932. Thomas Jefferson Parker lived until June 1940, when he was almost ninety.

JACOB MARION PAULK and
ANNIE CATHERINE REGISTER PAULK

Micajah Paulk, of North Carolina, was the first Paulk to come to Irwin County, Georgia. His wife was Mary C. Young. Their son, James, married Faithy Akerage. James and Faithy had a son, James, called Jeems, who married Milly Whiddon, June 1, 1865.

Jacob Marion Paulk, son of Jeems and Milly Whiddon Paulk, was born April 19, 1866, in Irwin County. When a small boy his mother died. Later his father married again and there was a large family by the second marriage.

Jacob attended the schools of Irwin County. He later was a student at the Florida Normal School at White Springs, Florida, and in 1882, when Dr. M. A. McNulty founded the South Georgia Male and Female College at Dawson, Georgia, he attended that institution of learning, where he remained in 1883. There he won three medals, one in mathematics, one in scholarship, and one for general excellence. A shy, studious youth, he never looked at a girl, and he always had a book. The S. G. M. and F. C. went out of existence in 1885, upon the death of Dr. McNulty.

After teaching in Wilcox County during his early manhood, Paulk was in the mercantile business in Rochelle before going to Alapaha where he and a Mr. Gaskins were partners in a general merchandise business.

In 1895 Mr. Paulk came from Alapaha to Tifton. Here, on Main Street, in the south side of what is now Friendlander's, he conducted a general merchandise business purchased from another Mr. Gaskins. This Paulk sold in 1899 and thereafter he opened a furniture business. This, located on Second Street, he sold to Kent when Paulk became cashier of the new Citizens' Bank, opened February 1st, 1903, where the Cigar Store now is. Paulk was a stockholder, and E. A. Buck was president.

On a Wednesday in November, 1899, Jacob Marion Paulk married Annie Catherine Register, daughter of James W. Register (born February 4, 1850, at Hamilton County, Florida; died, Jasper, Florida, June, 1929) and Florence Rainey Register (born March 11, 1851, Hamilton County; died June 1917, at Jasper). The ceremony was performed by the bride's pastor, the Reverend T. H. Bradford, of the Jasper Methodist Church, at the home of the bride's parents. Immediately after the ceremony the Paulks came to Tifton.

As bride and groom the Paulks, upon coming to Tifton, boarded with the Badger Murrows on Park Avenue until the home which the Paulks were building on Central Avenue could be finished. Then they moved there.

Years passed. Life to Marion was sweet. He had a beautiful and talented wife. He had a son and a pretty little daughter. He owned his home. He had a good position in the bank. He had everything—except health.

In search of health Marion went to Johns Hopkins, to Atlanta, to Mobile. At Mobile Dr. H. P. Cole was effecting cures by giving blood transfusions. He was the only physician in the Southeast giving them. Jacob Marion's brother, Edward, of Ocilla, went too and bared his arm. A five inch slit was made and a pint and a half of blood was drawn; but in those days few had heard of blood matching. After the transfusion Marion had a violent chill. He was able to travel, later, back to Tifton, but soon afterward he died, Saturday, March 26, 1910. Of him was written in the Tifton Gazette: "One of nature's noblemen, a man whose life was above reproach and whose dealings with his fellow-man were marked with sterling honesty and unflinching integrity, and whose life as a Christian, as a husband, a father and citizen, stands as a mark for emulation and praise, passed away —when Jacob Marion Paulk breathed his last."

Mrs. Paulk set herself to the business of rearing and educating her children. Back in Jasper she had played the organ in the Methodist Church from the time she was ten, until the time of her marriage. She had studied music at the Jasper Normal Institute, of which Mr. J. M. Guilliams was head. After her marriage she studied further at the Atlanta Conservatory and at Brenau. She taught music in Tifton and contributed much to the musical life of the town. She was a charter member and first president of the Tifton Music Club, organized by Mrs. Durrett, of Cordele.

Mrs. Paulk reared her children, and they would come back to Tifton and visit her. Her married daughter, who lived in Atlanta, would bring Mrs. Paulk's little grandchildren. White-haired Kate Register Paulk continued to play a large part in Tifton's life. She continued to teach music and had many piano pupils, both boys and girls.

One day in late August, 1947, Kate Paulk said, "I think I'll go over and go up stairs in the house where the Murrows used to live. I haven't been there for a long time. I think I'd like to see it again." She did. Afterward she was quiet for a little while. Her eyes were shiny and very blue, but she went about her duties as usual.

A few days later Tifton was grieved to learn that Kate had suddenly had a heart attack. She went immediately. Perhaps she wished to go to Marion.

Marion and Kate Register Paulk's children are Maudie (Mrs. Warren Maddox, of Atlanta), and Clarence, also of Atlanta.

JOHN A. PETERSON

John Atkinson Peterson, born in Douglas, Georgia, August 13, 1870, was educated in the schools of Coffee County, entered Emory College at Oxford where he took the literary course, and then went to Atlanta with an Emory professor and a group of Emory students who removed to the Capital City and became the beginning of Georgia School of Technology. Among his fellow students when still in Oxford were W. L. Harman, later superintendent of Tifton Schools, and James Clements, later Judge Clements, of Irwinville.

Young Peterson was skilled in working with cabinet makers tools and also was gifted as a metalurgist, but after remaining at the young Georgia Tech for a short time he left that college and entered upon the study of dentistry at the Atlanta College of Dentistry, from which he graduated, 1898.

John Peterson had first come to Tifton in 1894 when he came here to be with his brother, Dr. Nicholls Peterson, and it was while in Tifton that he decided upon being a dentist. While still a student he practiced here, during vacations, with Dr. Alexander, eminent Alapaha dentist who came to Tifton several days a week, and here had an office.

After his graduation, Dr. Peterson came to Tifton and took over the Alexander practice as well as continuing with his own.

Dr. John Peterson met and married Miss Mabel Haulbrook, a teacher, daughter of William Coleman Haulbrook and Susannah Mason Haulbrook, newcomers to Tifton from Calhoun, Georgia, where Mr. Haulbrook had been a merchant. Although the Haulbrooks later bought land here they at that time were living on the Morris Place on the Brookfield Road and there Mabel and John were wed, September 2, 1903. Thereafter they lived for a year at Hotel Sadie, then, with the Haulbrooks, at what is now the R. E. Hall Place on West Sixth Street. Then they moved into the cottage which later, at the time of his death, was the home of Chief of Police Joseph Henderson. Thence they moved to the Nicholls Peterson home on Love Avenue and there their son, John Haulbrook Peterson, was born.

After other moves the John Petersons built and for twenty-five years lived in the Central Avenue house now the home of the G. N. Herrings. To Dr. and Mrs. Peterson were born two other children, Clyde Mason and Rosalie Mason, both of whom died in infancy.

During all this time Dr. Peterson was practicing dentistry in Tifton, where he was highly regarded and greatly beloved. Also he was prominent in state and national dental societies. His son, John studied dentistry and practiced

HISTORY OF TIFT COUNTY   441

with him. John married a charming young woman, Mary Woody, daughter of Willis Gaines Woody, and Mary Reynolds Woody. To John and Mary were born sons whom they named John Haulbrook, Jr., and Nicholls Alton. A daughter, Mary Catherine, was born not long after her grandfather's death.

Dr. John Peterson died at Tift County Hospital, March 13, 1944. Burial was at Tifton.

NICHOLLS PETERSON

Nicholls Peterson was born near Douglas, Georgia, January 31, 1868, lived for a time in Kirkland, attended Southern Medical College, graduated from the University of Louisville, took post graduate work in New York. After practicing medicine for about a year at Irwinville, he came to Tifton, in 1891. Except for a few months at Douglas he continued to practice medicine in Tifton until ten days prior to his death at the Coastal Plain Hospital, Tifton, Friday morning, March 13, 1936. Burial was in Tifton, where a host of friends mourned his passing.

At Tifton, May 16, 1897, the Reverend C. E. Crawley, pastor of the Tifton Methodist Church, performing the ceremony, Dr. Peterson was married to Miss Edna McQueen, of Nashville, Tennessee. She had been teaching at the Tifton Institute (see article on Mrs. Peterson, in Education chapter, this book).

Nicholls Peterson was a member of the Tifton Board of Education from about 1904 until 1923, when he resigned at the end of Mr. J. C. Sirmans's term of office as school head. For many years Dr. Peterson was chairman of the Board.

Dr. Peterson served on Tifton's earliest Board of Health created at a meeting of Tifton City Council, March 2, 1891. Other members of the board were Dr. J. C. Goodman, Dr. J. A. McCrea, Messrs. T. M. Greer, H. H. Parker. At various times throughout many years Dr. Peterson served on the board of health. He was elected city physician of Tifton August 24, 1893 and in this capacity served at various times during many years. He was appointed, by Governor Terrell, a member of the Board of Public Welfare and continued on this board until 1911 when he resigned in order to accept appointment as a member of the Georgia Board of Medical Examiners, on which he continued until 1925. He was Tift County's representative to the state legislature for two years, 1925 and 1926. Soon after coming to Tifton he became a trustee of the Tifton Methodist Church and served in that capacity until his death.

Dr. Peterson began practicing in "the horse and buggy days." He loved fine horses and had a span said to be among the finest in the state. He and another Tifton man owned a livery stable here. His partner conducted the business.

Dr. Peterson began the House, which became the C. W. Fulwood home, for a hospital, but sold it instead to Fulwood. Dr. Peterson then opened a small hospital in other quarters. He later had a hospital in the home now occupied by Marion Holmes. Still later, with others, he conducted the Coastal

Plain Hospital which continued until the opening of Tift County Hospital. At the new hospital the nursery is a memorial to Dr. Peterson who brought into the world more than a thousand babies.

A person who did not live in Tifton and know Dr. Peterson when he practiced here can have no adequate conception of the esteem with which he was revered, nor the deep affection in which he was held by thousands of patients who not only respected him for his professional skill, but also loved him because of his spirit of kindliness.

After he passed to his long rest a memorial service was held for Nicholls Peterson at the Twentieth Century Library Club. At this service Dr. Orin Mixon read a long and high tribute to Dr. Peterson. This, which was written by Dr. C. W. Durden who knew Dr. Peterson in other years when Dr. Durden lived in Tifton, read in part:

"He was a most charitable man. He would forgive like a child, nor would he treasure a grievance to mar his peace of mind; nor conjure time or occasion to repay an injury. He pushed from his mind as pestiferous weeds hatred and malice, but cultivated with delight the flowers of brotherly love toward all men. This made him the guileless man he was as he walked among men."

J. J. L. PHILLIPS

J. J. L. Phillips, his brother, P. D., and two other children moved with their parents from Alabama to Louisiana, in 1873. There his father, who was a physician, and his mother died in August of 1874. In October of 1874 an uncle from Alabama came and carried all of the orphaned children to his farm in Alabama. Here the children learned to work and they attended an Old Field School several weeks of each year.

In 1893 J. J. L. and P. D. came to Chula and there set up a small saw mill which they operated jointly. Later they operated a larger mill at Eldorado. After some years as joint owners J. J. L. sold his interest in the mill to his brother P. D. and J. J. L. moved to Tifton, where he opened a wholesale lumber business. J. L. Padrick worked for him in the office of this business. Later J. J. L. engaged in farming on a large scale, and he was interested especially in the raising of Black Angus cattle. Buyers came from great distances to view his herds and buy his cattle. Also he was manager of a "long distance telephone company," in 1903. That year, also, he became the first president of the First National Bank of Tifton, which opened in February. O. D. Gorman was cashier.

J. J. L. was nearly blind. He could not see well enough to read a letter even, and everything had to be read to him. His secretary, from South Carolina, was a pleasant young person and he fell in love with her and they were married.

In the early days J. J. L. Phillips was a member of the Sam Clyatt Fishing Club which used to make annual excursions to Homasassa, Florida. Later he was a member of the Country Club, at Gun Lake.

Associated in business with J. J. L. were the Hollinsworths. Mrs. Hollinsworth, prior to her marriage, was a Dickerson, and the Phillipses, the Hollinsworths and the Dickersons and Dr. and Mrs. J. M. Price were close friends.

After his marriage J. J. L. Phillips built a large and handsome brick residence at the southwest corner of Central Avenue at Twelfth Street. There he and Mrs. Phillips lived for a number of years before moving to Florida where he engaged in further sawmill operations, before moving to Coral Gables where Mr. and Mrs. Phillips now make their home.

The beautiful Tifton home which J. J. L. built for Evie was sold to the W. T. Roughtons. Later, after the death of Mrs. Roughton, it was purchased by the Twentieth Century Library Club, and it has not only housed the library but has been the scene of many beautiful receptions and weddings.

JOHN A. PHILLIPS

John A. Phillips was born in Emanuel County, Georgia, July 28, 1836; served in the Confederate Army; married, in Emanuel County, Miss Margaret Elizabeth McArthur (born July 25, 1845—died December 18, 1932 Atlanta; buried at Tifton). To John and Margaret were born two daughters, Ida, and Sadie (born July 4, 1872).

Captain Phillips had made his fortune and had retired from business and his two daughters had graduated from Wesleyan, Macon, when he and Mrs. Phillips and Ida and Sadie came to Tifton, in the fall of 1889. He made large investments here, where he bought land and erected Tifton's first hotel of considerable size. This large hotel was in process of erection on the site now occupied by the Myon Hotel, when Sadie, about seventeen years old, was stricken with typhoid fever. She died on Christmas Eve, 1889, only a few months after her family had moved to Tifton. Sadie was buried at Tifton.

The new hotel was completed, and Captain Phillips called it "The Sadie Hotel," for his beloved daughter. This structure became famous in the social life of early Tifton.

The Phillips had an apartment at the Sadie and for a short time lived there, but they never operated the hotel, but leased it to I. J. Clements. Captain Phillips built and moved his family into the large frame house now called the Julian Apartments, at northwest corner of Central Avenue at Second Street. Next door to this house was the Methodist parsonage, occupied by the Reverend C. E. Crawley, pastor of the First Methodist Church. The parsonage burned and the lot on which it stood and the adjoining lot were bought by Captain Phillips and Jacob Marion Paulk, the Methodists buying a lot in the next block and erecting thereon a large two story house.

The Tifton Gazette on May 10, 1895 carried the following item: "Capt. John A. Phillips lost one of his cottages at Phillipsburg by fire early Wednesday morning. It was occupied by a family of negroes."

After living in Tifton only a few years, Captain Phillips sold his interests here and he, Mrs. Phillips, and Ida moved to Fitzgerald. He sold the Sadie to W. W. Timmons; he sold his large new home to Dr. George Julian, who made it his home until his death; he sold to J. M. Paulk his interest in the lots they had bought from the Methodists. Paulk built on these lots two homes the second of which he and his bride occupied, and in which Mrs. Paulk lived until her death in 1947.

Mrs. Irvine Myers later owned both the hotel site and one of the Paulk built houses. The Sadie burned in 1904 and was replaced by the Myon. Phillips was active in the founding of Fitzgerald where he remained until his death from a stroke of paralysis. He had first suffered a stroke in 1903, and had apparently recovered when he was again stricken on May 27, Saturday, 1905. He never rallied. Death came on Sunday evening at eight o'clock, at the home of his daughter and her husband, J. H. Harris, in Fitzgerald.

The body of Captain Phillips was brought to Tifton on a special train Wednesday morning. It is said that nearly half the population of Tifton joined in the procession to the Tifton cemetery where Captain Phillips was laid to rest beside his beloved daughter, Sadie.

Later Ida's husband was killed by a truck, in Fitzgerald. Following his death she and her children and her widowed mother moved to College Park. Mrs. Phillips died in Atlanta; and Mrs. Harris died in or about the year 1945.

Of Captain Phillips the Tifton Gazette in issue of June 3, 1905, wrote, in his obituary: "He was one of the first heavy investors in Tifton in the early days of its growth, and also one of the founders of Fitzgerald, to which city he contributed much of its growth."

P. D. PHILLIPS

P. D. Phillips was born in Calhoun County, Alabama, in 1860. He was son of a physician who, in 1873, moved his family to Louisiana. In August of the next year both P. D.'s parents died. In October an uncle came from North Alabama to Louisiana for P. D. and his brother, J. J. L., and the two other children and carried them back to his Alabama farm where he taught them to work. They attended an Old Field School for several weeks each year.

By hard work and economy young P. D. saved a little money and, when twenty-one years old, went to Texas where for $500.00 he purchased a half interest in a sawmill—the beginning of his sawmill activities.

In the fall of 1890 P. D. Phillips married his first cousin, Miss Willie Phillips, of Jacksonville, Ala. Of this union were four children; Joe, Clarence, Charles, Mary Lou.

Three years after his marriage P. D. and J. J. L. Phillips began sawing lumber with a small mill near Chula. About 1901 the Phillips brothers began operating a much larger mill at Eldorado. After a period of joint operation P. D. bought out J. J. L.'s interest, J. J. L. moved to Tifton and P. D. and his famiy continued in Eldorado, where P. D. operated the mill.

In 1909 P. D. was a member of Tift County's first Board of Education. Chairman of the board was Briggs Carson, and other members were W. R. Smith, Dr. B. F. Pickett, G. W. Crum, and J. N. Horne. Of Mr. Phillips the Tifton Gazette wrote at that time, "As a member of the Board of Education he has always been punctual, and his judgment, dispatch, and business ability have been recognized from the start.

"As a citizen he has been a firm friend of education and extremely generous to the church, the school, and to the Children's Home. Like other members of the Board of Education he takes great interest in agriculture and has demonstrated that two bales of cotton per acre can be raised on Tift County soil."

During that year, 1909, Mr. Phillips was still operating the Eldorado mill, he was president of the State Mutual Insurance Company, was president of the Phillips Lumber Company, was a director of the Bank of Tifton, a stockholder in various other Tifton enterprises, besides owning valuable real estate in Georgia, Alabama and Tennessee.

From Eldorado Mr. and Mrs. P. D. Phillips moved to Thomasville, where Mrs. Phillips still lives. P. D. died about two years ago.

THURSTON ELILIS PHILLIPS

Thurston Ellis Phillips, one of several children of Ellis and Elizabeth Lansdell Phillips, of Columbia County, Georgia, was born in Columbia County, October 4, 1868 and spent his boyhood on his father's large Columbia County plantation, not far from Augusta.

Aftar having finished his school in the educational institutions of the community, young Thurston, at the age of twenty-one, acquired a portable sawmill and began sawmill activities, first in Columbia County, and later in Burke, Jefferson, Johnson and other Georgia counties and in Edgefield County, South, Garolina. It was his wont to stay in one location for a fortnight or for several weeks and then move on to another.

At Darien, Georgia, February 8, 1898, Thurston Ellis Phillips was united in marriage with Mary D. Chappellear, an orphan, daughter of Reuben and Mozelle Patterson Chappellear, of Jefferson County. Miss Chappellear was, at the time of her marriage, living with a sister, Mrs. Robert E. Printup, in Darien. Of this marriage were four children, Mattie Lou, Ida, May, T. E. Jr., Mary.

Mr. Phillips bought land at Eldorado in what was then Berrien but now is Tift County. On January 1, 1900 he established there a sawmill and he also engaged on a large scale in the turpentine industry. Also he engaged in farming and increased his land holdings until he owned six thousand acres and was operating sixty-five plows.

The Phillips family remained at Eldorado for fourteen years and then, in order to avail themselves of better schools for the children, Mr. Phillips moved his family to Tifton where he built for their occupancy a large brick house at 410 Park Avenue, North, which is still the Phillips home.

In Tifton, Thurston Phillips took an active part in all worthwhile community projects. In 1916 he was elected to Tifton City Council, on which he served for about eight years. For about six years he was on the school board. He served as chairman of Tift County's first Board of County Commissioners, was off the board for a year, then returned and served as chairman for two terms, during which time, through his influence, the county's first concrete bridges were built. One was built over Little River and there were numerous smaller ones built. From 1927 to 1931 T. E. Phillips ably represented Tift County, for three terms, in the state legislature.

Walter G. Cooper, writing of Mr. Phillips in his "Story of Georgia," credits him with always standing for progress, and always being interested in economy and efficiency of government, striving to ease the taxpayers' burden and seeing that the taxpayer received a full measure of benefit for money expended.

Mr. Phillips is a director of the Bank of Tifton, of the Tifton Investment Company and of the Farmers' Bank of Tifton.

In partnership with Holmes Murray, Mr. Phillips operated for many years a grist mill at Tifton. Later he owned it outright, and still later in 1945 when the mill was incorporated he retained one-third interest and became president of the corporation.

Mr. Phillips is a deacon for life of the First Baptist Church, Tifton.

On October 6, 1938, Mary Chappellear Phillips died, at Tifton, where she is buried.

After six years, T. E. Phillips married again. His bride was Miss Sarah Dunbar, of Tifton, daughter of William Allen Dunbar and Emily Wright Dunbar, both deceased, of Dunbar, Georgia. The ceremony was performed at Druid Hills Baptist Church, Atlanta.

Re children of Thurston and Mary Chappellelar Phillips:

Mattie Lou attended Bessie Tift College for three years, and studied in Chicago one year. She married Dr. Earl Kilpatrick Lazenby, of Fayetteville, North Carolina. They have one daughter, Martha.

Ida May Phillips graduated from Bessie Tift College. She married Malcolm Kirk Smith. They have one daughter, Siska. They live in Jacksonville, Florida.

Thurston Ellis Phillips, Jr., married Vera Sport, a young woman of exceptional beauty and sweetness. They live in Tifton.

Mary Phillips graduated from Queens College. She was president of the Phi Mu Chapter there. She lives in North Carolina where, during World War II, she was with the American Red Cross.

FLORENCE WILLINGHAM PICKARD

Florence Martha Willingham was the daughter of Thomas Henry Willingham and Cecilia Baynard Willingham. She was born on Thomas's large South Carolina plantation, "Smyrna," near Old Allendale, March 7, 1862. When still very young she refugeed with her family from Smyrna to a Mitchell County, Georgia, plantation which Thomas owned. After a short residence there the family moved to the "Yancey Place" about four miles from Albany. On this large plantation which Thomas owned and where the Willingham family lived for many years, was beautiful Blue Springs, deep, clear and blue. It is now famous as Radium Springs.

Florie and Bess, when Florie was not more than twelve, were sent to Wesleyan College, where both were Adelphians. Later Florie attended a private school taught by Miss Sallie Reynolds in Albany, and Bess went to Monroe Female College in Forsyth, Georgia. The Willinghams have moved into Albany.

After Bess had graduated it was Florie's turn to go away to school; for of the seventeen Willingham children fourteen reached maturity and all fourteen were college students, and most of them graduated from college, and with honors. Florie went to Woman's College, Richmond, Virginia. She had loved art since childhood and while at Richmond she learned that at nearby Staunton Female Seminary was a very fine art teacher, Madam Garcia, a Parisian. Florie at the next term entered Staunton, of which Miss Mary Baldwin was at that time principal and for whom the college was later named. Florie studied there several years and received the highest honor in art.

Returning to Albany, Florie continued her painting and also conducted a private school of which she was principal and whose clientile were the elite of Albany.

Florie during vacations did much visiting to her older sisters and other relatives. While visiting her sister, Sallie, Mrs. Ed Bacon, in Eastman, Dodge County, she met a young divinity student from Mercer University. He was preaching at the Baptist Church of Eastman. His name was William Lowndes Yancey Pickard, of Upson County, Georgia. Later Will roomed at Mercer with Florie's brother, Winnie Joe. When Florie would visit her brother, Thomas, and his wife in Macon, Will would come with Winnie to see Florie. Thus the acquaintance ripened into friendship and later they became engaged. They were married at Albany, June 15, 1886.

Meanwhile, Florie nearly went blind. She had had to give up her school and also had to give up her painting. Her sister, Bessie, had to read her love letters to her and to write the answers too; but after Bess married Henry Tift and went to Tifton to live Florie did her own reading and writing, her eyes were by that time stronger.

To Will she bore four children, Julia, Florence, William L., Jr., and Elizabeth Belle, born after the death of the beloved only son, Will's namesake, who died of diphetheria when five years old, while Will was pastor of the Broadway Baptist Church, Louisville. All of the family found the Kentucky winters bitter and Florie and the children would come to Tifton and spend the coldest months, either with her sister, Bessie Tift, or with Will's brother, J. L. Pickard and his wife, Cornelia. This continued when Dr. Pickard went to the Cleveland Church, where he remained for nearly five years. So it was over a long period of years that the W. L. Pickards spent their winters in Tifton. The little girls would study out of the Cleveland school books, and be tutored by Tifton teachers, and send their exercises back to the Cleveland schools, where they never missed a grade. Julia studied Greek under W. L. Harman.

During 1905 when making their home in Lynchburg, Virginia, Florie went with Will to the First Baptist World's Alliance, which met in London. Bessie Tift went with them and after the convention the three toured Europe. At Paris Bessie bought a pearl hair ornament and crowned Florie. That night Florie had a dream which she later, after her return to America, transferred to canvas; for her eyesight had so improved that after eighteen years of not painting she had resumed her well-loved art, in which she achieved extraordinary success, and much renown. She also wrote five books, three of which were published during her lifetime. The other two have never been published. The three published books were: "The Ides of March," published in 1901; "Between Scarlet Thrones," published in 1919; "In The Palace of Amuhai," published in 1926.

In 1914 Florie moved with Will to Macon where he was president of Mercer University during World War I. There she was a member of the First Baptist Church. She took great interest in the life of the college, as she always did in all of her husband's work. She was a charter member and honorary member of the Macon Writers' Club, founded in 1915, by her Albany schoolgirl friend, Willie Oliver Moore. After Dr. Pickard resigned as president of Mercer he became pastor of the Central Baptist Church in Chattanooga, Tennessee, and there Florie lived seven happy years. She loved Chattanooga. Her children being grown, she had more leisure, than when they were young, and she was greatly beloved in the clubs in which she enjoyed membership: the Chattanooga Writers' Club, The Tennessee Writers' Club, the Chattanooga Chapter of the National Pen Woman's League, the Kiwanis Auxiliary, of which she was chaplain. In Chattanooga, as in all of Will's churches, she took an active part in the church work, and she had the gift of endearing her associates to her so that she received from them cooperation in whatever was undertaken. She would gather the women of the church together and they would sew for the poor, or would make gay quilts, which they would sell, and the proceeds from which would be given to missions. Her especial concern was the aged of the church and she often planned gay parties for their pleasure, and they were very brilliant, beautiful parties, into the spirit of which the younger women would enter with great enthusiasm and interest; and the happiness of the aged "Mothers in Israel" was compensation enough for all the trouble.

In 1925 Will's health began to fail, so that doctors said he must take life quietly or he could not live long. Florie's sister, dear Bessie Tift, told Florie that if she and Will would come to Tifton to live she would give them a house. They did and she did—415 Park Avenue, which was their home for the next five happy, brief years which soon had sped by. There Florie died, December 2, 1930.

Florie's body was taken to the First Baptist Church of Tifton, then to Albany, where a brief service was held in the Albany Baptist Church, before she was laid to rest beside her only son, William L. Pickard, Jr., in the Albany cemetery.

Both Will and Florie were survived by all three of their daughters:

Julia Baynard Pickard, married Ralph Edward Bailey.

Florence Martha Pickard, married Leverett Roland Harrison.

Elizabeth Belle Pickard, married Paul Daggett Karsten. (See Wire Grass Journalism chapter.)

For sketches of Julia and Florence Pickard, see elsewhere this chapter.

Elizabeth Pickard is the writer of the bigrophical sketches of the Tift County Pioneers contained in this book, except those designated as being the work of other writers.

WILLIAM LOWNDES YANCEY PICKARD

William L. Yancey Pickard, third son of James LaFayette Pickard and Anne Hasseltine Ross Pickard, was born in Upson County, Georgia, October 19, 1861.

James LaFayette Pickard was a planter of Upson County. He was son of Robert Micajah Pickard and his wife, Sarah Barksdale, daughter of William Barksdale, of English descent, who lived in Sparta, Georgia, and is buried in Pine Bluff Cemetery, east of Albany. The Yancey Place, where Florie Willingham, whom W. L. Y. Pickard married, spent her childhood, was owned by a Mr. Barksdale prior to its being owned by Thomas Willingham, Florie's father. Florie and Bessie (Willingham) Tift were sisters. The Barkdales are a distinguished family in and around Wilkes County, Georgia. They came from Abbeville District, South Carolina, and previously were from Albemarle or Hanover County, Virginia.

Anne Hasseltine Ross Pickard was daughter of the Reverend John Ross II (born Virginia, 1781; ordained to Baptist ministry, 1816; died June 17, 1837, Georgia), who came from Virginia to Columbia County, Georgia,

1798. A clergyman of note, John Ross was, at the convention meeting in Talbotton, in 1836, a strong advocate of the Baptist establishment of Mercer University. He also attended a ministers meeting in July following, at Forsyth where he was instrumental in accomplishing much good. Of John Ross was written, "His preaching talents were of a very respectable order, and he began exercising them about 1816." A sketch of the life of John Ross may be found in Jesse Campbell's "Georgia Baptists," published by H. K. Ellyson, Richmond, 1847; also in "History of Georgia Baptists," compiled for Christian Index, 1881. Anne's mother was Charity Mitchell, second wife of John Ross. After John's death, Charity married Captain Thomas Hall. Charity is buried on the Ross lot in Fort Valley.

James LaFayette Pickard was a soldier of the Confederacy. He died from exposure upon field of battle whither he had gone when still ill of measles of which there had been many cases in camp. He died at the Confederate Hospital which stood where the Hotel DeSoto, Savannah, now stands. James LaFayette Pickard was of the 32d Georgia Regiment.

After J. L. Pickard's death, Anne, left a widow with six children, married again. This marriage had the result of bringing it about that the children of her first marriage were reared in various homes by different of her own and her first husband's relatives. The Pickard children seldom saw their mother again.

William L. Y. Pickard, who was named for the great statesman, William L. Yancey, declared in after life that his earliest recollection was that of his father's funeral. His older brother, J. L., believed that he was too young at the time for him to remember—that he must have confused it with some decoration of the grave at some subsequent time. Howbeit, William and the eldest brother, John Pickard, made their home with their father's sister and her husband, James Pound, a scholarly planter, of near Talbotton, Georgia. Gifted as an educator, James taught Will, his own son Jerre Pound, and a neighbor lad, Charles Jenkins, and another neighbor's boy. Of these Charles Jenkins became president of Wesleyan College, Jerre Pound became president of Georgia Normal College, at Athens, and William L. Pickard became president of Mercer University. The fourth lad became an eminent ear, eye, nose and throat specialist of Atlanta.

From the age of twelve Will Pickard supported himself, working at first for his uncle, James Pound. He plowed and did other plantation work. As a reward for some of his labor Mr. Pound offered to give him a fine horse, bridle and saddle. Will asked that instead he might have the equivalent in money that he might have it as part of his college expenses, which was granted. He went first to celebrated College Temple, at Newnan, a famous school in its day, though now no longer existing. Most of its students were girls, but a few boys were there. Miss Annie Belle Clarke and an older sister were College Temple pupils, and the sister was there when Will Pickard was a student there.

From College Temple Will went to Mercer where he graduated with the A.B. degree in 1884. While there, he had been, in 1883, ordained to the

Baptist ministry, the ordination service being at the First Baptist Church of Macon. Will received his M.A. degree from Mercer in 1885 and in June of that year, at the First Baptist Church of Albany, he was married to Florence Martha Willingham, daughter of Thomas Henry Willingham and Cecilia Baynard Willingham.

While attending Mercer, Will preached at Thomaston, Georgia, on Sundays. From Mercer he went to the Southern Baptist Theological Seminary at Louisville, Kentucky, where he graduated in 1887. Other pastorates were: El Creek, and Normandy, Kentucky, while at the seminary; First Baptist Church, Eufaula, Alabama, 1887-1888; First Baptist Church, Birmingham, 1889-93; Broadway Baptist Church, Louisville, Kentucky, 1894-1898; First Baptist Church, Cleveland, Ohio, 1899-1902; First Baptist Church, Lynchburg, Virginia, 1903-07; Savannah Baptist Church, 1907-14; Central Baptist Church, Chattanooga, Tennessee, 1919-1926.

Between the Louisville and Cleveland pastorates Pickard went to Chicago as professor of New Testament Greek, at the Moody Bible Institute, where he went at invitation of Dr. Dwight Moody. Soon after Dr. Pickard went to the Institute, Dr. Moody died. Temporarily the institution ceased to function on the old schedule, and in that period the Cleveland church called Dr. Pickard and he accepted the call.

After the Savannah Pastorate, Dr. Pickard went to Macon as president Mr. and Mrs. Harrison have recently celebrated their thirty-third wedding anniversary.

Mrs. Harrison is the original of the girl in two of her mother's wellknown paintings, "Choosing the Crown," and "The Chosen Crown," the latter painting is in Tifton.

JAMES LaFAYETTE PICKARD

James LaFayette Pickard, Jr., son of James LaFa'yette Pickard and Anne Hasseltine Ross Pickard, of Upson County, Georgia, was born December 12, 1858. His mother's father was a well known Baptist preacher, the Reverend John Ross. James LaFayette, Sr., a soldier of the Confederacy, died at Confederate hospital at Savannah, during the War Between the States. After Anne's second marriage, James, Jr. was reared by a kinsman, a Mr. Willis.

James LaFayette Pickard married Victoria Thornton and to them were born four children, Novella (married Dr. Sam T. Vann), Lenwood, Willie, who was a little girl who was fatally burned during infancy, and Arlene (1891-1897). The Pickards lived for a time at Woodbury.

After Victoria's death James married Victoria's sister, Cornelia Thornton. They lived for about a 'year in Maitland, Florida, where Cornelia's family lived. Victoria and Cornelia were daughters of Seaborn Thornton, originally of Meriwether.

After the great freeze in Florida, J. L. Pickard and Cornelia moved to Tifton, in 1896. Here were born to them three children, Cornelia (married

Newton Dorsett), James LaFayette Pickard III (now of Miami), and Ralph Pickard (now of St. Petersburg).

In Tifton Mr. Pickard worked for H. H. Tift as manager of the Tift Commissary. This position he held for a long period of years, until the commissary closed with the closing of the mill. He then for a time had a grocery store of his own, and for a time he served as postmaster at Tifton.

The Pickards lived on Second Street next door to the H. H. Tifts. At first they occupied a house which formerly stood between the corner lot and the Tift home, and later they were the first occupants of the house which has recently been moved from the corner of Second Street and Tift Avenue. They occupied one apartment in the house, and a smaller apartment was occupied by Florie Pickard and her children, the wife and children of Dr. W. L. Pickard, Jimmy's brother. Florie was Bessie Tift's sister and in the early days of Tifton when she lived in the North she spent her winters in Tifton. James Pickard, called by everyone "Uncle Jimmy," loved roses and his garden contained many very fine specimens with which he was most generous.

J. L. Pickard was possessed of an exceptionally fine bass voice, and he had taught singing, and he had a gift for leading singing. He was instrumental in the formation of the Tift County Singing Convention and he served on its advisory board, and was in 1921 elected vice-president. He often was song leader at its conventions, and also he was much in demand as a song leader at many different churches, especially the country churches of Tift County.

J. L. Pickard was delegated to visit Governor Joseph M. Terrell in behalf of the establishment of an agricultural and mechanical school at Tifton. In this project he was successful and the Second District A. and M. School, the beginning of what is now Abraham Baldwin Agricultural College, was established at Tifton in 1908. This was secured to Tifton largely through the personal generosity of Henry Harding Tift, who gave large acreage of land and money to the school. James LaFayette Pickard served as the school's first trustee from Tift County, and he held the trusteeship for many years.

J. L. Pickard, and his younger brother, Dr. W. L. Pickard, whom he called "Little Bud" were great fishermen and W. L. tried to get to Tifton for a visit to Jimmie at least once each year even when he lived in other and distant states. Both of them were fine marksmen and they loved and owned some very fine bird dogs, notably an English Setter, Maude, and English Setter, Sport, son of Maude. Also, J. L. had a white and lemon pointer, Hal.

James L. Pickard was a man of sterling integrity of character. He was possessed of a sparkling wit and a keen humor, and he was kind and loved people; and everybody loved "Uncle Jimmy."

James LaFayette Pickard died in Tifton, May 13, 1927. Burial was in Tifton cemetery. His widow now lives in West Palm Beach, Florida.

Lenwood Pickard, eldest son of James LaFalette Pickard, was born at Woodbury, Georgia, July 8, 1883; attended Southern Shorthand Business College, Atlanta; was in World War I, in Service Park Unit No. 384. He moved to Tifton from Florida in 1896. He has held high office in the Tifton Chapter of the Masonic Order and at the Masonic Convention at Macon was consecrated to the High Priesthood, April 26, 1939.

JOHN MILTON PRICE
TIFTON FAIRY TALE

Once upon a time there lived a couple whose names were John and Minerva Emerson Price. They had two children. The girl, Lucy, grew up and married Mr. Kilby. The boy, born September 14, 1858, was named John Milton Price.

When John Milton Price was a small boy his father died. Young John assumed the responsibility of earning a living for the family. However, he loved learning, and eagerly attended the country schools for the three months' term each year.

When John was twenty-one years old he gathered his belongings and, tying them in a bandana handkerchief, he took them with him and walked forty miles to Dahlonega.

Arrived there, John contacted the president of the college. That gentleman discouraged John's entrance, but John, after much persuasion succeeded in being permitted to remain for a try-out.

After a few weeks John received an invitation from the president to come to his rooms nights so that he could help him with his studies. John was overjoyed. Later he graduated with honors.

Next John studied at Augusta, where he received his medical degree from the Augusta Medical College.

Young Dr. John Milton Price opened his first office in Orange, Georgia. Also he was physician to the Franklin Gold Mines, in Creighton, Georgia. Later he moved to Canton, Georgia, where he practiced medicine for several years and was prominent in both civic and professional life. He was president of the Medical Society there.

Dr. John Pirce married a young woman named Georgia Archer. They had two little daughters, Jene and Rebecca, who were their joy.

One day Dr. Price visited Tifton. He was delighted with the place. He called it, "The Garden Spot." Soon he moved him family there and there they lived happily ever after, until September 17, 1941 when Dr. Price died, but not until after celebrating his eighty-third birthday.

Dr. and Mrs. Price's little girls grew up and married and they still live in Tifton. They had a flower shop where they had so many beautiful flowers that seeing them reminded one of Dr. Price's words: "Tifton is the Garden Spot." Perhaps some day they will call the flower store "The Garden Spot."

S. G. SLACK

S. G. Slack, born about 1854, was one of seven brothers born to English parents who came from England to Canada and settled in Ontario. S. G. came to Tifton in the early 1890's; a brother, Ernest Edward, soon followed and settled in Tifton. Another brother settled in Alabama. The others remained in Canada.

As early as 1893 S. G. was already a well known and highly revered citizen of Tifton. A builder and contractor, he had established a reputation for doing high quality work. The houses he built were good houses and are today some of the best houses in Tifton. Among these is the Carson home, built by Slack for Elias Vickers at 315 W. Sixth Street. Slack loved good lumber and good workmanship, and it is told of him that one day when he stood in the door way of the Carson house he ran his hand over the beautiful carving of the woodwork and it was almost as though it were a caress.

Also from Canada was Tifton's first contractor, John C. Hind, to whom was issued the first contractor's license in Tifton, 1891.

In the spring of 1893 H. H. Tift, E. P. Bowen and S. G. Slack and others formed a stock company and built and operated a canning factory in Tifton. The building was begun on April 15. By May 15 the factory was in full operation. With a capacity of ten thousand cans a day, they employed one hundred and twenty hands during the busy season. The first season they canned peaches, pears, tomatoes. In 1895 they canned strawberries, dewberries, peaches, pears, okra, English peas, wax beans, sweet potatoes. With great success they shipped "all over the country."

In 1895 Mr. Slack completed erection of a ten thousand dollar church in Valdosta. Also, he was in August awarded contract for the inside work of a church erected in Quitman. That same year he opened in Tifton a hardware store which for many years was the leading hardware firm of the community. An advertisement of May 5, 1905 indicates that at that time the members of the firm were S. G. Slack, J. J. L. Phillips, A. B. Hollingsworth, E. E. Slack.

Early in the twentieth century S. G. Slack became interested in Tifton city politics. He was elected alderman to serve for two years, beginning 1902. Others elected to serve for the same period were H. H. Tift and E. P. Bowen. F. G. Boatright was mayor. Slack was at once placed upon various committees. With E. P. Bowen and W. T. Hargrett he served on the committee on streets. With J. M. Paulk and E. P. Bowen he served on the committee on accounts. He was on the committee of appraisers. S. G. Slack was on the Board of Aldermen when that body voted to accept the proposition of B. M. Griffin to "light the streets." Also when it voted to purchase from H. H. Tift a site for a school. The old school was located on the site of what is now that of the Primitive Baptist Church.

Slack continued to serve in 1903 under Mayor Boatright. He, Mr. Boatright, W. W. Timmons and E. P. Bowen were present at a call meeting of the council for the purpose of appointing managers and clerks to conduct the election of Judge and Solicitor of the City Court of Tifton. Appointed so to act as election managers were O. L. Chesnutt, J. P., T. J. Parker, J. K. Carswell. W. W. Webb, T. E. Phillips, S. S. Monk, William Whiddon and E. R. Gaulding were alternates. As a result of the election F. G. Boatright was elected judge and C. C. Hall solicitor. An offer of H. H. Tift to provide court room quarters at $17.00 per month was declined, and an offer of E. P. Bowen to provide them for $100.00 per year was accepted. Kent's offer to furnish the room was declined and that of F. C. Dynes was accepted.

In April of 1903 S. G. Slack was on a committee to arrange for a city engineer to make a map of the city. That same year, Mr. Slack, Briggs Carson and W. W. Timmons were tax assessors.

W. W. Timmons was mayor of Tifton in 1904 and councilmen elected to serve with him were S. G. Slack, H. H. Tift and E. P. Bowen. When W. W. Timmons resigned his place on council in order to become eligible as a candidate for mayor, J. J. Golden was elected to fill his unexpired term. This was on November 28, 1903.

Slack continued to serve on council in 1905 when Timmons was again mayor, and Slack served as councilman when Sam M. Clyatt became mayor in 1906. In 1906 S. G. Slack, J. J. Golden, Dr. N. Peterson were appointed by Mayor Clyatt to compile a sanitary code for the city. Slack, E. P. Bowen and J. J. Golden were appointed to draft a Tifton curfew ordinance. On November 6, 1905, Mr. Slack was on a committee which ordered an election held for bonds for water works and a school building. Bonds were voted.

In September of 1906 S. G. Slack, John Murrow, T. E. Phillips, J. A. Warren, H. H. Tift, J. J. Golden were appointed by Ordinary W. S. Walker to constitute an advisory board with the ordinary in selecting plans, making contract, and superintending the building of a courthouse. Mr. Slack continued to serve on various committees of city council for a great many years. In 1907 he, with H. H. Tift, favored passage of a cow ordinance but it failed of passage.

At a meeting at seven P. M. Tuesday, October 29, 1907, a volunteer fire department was organized in Tifton. S. G. Slack was chief of the department, which was divided into two companies. Captain of Company Number 1 was W. H. Spooner. Captain of Company Number 2 was L. Mask. Members of Company Number 1 were: W. H. Spooner, Capt., Z. T. Brown, A. C. Soule, B. J. Booth, R. S. Short, H. H. Tift, Jr., W. R. Walton, R. H. Murrow, W. H. Graham, J. B. Greene, W. N. Camp. Members of Company Number 2 were: Capt. L. Mask, C. B. Grugger, J. A. Ryals, J. L. Williams, G. B. Courtney, H. C. Carmichael, P. H. O'Quinn, D. L. Swindle, W. H. McClellan, T. J. Welch, W. P. Stipes.

Later S. G. Slack moved from Tifton to Union City where he made his home for many years and until his death there on Wednesday, October 23, 1940, at the age of eighty-six years. Funeral services and burial were at Union City on the Friday next.

S. G. Slack was survived by his widow, who has since then died, and by the following children: Mrs. Faust Dewitt, of Elkton, Md.; Mary Belle (Mrs. S. R. Smith) of Union City; Harry Slack of Boston, Georgia; Willard Slack, of Rome. Also surviving was one brother, Jule Slack, of Hagersville, Ontario, Canada.

A son, Lawrence Slack, who was very popular in Tifton, died in 1931, unmarried.

Ernest Edward Slack, brother of S. G., was born in Canada, came to

Tifton and spent the rest of his life here, where he died and is buried. Children of E. E. Slack are Eugene Slack, of Tifton, and Dorothy Slack, who was clerk of Tift County Draft Board during World War II.

JASON SCARBORO

Jason Scarboro, son of Absolom and Demarius Scarboro, was born in Bulloch County, Georgia, May 5, 1860. He came to Tifton from Moultrie.

Although Lucian Lamar Knight states that Jason Scarboro was head of Tifton's first high school in 1888, it appears that this must be a misprint, for it appears from local records that Mr. Scarboro came here at a later date. In 1902 he was head of Tifton schools which had an enrollment of 273, with an average attendance for the fall term of 223. On December 29, 1902 began the spring term for 1903. Professor Scarboro was principal and teachers were Misses Worrell, Smith, Ellis, Murray, Parham. In spring of 1906 the enrollment was the largest in the history of the school up to that time. Scarboro presented a commencement program in the new cotton warehouse "fitted up for the occasion." On the program were Reverend Henry Miller, Essie McDuffie, Adelaide Hargrett, Annie Barnes, Reverend J. W. Domingos, who pronounced the benediction, and Willingham Tift, who spoke on "The Right Start." The school was at this time housed in a small wooden building which stood where the Primitive Baptist Church now is.

On June 12, 1906, an election was held to decide whether or not Tifton would have public schools. Raleigh Eve, S. S. Monk, were clerks of the election, and O. L. Chesnutt, J. P., E. B. O'Neal, and Willard Gaulding were managers. The vote for schools was unanimous, and a new school building was erected in Tifton and first occupied on January 14, 1907, when Sam Clyatt was mayor. Mr. Scrboro was principal at this time and this new building then erected was what is now the Tifton Grammar School.

Mr. Scarboro was principal of schools here for many years, and was instrumental in securing the building of the present Tifton High School, but failing health prevented his continuing longer as school head. He owned a farm near Tifton, and he taught for a brief time in Adel, but was not physically equal to continuing the arduous duties of teaching, in which he had already served long, faithfully and efficiently. Hoping to improve his health, he went West, but there died, October 28, 1926. He was survived by his widow, a delightful and pious woman, who died in 1945 and is buried at Tifton. One son died in early boyhood. Surviving children are Effie Mae (Mrs. George Towns) of Long Island; Mary Belle (Mrs. Scott), of Tifton; Dr. Edwin Scarboro, of California.

In January, 1923, Jason Scarboro was elected chairman of the Board of Trade. In July of the same year he was elected to serve on the executive committee of the Tift County Singing Convention for the following year. Also, that year he worked to keep the A. and M. School in Tifton and was chairman of a committee who drew a resolution against removal. Their efforts were successful.

MATTHEW SYLVESTER SHAW

Matthew Sylvester Shaw, son of W. S. Shaw, was born in Berrien County, Georgia, October 24, 1873. He was in the mercantile business at Nashville, Gergia, and at Lenox, and then in the naval stores business at Crosland. About 1907 he moved to Tifton and while here engaged in the real estate business, especially pine lands. Also, from time to time he chartered a train and took large excursion parties on trips, and these excursions were a delightful feature of the lighter side of old Tifton. He was a great wit, and was always keeping his friends laughing by his humorous tales and quaint experiences. He was a great favorite with children and one tiny girl used to call him "Bess," by which nickname he was long called by a large circle of devoted friends.

Mr. Shaw married Miss Edna Cox, daughter of the Reverend W. F. Cox, of Omega, and Emma Royal Cox. Of this union were two sons, Roy and Fred. Fred, who attended Mercer and was a brilliant student, did much research for the Tift County Historical Society some years ago. He was assisted by Clem Carson, and their manuscript was one of the references used in the History of Tift County as written by Miss Ida Belle Williams, although she personally did much research in addition. Fred Shaw now teaches at the University of Miami. Clem Carson continues to live in Tifton where he is engaged in business. Fred and Clem were close friends when Fred lived in Tifton.

M. S. Shaw died at his Tifton home, corner of Chesnut Avenue and Sixth Street, April 16, 1929. Funeral was at the Baptist Church and burial in the Tifton cemetery.

Mrs. Shaw taught school in Tifton for many years. She was an excellent teacher, and was greatly beloved. She was found dead in her bed and it was believed she had died during her sleep. Her obituary was in the Tifton Gazette, issue of May 2, 1935. She was fifty-seven years old at the time of her death. Burial was in Tifton cemetery. Mrs. Pickens of Central Avenue, Tifton, is a sister of Mrs. Shaw.

LUTHER SMITH SHEPHERD AND LARKIN G. MAYNARD

Luther Smith Shepherd was born in Fayette County, Georgia, June 29, 1855. At Senoia, Georgia, on January 27, of 1885 or 1887, he married Miss Callie Gaulding, one of twin daughters of Joe and Mary Gaulding, and granddaughter of Archibald Alexander Gaulding, eminent newspaper editor and lawyer of Atlanta, prior to the War Between the States. Callie and her twin sister, Donie, were born at Ellaville, Hamilton County, Florida, January 23, 1865. Callie and Donie grew up in Pike County, Georgia. Donie married Larkin G. Maynard.

When Luther and Callie Shepherd had been married about ten years they moved to Tifton, and there Messrs. Luther Smith Shepherd and Larkin G. Maynard went into business together and, as the firm of Shepherd and Maynard, did business for many years. Both families lived on Love Avenue.

Mr. Maynard was a Tifton councilman in 1896, at which time F. G.

Boatright was mayor, and Holmes Murray was clerk and treasurer. Fellow councilmen were H. H. Tift, E. P. Bowen, W. W. Timmons, John A. Phillips, W. O. Padrick.

In 1926 Mr. Shepherd was stricken ill and he died on January 27, 1928, at his Love Avenue home in Tifton, on his wedding anniversary.

Mrs. Shepherd, a conscientious Methodist, was a woman "of culture, refinement, gentle and unassuming manner." Hers was a large circle of friends. An article from her pen appeared in the March 21, 1930 issue of the Tifton Gazette. It was on orchids grown by Dr. Meade at Oveida. Delightfully written, with graphic description and a light touch of humor, it indicates that the writer inherited some of the literary ability of her editor grandfather. At the time it was written Donie was visiting her daughter and her sister in Florida. She did not live much longer than a year afterward. She died Saturday night, June 27, 1931, at the Orange General Hospital, Orlando, Florida. Her body was brought to Tifton and funeral was from her Love Avenue home. At the time of the funeral her twin, Donie, lay ill in a hospital in Tampa, Florida. She, however, improved and lived until July 22, 1939.

Luther Smith Shepherd and his wife, Callie, and Larkin G. Maynard and Callie's twin, Donie, are buried on the same lot in Tifton cemetery. "They were together in life, and in death they were not separated."

GEORGE ALFRED BRANNON SMITH

George Alfred Brannon Smith, born at Columbus, Georgia, August 4, 1857, was son of George Bartlett Smith of the Bartletts and Smiths of Connecticut, and Laura Virginia Brannon, of Columbus, Georgia. George Bartlett Smith's family came to Columbus from Connecticut before the War Between the States. He graduated from Mercer with the A.B. degree and then went to Yale where he received his M.D. degree. Also he was a doctor of divinity. A great scholar, he spoke thirteen languages. At the time of his marriage he was cashier of a Columbus bank, but he resigned the bank position and later owned a drug store in Wetumka, Alabama, where he also was editor of a paper. He was editor of a Montgomery paper at one time.

At the outbreak of the War Between the States Smith's family returned to Connecticut but he entered the service of the Confederacy, and went into the army. His wife and children were living at his wife's birthplace, a large and handsome Columbus house called the "Lion House," because its entrance was guarded by large carved stone lions. The Union soldiers seized the house as officers' headquarters. Mrs. Smith locked herself and children in her room where she remained three days. When necessity drove her thence she was courteously treated by her uninvited guests. Her silver, which she had hidden in a secret passage under the house, was unmolested, and later was recovered safely. She sold her grand piano, sent the money to her husband, who, with it, paid for a substitute for military service and then became a secretary to Vice-President Jefferson Davis.

The four children of the above mentioned union were George Alfred

Brannon Smith, who was the eldest child, Freeman, Martin, and Jim. All except George grew up and died unmarried.

George A. B. Smith attended a school of pharmacy in Atlanta. On September 28, 1882, at the First Baptist Church at Wetumka, he married Lula E. Mann, daughter of Frances Marion Mann, who was second cousin of the renowned Horace Mann, for whom Horace Mann School was named, and governor of Massachusetts.

After completing his pharmaceutical course, Dr. Smith lived for about three years in Columbus but then went to Macon where he was manager of the wholesale house of Lamar, Taylor and Riley. In Macon his daughter, Laura, was born. From Macon the Smiths went to Athens, where little Lula Belle Smith was born. Thence the family went to Brunswick where Dr. Smith was manager of Lloyd and Adams, later Smith and Adams.

Dr. Smith was a very good druggist and it is said that he was the highest paid druggist in Georgia during his time. He came from Brunswick to Tifton in 1896.

Upon coming to Tifton, Dr. Smith built a large brick store to house his drug business, and a large frame dwelling to house his family. The store was the Main Street store now occupied by Wright, and the house was the large edifice at the northwest corner of Central Avenue at Sixth Street, which now houses Miss Tucker's business school. There for many years Dr. and Mrs. Smith and the two beautiful daughters, Laura and Lula Belle lived, and there were spent many happy days, for the girls were winsome and unusually pretty; especially so was Laura. Both girls attended Wesleyan, at Macon.

Dr. Smith looked upon his profession as a means of serving humanity and often he filled prescriptions for which he knew he would never be paid, and he did much charity work. He continued in the drug business in Tifton until 1906 when failure of his own health caused him to retire and seek improvement in the dry climate of Denver, Colorado. However, he was not successful in his search for health. In Denver he died, in 1908. His body was brought back to Tifton for burial and the large concourse of friends at the funeral service and at the grave attested the love and esteem in which he was held by this community.

Not many months after Dr. Smith's death, Lula Belle, at college, was stricken with typhoid fever and died. Mrs. Smith and Laura lived on at the Smith house for many years, and in 1918 Mrs. Smith built and moved into a brick bungalow next door, on Sixth Street. Laura was the first woman in Georgia to drive an automobile. The car was a big Rambler which her mother bought in 1908 from H. H. Tift, Jr., for $2,600. Mrs. Smith lived in the Sixth Street brick bungalow until her death in 1938.

Laura Smith married the late Keith Carson, Tifton real estate man, and son of Capt. Joseph Carson, C. S. A., and Charlotte Carson. Of this union were two children, a son, who died in childhood, and a daughter, Laura Smith, who married Sam Chastain and lives at Palm Beach. The Chastains have one son.

Laura Smith was by her second marriage Mrs. Edmund Walker. To

Laura and Edmund Walker of Madison, Georgia, was born a daughter, Lula.

On September 12, 1945, at the First Baptist Church at Folkston, Georgia, Laura Smith was united in marriage with Judge Albert Gallatin Foster, of Madison.

ROBLEY DUNGLISON SMITH

Robley Dunglison Smith, Jr., was born in Knoxville, Crawford County, Georgia, August 3, 1882, son of Robley Dunglison Smith, Sr. (born and died in Crawford County, Georgia, at Knoxville), and Nancy Missouri Persons Smith (born Crawford County, died Tifton), daughter of Thomas Persons. Nancy was a kinswoman of William Pinkney Persons and John Thaddeous Persons, brothers who married respectively, Susan Pickard and Sarah Pickard, sisters of Dr. William Lowndes Pickard of Tifton.

Robley Dunglison, in Tifton called "R. D." was grandson of Dr. Smith who went to Jefferson Medical College and named his son for his former professor at the college, Dr. Robley Dungleson, who was physician to Thomas Jefferson.

"R. D." received his schooling at Knoxville, Georgia; received his bachelor of law degree from the University of Georgia in 1904, and on August 20, of that same year, he came to Tifton, where he has continued to practice law from the time of his arrival until the present. He was attorney for Tift County for about five years. Keen minded and popular, he has a large practice.

In Senoia, April 28, 1907, R. D. Smith married Mary Carlton (died November, 1934), daughter of Mr. and Mrs. W. L. Carlton, of Senoia.

On March 28, 1936, R. D. Smith married Anna Hopkins, daughter of Judge W. H. Hopkins, of Thomasville.

R. D. Smith had two sisters and three brothers, the late Dr. W. T. Smith and Howard Smith, both of Tifton, and Northrop Smith, of Macon.

WILLIAM THOMAS SMITH

William Thomas Smith, born March 5, 1876, in Crawford County, Georgia, was son of Robley Dunglison Smith, a Knoxville, Georgia, lawyer, and Nancy Missouri Persons Smith, daughter of Thomas Persons. Robert Dunglison Smith was son of a physician who married a Pennsylvanian. W. T. spent his childhood in Knoxville, where he received his schooling prior to entering George Washington Medical School, at Washington, where he graduated in 1898. Thereafter he practiced medicine in Colloden, Georgia for one year and then went to Tallahassee, Florida, where he practiced medicine until he moved to Tifton in 1906.

A young woman named Maude Burns came from Tennessee to Tift County to teach. Dr. William T. Smith and Miss Maude Burns were married at Columbia, Tennessee, December 29, 1909.

During World War I, Dr. Smith, in 1917, entered the United States Medical Corps, in which he was first lieutenant.

After he returned from the war, Dr. Smith did post graduate work at Tulane University, where he specialized in ear, eye, nose and throat. Returing to Tifton he here practiced as a specialist until three days prior to his death at the Tift County Hospital, Saturday, at 1:15 A. M. December 8, 1945. Burial was at Tifton.

Dr. Smith was a member of the Tifton Methodist Church. He was a kind, cheerful man, who was highly esteemed and greatly beloved by a host of friends. He loved to fish, and went fishing on nearly every holiday.

Children of Dr. W. T. Smith and Maude Burns Smith are: Maude Burns Smith (Mrs. H. E. Killian, of Anniston, Alabama); Katherine (Mrs. Dave Howard, of Atlanta); William T. Smith, Jr.

Issue of Maude Burns Smith and Dr. H. E. Killian: Joyce and Claude Edward. Issue of Katherine Smith and Dave Howard: twins, Ann and David. Issue of Dr. William T. Smith, Jr., D.D.S., and Cecilia Travis Smith, daughter of Lieutenant-Colonel Travis, of Savannah: Gordon Burns Smith and Bruce Smith.

Dr. W. T. Smith had two sisters and three brothers. The brothers are: Robert D. Smith, Jr., Tifton lawyer, Howard Smith, of Tifton (who married a sister of Maude Burns); and Northrop Smith, of Macon, who married two Solomon sisters, the second wife being Elizabeth (Buff) Solomon, of Macon. Mr. and Mrs. Howard Smith have two sons, Howard Smith, Jr., and Robley Smith.

WALTER CRAWFORD SPURLIN

William Crawford Spurlin (born February 10, 1868, in Pulaski County, near Hawkinsville—died February 8, 1940, at Tifton; buried in Tifton cemetery), was son of Frances Bateman Spurlin and William H. Spurlin, a farmer who also owned and conducted a livery stable and blacksmith shop. When little William C. was about one year old his mother died. He was therefore reared by his older sister, Ella, and by his step-mother. He lived in or near Hawkinsville until nineteen years of age and then went to Sumner, Georgia, where he worked in a dry goods store, or commissary for a few months before coming to Tifton where he worked first at the Tift Commissary and later at the Tift Dry Goods Store. Later Spurlin's Store carried shoes and men's clothing.

Highly esteemed for his integrity of character and for his unfailing courtesy to all, W. C. Spurlin was "a gentleman of the old school."

Mr. Spurlin was twice married. His first wife was Allie O'Kelley. By this union were two children, William Francis Spurlin, of Miami (married Alline Bragg. Issue: W. F., Jr., and Florence), and an infant who died in 1900, when, also, Mrs. Spurlin died.

William C. Spurlin on September 7, 1904, at Sparks, Georgia, married Laura McKinney, daughter of J. W. McKinney, of Sparks, and Nancy McCrainie (McKinney), of Berrien County. Issue: Walter Crawford, who married Estelle Connor; James Raleigh, who died in 1909, aged eighteen months; Helen; Eunice.

Walter and Estelle Connor Spurlin have two children, James Kenneth and Laurel Ann.

In 1895 W. C. Spurlin was prelate of the Kinghts of Pythias, Piney Woods Lodge, No. 50. Other officers that year were: E. J. Williams, Jr., C. C., O. M. Tift, V. C., J. B. Green, M. of W., J. A. Peterson, M. of A., H. S. Murray, M. of F. and K. of R. and S., William Wilson, M. of E., H. F. Newton, I. G., J. A. Cole, O. G.

MRS. HENRY HARDING TIFT

NELSON TIFT

Tift County is named for Nelson Tift, founder of Albany, Georgia, and an uncle of Henry Harding Tift, Tifton's founder. Nelson sold Henry the land on which Tifton now stands. It was then covered with a mighty forest of virgin yellow pines.

Nelson Tift, born in Connecticut in 1810, lived in his native state until twenty years old. Long fascinated by tales of the South, he, at the age of twenty, came to Charleston, South Carolina, where he was with a mercantile house. In 1835 Nelson settled in Augusta.

In September, 1836, Nelson Tift received from a company of Augusta business men $1300.00 with which to come to the site now Albany and found a town. Those composing the company were John Rawls, Dr. R. N. Taylor, W. King, T. J. Watts, B. F. Watts.

HISTORY OF TIFT COUNTY 463

Traveling on horseback, Nelson arrived October 13, 1836 at the site now Albany. There he found Dr. Taylor and John Rawls directing white hands in construction of two log buildings. Next day the hands quit. After much search and travel Nelson secured others who completed these and other buildings.

On March 19, 1837 a steamboat, Mary Emeline, from Apalachiola, arrived with supplies for a store. Nelson Tift bought interests of the other pioneers. He had surveyed, cleared off timber and laid out a town site one mile square, the older portion of present Albany.

Nelson Tift, May, 1838, married Maria Mercer, a niece of Jesse Mercer for whom Mercer University was named. To Nelson and Maria Mercer Tift were born two sons and five daughters: Nelson, James M., Annie, Fannie, Isabel, Clara, Irene.

In 1841, the Georgia Legislature granted a charter for Albany, Georgia. One of the city's first commissioners was Nelson Tift. Also at that time Nelson Tift and J. C. Harris received a permit to build a bridge over the Flint River.

Albany, Georgia was named for Albany, New York.

During the War Between the States Nelson Tift and his brother, Asa, were Confederate sympathizers and materially aided the Confederacy by furnishing supplies of pork and beef, and by building boats. Also, they owned a hard-brick factory, a grist mill, and a barrel factory.

Nelson and Asa employed their nephew, Henry Tift, for a while in Albany before Henry moved to the site now Tifton where he established a sawmill, in 1872. The sawmill village became Tifton.

In Albany, Tift Avenue and Tift Park are named for Nelson Tift. He served as mayor of Albany and he was representative of his district in the Georgia Legislature. Nelson was active in Albany's development as well as with his personal business until shortly before his death at the age of eighty-one, in 1891.

HENRY HARDING TIFT, FOUNDER OF TIFTON

Henry Harding Tift was born in Mystic, Connecticut, March 16, 1841. He was one of seven children born to Phoebe Harding Tift and Amos Chapman Tift, a Mystic merchant, descendant of that Tift family of which John Tefft, of Portsmouth, Rhode Island, who died in 1676, and John Tifft, of Nassau, New York, were early American progenitors.

Henry Tift's schooling was in Mystic common schools. Thereafter he attended historic Greenwich Academy from which he was graduated, 1859. At eighteen he became an apprentice in a Mystic machine shop where he remained for three years. A MAN of VISION, he did not scorn to begin work at a dollar and a half a week in order to learn the things he wished to know, and the knowledge of which was a useful factor in his later success in life, when came the time for him to build an industry on which a town was founded and which led to development of a whole community.

After finishing his appenticeship, Henry Tift spent five years as steamship engineer in lines operating between Apalachicola and Key West, and on the C. H. Mallory Line. His brother, W. O. Tift, married the daughter of the owner of this line.

In 1870 Henry went to Albany, Georgia, where he became general manager of the N. and A. F. Tift Manufacturing Company two years before moving to the site of what is now Tifton, the town which is named for him and which he founded. Albany had been founded by Henry's uncle, Nelson Tift, and from Nelson Henry purchased his acreage in what was then Berrien, but is now Tift County. The land was then a vast unbroken tract of heavily wooded pine forest. The tall yellow pines were in their virgin growth. He acquired more and more land until he owned more than fifty-five thousand acres.

Some of the machinery for the lumber mill which Henry Tift bought he purchased from Thomas Henry Willingham, a prominent and wealthy South Carolinian who, since the War Between the States, had been living in the vicinity of Albany where he had large land holdings. Mr. Willingham owend a large tract of timber land at a post office station named Willingham, for him. At Willingham, T. H. Willingham owned a large sawmill and the surrounding mill village. Fire completely destroyed the village and the mill, except the machinery, which Henry Tift bought from Mr. Willingham and had hauled by an eight ox team, driven by a Negro named Louis Walker, through the pine wilderness which lay between Willingham and what is now Tifton. Here the mill was set up and soon there sprang up around the mill a village which grew into the town of Tifton.

Henry had an office and a commissary on the lower floor of a tall three-story building which stood near the mill. Above the office was a pleasant two-room apartment which he and one of his brothers, Eddie Tift, occupied, there for a while keeping bachelor quarters.

Later Henry met and paid court to Thomas Willingham's daugter, Elizabeth Willingham, of Albany. Better known as "Bessie," Miss Willingham was a young woman of unusual charm and beauty. She had attended Wesleyan College and later had graduated with honors at Monroe Female College, Forsyth. Mr. Tift first saw her in the Episcopal Church in Albany one Easter Sunday, and he later said that from the time he saw her he made up his mind that he would ask her to be his wife. They were wed in the First Baptist Church in Albany, on June 25, 1885, at eleven o'clock, the noted Baptist clergyman, Dr. M. B. Wharton, of Atlanta, performing the ceremony. The marriage had been preceded, on the evening before, by a banquet and family reunion held in honor of the bride and groom at the bride's parents' home, where relatives from Albany, Macon, Atlanta, and elsewhere came to attend the festivities.

Following the fashionable wedding, the couple left for a bridal trip to New York, Saratoga, Niagara, and Mystic, Henry's beloved home. At Mystic, Henry and his bride spent the summer with his people, and in the fall he brought her to Tifton where he had had his apartment in the tall building refurnished in the latest style for Bessie's reception. The fashionable wicker furniture was threaded with wide blue satin ribbon, tied in big bows.

Soon after bringing Bessie to Tifton, Henry began to build for her, across the street from the first quarters, a large, new house, made of heart pine lumber from his mill. It is said that Henry personally selected each board. Especially beautiful was the curly pine woodwork of hall, parlor and dining room, and a large built-in corner-cupboard. Henry and Bessie soon moved into the new home, which became notable for the large hospitality of its owners, ever generous, kind and upright.

For long the Tift mill was the industrial life of Tifton and all of Tifton savored of it. The Tift plant had a capacity of 50,000 feet of rough lumber per day. There were three large dry kilns, and a planing mill with a daily output of 30,000 feet of matched and planed lumber. Also there was a turpentine distillery with which to extract gum from trees before sawing the trees into lumber. There were three locomotives, eighteen miles of railroad, and two hundred hands constantly at work.

As years passed, Henry not only cut timber but he developed the rich farming lands from which the giant trees had been cut. Cotton became an increasingly important factor in the community and forward-looking Henry built and was president of the Tifton Cotton Mill, still the outstanding manufacturing plant of the town.

Tifton was incorporated as a city in 1890, by act of legislature approved December 29. The first regular meeting of the city council of Tifton was held January 9, 1891. The minutes of the first meeting follow: "'J. I.' Clements was requested to act as secretary of the meeting. Present, his honor, W. H. Love, Mayor. Councilmen H. H. Tift, J. C. Goodman, E. P. Bowen, John Pope, and J. I. Clements. Absent, Councilman M. A. Sexton. On motion of Alderman Bowen, Alderman J. I. Clements was elected mayor pro tem. On motion of Alderman Tift, A. J. McRea was elected marshal for the year. On motion of Alderman Clements, J. H. Goodman was elected clerk and treasurer for the year. Motion made and carried that the marshal's salary shall be thirty-three and one-third dollars per month and such other cost as he may be entitled to for him services. But in no case shall the city be liable for any fees whatever. On motion it was ordered that the marshal and the clerk and treasurer each give bond for one thousand dollars for the faithful performance of their duty. On motion it was ordered that the mayor be authorized to make arrangements to care for prisoners until a guard house can be built. On motion it was ordered that the regular meeting of Council be held on the first Monday night at 7 P.M. in each month.

"On motion it was ordered that the marshal shall procure him a dark blue suit and brass buttons. On motion it was ordered that the mayor be paid One Hundred Dollars per annum for his services. On motion Council adjourned.

"Signed J. I. Clements,
Clerk pro tem."

The mayor and councilmen took oath of office before Columbus W. Fulwood, N. P., of Berrien County.

The minutes of the City of Tifton do not indicate where the first meeting of council was held, nor is set forth the place of the second meeting, but the third meeting, which was on February 2, 1891, at 7 o'clock, was held in the office of H. H. Tift, and was the customary place of meeting of Council for several years.

Among the earliest activities of the City Council was the building of a guard house and for this Henry Tift advanced the sum of $685.51 to complete the project, the money to be repaid by the city, and at 8% interest.

Early the use of spiritous liquors was discouraged by the passing of an ordinance fixing the license "for selling spiritous, vinus, malt or intoxicating liquors, rice beer, cider, beer bitters or anything that will tend to intoxicate, at Ten Thousand Dollars per annum, Payable before Commencing business." This ordinance and others fixing various license fees was passed at a called meeting, held January 19, 1891, the second meeting of council.

Fines were set for anyone guilty of disturbing public worship, or public meetings, or for using profane or obscene language in a loud or boisterous manner upon the streets or in any public place. Fines were set for the violation of the Sabbath day; also for hitching a horse, mule, donkey or any other animal to shade tree or injuring the shade trees in any manner.

At a meeting of Council in H. H. Tift's office, September 7, 1891, Messrs. B. T. Allen, H. H. Tift and J. C. Goodman were appointed to constitute a committee to suggest a method of naming streets and appropriate names for same. E. P. Bowen, mayor pro tem., presided at this meeting. Present were Aldermen H. H. Tift, J. C. Goodman, John Pope, B. T. Allen.

At a meeting held in Henry's office November 2, 1891, at eight o'clock, W. H. Love, Mayor, presiding, the following present, Aldermen H. H. Tift, E. P. Bowen, J. C. Goodman, B. T. Allen, the matter of streets was discussed by council as a whole and it was agreed that all streets runing east and west should be called streets and numbered. Those on the north side of the B. and W. R. R. to have even numbers, beginning with the one next to the railroad as Second Street, and those on the south side of the railroad next to the railroad as First Street.

That all streets running north and south should be called avenues and named, with the exception of two which should be called streets and named. Thus, the street running between Messrs. Green and Knight's should be Mill Avenue; the one by the Institute, Tift Avenue, which ends at the B. and W. R. R., one by Dr. J. C. Goodman's, Central Avenue; the next one west of Central, Ridge Avenue.

"Exceptions: That the Street joining Love Avenue at the B. and W. R. R. and running by the Guard House be called Main Street, the one running by J. C. Goodman's drug store and parallel with the G. S. and F. R. R. should be called Railroad Street. It was moved and seconded that a committee be appointed to establish the city limits. The motion was carried and Messrs. H. H. Tift and B. T. Allen were appointed on that committee.

"J. H. Goodman, clerk and treasurer."

Among early settlers who came to occupy places of prominence in the community were Henry Tift's brothers, W. O. Tift and Edward Tift; principals of the school, W. L. Harman, and Jason Scarboro; Ben T. Allen, founder of the Tifton Gazette, in 1891; Reverend J. H. Foster, pastor of the Methodist Church; Captain John A. Phillips, who owned the Sadie Hotel; W. W. Pace; W. H. Love, Tifton's first mayor, for whom Love Avenue was named; E. P. Bowen, who later became president of the Bank of Tifton; M. A. Sexton; J. I. Clements; J. C. Goodman, beloved "family physician" of Tifton's early days; Reverend Charles M. Irwin, first pastor of the Baptist Church; John Pope, C. A. Williams; the Reverend W. W. Webb, who had presided over the meeting at which the Tifton Baptist Church was constituted, about 1888; James Overstreet, a farmer of the vicinity before Tifton became a town; Dr. J. A. McCrea, Dr. N. Peterson, J. L. Pickard; Raleigh Eve, J. L. Herring, C. W. Fulwood, Mr. Carswell, Briggs Carson, Dr. P. A. Jessup.

Henry Tift, his brother, W. O. Tift, and the Reverend L. A. Snow had extensive fruit plantings in the vicinity of Tifton in the early 1890's. H. H. Tift and Snow, Inc., was incorporated in 1891. The cultivation of Concord grapes was so extensive that many carloads of the luscious grapes were shipped to points far distant. Peaches and other fruits were cultivated on an extensive scale and were shipped throughout the country. Henry gave the land for an experimental farm, called Cycloneta, which was famous in its day. The Railroad company to which the land was given failed, and with it the experimental operations ceased. Henry personally owned numerous large farms and these, operated for him by J. Burwell Greene, were interesting and profitable ventures. With S. G. Slack and others H. H. Tift in 1892 began a canning factory in Tifton to can local produce, which was widely shipped. Tobacco was successfully grown and after the experiment had proved successful, it was abandoned by Mr. Tift who was more interested in other projects.

In 1896 Henry Tift founded and was a principal stockholder of the Bank of Tifton of which he was president from 1903 until his death in 1922.

Besides his local business interests, Henry was prominently associated with numerous important enterprises elsewhere in Georgia and in Florida.

Henry was vice-president of the Central Grocery Company, a director of the Planters' Cotton Oil Company, and of the Georgia, Southern and Florida Railroad. He was vice-president of the Bankers' Trust Company; president of the Piedmont Cotton Mills at Egan; vice-president of the Willingham Lumber Company, of Atlanta; president of the Tift Silicia Brick and Stone Company, of Albany. He organized the Georgia-Florida Saw Mill at Alton, Florida, and was for many years president of the Georgia-Florida Saw Mill Association. In 1896 he extended one of his logging roads to Fitzgerald and for a number of years owned and operated this road under name of the Tifton and Northeastern, which he later sold. It afterward became known as the Atlanta, Birmingham and Atlantic. He also built and owned the Tifton, Thomasville, and Gulf Railroad, the T. T. and G. The Negroes used to call it the "Turtle, Tappin and Gopher."

Through the vision of Henry Tift and his generosity the Abraham Baldwin Agricultural College and the Georgia Coastal Plain Experiment Station were located at Tifton. Henry personally gave the land for the original 315 acre campus and a large donation in money.

Henry Tift attended all trustee meetings and was the guiding spirit in the development of the institution. Later he became a trustee and so continued. He loved the school and once when at commencement the students presented him a silver loving cup he was so deeply touched that all he could say was: "Of all the investments I have ever made, this school has brought me the biggest dividends."

Henry also was a patron of the Georgia Coastal Plain Experiment Station and it was secured to Tifton largely through his personal effort and his personal generosity of several hundreds of acres of land and several thousands of dollars in money. It began operations in 1920.

The Fulwood Park also is the gift of Henry Tift to Tifton. Henry, with characteristic modesty, in its name honored not himself but his good friend who helped him draw up the papers for the park and who later served for many years as park commissioner—Columbus Wesley Fulwood. Col. Fulwood was for many years Henry's legal adviser and he held Mr. Fulwood in high esteem.

The land for the first church edifice erected in Tifton was a gift of Henry Tift. This, next to where the Methodist church now is, and toward where the Post Office now stands, was the site of a neat white frame chapel which was built for the worship of God and for the use of all denominations. The Methodists soon outnumbered any other denomination and the church being claimed by them as being in the majority it was turned over to them exclusively and Henry gave to the Baptists a site on which they built a church of their own—the edifice now owned by the Presbyterians. Henry also gave to the Episcopal denomination the site on which was built St. Anne's. When the Baptists first built on their North Park Avenue site they erected a frame building. Before a single service was held the building was destroyed by fire. Henry, who had given generously toward the first building suggested that they rebuild with brick and to make that possible, he gave generously, as he gave to all of the churches. When the Methodists built a larger church he bought back from them the original building, had it moved on rollers to the mill village and named it the Bessie Tift Chapel for his beloved wife. In it on Sunday afternoons she would teach the mill children the Word of God.

On August 17, 1905 the site of Tifton and its outlying lands, part of Worth and Berrien Counties, became by act of Legislature TIFT COUNTY. It is not customary to name a county for a living person and therefore Tift County honored Nelson Tift (born Groton, Connecticut, 1810; died Albany, Georgia, November 21, 1891), founder of Albany, and an uncle of Henry Tift, but it is generally conceded that the name was chosen not only to honor Nelson but also Henry because of the high esteem in which Henry Tift was held.

Though far from his boyhood home, Henry still loved it and he would spend his summers there. In 1906 he bought the old Pyncheon home on Meeting House Hill, Mystic. This had been in his family for ninety years, and there Henry and Bessie and their family would spend their summers thereafter. Henry loved sailing, and owned "The Annie" and "The Wasp," and was seldom happier than when, with his hand on the tiller, he was sailing over the waters of the Sound. Also there was swimming and there were clam-bakes. All these things Henry loved. His merry, blue eyes would twinkle with happiness as he saw everybody about him enjoying the fun. His sister and her family, the Bebees, usually were of the party occupying the old house each summer. Various members of Bessie's family would visit there at different times. The Mystic summers were happy times.

For many years Henry Tift made large and frequent donations to Monroe Female College, Forsyth, where Bessie had graduated in 1878. In recognition of Henry's and Bessie's generosity and in appreciation of their great service to the college the Board of Trustees changed the name of the institution to Bessie Tift College. This took place in 1907, when Dr. C. H. S. Jackson was president of the college.

Bessie became interested in the work of Tallulah Falls School, and returning from a meeting at which she had learned of the great need of the school, and at which she had been elected one of the first three trustees, she told Henry about the school and about how handicapped it was for lack of almost every needful thing. Impressed by the loftiness of the project and by the need, Henry sent a carload of lumber from his Tifton Mill to Tallulah Falls. There, with lumber from the Tifton mill was erected the school's first dormitory. It was built by the school boys, and the tools with which they worked were bought by money sent for the purpose by Henry Tift, Jr. This cottage, called the Lucy Willett Cottage, is now used as a hostess house.

Far-seeing Henry, in addition to giving Fulwood Park to Tifton, said that the town would need a hospital, and he provided that a certain choice lot near the park might be acquired by the city at a low price provided it were used as a hospital site. Also, he gave to the Twentieth Century Library Club a lot on which to build a library; but they sold it instead of using it as a building site, and later they purchased the handsome J. J. L. Phillips house in which the library is housed, and which provides spacious and beautiful rooms for club meetings.

Henry was a man of such shrewd judgment that he not only foresaw an opportunity for building, but he also was quick to perceive when a thing had fulfilled its usefulness. Therefore when the tall timber was cut and Henry realized that to continue to operate the mill would be to do so at a loss, he closed it down. This was in 1916, after forty-four years of operation. After that the town, to Henry's machinery accustomed ears, seemed strangely quiet.

"It seems quiet without the mill, doesn't it, Bess?" he asked. However, he turned his attention to fruit growing, live stock raising, pecan growing and to cotton seed oil. He felt that in these things lay Tifton's greatest opportunity of financial growth.

January 1, 1920, Henry became Tifton's last mayor. When the city changed its form of government to the commission form of government he became chairman of the commission, January 1, 1921.

Henry and Bessie had three sons, Henry Harding Tift, Jr., Thomas Willingham Tift, and Amos Chapman Tift, and Henry and Bessie had a number of grandchildren who were their pride and joy. Granddaddy'll take that boy!" Henry would say, and take his little grandson, Henry Tift III, whose mother had died and who was living with Bessie and Henry, where also the child's father, Henry, Jr. lived and Henry, Jr.'s little daughter, "Pres." Henry, Sr. would take little Henry II and walk with him up and down the room and sing to him, until the child slept.

Henry was eighty-three years old when, in 1922, he suffered a stroke of paralysis from which after a few days he died, on Saturday morning, February fourth. His last words were, "Take care of Bess."

In accordance with his previously expressed wish Henry's body was carried back to his beloved Mystic for burial. A number of devoted and sorrowing friends formed an escort of honor that went with his body on a special train from Tifton to Mystic. Besides his family those who went were R. W. Goodman, J. L. Pickard, J. J. Golden, I. W. Meyers, S. F. Fleetwood, E. P. Bowen, B. Y. Wallace, J. L. Herring, all of Tifton; J. D. Willingham and W. B. Willingham, both of Atlanta.

Words cannot express the kindness of Henry, with his twinkly blue eyes and benign smile. Though not large of physique, Henry was large in every other respect. His was a large heart, a large mind—and he was a man of large vision. Bessie always called him, "Big Henry," and perhaps her name for him aptly summed his character. Henry Tift was big in all that was good. He was a truly great man.

Although Henry received a financial rating of upward of seven million dollars, it was not because of his wealth that Henry Tift was esteemed, but rather because of his constant consideration of the welfare of his fellows. Perhaps he was greatest not on the day in which he made his largest sum of money, but rather on that day when, in his office, he fingered a stack of notes due him and said, "If I should call these notes, I would make a million dollars; but if I did, I'd break every man whose note I hold. Not a note shall be called!"

EDMUND HARDING TIFT

Edmund Harding Tift, born Mystic, Conn., was son of Amos Chapman Tift and Phoebe Harding Tift, and was brother of Henry Harding Tift, founder of Tifton. Edmund came to Tifton in 1885, the year of Henry's marriage, but prior to it.

Edmund Tift's wife was Catherine Ransome, a native of Mystic, Conn., and they had one daughter, Catherine, called Lassie.

When Eddie Tift arrived in Tifton another brother, Orville, was already here. For a number of years the three Tift brothers lived in a row, Henry being in a large house in the middle and one brother on each side, in a cottage. Later, Orville built a very large house, now the Hendricks' house, on Love Avenue, and Ed built a large house across the street, the house now the Frank Corry home.

Edmund, called "Uncle Eddie" was associated with Henry Tift in business. He was head of the Tift Dry Goods Store which occupied the building now housing the Wade-Corry Co. In the store was W. C. Spurlin, and

Mrs. Annie Bennett there had her fashionable dressmaking establishment where she with exceptionable skill fashioned smart and beautiful garments.

In addition to their other interests, all of the Tift brothers had farming interests. In August, 1895 the Tifton Gazette stated: "Capt. E. H. Tift has shipped 52,000 lbs. of grapes from his Mystic, Georgia vineyard up to yesterday and has more to ship." The big purple Concord bunch grapes of the Tifton of that day were a great delicacy, much in demand.

The home of Mrs. E. H. Tift was the birthplace of the Twentieth Century Library Club. The meeting had been planned and scheduled to be held in the home of Mrs. W. W. Banks. Mrs. Banks had a headache, and Mrs. Tift, at Mrs. Banks' request, offered her home. Mrs. W. O. Tift was first president of the club. Thereafter Mrs. H. H. Tift was president until her death. Through efforts of Mr. and Mrs. E. H. Tift Episcopal Church services were brought to Tifton, and St. Anne's Church was built, work on the building beginning March 20, 1898. Prior to that services had been held in the Methodist Church which had been built as a church to be used by all denominations. Henry for that purpose had donated the lot and a generous sum of money. At the beginning of the Episcopal Church here there were only four members and to augment their small group the Baptist and Methodist friends would meet with them. From the earliest days until they left Tifton, Mr. and Mrs. E. H. Tift usually would entertain in their home the Episcopal minister when he would come to Tifton to hold service. The minister came from Albany, Fitzgerald or Cordele, and services were held once or twice a month. Mrs. E. H. Tift played the organ and E. H. Tift sang in the choir. With the bishop, E. H. Tift planned the building and supervised its erection on a lot given by Henry Tift. The Bishop gave some financial aid and the small congregation was cooperative, and St. Anne's became a reality.

Mr. and Mrs. E. H. Tift were interested too in the social life of the community and gathered together the talent of the town of that early day and gave entertainments, a source of pleasure to those presenting the program and those who composed the audience.

In the summer of 1906 Mrs. E. H. Tift and Miss Catherine Tift visited Mrs. Tift's sister, Mrs. Sanford Starke, in Denver, Colorado. They returned to Tifton in September.

Mr. Tift built many cottages in Tifton, and also built the brick business block which, in 1917, was occupied by Kent & Son.

Mr. Tift was for a time exalted Ruler of Tifton Lodge of Elks.

Mrs. Tift was a woman of beauty of face and character. Mr. Tift, quiet and kind, was deeply interested in his home and church, and was capable in business. He lived in Tifton for thirty years, and he and Mrs. Tift had many friends here. For a time, Mrs. Tift's mother, Mrs. Ransome, lived with the E. H. Tift's. She was an invalid who sat in a wheelchair. Mrs. Tift was careful to have Mrs. Ransome always daintily clad and about her shoulders a pretty scarf, usually hand crochet. On her head would be a small lace cap, the fashion among elderly women of that day.

Catherine, only daughter of Edmund and Catherine Ransome Tift, married Edward Henry Bacon, Jr. (born Jan. 21, 1882; graduated Georgia

Tech, 1902), son of Sallie Willingham Bacon and Dr. Edward Henry Bacon of Eastman. Sallie was a sister of Bessie, and Ed, Jr. was a frequent visitor in the H. H. Tift household, in Tifton.

Catherine and Ed Bacon went to Manchester, England where they lived for five years. They later lived in Cambridge, Massachusetts. Thence they moved to Jacksonville, Fla., their present home. They have three daughters, Dorothy, Katherine and Betty.

In 1915 the E. H. Tifts went from Tifton to Massachusetts. In December, 1916, Mr. E. H. Tift visited Tifton friends by whom he was warmly received. He then returned to Massachusetts. There, shortly afterward, one Wednesday afternoon, at about six o'clock, he died of hardening of the arteries. Death occurred at Arlington, a suburb of Boston. Burial was in the Tift lot in Mystic, where the Tifts had been buried for many generations, E. H., at the time of his death was about 63 years old.

E. H. Tift was survived by his widow, his daughter, his brother, H. H. Tift, and three sisters, Mrs. William K. Holmes, of Mystic, Conn.; Mrs. S. E. Bebee, of New York City; Mrs. Frank Buckley, of Mystic, Conn.

At the exact hour of the Mystic service a memorial service for E. H. Tift was held in Tifton at St. Anne's, in the little white chapel which he had helped to build and which he had greatly loved. There his friends gathered at 2:30 in the afternoon of Thursday, January 25, 1917. The Vicar, W. W. Webster, was in charge of the service, but had recently come to Tifton and had not known Mr. Tift. He introduced Dr. C. W. Durden, pastor of the First Baptist Church of Tifton, and a friend of Mr. Tift. Dr. Durden preached the sermon, which was followed by the reading of the Episcopal burial service, the Lord's Prayer, and the singing of "Asleep In Jesus."

Mrs. E. H. Tift continues to live in Cambridge, Massachusetts. Mr. and Mrs. E. H. Bacon, Jr. continue to make their home in Jacksonville, Fla. Dorothy Bacon is a skilled technician. She has been in doctors' laboratories in Thomasville, and Jacksonville, and she now is in the far West. Katherine and Betty Bacon are married.

BESSIE WILLINGHAM TIFT

Bessie Willingham Tift moved to Tifton in the autumn of 1885 when she came here as bride of Henry Harding Tift after a honeymoon trip which included a visit to fashionable Saratoga, Niagara Falls, and New York City, and a sojourn with Henry's people in his boyhood home, Mystic, Connecticut. Bessie and Henry had been married at a ceremony performed by the Reverend W. B. Wharton of Atlanta, in the First Baptist Church, Albany, Georgia, June 15, 1885.

Bessie was one of seventeen children of Thomas Henry Willingham (born Lawtonville, South Carolina, July 12, 1825; educated, Penfield Academy, Penfield, Georgia and at Madison University, Hamilton, New York, now Colgate's, which he attended 1842-1844; married at Beaufort Baptist Church, Dr. Richard Fuller officiating; died May 29, 1891, Atlanta, Geor-

Top—Mrs. Henry Harding Tift, the beloved mother of Tifton prominent
Left—Mrs. H. H. Tift and three little sons, Willingham, Amos, Henry.
artist and writer.
Bottom—Mrs. Florence Willingham Pickard, prominent artist and writer, a sister of Mrs. H. H. Tift.

gia; buried, Albany, Georgia) and Cecelia Baynard Willingham (see sketch, this book).

Bessie's parents were natives of South Carolina, and Bess was born at their handsome South Carolina plantation home, "Smyrna," near Old Allendale, on June 30, 1860. When still very young she refugeed with her parents and brothers and sisters from South Carolina to a plantation her father owned near what is now Baconton, Georgia. Not long afterward she moved with her family to another place Thomas owned, the Yancey Place, comprising several hundred acres, on which was Blue Springs, now famous Radium Springs, a few miles from Albany.

When ten years old Bessie was baptized into membership of the Missionary Baptist Church, Albany; Dr. H. H. Witestt, pastor of the Albany Church and later president of the Southern Baptist Theological Seminary, performed the rite of baptism.

Bessie and her younger sister, Florie (see sketch, this book), attended in Albany a girls' private school conducted by R. D. Mallory. There they were prepared for college. Both entered Wesleyan in 1875, Bessie going into the Freshman class and Florie entering Sub-freshman. At Wesleyan both joined the Adelphian Sorority, which many years later became Alpha Delta Pi.

In January of 1877 Bess entered the upper Junior Class of Monroe Female College, Forsyth, from which she was graduated in 1878. During that period Florie remained in Albany but after Bess's graduation Florie went to college in Virginia.

During one of Florie's vacations Bess and Florie visited friends at a house-party at Louisa Courthouse, Virginia. There Bess fell in love with a brilliant young man to whom she became engaged. Later they had a misunderstanding, which made Bess deeply unhappy. Soon afterward she was shocked and grieved to learn that he had committed suicide.

Some time after this Bessie attended service at the Episcopal Church in Albany, one Easter Sunday. Bess had on a daring new hat, so new and so stylish that her married sister to whom it and another belonged had told Bess that she had not nerve to wear either alone but would wear one if Bess would wear the other. That day Henry Tift was present at the service. He saw Bess and was captivated. He later said that he made up his mind at once that if that young lady (Bess), was as good as she was pretty he was going to have her for his wife, if possible.

Bess soon after this received an invitation to attend a house-party given by the Nelson Tifts at St. Simons Island. Nelson Tift was Henry's uncle, and Henry, who had arranged the party for the purpose of meeting Bessie, was one of those present. Later, while driving near Blue Springs, Henry asked Bessie to marry him. At first Bess said "No," but he asked her why?

"There are two reasons," said Bess.

"What are they?" queried Henry.

"You will not go to church with me." Bessie told him.

"I will go to church with you every Sunday morning that I am not sick," Henry said, and then asked, "What is the other reason?"

"You are twenty years older than I am," said Bess.

Henry replied: "That is true, but I come of a family of great longevity, and it is probable that I shall live almost as long as you do."

Henry was highly regarded by Bess's father and by all who knew him. He was a man known to be of sterling character and he had accumulated great wealth. Bess decided to marry him; and she liked his sending from the jeweler's a whole tray of diamonds from which she might choose any ring she preferred.

Henry proved to be a kind and devoted husband and Bessie was deeply blessed in his great love for her.

When first Bessie and Henry arrived in Tifton in the fall of 1885, after their honeymoon in the North, they occupied the two-room apartment which had been Henry's before his marriage and which was over his office. He had had it completely newly furnished in readiness for Bess's coming.

Henry soon built for Bess a handsome new house into which they moved and which they continued to call home as long as they lived. The house in which they first lived is still standing, but it has been moved from its original location to a site about a block east on Second Street, and across the street. Its original location was the place where Twin Brick Warehouse now is. The new home that Henry built for Bess is that now occupied by Amos Tift, son of Henry.

To Bessie and Henry Tift were born three sons, Henry Harding Tift, Jr., Thomas Willingham Tift, and Amos Tift. They had no daughter, but they reared the daughter and also a son of Bess's sister, Belle, who died when her children, Cecilia and William Lawrence, were small. Bessie and Henry also reared Virginia Pound Tift, called "Prec," and Henry Harding Tift III, children of their eldest son, Henry, Jr., whose wife, Virginia Pound, died when the older child was still little more than a baby.

When Bessie came to Tifton she found no Baptist Church here. It was not long before she and a few other Baptists, about a dozen in all, banded together, and a church was constituted. The minister who constituted the church was the late Reverend William Wiley LaFayette Webb, better known as W. W. Webb, whose sons Henry D., Elias, and George, make their home in Tifton and are members of this church. Bessie was one of the charter members of the church and among the others were Reverend and Mrs. W. W. Webb, Mr. and Mrs. B. T. Allen and a Mrs. Adams. That first meeting was held in a small frame building which stood on a lot next to a cotton field which Bess owned behind their house lot. The building stood about where the Primitive Baptist Church now stands. This small building was used for a church, a school, and a courthouse, and for all public meetings. It was Tifton's only place of public meeting at that time. It was destroyed by fire in 1888, not long after the Baptist Church was constituted.

Soon after the destruction of this building, Baptists, Methodists and other Tifton church members desired to erect a new building to be used by all denominations as a church. Henry Tift for this purpose gave a lot and a part of the building fund and this dream became a reality. (See sketch of Henry Tift.)

Bessie was instrumental in organizing the first Woman's Missionary

Society in Tifton. Composed of women of different denominations, it met in Bessie's parlor early in 1891, and she became its first president. Miss Lena Knight (later Mrs. Williams), a Methodist, was the first secretary. Mrs. Wesley Thomas Hargrett, a Baptist, was the first treasurer. There were about ten charter members. Seven of these were: Bessie Tift, Lena Knight, Mrs. W. T. Hargrett, Mrs. I. W. Bowen, Mrs. E. P. Bowen, Mrs. Hargrett's sister, Mrs. A. S. Speight, Mrs. W. O. Tift. The Reverend C. M. Irwin, of the Baptist State Mission Board and first pastor of the Tifton Baptist Church, met with the ladies on the occasion of their organization meeting.

Bessie continued president of the Missionary Society until her death, a period of more than forty years; out of this society grew the Baptist Woman's Missionary Society of which Bessie was president from the time of its beginning until her death. As the various churches increased in membership, women of each denomination had their own society.

The year 1904 was brimful of excitement for Bess. Tifton was growing, and the world was doing things hitherto little heard of, or on a scale unprecedented. On Tuesday afternoon, of the first week of January, 1904, the first south bound train of the "Millionaire's Special" steamed into Tifton. Its "elegance" and convenience was town talk, for at that time its two Pullman cars, dining car and observation car were a marvel of luxury. It was "lighted by electricity by a special, patented device." The cars were the El Dorado, the Persian, the Falls City, and the Wellington. Bess looked forward happily to the exciting pleasure of travel under such conditions as these.

The tenth of January was the brithday anniversary of Cecilia Willingham. As the day of seventy-fifth year approached Bess was busy in preparation for a family reunion in honor of Cecilia. She and Henry were hosts at the hospitable Tift home to a great gathering of Cecilia's children, grandchildren, and great-grandchildren, and the wives or husbands of the descendants. It was a brilliant occasion. The Tift home was flower-decked, the great seated dining in the dining room was a veritable feast of turkey, cranberry, home-made rolls, steaming hot vegetables, ice cream, whipped cream, and home-made cake. Following this was a heart-stirring program rendered amid tears of joy, or mirthful laughter in the candle-lighted parlor, cheerful with its great logs upon the tall brightly polished brass andirons. These reunions were held almost every year from the time Cecilia was seventy-five until the year of her death, at 86, in 1914, at Easter time.

The St. Louis World's Fair was held in the year of 1904. At the exposition grounds was a Georgia building, a replica of the General John B. Gordon home. Into its building went the finest of lumber and Henry Tift was in charge of furnishing that lumber. He personally selected for the interior especially beautiful lumber from his Tifton mill.

Henry went up to the Fair, and Bess journeyed there with him. It was great fun. The Georgia building, on the highest place of the fair grounds, was beautiful. It was the scene of a number of receptions arranged for Georgians attending the Exposition. At one of these Bess wished to summon a maid. She pushed a button and awaited the maid's arrival, but she did not appear. Suddenly, Bess heard the loud commotion of the arrival of the fire department. It stopped at the Georgia building. To her consternation and embarrassment Bess realized that she had not summoned a maid but had turned in a fire alarm!

One of the most interesting trips of Bess's whole life was in the summer of 1905 when she accompanied her sister, Florie and Florie's husband, the Reverend William Lowndes Pickard, to Europe where Will Pickard went as a delegate from the church of which he was pastor, the First Baptist Church of Lynchburg, Virginia, to the first Baptist World's Alliance, held at Exeter Hall, London, July 11 to 18, 1905. The venerable Dr. Alexander McLaren, then in his eightieth year, presided over the congress. Dr. Pickard preached at one of the Baptist churches of London on Sunday.

After the congress was over, Bess and Florie and Will toured Europe, visiting England, Scotland, France, Germany, Switzerland and Italy. It was on that trip that occurred an incident out of which grew the inspiration of two large pictures painted by Florie. One of these, "Choosing the Crown" was dedicated to Bessie. The other, "The Chosen Crown," was dedicated to her sister, Belle.

In 1905 came the long hoped for creation of a new County of which Tifton was to be the County Seat. It made Bess very happy that it was named Tift, partly for Nelson and much for Henry. Everyone knew that though the county was officially named for Nelson, it was in large degree Henry's popularity that prompted it and the name was chosen to do honor to him as well as to his uncle.

Nearly every summer Bess and Henry spent at Henry's boyhood home, beloved Mystic, Connecticut. After the death of one of Henry's aged relatives, Frances Pyncheon, who had owned the old Tift homestead, Henry bought the old home, and thereafter he and Bess spent most of their summers there. The summers were given over to house-parties, and Henry's relatives, the Beebees, and many of Bessie's relatives were their guests on more than one occasion. Those were happy days, begun with prayer and Bible reading, and given over to rest and recreation. There were clambakes, swimming parties, sailing and picnics. The Tifts loved those summers at Mystic, but they also looked forward to the return to Tifton in the fall.

In 1906, through Henry's suggestion, Mrs. N. Peterson interested Bessie in the one-year-old Twentieth Century Library Club. Bess was not a member nor had she ever attended a meeting. She said she did not have time for the work.

"My church work keeps me so busy—my Sunday School class and the Missionary Society. I just haven't time for club work," Bess said.

Nevertheless, the club announced to Bess that she had been elected president, provided she would join the club and so serve. She accepted the office, which she held, with the exception of a few months, until her death, thirty years later. She became interested in other clubs, also. About the time that Bessie became president of the Library Club the organization affiliated with other state clubs, and the State Federation of Clubs met in Tifton in 1907, at the new school, at present Tifton Grammar School, but then housing all of the grades through high school. Social functions were at the then recently completed Hotel Myon. The delegates were entertained in the homes of the Tifton club members.

In 1907 Bess became a vice-president of the Georgia Federation of clubs. This position she held for many years. Also she was a life director of the Federation.

Bess was one of the first three trustees of Tallulah Falls School. Through her interest in that school Henry gave the lumber with which the school's first dormitory was erected, and her son, Henry, Jr., gave the money for the purchase of tools with which it was built. The students did the labor. That cottage is now called the Lucy Willett Hall.

Bessie Tift taught the Bessie Tift Bible Class from the time of its organization until her death, a period of many years. She was for five years president of the Tifton Woman's Temperance Union.

Bess was a charter member of the Charlotte Carson Chapter of the United Daughters of the Confederacy, and she was a member of the Thronateeskee Chapter of the Daughters of the American Revolution.

After Bess's graduation from Monroe Female College she continued deeply interested in the work of the college. Henry became interested, too. This resulted in Henry's making numerous large gifts to the college. The gifts were so generous, that the college trustees, to show appreciation, changed the name of the college to Bessie Tift College. This took place at a Trustee meeting held at Cartersville, Georgia, November 21, 1906. J. L. White was president of the Board of Trustees at that time and Dr. C. H. S. Jackson was president of the college.

Bessie was a woman of exceptional charm and beauty and she was a gifted and persuasive speaker. Besides teaching the Bessie Tift Sunday School Class, Bessie taught a Sunday School class which she organized at the Second District Agricultural School. Also, she for a time taught a Sunday School class at the Bessie Tift Chapel. She was a consecrated, pious woman and gave much of her time to Bible study and to the study of the Sunday School lesson, and to prayer. Throughout the years daily family devotions were held in the Tift home each early morning. To prayer came all members of the household—the family, guests, Negro servants. Scripture was read, Bess or Bess's mother, Cecilia, if she were there, led in prayer and then all joined in the repetition of the Lord's Prayer. It was a sweet and blessed devotion whose influence reached out into the days and years ahead.

Bessie lived in terms of her church, her family and clubs. She was deeply devoted to her husband and to her sons, Henry, Jr., Willingham, and Amos; and she loved to visit her kinspeople and to have them visit her. Hospitality had a large share in hers and Henry's lives. Bess's brothers and sisters with their wives or husbands, and her many nieces and nephews were frequent visitors, and it was seldom that there was not one or another of these present. The household was blessed with faithful and efficient Negro servitors, and among these were Aunt Jane, an artist in cookery, Jerry, Julia, both excellent cooks, Old Uncle Herbert, for many years the gardener; kind Bertha, nurse and sometimes house-maid; Flora, who as a laundress was unexcelled, and faithful Jeff Mathis.

Bessie Tift often visited her brothers, Ben and Will in Atlanta, Baynard, in College Park, and her sisters, Fetie (Mrs. Cornelius Daniel), in Atlanta; Florie (Mrs. W. L. Pickard, who lived in many places where Dr. Pickard's church pastorates took him); Julia (wife of Dr. Wallace Winn Bacon), in Albany; and Sallie (wife of Dr. E. H. Bacon, brother of W. W. B.), Eastman. Bessie's sisters, Maggie (Mrs. T. O. B. Wood), Pearl (Mrs. Irvine Myers), and Belle (Mrs. William Lawrence), lived in Tifton. Bessie's brother, W. J. Willingham, was a frequent Tifton visitor.

The Bacon brothers, Wallace and Edwin, whom Bessie's sisters Julia and Sallie, respectively, married, were descendants of the Bacons who were among the earliest settlers of famous Midway, in Liberty County. History relates that on 6th of December, 1752 Mr. Benjamin Baker and family and Mr. Samuel Bacon and family arrived at Midway and proceeded to form a settlement. (White's Statistics of Georgia, p. 370.) Wallace and Edwin were first cousins of Senator A. O. Bacon, who, early orphaned, was reared in their father's home. Julia Bacon (Mrs. Jim Osburn), daughter of Dr. and Mrs. W. W. Bacon, was a member of the Tift household for a time when she taught school in Tifton, when a young woman just out of college. Belle Willingham, Bess's sister, made her home with Bessie for several years prior to her marriage. Bessie's mother, Cecilia Willingham, made her home with Bessie from a few years after Bessie's father's death until Cecilia died.

All three of Bessie's sons married. Henry, Jr. married charming Virginia Pound, daughter of J. B. Pound, of Chattanooga; Willingham married lovely blond Catherine Terrell, niece of former Governor Terrell, of Georgia; Amos married beautiful Titian haired Lutrelle McLennard, who is a ministering angel to the bereaved when death visits a household. Bess took great joy in her grandchildren, Henry's and Virginia's Virginia and Henry III; Willingham's and Catherine's Catherine Hill and Thomas Willingham, Jr.; and Amos's and Lutrelle's children, Lutrelle, Amos Tift V, and David Tift.

Bess was deeply interested in Tifton's growth, and she was delighted whenever a new building was erected. It made her happy when Henry, Jr., built his pretty bungalow, and next to it Amos, his. It pleased her when Willingham put up a number of houses for sale, and store buildings, and when Amos erected business edifices. It pleased her, too, that Henry, Jr. took great interest in Tifton's civic affairs, and was in demand as a speaker at club meetings and at the college in the founding of which his father took prominent part. She loved the park which Henry had given to Tifton.

In February of 1922 Bess saw her beloved husband, Henry, Sr., buried, at Mystic, Connecticut, whither a large group of sorrowing relatives and friends took his body to be placed, according to his request, in his native soil.

After Henry, Sr.'s death, Bess leaned more and more upon her son, Henry, Jr., ever loving and considerate of her welfare and happiness. She derived happiness also from the companionship of her beloved sister Florie, whom Bess called her "Other Self." Florie and Will, after his retirement because of failing health were making their home in Tifton, and Bess and Florie saw each other every day.

Bess bravely accepted giving up her precious Henry, Jr., who was tragically killed in an automobile accident. He died June 13, 1929, at Tifton. Florie lived only a short time after this. She died December 2, 1930. Bess also in the time soon after this gave up two brothers claimed by death, Will, and Baynard. Through all of this sorrow she continued in the sweetness which had endeared her to all. She progressed also in spirituality and in consecration, which made her life a power in its influence for good.

Bessie Tift died at dawn, Tuesday, December 8, 1936 in her bedroom of the home that Big Henry had built for her. Willingham and Amos were with her when she went, as were her sister Pearl, her daughters-in-law, Lutrelle and Catherine, her brothers-in-law, Irvine Myers and Will Lawrence, her nieces, Telie Daniel Fleetwood, Marguerite Myers and Bessie Belle Pickard. Telie's husband, Shine Fleetwood was present, and a trained nurse, and Dr. Carlton Fleming.

In another room in the house lay desperately ill Marion Ragan, who with her mother, Mrs. Dan Ragan, had been Bessie's companions since Bessie's grandchildren had been away at school and her sons were living in their own homes.

In Bessie's room the fire, forgotten, burned low in the big fire place. In the garden outside birds sent up a chorus of song, a strange, excited and unwonted persistent twittering. When the doctor announced that Bessie was dead, the sorrowing loved ones passed about the bed, a weeping procession, each pausing for the last farewell. Willingham and Amos, shaken by silent sobs, turned away from the bed where their mother lay and placed their arms about each other's shoulders. One of them said: "Let's say the Lord's Prayer. She would want it so!" All joined in the familiar, blessed words of our Lord Jesus:

> "Our Father, who art in Heaven,
> Hallowed be Thy name.
> Thy kingdom come;
> Thy will be done
> On earth as it is in heaven.
> Give us this day
> Our daily bread;
> And forgive us our debts
> As we forgive our debtors.
> Lead us not into temptation
> But deliver us from evil.
> Thine is the kingdom,
> The power and the glory.
>   Amen."

Funeral services for Bessie Tift were held at the First Baptist Church, Tifton. Burial was in Tifton Cemetery, by her beloved first-born son, Henry

Tift, Jr. Bessie's pastor, Dr. Orion Mixon, conducted the services at the church and at the grave, and he was assisted by Dr. Aquila Chamlee, President of Bessie Tift College, and two former pastors, Dr. C. W. Durden, of Charlotte, North Carolina, and Dr. F. C. McConnell. Present was a delegation of faculty members and students from Bessie Tift College.

All of Tifton and a host of friends elsewhere mourned Bessie's passing; for all felt somewhat as did an old friend who said of her: "She was the sweetest person I ever knew."

Indeed, to her family, Bess was long known as "Sweet Bess."

HENRY HARDING TIFT, JR.

Henry Harding Tift, Jr., eldest of three sons of Henry Harding Tift, Tifton's founder, and Bessie Willingham Tift, was born October 1, 1886, in a private Pullman car, in, or near, Washington, D. C. when Bessie was coming to Tifton from her husband's old home, Mystic, Conn., where she and Henry, Sr. had spent the summer.

Henry, Sr. and Bessie, rejoicing at the advent of the fine boy, gave, as a thank offering, $1,000.00 to Baptist Foreign Missions.

Early the child's Christian education began. He received also public speaking instruction. Though not yet nine years old at the time of the laying of the corner stone of the Tifton Baptist Church in 1895, he took part in the ceremony. After an inclement Sunday, Monday was bright and beautiful and the Baptists had a fair day for laying the corner stone of their edifice. At the exercises, music was led by Miss Ella Bacon and Prof. E. J. Williams. The address was by the Reverend E. Z. F. Golden, of Cuthbert. Miss Gertrude Patrick recited. Dr. J. B. Gambrell, Macon, President of Mercer University, and Messrs. B. T. Allen, Carswell, and Cole spoke. Master Henry Tift, in behalf of the Little Helpers, having laid the corner stone solid and firm, pronounced it " 'well and truly laid'."

This was the brick church, with amber colored windows, on North Park Avenue, and now used by the Presbyterians. When first built it had a spire 140 feet high. The contractor was John C. Hind, from Ontario, Canada, and Tifton's earliest contractor and builder. Henry, Sr., had given much of the cost of the church, of which his beloved wife, Bessie, was one of the charter members. Henry, Jr., attended Tifton public schools under W. L. Harmon and Jason Scarboro. He then entered Mercer University. There he became a close friend of Bobo Murray, nephew of the distinguished Greek scholar, Dr. John Scott Murray, for quarter of a century professor of Greek at Mercer, and later at Furman. Henry and Bobo one summer toured Europe together. This was a rollicking, happy journey. This was Bobo's first European travel but he subsequently took numerous other trips, conducting large parties on European tours. Later Bobo was professor of French at Mercer where he taught when Henry's uncle, W. L. Pickard, was president of Mercer. Henry became a Mercer trustee. Later Bobo went as consul to South America, where he died soon after arrival.

At Mercer both Henry and Bobo were Phi Delta Thetas.

After graduation from Mercer in 1906, Henry Tift, Jr. attended Eastman

Business College, Poughkeepsie, N. Y. While playing ice hockey there he fell and received a severe blow on his head. However, he continued his studies and graduated.

Henry, Sr. and Bess were delighted at Henry, Jr.'s decision to locate in Tifton. He took a position with the Tifton Cotton Mills, of which Henry, Sr. was president. Henry, Jr. was doing well but one hot summer day while at the mill he suddenly fell over in a fainting spell, the first indication that the severe blow received the previous winter had caused a permanent injury. From then on life was an alternation of apparent good health and serious illness, but Henry was diligent and enterprising in business in which he was markedly successful; and his was a radiant personality which endeared to him many friends. Bessie Tift had a first cousin, Caroline Willingham, who became second wife of Jerome Balaam Pound, of Chattanooga, Tenn. J. B. Pound, by his first wife, has several daughters, of whom one, Virginia, was a person of rare sweetness and charm. Henry Tift, Jr., and Virginia Pound were married in Chattanooga, November 4, 1914.

To Virginia and Henry Tift, Jr. were born two children, Virginia (called "Prec"), born at Tifton, December 10, 1915, and Henry Tift III, born February 4, 1917, at Tifton.

Henry, Jr., built for his wife, whom little Prec called "Big Dolly," a large bungalow on College Street. Next door Amos, Henry, Jr.'s brother, built one for his beautiful wife, Lutrelle.

Henry, Jr. also had a large and valuable farm (now the Fulwood Plant Farms) and he owned extensive acreage on the Alapaha River, on the bank of which he built a large cabin, the scene of numerous merry-makings when he and his friends repaired there for an evening following a supper of freshly caught fish.

When Henry and Virginia had been married only a few years Virginia became ill. She was taken for her health to North Carolina but instead of improving she died there in 1918. She is buried on the Pound lot, Chattanooga. Henry, grief-stricken, moved his two babies to the home of his parents where they were reared by his mother. The Lennon Bowens moved into the Henry Tift bungalow.

The first automobile in Tifton was owned by Mr. Johns, of Tifton Heights. He had the car for hire. Henry, Jr. was one of Mr. Johns' best patrons. At the St. Louis Exposition Henry was greatly interested in the automobile display. He urged his father to buy a car, which Henry, Sr. did. His was the first private automobile in Tifton.

Later Henry, Jr. always had a beautiful car. He also went in to the automobile business and had an automobile agency. He was an excellent driver and enjoyed high speed. He liked to drive, but because he was often ill he usually took his colored chauffeur, Jeff Mathis, with him and if Henry felt ill Jeff would drive.

Henry attended an automobile show in New York City, and greatly enjoyed it. At the time of the Glidden Tour in interest of better roads, he hastened all the way from New England in order to drive in the procession of cars on the tour.

Henry was greatly beloved in Tifton, and was much in command as a public speaker. He was a member of Tifton Chamber of Commerce and at one meeting said that Tifton should have an airport and he offered the use of some of his land to be used as a landing field. This was in a day when aviation was not so general as it now is.

Henry, Jr. loved the beautiful virgin growth pines and he was happy over his father's gift of Fulwood Park to the city. He also loved roses, perhaps because from earliest childhood he had seen beautiful and choice ones in his mother's garden and in that of his next door neighbor, J. L. Pickard, who was a great lover of roses. Henry, Jr. gave funds with which to buy rose bushes for the establishment of a rose garden in Fullwood Park.

"Now," said Henry, "everybody can enjoy the pine trees and everybody can enjoy roses."

Like his great and good father, Henry was generous hearted. The first dormitory at the Tallulah Falls School was made of lumber donated by Henry, Sr., and it was built by the students with tools bought with $250.00 donated by Henry, Jr.

Like his father also was Henry, Jr. in his great interest in the Second District Agricultural School. On June 11, 1929, Prof. S. L. Lewis, president of the school, was to be presented a gold watch in appreciation of his work at the college. Henry, Jr. made the speech of presentation at exercises held in the auditorium of the Tifton High School. Bess attended, and later left for Bessie Tift College, to attend a mission meeting. Henry, Jr. drove her to the train. He had a brand new, beautiful car.

Next day Henry, Jr. did not feel very well, but he was enjoying his new car so much that he did not get Jeff to drive, but drove it himself. He liked to feel the engine respond to his slightest touch.

When after supper, he left the house, his namesake, Henry III, wished to go with him as far as Aunt Florie Pickard's where their cousin, "Kewpie," had arrived that day for a visit. Henry, Jr. let Henry III out there, and then drove on. He turned and drove up Sixth Street. He did not take the familiar turn onto College Avenue where he and Virginia had been so happy. He drove on past, straight out Sixth Street. At the end of the street instead of making the turn the car shot forward at a terrific speed. There was a splintering crash. The car telescoped against a giant pine tree.

Those who rushed to the scene found Henry's body completely crushed. He was still alive, though unconscious. Dr. N. Peterson, hastily summoned, rushed to his aid but said afterward that there probably was not a bone in Henry's body that was not broken. Henry was taken to the Coastal Plain Hospital. By God's mercy Henry died without ever regaining consciousness. He died in the first minutes of the morning of June 13, 1929.

All of Tifton mourned Henry's passing. His personality had been one of rare radiance, and his spirit was ever one of generosity and thoughtful and loving service to others.

Burial was in Tifton cemetery, where a lone pine stands sentinel near where he sleeps.

"Henry always loved the pine trees," said Bess, one Easter day after she had placed at the head of Henry's resting place some Easter lilies sent by Henry III. Henry III was at Harvard where he was studying to be a physician.

AMOS CHAPMAN TIFT

Amos Chapman Tift, third son of Bessie Willingham Tift and Henry Harding Tift, Tifton's founder, was born in Atlanta, Georgia, August 24, 1891.

A member of the First Baptist Church of Tifton, he was for a great many years song leader in the First Baptist Sunday School, of which also he was a loyal and faithful and useful member.

Amos attended Tifton public schools and the Virginia Military Institute, and graduated from Mercer University. There he was a Phi Delta Theta. Also he was 1911 manager of the Mercer Cauldron and in 1912 he was prominent in baseball.

Amos Tift was wont to spend the summers with his parents at their summer home, Mystic, Connecticut, where he learned to handle a boat skillfully, and grew to love the water.

Returning to Tifton after graduation from Mercer, Amos engaged in the automobile and garage business and erected some of Tifton's handsomest business edifices. He also has farming and other real estate interests.

On July 5, 1918 Amos Tift married beautiful Titian-haired Lutrelle McLennan, daughter of David Charles and Lina Roberson McLennan, the Reverend Ward performing the ceremony at Bainbridge, Georgia.

Of this union are three children, Lutrelle Tift, born April 15, 1919; married Homer Meade Rankin (born New Orleans);

Amos Chapman Tift, born January 19, 1921;

David Harding Tift, born December 19, 1923.

All were born in Tifton and all served in the armed forces of their country during World War II. Prior to the war, and after her graduation from the University of Georgia, Lutrelle, Jr., was founder and editor of a weekly newspaper at St. Simons Island, "The St. Simons Star."

Amos built and for many years occupied a house on College Avenue, but after his mother's death he bought and moved into the H. H. Tift homestead on Second Street, where he now lives. He owns a summer home at St. Simons Island.

His love of the water and water sports has influenced him to have a large part in the construction of the old swimming pool which through the years has furnished a wholesome recreation for Tifton people and he has been one of the most generous donors to the fund for the construction of the new swimming pool, also he has built two beautiful artificial lakes near Tifton, Tift's Pond, now called Lake Mary, after Mary Carmichael, the beautiful deceased daughter of the present owners of the lake, Mr. and Mrs. Homer Carmichael; and another lake not far from the Ocilla Road near Tifton. This is as yet unnamed.

A friendly, kind man of few words, Amos combines many of the excellent

THOMAS WILLINGHAM TIFT, of Atlanta and Tifton
Large owner of Tifton property and oldest son of Tifton's founder

traits of both his parents. He is a trustee of Bessie Tift College and is a member of the Tifton City Commission. He enjoys golf and is a member of the Tifton Country Club.

All three of Mr. and Mrs. Amos Tift's children have returned safely from the war, though Amos, Jr. was in the European Theatre of Operations, and David was in the hazardous undersea duty in the far Pacific. They are now with their parents in the old Tift homestead, and Lutrelle, Jr. is married and lives next door.

THOMAS WILLINGHAM TIFT

Thomas Willingham Tift, second son of Henry Harding Tift, Tifton's founder, and Bessie Willingham Tift, was born September 15, 1889 at Albany, Georgia, at the home of Bessie's sister, Julia Bacon, where Henry had taken Bess that she might be under the care of Julia's husband, Dr. Wallace Winn Bacon, an eminent physician. The child spent his boyhood in Tifton where he was called Willingham, but at Mercer University, from which he was graduated in 1910, he was called Tommie. At Mercer he roomed with Ralph Bailey, clergyman and writer, who married Tommie's cousin, Julia Baynard Pickard. At Mercer, Tommie was a Phi Delta Theta. After graduation from Mercer he went to Yale where he was graduated from the Law School, in 1912.

Mr. Tift possesses great business acumen and he engaged in farming interests near Tifton, and also built a number of houses and stores in Tifton, some for rent, some for sale.

April 16, 1921, at Greenville, Georgia, his uncle, Dr. W. L. Pickard, performing the ceremony, he was married to Catherine Hill Terrell, daughter of Dr. Terrell, and a niece of former Governor Terrell, of Georgia. She had been a room-mate at Washington Seminary, Atlanta, of Dr. Pickard's daughter, Elizabeth Belle, name-sake of Willingham's mother and of Elizabeth's and Tommie's Aunt Belle.

In addition to his Tifton holdings Willingham Tift acquired valuable interests in Atlanta and moved there to make his home. He continues to have large Tifton holdings and makes frequent sojourns there where he maintains a country home.

Willingham Tift is president of the Westside Land Co., Chattanooga, Tenn.; president of the Piedmont Cotton Mills, Egan, Georgia; vice-president of the Bank of Tifton; president of the Tifton Chennille Co.; is a director of the Willingham-Tift Lumber Co., Atlanta; is a member of the Board of Trustees of Bessie Tift College, which is named for his mother; is on the Board of Trustees of the Tifton Investment Co.

Willingham Tift is a member of the First Baptist Church of Tifton, of which his mother was a charter member and to which his father gave the original church site, and which Willingham joined in early boyhood.

Willingham Tift is a member of the Atlanta Rotary Club; the Capitol City Club; Atlanta Piedmont Driving Club; Tifton Country Club.

Thomas Willingham Tift and Catherine Terrell Tift have two children: Catherine Hill Tift and Thomas Willingham Tift, Jr.

Catherine Hill Tift was born Atlanta, Georgia, July 15, 1922, and married James Tinsley Porter, December 7, 1945.

Thomas Willingham Tift, Jr. was born January 8, 1927. He is a cadet at the United States Naval Academy, Annapolis, Md.

WILLIAM ORVILLE TIFT

William Orville Tift was the second son of Amos and Phoebe Harding Tift born in Mystic, Conn. in the year 1843. He was educated in the Mystic public school and joined the Army at the age of nineteen.

At the close of the War he took a position as purser with the Mallory Steamship Lines sailing to Galveston, Texas and Key West, where his uncle, Asa, had gone some years before.

In Texas, he made connections and went into the business of cattle raising, and became the junior partner on one of the largest cattle ranches in the state.

In the meantime he had married Eliza Catherine Mallory, eldest daughter of David and Sarah Stark Mallory, also of Mystic, Conn. She was born in the year 1848, also in Mystic. All went well with the young couple until one summer when yellow fever broke out in Galveston and a tidal wave swept hundreds of head of cattle into the Gulf. This meant the failure of the firm.

In the meantime his brother, Henry Harding Tift, had come to South Georgia and sent for him to join him. It took great courage, for at that time South Georgia was virgin territory; there was nothing here but the pine woods,—no schools, no churches save the little log cabins where the Primitive Baptists and Primitive Methodists held forth. I have heard my mother say that, unless she had guests, six months would go by and she wouldldn't see a white face save that of Uncle Henry, Father and Mr. Hall, who was overseer of the saw mill.

But they stayed, believing in the future of this part of the state.

My father was a visionary—he saw that the state must get away from cotton, and he introduced tobacco, peaches and grapes into what is now Tift County. He planted most of the trees in Tifton and believed in its future.

He died in 1909 of hardening of the arteries, in Mystic, Conn., in the house where he was born.

His wife survived him by a number of years.

Two children were born of their union—a son, William Orville Tift, Jr., and a daughter, Katherine Stark Tift.

> (Editor's Note: Mrs. Katherine Stark Tift Jones, the writer of the above sketch of her parents, has established a wide reputation as a gifted reader, particularly of Negro dialect sketches. She is a radio speaker, and at present is with the Tifton broadcasting station.)

WILLIAM WHITFIELD TIMMONS
(Contributed)

William Whitfield Timmons, who was born in Marion County, South Carolina on July 15, 1852, moved to Tifton (then Berrien County) in July, 1891. He and his wife, the former Mary Frances McWhite, to whom he was married on December 27, 1876, first lived in a house on the corner of Love Avenue and Second Street. After this house burned with all its contents in 1904, he bought the house immediately next door on the north side.

After moving to Tifton, he spent the rest of his life engaged in the production of turpentine. He was in this business, which was on a large scale, both singly and in partnership. He also owned and operated several farms of considerable size. Mr. Timmons was one of the important men of his time and section: he was public spirited, generous, and active in anything for the good of his community. He was a Mason, a member of the Tifton Lodge, and of the Baptist Church, and was for twenty years prior to his death, Chairman of the Baptist Board of Deacons. He served as councilman for several years in Tifton and was at one time mayor of the city. He was in every respect a good citizen who died in 1924 with the love of all who knew him.

ELIAS L. VICKERS

Elias L. Vickers, son of Henry Vickers, a farmer, and his wife, Ellen Sears Vickers, was born June 21, 1861, in a large six or seven-room log house on his father's farm in Coffee County about six miles west of Douglas. In this house red-haired Elias lived for several years and there were born to his parents several other children before the family moved into a new clapboard house built in front of the older log house.

An alligator bit Elias's leg when the boy was ten, and it was a problem to know how to extract the leg from the creature's jaws without hurting the boy more than he was already hurt. Finally a fire was placed under the reptile's jaws, and when he then opened them a rope was slung around the upper jaw to prevent him again closing his mouth and the boy's leg was thus freed. Mrs. Vickers insisted that the alligator's head be cut off, which was done, but he walked about without his head and this horrible and gruesome sight haunted Elias even when he was grown; also, even when he was grown he carried the scars made by the teeth of the creature. He said he was not so much hurt as that the pressure was terrific and the blood circulation was cut off, so that he felt numb.

Elias after finishing the schools near Douglas went to Eastman Business College, at Poughkeepsie, New York. Thereafter he went to Willacoochee where he engaged in turpentining. There he met Charles Goodman, son of Dr. J. C. Goodman, later a well-known Tifton physician. Elias met Charles's sister, Mary Etta Goodman, who was living with her parents at Jacksonville, Georgia. The Goodmans soon after this moved to Tifton and there Elias Vickers and Mary Etta Goodman were married, the first couple to be married in the little white chapel, then newly built and Tifton's only church edifice, the same now known as Bessie Tift Chapel, but at that time it stood near the present site of the Methodist church. Later, Etta's sister, Harriet, and George Evans were the last couple to be married in this church before it was moved to the mill village.

About 1894 Mr. Vickers had a large house built for his family at 315 West Sixth Street, the same now owned by Mrs. Briggs Carson, Sr. It was built by S. G. Slack and was then and still is one of Tifton's most beautiful and interesting residences. It was at one time occupied by Mrs. T. O. B. Wood, sister of Bessie Tift. Elias Vickers also built homes for his family at Arabi and at Old Field. He had turpentine stills at those places and at Adel, and at Panama City, Florida. Mr. Vickers moved his family to Tifton in 1910.

When the Vickers house was built it stood in a woodland, and there were only two houses between it and the home of the Goodmans on Central Avenue and Second Street. The two houses were the C. W. Fulwood house, and the Dinamore house, then occupied by a Northern man who tended the fruit at Cycloneta.

At the Vickers's house was written, by a friend of Mr. Vickers, a book entitled "The Negro Is a Man," written to offset the then recently published book, "The Negro Is a Beast," which book sorely angered Mr. Vickers, who loved the negroes and would never work convict labor as was sometimes customary at that time among turpentine men.

Elias Vickers invented what is said to have been the first turpentine cup to fit a tree. Formerly the trees had merely had a trough cut in them. Vickers's cups were first made of wood, later of papier-mache.

In 1910 Elias and his family moved to Macon, where they lived on a farm across the Spring Street bridge. There, on December 14, 1910 his daughter, Ruth, was married to Paul Fulwood, of Tifton. Later Elias sold the farm, and lived in the old Joe Hill Hall place in Macon, where he continued until his son, John had graduated from Georgia Tech. Mr. Vickers live in Atlanta for a while.

Another son, Hawkins Ladson Vickers, had a position with the Ballard Plant Company, at Hattiesburg, Mississippi, and Mr. and Mrs. Elias Vickers moved to Hattiesburg in 1925. There Mr. Vickers died September 7, 1933. He is buried in the Tifton cemetery.

Mr. Vickers was a staunch Methodist. He was a trustee of Sparks Collegiate Institute, at Sparks, Georgia, and of Wesley Memorial Hospital, until it was consolidated with Emory University. He was a lay leader of the South Georgia Conference of the Methodist Church.

Mrs. Vickers, Mary Etta Goodman, was born March 10, 1866, at Somerton, Virginia. She was graduated from Wesleyan College. She died at Charlotte, North Carolina, April 28, 1947. Burial was at Tifton.

To Elias and Mary Etta G. Vickers were born ten children. Those who survive are Mrs. P. D. Fulwood of Tifton; Mrs. E. H. Cardwell, Mrs. Paul Bankston, Miami; Mrs. S. J. Evans, Washington; John H. Vickers, Charlotte, North Carolina; Hawkins L. Vickers, Hattiesburg, Miss.

Mrs. W. L. Harman, of Tifton, is a sister of Mrs. Vickers. Another sister, Mrs. W. M. Thurman, died March, 1947.

JONATHAN WALKER

Hezikiah, Jonathan, Jack and Wash Walker came from South Carolina to Irwin County in the early days of Irwin County.

Of the above, Jack was living near Bones Mill Pond (now Crystal Lake) during the War Between the States. Jack married Sarah (Sabry) Clements, sister of Abraham Clements, of Irwin County. Jack's and Sarah's children were: Abram, John, Sarah, Melanchthon, who was called Dink, Jim, Joe, Sam, Rachel, Jane, and Jonathon.

Bones Mill Pond was one of the most picturesque inland bodies of water to be found. Its waters are of an amazing clarity, and though far from the coast, the hard sandy beach is as dazzling in whiteness as the ocean strand. The whole is surrounded by a dense forest wherein are choice and rare flora. In one place near the lake is a peat bog, in another the trembling earth. In still another place beneath the near Stygian shade of forest giants the water is unfathomed. This weird, secluded, dangerous and dark water is known as Devil's Den.

During those troublous times of war the sad plight of runaway slaves was one of the gravest problems of the time. One such was known to be at large, and Jack saw him on his neighbor's land, near the lake. Jack went to capture the slave, but Jack and his neighbor became engaged in a struggle and Jack disappeared, as also did the Negro. Later Jack's body was found buried near the lake edge, and irate citizens seized and tried the owner of the lake and hanged him to a limb of a tall oak tree which still stands a gaunt, bare, white skeleton of a dead tree rising spectre-like above the lesser trees of the forest.

A mere lad at the time of his father's death, Jonathan Walker, born February 12 (or 7), 1852, grew to manhood in his native Irwin County. On February 23, 1881, he married Margaret Fletcher, called Gally, daughter of Black Jim Fletcher, Irwin County's representative to the Legislature. Gally was born January 6, 1862. She was niece of Elbert Fletcher, whose son Danny Fletcher married Mattie Churchwell. Gally's mother was Melissa Paulk.

Jonathan Walker and Gally settled on a large plantation which he cleared in the pine wilderness. He farmed, cut timber and ran a grist mill. Also he owned a wooded tract on the Alapaha river where he loved to fish. This place he sold to a corporation which in 1912 formed the Country Club at Gun Lake, of which Jonathan was a charter member. The club has numbered among its membership some of the most prominent citizens of the county.

An accident left Jonathan Walker crippled, but despite this his was a sunny, cheerful disposition, and his was a large circle of friends. Jonathan died at his plantation home near Tifton, October 1, 1917. To him and Gally were born four children: Alice (Mrs. George Edd Clements); Edna (Mrs. W. B. Hitchcock); Kate (married first, Robert Land; second, Loften Hitchcock; third, George Paulk); James, who married and has several children, of whom Elsie was voted the prettiest girl in the Senior Class at Tifton

High School in 1942. James Walker is Sheriff of Tift County. He loves to shoot and often in season brings home a fat deer, and he, his family and friends have a feast of venison.

THE WARRENS

William Warren was the first of the Warren family to locate in what is now Tift County. He was born in Irwin County, December 8, 1846, and was son of George Washington Warren, Sr., and Sallie Ross Warren, both of Irwin County. George and Sallie Warren are buried on the Macajah Young private burial ground, Tift County. Micajah Young's mother was Hester, a sister of William Warren.

Children of George and Sallie Ross Warren were William, who married Sarah Clements; James, who married Martha Gibbs (an aunt of Earl Gibbs, clerk of Superior Court of Tift County); Lott, who married Millie Sumner, of Irwin County; George Washington, Jr., who married Ellen Fox, of Tifton (their daughter married William Bruce Donaldson, Sr., father of Bruce Donaldson, Jr., of Tifton); Bettsie Warren, who married William Sumner, of near Moultrie; Hester Warren who married first, Macajah Young; and second, Aaron Tyson; Sallie Warren, who married Allen Gibbs (a brother of Martha); Pollie, who married Reverend James Gibbs, Primitive Baptist Elder, who was at Hickory Springs Church and other churches. Polly and James Gibbs are buried at Hickory Springs.

Wm. Warren and Sarah Clements (born July 7, 1851) were married January 6, 1870 and came to what was then Worth but now is Tift County. Sarah was a sister of R. Walton Clements, father of Judge James Clements who deeded to Georgia the land which comprises the Jefferson Davis National Park, which project came into being largely through the untiring efforts of Mrs. Ralph Johnston, of Tifton, formerly of Ocilla. William, a farmer, lived on the place where he settled soon after his marriage until his death there, May 3, 1914. Sarah died Tuesday night, March 30, 1909. Burial was at Hickory Springs, where Elder James Gibbs conducted the services.

To William and Sarah Clements Warren were born the following children: George Washington Warren, born Irwin County, May 5, 1872; died July 26, 1872. Lott Warren, born Irwin County, July 19, 1873; died July, 1875. William Jelks Warren, born Worth County, April 2, 1875; Lula Alice Warren, born Worth County, August 7, 1877 (Mrs. Will W. Willis, of Willacoochee); Luna Warren, born Worth County, February 11, 1880 (Mrs. John Henry Pitts, of Tifton); Thomas Lawrence Warren, born Worth County, June 10, 1882; Lillie Warren, born Worth County, June 17, 1884 (Mrs. George Washington Peters, of Tifton).

William Jelks Warren has for many years been tax collector of Tift County.

Jimmie Clements was one of six brothers of Sarah Clements Warren. Jimmie married Sarah Henderson, and was prominent in the life of early Tifton where he leased the Hotel Sadie from Captain John Phillips, who built it. Sarah Clements Warren also had four sisters.

WILLIAM WILEY LaFAYETTE WEBB

William Wiley LaFayette Webb, son of James I. Webb and Mary Sandifer Webb, was born in Crawford County, Georgia, April 25, 1838. He grew up on his father's farm, moved to Sumter County in 1846 and to Dooly County in 1858. To most people he was known as W. W. Webb.

On March 4, 1862 at Vienna, W. W. Webb joined Company C, under Captain W. C. Carter, 4th Regiment of Georgia Volunteers, of the Confederate Army. He was mustered into service at Griffin, left May, 1862, and the first battle in which he took part was the Seven Days Battle at Richmond. Next he was in the second Battle of Manassas, then at Harper's Ferry, next at Chancellorsville, and he was in the terrific Battle of Gettysburg, the bloodiest battle of the war. At Gettysburg he was shot and wounded, one finger being burst by a minnie ball. After a brief furlough he was in the Battle of the Wilderness, on the Plank Road, May 6, 1864. In this engagement he was shot in the heel and the heel string was cut one third. After two months in a hospital he returned to service and was in the Battle of Petersburg and Weldon Railroad. On July 31, 1864 he fought in his last battle when the mines were sprung in front of Petersburg. Thereafter he was confined by rheumatism to a hospital, received a furlough, at the end of which he reported to a hospital at Macon, where he was pronounced disabled for service. Sent to a Fort Valley Hospital, he was transferred thence to a hospital at Eufaula in order to make room at Fort Valley for the wounded. He remained at Eufaula until the end of the war. He was paroled in May or June, 1865.

On February 28, 1865 W. W. Webb married Miss Laura Daniels. Of this union were four children: Joseph T., Ella Assenith, James I., Jr., L. Timothy. Laura Daniels Webb died June 16, 1873.

On August 20, 1876 W. W. Webb married Sarah Catherine Sinclair, at the Sinclair homestead two miles north of Tifton. She was daughter of Dr. Robert D. Sinclair and Mary Culpepper Sinclair. Of this union were eleven children: William E., John T., Henry D., Thomas T., Robert F., Mary C., Margaret E., Louise Lee, Elias L., Jacy J., George G. Of these Henry D. was for many years clerk of the Superior Court of Tift County. He also was for many years chairman of the Board of Deacons of the First Baptist Church; and he is secretary of the Country Club, at Gun Lake. Elias and George engage in the plant business on a large scale, and have other business interests in Tifton, where they are well known and highly regarded. Elias was for a time secretary and treasurer of the Tift County Historical Society. Also he is on many committees of the First Baptist Church of Tifton.

W. W. Webb was ordained to the Baptist ministry in 1870. He served at Lake View, Staunton, both in what is now Cook County; Macedonia, in what is now Turner County; Willacoochee, in what is now Atkinson.

Mr. Webb moved to Irwin County in February, 1878, and to near the Tifton site that fall. In what is now Tift County he served Zion Hope, Mt. Zion, Mt. Olive, Liberty; in Berrien County he served at Enigma, Alapaha, and at Brushy Creek.

His was a service of deed as well as of word. Many times he walked from his farm south of Tifton to his church many miles north of Tifton, and when one church was in the building he helped carry the logs and set them in place. His influence for good cannot be expressed in words. He it was who constituted the First Baptist Crurch of Tifton, in 1888, when about a dozen Baptists met in a small frame building used in Tifton as a place for all types of public meetings, before a real church edifice was constructed here. About a dozen Baptists banded together to form the Baptist Church. These were the Reverend and Mrs. W. W. Webb, Mr. and Mrs. B. T. Allen, Bessie W. Tift, Mr. and Mrs. E. E. Youmans, Mrs. Adams, and several others. Soon after this meeting, this meeting place was destroyed by fire, and not long thereafter Henry Tift gave a site on which a church was built to be used by all denominations. This formerly stood about where the post office is, but nearer to where the present Methodist Church is, and the building was that now known as Bessie Tift Chapel, in the mill village, where it was moved by Henry Tift after the Methodists built a new edifice. (See article on Henry Tift.)

W. W. Webb died on July 5, 1917, and burial was the following day at Zion Hope. Of him has been said "As a soldier, minister and citizen, he measured to the full statue of a man."

WHIDDON FAMILY

By Mrs. Clifford Whiddon

James W. Whiddon, son of Juda Dominey Whiddon and Lott Whiddon, was born April 20, 1834, in a settlement since named Sycamore, Ga. His father, Lott Whiddon, came from South Carolina to Emanuel County, Georgia, where he married and later moved to Sycamore, Georgia. Lott Whiddon served with Company F, 59th Georgia Regiment in the War Between the States, and died of fever, near Gettysburg, Pennsylvania, in 1863. His was the first grave in Hickory Springs Cemetery. In 1796, James W. Whiddon's mother, Juda Dominey Whiddon, was given a small sycamore limb, used as a riding switch, by a man who spent the night in their home. She planted that switch and it grew. Thus the town of Sycamore received its name. The old dead stump of the tree stands today.

James W. Whiddon was the youngest boy in a family of nine children. When a small boy he lost one eye while he was threading an old-time homemade, harmonium. He played the harmonium well. My great-grandfather, James W. Whiddon was married to Lucy Branch, April 10, 1856, in Waterloo, by Mr. Abram Clements. Thirteen children were born to this union. They lived in Waterloo for twelve years, then moved nine miles south of Sycamore to the Whiddon Mill home, a log house built near the mill in 1868. This 1500-acre tract of land was purchased from Mr. Jesse Sumner. Here, great-grandfather, with the help of his two oldest boys, John and William, built a dam on what is known as Mill Creek. They used a horse cart, wheel barrow, and shovels to do the work. Great-grandfather put up a saw mill and grist mill at the west end of the dam and later a flour mill and rice mill at the east end. All the mills were powered by water. Trees were cut from the land and floated down the pond to the sawmill. In 1880 a new house was built. Today, the house is the beautiful country home of J. O. Ross and family. Mr. Ross, a nephew of Mr. Whiddon, purchased the home from the Whiddon estate after the death of Mr. Whiddon. Mr. Ross and Doctors W. F. and Charles Zimmerman own the Whiddon Mill Pond. The house is a large one and every piece, even the molding, was planed by hand. Great-grandfather was considered one of the best woodworkmen in the country. He cut, dressed and carved out his lumber. He told that he could shut his eyes and see a building finished in every detail before he built it. Farming and stock raising provided his livelihood.

In 1890 great-grandfather with the help of his children and other families in the church, built Little River Church, which is today known as Hickory Spring Primitive Baptist Church. The large hickory tree standing today in the cemetery grounds was his hitching post.

For several years the children attended school three months out of the year at Muddy Head, a one-room log school house near the Mill Pond. Later a private teacher was employed who lived in the home.

The home life of the family of James W. Whiddon was simple. They had no luxuries as we have today. For tubs to do the family washing, and to hold flour, meal, and syrup, large troughs were hewn from cypress trees. For light, string was spun for candles made from home grown wax. Practically all food was grown and raised at home. Granulated sugar was unknown, but rock sugar from syrup barrels was eaten. Most of their clothes and household linens were spun and woven at home. A few items such as coffee and matches were bought from foot and horseback peddlers, or in the nearest towns, Ty Ty, Albany, and Hawkinsville. Trading in the towns was done only in the spring of the year. Crops were laid by in June, and wild game was hunted until time to gather the corn. Square dances, "run and jump" and stone marbles gave fun for their little leisure time.

For many years the rural letter carrier rode horseback from Deep Creek post office in Dooley County (now Crisp County) three times a week to Hat post office, which was in the Whiddon home. During this time great-grandfather served as postmaster. Later David Whiddon my grandfather, and the third son of great-grandfather, became postmaster. He held this office for many years. During this time the post office was moved to Ruby, Ga. (now Chula, Ga.), and the name was changed to Ruby post office, and later to Chula post office.

Albert Whiddon, David's oldest son, was postmaster for many years. For the past thirty years Alonzo E. Whiddon, David's second son, has served as postmaster at the office in Chula, Ga.

Great-grandmother, Lucy Branch Whiddon, was a woman of large statue. Those who knew her say that she was very sympathetic, kind, generous and very talkative. She was always ready to lay aside her work to administer to the sick. She knew all the locally grown healing herbs from which she made salves and ointments. She was a good old-time cook, and when her grandchildren visited in her home she took them to her cupboard at once.

Great-grandfather was a tall well-built man. He was a man of few words.

He had a way of finding out all anyone knew by telling little of what he knew. He refused to make a reply when asked a foolish question. He believed in justice and peace. He was very ambitious for the education of his children. He kept lumber seasoned ready for caskets, which he made and gave to both white and colored.

Lucy Branch Whiddon died October 25, 1916, and James W. Whiddon died June 7, 1924. Their graves are in Hickory Springs Cemetery.

Following are the names of the children of James W. Whiddon and Lucy Branch Whiddon:

John J. Whiddon, born March 19, 1857, married Jane Sumner.
William Whiddon, born January 31, 1859, married Jane Easters.
David Whiddon, born December 18, 1860, married Priscilla Young.
Una Whiddon, born January 25, 1863, married John Vickers.
Dempsey Whiddon, born January 25, 1863, married Ava J. Vickers.
Georgia Ann Whiddon, born June 9, 1865, married George Cravey.
James B. Whiddon, born July 7, 1867, married Mollie Paulk.
Lula Whiddon, born June 21, 1869, married Tom Perry.
Reecy Whiddon, born December 1, 1871, married James Goodwin.
Lott Whiddon, born March 12, 1874, married Emma Fletcher.
Lucy Whiddon, born March 4, 1876.
Annibell Whiddon, born August 20, 1878.
Benjamin F. Whiddon, born May 27, 1882, married Mary Young.

Following are the names of the grandchildren living in Tift County:

Emmill Haywood Whiddon, born July 1, 1897, married Ethel McGill.
John Edward Whiddon, born February 16, 1888, married Mattie Godboldt.
W. Nichols Whiddon, born August 17, 1892, married Ocie Bell McCord.
Alonzo E. Whiddon, born October 11, 1885, married Annie Lou Leach.
Alice L. Whiddon, born October 23, 1887, married Dr. W. E. Tyson.
Clifford G. Whiddon, born August 22, 1897, married Cora Louise Buchanan.
Arthur Jack Whiddon, born March 25, 1886, married Nora Phillips.
Martha Van Whiddon, born July 30, 1887, married Tullie Sutton, and Tom Stowers.
Ave Jane Whiddon, born July 7, 1893, married James A. Akins.
David C. Whiddon, born December 23, 1900, married Blanche Clyatt.
Ora E. Cravey, born in 1891, married Bill Branch.
Abie J. Cravey, born in August, 1898, married Bessie Payne.
Joe L. Cravey, born in 1901, married Iva Cox.
James Richard Goodwin, born February 6, 1894, married Edna Dewey Smith.
Jacob Vinson Goodwin, born January 11, 1897, married Minnie Douglas.
Otis Grady Goodwin, born May 9, 1905, married Naomi ....
Lucile Whiddon Goodwin, born April 12 1907, married Omar Shiver.
Frankie L. Goodwin, born January 29, 1913, married Harold Turk.
Clarence Orvin Whiddon, born February 14, 1904.

Those grandchildren who served from Tift County in World War I, are as follows: Clifford Grady Whiddon, Quarmaster Corps, Army, overseas.

Emmill Haywood Whiddon, navy; John Edward Whiddon, army; Lemmie M. Whiddon, army; Claude Whiddon, navy; James Richard Goodwin, army; Vincent Goodwin, army; Leon D. Whiddon served in the army in World War II.

The great-grandchildren from Tift County who served in World War II are as follows: Hinton Goodwin, army; Wayne Goodwin, merchant marine; Donald Tyson, marines (overseas); Orman Whiddon, army (overseas); Raymond Whiddon, army; Ralph Whiddon, army; Oslin D. Whiddon, army; Ordway Whiddon, army (overseas); Haywood Whiddon, son of Emmill Haywood Whiddon and Ethel McGill Whiddon, joined the army in April 1942. He was Technician 5th Grade, in the Medical Corps. He died January 28, 1945 on Luzon Island, where he had served for three years.

Numbers of other great-grandsons, who lived in other parts of the state, served in World War II.

The Whiddon family were of substantial, common, people, the backbone of the country. This large family is, and has been, represented in many walks of life. They have been invariably a people simple in their life and tastes, but useful to the community.

CHESLEY ANDERSON WILLIAMS

In the early part of the nineteenth century there lived in Akin County, South Carolina, a veteran of the Revolutionary War. To him and his wife was born, in Akin County, on October 15, 1815, a son whom they named Hiram Williams.

When twenty-five years old, Hiram went from Akin County to Dooly County, Georgia, where his first Georgia land purchase was Lot 233 in the Tenth District of Dooly. This he bought from the Collins, and thereon he built his rift board home at the site later that of the refugee home of Governor Joseph E. Brown, and still later that of the Cordele hotel called the Suannee House.

Hiram upon arrival in Georgia taught school. Thereafter he represented Dooly County in the Legislature in 1865-6, 1868-9, 1873-4. A dauntless and courageous man, he was loyal to the South at a time when loyalty required courage.

In 1841, Hiram Williams married Sarah Jane Warren, daughter of James Warren, whose wife prior to her marriage, had been a Miss Stedman, of South Carolina. Sarah's ancestors had migrated to America from Ireland, soon after the Revolutionary War, and were of a high social standing and of "integrity of purpose." Hiram and Sarah lived at what was later known as the old C. C. Greer, Sr., place near Cordele. To them were born eleven children, all of whom lived to maturity and all of whom survived their father, who died in Dooly County, now Crisp, November 7, 1899. These children were Senator Isaiah Williams, Chesley Anderson Williams, Hiram Williams, Jr., Lydia Williams (Mrs. Wheller), Warren Williams (D.D.S.), Grovan Williams, C. C. Williams, Jane Williams (Mrs. McKinney), Joseph R. Williams, D. J. Williams (D.D.S.) Nannie Williams (Mrs. Fenn), whose husband was of that Fenn family of which "Uncle

Buddy Fenn" was a celebrated character, in Dooly.

Of the above mentioned children, the second son, Chesley Anderson Williams, came to what is now Tift County and here he carved for himself a permanent place in the annals of this community, where he was highly esteemed and much beloved.

Born March 3, 1848, in Dooly County on the site now that of the Suannee House, Cordele, he lived in one of the only three houses within a radius of nearly fifteen miles. The other homes were those of the Hamiltons and the Smiths. His boyhood days were spent on his father's farm which was in the midst of a vast pine forest spreading over what is now Cordele and environs. Deer and many kinds of wild beasts roamed the forests, in which also dwelt Indians. Far from civilization, nails were not easily obtained and the floor boards were not nailed in place; and often little Chesley would be awakened by the noise of the floor planks being displaced by wolves fighting beneath the house; for the house stood near what was called "Wolf Thicket."

Chesley, with his elder brother, Isaiah, and his younger brothers, Hiram, Warren and Grovan, and his sister, Lydia, attended famous "Oliver School," the only Old Field School prior to the Sixties, in what is now Crisp County. It was near Coney, and was east of Gum Creek, at what was later the Oscar McKinney farm. The first teacher was Miss Amanda Fitzpatrick, of Crawford County. Many Oliver pupils became distinguished in the community. Among these were John S. Pate, father of Ella Pate Carson, who married Briggs Carson, of Tifton. Mr. Pate was a boarding pupil at Oliver's.

Ches Williams was but a lad when the War Between the States broke. In those stirring times, in that wilderness, there remained little opportunity for formal school. His father was captain of the Militia of the Tenth District. Isaiah was in the war and was orderly sergeant of his company. Much work fell to the lot of Chesley, now the man at the home. He had to make the needed crops; but as he plowed he would prop his Blue Back Speller or some other book upon the cross bar of the plow and as he plowed would study.

In 1864 both Chesley and his younger brother, Hiram, Jr., joined the Confederate Army. Hiram was in Company H, 5th Georgia Reserves.

Chesley Williams was in Company G, 60th Georgia Infantry, and was with the Army of Virginia, under General Robert E. Lee. He was under "Stonewall" Jackson, General John B. Gordon, and General Jubal Early. A lieutenant, Chesley kept a diary of his war experiences. Wounded at the Battle of Gettysburg, he lay hour upon hour in the relentless downpour of rain. He bore valiantly the pain of the wounded leg, but he long mourned the theft of his diary at that time.

After partial recovery Lieutenant Williams in the last year of the war enlisted in the cavalry at Savannah. He was on his way to join General Lee when Lee surrendered, at Appomattox.

The war over, C. A. Williams returned to his home and resumed farming. In 1867 he married Miss Martha Jane McMercer, whose name, in later times, was spelled Mercer. In 1880 or 1881 they moved to Sumner where he was in the mercantile business until 1889, at which time he moved to Tifton. In 1890 he built at Tifton the brick sales stable and livery stable, the town's first brick building.

Devoted to his mother, C. A. Williams provided her with articles considered wonderful in that day in that remote community. They were the first cook stove, the first sewing machine and the first buggy owned by any of the family. These were treasures. Sarah had spun the thread for cloth which she had woven, and friends and relatives came great distances to watch her sew on the treasured new sewing machine.

Fox hunts were the order of the day in Chesley's time and he loved the chase. His granddaughter, Miss Eloise Roughton, of Tifton, owns an ingeniously carved cow-horn which belonged to her grandfather, C. A. Williams. The carving, done with a pocket knife, depicts deer, fish, a man on horseback, and a man hunting, and dogs. Also the dogs' names are carved: Pomp, Blue, Buck and Bully. The first three belonged to Williams. The horn was a gift to Williams by J. J. Garrett, Christmas, 1894.

C. A. Williams, and Martha Jane McMercer Williams had an only daughter, Antoinette Tallulah, born February 1, 1868, about nine miles from Cordele. She was called Lula. She married Willie Thaddeus Roughton (born near Sandersville, Washington County, Georgia, died November, 1896). When a small boy Willie and his mother were left at home when his father was in the Confederate Army. During Sherman's march, their house was raided, their stock taken. In a search for hidden valuables the commanding officer saw in a trunk in the attic Willie's father's Masonic paraphernalia. The officer was a Mason, and he ordered that the stock be returned, the house and its occupants be left unmolested; and he threw a guard around the house to see that his orders were carried out faithfully. Willie was a railroad engineer, and he and Lula Williams had two children, Eloise and Willie T., Jr., Willie T., Sr. was killed when struck by a train in a Savannah railroad yard.

Chesley Williams was local commander of the Confederate veterans. Governor Nathaniel Harris visited Titfon in September of 1916, and C. A. Williams was chosen to introduce the speaker. This he did, at the large assembly at the courthouse. It was a glorious hour for the gallant veteran of more than seventy-two years; but it also was his last public appearance. The excitement was too much. Later that day he was stricken ill, and he died, at his home in Tifton Heights, November 4, 1916. A long procession of friends and loved ones followed him to his last resting place. The Charlotte Carson Chapter of the Daughters of the Confederacy were in attendance; the old Confederate soldiers were present; and his pall-bearers were his former brothers-in-arms: R. A. Patrick, J. W. Bolton, B. N. Bowen, G. W. Montgomery, J. J. Baker, J. L. Rousseau. The casket was lowered into the grave just at sunset.

When Chesley died Martha McMercer Williams became ill. She survived her husband but three weeks, dying at their home, December 11, 1916.

Lula Williams Roughton and her children, Eloise and Willie T., Jr., bought the house which had been the J. J. L. Phillips' Tifton home. There they lived until Lula's death, January 16, 1926. This house was later purchased by the Twentieth Century Library Club and is now the Club House and Library.

Eloise Roughton attended Wesleyan College. There she studied china painting, in which she has exceptional skill and artistry. She is otherwise gifted, especially in needle work and knitting.

Willie T. Roughton, Jr., married Fannie Sue Stone. They live at Thomasville.

CECILIA MATILDA BAYNARD WILLINGHAM

Cecilia Matilda Baynard, born in Beaufort District, South Carolina, January 10, 1829, was one of five daughters of Archibald Calder Baynard (born Edisto Island, South Carolina, about 1797; honor graduate, University of South Carolina, 1817; married, 1820; died 1865 or 1866, at Jerico Place, near Beaufort) and beautiful Martha Sarah Chaplin (born near Beaufort, November 5, 1805; died Tuesday morning April 23, 1889, Chattanooga, Tennessee; buried on Pound lot, Forest Hill Cemetery, Chattanooga). Archibald was a man of great scholarship and brilliance of mind, and was a member of the South Carolina Legislature. He was son of Thomas Baynard and Sarah Calder Baynard, and was a brother of John, William and Ephraim Mikell Baynard, the last, a liberal patron of Charleston College. Cecilia's mother, Martha Sarah, was daughter of Benjamin Chaplin II, who was son of Benjamin Chaplin I, owner of Jerico Creek Plantation, Saint Helena's Parish, now Beaufort County, South Carolina. She was noted for her beauty, and she inherited from her father a large landed estate.

Cecilia attended the Charleston boarding school of Madamoiselle Bonne, a French woman, with an elite clientele. In later years Cecilia treasured a letter from her old teacher who wrote that Cecilia "was possessed of the most brilliant mind, and was the most thorough pupil" she had ever taught.

Thomas Willingham (born July 12, 1825, at Lawtonville, South Carolina; attended Penfield Academy; attended Hamilton College, now Colgate University, New York) and Cecilia set up housekeeping in a small new house which Thomas built on his plantation known as Mill Place, in Barnwell District. In about 1853 he built for Cecilia a large and handsome three-story mansion at Smyrna. Here was born to them on June 30, 1860, a dughter, Elizabeth, named for Cecilia's sister who married Thomas's brother, Benjamin Willingham. Bessie, as Elizabeth was called, was Thomas's and Cecilia's sixth daughter. When grown she married H. H. Tift, the founder of Tifton. At Smyrna was born on March 7, 1862, Florene Martha Willingham, who was named for Cecilia's sister who married another brother of Thomas, Winborn Joseph Willingham. Florie Willingham married Dr. W. L. Pickard, eminent Baptist preacher and president of Mercer University.

Cecilia and Thomas and their children, near the end of the War Between the States, refugeed from Smyrna to a plantation which Thomas owned in Mitchell County, Georgia, near what is now Baconton. Later Thomas's and Cecilia's eldest daughter, Sallie, married Dr. Edwin H. Bacon, and they lived at Eastman. Sallie's sister, Julia, married Ed's brother, Wallace Winn Bacon, afterward prominent as a physician in Albany. Ed and Wallace were first cousins of the distinguished Senator A. O. Bacon who was partly reared by their father, because, A. O.'s parents had died during his infancy. A. O. spent part of the time with another uncle, the head of a Georgia school famous in its day, but now no longer existing. A. O.'s parents are buried at Midway.

From Mitchell County the Willinghams moved to another plantation which Thomas owned in Daugherty County. Near Albany, this was formerly owned by the Barksdales, and on it was the beautiful Blue Springs, at present widely known as Radium Springs.

Before the War Between the States Thomas was said to be the third wealthiest man in South Carolina. Cecilia's uncle, Ephriam Mikell Baynard, was reputed second wealthiest. By the war, which freed the slaves, Thomas lost heavily, but he afterward made another substantial fortune. He had extensive land holdings in South Carolina and near Albany. Much of his land he sold and invested heavily in large bearing orange groves in Florida. Almost immediately afterward came the Florida freeze which killed his trees. Overnight he lost a fortune.

In ill health, Thomas and Cecilia and their youngest child, Pearl, went to Atlanta, although they still maintained their Albany home. They stayed with Thomas's and Cecilia's daughter, Fetie, and her husband, Cornelius Daniel, at their home, at 100 Forest Avenue.

It had long been the wont of the Willinghams to hold daily family prayer. On May 29, 1891, at Fetie's, Thomas and Cecilia had been praying. Then Cecilia spoke to Thomas. He made no answer. Touching him, she realized he was dead.

Cecelia made her home in Atlanta for a time with her eldest son, Thomas Willingham, C. S. A., who after the war, practiced law in Macon, in Atlanta and at Dallas, Texas. After his death his orphaned children moved to Eastman where they were reared by the Ed Bacons. Cecilia then visited among her numerous offspring, but soon began to call the home of her daughter, Bessie Tift, at Tifton, HOME. There she lived many happy years. She was gifted in all the household arts, was a convincing speaker, and in her early days was an accomplished equestrienne, and swimmer, in a day when most women did not swim. (Her handwriting was so beautiful and her letters were so neat and her phrases so felicitously turned and her English so smoothly flowing that one would need see her letters to appreciate her ease with the pen.) Yet it was not altogether her accomplishments which won for Cecilia the high esteem received from all who knew her. Hers was a strength of character not often met, and in her latter days she was a woman of deep piety.

In March of 1914, Cecilia had visited her friend Mrs. Briggs Carson. She crossed the street intending to call on a sick friend, Mrs. Goodman, wife of Tifton's pioneer physician. There was a step down into the yard. Cecilia missed her footing and fell. Her hip was broken. She was rushed on a special train to Atlanta, but she died there, in the Piedmont Sanitarium, on April 11, 1914, about two weeks after the accident. Burial was beside Thomas, in Albany.

To Thomas and Cecilia Baynard Willingham were born seventeen children. Fourteen grew to maturity and all of these attended private schools and college. Most of them were graduated from college, and many of them with highest honor.

Children of Thomas Henry Willingham and Cecilia Baynard Willingham were: 1, Thomas Willingham IV (married Mildred Lawton); 2, Sarah Jane (marriel Dr. Edwin H. Bacon, of Eastman); 3, Margaret (married T. O. B. Wood, of South Carolina); 4, Julia Baynard (married Dr. Wallace Winn Bacon, of Albany); 5, Anna Cornelia (married Cornelius J. Daniel, of Atlanta); 6, Cecilia Matilda (at birth so small that she slept in her mother's key basket, lived to be a normal-sized child, died of diphtheria, aged twelve years); 7, Benjamin Lawton (married Margaret Wood); 8, William Baynard (married Emma Davis, of Albany); 9, Elizabeth (called Bessie, married Henry Harding Tift, founder of Tifton); 10, Florence Martha (called Florie, married William Lowndes Pickard, D.D., LL.D.); 11, John Calhoun (died young); 12, Mamie (died young); 13, Belle Tift (married William Lawrence, skilled on the violin); 14, Winborn Joseph (married Katherine Couric, niece of Governor Shorter, of Alabama); 15, Baynard (married Lucile Doty, musician); 16, Calder (died young); 17, Pearl (married Irvine W. Myers, of Tifton).

MARGARET WILLINGHAM WOOD

Margaret Willingham, daughter of Thomas III, and Cecilia Baynard Willingham, was born at Smyrna, near Allendale, South Carolina, March 26, 1850. She attended Monroe Female College, Forsyth, and Andrews Female College, Cuthbert, where she graduated with first honor. Soon afterward she married handsome and dashing Thomas O. B. Wood, of South Carolina, her marriage being considered the brilliant social event of that season. The Woods lived at Smyrna, Thomas's former home, until it was destroyed by fire. They later lived in Atlanta, and then moved to Tifton where they leased the Vickers' house (now the Briggs Carson, Sr. home) on Sixth Street. They later bought the large A. O. Tift home on Love Avenue (now the Hendricks' home). Mr. Wood died and T. J., who managed his mother's business, sold the home. Maggie moved into Bessie Tift's guest apartment which was next door to the H. H. Tifts on Second Street. Here Maggie remained until her death in Tifton, March 28, 1926. Burial was at Tifton.

Children of Margaret and T. O. B. Wood were: 1, Thomas J. Wood; 2, Margaret (Marg. married Waring Lawton); 3, Cecilia (married Joseph Tabor); 4, Anna Cornelia (died unmarried).

ELBERT EDMUND YOUMANS

Elbert Edmund Youmans, son of James Stephen Youmans and Elizabeth Cleland Youmans, was born near Beaufort, South Carolina, January 12,

1851. When four years old he moved with his parents to Pierce County, Georgia. Later he moved to Appling County, Georgia, where he married Miss Mary Elizabeth O'Quinn, of Appling County, daughter of Jackson and Delilah McCall O'Quinn, both of whom were born, died and are buried in Appling County. Mary Elizabeth O'Quinn was born August 31, 1848. She and E. E. Youmans were married February 5, 1871.

E. E. farmed at Jesup, then moved to Screven, in Wayne County, Georgia, where he was in the mercantile business, in which he also engaged when he moved to Alapaha, and thence to Nashville, whence he came to Tifton, about 1890. At Tifton Mr. Youmans was with Love and Buck, a firm of wholesale grocers. The Youmans lived on Love Avenue, Tifton.

About 1893 E. E. Youmans built, several miles from town, a large white two-story house which thereafter for many years was the Youmans home. This home was later sold to Miss Ida Dickerson who operated a dairy farm. Later still it was bought by Ralph Walton, a farmer, and while he was living there the place was destroyed by fire. At that large country house was dispensed a hearty and gracious hospitality, and the rooms were filled with the laughter of jolly young people; for Mr. and Mrs. Youmans had twelve children, a jolly brood, and their parents delighted in providing those things which would contribute to their happiness.

After several years with Love and Buck, E. E. Youmans opened in Tifton his own market which he operated for about twenty years. In his old age he sold the market and thereafter served as Justice of the Peace until his death, August 27, 1933, at Tifton. Burial was at Tifton. Mary Elizabeth O'Quinn died at Tifton, March 13, 1938.

Mr. and Mrs. E. E. Youmans were a devoted couple and their golden wedding anniversary was a family event of outstanding importance. It was celebrated by a large reception tendered them by their daughters, Mrs. George Coleman, Mrs. Leonidas Clifton Spires, and their son, Stephen A. Youmans, at the home of Mrs. Spires.

Other anniversaries were celebrated. On the sixtieth wedding anniversary, Mr. and Mrs. G. W. Coleman entertained with a large reception at their Tifton home. On the sixty-second wedding anniversary Mrs. Spires honored them with a large turkey dinner at her home where many friends and relatives assembled.

Children of E. E. and Mary Elizabeth O'Quinn Youmans are: 1, Stephen A. Youmans (who became Tifton's City Manager); 2, Laura Elizabeth, who married William Henry Sneed (they celebrated their golden wedding at a reception at the Woman's Club, in Nashville, Georgia, 1938); 3, Carl Jackson (died, aged two years); 4, Minnie Belle (married Leonidas Clifton Spires); 5, Nettie Florence (married J. L. Mathis); 6, Sarah (married J. T. Mathis); 7, Lester Grace, a Valdosta dentist; 8, Ella Callie (married George Washington Coleman, Tifton City Manager); 9, Edmund Bryant (lives at Miami); 10, Thomas Gelzer (lives at Miami); 11, Elbert James (lives at Miami); 12, Henry Oswald (died in Valdosta, September 26, 1936).

J. L. Mathis and J. T. Mathis, husbands of Nettie and Sarah Youmans, were not related. Mary Elizabeth O'Quinn was not of the immediate family of the school-teacher John O'Quinn, here in Tifton's early days. The Tift County farmers, Elias and Silas, were very distant cousins. John moved away, but Silas and Elias continued in Tift County where their descendants still live.

ALLEN, Benjamin T....364	HOLMES, Charlton B. ..414
BAKER, Joseph J......365	HUTCHINSON, Bailus C.415
BANKS, William W. ...365	John H. 415
Mary E.T. 365	JAY, J.L. 416
BENNETT, Annie F.....367	JONES, Katherine T. .417
BOATWRIGHT, Frederick 368	JULIAN, George W. ...417
BOWEN, George W......369	KENT, The Family 418
Enoch P. 369	LAWRENCE Belle W. ...419
Irwin W. 371	LOVE, Willard H. 420
Isaac S. 371	MATHIS, John T. 421
BRANCH, The Family ..372	MAYNARD, Larkin G. ...457
Elias 373	McCREA, John Arch ...422
BRITT, The Family 374	McLEOD, Benjamin H. .430
BUCK, Edward A. 378	McMILLAN, The Family 431
CARMICHAEL, Patrick .379	MOORE, Perryman 426
CARSON, Briggs 380	Susie T. 426
Charlotte 383	MURRAY, Holmes S. ...427
CHESTNUT, Owen L. ...385	MURROW, Tillou B. ...428
CLYATT, Samuel M. ...387	MYERS, Irvine W. 429
CHURCHWELLS, The 388	O'QUINN, Silas 432
COCHRAN, James E. ...389	Duncan 432
CONGER, Abraham B. ..390	OVERSTREETS, The 433
DINSMORE, Virgil F. .392	PADRICKS, Brother ...436
DUFF, John M. 393	PARKER, Thomas J. ...436
EVE, Raleigh 394	PAULK, Jacob M. 438
FLETCHERS, The 396	Annie C. 438
FULWOOD, Daniel A. ..396	PETERSON, John A. ...440
Columbus W. 397	Nicholas 441
GAULDING, James S. ..400	PHILLIPS, J.J.L. 442
GREENE, James L. 402	John A. 443
John B. 402	P.D. 444
Leola J. 402	Thurston E. 445
GIBBS, The Family ...403	PICKARD, Florence W. .446
GOLDEN, Joseph J. ...404	William L. 449
GOODMAN, John C. 405	James L. 451
GUEST, Charles C. ...407	PRICE, John M. 453
HALL, Robert E. 408	Tifton F. 453
HARGRETT, Wesley T. .410	SCARBORO, Jason 456
HAKMAN, Willard L. ..411	SHAW, Matthew S. 457
HENDRICKS, William H.412	SHEPHERD, Luther S. .457
HERRING, John L. 413	SLACK, S.G. 453

SMITH, George A.B. ..458
      Robley D. 460
      William T. 460
SPURLIN, Walter C. ..461
TIFT, Amos C. 484
      Bessie W. 472
      Nelson 462
      Henry H. 463
      Henry H.T. 481
      Edmund H. 470
      Thomas W. 486
      William O. 487
TIMMONS, William W. ..488
VICKERS, Elias L. 488
WALKER, Jonathan 490
WARRENS, The 491
WEBB, William W.L. ..492
WHIDDON, Family 493
WILLIAMS. Charles A. .496
WILLINGHAM, Cecilia .499
WOOD, Margaret W. ...501
YOUMANS, Elbert E. ..501

www.ingramcontent.com/pod-product-compliance
Lightning Source LLC
Chambersburg PA
CBHW030538080526
44585CB00012B/190